Due Return	Due Return
Date Date	Date Date

BYRON

Byron
from the engraving by T. Lupton
after the painting by Thomas Phillips, R.A.

BYRON

BY

ETHEL COLBURN MAYNE

WITH TWO ILLUSTRATIONS

SECOND EDITION. REVISED

BARNES & NOBLE, Inc.
New York
METHUEN & CO. Ltd
London

First Published in Two Volumes . . . October 17th, 1912
Second and Revised Edition in One Volume . . . 1924

Reprinted, 1969
by
Barnes & Noble, Inc., New York
and
Methuen & Co. Ltd, London

Barnes & Noble SBN 389 01071 5
Methuen SBN 416 15630 4

Printed in the United States of America

PREFACE TO NEW EDITION

SINCE the first publication of this book in 1912, some import-
ant additions have been made to our knowledge of Byron.
The most remarkable of these are *Lord Byron's Corre-
spondence*, published by Mr. John Murray in 1922 (2 vols), and
the new edition of Lord Lovelace's privately-printed *Astarte*,
which with many additions and notes was published in the
usual way by his widow, Mary, Countess of Lovelace, in 1921.
On these two books I have a few remarks to make.

Lord Byron's Correspondence consists of many hitherto un-
published letters which had passed on Hobhouse's (Lord
Broughton's) death, to his daughter, Lady Dorchester. On her
death, she bequeathed these papers to Mr. John Murray. The
letters were written at all the outstanding periods of Byron's
life; and in those to Lady Melbourne between 1812 and
1815, there is much highly detailed information about his
love-affairs with Lady Caroline Lamb, Lady Oxford, and
Lady Frances Wedderburn Webster. The last of these is
reported almost hourly, and in its mingling of ribaldry, humour,
and sentiment is as characteristic a Byron document as we
possess.

Byron's offer of marriage to Annabella Milbanke, who
afterwards became his wife, is prominent among the sub-
jects of these letters; and closely connected with this by the
tragic issue, there are in the letters to Lady Melbourne many
references, more or less veiled but unmistakable, to his relations
with Augusta Leigh. These are so remarkable as to have made
at least one distinguished convert, Mr. G. S. Street, to the *Astarte*
theory of the Byron Separation Mystery. Mr. Street's view is
that we *can* escape from the *Astarte* documents, but not from the
allusions in the Melbourne letters.

To the relief of many—myself among the number—there is
also in the 1922 *Correspondence* a light thrown upon the much-
debated question of the " Hoppner Letter ", which enables us
at least to hope that Byron did send Mary Shelley's fervent
repudiation of the scandal to Mrs. Hoppner. It is no more than
a hope—but, as such, we welcome the testimony of the broken
seal and adherent morsel of paper. For this was, to the sense
of many of us, the worst thing we feared to have to think of
Byron. Since, however, the new light cannot be regarded as

more than a hope, I have left my text as it stands, and added a note embodying the information.

The 1921 edition of *Astarte* contains a great deal of hitherto unpublished matter bearing on the question of Augusta Leigh's relation to Byron, and to those most intimately connected with her life after his departure from England—namely, Lady Byron and Augusta's friend, the Hon. Mrs. Villiers. A quantity of letters from and to Augusta, which Lord Lovelace held from publication by the advice of the late Sir Leslie Stephen, are now displayed. Much of this new matter will be found in the text and notes of my present volume. The page-references throughout are to the new *Astarte*.

I should add that the 1921 *Astarte* has been edited with scrupulous care by Mary, Countess of Lovelace—a commendation which cannot be extended to the editing of *Lord Byron's Correspondence*, where errors in the text are numerous and often glaring, despite the services of two such eminent authorities as Lord Ernle and Mr. Richard Edgcumbe, who are stated to have read the proofs. Some of the more perplexing slips were pointed out and corrected by Mr. Edward Marsh, in a letter to the *London Mercury* for May, 1922. One, very notable, occurs in a letter from Byron to Lady Melbourne of October 4, 1814. At this time, Annabella Milbanke had accepted him; and he had been invited to Seaham on a visit. He had delayed to start, and this had called forth comment from Lady Melbourne, who had been all along his confidante in this affair, as well as in that with Augusta Leigh. Byron, writing to excuse himself, began his letter of October 4 with these words: " X never threw obstacles in the way ". In *Lord Byron's Correspondence*, the letter is shown as beginning: " I never threw obstacles in the way ". The phrase is evidently meaningless as it appears in the *Correspondence*; and it is not the only instance in the book where the significant " X " has been left out. Significant, because this " X " was the symbol used for Augusta by Byron and others. In this connection it may be as well to refer the reader to a book published by Mary, Countess of Lovelace in 1920, entitled *Ralph, Earl of Lovelace*, where an account is given of the various difficulties standing in Lord Lovelace's way in 1905.

Other new publications since 1912 are *In Whig Society* (1921) by Mabell, Countess of Airlie, where there are many letters from Lady Melbourne in her part of Byron's confidante; *The Journal of Henry Edward Fox* (1924), which gives us side-lights upon Byron and Teresa Guiccioli; and—for the Greek adventure— Mr. Harold Nicolson's *Byron; The Last Phase* (1924), a book with which no future biographer of Byron will be able to dispense.

I have revised the present work in the light of all these publications. Some compression of my text has seemed desirable, and has been made. In only one instance have I seen cause to abandon a position taken up in 1912. This is concerning Trelawny, of whom I have learnt more than I then knew, especially from Mr. Nicolson's book, and Mrs. Olwen Campbell's *Shelley and the Unromantics* (1924), where there are some arresting pages on the friends of Shelley and a vivid portrait of Trelawny. That " more " has caused me to remove from my pages some expressions of a sympathy which I no longer feel. Trelawny was a puzzle, and remains one. His appreciation of Shelley, and his devotion to that radiant memory, forbid us to appraise him as he appeared in every other relation of life. Something there must have been in him which answered to the beauty of Shelley's nature ; and though we have no proof at all that Shelley liked Trelawny, that does not do away with, but rather even brings into relief, the ardour and the reverence which Trelawny felt so deeply that at the end of his life he wrote : " In my love for Shelley, and so rarely speaking to anyone that knew him, everything else vanishes from my mind." And he was buried, as he persistently had purposed, beside the grave that holds Shelley's ashes in the Roman cemetery.

It seemed written that for Byron human nature should be constantly revealed at its most complex. Complex himself, he drew to himself the puzzling, the unaccountable, in every kind. Among his intimates the only simple propositions were Moore and Hobhouse ; and it is worth observing that these two were more dear to him than all the rest. In his friendships, as in other ways, he seldom found the " very thing " he wanted. Moore and Hobhouse, strongly contrasted as they were, yet were alike in this—that they were single-natured ; and for Byron, to be single-natured was to offer that seductive difference, that complementariness, which psychology declares to be among our deepest emotional needs. His other intimates, like Shelley, Trelawny, even Medwin, were beings not to be explained by normal standards of appraisal; and for the earlier years, Scrope Davies and the dazzling Matthews play the same disturbing part. The little group of clergymen which figured so amusingly among his intimacies at one time bears, in a measure, the mark of " queerness " ; while Dallas—quaint, portentous, but discerning Dallas —only by his tediousness escapes the crown of queerest of the early lot. Again, of mere acquaintances, none was more drawn to Byron than Galt ; and Galt, in every word he wrote of him, reveals himself as gloriously eccentric. And then the women ! We might say that till Teresa Guiccioli appeared, he never was concerned with one who was not unaccountable beyond—far,

*b**

far beyond—the fabled unaccountability of women. Even the boyish affair with Mary Chaworth shows a girl more variable, more wayward than most girls; and Mary Chaworth's end was madness. Then came Caroline Lamb, the queen of fashionable oddities, and she too ended in mental disorder; then Claire Clairmont, never to be held entirely sane; then that Augusta who by all was felt to be an enigmatic creature, and who became, with him, the great enigma of their period. The sentimental Lady Frances Webster, whose affair with Byron ran alongside, as it were, that with Augusta Leigh, is surely in her fashion a strange figure—taking the first step in their relation, drawing back with floods of tears and prayers for mercy, then to prove an adept at the furtive interchange of notes, so much so that she quite outdid all Byron's experience of the kind, and finally appealing so successfully to his (hitherto untampered-with) supply of sentimental chivalry that she escaped unscathed, soon afterwards regretted that escape, and vainly sought to enter once again the perilous dark region of his spell. And then came Annabella, whom we still exhaust ourselves to comprehend, and after all must give up as incomprehensible. Who shall account for the extreme of her implacability, when joined, as it must be, to the intensity of her love? The Guiccioli alone is easy reading. Byron remained with her because he could not get away—until he got away for ever from them all; and, doing so, gave up his life for Greece, an Unaccountable among the nations then and now.

But, for all that, the nation which in almost fairytalelike fashion has made Byron's dream of immortality in fame come true. In this Centenary year of 1924, letters from Athens bear a Byron stamp. It *carries* the letter—the splendid head, more kingly than a king's, does this year what a king's head does : it franks the letters from his Greece. "To be popular in a rising and far country has a kind of *posthumous feel*". So Byron wrote in 1813, on hearing of his fame in America. Could he have known that Greece would send her letters under his image and superscription a hundred years after his death, what would have been his feeling?

An answer is not lacking to that question. Let me end this second preface as I ended the first, with his own proud, prophetic words :—

> " But there is that within me that shall tire
> Torture and Time, and breathe when I expire."

ETHEL COLBURN MAYNE

ACKNOWLEDGMENTS

I WISH to give very grateful thanks to those who have helped me in my work, and to those who have, by their kindness, added a value to this book which it could not otherwise have boasted. Of the former, I am especially indebted to Mr. Roger Ingpen for the most generous of aid, and for the loan of many books. Of the latter, I would name particularly Mr. John Murray, who has allowed me to quote freely from his inestimable editions of the *Letters and Journals* by Mr. Rowland E. Prothero, and of the *Poems* by Mr. Ernest Hartley Coleridge, and has also permitted the use of several pictures ; Mr. Horatio F. Brown, to whom I owe the reproduction of Ruckard's picture (" Byron in Venice ") ; and Mary, Countess of Lovelace, who, after my work was finished, read the proofs, and finding my view of the Separation-episode in agreement with her own and that of her family, accorded me the right of reproducing Hayter's miniature of Lady Byron. Lady Lovelace asks me to state, in this connection, that in the opinion of the family, the portrait by Ramsay, in vol. iv. of *Letters and Journals* (said to be that of Lady Byron), is not authentic.

Mr. Buxton Forman was kind enough to give his opinion against the authenticity of a picture which I had hoped might prove to be one of Allegra. It is therefore not included.

E. C. M.

1912.

CONTENTS

LIST OF ILLUSTRATIONS

INTRODUCTORY

THERE is only one full-length *Life and Letters* of Byron in English, and that was published in 1830. I imagine that this statement will astonish a good many people, for most of us have had—I certainly had—a vague impression that Lives of Byron were too numerous. Writings about Byron have been at times too numerous, it is true. In 1869–70, for example, periodical literature was infested by his name; but those writings were only in a very restricted sense biographical. Pathological would be their juster description, for they were concerned with what was called " the Beecher Stowe revelation ", and the whirlwind of controversy to which they contributed raged round one point only. I hope it will be as pleasant a surprise to my readers as it was to myself to find how very little else we knew about Byron, and how enthrallingly interesting, from its beginning to its end, his story is. The first act of a drama is sometimes seen, as the action develops, to have been too powerful. It has tuned the mind for events which, in the actual happening, fail to fulfil such radiant or such sinister promise. We who watch the play called " Byron " need fear no like deception. The first act seizes us, but when we rouse ourselves to attention for the next, we find no element of excitement wanting, and the third and fourth keep us not less enthralled. There is hardly another life-drama of which the same can be said. That one to which we turn as instinctively as he turned himself for a parallel—the life-drama of Napoleon—falls below Byron's by reason of the hero's sterility in defeat. The sick eagle of St. Helena, the sick eagle of Italy and Greece—which had the unconquerable mind? If we measure men by their reaction to misfortune, there can be little doubt of the answer.

Thus, like many another writer of many another nation, I (the countrywoman of Thomas Moore, his first biographer) " felt the call "—I longed to write a book about Byron. The coveted opportunity was afforded, and then for the first time realising the task which lay before me, I realised also for the first time the delight. If any degree of the joy I have felt in the work be transmitted to my readers, I shall count myself a fortunate woman. But perhaps I ought to apologise, as Byron's

biographer, for being a woman at all. Assuredly *he* would have
thought so. " You should recollect ", he wrote of some critical
severity on Lady Morgan, " that she is a woman ; though, to
be sure, they are now and then very provoking, still, as authoresses,
they can do no great harm ". The indulgence, scathing as it is,
would not have been extended to her who dared to ply her pen
upon the subject of himself.

Much water has run, since Byron's day, under the bridge
between authors and authoresses ; it seemed high time that
a woman should write of this " victim of her sex ", as he loved
to call himself. There might appear, were I to cite all the argu-
ments in such a biographer's favour, something too much of that
sex-vanity which many of us feel to be losing in subtlety of
effect what it has gained in candour ; and indeed I think that
the extremely articulate method is here, as elsewhere, superfluous.
Those who have not already the arguments at their fingers'
ends, will, I humbly hope, discover them as they read.

A word about the books on Byron.

Moore's *Life*, published in 1830, is the foundation-stone for
all ; and if we often wish that it had been more soundly laid,
we nevertheless must recognise that it has enabled two structures
of supreme value to be erected. I allude to the editions of the
Letters and Journals, and of the *Poetry*, by Mr. Rowland E.
Prothero[1] and Mr. Ernest Hartley Coleridge respectively. Both
are published by Mr. John Murray. Praise of such works from
me would be an absurdity : I offer my sincerest gratitude and
admiration.

John Cordy Jeaffreson's book, *The Real Lord Byron* (1883),
which is by way of being a " full-dress " biography, is, rather,
a full-dress debate. All through the author argues interminably
against now an actual, now an imagined, opponent, and we rise
from our perusal with brain battered and image shattered.
Neither a " real " nor an unreal Byron emerges from these wordy
pages, wherein there is an occasional shrewdness, an intermittent
flash of insight, a love of truth that pulses, however, chiefly for
the sake of defeating some one else's. Further, the book was
written at a time when guesswork had to supply the place of
knowledge ; and Jeaffreson, like many another, guessed badly.

Of the late Lord Lovelace's *Astarte* [2] the text of this book says
enough. *Astarte* gives us vivid evocations of Lady Byron and
Mrs. Leigh ; and it has, besides, the supreme merit of unassailable

---

[1] Now Lord Ernle.

[2] Privately published 1905. In 1921 his widow, Mary, Countess of
Lovelace, re-edited the volume, adding much new material ; and this was
published in the usual way by Messrs. Christophers.

documents—to a degree which makes the sole attempt at refutation
entirely unconvincing. (See Appendix III. : Medora Leigh.)

These are the chief sources. Of the rest, I may mention
Galt's short *Life* (1830) and Lady Blessington's *Recollections*
(1834). W. E. Henley's notes to the single volume of letters with
which he dealt (1897) have been, I cannot but think, a good deal
overpraised. His inaccuracies are flagrant ; his devotion to the
prize-ring aspect of society is exaggerated to a degree which
destroys the values of his picture ; while his animus against all
the women concerned is so great as to make him a mere special
pleader in the record of Byronic basenesses.

Of Lord Broughton's *Recollections*, the value, less though it
be than fond expectation had long looked forward to, is still
considerable, especially as regards the highly controversial topic
of the burnt Memoirs.

In writing of Byron, we write of quintessential humanity.
" My pang shall find a voice " : that cry in *Manfred* is the word,
as it were, of his life ; and he uttered it hardly more for himself
than for us all. We need that utterance, for scarce one of us
would have the honesty, had we the power, to crystallise our
feelings into the phrases he has made for us. Humour we
love to term our lesser form of self-consciousness; but Byron's
self-consciousness was supreme, and towered high above the
subterfuge of humour. Through its excess it became its own
antithesis—it became unconscious. He " did not know when he
was doing it ". Each time we use that pedestrian saying, we
define the last triumph of expression. Yes : the vanity of
suffering, which every one possesses in a greater or less degree,
Byron possessed in a degree which has made him mankind's
most fearless mouthpiece—for courage also is needed for such
spontaneity as his.

That he was, besides the Byron of Byronism, the Byron of
whom his intimate friend could write (in a travesty of one of
his saddest poems) that " Momus himself never painted A livelier
creature than thee ", alters nothing in the case. The paradox
was part of the pose, using pose in its true sense of poise—the
way in which you have to stand if *you* are to stand at all. We
hear too much of his " chameleon " character. His character
was not chameleon, but strikingly the reverse. Byron never
changed ; in all surroundings he remained the same. " Every-
thing that he did is implicit in everything else that he did." I
have written that elsewhere of him ; and it is, in truth, from his
invariability that the whole Byronic legend has grown. So far
from not being able to guess what he will do, we know on the
instant what he will do and—still more accurately—what he

will say. We could not have imagined the words, but we can imagine the sense. Did he ever fail to say it? Not once. " My pang shall find a voice "—and it was always the same voice. The songs, with growing powers, became more complex ; even as a De Reszke advances from singing scales to singing *Tristan*, so Byron advanced from the vibrant monotony of the early narratives to the vibrant variety of his World-poem. What is *Lara*, after all, but an inarticulate Juan? And in *Juan*, again, we find further proof of his invariability—for how persistently, in *Juan*, the imperishable boy that Byron was flames forth ! Men are not so intoxicated with knowing. Goethe perceived this puerile strain in him : " As soon as he reflects, he is a child " (*Sobald er reflectirt, ist er ein Kind*).

Thus, in the continual portrayal of himself, he was in reality portraying a recurrent aspect of young manhood. The mode, to be sure, is for the hour altered : young men nowadays are morbidly cheerful, amused as never children were by children's toys—and does not the much-paraded bloom seem often to be only painted on the peach? Byron's pallor, Byron's wild-eyed woe, histrionic though they be, convince us of some profound unseizable sincerity. The *sunt lacrimæ rerum* is somewhere therein affirmed—with all the crudeness of half-comprehension, it is true, yet with a quality in the utterance which persuades the soul. And if ever the child was father of the man, Byron's youth was father of the wildfire Byron whose stone is not, and never will be, in Westminster Abbey ; yet whose memory tingles so keenly through the veins of England that, forgotten as he is often said to be, there is rarely a day even now on which in one connection or another we do not find, as they found when he was alive, his name in the newspaper.

> " But there is that within me that shall tire
> Torture and Time, and breathe when I expire."

11 HOLLAND ROAD, KENSINGTON
April 22, 1912

BYRON

CHAPTER I

CHILDHOOD—1788-1798

Byron's forebears—Foulweather Jack—The Wicked Lord—Byron's father and mother—A miserable marriage—The heiress despoiled—Birth of Byron—His only childism—The twisted foot—Life in Aberdeen—Death of Captain Byron—Childish traits—First lessons—The Highlands—Mary Duff—Precocity in love—He succeeds to the title

WILDFIRE leaped about his cradle, as it were. Of a "dark and ominous type", says his German biographer, Karl Elze, were his immediate forebears. "Unbridled passions, defiant self-will, arrogant contempt for the accepted order of things, together with high endowments of energy—these made an inauspicious heritage"; and his grandfather, by marrying a Cornish woman,[1] had added to the cup an infusion of the Celtic melancholy—as notorious in our own days as was the Byronic variety in those of which I am to write. The grandfather was that Admiral John Byron who was known to his companions in service by the nickname of Foulweather Jack, because he never could make a voyage without encountering a hurricane. From a word let fall by Mrs. Piozzi, who was an intimate friend of his wife, we gather that the Admiral made his hurricanes for himself when he was at home.[2] His first cousin, Sophia Trevanion, whom he married in 1748, gave him two sons and four daughters.[3] From the list of these, Juliana

---

[1] She was his first cousin as well. William, fourth Baron Byron, married Frances, second daughter of the fourth Baron Berkeley of Stratton, and had by her the two sons known as the Wicked Lord (William, fifth Baron) and Foulweather Jack. Her sister married John Trevanion of Caerhayes, Cornwall, and had by her that daughter, Sophia, who, marrying Foulweather Jack, became the mother of John Byron (" Mad Jack ") and grandmother of the poet. To the Berkeley strain John Cordy Jeaffreson attributes " the impulsiveness and vehemence of Jack Byron and his son " (*The Real Lord Byron*, i. 28).

[2] Mrs. Piozzi wrote of Mrs. Byron, " She is wife to the Admiral, *pour ses péchés* " (*Life and Writings of Mrs. Piozzi*, ii. 456).

[3] They were : (1) John, eldest son ; father of the poet. (2) George,

and John stand forth as the stormy petrels. Juliana qualified
for the typical Byronic part by marriage with *her* first cousin,
William Byron. This was violently opposed by his father, the
legendary Wicked Lord—otherwise William, fifth Baron Byron,
hero of the Chaworth Duel tragedy. His dislike to the union
brought about the devastation of the family property from which
it never, in the Byron days, wholly recovered ; for this fifth lord
was so infuriated by the marriage of his son with one thus near
in blood that—very nearly insane as he was, and to that extent
justified of his wrath against the Byronic tendency to in-breeding
—he resolved to hand that heir a ruined heritage. The heritage
was ruined, but the son never received it. He died before the
father in 1788 ; and *his* son, too, died in 1794,[1] when our Byron
was six years old—leaving the child heir to the barony.

John, father of the poet, and elder son of Foulweather Jack,
was the other stormy petrel. At twenty-two, a dazzlingly hand-
some and very dissipated Guardsman, he ran away with, and in
a year married, the Marchioness of Carmarthen [2]—born Amelia
d'Arcy, only child and heiress of the last Earl of Holderness, and,
moreover, Baroness Conyers in her own right. They lived in
France and had three children, of whom only the last-born,
Augusta, survived. This was the girl who in 1807 married her
first cousin, George Leigh, and thus became the Augusta Leigh
whose name runs through the whole Byron story.

In 1784, the year after Augusta's birth, Lady Conyers [3] died,
and Captain Byron returned to England, head over ears in debt,
and avowedly on the look-out for what his son, in after years,
was to describe as a " Golden Dolly ". He found her quickly in

who married Henrietta Dallas. Their son, George (R.N.), succeeded the
poet in 1824 as seventh lord. (3) Frances, who married Colonel Charles
Leigh. Their son, George, married his first cousin, Augusta Byron (Hon.
Augusta Leigh), daughter of John Byron by his first marriage. (4)
Juliana-Elizabeth, who married her first cousin, the Hon. William Byron,
only son and heir of William, fifth lord, whom the poet (his grand-nephew)
succeeded in 1798—the son having died before his father. (5) Sophia-
Mary, who died unmarried. (6) Charlotte-Augusta, who married Vice-
Admiral Parker.

[1] This son was killed fighting at the siege of Calvi, in Corsica.
[2] Wife of Francis, Marquis of Carmarthen, afterwards fifth Duke of
Leeds.
[3] Lord Lovelace, in *Astarte*, says that she died in giving birth to
Augusta, in 1784. Her death deprived her husband of £4000 a year.
She is said to have died of grief caused by his vices and brutalities. This
was strenuously denied by the poet in a letter written to a Swiss admirer
in 1823. " So far from [my father's] being ' brutal,' he was of an extremely
amiable and joyous character, though careless and dissipated. . . . It is
not by brutality that a young officer in the Guards seduces and carries off
a Marchioness, and marries two heiresses ". Elze pours contempt on this
letter : " it is either self-delusion, or deliberate falsehood."

Miss Catherine Gordon of Gight,[1] a direct descendant of the Royal House of Scotland—for Annabella Stewart, daughter of James I of Scotland, had married the second Earl of Huntley, and their third son became Sir William Gordon of Gight. The lairds of Gight were a " hot-headed, hasty-handed race, sufficiently notable to be commemorated by Thomas the Rhymer " ; and Catherine's father, George Gordon, was the fifth who bore the two names which his grandson was to make immortal. He married one Catherine Innes of Rosieburn ; the daughter was born in 1765, and was their only child. Both her parents died early, and she was brought up by her grandmother—a Duff of the Fife family—who lived at Banff, and was commonly called Lady Gight. This was a very parsimonious great lady, and an illiterate one as well ; but, aware of the disadvantages of illiteracy, she was solicitous that the little girl should be better educated than herself. Her solicitude bore fruit. Catherine Gordon— destined to be the mother of a great poet—was all her life particularly fond of reading, and read good literature ; she wrote vivid though inelegant letters ; and she could criticise shrewdly, in after years, not only her son's poems (those which she saw, for she died before his notable works were published),[2] but the discrepant reviews of them. On the other hand, she never lost the provinciality, the uncouthness even, of the atmosphere wherein she had grown up; and to this defect was added the far more distressing one of a violent temper which had never known control, and which expressed itself not only in speech, but in all too appropriate action. China as well as " words " flew at her victims' heads ; with fire-irons no less than with opprobrium were they pursued. . . . In this undisciplined personality an evident and overweening pride of birth, justified though it was by facts, made a ludicrous impression. She seemed of the soil —nay, of the slums (had the word then been in vogue) ; yet in her the observer was enjoined to honour a " gentlewoman".

It was in Catherine Gordon's twentieth year that, for her sins, she met and married John Byron. Bath was the scene of both events—Bath where, some years earlier, her father had

---

[1] She had a fortune of £23,000, " doubled by rumour " (*Dict. Nat. Biog.*). In 1784, the year of Lady Conyers' death, before Miss Gordon met Jack Byron, she saw at Edinburgh Mrs. Siddons act the character of Isabella in Southerne's *Fatal Marriage*, and was so overcome that she fell into convulsions and had to be carried out, uttering with a loud cry—an exclamation belonging to the character acted by Mrs. Siddons—" Oh, my Biron, my Biron " ! (*Moore* ; 1838, p. 3).

[2] With the exception of *English Bards and Scotch Reviewers*. There is said to be in existence a book in which she collected all the criticisms of his early poems, and inserted on blank pages interleaved her own comments, which were written with wit and ability. The whereabouts of the volume is unknown (*Notes and Queries*, 4th series, December 1869, p. 495).

drowned himself.[1] In a girl so superstitious as was the heiress of Gight, it seems a reckless ruffling of destiny to have fixed her wedding-day, in Bath, for the thirteenth of May. But that was what she did, that was how she " defied augury "—and all the world knows whether augury or she prevailed. The union was unimaginably wretched. She had been married for her money—as an anonymous Scottish rhymer had warned her on her wedding-day, in a ballad openly addressed to Miss Gordon of Gight ; and her money was instantly snatched from her. In two years (1784–86) the heiress was landless and almost penni-less ; she had nothing of her own in the world but a pittance of £150 a year.

> " When the heron leaves the tree
> The laird of Gight shall landless be."

So ran an old saw of the Gordons ; and legend affirms that on that sinister Thirteenth of May the heronry of Gight flew over to Haddo, the property of the Earl of Aberdeen. Lord Haddo, the eldest son, on hearing it said calmly : " The land will soon follow ". . . . For a few months the Byron-Gordons (her husband assumed the name) lived at beautiful Gight. But quickly the truth came out. Captain Byron was assailed on every side by clamorous creditors ; all available cash was engulfed, the timber on the estate was cut down, the farms, the salmon-fishery rights, were sold, £8000 was borrowed on mortgage. It was in vain. The debts were still but half paid. In 1786 the Byrons left Gight ; in 1787 (almost unbelievable, were it not that such things seem constantly to happen) Lord Haddo bought the estate. The land had followed.

[1] " You know, or you do *not* know, that my maternal grandfather * (a very clever man, and amiable, I am told) was strongly suspected of suicide . . . and that another very near relative of the same branch took poison, and was merely saved by antidotes. For the first of these events there was no apparent cause, as he was rich, respected, and of considerable intellectual resources, hardly forty years of age, and not at all addicted to any unhinging vice. It was, however, but a strong suspicion, owing to . . . his melancholy temper. *The second had* a cause, but it does not become me to touch upon it ; it happened when I was far too young to be aware of it, and I never heard of it till after the death of that relative, many years afterwards. I think, then, that I may call this dejection *constitu-tional.* I had always been told that in *temper* I more resembled my mater-nal grandfather than any of my *father's* family—that is, in the gloomier part of his temper, for he was what you call a good-natured man, and I am not " (Letter to John Murray ; Moore, ed. 1838, p. 531).

* Byron's grandfather, George Gordon, was found drowned in the canal at Bath in 1779. His great-grandfather, Alexander Davidson Gordon, was drowned in the Ythan, a river of Aberdeenshire, in 1760. In both cases there was sus-picion of suicide.

" Ye've married, ye've married wi' Johnny Byron,
    To squander the lands of Gight away " ;

the doggerel must have jingled in Catherine Gordon's ears, but Johnny Byron was still enthroned in her heart. " *His foibles—they deserve no worse name* " : thus she wrote, after his death, of the courses which had disinherited her house ; and indeed this wife, who could storm the roof off for a whimsy, bore her financial ruin with dignity and composure. The purchase-money of Gight was thrown, after the rest, into the abyss of her husband's debts ; but Catherine could live on her pittance of £150 a year without incurring any. At first it was in France, with him ; then at the end of 1787, returning alone to England, she soon afterwards—on January 22, 1788—gave birth, at 16 Holles Street, London,[1] to her first and only child, George Gordon Byron.

He was born with a caul. The fabled talisman against drowning was sold by his nurse to one Captain Hanson, brother of Mrs. Byron's family lawyer, John Hanson ; and two years after buying it, Captain Hanson was drowned. It is strange that Byron should never have commented on this little irony, and the more so because tragedies of drowning entered with unusual frequency into the story of his life. He had much to say, on the other hand, of the two remaining peculiarities of his birth : his only childism, and his twisted foot. Of the former he made a subject for vanity. " I have been thinking", he says in his *Detached Thoughts*,[2] " of an odd circumstance. My daughter, wife, half-sister,[3] mother, sister's mother, natural daughter, and myself, are or were all *only* children. . . . Such a complication of *only* children, all tending to *one* family, is singular enough, and looks like fatality almost. But the fiercest animals have the fewest numbers in their litters ". Not many passages of his characteristic prose are more characteristic than this one, wherein his constant brooding over the family history is mingled with the special form to which his vanity tended. He would be exceptional at any cost, fierce at any cost : thus horses (the one-litter animal *par excellence*) are omitted from a list in which " lions, tigers, and even elephants, which are mild in comparison ", are eagerly displayed. Horses, though spirited, are not fierce—and horses are ignored.

Of the other circumstance—the twisted foot—vanity possessed

---

[1] Since numbered 24, and now destroyed.
[2] Prothero, *Letters and Journals*, v. 467.
[3] In this instance he thought erroneously. Augusta Leigh was not an only child, except in the sense that the two other children of Captain Byron's first marriage died before her birth.

itself also, but this time with a morbid intensity which turned it into one of the keynotes of his life. It is as well one of the puzzles of his story. Inured as the student of biography must needs become to conflicting evidence, the discrepancies here afford a fresh amazement. Of all things, *this*—a question of visible and tactual fact—would seem the easiest to establish ; yet even in the Byron legend no point is more debated. I shall not summon the cloud of witnesses, for they witness only to the enigma ; what this one positively affirms, that one as positively contradicts ; what the lasts on which his shoes were made [1] would seem to prove—that both feet were perfect—is powerless to convince when set against the observation of all who knew him, and the (perhaps less cogent) testimony of his own incessant mental suffering. . . . From the maze, one certainty alone emerges. The foot was not a club-foot. But he, in the histrionic heats of his imagination, fanned as they were by the continuous actual drama which his (in all other respects) surpassing personal beauty kept ablaze—he would be satisfied, so to speak, with nothing less than the worst, the ugliest aspect. *He had a club-foot :* only the big word would do, and it must be in the biggest letters, and the limelight must illume them. It is not difficult to understand. Dowered as he was with almost everything else that the fairies can bring to the christening, this was, as Macaulay said, the bad fairy's bundle. She flung it into his cradle, and she flung a curse with it : he was to attribute it to his mother. The allusion (made by himself) to that mother's " false modesty " remains obscure, but we can conjecture its meaning ; and his persuasion of its truth embittered hopelessly a relationship which nothing could have made an even tolerable one. We shall learn later what his life with her contained of mental torture —and we shall not forget, while learning it, that her offences against him dated, as he came to believe, from before his conscious existence. Once, in a fit of her unhappy fury, she called him a lame brat. He answered, " I was born so, mother " ; and the boyish face was white with such anguish as permits no further analysis. . . . Words ! No blows have ever shown men hell as words can show it.

When the little boy was two years old, Mrs. Byron left London for Aberdeen,[2] where her husband joined her. They lived

---

[1] Preserved in Nottingham Museum.

[2] A fine bronze statue has been erected (1923) in Aberdeen. Byron is shown at about 20, in a cloak of the period. The statue is the work of Dr. Pittendrigh Macgillivray, R.S.A., King's Sculptor, of Edinburgh. No other sculpture of Byron is comparable to this one in vitality and nobility. It is at a glance " Byronic ".

together for a short time in lodgings in Queen Street, but domesticity with this latter-day Catherine the Curst was out of the question. Jack Byron—then safely self-exiled in Valenciennes—wrote of her in 1791 to his sister, Mrs. Charles Leigh, with whom he corresponded : " She is very amiable at a distance ; but I defy you and all the Apostles to live with her two months, for if anybody could live with her, it was me ". Nor had *he* given it up without a fair trial. If they could by no means agree in the same house, perhaps they might contrive to do so if it were only in the same street. So the lady flitted to the farther end of Queen Street, bearing all expenses of the move herself ; and they visited one another, drank tea with one another —but even this soon proved to be more than could be tranquilly got through, and they agreed to meet not at all. Captain Byron still lingered a while in Aberdeen—his wife occasionally possessed small sums of ready money which could be wrested from her by letter—and in his walks he often met the little son, out for an airing with his nurse. The father would stop and chat with his offspring, and at last he expressed a wish to have the child on a couple of days' visit. Mrs. Byron demurred, but the nurse declared that if his father kept the boy *one* night, he would certainly not keep him another. Her presage was fulfilled. When she went next morning to inquire about her charge, Captain Byron earnestly requested her to take him home at once. Moore pleads for his darling that since the nurse (Mrs. Byron having only that one servant) could not stay with him, the little boy was naturally upset, and hence naughty. No doubt of it ; and a still more forcible defence should occur to any one who has ever beheld a man (and a fashionable and dissipated young man at that) helpless before the indomitable will of a child of two years old—to say nothing of its complicated toilet and feeding arrangements.

After this exploit Jack Byron, probably feeling that he had done all that could be required of him, fled to France and lived at Valenciennes on his wife's money, until he died in the summer of the following year (1791), aged only thirty-six.

Little though the visit to his father may prove concerning the character of the small Geordie (as our poet was called during his Scottish period), there can be no question that he inherited the passionate temper which came to him, as it were, from every side. He was once scolded for having soiled a new frock in which he had just been dressed. The tiny creature, in speechless resentment (" one of my silent rages "), seized the frock in both hands and tore it from top to bottom. He had many times seen his mother do the same with her gowns and caps ; but we must hope that he had not seen her commit the further delin-

quency which a relic, treasured in Aberdeen, was still attesting
when Moore published his biography in 1830. This was a china
saucer, out of which, in another silent rage, the baby Byron had
bitten a large piece.

In such manner was the stage set for his existence with his
mother. That rent gown and bitten saucer were sufficiently
significant properties, and the drama proceeded in their sense.
What was there not to intensify it! There was soon even
aggravated poverty. While Jack Byron lived, his wife had
been obliged to pay all his expenses ; and now that he was dead
—now that her characteristic shrieks of grief at that news (they
had been heard all over the street) had sunk into silence—the
woman who had been the victim of those foibles which deserved
no worse name, found herself heavily involved in debt. For since
he to the last had snatched all such ready money as she might
have painfully saved out of her very hands, she was forced to
procure on credit the furnishing for the flat to which she moved
after his death. This was in Broad Street ; her expenses in
connection with it, joined to the continuous drain that had gone
on in the past, now loaded her down with a debt of £300.[1] She
was a woman who worried herself vehemently over money-
matters ; and the incessant strain of grinding penury exacerbated
all her natural feelings. Catherine the Curst may claim, in the
early days of her motherhood at any rate, some sympathy.
An heretofore considerable heiress, totally despoiled, living in
a scrubby flat in a depressing northern town, cuts a deplorable
figure enough, though she be of docile temper ; what the ordeal
must have been to this one, fancy hesitates to grasp. She was
only twenty-seven years old ; she had been, besides a notable
heiress, a vain capricious girl, " as proud as Lucifer " : now
here she was, a disclassed, unfriended widow, beggared to such a
degree that she saw herself obliged to send her spirited and
sensitive child to a cheap and nasty day-school in the Long
Acre of Aberdeen !

Day-schools, one gathers, were always nasty in those days,
and this one was abnormally cheap—only five shillings a quarter.
Learning, even of the simplest kind, can hardly have been looked
for at the price, and Byron himself has told us how much the
year of his attendance taught him : " not even my letters ".
When his mother found this out, she first soundly boxed his ears,
and then got a private tutor for him, " a very devout, clever little
clergyman, named Ross ". Under Ross the boy discovered

---

[1] The payment of interest on this debt and of her grandmother's
annuity reduced her annual income to £135. On such a sum, however,
she contrived to live without increasing her obligations, and on the death
of her grandmother she discharged them all.

the passionate delight in historical reading which remained with him to the end. Next came Paterson, the " very serious, saturnine, but kind young man, the son of my shoemaker "— who was nevertheless a good scholar, and initiated him into Latin. From Paterson's hands he passed into the Aberdeen Grammar School, where he remained till he was ten years old.

In 1796, after an attack of scarlet fever, Mrs. Byron took him to the Highlands, and either in that year or the following one they lived at a farmhouse near Ballater. " From this period ", he wrote long afterwards, " I date my love of mountainous countries ". . . . It is said that our earliest clear memory of anything in Nature is always connected with that aspect which in later life is to prove the nearest to our hearts. Byron's joy was tardy in arrival : he was eight years old before he ever saw a mountain ; but the first vision was remembered as only the destined vision is—and, to account for its immanent vividity, we need no thin-spun theorising (such as Moore and Christopher North resort to) but merely the knowledge that these are something more than revocations, and shine for their possessors in the light that never was on sea or land. Such to me is my first outdoor memory—and each will find, on reflection, that the First-Remembered is, as well, the heart of all dreaming.

In Byron's boyish volume there are two poems relating to the Highland sojourn.[1] Of the first, the subject is the mountain of Loch-na-gar (or Lachin-y-gair) near Invercauld ; one Mary— " sweet Mary " with " the long flowing ringlets of gold "—is the inspiration of the second. " Byron ", says Mr. E. H. Coleridge, " was in early youth ' unco' wastefu' ' of Marys ". Between the ages of eight and ten we find two—this evanescent Highland nymph,[2] and the dark-haired, hazel-eyed little cousin and beauty, whose " very dress " he remembered sixteen years later when, in 1813, he wrote the famous passage in his journal for November 26 : " I have been thinking a good deal lately of Mary Duff ".

Precocity in love is not uncommon among ordinary mortals, though Alfieri considered such youthful sensibility to be an unerring sign of the artistic soul. He himself fell in love at nine years old ; Dante is so conspicuous an instance as hardly to permit of citation ; Heine, at eleven, began his career of

---

[1] See also the famous lines in *The Island :*

" The infant rapture still survived the boy,
And Loch-na-gar with Ida looked o'er Troy."
(*Poems*, 1903, v. 609.)

[2] This is the Highland Mary of local tradition. She was the daughter of James Robertson, a farmer of Deeside, and was of gentle birth through her mother—tracing her descent, indeed, to Macdonald the Lord of the Isles. " She died at Aberdeen, in 1867, aged eighty-five " (*Poems*, i. 192).

passion with the idyll of Little Veronica. Like Byron, Heine never forgot his childish love; but, unlike Byron, he beheld her die while she was still a child. Hazel-eyed Mary Duff married, at eighteen, an eminent wine-merchant [1]; and it is Byron's narrative of his reception of that news which makes the episode so singularly differ from other records of precocious passion. When he was sixteen (1804) his mother one day told him that she had had a letter from Edinburgh saying that his old sweetheart, Mary Duff, was married. "And what was my answer? I really cannot explain or account for my feelings at that moment; but they nearly threw me into convulsions, and alarmed my mother so much that, after I grew better, she generally avoided the subject—to *me*—and contented herself with telling all her acquaintance. . . . We were both the merest children. I had and have been attached fifty times since that period; yet I recollect all we said to each other, all our caresses, her features, my restlessness, sleeplessness, my tormenting my mother's maid to write for me to her, which she at last did, to quiet me. . . . I remember, too, our walks, and the happiness of sitting by Mary, in the children's apartment, at their house not far from the Plain-stones at Aberdeen, while her lesser sister Helen played with the doll, and we sat gravely making love, in our way.

"How the deuce did all this occur so early? where could it originate? I certainly had no sexual ideas for years afterwards; and yet my misery, my love for that girl were so violent that I sometimes doubt if I have ever been really attached since. . . . Hearing of her marriage . . . was like a thunderstroke—it nearly choked me—to the horror of my mother and the astonishment and almost incredulity of everybody. . . . How very pretty is the perfect image of her in my memory—her brown, dark hair, and hazel eyes; her very dress! I should be quite grieved to see *her now*; the reality, however beautiful, would destroy, or at least confuse, the features of the lovely Peri which then existed in her, and still lives in my imagination, at the distance of more than sixteen years".

Again, in 1815, writing to one Mrs. Hay, a cousin of Mary, he says, "I never forgot her, and never can. . . . I have the most perfect idea of her as a child"; and a year later Major Pryse Lockhart Gordon heard the same confidence. "We met at the dancing-school", [2] added Byron—and most of us have pirouetted through a similar idyll.

What the episode demonstrates, then, is not so much unusual precocity of feeling, as unusual violence in the expression of that

---

[1] Mr. Robert Cockburn, of Edinburgh and London. There is a long reference to Mary Duff in Ruskin's *Prӕterita*, i. 169.

[2] P. L. Gordon, *Personal Memoirs*, ii. 321–22.

instinctive masculine egotism which revolts at the capture by another of the once desired woman. Most boys of sixteen would have felt and looked for the moment mortified ; Byron was " thrown nearly into convulsions ". His sensibility was at any time excessive ; we shall see that, at this time, he was in the throes of Mary Chaworth's rejection of him for John Musters. Now here was another beloved Mary, and another proof that he could be forgotten. With remembrance of our own young vanities and their frequent wounds, even feminine readers will refuse to wonder with him over the intensity of his childish love. Not *that* was wonderful—but the intensity of his vanity, and of his generic masculine egotism.

In 1794 he had become heir to the title. In May 1798, his grand-uncle died at Newstead Abbey, and he became George Gordon, sixth Lord Byron.

CHAPTER II

EARLY BOYHOOD—1798–1801

The Chaworth Duel—Byron's inheritance—Rochdale and Newstead Abbey—Arrival at Newstead—May Gray—Nottingham : Lavender and Rogers—Move to London—Care of the twisted foot—Dr. Glennie of Dulwich—Mrs. Byron's character—The first dash into poetry—Margaret Parker

HE ran up to his mother on the day after his accession to the peerage and asked her if she saw any difference in him since he had been made a lord, for he could see none himself. But he was soon to feel acutely one difference. On the morning that his name was first called at the Grammar School with the title of *dominus* attached, he found himself so pierced by emotion as to be unable to give the " adsum ". The round-eyed amazement of his schoolfellows added to the drama ; speechless still, the small Baron at last burst into tears. In its intensity, and its departure from the national ideal in such matters, this (like many other things that he did) is a complete epitome of his relations with " the world ".

No communication of any kind had been held with the former lord, who on the few occasions of mentioning his heir at all would speak of him as " the little boy at Aberdeen ". Acquaintance with William, fifth Baron Byron, would, however, have afforded scant enjoyment to any one. He had lived under a cloud since the notorious Chaworth Duel in 1765 ; and the cloud was not only black, but charged with the lightning of every kind of scandal. His wife [1] had been unable to live with him ; and however exaggerated the tales of his brutalities to her (they were still current in the neighbourhood in 1830) there must have been some foundation of misery on which to build them. " He had thrown her into the pond at Newstead " ; " he had shot his coachman in a fit of fury, flung the body into the carriage where his wife sat alone ; then had mounted the box and driven her for miles through the darkness in that companionship ". These things are not to be believed ; but about what type of

---

[1] She was the daughter and heiress of Mr. Charles Shaw, of Besthorpe Hall, Norfolk. She married him in 1747, and died in 1788, the year of our Byron's birth.

12

man are they invented ?   Something gives rise to the fell imaginings ; it may be excusable when all is known ; but it is there.
The Calumniated Angel is a myth.

The Chaworth Duel had been more or less forced upon him.
Mr. Chaworth [1] was a fire-eater ; and the subject of their quarrel
was one which has ever, in the hearts of country gentlemen,
aroused strong passions—namely, the preservation of game.
Chaworth was of the most stringent severity for poachers ; Lord
Byron (very characteristically) maintained that the way to
have game was not to preserve at all.   It came to a wager ;
Chaworth declared that he had more birds on five acres than his
neighbour on all his estates, and Lord Byron proposed a bet of
one hundred guineas.   A third person intervened : " such a
bet could never be decided " ; and the conversation seemed
to diverge.   But Chaworth soon broke out again, and this time,
instead of a wager, it was a challenge.   He then left the room
much excited.   " Had he been hasty ? " he demanded of a friend,
and seemed uneasy ; but Lord Byron had followed.   The angry
men ordered a waiter—the quarrel took place [2] on the occasion
of the Notts Club Dinner at the Star and Garter Tavern, Pall
Mall—to show them to an empty room.   He did so, and placed
on the table one small tallow candle.   By this light they fought,
with swords.   In a few minutes the bell rang ; the waiter
entered, and found Mr. Chaworth supported in Lord Byron's
arms, and mortally wounded.   Chaworth had made the first
pass, through his opponent's waistcoat, and thought he had
killed *him* ; but while he was asking the peer if he were in truth
so sorely hurt, "Lord Byron shortened his sword, and stabbed
him in the belly ".   Chaworth was carried to his own house,
where he died, lamenting his folly in fighting in the dark, for
that was what had led to his mistake : his sword, instead of
being in Lord Byron's breast, had been merely entangled in the
waistcoat.   Lord Byron was tried by his peers at Westminster
Hall in April of the same year, and found guilty of manslaughter [3] ;
but by an old statute ordaining that " in all cases where clergy
are allowed, a Peer is to be dismissed without burning in the hand,
loss of inheritance, or corruption of blood ", this Peer escaped
all punishment, and was immediately dismissed " on paying
his fees ".

Such is one version of the famous Chaworth Duel, over which

[1] He was the great-grandson of George Chaworth, created (1627)
Viscount Chaworth of Armagh, whose daughter Elizabeth married William,
third Lord Byron, grandfather of the Wicked Lord.   See note at end of
chapter with reference to the Duel.

[2] On January 26, 1765.

[3] The coroner's jury had given a verdict of wilful murder.   Lord
Byron was consequently imprisoned in the Tower.

the slayer's grand-nephew was to ponder so moodily when, in
process of time, he fell in love with the victim's grand-niece.

William, fifth lord, called by the country-folk The Wicked,
lived thenceforth in utter seclusion for twenty-four years.[1]
He always went armed ; and when, by a particular exception,
an old friend once dined with him, a case of pistols was placed
on the table, as if it were part of the dinner-service and as probably
to be used. He kept but two servants : old Joe Murray, after-
wards to be the favourite of our sixth lord ; and a woman who was
dubbed by the neighbourhood Lady Betty—a nickname obvious
in its implication. The only other inmates of Newstead Abbey
were a colony of crickets, which he spent much time in feeding
and training. They did come to know his voice, and would even
obey his call ; and our Byron used to relate, on the authority of
Joe Murray and Lady Betty, that on the day of the fifth lord's
death the crickets left the house in a body and in such numbers
that " you could not cross the hall without treading on them ".

To such a being did the boy succeed—and to what inherit-
ance ? To an inheritance which had been deliberately ruined
for revenge upon an only son. The grounds and house of New-
stead had been allowed to fall into helpless decay ; five thousand
pounds' worth of oaks [2] had been cut down (for the old lord,
despite his sordid way of life, had the family knack of impecuni-
osity) ; worst of all, the Lancashire estate of Rochdale had been
sold—and sold illegally, both sellers and buyers being perfectly
aware of the inability to make out a title. But Lord Byron did
not care, and the purchasers shrewdly calculated that by the
time the tort could be set aside, they would have indemnified
themselves for any pecuniary loss which their dispossession
might then bring about.[3] For Rochdale was very rich in coal.

---

[1] " When compelled by business to go to London, he travelled as
Mr. Waters " (Dallas, *Recollections*, etc., 1824).

[2] One splendid oak, known as the Pilgrim's, which stood and stands
near the north lodge of the park, was bought in by the neighbouring gentry
and made over to the estate. " Perhaps " (says Mr. E. H. Coleridge,
Poems, vi. 497) " by the Druid oak [in *Don Juan*, xiii. 56] Byron meant to
celebrate this ' last of the clan ', which, in his day, before the woods were
replanted, must have stood out in solitary grandeur ".

[3] The Rochdale estate had been in the Byron family since the time
of Edward I. When Sir John Byron was, under Charles I (1643), raised
to the peerage, he was entitled Baron Byron of Rochdale in the county
of Lancaster. He had been a devoted partisan of the King. " Sir John
Biron," says the writer of Colonel Hutchinson's Memoirs, " . . . and all
his brothers, bred up in arms, and valiant men in their own persons, were
all passionately the King's." Seven brothers of the family, indeed, had
fought at Edgehill. Newstead was besieged by the Parliamentarians ; at
Charles I's death, the Parliament sequestered the Byron estates, but they
were restored immediately on the accession of Charles II.

Legal proceedings to recover the estate were begun by Byron's advisers in 1805. It may be said at once that the delays were so interminable—fresh points arising at every stage—that he found himself obliged to sell Newstead long before he regained Rochdale, which, according to his solicitor and agent, John Hanson, was worth three Newsteads. How harassing these postponements were can best be displayed by passages from his many adjurations to that agent, whose probity was only equalled by his dilatoriness. One letter bears date July 19, 1814. " Pray think of Rochdale ; it is the delay which drives me mad. I declare to God, I would rather have but ten thousand pounds clear and out of debt, than drag on the cursed existence of expectation and disappointment which I have endured for the last six years, for six months longer, though a million came at the end of them ". And again in a letter to John Murray, referring to Hanson, and dated August 21, 1817, he wrote : " The devil take everybody : I never can get any person to be explicit about anything or anybody, and my whole life is passed in conjectures of what people mean ".

In 1823, the year before his death, having at last regained the estate, he sold it to Mr. James Dearden—with whom he had been in litigation all along, for Dearden was the lessee of the coal-pits—for thirty-four thousand pounds, " a very low price ", as the *Blackburn Mail* for March 10, 1824, commented. The money was devoted to the Greek cause.

So much for one inheritance. And what of Newstead, the inheritance of the heart, as Rochdale should have been of the pocket ? Newstead Abbey, Notts, in the heart of the Sherwood Forest, the Robin Hood country,[1] had been with the Byrons since the time of Henry VIII. The priory had been founded and dedicated to God and the Virgin by Henry II, in expiation for the murder of Thomas à Becket, and its monks were of the order of St. Augustine.[2] They surrendered in July 1539,

---

[1] About five miles south-west of Mansfield, " whose size, antiquity, and ancient privileges make it the capital of the Forest".

[2] They appear to have been high in the Royal favour, no less in spiritual than in temporal concerns. In the fifth lord's lifetime there was found in the lake at Newstead a large brass eagle, in the body of which was discovered a secret aperture, containing many legal deeds of rights and privileges. One was a grant of full pardon by Henry V for every possible crime (and there is added a long catalogue of such) which the monks might have committed previous to the 8th of December preceding ! At the sale of the old lord's effects in 1776–77, this eagle, together with three candelabra found at the same time, was purchased by a watchmaker of Nottingham, and passed from his hands into those of Sir Richard Kaye, who was a prebendary of Southwell Minster. It now serves as a lectern in that church.

the thirty-first year of Henry VIII's reign ; and in May 1540, the King granted Newstead and all its appurtenances to Sir John Byron, " little Sir John with the Great Beard ". Sir John made it into a " castellated dwelling ", and preferred it to the Lancashire house. Horace Walpole visited Newstead in 1760 (during the less insane years of the fifth lord's reign) and wrote : " It is the very Abbey. The great East window of the church remains and connects with the house ; the hall entire, the refectory entire, the cloister untouched, with the eastern cistern of the convent, and their arms upon it ; a private chapel quite perfect. The park, which is still charming, has not been so much unprofaned ; the present lord has lost large sums, and paid part in old oaks, five thousand pounds' worth of which have been cut near the house. In recompense he has built two baby forts, to pay his country in castles for the damage done to the navy, and planted a handful of Scotch firs that look like ploughboys dressed in old family liveries for a public day. . . . Newstead delighted me. There is grace and Gothic indeed ".

Walpole wrote before the days of deliberate despoilment, in which the oaks were sacrificed to malice rather than to necessity ; but already one of the many saws about the Byrons had been brought to an early stage of fulfilment through the hatred of the country-side for the fifth lord. Mother Shipton had declared that " when a ship laden with *ling* should cross over Sherwood Forest, the Newstead estate would pass from the Byron family ". This might well have seemed a promise of their keeping it for ever—since what could be more improbable than the necessary concatenation ? But Lord Byron, to get the full enjoyment of his naval forts upon the lake, used in his more sociable days to amuse himself with sham fights, and for these had vessels built for him at a seaport on the eastern coast. The largest of them was brought on wheels through the Forest to Newstead ; and in order to bear out Mother Shipton and spite the detested owner, the people ran beside the ship, heaping it with heather (for which ling is the Nottinghamshire word) all the way along. *They* did their part ; but who shall name the agent for the rest of that fulfilment ?

In the late summer of 1798, Mrs. Byron and her son left Aberdeen for Newstead. So ended the Scottish sojourn, which was never repeated—though he kept alive to the last an affection for the Auld Lang Syne of it all. The first tour in Greece " carried me back to Morven " [1] ; and in the second expedition (says Moore)

---

[1] A lofty mountain in Aberdeenshire.

the dress chiefly worn at Cephalonia included a jacket of the Gordon tartan.[1] But what of the other association which Scotland came to have for him—what of the *Edinburgh Review* ? Can we doubt, on even slender knowledge of him, that during that turmoil Scotland became the very Hades ? A girl, at the time of the notorious article, happened to observe that she thought he had a slight Scotch accent. " Good God ! " he cried, on hearing of it, " I hope not. I would rather the d——d country was sunk in the sea. *I*, the Scotch accent ! "

" He passed ", said a writer in the *Quarterly Review* for 1831, " as at the changing of a theatrical scene . . . from a shabby Scotch flat to a palace ". Well, if not to a palace, at least to something almost as fairy-tale-like in its difference from that abode whose furnishing, when sold on their departure, fetched £74. 7s. 7d. ! At the Newstead toll-house, Mrs. Byron, savouring the drama of the moment, asked the woman in charge to whom these woods might belong ?

" The owner, Lord Byron, has been dead some weeks ".

" And who is the next heir ? "

" They say it is a little boy who lives at Aberdeen ".

" And here he is, bless him " ! broke in the nurse—that May Gray around whom Moore hangs a garland of pathos, and whom John Hanson (in a letter to Mrs. Byron of September 1, 1799) [2] despoils of it with blunt and all too convincing hand. Let us compare the accounts, for this child's childhood is of poignant interest. If his nurse were really " another mother " to him, no overcharged fiction of young mental suffering surpasses his reality. " Such is his dread of the woman that I really believe he would forego the satisfaction of seeing you if he thought he was to meet her again. He told me that she was perpetually beating him . . . that she brought all sorts of company of the very lowest description into his apartments ; that she was out late at nights, and he was frequently left to put himself to bed ; that she would take the Chaise-boys into the Chaise with her, and stopped at every little Ale-house to drink with them " ; and Hanson adds that her conduct towards the boy was so shocking that it was the general topic of conversation among " dispassionate persons " at Nottingham.

When we examine Moore's garland in connection with this unmistakably truthful tale, we find him, perhaps, at nothing worse than his darling trick of the *suppressio veri*. In the very early days (he tells us), " she gained an influence over the boy's mind against which he rarely rebelled "—and this will, to the reader enlightened by Hanson, seem a not wholly ingenuous

---

[1] And see the famous *Don Juan* stanza (x. 18).
[2] *Letters and Journals*, i. 10.

statement of the possible case. Again, when putting on the appliances which the little twisted limb required, the woman "would . . . teach him to repeat the first and twenty-third Psalms ". Such teachings may be, have often been, associated with personal cruelties; and we read elsewhere that in the Aberdeen days, after the first and twenty-third Psalms had been duly repeated, the woman, leaving the child alone in that darkness which is so easily filled with every chosen horror of the mind, would slip out to her lover; while "Geordie," who was persuaded that the house was haunted, would get out of bed and run along the lobby till he saw a light, there to stand until he got so cold that he was obliged to go back to the warmth of the dreaded bedroom. And of course, in the mysterious and pathetic secrecy of babyhood, he never spoke of all this suffering to his mother until after May Gray had left them. Moore's wreath was twined of flowers supplied by herself to the doctor who attended her when she died in 1827—three years after the death in Greece. Dr. Ewing of Aberdeen was an ardent admirer of Byron, whose name just then was haloed like a saint's. May Gray would hardly have been human if she had not enskied herself. The doctor may be excused for his credulity, and all the more because she could show him keepsakes given her by the boy when she left Mrs. Byron's service in 1799, a date coinciding too well with Hanson's accusatory letter. The keepsakes were a watch—the first that he had ever possessed—and a full-length miniature of himself, painted by Kay of Edinburgh in 1795 (when he was six years old), which shows him with a bow and arrows in his hand, and long, curly hair falling over his shoulders. Both these treasures were given by May Gray's husband, after her death, to Dr. Ewing.

Thus stands the case for and against the nurse : and unfortunately Moore is a witness too often convicted of amiable evasions for us to take his word against the damning bluntness of the Hanson letter. I fear that the garland must be scattered, and a new pang added to the heartache with which we ponder on Byron's childhood.

They did not live at Newstead Abbey. Inured though Mrs. Byron was to poverty and hardship, the unspeakable desolation wrought by the fifth lord was more than she could face. Nottingham was chosen for their first home in the neighbourhood ; and there, in the hope of curing his lameness, the boy was placed in the hands of a man named Lavender, "trussmaker to the General Hospital". Again the doom ! Assuredly it seems that this child was singled out for misery. Lavender was the merest quack, and the merest brute as well, if we are to believe the earnest and reiterated testimony of a writer in *Notes and*

Queries, who says that when the boy was *living* [1] with him (and undergoing tortures from the maltreatment of the defective limb) " he was frequently sent across the street for Lavender's beer ".[2] The method adopted for the " cure " was to rub the foot with oil, then forcibly twist it round and screw it up in a wooden machine. This caused frightful suffering, visible to any one present, despite the bravery with which the boy endured it. Byron's teacher at this time was one Dummer Rogers,[3] who read Latin with him ; and Rogers one day broke out in urgent sympathy. . . . " Such pain as I *know* you must be suffering, my Lord ! " " Never mind, Mr. Rogers," said the boy. " You shall not see any signs of it in *me* ". He was fond of the kindly man ; and many years afterwards, when in the neighbourhood of Nottingham, sent him a message to say that he could still recite some lines of Virgil which he had read during the period of Lavender's torture. For the latter he had a burning contempt. One day he scribbled all the letters of the alphabet on a sheet of paper, combined them anyhow into words and sentences, and asked Lavender what language that was.

" Italian ", pronounced he—for he never could own to any ignorance ; and the boy burst into a shout of rapturous laughter.

Mrs. Byron was soon shown that Lavender's cure was merely the infliction of useless torture, and she then took her son to London to consult the renowned Dr. Baillie—brother of the still more renowned Joanna Baillie. She left Nottingham in the summer of 1799, and took a house in Sloane Terrace. From that time until the end of 1802 Byron was attended by Dr. Baillie, in consultation with Dr. Laurie, of 2 St. Bartholomew's Close, and special boots were made for him by an expert named Sheldrake in the Strand.[4] No cure was effected ; and judging by Laurie's letters to Mrs. Byron, it is not astonishing that the foot remained as it was. " I much fear his Extreme Inattention will counteract

---

[1] The " living " must have been during temporary absences of Mrs. Byron (that these took place is attested by Hanson's letter about May Gray), and the abode was at a Mrs. Giles's, in St. James's Lane (*Notes and Queries*, 4th series, iii. 284, 418, 561). The writer signed himself " Ellcee."

[2] " Lord Byron going to fetch a tankard of ale with one of Lavender's sixpences" was, says " Ellcee," one of the familiar sights of the locality. Lavender was what was termed a *sixpence-maker*. " Whenever he met with a pretty good half-crown, he would hammer it out to make sixpences from it " (*Notes and Queries*, 4th series, iii. 284).

[3] Rogers was an American Loyalist who was pensioned by the English Government. He lived at Hen Cross, Nottingham.

[4] In *The Lancet* for 1827–28 (ii. 779) Mr. T. Sheldrake describes " Lord Byron's case ", giving an illustration of the foot. But his account is as discrepant with the rest as they all are with each other. For a résumé of the opinions see *Letters and Journals*, i. 11–12.

every exertion on my part to make him better"; "I cannot
help lamenting he has so little sense of the Benefit he has already
received as to be so apparently neglectful "—for in the second
letter, written on October 2, 1802, Laurie had to complain that
the boy (who was then at Harrow) had spent several days in
London without seeing him. This was the last attempt made
at a cure; but Sheldrake, in later years, contrived a sort of
shoe which did away with the worst inconveniences.

While the two surgeons were tending the foot, Dr. Glennie
of Dulwich was doing his best to develop the head. In the
Lordship Lane of that pretty suburb stood the private school
of this first serious teacher of Byron, who was to be the first also
to form any well-considered view of his character. But Glennie
was in addition to learn the full force of Mrs. Byron's. Every-
thing that he thought desirable she opposed; she interfered with
his instruction, and when the master tried to stop the foolish
system of Saturday-to-Monday sojourns in London, Mrs. Byron
retorted by making them into weeks instead of week-ends.
With any tolerable opportunity, Glennie could have done
much; as things were, he could do almost nothing. Nor did
even the injunctions of Lord Carlisle,[1] the boy's guardian, avail
to influence Mrs. Byron. To every remonstrance from the
master she would reply by one of her paroxysms of passion,
and these, unlike her son's rages, were audible over the whole
school. Glennie overheard one day a painful morsel of dialogue.
One of the boy's companions bluntly came out with: "Byron,
your mother is a fool". "I know it ", he answered gloomily,
not knowing to what a degree the worse than folly was to injure
him in later life. For Lord Carlisle was soon irretrievably
alienated. He ceased to have any intercourse with his ward's
mother, and when Glennie once again implored his intervention,
he replied, "I can have nothing more to do with Mrs. Byron.
You must manage her as you can ". No one had ever succeeded
in managing her, and Glennie failed with the rest. . . . Natures
like hers make the constant problem of the observer. She
had a warm heart, courage, generosity, some shrewdness, and
a crazy kind of devotion. Yet she made the misery, and
might easily have made the ruin, of her only child. What
practical care, after all, had she ever given him ? None in
his babyhood : where was the mother on all those haunted
nights in Aberdeen ? None, or far too little, in his physical
distress, or Lavender's peer beer-boy could not have been the
common gapeseed of St. James's Lane in Nottingham. None,
and worse than none, in his first really vital contact with the

---

[1] He was the son of Isabella Byron, daughter of the fourth Lord Byron,
by her marriage with the fourth Earl of Carlisle.

outer world, or Glennie would have been permitted to do what
he could, and the guardian, influential and prepared at least
for duty-kindness, would not have been fatally estranged. It
would have been better for Byron, as Elze comments, to be
a " double " orphan. No relative could have proved a more
infelicitous guardian than his mother proved. Her sudden
gusts of maudlin tenderness (in which his eyes were pronounced
to be as beautiful as his father's) became, we may well suppose,
as abhorrent as her gusts of loud-mouthed fury—and yet the
boy was warm-hearted, generous, kind. As he grew up, he
was forced into deception that she might not haunt and disgrace
him ; he wrote to her, when he did write (but it is remarkable
how dutiful he was in that respect), with frequent cold rejection
of advances which would end, as he knew, in only one way.
His deep and bitter suffering shows itself in various forms through-
out his letters to the one woman who did, for a time, retain him
by the proverbial silken thread—his half-sister, Augusta Leigh,
then Augusta Byron. But what profound, what inexpressive,
anguish lay beneath the brilliant mockery, and the stinging
satire, and the outraged accusations of destiny, only those
whose experience has been similar can in any degree compute.
No pain is like it, since (as he was himself to cry when she lay
dead—and what must not the words have carried beyond the
hackneyed surface pathos ?) " We have only *one* mother."

The year 1800 is a notable one to Byron's biographer, for in
it he made his " first dash into poetry ". This adventure was
in honour of his second first love—if one may use a term which
occupation with his early history soon makes indispensable.
The result of the dash has perished, but the name of its victim
remains. She was his first cousin, Margaret Parker,[1] " one of
the most beautiful of evanescent beings ". Few girls, indeed,
have left a more exquisite memory in a lover's heart. " She looked
as if she had been made of a rainbow, all beauty and peace ".
So he wrote in a diary of 1821. Margaret died at fifteen of
consumption, two years after their meeting ; and Augusta Byron
went to see her shortly before the end. Augusta happened
casually to mention his name. He knew nothing of Margaret's
illness (" being at Harrow and in the country at the time ") ;
it was plainly not a continued episode—but as the sister spoke,
the girl's shadowed face flushed into vivid, lovely colour to the
very eyelids. No wonder that he never forgot her ! But the
elegiac verses which he wrote in 1802, the year of her death

[1] Charlotte Augusta, daughter of Admiral, and sister of Captain " Jack ",
Byron, married Christopher Parker, son of Admiral of the Fleet Sir Peter
Parker, Bart. ; and this Margaret was her daughter.

(though he, in the diary, says " Some years after "), are deplorable.
Frigidly correct in such technique and such sentiment as they
aspire to, they are the one dull element in an idyll as transparent
in its beauty as the memory she left behind.

Note on the Chaworth Duel

" The Coroner's jury brought in a verdict of Wilful Murder, and on
the presentation of their testimony to the House of Lords, Byron
pleaded for a trial ' by God and his peers,' whereupon he was arrested
and sent to the Tower.   The case was tried by the Lords Temporal
(the Lords Spiritual asked permission to withdraw), and after a defence
had been read by the prisoner, 119 peers brought in a verdict of ' Not
guilty of murder ; guilty of manslaughter, on my honour '.   Four peers
only returned a verdict of ' Not guilty '.   The result of the verdict was
that Lord Byron claimed the benefit of the statute of Edward VI, and
was discharged on paying the fees.

" The defence . . . is able and convincing . . . the accused con-
trived to throw the onus of criminality upon his antagonist.   It was Mr.
Chaworth who began the quarrel . . . it was he who insisted on an
interview, not on the stairs but in a private room, who locked the door,
and whose demeanour made a challenge ' to draw ' inevitable . . . Lord
Byron came to close quarters with his adversary, and ' as he supposed,
gave the unlucky wound which he would ever reflect upon with the
utmost regret ' " (Poems, iv. note to p. 542).

The poet, in his famous letter to Coulmann of 1823, said that so
far from feeling any remorse for having killed Mr. Chaworth, who was a
fire-eater (spadassin) . . . his grand-uncle " always kept the sword
. . . in his bed-chamber, where it still was when he died " (Elze, Life of
Byron, Authorised translation, 1872, Appendix, p. 445).

CHAPTER III

HARROW—1801–1805

Dr. Drury of Harrow—Lord Carlisle—Friendships : Clare, Delawarr, Wingfield, Long—Intellectual development—Oratory—First letters—Turbulence at Harrow—The quarrel with Dr. Butler—End of schooldays

HE had been two years with Dr. Glennie when Mrs. Byron finally flamed forth. She declared herself dissatisfied with his progress : he must go to a public school. Lord Carlisle was appealed to, and, remembering former encounters, he hastily acquiesced. And so, at thirteen (April 1801), the boy entered at last upon the manner of life which properly belonged to his rank, and entered upon it dispossessed of every advantage—for, peer of the realm [1] though he was, he came (and his schoolfellows knew he came) from social circles wholly undistinguished, with a fortune that corresponded in no way to his title, and, despite a rich store of odd general knowledge, as half-baked in the formal school education as he was in everything else. When to all this is added his lameness, we can figure to ourselves the state of mind which made him write in later life : " I always *hated* Harrow till the last year and a half ".

John Hanson, on bringing him to the school, had warned the Head Master, Dr. Joseph Drury, that his education had been much neglected, but " thought there was a *cleverness* about him." Drury was at once convinced not only of that —" there was mind in his eye "—but of something far more valid for the boy's immediate happiness. He perceived that it was a wild mountain-colt that Hanson had left behind, but the colt, he thought, was " to be led by a silken string rather than by a cable "—and he obeyed the intuition. Wisest of his indulgences was that for the supersensitive vanity which was so marked a trait in Byron. The new boy, hearing from a comrade that many younger than himself were immensely more advanced in learning, fell into a mood of deep dejection. He would be placed in a class below these juniors—he would be

---

[1] At Dulwich School he had been nicknamed the Old English Baron from his " frequent boast of the superiority of an old English Barony over later creations " : a kind of vapouring soon cut short at Harrow.

humbled and degraded—everything would be hopeless! Drury divined the apprehensive misery, and promised him that he should not be placed at all until it could be with boys of his own age. From that moment he revived, and soon his shyness (he suffered much through life from shyness) began to give way. The master kept a discreet look-out, and found some of his first impressions confirming themselves. When, not long afterwards, Lord Carlisle expressed a wish to see him, Drury hastened up to London. Carlisle was anxious to discuss future prospects, and to hear his view of the boy's abilities. " He will never be a rich man," said the guardian. Drury made no comment on that, but remarked with emphasis, " He has talents, my lord, *which will add lustre to his rank.*"

Lord Carlisle raised his eyebrows. " Indeed ! " said he coldly ; and Drury, with some repugnance, felt that he would rather have been told of mediocrity in mind as well as in fortune.

The truth was that Mrs. Byron had left an indelible impression on Frederick Howard, Earl of Carlisle—at one time among the most prodigious dandies of his period, and now a perfect type of the reformed rake. He desired to be kind ; but to *like* the son of such a woman, even to wish him well in any but the most conventional sense, was more than he could achieve. And probably he had disturbing memories of his own mother —that Isabella Byron (sister of the notorious fifth lord) whom Fox had satirised as " a recluse in pride and rags ", and who, when her eldest son was ten years old, had taken for second husband a mere baronet.[1] Isabella was, indeed, of the pure Byron tradition. She wrote *Maxims for Young Ladies*, and she also wrote an answer to one Mrs. Greville's *Ode on Indifference.* The answer contained two stanzas which most of her near relatives might have signed :

> " Let me drink deep the dang'rous cup
> In hopes the prize to gain,
> Nor tamely give the pleasure up,
> For fear to share the pain.
>
> Give me, whatever I possess,
> To know and feel it all ;
> When youth and love no more may bless,
> Let death obey my call." [2]

By the time her son comes on the stage of our story, he had been thoroughly sobered by much public office—Treasurer of the Household, Lord Lieutenant of Ireland, and so forth. He was also a renowned collector of pictures and statuary, and a poet to the extent of writing and publishing an enormous quan-

[1] This was Sir William Musgrave, of Heaton Castle, Cumberland.
[2] *L. and J.*, I. 36.

tity of mediocre verse—which, in process of time, became the
object of his young ward's savage satire.

The Byronic doom, then, had followed our youth in this
relationship as in so many others ; but now at last, as the school-
life developed, he was to know what kindness and judicious
authority and (above all) passionate friendship could mean. For
Dr. Drury he had a deep and reverent affection. In his letters
to Augusta at this period, and in his later diaries, there are
many warm tributes ; and Drury himself told Moore an enter-
taining anecdote of the later days of renown. None of the
publications of which the world was talking had ever been pre-
sented to him ; and, meeting in London just after *The Corsair*
had appeared in 1814, he asked Byron why, " as in duty bound ",
he had never sent his old master any of his books. " Because
you are the only man I never wish to read them ", Byron answered,
delightfully in the tone of them all ; but then, forgetting the
pose of a profligate abashed before the beloved mentor of youth,
he added eagerly, " What do you think of *The Corsair* ? "

Truly he could do nothing that did not epitomise himself
—all pose yet all spontaneity as he inveterately was ! *The
Corsair* was selling at " a perfectly unprecedented rate " (as
Murray had already panted), and not only so, but glorious whis-
perings were rife. " Its author was the veritable Conrad, the
actual Corsair ; part of his travels had been spent in real piracy " ;
and that author was helping on the craze with beautiful dark
hints ; and Drury was sure to have read it, and this would the
more deeply move him since he was sure to have been shocked ;
and above all, beyond all, *had* Drury read it, and read the others ?
. . . We may not mock overmuch—not those of us, at any
rate, who have published, and met old friends afterwards. And
he was, with Napoleon Buonaparte, the most talked-of creature
at that time alive !

But the joy of all others that Harrow brought about was
the discovery of the passionate heart. There had been the
love-affairs, to be sure, but the delights of comradeship were
of a happier order than such fervid heats. Not that the friend-
ships lacked ardour. " They were with me *passions* (for I was
always violent) " ; and indeed one hardly knows whether the
traits displayed are matter for smiles or sighs. Jealousy, flaming
perpetually, flamed mutually too. If *he* could take offence at
being addressed in a letter as my dear instead of my dearest,
and sulk because his correspondent said he was sorry another
boy had gone abroad—that correspondent could write *him* a
letter so extraordinary in its matter, so striking in its manner,
as to demand reproduction here.

To the Lord Byron

HARROW-ON-THE-HILL, *July* 28, 1805.

" Since you have been so unusually unkind to me, in calling me names whenever you met me, of late, I must beg an explanation, wishing to know whether you choose to be as good friends with me as ever. I must own that, for this last month, you have entirely cut me—for, I suppose, your new cronies. But think not that I will (because you choose to take into your head some whim or other) be always giving up to you, nor do, as I observe other fellows doing, to regain your friendship ; nor think that I am your friend either through interest, or because you are bigger and older than I am. No—it never was so, nor ever shall be so. I was only your friend, and am so still—unless you go on in this way, calling me names whenever you see me. I am sure you may easily perceive I do not like it ; therefore, why should you do it, unless you wish that I should no longer be your friend ? . . . Though you do not let the boys bully me, yet if *you* treat me unkindly, that is to me a great deal worse.

" I am no hypocrite, Byron, nor will I, for your pleasure, ever suffer you to call me names, if you wish me to be your friend. . . . I am sure no one can say that I will cringe to regain a friendship that you have rejected. Why should I do so ? Am I not your equal ? Therefore, what interest can I have in doing so ? When we meet again in the world (that is, if you choose it) *you* cannot advance or promote *me*, nor I you. Therefore I beg and intreat of you if you value my friendship—which, by your conduct, I am sure I cannot think you do—not to call me the names you do, nor abuse me. Till that time, it will be out of my power to call you friend. I shall be obliged for an answer as soon as it is convenient ; till then, I remain yours,

CLARE
" I cannot say your friend ".

The writer was thirteen, Byron seventeen, for the incident belongs to his last year at Harrow ; and what a picture does the letter set before us, of the handsome, cross youth (for his beauty was, at times, already remarkable), passing with his " new cronies," and breathing flame as he went on the small, hot-hearted Forsaken ! The quarrel was of short duration ; " our first and last ", he commented in an endorsement (he kept the letter all his life)—but later reproaches from the same pen seem to contradict that assertion.[1]

---

[1] Another school-friend, William Harness, said of his attachments at Harrow : " He required a great deal from [his friends]—not more, perhaps, than he, from the abundance of his love, freely and fully gave—but more than they had to return ".

The boy was John FitzGibbon, second Earl of Clare,[1] the Lycus of *Childish Recollections*, and the most beloved of all friends through all Byron's life. Not that they met often ; but the feeling for this " earliest and dearest " was one of those shrined things which can almost disdain the personal contact—though that, when it was vouchsafed, caused joy so uplifting that it was " like rising from the grave ". In the quasi-journal of 1821 there are two mentions of this friendship. " I never hear the word ' Clare ' without a beating of the heart even *now* ". The word, one may observe in passing, is eminent among the lovely both in sound and aspect ; this, when the dear memories were added, may have played some part in the emotion ; but it was rooted in genuine feeling, as the subsequent entry, which speaks of their meeting, strikingly demonstrates.

PISA, *November* 5, 1821

" [In] this collection of scattered things, I had alluded to my friend Lord Clare in terms such as my feelings suggested. About a week or two afterwards, I met him on the road between Imola and Bologna, after not having met for seven or eight years. . . .

" This meeting annihilated for a moment all the years between the present time and the days of *Harrow*. It was a new and inexplicable feeling, like rising from the grave, to me. Clare, too, was much agitated—more in appearance than even myself ; for I could feel his heart beat to his fingers' ends, unless, indeed, it was the pulse of my own which made me think so. . . . We were but five minutes together, and in the public road ; but I hardly recollect an hour of my existence which could be weighed against them ".

They met once more. In the following year Clare came for one day only to the salmon-coloured Villa Dupuy at Leghorn. " I have a presentiment that I shall never see him again ", Byron said when they parted, and his eyes filled with tears. He never did see him again, but one of the last letters from Missolonghi (March 31, 1824) was written to this dearest Clare, whom he had " always loved better than any (*male*) thing in the world ", who indeed was the only *male* human being for whom he felt anything that deserved the name of friendship.[2] " All my others were men-of-the-world friendships ".

But Clare, though the dearest, was not by any means the only Harrow intimate. Lord Delawarr [3] at first was given pride

---

[1] This earl's brother, Richard, succeeded him in 1851 as third and last Earl of Clare.

[2] This phrase occurs in an undated letter, presumably, from the context to Mrs. Shelley, of 1823 (Moore, p. 574).

[3] George John, fifth Earl Delawarr. He married, in 1813, Lady Elizabeth Sackville.

of place : " the most good-tempered, amiable, clever fellow in
the universe. To all which he adds the quality . . . of being
remarkably handsome, almost too much so for a boy ". Delawarr
was only nine years old at this time (1804), but already in the
preceding year a copy of verses had been addressed to him.

> " In thee I fondly hoped to clasp
> A friend whom death alone could sever ;
> Till envy, with malignant grasp,
> Detach'd thee from my heart for ever."

Envy seems to have treated the handsome little boy like a
shuttlecock, and tossed him back to Byron—quickly, however,
to receive him again with another lyric tagged on like one of the
feathers ; for a later address, still more poignant, is balanced
throughout between passionate reproach and freezing politeness :

> " For the present we part—I will hope not for ever ;
> For time and regret will restore you at last " . . .

Poor Delawarr was unequal, all along, to the strain.[1] Before
Byron left Harrow, a definite breach had taken place ; and
though he ultimately figured as Euryalus in *Childish Recollections*,
there *had* been a peremptory order to the publisher to omit the
whole character. They must have renewed their intercourse
in London, for the old schoolfellow who refused to spend with
him the day before he set out on his Albanian travels in 1809,
on the plea that he was engaged to go shopping with some ladies,
is believed by most of the biographers to have been Delawarr,
" who had recently in a marked manner withdrawn from him ".[2]
Byron was bitterly angry ; but it suggested a picturesque stanza
for *Childe Harold*.

> " And none did love him—though to hall and bower
> He gathered revellers from far and near,
> He knew them flatterers of the festal hour,
> The heartless Parasites of present cheer."

---

[1] In the *Life of the Rev. W. Harness* we find the following reference
(in a letter of 1869) to Lord Delawarr, who had lately died : " I believe
there was no actual quarrel with Byron. It was simply a case of incom-
patibility. The ardour of B. was more than D. could adequately meet "
(*Literary Life of the Rev. William Harness*, by the Rev. A. G. L'Estrange).

[2] They were in a way connected, for the families had twice inter-
married in the time of Charles I, the third Lord Delawarr's daughters,
Cecilie and Lucy, having both married Byrons. Cecilie's husband was
that Sir John who became the first Baron Byron. He left no heirs, and
his brother Richard succeeded. The first Lord Byron's *second* wife, by the
way, was a daughter of Lord Kilmorey, and the widow of Peter Warburton.
Of her Pepys, in his Journal, relates that she was the seventeenth mistress
of Charles II when abroad, and did not leave him till she had extorted
from him an assignment of silver plate to the value of £4000, " but by
delays, thanks be to God, she died before she had it."

Two other Harrovians, very dear, were the Hon. John Wingfield and Edward Noel Long, the Cleon of *Childish Recollections* :

> "On the same day our studious race begun,
> On the same day our studious race was run " ;

—and Long was the only intimate who went with him to Cambridge. Wingfield was one of the " juniors and favourites whom I spoilt by indulgence ". " Of all human beings I was perhaps at one time the most attached to poor Wingfield ". This friend, indeed, in one letter usurps Clare's title of earliest and dearest. Two stanzas of *Childe Harold* were consecrated to his memory [1] ; he died of fever at Coimbra, Portugal, on May 14, 1811, in his twentieth year. " One of the few one could never repent of having loved " ; " one whom I could have wished to have preceded in his long journey ".

Edward Noel Long, John Wingfield, and George, Duke of Dorset (who was Byron's fag at Harrow, and in the early days much beloved), all died in the early twenties. Dorset was killed by a fall in the hunting-field. This was in 1815, and Byron wrote to Moore a strange, morbid letter.

" I have just been—or, rather, ought to be—very much shocked by the death of the Duke of Dorset. We were at school together, and there I was passionately attached to him. Since, we have never met . . . and it would be a paltry affectation to pretend that I had any feeling for him worthy the name. But there was a time in my life when this event would have broken my heart ; and all I can say for it now is that—it is not worth breaking ".

Enclosed in his next letter were the well-known verses :

> " There's not a joy the world can give " . . .

—of which he " flattered himself " that they might pass for an imitation of the Irish poet. He must have written at the same time the lines beginning :

> " I heard thy fate without a tear." [2]

They are among the worst he ever composed, which is not surprising, since they were written expressly to declare the lack of any feeling.

---

[1] " And thou, my friend !—since unavailing woe " . . .
(Canto i. stanzas 91, 92.)

[2] These verses have been by some writers (myself among them) erroneously attributed to a later period—the Teresa Guiccioli period ; and said to have been written during her illness at Ravenna, when Byron thought she was going into consumption. They were not published until two years after his death, in a Paris edition of his poems.

If I have dwelt long upon the school-friendships, my reason for doing so is that they seem to me of great importance in reviewing his character ; and this not only because the Harrow period was formative in a high degree, but because (whatever they may have signified) these boyish experiences were, each in its varying development, recurrent through Byron's life. The brooding emotion of the attachment to Clare was repeated in the Mary Chaworth romance ; the distrust, reaction from distrust, and final loss of all illusion, which mark the Delawarr affair, are still more characteristic, are indeed a kind of epitome of Byronism ; while the grief of early and tragically sudden death —as in the cases of Long, Wingfield, and Dorset—is one of the sadnesses that haunted his career. He noted this himself. "Some curse hangs over me ", he wrote at twenty-three in recounting the death of a later friend; and again at thirty-one, " I never could keep alive even a dog that I liked, or that liked me ".

While all this luxuriance of emotion was unfolding itself, the intellectual growth was taking as determined a personal note. His general information on modern topics was " so great as to induce a suspicion that I could only collect so much information from *Reviews*, because I was never *seen* reading ; but always idle, and in mischief, or at play. The truth is that I read eating, read in bed, read when no one else read, and had read all sorts of reading since I was five years old ". He drew up, in 1807 at Cambridge, a list of the books he had been through : " the greater part of them before the age of fifteen ". It oppresses the imagination. Of historical writers the number cited would be by itself overwhelming ; his mind must have been gorged, the half undigested. " There is a way of *scouting* through books ", remarked the *Westminster Review* in 1830, commenting on Moore's infatuated awe before the list, " which some people call reading, and we are afraid much of the reading here set down was of that description ". History was the passion of his mind, we should remember [1]; but the biographical muster is also stupendous, for, after setting down many names, he adds, " with thousands not to be detailed ". Poetry came next ; philosophy was a bad fourth ; law, geography, " eloquence ", and divinity were comparatively nowhere. The note on divinity is frank. " Blair, Porteous, Tillotson, Hooker ", he enumerates, " —all very tiresome. I abhor books of religion ". There is a summing-up and a confession : " Since I left Harrow, I have

[1] Next to history, descriptions of travels in the East particularly interested him. " All books upon the East I could meet with I had read before I was ten years old ".

become idle and conceited, from scribbling rhyme and making love to women ".

At school his destiny was believed to be that of an orator. He was copious in declamation ; he selected always for speech-days the most vehement passages—such as Lear's address to the storm, and the tirade of Zanga in Young's *Revenge*. Drury was struck by all this, but the instance which led him to foretell an orator's destiny was a declamatory exercise composed by the boy himself. These efforts were always rehearsed, before public delivery, to the Head-Master ; and at the rehearsal Drury was already pleased with Byron's display. The day came ; all the other boys delivered the words that had been already " passed ", and Byron did the same in the beginning of his speech. But suddenly Drury realised that he was reciting something quite different from the draft—and reciting it with such boldness and rapidity as to alarm the listener. Surely he must break down ! But he went on to the end ; there was not a falter nor a stumble, and the whole seemed far more striking than the original. . . . When all was over, Drury inquired of him why he had altered the speech. He declared that he had not altered it. Drury pressed him for the truth. " I did not know that I had deviated by a letter ", the boy reiterated ; and the observant master believed and understood. " He was so impressed by the subject that he hurried on to expressions and colourings more striking than his pen had expressed ".

He was very idle. " Always in scrapes " ; " I rarely knew my lesson, but when I did know it, I knew it well ". His school-books were scribbled over with clumsy interlined translations . . . " the most ordinary Greek words had their English significa-tion scrawled under them ". His incorrigible laziness, joined to " his propensity to make others laugh and disregard their Employ-ments as much as himself ", soon got him into serious trouble. On his entrance to the school he had been placed in the house of Henry Drury, the Doctor's eldest son, who was an assistant-master. When the Christmas holidays of the 1802 term were over, Byron refused to return to Harrow unless he were removed from this care. Henry was quite as eager to get rid of him as he could be to go, but the Head had hesitated to consent until the boy's request was thus urgently made. He was then placed (January 1803) in Mr. Evans's house, and every one hoped that this was the dawn of a new era. By May 1 those hopes were dead. The date is interesting, for upon it the first of the vivid, pulsating things that we know as Byron's letters came into the world.[1] It is to his mother ; he was fifteen.

---

[1] In the *Letters and Journals* there are three of earlier date. The second to his mother, dated March 13, 1799, when he was eleven, has a hint of his

" I am sorry to say that Mr. Henry Drury has behaved to me in a manner that I neither *can* nor *will* bear. He has seized now an opportunity of showing his resentment towards me. To-day in church I was talking to a Boy who was sitting next me ; *that* perhaps was not right, but hear what followed. After church he spoke not a word to me, but he took this Boy to his pupil-room, where he abused me in a most violent manner, called me *blackguard,* said he *would* and *could* have me expelled from the School, and bade me thank his *Charity* that *prevented* him ; this is the message he sent me, to which I shall return no answer, but submit my case to *you* and those you may think *fit* to *consult.* Is this fit usage for anybody ? had I *stole* or behaved in the most *abominable* way to him, his language could not have been more outrageous. What must the boys think of me to hear such a message ordered to be delivered to me by a *Master* ? Better let him take away my life than ruin my *Character.* . . . Among other things I forgot to tell you he said he had a great mind to expel the Boy for speaking to me, and that if he ever again spoke to me he would expel him. Let him explain his meaning ; he abused me, but he neither did nor can mention anything bad of me, further than what every boy else in the School has done. . . . If you do not take notice of this, I will leave the School myself . . . better that I should suffer anything than this. . . . If you love me, you will now show it ".

Mrs. Byron sent this explosive to Hanson, who sent it to Drury. The result was little short of a formal apology for Henry's hasty word. " I am sorry ", wrote his father, " that it was ever uttered ; but certainly it was never intended to make so deep a wound ". He continued in a strain of particular and anxious affection for the boy. " He possesses, as his letter shows, a mind that feels, and that can discriminate reasonably on points in which it conceives itself injured. . . . I feel particularly hurt to see him idle, and negligent, and apparently indifferent ". . . . But even this letter ends on a hopeful note.

That Byron really was—as Drury had at first believed—the proverbial creature to be led with a silken thread is, I think, more than doubtful. The thread could draw him only so far as his heart would go too ; and his heart was hot, turbulent, and as easily drawn in the wrong as in the right direction. Reason

peculiar vivacity : " Mr. Rogers could attend me every night at a separate hour from the Miss Parkynses, and I am astonished you do not acquiesce in this Scheme, which would keep me in mind of what I have almost entirely forgot. . . . If some plan of this kind is not adopted I shall be called, or rather branded with the name of a dunce, which you know I never could bear " (i. 8).

rarely spoke, and when it did, was most often silenced. No matter how gentle it be, authority must ever smack of discipline ; and discipline had, for Byron, as little attraction as it is possible to conceive. There was something in the nature of the boy, as of the man, that was at bottom wholly unmalleable. He would learn and submit when he chose, and at no other hour ; and there was arrogance even in the submission. So *he*, Byron, had elected to act. When he did not so elect, all trouble must take its course, for the only thing that mattered was his election. Drury, in the end, sadly realised this—to the extent of desiring him to leave the school ; moreover, as we shall see, his very affection for Drury caused the final months at Harrow (under Dr. Butler) to be one long scene of violent insolence. Such a tribute could not gratify ; nor did it reflect any honour on Drury's training. But these were not the aspects to influence Byron. We may suspect that the picturesque, here as elsewhere, was the snare ; how scenic to hate and despise Butler because one had loved and respected Drury, and because Drury's brother had been a candidate for the prize that Butler won ! . . . I think there is no doubt that Drury, for all his sagacity, failed to comprehend the innate rebelliousness of his pupil's nature. The charm, the brilliancy, the quick warm heart—these he understood, and as it were succumbed to ; we might call the Head-Master of Harrow Byron's first conquest.

By the time the Christmas holidays of 1804-5 arrived, matters had come to a crisis. Byron spent the vacation with John Hanson's family in London, and told Hanson that he wished to leave Harrow. Hanson wrote to Drury, urging that the boy was too young to finish with school. Drury's reply, dated December 29, 1804, puts a startling gloss on the matter. " The wish ", he wrote, " originated with me. During his last residence . . . his conduct gave me much trouble and uneasiness. . . . If we part now, we may entertain affectionate dispositions towards each other, and his Lordship will have left the school with credit ". The Doctor's urgent advice was that he should go to a private tutor ; but Lord Carlisle and Hanson joined in an appeal to allow him to return to Harrow. Drury yielded, and Byron remained there till July 1805 ; " always ", as he confessed himself, " cricketing, rebelling, *rowing*—(from *row*, not boat-rowing, a different practice) and in all manner of mischiefs ". The rebelling came to a head on Drury's retirement from the head-mastership in March 1805. There were three candidates for the vacant chair—Mark Drury (his brother), Mr. Evans, and the Rev. George Butler, then Fellow, tutor, and classical lecturer at Sydney Sussex College, Cambridge. A strong party was formed for Mark Drury. At its head was at first young Wildman [1]; Byron had not then declared himself for any of the candidates. The Mark Drury faction was anxious to attach him, and one of the boys said to Wildman, " Byron, I know, won't join, because he doesn't choose to act second to any one ; but, by giving up the leadership to him, you may at once secure him ". Wildman, surprisingly enough, gave it up; and Byron " at once " took command.

Dr. Butler, who was only thirty-one, [2] prevailed ; and paid for his victory by becoming the Pomposus of two poetical attacks. Not only so, but he found himself faced by a fierce personal enemy in the boy, who was now a resident in his House. One day Butler found the iron gratings gone from the hall window. Byron had torn them down in a fit of rage. When summoned to give a reason for such violence, he answered coolly that they darkened the hall. Again, at the end of term, Butler, according to custom, invited the upper form to dine with him—a kind of royal command. Byron refused. He was asked, in the presence of other boys of the same standing, his reason for this second insolence.

" Why, Dr. Butler ", he replied, " if you should happen to come into my neighbourhood when I was staying at Newstead, I certainly should not ask you to dine with me, and therefore I feel that I ought not to dine with you ".[3]

The Pomposus portraits were mere caricatures, as he afterwards admitted, although the feeling of enmity endured for some time after he left Harrow. He wrote to his ancient foe, Henry Drury (by that time a close personal friend), in 1808, alluding to Butler : " We have only spoken once since my departure from Harrow in 1805, and then he politely told Tatersall [4] that I was not a proper associate for his pupils ". On February 21 of the same year, however, we find him reconciled to Butler ; and when in 1809 he went on his Albanian tour, he took with him a gold pen given him by the Doctor, and " a treasure of a German servant, named Fritz ", who had been recommended by Pomposus himself !

Thus, under a cloud, Byron left Harrow in July 1805— seventeen and a half years old. What did he bring away from the life which he had entered on so ill equipped ? He brought

---

[1] Many years later, when Colonel Wildman, he bought Newstead Abbey from Byron.

[2] " A Boy, o'er Boys he holds a trembling reign,
More fit than they to seek some school again."
These lines were in the MS. draft of *Childish Recollections*.

[3] Moore, on quoting this in his second edition, added a note to say that Dr. Butler assured him it had very little foundation in fact.

[4] John Cecil Tatersall was the Davus of *Childish Recollections* : " the laughing herald of the harmless pun." He died at twenty-four.

at any rate a much developed heart and body. Of the mind
we may suppose that the progress had followed inevitable lines.
Wherever he had been he would have learned what suited him,
and learned that only. . . . There was ground for some appre-
hension. Nearly all his close friends at Harrow had been much
younger than himself ; and outside the school, his chosen comrade-
ship had hitherto been with the son of one of his tenants at
Newstead, immeasurably his inferior in rank—and, again, years
younger. The misery of his home-life would oppress him the
more heavily now because his heart *was* developed—and because,
within these last two years, it had been much wounded as well.
The Mary Chaworth episode had begun in 1803 during the summer
holidays. . . . On the other hand, there was the University to
look forward to. Intimacies would spring up there, and though
individual ones might throb and smart as they had done at
Harrow, the boy now knew besides what comradeship was.
And there was hope in the great increase of his bodily activities.
He had given proofs of capacity for many athletic exercises.
" At Harrow I fought my way very fairly. I think I lost but
one battle out of seven ". He was noted for feats in swimming
—could mount a younger boy on his shoulders and dive thus
into the water. Cricket, too, he enjoyed ; his reputation for
the game rests on the match between Eton and Harrow on August
2, 1805,[1] when, says a note in the *Letters and Journals* : " Lord
Stratford de Redcliffe remembered seeing a 'moody-looking
boy' dismissed for a small score. The boy was Byron ".[2]

Despite the enmity with Butler, he was so unhappy at leaving
school that " it broke my very rest for the last quarter, counting
the days that remained. . . . One of the deadliest and heaviest
feelings of my life was to feel that I was no longer a boy " ; and
Harrow was sung in several poems of the earliest volume.

> " Again I behold where for hours I have pondered,
>   As reclining, at eve, on yon tombstone I lay "—

the famous Peachey grave in the pretty little churchyard that
adjoins the school, so well known to be his favourite resting-
place that the boys called it Byron's tomb. Here he would some-
times lie for hours, gazing over the wide and radiant prospect,
where the battlements of Windsor shone in the evening light,
and London rose, as it were, from the sea : " A fairy city of the
heart ", as he was to write in later years of a lovelier town.

Before the tomb, on the side looking towards Windsor,
there now stands a tablet inscribed with the opening of the *Lines*

---

[1] Played in the old cricket-ground in Dorset Square.
[2] Lord Stratford de Redcliffe also said that another boy " ran " for
Byron in this match (*Dict. Nat. Biog.*).

written beneath an Elm in the Churchyard at Harrow. The elm
(no doubt to preserve what may be still preserved of so historic
a tree) has been cut down to within a few feet of the ground;
there are no branches to droop or moan,

> " And seem to whisper, as they gently swell,
> ' Take, while thou canst, a lingering last farewell ' ".

But the thought of him follows every footstep that one takes
in the place. From the first sight of the high-set spires to the
climbing of the hill ; in the hall where he thrice stood to declaim
the " passionate speech " he loved : in the church where gleam
the tablets of the Drury family [1] and of Pomposus and his wife ;
in the churchyard, above all, where the air blows embalmed
with the scent of many crimson rose trees—Harrow-on-the-Hill is
lyrical of Byron. He found there, and there only throughout
all his life, " a home, a world, a paradise "—

> " Where friendship bow'd before the shrine of truth,
> And Love, without his pinion, smil'd on Youth."

---

[1] One of Henry Drury's sons was named Byron. His tablet is in the
church.

CHAPTER IV

MARY CHAWORTH

The Dream—The heiress of Annesley—Byron's rival—The trip to Matlock—John Musters prevails—The farewell—Meeting again : letters and verses—Mary's misery—Her death

ALONG with the school-life there had run, since the summer of 1803, the course of that love-affair whose influence upon him has been so grossly exaggerated by his biographers. But this has been because it was so grossly exaggerated by himself, in that most deceptive of all moods—the sentimental-reminiscent one. That *he* believed in the tears which, long after it had been for anything but sentimentality forgotten, the revocation of this episode could draw from him, adds no tincture of reality to the flow. *The Dream* (he said) " was written at Diodati in 1816, amid a flood of tears ". Yes ; and with just such tears every one of us can blot the page when we enter the region of self-pity. It is a mood most incident to, most fruitful for, poets ; let us rejoice that they enjoy it, and let us, for our part, see it as it is—sincere, but sincere through its very insincerity. If, through the thirteen years that had swept by since that boyish passion absorbed him, Byron had been constantly occupied with its remembrance, *The Dream* could never have been written. Just because it crept back into his consciousness, after many years of oblivion, in an hour of deep and ever-deepening bitterness, did those memories take substance with such authentic accent, such limpid truth and purity. They were almost as fresh to him as to his readers !

He had met Mary Chaworth first, probably, in London ; and during the summer holidays of 1803 the acquaintance was renewed at Nottingham. Mrs. Byron was at that time lodging in the town, awaiting her move to Southwell, where, in the latter part of the same year, she took up a fixed residence at Burgage Manor, on the Green. Newstead was let, in March 1803, to Lord Grey de Ruthyn, whom Byron came so passionately and mysteriously to detest ;[1] but at this time they were great friends, and he often slept at the Abbey. About three miles from New-stead, and nine from Nottingham,[2] stood (and stands) Annesley Hall, where Mary Chaworth lived with her mother, Mrs. Clarke. She was heiress to the estate, she was two years older than her boy-lover, and she was grand-niece of the Mr. Chaworth whom William, fifth Lord Byron, had killed. There was a Romeo and Juliet flavour in the situation which would have been enough in itself to attract Byron, overflowing as he was at this time with newly awakened sensibilities ; and the heiress of Annesley was plainly something of a coquette. A girl of seventeen and a schoolboy ; she in the dawning days of power, he still under discipline ; she volatile and he serious (as he said in later years)—the position is familiar, and its effects are almost invariable. Mary was considered handsome—a pronounced brunette, with dark eyes and clouds of dense black hair. Something of *espièglerie* lurks in the little oval face, which to modern eyes is barely pretty, though we can guess at a mobile charm when laughter lit it. Byron, on the other hand, is at fifteen not to be figured as attractive. He had a tendency to fatness (his mother was by this time monstrously corpulent), and his features had not yet refined and kindled into the beauty which was soon to reveal itself.[3] Moreover, he was lame, and Miss Chaworth loved dancing. She accepted his adoration; she may even, in very romantic moonlit hours, have imagined herself into a kind of reciprocity ; which of us has not passed through the melting moments of such a relationship ? She did give him her picture—which meant something in those days ; there is a tradition that she gave him a ring.[4] If she did, the instant consequence of her gift was the announcement of her engagement to " another ". The story goes that this Mr. John Musters—a fox-hunting squire of the neighbourhood—was bathing with Byron in the river which ran through his estate of Colwick Hall, and suddenly

---

[1] " I am not reconciled to Lord Grey, *and I never will*. He was once my *Greatest Friend*, my reasons for ceasing that Friendship are such as I cannot explain. . . . They are Good ones, however. He has forfeited all title to my esteem, but I hold him in too much *contempt* ever to *hate him* " (*L. and J.* i. 23).

[2] Newstead, Annesley, and Hucknall Torkard (his burial-place)form the three points of a triangle, each of whose sides may be about two miles in length (see " A Byronian Ramble ", *Athenæum*, August 23 and 30, 1834).

[3] Elizabeth Pigot, the platonic friend of later Southwell days, described him, at their first meeting in 1804, as " a fat, bashful boy, with his hair combed straight over his forehead ".

[4] This rests on the authority of the Countess Guiccioli, to whom Byron must of course have told it. But a ring is a more flattering token than a picture ; and pictures had turned into rings before then, and will so turn again.

perceived among the boy's clothes, scattered on the bank, a
ring which he recognised as Mary's. He at once took possession ;
Byron claimed it, but Musters refused to restore. They con-
tended hotly, and soon Musters mounted his horse and galloped
to Annesley Hall, there to confront the girl with the disputed
token. She confessed that Byron wore it as her gift—but she
solaced the rival by promising to declare without delay her
engagement to himself.

There is nothing very reprehensible in all this ; it merely
gives an impression of shallowness of feeling. She cannot have
cared much for either lover, one judges. More than probably
she did not ; of Mary Chaworth's real calibre we know practically
nothing. She was the bright Morning-Star of Annesley, and
she was the Lady of the Dream ; beyond that, she scarcely
exists for us, except as, in later years, a miserably unhappy wife.
. . . But let us see what effects her coquetry had upon the boy
who now for the first time met, on intimate terms, a " grown-up
young lady ". The earliest one was as violent as most things
were with Byron. After the summer vacation of 1803, he refused
to go back to school. Drury wrote to ask for an explanation,
got no answer, and then applied to Hanson. Hanson wrote
to Mrs. Byron, and on October 30 received the following answer,
which enclosed a letter to herself from the boy.

" The truth is, I cannot get him to return to school, though
I have done all in my power for six weeks past. He has no
indisposition that I know of, but love, desperate love, the *worst*
of all *maladies* in my opinion. In short, the Boy is distractedly
in love with Miss Chaworth, and he has not been with me three
weeks all the time he has been in this County, but spent all
his time at Annesley. If my son was of a proper age, and the
lady *disengaged*, it is the last of all connexions that I would wish
to take place ; it has given me much uneasiness ".[1]

This was the period during which he still hated Harrow ;
he hated Nottingham too, where his mother was then lodging ;
so that everything combined to keep him at Annesley and New-
stead as much as might be, and it is evident that Mary Chaworth
(though even then, apparently, known to be pledged to Musters)
showed him favour enough to keep him dangling at her side.
The Morning-Star here loses some of the lustre which Moore
lavishly assigns her as the paramount good influence of Byron's
life. She seems to emerge as an ordinary young lady of the
drawing-rooms, in love with a good-looking country clown, but
very willing to have a *soupirant*, however negligible, at her beck
and call. For we may safely conjecture that if Mary had told
her adorer to go back to Harrow, he would have gone. He

[1] *L. and J.* i. 16.

did not return until January 1804—missing the whole autumn term.

The summer holidays had been vibrant both with joy and anguish. There had been a trip with her party to Matlock and a *tête-à-tête* in a boat, during which they crossed, in a cavern, a stream which followed so close under a rock that the boat could only be pushed along by a stooping ferryman who waded at the stern. More than two people could not go in a boat ; and they must lie down. " I recollect my sensations ", he wrote in 1821, " but cannot describe them, and it is as well ". They were of a different kind in the evening, when the party went to one of the balls which were held in the Assembly Rooms at Matlock. Here the sources of pain were manifold, for Mary excelled in the dance, and it was the custom to accept as partners total strangers ; while he, forcibly excluded from all active share in the festivity, felt the old wound reopening with a pang that made all former pangs mere nothings.[1] He attacked her bitterly ; of course she laughed at him ; and, to complete his humiliation, a terrible guy of a Scotchwoman came up and loudly claimed him as a cousin. . . . " I hope you like your friend ! " he had hissed in Mary's ear as she came back from dancing with her stranger ; now she contrived to pass close to him in the throng, and to murmur mockingly, with a girlish grimace, " I hope you like *yours* ! "

But away from the Assembly Rooms all was bliss. He passed the summer vacation among the Malvern Hills—already familiar, for in 1801 he had spent the summer at Cheltenham with his mother, and had " watched the hills every afternoon at sunset with a sensation I cannot describe ". They were the first mountains he had seen since Lachin-y-gair and Morven ; and now, in 1803, he was looking at them with Mary. " Those were the days of romance ! " he said to Medwin in 1822. " She was the *beau idéal* of all that my youthful fancy could paint of beautiful ; and I have taken all my fables about the celestial nature of women from the perfection my imagination created in her—I say created, for I found her, like the rest of the sex, anything but angelic ".

In 1821 he wrote in the *Detached Thoughts*, recalling this sojourn : " We were a party—a Mr. W., two Miss W.'s, Mr. and Mrs. Cl—ke " (her mother and stepfather), " Miss M. and *my* M. A. C. Alas ! why do I say *My* ? Our union would have healed feuds, in which blood had been shed by our fathers ; it would have joined lands, broad and rich ; it would have joined at least *one* heart, and two persons not ill-matched in years (she

[1] Elze compares this with a " strikingly similar " incident in Scott's life ; but Scott " had the satisfaction of leading his fair one in to supper."

is two years my elder) ; and—and—what has been the result ?
She has married a man older than herself, been wretched, and
separated. I have married, and am separated ; and yet *we* are
not united ".

But the probabilities are as strong in one direction as in the
other. Elsewhere in the same quasi-diary, he says : " I doubt
sometimes, after all, whether a quiet and unagitated life would
have suited me." We may go further, and say that a quiet
and unagitated life not only would not have suited him, but was
unthinkable for him—wedded to mere routine though he often
showed himself. But that routine had to be of his own choosing,
and was most followed when living alone. No wife, at any rate,
could have shared it. And moreover, it was sometimes open
to interpretations which are foreign to the word. " If I stay
six weeks in a place, I require six months to get out of it "
—and what did he do, in some of the places !

Back at Annesley, after the Derbyshire excursion, he now
—having conquered a superstitious dread of the family pictures,
which he fancied to have " a grudge against him because of the
Duel, and to be ready to come out of their frames and haunt
him "—became almost a fixture in the house. The days were
spent in riding with Mary and her cousin, in sitting lost in dreams
beside her, and in shooting at a door which opened on the terrace
of the Hall, and which, when Moore wrote, still bore the marks
of his shots. There was music too ; Mary could play and sing,
and one of her ditties, the Welsh air " Mary Anne ", was very
often pleaded for. Mary Anne was her full name, not then so
overlaid with unromantic associations as we now have it—a
love-sick boy could gloat upon it without being more ridiculous
than usual. Very love-sick he must have been by this time,
for now there was no doubt that she was in love with " hand-
some Jack Musters ". " He was one of the most eminent sports-
men of his day ", said a writer [1] in the *Athenæum* in 1834 ; and
he was also, in a florid, stupid sort of way, very good-looking.
(A portrait of him by Reynolds, belonging to Lt.-Col. W. H. Poë,
was shown in the Japanese-British Exhibition of 1910.) She
had seen him first at a fox-hunt—" the Unspeakable in pursuit
of the Uneatable " ; but it was not so that she would, in those
days at any rate, have characterised him. No ; for she would
stand, on the famed Diadem Hill,[2]

> " Looking afar if yet her lover's steed
> Kept pace with her expectancy, and flew."

---

[1] " A Byronian Ramble," *Athenæum*, August 23 and 30, 1834.
[2] The spur of the long ridge of Howatt Hill, which lies about a mile to
the south-east of Annesley Hall.

The steed would have come along the road that winds up the common from Hucknall, says the same *Athenæum* writer ; and thither Mary's dark eyes gazed, and Byron's too :

" For his eye followed hers, and saw with hers "—

though not, we may suppose, with the same admiration for Jack Musters. To show the absorbed maiden a locket which an earlier love had given him (Moore thinks it may have been the exquisite dead cousin, Margaret Parker) can have availed little for solace against these hours of boyish jealousy ; we may conjecture that her attention and interest were perfunctory. And indeed it was during the latter part of the same holidays that the most poignant incident of the affair occurred. " He either was told of, or overheard, Miss Chaworth saying to her maid, ' Do you think I could care anything for that lame boy ? ' This speech " (says Moore, on the authority of Byron's own Memoranda) " was like a shot through the heart. Though late at night when he heard it, he instantly darted out of the house, and scarcely knowing whither he ran, never stopped till he found himself at Newstead "—three miles away. It gives us the measure of his young infatuation that so agonising a stab could be forgotten.

He went back to Harrow in January 1804, more deeply enamoured than ever, and passed the next holidays too in her neighbourhood. " I now began to fancy myself a man, and to make love in earnest ", he told Medwin—to whom, however, he told many a fib. For Medwin (John Cordy Jeaffreson's " perplexing simpleton ") was the dedicated victim of Byron's favourite game of mystification : Medwin would swallow anything. The story he heard differs considerably from Moore's, who assigns only six weeks to the whole of the Chaworth love-affair. Medwin heard that, in the holidays of 1804, " Our meetings were stolen ones, and my letters passed through the medium of a confidant. A gate leading from Mr. Chaworth's grounds to those of my mother " (plainly a fib, for Southwell and Annesley are several miles apart) " was the place of our interviews. But the ardour was all on my side. I was serious ; she was volatile. She liked me as a younger brother, and treated me and laughed at me as a boy. She, however, gave me her picture, and that was something to make verses on ".

With his return to Harrow in the end of 1804, the dream— if it could be called a dream—was over. He said his good-bye to her on the historic hill. With quiet voice and quiet face he spoke. " The next time I see you, I suppose you will be Mrs. Chaworth ".[1]

[1] Her husband, for some time, assumed her name.

" I hope so ", she replied.

That is Moore's account ; *The Dream* gives a different setting to the farewell.

> " Within an antique oratory [1] stood
> The Boy of whom I spake " . . .

and when the interview with " the Lady of his love " was over,

> " . . . he passed
> From out the massy gate of that old Hall,
> And mounting on his steed he went his way ;
> And ne'er repassed that hoary threshold more."

In the following year (August 1805) Mary was married to John Musters. There had been a letter from Byron to Augusta in June : " The later one makes one's self miserable with the matrimonial clog, the better " ; and to all correspondents he complained of utter ennui, besides the never-ending strain of the quarrels with his mother. He wrote, in after years, of Mary's marriage : " *This* threw me out again ' alone on a wide, wide sea.' In the year 1804, I recollect meeting my sister at General Harcourt's in Portland Place. I was then *one* thing, and *as* she had always till then found me. When we met again in 1805 (she told me since) my temper and disposition were so completely altered that I was hardly to be recognised. I was not then sensible of the change, but I can believe it, and account for it ". We may remind ourselves that between 1804 and 1805 had come the great change from school to university life—from boyhood to young manhood ; and also a prolonged residence with Mrs. Byron, which could not leave any temper unaltered for the worse.

Moore's account of Byron's hearing the news of the marriage is well known, and is told on the authority of " a friend who was present ". But John Cordy Jeaffreson pours contempt on the story, pointing out the similarity between it and the hearing of the same news about his child-love, Mary Duff—an incident, moreover, which had happened only the year before. [2] Mrs. Byron had then been sufficiently alarmed by her son's demeanour ; is it likely (asks Jeaffreson) that she would have repeated her— in the first instance unconscious—cruelty at so short an interval ? Moreover, the news can scarcely have been news ; the boy would either have known it already or have been hourly expecting to hear it, of neighbours so near, so intimate, and so prominent in

---

[1] " A small room built over the porch . . . and looking into the court-yard " (E. H. Coleridge, Introduction to *The Dream. Poems*, iv. 31).

[2] " When I was sixteen " (1804).

the social life of the place. Jeaffreson's point is striking. More
than probably, almost certainly, his explanation is the just one :
the name of Mary Duff got mixed, in the gossip of the tattling
little town, with the name of Mary Chaworth.

He met her again in 1808, when she had been for two years
a mother.[1] Mr. Chaworth-Musters invited him to dine at An-
nesley not long before he left England on his Albanian tour.
He did, then, revisit Annesley Hall ; " but " (says Mr. E. H.
Coleridge) " it is possible that he avoided the ' massy gate ' of
set purpose, and entered by another way ".[2] He has left three
descriptions of his feelings—one in prose, the others in verse.
The former was contained in a letter of November 3, 1808. " You
know, laughing is the sign of a rational animal . . . I think so,
too, but unluckily my spirits don't always keep pace with my
opinions. I had not so much scope for risibility the other day
as I could have wished, for I was seated near a woman to whom,
when a boy, I was as much attached as boys generally are, and
more than a man should be. I knew this before I went, and
was determined to be valiant and converse with *sang froid* ;
but instead I forgot my valour and my nonchalance, and never
opened my lips even to laugh, far less to speak, and the lady was
almost as absurd as myself. . . . You will think all this great
nonsense ; if you had seen it, you would have thought it still
more ridiculous. What fools we are ! We cry for a plaything,
which, like children, we are never satisfied with till we break
open, though like them we cannot get rid of it by putting it on
the fire ".[3]

The poems are the stanzas *To a Lady on being asked my
Reason for Quitting England in the Spring*, and the better-known
verses, " Well ! thou art happy ". The two-year-old daughter
had been exhibited—was it the conscious cruelty of the coquette,
or the unconscious cruelty of the new-made mother ?—and he
had found it hard to conceal his emotion.

> " When late I saw thy favourite child,
>   I thought my jealous heart would break ;
> But when the unconscious infant smil'd,
>   I kiss'd it for its mother's sake.

---

[1] Her eldest child, a daughter, was born in 1806. This daughter mar-
ried a Mr. Hamond of Westacre, Norfolk, and was living in January 1898,
aged ninety-two (*Poems*, i. 277).

[2] But is it certain that the dinner-party was at Annesley Hall ? It may
have been at John Musters's own place, Colwick Hall, which was also in the
near neighbourhood. There is nothing in Byron's letters to indicate which ;
and Mary seems to have " gone " to Annesley when she separated from her
husband.

[3] *Memoir of Rev. Francis Hodgson*, i. 105.

I kiss'd it—and repress'd my sighs,
  Its father in its face to see ;
But then it had its mother's eyes,
  And they were all to love and me.

> . . . . .

I deem'd that Time, I deem'd that Pride,
  Had quenched at length my boyish flame ;
Nor knew, till seated by thy side,
  My heart in all—save hope—the same.

Yet was I calm ; I knew the time
  My heart would thrill before thy look ;
But now to tremble were a crime—
  We met—and not a nerve was shook.

I saw thee gaze upon my face,
  Yet meet with no confusion there :
One only feeling couldst thou trace—
  The sullen calmness of despair."

Was she happy ? These verses are discrepant with the letter to Hodgson ; and when he tells her, in the other lyric, that he leaves England because he " could not view his Paradise, without the wish of dwelling there ", that while near her " he sighs for all he knew before "—we can hardly avoid asking ourselves, " What did *she* sigh for ? " . . . By this time, the jilted schoolboy was a dazzlingly handsome and experienced young man, against whom, too, as a budding poet, the mighty *Edinburgh Review* had thought it worth while to use all its thunder. What such a youth would have thought of John Musters we can well divine ; was there, that evening, already an indication that Mary had come to think something not greatly different ? She became, at any rate, a miserably unhappy wife. In 1813 she separated from Musters—whose infidelities and cruelties were flagrant—and went, with her children and a friend, Miss Radford, to live at Annesley. During this sojourn there was a proposal of a visit from Byron. He gives two accounts of it, which contradict one another. To Medwin he said, " She was at length separated from Mr. M——, and proposed an interview with me, but by the advice of my sister I declined it." In the letter to M. J. J. Coulmann (in 1823) this is the altered aspect which the incident acquires. " I had not seen her for many years when an occasion offered to me, January 1814.[1] I was upon the point, with her consent, of paying her a visit, when my sister, who has always had more influence over me than any one else, persuaded me not to do it ; ' for ', said she, ' if you go,

---

[1] I quote from *Poems*, 1903, i. note to p. 283, where Mr. Coleridge refers to *Letters and Journals*, in the edition of 1901. In the edition of 1904 of *Letters and Journals*, the passage runs : " I had not seen her for many years. When an occasion offered, I was on the point, etc." (vi. 234).

you will fall in love again, and then there will be a scene ; one step will lead to another, *et cela fera un éclat* '. I was guided by these reasons ".

An undated letter from Mary herself, preserved among the Byron papers,[1] leaves the point undecided. " If you come down to Newstead before we leave Annesley, [I] *see* no *reason* why you should not call on us. . . . We are very anxious to see you, and yet know how we shall feel on the occasion—*formal*, I dare say, at the *first* ; but our meeting must be confined to our *trio*, and then I think we shall be more at our ease. *Do write* me, and make a *sacrifice* to *friendship*, which I shall consider your visit ". She either wrote to him again or had written before, for he says to Augusta in an undated letter (certainly, however, of January 1814) : " M. has written again—*all friendship* —and really very simple and pathetic—*bad usage—paleness—ill-health*—old *friendship—once—good motive*—virtue—and so forth ". That would be a very exaggerated gloss to put upon any phrase in the letter from which I have quoted. Again, on January 12, he writes to Augusta : " More news from Mrs. *—all friendship* ; you shall see her ". Augusta was about to pay him a visit at Newstead. She stayed three weeks, " sauntering and dozing very quietly, and not unhappily ".[2] If he kept his promise of her seeing Mrs. Chaworth-Musters, there is no reference to the meeting.

In 1817 (when Byron had left England for ever) a reconciliation took place between Mary and her husband ; but she had been so bitterly wretched that she never regained health and spirits—she was, indeed, for some time in 1816 out of her mind, " and would sit for days and weeks alone and secluded, weeping over the poems which Byron had written to her ". In 1832, when rioters from Nottingham plundered Colwick Hall (the estate of Musters), she and her daughter were obliged to rush out and hide themselves in the shrubbery. The cold and the terror so shattered her that in February she died, at Wiverton Hall, near Nottingham. John Musters lived until 1850, and after his death every relic of his wife and her ancient family was sold by public auction.[3]

The " peculiar diadem of trees " had long been destroyed. In a fit of rage at the publication of *The Dream*, and the blazing publicity into which it brought his name (his wife was then living away from him in her own home at Annesley Hall), John Musters had them all cut down. The *Athenæum* pilgrim of 1834 spoke to a mechanic of the neighbourhood about this sacrifice.

" Trees that might be seen so far ! "

[1] See *L. and J.* iii. note to p. 7.   [2] *L. and J.* iii. 24 and 32.
[3] Karl Elze, *Life of Lord Byron*.

" Seen, sir ! " exclaimed the man ; " those trees were seen all over the world ".

This is all we know [1] of the relations between Byron and Mary Chaworth. His remark to Medwin that he found her, like the rest of the sex, anything but angelic, may well have no bearing except upon the early coquetries. She drew her own character, shortly before her death in 1832 (aged only thirty-six), in a letter to one of her daughters. " Soon led, easily pleased, very hasty, and very relenting, with a heart moulded in warm and affectionate fashion ". So she may indeed have been— that bright Morning-Star of Annesley, whose light was to be so clouded.

> " . . . —Oh ! she was changed
> As by the sickness of the soul ; her mind
> Had wandered from its dwelling, and her eyes,
> They had not their own lustre, but the look
> Which is not of the earth ; she was become
> The Queen of a fantastic realm ; her thoughts
> Were combinations of disjointed things ;
>
> .   .   .   .
>
> And this the world calls frenzy ; but the wise
> Have a far deeper madness. . . .
>
> .   .   .   .
>
> My dream was past ; it had no further change.
> It was of a strange order, that the doom
> Of these two creatures should be thus traced out
> Almost like a reality—the one
> To end in madness—both in misery."

---

[1] For allusion to a recent theory of Byron's later relations with Mrs. Musters, see Appendix III. : " Medora Leigh ".

CHAPTER V

SOUTHWELL—1804–1807

Burgage Manor—Augusta Leigh—Byron's letters from Southwell—
The Pigots—Social relations—His unhappy home-life—Flight to London
and Littlehampton—Harrogate—Theatricals at Southwell—Flirtation and
platonics—Life at Southwell—He leaves Southwell, and forgets old friends

HIS first stay at Mrs. Byron's new abode, Burgage Manor,
Southwell, was during the Easter holidays of 1804. It
was a square, homely-looking house, which she had
evidently taken furnished, for Moore speaks of the good library
belonging to the owner. Southwell is the typical small English
country town—very small, for at the present day it has a popula-
tion of only just over three thousand.[1] It stands, a few miles
north of Nottingham and east of Newstead, in an undulating
plain, rich in pasture-land ; and possesses two show buildings
—the fine old Norman Minster (where the Newstead monks'
brass eagle serves as lectern), and the ruins of a former palace
of the Archbishops of York. In this palace Charles I once took
refuge ; Cromwell besieged it, and quartered his cavalry in the
Minster. The Green is an open grassy space ; across it Burgage
Manor [2] and Mrs. Pigot's house faced one another. . . . Byron's
first letter thence is dated March 22, 1804. He had arrived
from Harrow that very day, and his mother having gone out
to " an assembly ", he seized the occasion to write to his half-
sister, with whom since 1802 he had been on affectionate terms.

Augusta Mary Byron was born in 1783, according to most
authorities, who state also that her mother died a year after-
wards. Lord Lovelace, in *Astarte*, gives (in the list of dates
appended to the volume) the year 1784 as that of her birth,
and says that Lady Conyers died in the confinement. Augusta
bore the courtesy title of the Honourable through her mother's
barony of Conyers. The little girl lived with her father and
stepmother while they were at Chantilly. Mrs. Byron brought

[1] When Elze wrote in 1872, the population was a little larger—3500 as
against 3161 to-day (1912).

[2] Said to be the house occupied—in 1905—by Mrs. Birdmere (*Poems*,
vii. 2).

her to London in 1788 ; but she was then (probably in view of
the expected confinement) handed over to the care of her maternal
grandmother, Lady Holderness,[1] and Mrs. Byron lost sight of
her, for Lady Holderness would have nothing to do with the
second wife of Mad Jack. Until 1801, the year of her grand-
mother's death, Augusta was wholly estranged from her father's
family. She lived with various maternal relatives until her
marriage in 1807 with her first cousin, Colonel George Leigh, of
the Tenth Dragoons, son of General Charles Leigh by Frances,
daughter of Admiral Byron. But in 1801 Mrs. Byron wrote to
her, condoling on the death of her grandmother, offering to bury
the past in oblivion, yet recalling, pathetically enough, a severe
childish illness through which she had nursed her. " These days
you cannot remember, but I never will forget them ". She
added that her son was at Harrow, " and I have now no desire
to keep you asunder ".[2]

He did not delay to give Augusta his impressions of South-
well. On March 26, " my ever dear sister " hears of overwhelming
dulness and ennui. Newstead is avoided, for the deadly and
mysterious detestation of Lord Grey de Ruthyn is in full swing,
and forms one among the many bones of contention with Mrs.
Byron, who understands it no more than any one else. " My
reasons will ever remain hidden in my own breast ". By April 2,
Southwell is a horrid place ; there is no society but old parsons
and old maids; he shoots a good deal, " but, thank God, I have
not so far lost my reason as to make shooting my only amuse-
ment ". Many of his neighbours do, " but they are only one
degree removed from the brute creation ". His mother's con-
versation, " though sometimes very *edifying*, is not always very
agreeable ". This is the first entrance of a theme which, in later
letters, develops all too brilliantly. On April 9, he informs her
that they are giving a party that night. " The principal *Southwell
Belles* will be present, with one of which, although I don't as
yet know whom I shall so far *honour, having never seen them*,
I intend to fall violently in love ". That will " at least have
the charm of novelty to recommend it ".

This party of Mrs. Byron's was probably the occasion of his
first meeting with Elizabeth Pigot, who became the Egeria—
wholly platonic—of later Southwell days. She thus described
to Moore [3] their introduction. " He was so shy that [Mrs.

[1] She had been renowned as " the lovely Dutch girl " (daughter of a
M. Doublette, of The Hague), and had married, in 1743, Robert d'Arcy,
fourth and last Earl of Holderness. Their only child was that Marchioness
of Carmarthen whom Jack Byron seduced.

[2] *L. and J.* i. 18.

[3] Moore, under the wing of the Rev. John Becher (another close friend of
Byron), called on the Pigots to collect material on January 22, 1828. It

4

Byron] was forced to send for him three times before she could persuade him to come into the drawing-room to play with the young people at a round game. He was then a fat, bashful boy with his hair combed straight over his forehead, and extremely like a miniature portrait that his mother had painted by M. de Chambruland. The next morning Mrs. Byron brought him to call at our house, when he still continued shy and formal in his manner. The conversation turned upon Cheltenham, where we had been staying, the amusements there, the plays, etc. ; and I mentioned that I had seen the character of Gabriel Lackbrain [1] very well performed. His mother getting up to go, he accompanied her, making a formal bow, and I, in allusion to the play, said ' Good-bye, Gaby '. His countenance lighted up, his handsome mouth displayed a broad grin, all his shyness vanished, never to return, and, upon his mother's saying, ' Come, Byron, are you ready ? '—no, she might go by herself, he would stay and talk a little longer ; and from that moment, he used to come in and go out at all hours, as it suited him, and in our house considered himself perfectly at home."

The Byrons all suffered more or less from shyness, and he, though with the Pigot household it was cast aside, preserved for long his dread of strangers. He would jump out of the window to avoid visitors ; he was often not less than rude to the other young men of the neighbourhood, and would leave their visits to him unreturned. But pride as well as shyness had something to do with this latter mode of behaviour. Sometimes the calls had been too long delayed ; sometimes the ladies of the family had neglected to visit Mrs. Byron, whom we may easily suppose to have been a great deal talked about, and whose narrow means [2] put her at a disadvantage in hospitalities. Her son perceived the position, which is a common one in English provincial society : the County was putting on airs, and the Town was putting out feelers. There were many pleasant

was a curious, if an undesigned, coincidence that the date should have been that of Byron's birthday. The Pigots remarked on it : " he would to-day have been forty ". Moore found Mrs. Pigot " a fine, intelligent old lady " ; on parting, she kissed his hand most affectionately, and, with a compliment to his own renown, said that it was as the friend of Byron that she valued him most. " She seems unwilling to allow that he had a single fault " (*Diary of Thomas Moore*, v. 249).

[1] The character occurs in *Life*, a comedy of F. Reynolds (*L. and J.* i. 32).

[2] She had been awarded, in 1799, a Civil List Pension—" on what grounds I know not ", says Moore—of £300 a year. (This was afterwards reduced to £200, and at all times most irregularly paid.) During Byron's schooldays she received £500 a year from the Court of Chancery for his education. When he went to Cambridge, she gave up this allowance to him, and at the same time applied for a personal allowance of £200 a year, but in 1807 this had not yet been granted (*L. and J.* i. 76).

houses open to them both in the latter ; the former disdained
his mother, and would soon weary *him* with the field-sports
which removed them so little from the brutes. He chose the
Town ; and having done so, soon cast off his misanthropy, was
to be counted on for all gaieties, and felt mortified and angry
if he were left out of any. Soon too (in the August of 1804) an
agreeable tribute to that dubious social position offered itself.
A strolling company of actors came to Southwell, and finding
that a nobleman was living in the place, at once approached
him for patronage. On August 8, he had the glory of attending
at a performance " bespoke " by his mother and himself. We
need not question his enjoyment : the patron, even at sixty, is
perennially blissful. What must sixteen—and a sixteen that
had suffered the scorns of the unworthy—have felt !

The principal people in Southwell were the Pigots, Leacrofts,
Housons, and of course the clergyman, Mr. Becher. At the
Pigots', as we have seen, Byron had a second home. There
were sons and daughters, and Elizabeth, his friend, was, we
gather, a good deal older than her Gaby.[1] His first letter to her
—she kept all from him that she or her family ever had, and
was the only one of his early correspondents who had the fore-
sight to do so—is dated August 29, 1804, from Burgage Manor.
She was evidently already devoted to his service—for she had
done a book-plate for him, and was knitting him a watch-riband
and a purse. Moore points out, in this letter, two characteristics.
His punctuality in answering : " Your note was given me by
Harry at the play . . . and now I have sat down to answer it
before I go to bed " ; and his love for simple ballad-music : " I
shall be happy to hear you sing my favourite, ' The Maid of
Lodi ' ". These two traits he preserved unaltered during the
remainder of his life. Of the choice in music we have already

---

[1] The Pigots followed Byron's career with enthusiastic interest. Eliza-
beth " regarded it as the business of her life and heart to preserve his
memory ". She died in 1866, at a good old age, still in Southwell. Her
eldest brother John, who was very intimate with Byron in 1806–7, lived
until 1871, when he died at Ruddington, Notts, aged eighty-six. Harry
Pigot, the younger brother, was Byron's godson—or, as they loved to say,
grandson. He entered the East India Company, and died in 1830. He
was once on board a ship which suddenly sank, on the river Coosy—so sud-
denly that the only thing Pigot could save was the book he happened to
be reading at the moment. It was a copy of the second impression of
Byron's early poems—the small octavo of January 1807, entitled *Poems
on Various Occasions*. Byron had given him a copy with this inscription :
" Harry Edward Pigot : the gift of his grandfather, George Gordon
Byron, 1807 ". When Pigot died, his daughter brought it back to Eng-
land, " where, in September 1862, it formed the ornament of a bazaar on
behalf of the volunteers in East Retford, and was sold by auction for £25 "
(Karl Elze, referring to *Notes and Queries*, November 1, 1862, p. 346).

had an indication in the Mary Chaworth days, when " Mary Anne " was always pleaded for. He liked " Robin Adair " too, and he sang, with Elizabeth Pigot, many other naïve ditties. " It is very odd ", he once said to her, " that I sing much better to your playing than to any one else's ". " That ", she answered, " is because I play to your singing ". He probably sang very badly. Rogers [1] said that one could tell from a poet's versification whether he had an ear for music or not. " From Bowles's and Moore's I should know that they had fine ears . . . ; from Southey's, Wordsworth's, and Byron's, that they had no ears for it ".

He did not spend the Christmas holidays of 1804–5 at Southwell, but in London with the Hansons.[2] This was arranged for him by Augusta, in consequence of the burning letters she had been getting for some time about his relations with his mother. " I dread the approach of the holidays ", he wrote from Harrow in November. The sinister Lord Grey de Ruthyn seems to have been one reason for these aggravated terrors. He had called during the summer holidays, and there had been a scene. The boy would not see him ; and Mrs. Byron was so inordinately angry that he began to suspect her of a " penchant for his lordship ". " But I am confident that he does not return it. . . . She has an excellent opinion of her personal attractions, sinks her age a good six years, and avers that when I was born, she was only eighteen. . . . But vanity is the weakness of *your sex* ",[3] sums up the youthful philosopher who was so wholly free from it ; and he adds that he could forgive these foibles, did not worse remain behind.

In this letter we hear the first of those cries of veritable anguish which ring through many belonging to the Southwell period. " Am I to call this woman mother ? . . . am I to be goaded with insult, loaded with obloquy, and suffer my feelings to be outraged on the most trivial occasions ? I owe her respect as a Son, but I renounce her as a Friend. What example does she show me ! I hope in God I shall never follow it ".[4] His own anger was of different calibre, for the worst rages were the silent ones ; but his demeanour towards the unhappy woman, during these scenes, was of a very provocative kind. He would

---

[1] *Table Talk*, pp. 224, 225.

[2] Be it remembered that this was the time of that crisis at Harrow when Dr. Drury wished him to leave the school.

[3] *L. and J.* i. 46.

[4] A painful, yet farcical, story (vouched for by Moore) is told of one of these encounters. Late one evening, Byron went to their chemist and begged him on no account to supply Mrs. Byron with the means for suicide. He had scarcely left the shop, before his mother entered—not to buy the poison, but to make the same request about her son.

make her low mocking bows, would listen with an interest
burlesqued to insolence, as she screamed and choked out her
abuse, her accusations, her indictments of the "Byrrones".
She would then dash the household china to the ground, or
catch up the poker and tongs and pursue him round the room ;
but for all his lameness, he could usually prevail against her
slow-moving corpulency. Once, indeed, she did overtake him,
brandishing her heavy cut-steel weapons, and in the madness
of her fury his actual personal danger was supreme ; but he
contrived to evade the blow, and fled not only from the room
but from the house. He went to the Pigots', and, with their
connivance, escaped to London next day. She followed him
there, and "after an obstinate engagement of some hours " (as
he wrote to John Pigot), returned to Southwell, while he " pro-
ceeded with all my laurels, to Worthing, on the Sussex coast ".
What scathing truths he spoke to her on that occasion we
may imagine only if we know something of the feelings which
such monstrous episodes can generate. He might write, and he
did write, pages of vivid satire, and invective, and lamenta-
tion, to his sister and his friends ; but what he must have felt
at heart was something bitterer than any form of utterance
could express. " Such scenes ", wrote Augusta Byron to Hanson,
" are enough to spoil the very best temper and disposition in
the universe ".[1] The sense of irreplaceable ignorance of one
deep emotion—a son's love for a mother—that he could never
truly feel ; the sense of personal degradation, and of almost
open shame (there are phrases, here and in later letters, that
hint at Mrs. Byron's intemperance) ; and possibly the abominable
sense of actual physical fear . . . these must have mingled into
wretchedness inexpressible—though so dazzlingly, so irresistibly
expressed ! For with aching heart though we must read his
Southwell letters, we must read them with laughing lips as well.
The traits are so lifelike, the picture drawn with a *brio* so amazing,
that sheer pleasure in the thing well done brings the light of
exultation to our eyes. We lie back and laugh, for all our pity
—because we know that he must have done the same, because
genius cannot show us its vast compensations without awakening
the old, the ever-new, delight in that " glory, jest, and riddle "
which is Man.

He left Harrow, as we have seen, in July 1805, and on the
first day of that month entered himself at Trinity College,
Cambridge, though he did not go into residence until the follow-
ing October. The interval was spent at Southwell, " which . . .
I wish was swallowed up by an earthquake " ; but though unhappy

[1] *L. and J.* i. 46.

to think he was no longer a boy, inevitably he was looking forward to the life in which he would be, for the first time, his own master. That life will be dealt with later; at present the sojourns at Southwell claim our attention. He spent a year there in 1806-7, from one June to the next; it was a retreat from the University rendered desirable, even indispensable, by his extravagance.

The great scene of the Flight from the Fireirons took place in the August of this stay. " Oh! for the pen of Ariosto to rehearse, in epic, the scolding of that momentous eve—or rather, let me invoke the shade of Dante to inspire me, for none but the author of the *Inferno* could properly preside over such an attempt. . . . What a group! Mrs. B. the principal figure; *you* cramming your ears with cotton, as the only antidote to total deafness; Mrs. —— in vain endeavouring to mitigate the wrath of the lioness robbed of her whelp; and last, though not least, Elizabeth and *Wousky*—wonderful to relate!—both deprived of their parts of speech, and bringing up the rear in mute astonishment ". This letter is to John Pigot, and is dated from 16 Piccadilly. Next day came the engagement of some hours with his mother; on the 18th (she having returned to Southwell), Byron went on to Worthing and Littlehampton, begging Pigot to send " that *idle scoundrel* Charles " after him with his horses; and in September, after a victorious flying visit to Burgage Manor, Byron and John Pigot went to Harrogate together. Both were delightfully busy with " poetics ", and with a project for amateur theatricals at Southwell. They were shy and reclusive; yet they no doubt attracted attention in Harrogate, extremely full though the place still was; for they had arrived in " Lord Byron's own carriage with post-horses; and he sent his groom with two saddle-horses, and a beautifully formed, very ferocious bull-mastiff, called Nelson, to meet us there ". The groom was the idle scoundrel Charles; and there was a valet as well, who went on the box of the carriage, " with Boatswain beside him ".[1] Boatswain the Newfoundland is, as Henley said, one of the world's dogs, and will reappear in this narrative; poor Nelson ended his tempestuous days during the Harrogate sojourn.

Byron and Pigot were at the Crown Inn—dining nightly in its public room, but retiring immediately afterwards to their private one, " for Byron was no more a friend to drinking than myself. We lived retired, and made few acquaintance, for he was naturally shy, *very* shy; which people who did not know him mistook for pride. Few people ", adds John Pigot, " under-

[1] From a letter written by John Pigot to his sister; and from his account given verbally to Moore in 1828.

stood Byron, but I know that he had naturally a kind and feeling heart, and that there was not a single spark of malice in his composition."

He had been nearly a year in residence at Cambridge when this visit to Harrogate took place, so that we behold the young man launched, as it were : private carriage, two men-servants, two saddle-horses, and two notable dogs. Poetics were in full swing, and the Pigots and Mr. Becher were in the secret ; the first quarto was indeed actually in the press, but the more absorbing interest of the moment seems to have been the projected theatricals. " They were ", says Moore, " a source of infinite delight to him ", while the excitement at Southwell was of course intense.

They started in good time for the rehearsals from Harrogate, and the journey was beguiled by the composition of the Prologue. " On getting into the carriage at Chesterfield, Byron said, ' Now, Pigot, I'll spin a prologue for our play ' " ; and before they reached Mansfield, he had spun it, with but one interruption : " How do you pronounce *début* ? " Reinforced by Pigot's opinion, he exclaimed, "Aye, that will do for a rhyme to *new* " ; leaving us to ponder (for the deed was perpetrated) on the teaching of French—or rhyme—in those days.

The great event came off in the end of September, at Mr. Leacroft's, whose pretty daughter Julia played a part in the first piece. The plays were Cumberland's *Wheel of Fortune*, and Allingham's *Weathercock*. Byron's parts in both were the star parts. He repeatedly brought down the house ; and it was either very odd, or very natural, that the pair of characters should figure his own renowned duality, for Penruddock in the *Wheel* was gloom incarnate, while Tristram in the *Weathercock* was the embodiment of whim—a Hawtrey part, as we should say to-day.

The memorable evening had consequences, and unpleasant ones. We have seen that Miss Julia Leacroft played a girl's part in the *Wheel of Fortune*, probably that of Penruddock's *inamorata*. Byron stayed in Southwell during the ensuing winter,[1] and it is clear that the mimic passion was prolonged. Southwell soon began to gossip ; and on the last day of January there is a note to Julia's brother, Captain John Leacroft, which proves that the girl's menkind had grown uneasy. Moore [2]

---

[1] Despite his assertion (*Poems*, i. 38) that he never passed a winter there, we find letters dated from Southwell on December 7, 1806, and through the January and February of 1807.

[2] Not in the Life of Byron, but in the *Prose and Verse of Thomas Moore*, edited by Richard Herne Shepherd (London, 1878), p. 420, is this reference to be found.

stated that the brother sent Byron a challenge, but that is inaccurate ; Mr. Prothero thinks that probably Mr. Becher advised him to write as he did to Captain Leacroft. What he wrote was that the only way, so far as he could see, of " crushing the animadversions of officious malevolence " was for him to " decline all further intercourse with those whom my acquaintance has unintentionally injured ". This was agreed to by the Leacrofts—and another pretext afforded for Byron's hearty hatred of Southwell. Most of us would find such an one irresistible. He was evidently the talk of the town at this time, and he was, as evidently, ready for any diversion that the young ladies in it could supply. Miss Julia Leacroft and Miss Anne Houson were the rival belles. Julia was first in the field ; their flirtation dated from before the theatricals, as the earliest set of verses addressed to her in 1806 attests. They are affronting —not to say insulting—in tone.

> " Sixteen was then our utmost age,
> Two years have lingering passed away, love !
> And now new thoughts our minds engage,
> At least, I feel disposed to stray, love ! "

Few families would take that quietly, for Miss Leacroft was unmistakably designated ; and so we have seen that whether disposed to stray or not, the young man was obliged to take his impertinences elsewhere. He took them—and took them in full force—to Miss Anne Houson, who inspired no less than six poems. She was the daughter of a clergyman, and she married a clergyman.[1] Evidently very beautiful, she was very vain as well, and given to boasting of her many conquests. A truly awful warning was addressed to her on this count in January 1807.

> " Dost thou repeat, in childish boast,
> The words man utters to deceive ?
> Thy peace, thy hope, thy all, is lost,
> If thou canst venture to believe " . . .

This, from nineteen, is surely one of the most humorous adjurations which that much-adjured being, Woman, has ever received. But Anne never saw it, for it was not published until 1832.

Meanwhile the calm current of his friendship with Elizabeth Pigot flowed on—a part of the routine of life. He had settled down into a groove—he could often do that, as we shall see ; and Southwell favoured such regularities. Not that his were wholly in the cathedral-town tradition. He was a sluggard, for instance, of the incorrigible hereditary type. Mrs. Byron

---

[1] The Rev. Luke Jackson. She died on Christmas Day 1821, and her monument is in Hucknall Torkard church.

could never be got out of bed at a decent hour, and her son followed her example—to the end of his life, be it said. He wrote at night, and the Muse was gracious ; every morning he had a sheaf to carry down to Elizabeth, who acted as his amanuensis. Thence he would proceed to Mr. Becher's, and after that would look in on the Housons or Leacrofts (before the animadversions of officious malevolence), and after this lounging sort of morning, he would devote himself to his favourite exercises. These were swimming, sparring, firing at a mark, and riding. Oddly enough, he still played cricket ; there is a letter from Elizabeth to John Pigot in which she says : " Lord Byron has just gone past the window with his bat on his shoulder to cricket, which he is as fond of as ever ". But swimming and diving were real proficiencies. Elizabeth Pigot, when Moore was writing the biography, still kept as a precious relic a thimble which Byron borrowed from her one morning, and which her brother (who was his companion) testified to his having brought up three times successively from the bottom of the river. To dive in the little Grete, which ran through Southwell, was child's play to one of Cambridge's most renowned performers —for Byron and his friend Noel Long were brilliant rivals, and used to practise in a part where the Cam is fourteen feet deep.

Byron's riding was never remarkable, nor did he ever acquire true horsiness. A spirited pair passed by his window one day. " What beautiful horses ! " he exclaimed. " I should like to buy them ". " Why, they are your own, my lord ", said a servant who was present.

He inherited—or imitated—from the Wicked Lord a passion for weapons of all kinds. His pistol was as dear to him as most men make their pipes ; and beside his bed there lay always a small sword with which he used to amuse himself, when he awoke, by thrusting it through the hangings. The tattered condition of these added a high value to the bed when Mrs. Byron sold it on her removal to Newstead ; for the purchaser loved to persuade herself and all her acquaintances that the sword was the very one which had killed Mr. Chaworth in the famous duel. It was not ; but an innocent and stainless weapon, which did not even belong to Byron, for he used to borrow it from a friend during his visits to Southwell.

Despite his detestation of the place, he left many endearing memories behind him. Not to reckon the ever-devoted attachment of the Pigots, there were humbler celebrants of his warm heart and quick, picturesque generosity. Moore tells a charming little tale of a poor woman who came into the bookseller's shop one day to buy a Bible. Byron was there, and overheard the colloquy between her and the shopman. The cost proved to be beyond her means : it was eight shillings. " Ah, dear sir ", she cried, " I cannot pay such a price ; I did not think it would be half the money " ; and she was going away, much cast down, when the boy (for this was in the early days of durance) called her back, bought the Bible, and made her a present of it.   The incident counted as a good omen through the day, for he was at that time (and indeed all through life) very superstitious—like his mother, who was steeped in the lore of second-sight, had ever haunted fortune-tellers, and could reel off tale after tale of occult faculties and presentiments.   A lady in Southwell told Moore an amusing anecdote of the lighter side of this trait in Byron.   She had a large agate bead with a wire through it in her work-box, and when he asked what the strange object might be, she told him that it was a charm against love, and that as long as she had it she was immune from that malady.   " Oh, give it to me ", he cried, " it's just what I want ".   She refused ; but ere long found herself bereft of the bead.   " Did you take it ? " she asked, and he confessed that he had, adding that she should never see it again.   A little flirtation may have been mingled with this theft ; but Mary Chaworth, in whose epoch it took place, most probably was accountable for his desire to be protected against love.

So, half-fledged as man and as poet, he left Southwell behind him in the June of 1807.   His last letter to Elizabeth Pigot is dated October 26, 1807, and though it closes with the adjuration, " Write, write, write ! ! ! " she plainly got no answers if she did. He was " grown-up " then, and life was branching out in many directions.   The early poems had attracted some notable attention ;   he was making friends at the University among men of his own standing, brilliant, dissipated, sceptical—" young pride-lings of intellect " (to use the delightful phrase of Dallas) ;   and John Pigot, the steady young provincial doctor, was receding into a dim background.   Elizabeth Pigot, wise and humorous, must for long have been aware that the end of her close inter-course with Gaby was approaching.   With that want of tact, of any perception of, or care for, their probable feelings, which was one of the constant defects in Byron's attitude towards women, he had now adopted a tone in his letters to her which a girl of spirit and intelligence can scarcely have found agreeable. And when, leaving Cambridge, he went to London, the poor Egeria had to endure being told that the news of the metropolis could not be interesting to *her*, who had rusticated all her life, and had insulated ideas of decorum.   By August the note of patronage had grown still more strident, and was mingled with a lamentable note of bragging. " A man whose works are praised by *reviewers*, admired by *duchesses*, and sold by every bookseller of the metropolis, does not dedicate much consideration to *rustic readers* ". The letter closes with what in those days would have been called a handsome tribute to her steady and devoted friendship ; but he was plainly forgetting, and, inevitable as the Pigots must have known this to be, such driftings apart bring pain and mortification into hearts as kindly, and lives as monotonous, as theirs. Mrs. Pigot—not Elizabeth —and John were each to hear once more, in 1811 ; but these messages merely emphasised the distance between the past and the present ; and we see the very end of the end in a word to his mother before starting for the Albanian tour in 1809. " I wish the Miss Pigots had something better to do than carry my miniatures to Nottingham to copy ".[1]

[1] What was not good enough for himself, however, was good enough for Dallas, his friend, connection, and literary agent in later days; for we find him in a letter of October 11, 1811, cordially recommending Southwell as a place in which to settle down. Dallas's family would have the advantage of very genteel society ; and Byron had " friends there to whom I should be proud to introduce you". Dallas did not act on the advice, but went (at that time) to live at Mortlake, Surrey (see Byron's Will of 1811, *L. and J.* i. 329).

Elizabeth Pigot never married. She lived in Southwell till her death in 1866, much visited by Byron pilgrims. " Her friendship with him was the great romance of her life," says Mrs. Fraser (daughter of the Mr. Webb who bought Newstead in 1862) ; and to Mrs. Webb she bequeathed all her Byron relics, letters, and copies of verses. One of these consisted of an epitaph on his mother, composed in a game which he was playing at the Pigots. It has never been published.

CHAPTER VI

CAMBRIDGE—1805–1808

HE went up to Cambridge in the October of 1805, feeling miserable. To go there at all had been a great disappointment. He had chosen Oxford, but there proved to be no vacancy at Christ Church, the desired college—and moreover, Dr. Drury strongly recommended Cambridge, which had been his own University. Byron acquiesced, but the decision was unfortunate. Oxford would have suited him better—being, as Mr. E. M. Forster has amusingly said, " not a mere receptacle for youth, like Cambridge ". There, too, he might have read for Honours, while at Cambridge the rule then prevailed that Honours were only for mathematicians—and Byron as a mathematician is unthinkable. But Elze maintains that neither would Oxford have suited him: " his mind, with its universal tendency, could never be attracted by either of the two centres "; and Moore, more wordily, has much the same judgment to deliver. It is probably a just one. He was impatient, wilful, avid of experience —that is not the stuff of which scholars are made.

In his diary he recorded the mood of dejection in which he entered University life. " I was so completely alone in this new world that it half broke my spirits. . . . It was one of the deadliest and heaviest feelings of my life that I was no longer a boy ". Yet with him to Cambridge went an old and dear Harrow intimate, that Edward Noel Long who was the Cleon of *Childish Recollections* ; they lived in close intercourse until the summer of 1806 [1] ; and in the Ravenna Journal of 1821 Byron

---

[1] Long was Byron's companion in the visits to Littlehampton and Worthing, which followed the Flight from the Fireirons and from Southwell in that August. He left college then, went into the Guards, and was drowned early in 1809 on his passage to Lisbon with his regiment.

spoke of that time as the happiest days of his life. In November 1805, he wrote to Augusta in enthusiastic praise of college life. The initiatory melancholy, then, seems to have quickly disappeared ; but with closer knowledge his critical spirit awoke, and he poured contempt on the place. " It is the *Devil* or at least his principal residence. They call it the University, but any other appellation would have suited it better, for Study is the last pursuit of the Society ; the Master [1] eats, drinks, and sleeps, the Fellows *drink, dispute, and pun* ; the employment of the Undergraduates you will probably conjecture without any description ".

Long, at Harrow, had been a milder spirit than Byron, but now (as Byron said) either Long had roughened or he had softened, for they met on equal terms of behaviour. They were rival swimmers, " fond of riding—reading—and of conviviality ". The last they seem to have abjured in their own intercourse. When we read the tale of their tête-à-tête evenings, we mentally exclaim that it must indeed have been Byron who had softened. They spent the hours in music, Long performing on the violoncello or the flute, and his friend meekly doing audience to the accompaniment of " our chief beverage, soda-water ". The depressive drink was, however, part of a régime—certainly in Byron's case, probably in Long's ; for this was the earliest period of the great Thinning Campaign which lasted all the former's life. We have already seen that a tendency to put on flesh— to become, indeed, as Moore frankly expresses it, enormously fat—had for some time worried him ; now that he was growing vain of his looks, solicitous about the becoming arrangement of his hair and so forth, that tendency had become a haunting horror against which he fought untiringly. His letters from Cambridge are threaded with allusions to it ; and always he was able to announce his triumph—always he was " *thinner* ", and thinner was always gleefully underlined.

The young anchorites of vanity solaced themselves mentally for this bodily discipline. " I remember our buying, with vast alacrity, Moore's new quarto [2] (in 1806) and reading it together in the evenings ".

---

[1] William Lort Mansel, then Master of Trinity, was the chief wit of Cambridge in his day. Rogers wished that somebody would collect his epigrams ; " they are remarkably neat and clever ". As Master, he was a severe disciplinarian and extremely tenacious of his dignity (*L. and J.* i. note to p. 84).

[2] This was the *Epistles, Odes, and other Poems ;* but Byron was already a confirmed reader of Thomas Little. In later years he often used the Little volumes as texts for the hypocrisy of that public which refused to accept *Don Juan.*

" 'Tis LITTLE ! young Catullus of his day,
As sweet, but as immoral in his Lay !
Grieved to condemn, the Muse must needs be just,
Nor spare melodious advocates of lust ".

Strangford's Camoëns [1] was another much-read book, and
this poet was to be, in the future, still more stringently rebuked.
But whatever the young satirist-moralist of 1809 might say, we
may be sure that the soda-water drinkers of 1806 found Little
and Strangford a good deal more to their taste than the austere
refreshment which stood, chillingly, within reach of their in-
frequent hands.

Another friendship ran alongside this. In July 1807, Byron
wrote to Elizabeth Pigot of one who " has been my *almost constant*
associate since October 1805. His *voice* first attracted my atten-
tion, his *countenance* fixed it, and his *manners* attached me to
him for ever ". He was a young man named Edleston, who was
one of the Cambridge choristers ; two years younger than Byron,
" nearly my height, very *thin*, very fair complexion, dark eyes,
and light locks ". Their acquaintance (as another friend [2] has
recorded in a MS note) began by his saving Edleston from drown-
ing. The key was thus dramatically set for a kind of relation
which, in its departure from a normal choice of intimates, was
(in youth, at any rate,) profoundly characteristic of him. The
paradoxical nature of these dual types of intercourse—that with
" men of my own rank " (a favourite phrase) and men, like
Edleston, of no social rank at all—is more apparent than real.
Each has its origin in the consciousness of that " own rank "
from which Byron suffered so much more than do the generality
of lordlings. It was born of the long poverty and disclassment,
and kept alive, we may conjecture, by the perpetual sense of
Mrs. Byron's irrelevancy as the mother of an old English Baron.
These things, making self-assertion often necessary, pushed for-
ward in his mind a circumstance usually unapparent by reason
of the very atmosphere of recognition which surrounds it.

At any rate, the Edleston friendship became a very senti-
mental one. The chorister gave him a cornelian heart as a
keepsake ; and Byron entrusted it to Elizabeth Pigot to keep
for him. In 1807, writing to her about the "hero of *my corne-
lian* ", he propounded a fantastic scheme for living with Edleston
when he should come of age. If it was carried out, they were

[1] *Translations from the Portuguese of Luis de Camoëns*, by Lord Strang-
ford. The " translations " were not translations ; " no more to be found
in the original Portuguese than in the Song of Solomon " (Byron's note to
English Bards and Scotch Reviewers. *Poems*, i. 320).
[2] The Rev. William Harness, whom Byron (at Harrow) had pitied and
protected. Harness was, after Byron had left Cambridge, at Christ's
College.

to " put the ' Ladies of Llangollen ' to the blush ".[1] It never was carried out, nor even attempted. Whether the friends met again at all is indeed uncertain ; no further mention of Edleston occurs until 1811. In the May of that year he died of consumption. Byron wrote at once to Mrs. Pigot, asking for the return of the cornelian, which he now had a confused memory of having *given* to Elizabeth. The cornelian was returned at once ; he was reminded that he had left it as a deposit, not as a gift ; but it was returned—broken.[2] The omen haunted him for long.

Byron, in the Ravenna Diary of 1821, thus summed up the emotional content of this summer of 1806. " [Long's] friendship, and a violent, though *pure*, love and passion—which held me at that period—were the then romance of the most romantic period of my life ". It is noteworthy that in all his recallings of the days at Cambridge there is no explicit allusion to the once beloved Edleston.

He showed no originality in his mode of life at college. What all the rest did, he did—neither more nor less, neither better nor worse ; and that, I think, is the mark of Byron which best helps to explain him. Wholly incapable as he was of any real originality in the conduct of the daily round, yet with a native impulse to scorn the multitude developed by every circumstance,

---

[1] These were Lady Eleanor Butler and Miss Sarah Ponsonby, who lived together in the Vale of Llangollen for upwards of half a century. They were immensely talked of and run after ; there was no person of rank, talent, and importance, said John Murray in a letter to his son in 1829 (*Memoir of John Murray*, ii. 304), who did not procure introductions to them. Charles Mathews saw " the dear inseparable inimitables " in the theatre at Oswestry in 1820. " They came twelve miles from Llangollen, and returned, as they never sleep from home. . . . Oh, such curiosities ! As they are seated, there is not one point to distinguish them from men. . . . They look exactly like two respectable superannuated clergymen. . . . I was highly flattered, as they never were in the theatre before ". Lady Eleanor died in June 1829 ; Miss Ponsonby survived her until December 1831.

[2] There is a theory, held by a few commentators, that the mysterious group of *Thyrza* poems refers to Edleston. I cannot find anything which accounts for it, either in the poems themselves, or in the stanzas in canto ii of *Childe Harold* (9 and 95–96) which Byron himself expressly related to the first *Thyrza* poem. By his manner of doing so, he removed (one would have thought) all possibility of such a theory ever coming into existence. See the letters to Dallas of October 14 and 31, 1811 (*L. and J.* ii. pp. 57 and 65). In the former he says, " . . . this stanza " (No. 9 of canto ii) " alludes to an event which has taken place since my arrival here, and not to the death of any *male* friend ". But great are the ingenuities of the commentator. In *Astarte*, we read that he occasionally spoke of Thyrza to Lady Byron, " always with strong but concealed emotion ". He once showed her a beautiful tress of hair which he said was Thyrza's, but he never mentioned her real name (p. 42).

hereditary and accidental, of his being he kicked, as it were, for ever against the pricks of his own uninventiveness. We frequently watch such a struggle : Byron is its great epitome. The sense of what genuine originality signifies is slow to dawn in natures like his ; a fitful eccentricity in trifles (such as he often achieved) masquerades for them as the trait which carries with it their admired privilege of disdain. They do not see that true originality is unaware of itself, and embroiders no tag of scorn on its banner. Thus, for example, Byron's dearest freak at Cambridge was the keeping of a tame bear " to sit for a fellowship ". The dullard of the year could have done and said as brilliantly. . . . For the rest, it was an aimless oscillation between the University and London—entirely alone in the sense of enjoying any vestige of domesticity, for it may be said almost without qualification that there was not a single private house which he could enter as an intimate. His guardian stood aloof ; with the Hansons his relations were at that time often strained ; Augusta Byron was scarcely ever in London ; while to go home was to go to purgatory.

The result was the inevitable one. " I took my gradations in the vices with great promptitude . . . but though my temperament was naturally burning, I could not share in the commonplace libertinism of the place and time without disgust. And yet this very disgust, and my heart thrown back upon itself, threw me into excesses perhaps more fatal than those from which I shrunk, as fixing upon one (at a time) the passions which, spread amongst many, would have hurt only myself ".[1] Is not that the very struggle of which I spoke but now ? And we see this the more clearly when we scan the record of that period's passion, and the one (at a time) upon whom it was fixed. He told Medwin that he used to dress up a certain Mrs. ——, and pass her off as his brother Gordon, in order that his mother might not hear of his having such a female companion. She lived with him in Brompton lodgings, and they went to Brighton for week-ends—she riding about there in her male attire. Somebody, whose name Moore gives as the late Lady P., met them, and remarked on the beauty of her horse. " Yes ", she answered, " it was *gave* me by my brother ". Already (by Moore's account) suspicious, Lady P. must have offered an interesting study in expression as she lent an ear to the English of Lord Byron's brother.[2]

Other delights were pugilism and fencing, and here he was blessed by the accident of time, for the chief exponents of both arts were of an unusually good type. John Jackson, better

[1] *Detached Thoughts. L. and J.* v. 445.
[2] The affair lasted, for in 1808 the lady was taken on a visit to Newstead.

known as Gentleman Jackson, was, says Henley in his notes to the one volume of Letters with which he dealt—notes which are at their most vivid in describing the Fancy—" the most picturesque and commanding figure in the sporting-world, and exercised an influence unique in its annals. The truth is, he was a vast deal more than an accomplished boxer and teacher of boxing and a brilliant all-round athlete. He was also a man of character and integrity—polite, agreeable, reputable, a capital talker, a person of tact and energy and charm ".

In 1806 this paragon had rooms at 13 Bond Street with Henry Angelo, the equally remarkable fencing-master, and they formed the most attractive lounge in the West End. Angelo was even more popular than the Emperor of Pugilism. He had dined at the same table with the Prince of Wales, acted with Lord Barrymore, played the flute to Lady Melfort's accompaniment. His acquaintance with Byron had begun at Harrow. " From his lordship's affability and pleasant manners, I knew more of him than of many I attended there at the time ". So the fencing-master wrote in his Reminiscences in 1830.[1] On one occasion, Byron drove Angelo down to Cambridge—Theodore Hook being of the party—gave him dinner, saw him and Hook to the coach, and " sent to St. John's College for the good beer it was noted for, when, filling two tumblers, he handed them up himself to us, laughing at the many people who were wondering at his being so very busy waiting on the outside passengers ".

By this time, in the development of the liberty which they at first had touched with so gingerly a hand, Byron's and Long's evenings at Cambridge had quite forgotten the flute and the soda-water. But Long left after the summer of 1806 ; and when Byron came back from his year's sojourn at Southwell, he made a new set of friends. One of these was John Cam Hobhouse,[2] destined to remain his close and unchanging intimate and ally through all that was to come. Hobhouse had cherished a keen dislike for him during the first two years at Cambridge. He also was at Trinity ; and the young man in the white hat and grey coat, riding a grey horse, who was George Gordon, sixth Lord Byron, had been one of his pet prejudices. They had become acquainted, had even got drunk together, but Hobhouse had remained orbed in his isolation for all other modes of intercourse. In 1807, however, there came an ex-

[1] Angelo collected portraits of pugilists and players, and made a screen with these for Byron. " John Murray the Second bought it at the sale in Piccadilly, and it abides in Albemarle Street to this day " (W. E. Henley).
[2] He was the eldest son of Mr. Benjamin Hobhouse, created a baronet in 1812. In 1851, John Cam Hobhouse was created Baron Broughton de Gyfford. He died in 1869.

5

pansion. The offensively dressed and mounted youth had pub-
lished a volume of poetry. This hinted at better things than
those more immediately apparent, and Lord Byron was graciously
admitted to intimacy : " We became really friends in a morn-
ing ".

William Bankes [1] was gone—he who had originally brought
them together, but had suffered the frustration of Hobhouse's
caprice. Bankes himself may have distressed this meticulous
censor a little. While he stayed, he had " ruled the roast—
or rather the *roasting*—and was father of all mischiefs " ; he
had been Byron's " collegiate pastor, and master, and patron ",
and had done his best to popularise him ; but those were the
days of that shyness which beset all Byrons in the beginning
of relationships, and Bankes had finally resigned himself to
" tolerating my ferocities ". By 1807 these had died down ;
and there was, moreover, a good opening for intimacy with the
dazzling Charles Skinner Matthews, who had occupied Byron's
rooms at Trinity during the Southwell sojourn.

Two circumstances of his tenancy had delighted this marvel-
lous youth. On his taking possession of the rooms, Mr. Jones,
the tutor, had urged upon him a great solicitude for the furniture,
" for Lord Byron, Sir, is a young man of tumultuous passions ".
The enchanted Matthews thenceforward enjoined his friends to
handle the very door with caution—and Jones's voice and manner
he was famed for his oddity) were faithfully reproduced in the
(corollary : " Lord Byron, Sir, is a young man . . ." The door
safely passed, visitors found themselves before a large looking-
glass, and this—evidently a rare luxury—so distracted their
minds by its generous reflections that Matthews soon complained
that they did not come to see him, but themselves. The stage
was thus set for friendliness, and " Matthews and I . . . became
great cronies ". Byron had a very high enthusiasm for the
starry Charles. Over and over again it sounds in his letters ;
and in a note to stanza 91 (canto i.) of *Childe Harold*, he expressed
it with a humility which caused another friend to protest. " I
should have ventured a verse to the memory of the late Charles
Skinner Matthews, Fellow of Downing College,[2] Cambridge, were
he not too much above all praise of mine ". Dallas (the friend
in question) thought this excessive, but Byron answered, " I
was so sincere . . . and do feel myself so totally unable to do
justice to his talents, that the passage must stand. . . . To
him all the men I ever knew were pigmies. He was an intellectual

---

[1] Bankes became celebrated as a traveller, explorer, and discoverer.
" Bankes has done miracles of research and enterprise ", wrote Byron in
1820 to John Murray.
[2] This honour fell to Matthews in 1808.

giant. It is true I loved Wingfield better [1] . . . but in ability —ah! you did not know Matthews ". And again, " None of us ever thought of being at all near him ".

To the influence of this potent spirit Dallas ascribed Byron's infidelity. Matthews was a pronounced sceptic, and a master of ironic japes as well ; the two minds, once any kind of intimacy began, were of necessity drawn together by their close intellectual affinity—they " spoke the same language ". The undoubted influence which Matthews had, consisted in that affinity ; he originated no scepticism in Byron, who had from boyhood abjured any orthodoxy in religious belief. Moreover (for all the ardent admiration), with this friend the chiefest spell was not at work: Matthews did not inspire Byron's love. " I did not love him so much as I honoured him ; I was indeed so sensible of his infinite superiority that though I did not envy, I stood in awe of it ".

Another member of the Byron Set was that Scrope Berdmore Davies whose name occurs so often not only in Byron's letters and journals, but in all social chronicles of the time. " One of the cleverest men I ever knew, in conversation. . . . Scrope was always ready, and often witty ". So wrote Byron in the Ravenna Journal ; but Davies belongs more intimately to his later life in London, when the clubs and gambling-dens saw him oftener than during the Cambridge period. At the University they counted for one another more as rival swimmers and divers than as anything else; and, criticising Matthews's less expert performances, " always told him that he would be drowned if ever he came to a difficult pass in the water ".

Byron took his M.A. degree on July 4, 1808, and ended then his living connection with the University. He thus summed up his feelings in a letter to Harness of March 18, 1809 : " *Alma Mater* was to me *injusta noverca* ; and the old beldam only gave me my M.A. degree because she could not avoid it ". He acknowledged, however, in another letter to the same correspondent, that he was " but an untoward child himself ". If idleness and absence be claims on the affection of an *Alma Mater*, Cambridge might have loved him—but not otherwise ; for though in his inveterate vein, he exaggerated the degree of his dissipations, the amount of them must have been considerable to plunge him in the slough of financial difficulties wherein he weltered (and caused his mother to welter) from almost the earliest days of his undergraduate life. He said in his first letter to Augusta from Trinity that his allowance—£500 a year

---

[1] Wingfield's death was commemorated in the stanza to which the note in question was attached.

—was one of the best in college. This, which Mrs. Byron received from the Court of Chancery for his education, she yielded wholly to him when he went to Cambridge; and Chancery further sanctioned the expenditure of a certain sum for furniture, clothes, plate, and so forth. But he had not been in residence a month before Hanson received a letter: " As the time of paying my Bills now approaches, the remaining £50 will be very agreeable. You need not make any deduction, as I shall want most of it ; I will settle with you for the Saddle and Accoutrements *next* quarter ". This letter is of November 23. On November 30, in reading his answer to Hanson's answer, we find ourselves whirled into the midst of a tornado of wrath. It arose from a misunderstanding of what the solicitor had said, but the form of nervous irritation which produces such unreasoned attacks belongs peculiarly to the spendthrift. Hanson remonstrated and explained ; the fifty pounds were sent ; but by December a further crisis was imminent. He wrote to Augusta, at the end of the year, asking her to go security—joint-security of course with him—for £800. " One of the money-lending tribe " had offered to advance it. He applied to her because—because he could think of no one else. She evidently consented to go security, for in February 1806 he wrote to his mother to say that he had paid his Harrow debts and college-bills, and happened to have a few hundreds in ready cash by him.

Poor Mrs. Byron had spent weeks of anguish. On January 11, she had written to tell Hanson that the bills were coming in thick upon her to double the amount she had expected. The news of the few hundreds in ready cash alarmed her. " Where can he get Hundreds ? . . . My idea is that he has inveigled himself with some woman that he wishes to get rid of and finds it difficult. . . . He has no feeling, no Heart. This I have long known . . . this bitter truth I can no longer conceal ; it is wrung from me by *heart-rending agony* ".

She had, indeed, a sufficiently unlovable letter before her. It was the February of 1806, and already he wished to leave college, and pass a couple of years abroad. He presumed she would agree, but he was going whether she did or not. He was remaining in town a month longer, when perhaps he would bring his horses and himself down to " that *execrable* Kennel ", Southwell. " I hope " (as his last word) " you have engaged a Man Servant, else it will be impossible for me to visit you, since my Servant must attend chiefly to his horses ; at the same time, you must cut an indifferent Figure with only maids in your establishment ". Mrs. Byron had at that time about £400 a year, while her son's personal allowance was £500. This is one of the moments in which she takes the stage with authority

as an injured mother. " I am well rewarded ", she writes to
Hanson of this letter. " I came to Nottingham to please him,
and now he hates it.   He knows that I am doing everything
in my power to pay his Debts, and he writes to me about hiring
servants ".

On March 10, Hanson's letter-bag was again Byronic, and
this time to the tune of a confession and a demand from the
culprit himself. " I confess I have borrowed a trifling sum and
now wish to raise £500 to discharge some Debts I have con-
tracted ".   Another quarrel with Hanson was the immediate
result of the answer he received, and it was the summer of that
year (1806) which was spent at Southwell.   An attempt was
made to compel him to return by cutting off supplies ; it failed,
for he did not reappear at Cambridge until the Summer Term of
1807.

Mrs. Byron again wrote to Hanson on March 19, 1807. " Lord
Byron has now been with me seven months, with two Men-
Servants, for which I have never received one farthing, as he
requires the £500 a year for himself.   Therefore it is impossible
I can keep him and them out of my small income of £400 a
year—two in Scotland,[1] and the pension is now reduced to £200
a year.   But if the Court allows the additional two hundred,
I shall be perfectly satisfied.   I do not know what to say about
Byron's returning to Cambridge.   When he was there, I believe
he did nothing but drink, gamble, and spend money ".   Finally,
£1000 was borrowed : £200 from bankers at Southwell, and the
remainder from old friends of his mother, the Misses Parkyns
of Nottingham, and from his great-aunt, Mrs. George Byron.
For this debt his mother made herself liable.   He promised her
a mortgage on one of the farms, but none was given.   Mrs.
Byron, in 1809, before Byron's departure on the Albanian tour,
begged Hanson to see that he gave some security for this
debt.   He did not give any ; and Mr. Prothero[2] says that her
death in 1811 was doubtless accelerated by anxiety from these
causes.

Young men are from of old privileged to be selfish, above
all with their mothers.   Let us then condemn our undergradu-
ate no further than by remarking that he used his privilege
bravely.

Cambridge, unloved and unloving in life, did him honour,
though tardily, in death.   Trinity College has placed Thor-
waldsen's statue of him in her Library, and preserves there also

[1] Mrs. Gordon of Gight, whose annuity had been charged on Mrs.
Byron's income, was now dead.
[2] *L. and J.* i. note to p. 221.

the first letter he ever wrote.[1] The statue was subscribed for
by a number of his admirers, with Hobhouse at their head.
They raised a sum of £1000, which proved inadequate to secure
any eminent British sculptor; Thorwaldsen, who had done
a bust of him in 1817,[2] offered to undertake the work for the
sum subscribed, and the Committee closed with his generous
proposal. The work was begun in 1829, but was not sent to
England until 1834—ten years after Byron's death. " West-
minster Abbey, St. Paul's, the British Museum, the National
Gallery, were each in turn considered as appropriate places for
its reception ; but all, even the secular institutions, refused to
receive it, and the statue remained for ten years or longer un-
packed in the cellars of the Custom-House ".[3]

[1] It is apparently addressed to his aunt, Mrs. Parker, and was written
when he was ten years and ten months old. It is dated from Newstead,
November 8, 1798 (*L. and J.* i. 6).
[2] This was, until her death, in the possession of Lady Dorchester. It
now (1924) belongs to the Right Hon. Henry Hobhouse.
[3] Elze, *Life of Byron*, Authorised translation, p. 66. There is a
statue of Byron in Hamilton Gardens, London, separated only by a railing
from the broad drive in Hyde Park.   On April 19 in each year a wreath of
Gloire de Dijon roses is placed at the foot, under the bequest of Mrs. Rose
Mary Crawshay, who left a legacy for this purpose, and for the insertion
of a memorial notice in *The Times*, until the day that the Dean of West-
minster shall allow Byron's name to be inscribed in the Poets' Corner of
the Abbey.

CHAPTER VII

THE FIRST BOOK AND THE SECOND—1806 AND 1809

Byron's Egeria—The *Fugitive Pieces*—The Rev. John Becher, and the burning of the first quarto—*Poems on Various Occasions*—Bankes, and a Byron letter—*Hours of Idleness*—Success—Robert Charles Dallas—William Harness—The *Edinburgh Review*—*English Bards and Scotch Reviewers*—Fame—Remorse—" A kind of posthumous feel "

D URING the early Southwell period of 1804, Byron and Elizabeth Pigot were one day studying Burns together in the parlour of her mother's house. She had been reading aloud, and had just finished the *Farewell to Ayrshire* : [1]

> " Scenes of woe and scenes of pleasure,
> Scenes that former thoughts renew,
> Scenes of woe and scenes of pleasure,
> Now a sad and last Adieu ".

Her companion exclaimed " I like that metre : let me try it "—and taking a pencil, he wrote on the instant those two stanzas, beginning

> " Hills of Annesley, bleak and barren "

—which, when they were published for the first time in Moore's *Letters and Journals of Lord Byron*, 1830, appeared with the legend : " Written shortly after the marriage of Miss Chaworth ".[2]

The ice broken by this impromptu, Elizabeth heard of his long meditation of the muse. Ever since 1802 it had gone on. He was persuaded to inscribe for• her one infant effort ;

---

[1] " It may be noted " (says Mr. E. H. Coleridge) " that these verses were not written by Burns, though included until recently among his poems ". They are by one Richard Gall, who died in 1801 (*Poems*, i. 211).

[2] Mary Chaworth was not married until August 1805 ; so we have here a case for strong suspicion of Moore's ingenuousness. It was certainly more ingenious than ingenuous thus to head the stanzas ; for Elizabeth Pigot, who copied them for him, can hardly have failed to tell him what in 1859—correctly or incorrectly—she stated " under her hand and seal " respecting the date of their composition (see *Poems*, i. 210-11).

and so she read (more respectfully no doubt than we have done) the lines to Lord Delawarr of February 1803 :

"In thee I fondly hoped to clasp".

She must have encouraged him, for he then had the hardihood to recite another effusion. This too had been written in 1803, and in it he exclaimed :

"My epitaph shall be my name alone;
If that with honour fail to crown my clay,
Oh! may no other fame my deeds repay!
That, only that, shall single out the spot,
By that remembered, or with that forgot."

She might excusably kindle at this achievement for fifteen ; and then, no doubt, she heard of the " first dash into poetry " —the forgotten verses to his exquisite cousin Margaret—in 1800 ; was perhaps regaled with a recital of the frigid elegiac stanzas of 1802, in memory of the same girl. But whatever reserves there may have been and whatever criticisms, the day marked an epoch for them both—and for the world ; since from that moment the desire to appear in print took possession of him.

His ambition went no further, at the time, than a small volume for private circulation. He began to collect what he had scribbled, to scribble more and more ; and by August 1806 his first book was in the press. Messrs. S. & J. Ridge, booksellers and printers of Newark, were the recipients of his MS., and he did not delay to adopt the sanctioned attitude of disdain for his typographer. Ridge figured instantly as "that blockhead " ; but, daily flooded as he was with corrections, alterations, additions, and wholly fresh material, the blockhead managed to be ready by November. It was a quarto volume of sixty-six pages, and contained thirty-eight pieces. The first copy was presented to the Rev. John Becher, "Vicar of Rympton, Notts, and Midsomer Norton "—which evidently meant that he lived at Southwell, for he had long been an intimate friend, and now appeared as a judicious counsellor. We have seen that the summer of 1806 was the period of Little [1] and Strangford as literary influences. Becher had from the first frowned on such readings (nothing in Moore [2] is more engaging than the manner in which he records this condemnation of his early muse), and had recommended, as might be expected, the study of Shakespere, Milton, and the Bible instead. He now opened his

---

[1] In a letter to Moore of June 9, 1820, Byron wrote : " I have just been turning over Little, which I knew by heart in 1803, being then in my fifteenth summer. Heigho! I believe all the mischief I have ever done, or sung, has been owing to that confounded book of yours ".

[2] *Life of Lord Byron* (ed. 1838), p. 40.

quarto ; and among the harmless puerilities and the first adumbrations of that destined wonder of the world called Byronism, he found those verses *To Mary* which have become notorious by dint of resolute suppression. He read them, frowned again, and then sat down and wrote to the boy (" as the most gentle mode of conveying his opinion ") some expostulatory couplets. Byron answered without delay, and doubly. First in a copy of verses :

" The artless Helicon I boast is youth ;—
My Lyre, the Heart—my Muse, the simple Truth " ;

then in a note, which promised that rather than allow the condemned poem to circulate, he would destroy[1] the whole impression. That evening he kept his promise. Becher watched every copy of the quarto burn, except one which had already gone to John Pigot at Edinburgh—and his own.[2] There is something irresistibly humorous in Becher's salvage of his own, but it was probably prompted by admiring pity for the generous boy who had been so proud of his first book—and now beheld it burn, unread, unseen, by all but two. Few of us could have done it, I think ; and though the drama of the scene, and the vanity of stoicism, and, vaguely, that dear scorn for the multitude, may have mingled into a mitigation of the sacrifice, it remained no less a sacrifice and an ordeal. Without straining at sentiment, we may surely see in imagination a dimming of the eye, a quivering of the lip, as eighteen-yeared Byron watched his first-born sink into a squalid little heap of ashes.

But his enthusiasm survived, and no sooner was the burning over than he began to prepare an expurgated and enlarged edition. For the next six weeks he and Ridge (who was again employed) were wholly absorbed in this task ; and by January 1807 the second volume for private circulation was ready. The quarto had been entitled *Fugitive Pieces* ; this edition was in small octavo and was called *Poems on Various Occasions*. Both were

[1] A facsimile reprint of the quarto, limited to a hundred copies, was issued, for private circulation only, by the Chiswick Press in 1886. In it the suppressed verses of course appear ; but Byron himself never allowed them to see the light after the destruction of the first edition.

[2] These copies still survive. John Pigot's came into the possession of his sister Elizabeth, who bequeathed it, with her other Byron relics, to Mrs. Webb of Newstead Abbey. This copy is defective. Two of the leaves (pp. 17–20) wanting are those which contain the offending poem " to that naughty Mary " (as Elizabeth Pigot adds in a note attached to the copy) . . . " which excited such a commotion in the state ". The second copy was long preserved by the Becher family, and is now in the possession of Mr. T. J. Wise. Not a single biographer (including myself) who has seen the lines *To Mary* has anything but condemnation for them. " There is nothing ", says Elze, " to compensate for their silly viciousness —not one felicity of thought or expression ".

anonymous.[1] The octavo numbered one hundred and forty-four pages, and contained forty-eight pieces. Only a hundred copies were printed. John Pigot was again one of the earliest recipients, and was begged to destroy at once his copy of the quarto. Apparently he compromised by tearing out those leaves which held the " unlucky poem to my poor Mary ".[2] " This volume ", adds the hero of the Burning, " is *vastly* correct, and miraculously chaste "—and then, as if to indemnify himself for the restraint shown in it, he goes on to say, " Apropos, talking of love " . . . but we are not permitted to know the à propos, for Moore flinched before it, and snook out asterisks with a lavish hand.

The publication of *Poems on Various Occasions* produced a letter from Cambridge. The writer was William Bankes. This did not happen till March ; and on the same day Byron had a gratifying compliment from Henry Mackenzie, author of that rather foolish book, *A Man of Feeling*, but nevertheless a shrewd critic, and one whose praise was well worth having. Bankes, on the other hand, wrote in a spirit of severe criticism ; and to me the answer from Byron is one of the most delightful displays of human nature which even *his* letters afford.

SOUTHWELL, *March* 6, 1807

" DEAR BANKES,—Your critique is valuable for many reasons : in the first place, it is the only one in which flattery has borne so slight a part ; in the *next*, I am *cloyed* with insipid compliments. I have a better opinion of your judgment and ability than your *feelings*.[3] . . . I feel no hesitation in saying I was more anxious to hear your critique, however severe, than the praises of the *million*. On the same day I was honoured with the encomiums of *Mackenzie*, the celebrated author of the *Man of Feeling*. Whether his approbation or *yours* elated me most, I cannot decide. . . . Your further remarks, however *caustic* or bitter, to a palate vitiated with the sweets of *adulation*, will be of service ".

In the June or July of 1807 there appeared, still printed and

---

[1] Two of the poems in the quarto were signed BYRON ; but the volume itself, which is without a title-page, was anonymous.

[2] This Mary is not to be confounded with the heiress of Annesley, nor with Mary of Aberdeen. She was of humble, " if not equivocal ", station in life ; and had long fair hair, a lock of which, as well as her picture, Byron used to show among his friends. The early verses *To Mary on receiving her Picture* (*Poems*, i. 32) were also addressed to her.

[3] In another letter to Bankes in 1809, this impression of heartlessness is again referred to. " Believe me, with that deference which I have always from my childhood paid to your *talents*, and with a somewhat better opinion of your heart than I have hitherto entertained,—Yours ever, etc."

sold by Ridge of Newark, but now to be had from four London booksellers besides, a small octavo volume, entitled *Hours of Idleness* :[1] *a Series of Poems Original and Translated*, " By George Gordon, Lord Byron, a Minor ". Ridge sold fifty in a fortnight, before the advertisements. In the earlier form of *Childish Recollections* (the long Harrow piece which first appeared in *Poems on Various Occasions*) the young singer had groaned :

> " Weary of love, of life, devour'd with spleen,
> I rest, a perfect Timon, not nineteen ;
> World ! I renounce thee ! all my hope's o'ercast,
> One sigh I give thee, but that sigh's the last ".

Yet never did ordinary mortal watch more eagerly his effect upon that rejected world than did our perfect Timon, not nineteen. And soon there came a flamboyant epistle—already alluded to. " Ridge does not proceed rapidly in Notts—very possibly. In town things wear a more promising aspect, and a man whose works are praised by *reviewers*, admired by *duchesses*, and sold by every bookseller of the metropolis, does not dedicate much consideration to *rustic readers* ". There had been a long notice in Crosby's magazine, *Literary Recreations* (he omitted to say that Crosby was Ridge's London agent, and that this was mere booming), and Elizabeth was advised to order the number for July —especially as it contained, besides, his own maiden essay in criticism.[2]   He continues : " My cousin, Lord Alexander Gordon . . . told me his mother, her Grace of Gordon,[3] requested he would introduce my *Poetical* Lordship to her Highness, as she had bought my volume, admired it exceedingly, in common with the rest of the fashionable world, and wished to claim her relationship with the author ". But the meeting failed to

---

[1] This title is now associated with Byron's *Juvenilia*. The collection of minor poetry so named (which has been included in every edition of Byron's Poetical Works issued by John Murray since 1831) consists of seventy pieces, being the aggregate of the poems published in the three issues— those of January and June 1807, and the final collection of 1808 (*Poems*, i. 12).

[2] This was a review of Wordsworth's *Poems* (2 vols. 1807). It would be difficult to imagine anything more banal. The ready-made phrase glides from his pen without intermission ; nor is any kind of penetration displayed in the criticism.

[3] She was " the witty Duchess of Gordon ", born Miss Jean Maxwell, of Monreith. The most successful matchmaker of her age, she married three of her daughters to three dukes. She had five, and married them all, though not invariably as she dreamed. She had wanted Pitt for Lady Charlotte, and Eugène Beauharnais for Georgiana, who became Duchess of Bedford. She attacked " Vathek " Beckford too, and stayed more than a week at Fonthill, magnificently entertained—but without ever seeing the master of the house.

be arranged, and " Gordon's broad and brawny Grace " never encountered her young kinsman.

Crosby had now sold two importations, and had sent to Ridge for a third. " In every bookseller's window I see my *own name* and *say nothing*, but enjoy my fame in secret ". There were two critics at least who wanted more ; and he was preparing to gratify them by writing a long poem in blank verse on Bosworth Field. If it was ever finished, it was never published ; and the same fate awaited a novel of which 214 pages were written. But yet another piece of work was in hand : " a poem of 380 lines, to be published (without my name) in a few weeks, with notes . . . a Satire ". Of this there will presently be much to say.

In November Ridge resolved on printing a second edition ; and a new critic sprang up in the person of one Robert Charles Dallas, who was a connection by marriage,[1] and now took the opportunity of introducing himself by writing a complimentary letter about *Hours of Idleness* He was himself a voluminous writer of poetry and novels, all without exception forgotten —and he was destined, later in their connection, to prove himself a critic of value. But Dallas, though kindly and affectionate, was without a spark of humour ; and Byron, to whom he from the first dealt forth every solemnity of his excellence, soon perceived the fun that was to be had out of it, and responded with his most strident *fanfaronnade des vices*. His first answer was serious, but even in that he failed not to calumniate himself. " The events of my short life have been of so singular a nature. . . . I have been already held up as the votary of licentiousness and the disciple of infidelity. . . . My hand is almost as bad as my character ". Dallas, who had specially eulogised the moral qualities displayed in *Hours of Idleness*, was much distressed by this revelation, for he believed every word of it. He wrote at once, commending this time instead of the morality the candour of his kinsman ; and Byron, now fully alive to the darling opportunity, responded with a mystification in his best vein. He laid his soul bare : his erudition and his illiteracy, his folly and his cynicism, his immorality, infidelity—*toute la lyre* ! " You have here a brief compendium of the sentiments of the wicked George, Lord Byron ; and till I get a new suit, you will perceive I am badly clothed ". They continued their intercourse, nevertheless, and Dallas[2] proved, in the future, very useful—though not more so than Byron was generous to him.

---

[1] His sister, Henrietta Dallas, married George Anson Byron (second son of Admiral Byron), who was the poet's uncle. Their son succeeded our Byron in the title.

[2] Dallas, after Byron's death, wrote *Recollections of the Life of Lord*

There was a revival, too, of an old but lapsed friendship
—that with William Harness, who had been with him at Harrow.
Harness, when at ten years old he entered the school, was lame
(and always remained so) from an accident in childhood, and
was only just recovering from a severe illness. Byron, seeing
him attacked by a boy bigger than himself, interfered and took
his part ; and next day, finding the child standing alone, went
up to him and said, " If any one bullies you, tell me, and I'll
thrash him if I can ". That was a kind of relationship dear,
as we have learnt, to the young patron ; and Harness and he
were for a time inseparable. Later a coolness arose between
them—from absence (the truancy of the Mary Chaworth period)
and " the difference in our conduct ", as Byron wrote in February
1808, in a letter full of reminiscence and sentiment. " The
first lines I ever attempted at Harrow were addressed to you.
You were to have seen them ; but Sinclair[1] had the copy in his
possession when we went home ; —and, on our return, we were
strangers ". They never indeed spoke during Byron's last
year at school, nor till after the publication of *Hours of Idleness*.
Harness was then eighteen, and in one of the upper forms at
Harrow. He gave Moore the following account of their renewal
of intercourse. " In an English theme " [at Harrow] " I hap-
pened to quote from the volume,[2] and mention it with praise.
It was reported to Byron that I had, on the contrary, spoken
slightingly of his work and of himself . . . Wingfield . . . a
mutual friend of Byron and myself, disabused him of the error
into which he had been led, and this was the occasion of the
first letter "—that from which a passage has been quoted. " Our
intimacy was renewed, and continued from that time till his
going abroad. Whatever faults Byron might have had towards
others, to myself he was always uniformly affectionate. I have
many slights and neglects towards him to reproach myself with ;
but I cannot call to mind a single instance of caprice or unkind-

Byron from the year 1808 *to the end of* 1814, but the publication was stopped
by a decree (obtained by Byron's executors) in the Court of Chancery,
August 23, 1824—on the strength of certain letters to Mrs. Byron which it
contained. The book was republished in Paris, edited by the writer's son,
in 1825 (Galignani).

[1] " The prodigy of our schooldays was George Sinclair (son of Sir John) :
he made exercises for half the school (*literally*), verses at will, and themes
without it. . . . He was a friend of mine, and in the same remove, and
used at times to beg me to let him do my exercises—a request always most
readily accorded. . . . On the other hand, he was pacific, and I savage;
so I fought for him, or thrashed others for him, or thrashed himself to make
him thrash others. . . . I have some of his letters, written to me from
School, still " (Moore, p. 21).

[2] *Hours of Idleness*.

ness in the whole course of our friendship, to allege against
him ". [1]

Harness was among those friends whose portraits Byron
collected when he went abroad in 1809. He employed George
Sanders, one of the first miniature painters of the day (and
the painter also of several portraits of Byron, two of which
have been often engraved), to take them, " of course, at my
expense, as I never allow my acquaintance to incur the least
expenditure to gratify a whim of mine. . . . Just now " he
continued, " it seems foolish enough; but in a few years,
when some of us are dead, and others are separated . . . it
will be a kind of satisfaction to retain in these images of
the living the idea of our former selves, and to contemplate,
in the resemblances of the dead, all that remains of judgment,
feeling, and a host of passions." [2]

Thus, until the spring of 1808, the First Book brought him
nothing but good—new friendship and the revival of an old
one, flattery, and a little graceful renown. So high were his
spirits that two trips were projected. August 11, 1807, saw a
letter to Elizabeth : " On Sunday next I set off for the High-
lands ". Everything was minutely planned, Iceland was in-
cluded in the itinerary ; and all the Erse traditions were to be
collected into a volume to appear next spring. . . . Already,
in the August of 1805, the same dream had been dreamed, and
the Highlands had become a joke among his friends. Eliza-
beth Pigot now wrote to John : " How can you ask if Lord B.
is going to visit the Highlands in the summer ? Why, don't
you know that he never knows his own mind for ten minutes
together ? I tell him he is as fickle as the winds, and as uncertain
as the waves ". And sure enough, the Highlands were aban-
doned ; in October a fresh plan held the stage. " Next January
I am going to *sea* for four or five months with my cousin Captain

[1] Harness went to Christ's College, Cambridge, but this was after Byron
had left. He was ordained in 1812, and forms one of the group of clergy-
men who were, somewhat unexpectedly, among Byron's intimates. He
was a great friend of Mary Russell Mitford, who had an enthusiastic admira-
tion for him. He wrote her Life in collaboration with the Rev. A. G.
L'Estrange, whose *Life of the Rev. W. Harness* is the chief authority for his
career. To Harness Byron had intended to dedicate *Childe Harold*, but
feared to do so, " lest it should injure him in his profession " (*L. and J.*
i. 1177–80).

[2] It is interesting to discover here that Byron, like many another of us,
fell in love with his own phrases. This is shown by the reappearance of
" all that remains, etc." in his note to line 686 of *English Bards*,
which refers to his friend Lord Falkland's death in a duel (*Poems*, i.
351).

Bettesworth[1] who commands the *Tartar*, the finest frigate in the navy ". Mrs. Byron was to be kept in ignorance, " or she will be throwing her tomahawk at my curious projects ". They were going to the Mediterranean, or the West Indies, or the devil. But once again he failed to start for any of the destinations.

This was a time of great impecuniosity, and the financial strait induced some hours of deep depression. Hanson's letter-bag became again Byronic, in every sense of the word. And with the New Year of 1808 there came another turn of Fortune's wheel in the wrong direction. Byron heard that the *Edinburgh Review* was preparing to notice *Hours of Idleness*.

At that stage of its development, it was hardly possible for the *Edinburgh Review* to notice anything without truculently attacking it. " They had become *feræ naturæ* " said the author[2], of an anonymously published Memoir of Byron in 1822 ; and it was one of the few truths which his book contained. . . . Byron heard of the attack which was preparing, through a friend who had seen the critic's MS. and proof. He wrote to Becher, half-alarmed, half-gratified, at being of so much importance, " as they profess to pass judgment only on works requiring the public attention. They defeat their object by indiscriminate abuse, and they never praise except the partisans of Lord Holland and Co.". " That is to say ", notes Mr. Prothero, " the *Edinburgh Review* praised only Whigs."

The January number of the Wild Beast did not appear until the end of February. The article was there—the true, abominable article. He read it in one panting moment ; and just as he finished, a visitor was announced.[3] He raised his head as this friend entered. " Have you received a challenge, Byron ? " exclaimed the latter, so startled was he by the fierce defiance of the face. . . . Anger of such calibre is potent for beauty. That flashing face assails the imagination.

And what of the article ? The article was abominable ; the judgment was true. If a great critical journal were to notice

---

[1] Captain George Edmund Byron Bettesworth was, through his grand-mother, Sophia Trevanion " of Carhais, in Cornwall ", Byron's cousin. He was killed off Bergen in this year 1808, while in command of the *Tartar*.

[2] He was one John Watkins, LL.D. In a letter from Isaac d'Israeli to Byron, in 1822, we find an allusion to this extraordinary performance. " There was a shameless imposition practised by Colburn, who announced THE life of Lord Byron . . . by a heavy garrettier *en chef*, a Dr. Watkins, who is a dead hand at a Life ! And if your Lordship received your own life, it was enough to have deprived you of it !—for some have died of laughter " (*L. and J.* vi. 86). It was entitled *Memoirs Historical and Critical of the Life of Lord Byron, with anecdotes of some of his Contemporaries*. London, 1822.

[3] Moore, who tells the anecdote, does not give the visitor's name.

Hours of Idleness at all . . . But there precisely was the wrong. For the *Edinburgh Review* to notice *Hours of Idleness* at all was a confession of malice. Supreme as they were, and knew themselves to be, the Reviewers fell upon this garland of boyish verse—one out of a hundred volumes, neither worse nor better, of the year 1807—and tore it to pieces. And why *this* volume ? All the world knew why. Only this one bore a noble name on the title-page. " The opportunity " (said the *Quarterly* in 1831, reviewing Moore) " of insulting a lord, under pretext of admonishing a poetaster, was too tempting to be resisted, in a particular quarter, at that particular time ".[1]

For long Byron believed the author to have been Jeffrey, who edited the Review. The author was in reality—by his own acknowledgment, after denying it for thirty years[2]—Henry, Lord Brougham.[3] . . . By an odd turn of destiny, Byron in later life conceived for him a profound and bitter hatred. In *Don Juan* he wrote seven stanzas so depreciatory that he himself forbade Murray to print them. " But I by no means wish *him* not to *know* their existence or their tenor."

The day went by ; and he used always to narrate, in recalling it, that he drank three bottles of claret to his own share after dinner. But nothing relieved him till he had given vent to his indignation in rhyme, and after the first twenty lines, he felt considerably better. He wrote to Shelley, thirteen years later, " I recollect the effect on me . . . it was rage and resistance and redress ; but not despondency nor despair ". And on the same date to Murray, " [It] knocked me down, but I got up again ". He " got up again " with *English Bards and Scotch Reviewers*. But not until the March of 1809 ; for a year was spent in polishing weapons which had been already in order for attack, and were now retained to be made more deadly for defence. We have seen that in the October of 1807 he had told

---

[1] H. Crabb Robinson told De Morgan that at that time he was one day sitting with Charles Lamb when Wordsworth came in, " with fume in his countenance, and the *Edinburgh Review* in his hand. ' I have no patience with these Reviewers ', he said ; ' here is a young man, a lord, and a minor, it appears, who publishes a little volume of poetry, and these fellows attack him, as if no one may write poetry unless he lives in a garret. The young man will do something, if he goes on ' ".·

[2] Sir M. E. Grant-Duff, *Notes from a Diary*, ii. 189.

[3] In Medwin's *Conversations* Byron is represented as saying : " [Jeffrey] disowned it, and though he would not give up the aggressor, he said he would convince me, if I ever came to Scotland, who the person was. I have every reason to believe it was a certain lawyer, who hated me for something I had once said of Mrs. [George Lamb]. The technical language about ' minority pleas ', ' plaintiffs ', ' grounds of action ', etc., a jargon only intelligible to a lawyer, leaves no doubt in my mind on the subject ". The further context proves the suspected lawyer to have been Brougham.

Elizabeth Pigot of a Satire. It was entitled *British Bards* ; and now the 520 lines to which it ran were printed in book form, for convenience probably, by Ridge of Newark. After the *Edinburgh's* review, he set to work at enlarging and recasting this piece ; [1] and on March 16, 1809, the Satire, then and now entitled *English Bards and Scotch Reviewers*, appeared anonymously.

This delay in revenge is one of the very few actions of Byron which are unlike him. Excited as he had been, and rapid in composition as he was, it might well have been supposed that he would flame forth instantly. But for once he calculated. He perceived that his next move would be decisive for his future fame. *British Bards* was already a work of brilliant technique and pungent satire ; now the technique must be made dazzling, and the satire vitriolic. He concentrated on the task with all the force of his mind and of his burning anger ; and among the tools that he found ready to his hand were not only the recent swarm of literary and political lampoons—the *Baviad, Mœviad, Rolliad* ; Canning's *New Morality,* Mathias's *Pursuits of Literature,* Wolcot's (Peter Pindar's) brutalities—but another, older model, world-renowned and immortal as his own was to become : the filthy, glittering *Dunciad* of Alexander Pope. [2]

He studied it eagerly and profoundly, and caught the glitter, leaving the filth untouched. By the New Year of 1809 he thought his work finished, and took it up to London from Newstead— where by this time he was more or less installed, Lord Grey de Ruthyn's tenancy having ended in the April of 1808. But no sooner had the sheets gone to press than fresh matter occurred to him ; having once begun to add, the fever grew, and he increased the length by more than a hundred lines. Alterations, too, poured in on Dallas every day—for Dallas had undertaken to see it through the press. In one of his covering notes, Byron said, " Print soon, or I shall overflow with more rhyme " ; and this habit of feeding the printers to the very last moment remained with him as long as he remained within reach of them. Everything came in, as it were, for the Satire : a visit to the opera drove the young moralist to denounce its licentiousness. " A cut at the opera ! " he wrote gleefully to Dallas. " *Ecce signum !* from last night's observations ".[3] The twenty lines in question were struck off after his return, and sent next morning

---

[1] A single copy, which he kept for corrections and additions, was preserved by Dallas, and is now in the British Museum.

[2] Moore thought that from this period dated " the enthusiastic admiration which he ever afterwards cherished for this great poet ".

[3] The piece which provoked the outburst was *I Villeggiatori Rezzani*, at the King's Theatre, February 21, 1809. Naldi and Catalani were the principal singers.

for the printer. . . . So it went on ; but at last he was ready, and on March 16 (just after taking his seat in the House of Lords) *English Bards and Scotch Reviewers* burst upon the town. Its success was instantaneous. James Cawthorn, of the British Library, 24 Cockspur Street, London, was the publisher[1] (*vice* Ridge of Newark, deposed), and printed an edition of a thousand. Byron had modestly protested : " We shall never sell a thousand ; then why print so many ? "—but the work was seen at once to be of genius, and moreover, conjecture fastened eagerly upon the author's name. London was soon murmurous with the right one ; and Dallas, visiting Hatchard's, heard the kind of report which makes, for its delightful moment, an author's life seem truly worth the living. Hatchard had sold a great many, had none left, was sending for more—and on being asked by the wily friend for the author's name, said that a lady of distinction had, without hesitation, asked for the Satire as Lord Byron's. This was good, but Hatchard had a still keener bliss to impart. " Gifford had spoken very highly of it " . . . . In Byron's literary character there are few features more singular than the immense, (and, says Henley, very fatuous) respect which he entertained for Gifford. He called him his Magnus Apollo, and a little while before his death wrote : " I have always considered him as my literary father, and myself as his prodigal son ". The prodigal sonship was the outcome of remorse for his own departure from the methods of Pope—of whom, as we have seen and shall see, he was a worshipper. Gifford was now the high priest of the Alexandrine tradition, and *English Bards* was frankly modelled on the *Dunciad*. He had apparently seen it in MS., for it was before its publication that Byron, hearing of his comments, wrote hysterically to their common friend, Hodgson, that " it was too good to be true . . . . but even the idea was too precious to part with ".[2]

[1] The house of Longman & Co. refused it, together (as Byron wrote in 1822) with " half the trade " in London, " though *no* demand was made ". " *They know nothing* ", was his comment on this timidity.

[2] Henley's note on Gifford is too vivid to be passed over. " His literary temper is atrocious ; his criticisms, whether aggressive or corrective, seem the effect of downright malignity ; in the long-run you are tempted to side with his victims. . . . Monstrous though it seem to us now . . . this alliance " [Byron's and Gifford's] " between Leviathan and a blind-worm (so to speak) was genuine, and the sincerity of neither party to it can be impugned ". Swinburne called Gifford an asp ; but he did good service to literature in the *Baviad*, the *Mæviad*, and the *Epistle to Peter Pindar*—in the two first, utterly annihilating the Della-Cruscan school of poetry, and in the last, " checking the insolence of as bold and hard-hitting a ruffian as the journalism of the time could boast " (Henley). Gifford's physical deformity may have had something to do with his attraction for Byron.

Thus did he achieve his revenge—and such a revenge as
author never had before nor since. The town rang with his
name, and the triumph was no flash in the pan, no success of
scandal (as it might well have been with mere personal satire
for the theme) ; but the unmistakable emergence of genius—
genius that had come to stay. In 1809 *English Bards and
Scotch Reviewers* was read with glee and admiration, and neither
emotion hesitates as we turn the leaves to-day. Every page
must be heavily fringed with notes ere we may grasp the point
of the gibes, yet it is with eyes already mirthful that we seek
the margin. Praise of topical satire can go no further. If after
the lapse of a hundred years it can do this, it has done all. Here
first, then, but again and again to be reckoned with, we encounter
that spell of personality which may be called the secret of
Byronism. He struck such fire into everything he did that, in
a sense, it hardly mattered what he did or how he did it. The
words (sometimes well, but seldom supremely well, chosen)
ring with the very sound of him—the voice of his being, as it
were—and are more stirring than the better chosen words of
others. The *Dunciad* is a case in point. It was his chief model
for the Satire, and is superior in every kind of accomplishment ;
but accomplishment is just what Byron seemed so miraculously
able to dispense with. We read the *Dunciad* now, and smile
a little, dimly, when we do not yawn. We see the glitter and the
high technique (though the opening seems to me the dullest of
things readable), and for their sakes condone the filth ; but our
eyes do not light nor our spirits unaccountably rise—we do
not, in short, feel that we have enjoyed ourselves. That is
what we do feel as we close the *English Bards*, with its inimitably
vivid opening, its bold quick flights, its lines (hackneyed now)
that have the very accent of the master :

> " 'Tis pleasant, sure, to see one's name in print,
>   A book's a book, altho' there's nothing in't " ;

> " Oh, Amos Cottle ! Phœbus ! what a name
>   To fill the speaking-trump of future fame ! "

and that amusing one, cancelled for an inferior in the fifth
edition :[1]

> " In many marble-covered volumes view
>   *Hayley, in vain attempting something new* ".

If such enjoyment of so faulty a performance remains inex-
plicable, it is because nearly everything about Byron remains

---

[1] The fifth edition was suppressed by himself.   It passed under his own
supervision, and from it the text in the Coleridge edition of the *Poems* has
been printed.

so—and that by reason of the personal magic which has itself from all time baffled its shrewdest analysts.

The Reviewers had called forth this, its earliest manifestation ; and though it must in any case have emerged, we feel that it is possible to close the account of English literature with the Scottish Wild Beast in a spirit of gratitude. Jeffrey—" dear d——d contemner of my early Muse "—became one of his kindliest critics ; and when the tumult and the shouting had died, the editor probably read again the Review's initiatory trumpet-blast and its far-echoing answer, and decided to be unremorseful for a sin which had had so exhilarating a retribution.

But Byron, already in 1811, regretted having written *English Bards*. On his way home from the Albanian tour, writing to Dallas of the fourth edition, he said his *mea culpa* ; and when, a year later, he became intimate with Lord and Lady Holland —therein bitterly attacked—and heard through Samuel Rogers that they would be glad if the Satire were withdrawn, he gave instant orders to Cawthorn to burn the whole impression, then being printed, of the fifth edition.[1] Not only so, but in 1816 at Diodati, reading it over in a copy of the fourth edition,[2] he recorded his own severe judgment of himself in the pages. On the first leaf we find :

" The binding of this volume is considerably too valuable for its contents.
" Nothing but the consideration of its being the property of another prevents me from consigning this miserable record of misplaced anger and indiscriminate acrimony to the flames ".

All through the copy ran his comments, mostly adverse. " Unjust " (to the lines on Wordsworth and Coleridge) ; " too savage all this on Bowles " ; " too ferocious—this is mere insanity ", on the margin of the page containing the truly ferocious attack upon the *Edinburgh Review* and Jeffrey ; while in the verses on Lord Carlisle he perceived also an undue violence. " The provocation was not sufficient " ; " much too savage, whatever the foundation may be ". Yet his feeling for that nobleman had altered little, and had had little reason to alter. His concluding remark on the whole performance is : " The greater part of this Satire I most sincerely wish had never been written ; not only on account of the injustice of much of the critical and

[1] A few copies escaped. Dallas kept two ; one belongs to Mr. John Murray, and the other is in the British Museum.
[2] This now belongs to the house of Murray.

some of the personal part of it, but the tone and temper are such as I cannot approve ". In his letters and journals, too, there are many entries of the same kind : " that confounded Satire " ; " that plaguy Satire "—and he strictly forbade Murray, when in 1817 a large edition of his Collected Works was in contemplation, to republish *English Bards*. " I would not reprint them on any consideration ".[1] In 1815 he sent Leigh Hunt a copy containing some manuscript corrections previous to an edition which was printed, but not published. It was the only one he himself possessed, though Lady Byron had a copy ; and he added a postscript to say that it was not in print for sale, nor ever would be (if he could help it) again.

We can the more cordially admire this remorse because we rejoice in the impotence of great renown. The name is supreme, and the cry of posterity is urgent—and posterity wins always at that tussle. . . . In 1813 they were reading and praising the plaguy Satire in America ; and he wrote : " To be popular in a rising and far country has a kind of *posthumous feel* ". As one copies those ingenuous words, writing of him in this nineteen-hundred-and-ten, one is conscious of an emotion that annihilates comment.

[1] During his lifetime no English edition (but several unauthorised American and foreign ones) appeared until 1823, when one Benbow, dating from the notorious Byron's Head—which Southey described as " a preparatory school for the brothel and the gallows "—brought out a pirated impression. Byron was then in Greece, and probably knew nothing of it.

CHAPTER VIII

NEWSTEAD—1808–1809

The Abbey—The Byron Oak—Early days at Newstead—Boatswain —Francis Hodgson—Hobhouse and Byron—Money troubles—His majority—" Thinness "—Byron's personal beauty—Lord Carlisle, and the introduction to the House of Lords—The attack on Carlisle—A bachelor party at Newstead—The Paphian Girls—Preparations for the Albanian tour

WHEN in the April of 1808, Lord Grey de Ruthyn's lease of Newstead Abbey terminated, Byron was already head over ears in debt. " *Entre nous*, I am cursedly dipped ", he wrote to Mr. Becher at the end of March. " My debts, *everything* included, will be nine or ten thousand before I am twenty-one ". With such a burden on his shoulders, he was thinking seriously at that time of selling the Abbey ; for Rochdale, the Lancashire estate, was (once he could make his title clear) worth three Newsteads. But though he might calmly plan, before revisiting it, such alienation of his heritage of the heart, he needed only to see it again for all thought of selling to be scattered to the winds. Here is a letter to Mrs. Byron, in March 1809, after he had lived at the Abbey for half a year. " . . . Come what may, *Newstead* and I *stand* or fall together. I have now lived on the spot, I have fixed my heart upon it, and no pressure, present or future, shall induce me to barter the last vestige of our inheritance. I have that pride within me which will enable me to support difficulties. I can endure privations ; but could I obtain in exchange for Newstead Abbey the first fortune in the country, I would reject the proposition. Set your mind at ease on that score ; Mr. Hanson talks like a man of business. . . . I feel like a man of honour, and I will not sell Newstead ".[1]

The Abbey laid a threefold spell upon him. It appealed to his pride of ancestry, his poetic imagination, and (never to

---

[1] We shall see that in 1812 he found himself obliged to put the Abbey up for auction. No sale was effected. Later in the same year another attempt was made, but this, too, ultimately failed. Not until November 1817 was the estate actually sold.

be omitted from any reckoning in which Byron is concerned) his vanity—for the lovely place conferred prestige in fullest measure. William, fifth Baron, had cruelly marred, and Grey de Ruthyn, leaseholder, had basely neglected; but Newstead emerged from both ordeals as it were with the imperishable beauty of the soul, to pierce him as such beauty always could —and never more than in absence from its spell! For though to the spirit of the place he paid little outward tribute—his way of life there was as uninspired as elsewhere—yet the long revocation in *Juan* of that " Norman Abbey " leaves no doubt that Newstead was one of the great affections of Byron's heart. He brooded on it, as he brooded on the Lady of the Dream, and could never have loved either so well if he had not lost them. Directly love in any form appears, he is the Sentimentalist— ready to feel everything, and to do nothing. For friendship, fame, and freedom he could act; for love he could only dream.

He took up residence at the Abbey in September 1808, after having obtained his M.A. degree at Cambridge; and he found the house and grounds unimaginably neglected. Long, long ago, when the little boy from Aberdeen arrived at the place of his inheritance, he had planted a sapling oak in the park, and had made it into an omen of his own destiny: as the tree flourished, so should he. Already in 1807 Fate, in that shape, had menaced. He had gone to see the oak, and had found it choked with weeds, almost destroyed. In the early volume of poems he recorded the experience, but not without a hope for the future, since as soon as he should again possess the " land of his fathers " the tree was to know such care as must restore it. Now it was among the earliest matters to be seen to, and it responded to his hope; for when Colonel Wildman bought the Abbey in 1817, he noticed a fine young oak—which nevertheless he designed to cut down, for it grew in an improper place. But a servant who was with him on the tour of inspection pleaded that " my lord was very fond of it, because he set it himself "; and Colonel Wildman at once yielded. The oak was thereafter especially cherished, and to this day forms one of the sights of the place.

The house was almost unfit for habitation. Repairs were instantly begun, for not only did Byron mean to live there himself until the spring of 1809, but he wished the Abbey to be his mother's home when he was away. A foreign tour was this time positively decided on, but as usual there were conflicting projects: Persia, India, " in March or May at farthest ". They crystallised into the Albanian tour of 1809-11, on which he did not start until the end of June. Mrs. Byron had long desired to enjoy a sojourn at Newstead, but her son was resolute that she should not be installed until *he* had left. Her infirmities of temper were not alone the reason for this. He had now a little knot of friends and acquaintances whom he looked forward to entertaining, and the courses which suited them and him were not such as could be pursued under any maternal eye. Charles Skinner Matthews, Scrope Davies, Hobhouse, were the centre-pieces ; but there were to be others, and among them that brother to whom Lady P—— had listened at Brighton. All such projects, however, had to be put off, for at first the Abbey was the prey of the British workman.

In November he lost his dear Boatswain. Byron's love for dogs—for animals of all kinds—was remarkable ; and now, with the Newfoundland's death, he was to display it in a violently exaggerated form. He wrote the tidings to a new friend, Francis Hodgson. " Boatswain is dead ! He expired in a state of mad-ness on the 18th, after suffering much, yet retaining all the gentleness of his nature to the last, never attempting to do the least injury to any one near him. I have now lost everything except old Murray." What he did not tell Hodgson was that he had himself more than once with his bare hand wiped away slaver from the lips during the paroxysms. The whole world knows of the dog's monument, which is a conspicuous feature of the gardens at Newstead ; and Byron long desired to be buried in the same vault.[1] The strange Will of 1811 enshrined this sick fancy—which was twice emphatically expressed. The solicitors protested ; his answer was, " It must stand ". For the monument he wrote an inscription, which, together with some lines to Boatswain's memory, adorns the stone.

NEAR this spot
Are deposited the remains of one
Who possessed Beauty without Vanity
Strength without Insolence
Courage without Ferocity
And all the Virtues of Man without his Vices.
This praise which would be unmeaning Flattery
If inscribed over human ashes
Is but a just tribute to the Memory of
BOATSWAIN, a Dog
Who was born at Newfoundland, May 1803,
And died at Newstead Abbey, November 18, 1808.

The lines,[2] which breathe the same spirit, contain one couplet as familiar as anything he ever wrote :

[1] His " old Murray " was to be there too ; but Joe had his misgivings on the point. To a gentleman viewing the tomb, he once said, " If I was sure his lordship would come here, I should like it well enough, but I should not like to lie alone with the dog ".

[2] It is at least disconcerting to find, on the authority of Byron's own

" To mark a friend's remains these stones arise ;
I never knew but one—and here he lies ".

John Cordy Jeaffreson, with that shrewdness which often
redeems his oftener foolish book, comments thus on the Boat-
swain incident : " [Byron's] loves, hatreds, friendships, griefs,
were so passionate that as long as any one of them was in full
force . . . it possessed him completely, and caused him for the
moment to imagine he had never loved or abhorred any one else.
Touched by grief for the death of his . . . dog, the young man
who could not go abroad for a couple of years without taking
miniatures of his Harrow ' favourites ' with him, wrote of the
animal . . . ' *I never knew but one,* etc.' " ; and he gives two or
three further instances as characteristic in their exaggeration
of the moment's feeling. Thus—for an example of my own—
Byron had with him at this very time his then dearest friend,
John Cam Hobhouse. " Hobhouse hunts as usual, and your
humble servant ' drags at each remove a lengthened chain ' ".
This rather enigmatic quotation of Goldsmith might well (if it
actually does not) refer to the chain of *English Bards and Scotch
Reviewers.* He was deep in that affair, and was keeping his
hand in at lyrics too, for this is the time of the dinner with Mary
Chaworth-Musters [1] which was twice celebrated in verse, and
described in a letter to Francis Hodgson.

That new crony had come upon the scene in 1807. He was
then just about to take up the position of resident tutor at King's
College, Cambridge, and was an intimate of Henry Drury—the
one-time Harrow foe, but now, with mellowed tempers on both
sides, become a familiar friend. There was soon a far more
powerful magnet than this to draw Hodgson and Byron together.
Hodgson, in 1807, published a translation of Juvenal, and was
set upon by the *Edinburgh Review.* When Byron first met him
he was meditating a Satire to be called *Gentle Alterative for the
Reviewers,* while the other, as yet unscathed, was nevertheless
engaged on *British Bards.* The new year of 1808 brought, on
its twenty-seventh of February, Byron's baptism of vitriol—and
at once the pair of victims rushed into one another's arms. To
make the gesture still more passionate on Byron's part, Hodgson
was a friend of Gifford. Gifford had praised the Juvenal (gener-

dating, that these lines to Boatswain's memory were written nearly three
weeks before the dog died. Mr. Prothero (*L. and J.* iii. 170) refers for the
date—October 30, 1808—to a note inserted in Mrs. Byron's copy of
Imitations and Translations, a miscellany of Hobhouse's which was pub-
lished in 1809. (See *Imitations and Translations from the Antient and
Modern Classics : Together with Original Poems never before Published,*
1809, p. 191.) The lines on Boatswain were first published in this.
  [1] See Chapter IV.

ously, for had he not done one himself ?) ; Gifford corresponded with the lucky translator ; moreover, Hodgson was unorthodox in the Alexandrine religion only so far as to admire Dryden a little more fervently than Pope. An acquaintance so haloed was golden with promise, and the link between them grew stronger through the next few years. Hodgson was a potent rhymester ; one of his critics said that he appeared literally to think in verse.

Hobhouse, hunting as usual, must nevertheless have spent some hours in rhyming like the rest—for in 1809 he published that *Miscellany* which Charles Skinner Matthews would never call anything but the Miss-sell-any. The austerity which had made Hobhouse recoil from the white hat and grey horse at Cambridge evidently still lingered—for when Byron wrote the *Lines to a Lady on being asked my Reason for Quitting England in the Spring*, he did not dare to show them to his guest, but sent them to Hodgson as the first reader, for " Hobhouse hates everything of the kind." This censor's view of other mani-festations continued to be repressive ; for exuberance of any kind he had no love. In May he had written from Cambridge to the young man about town : " I learn with delight from Scrope Davies that you have totally given up dice. To be sure you must give it up ; for you to be seen every night in the very vilest company in town—could anything be more shocking, any-thing more unfit ? I speak feelingly on this occasion, *non ignoro mali miseris*, etc. I know of nothing that should bribe me to be present once more at such horrible scenes ". . . .[1] But Byron, with an unconquerable zest for experience joined to a vast capacity for self-delusion, was the victim of chance's glamour to a degree which Hobhouse, more serene and lucid in spirit, could not even imagine. In the quasi-journal of 1821—*Detached Thoughts*—he wrote : " I have a notion that gamblers are as happy as many people, being always *excited*. Women, wine, fame, the table—even ambition, *sate* now and then ; but every turn of the card and cast of the dice keeps the gamester alive ; besides, one can game ten times longer than one can do anything else. I was very fond of it when young, that is to say of hazard, for I hate all *card* games—even faro. When macco (or whatever they spell it) was introduced, I gave up the whole thing, for I loved and missed the *rattle* and *dash* of the box and dice, and the glorious uncertainty, not only of good luck or bad luck, but *of any luck at all*, as one had sometimes to throw *often* to decide at all. I have thrown as many as fourteen mains running, and carried off all the cash upon the table . . . but I had no coolness, or judgment, or calculation. It was the delight of the thing that pleased me. Upon the whole, I left off in time, without

[1] *L. and J.* i. note to p. 219.

being much of a winner or a loser. Since one-and-twenty years of age I played but little, and then never above a hundred, or two, or three ". On this topic, Jeaffreson again displays his flickering shrewdness : " When a gamester prates of ' having left off in time, etc. ', it may be taken for certain that he did not leave off in time." And Byron's ten thousand pounds' worth of liabilities, contracted in two years, puts a startling gloss on the maxim.

In that extract, we see part of the reason for Hobhouse's failure to influence Byron. He had force, lucidity, and kindness ; he loved and was loved ; yet he never prevailed in even minor matters. The reason was that these friends, when they turned the same leaf in the primer of experience, learned wholly different lessons from it. Byron's definition of happiness was (as we have just seen) excitement. Hobhouse found such excitement merely a weariness—and knew it. Byron, in the long run, found it a weariness too, but seemed unable to realise that he did. When he was bored, he arraigned the world, the heavens, the Deity —anything but the thing that was actually depressing him. No error is more common ; but he made it seem uncommon by the passion of his perplexed resentment.

Soon he was alone at the Abbey. " I could not bear the company of my best friend above a month ", he wrote to Augusta. The Rochdale litigation was lagging ; he had suggested a compromise to Hanson, but felt himself too ignorant of such things to be anything but a reed before the wind. " I suppose it will end in my marrying a *Golden Dolly*, or blowing my brains out ; it does not much matter which, the remedies are nearly alike."

This was another season of Byronism for Hanson, for from the mother also letters poured into his hands. She was in the same dark mood. " I can see nothing but the Road to Ruin in all this . . . unless, indeed, Coal Mines turn to Gold Mines, or that he mends his fortune in the old and usual way by marrying a Woman with two or three hundred thousand pounds ". . . . It was in such condition of mind and pocket that he celebrated his majority on January 22, 1809.[1] The Newstead festivities were pathetic ; he was absent, and money and friends were absent too. An ox was roasted for the farmers and peasantry of the estate, and in the evening there was something in the nature of a ball— but the only thing Moore could discover about it was that John Hanson was among the dancers. The hero of the day had his own method of commemorating it. In a letter to John Murray,

[1] He spent the day in London at Reddish's Hotel, and Dallas found him in high spirits (*Recollections*, p. 161).

written from Genoa in 1822, he says : " Did I ever tell you that
the day I came of age I dined on eggs and bacon and a bottle
of ale for once in a way ?　They are my favourite dish and
drinkable ; but as neither of them agree with me, I never use
them but on great jubilees—once in four or five years or so."

The Thinning Campaign was still going on.　It was to go on
all his life, for though vanity was one reason—and in his case,
because of the form his corpulency took, a sufficient one—mere
common-sense as well demanded an increasing vigilance in the
matter of food.　Whenever he ate largely, he suffered madden-
ing torments ; and though at this age the worst of such troubles
were still in the future, he never was able, at any age, to eat as
other people do.　At twenty-one, he had attained his full stature
of " five feet eight *and a half* inches ".　Jeaffreson is gnomic
again : " In questions of height, it may be laid down as a sure
maxim that the man who claims credit for the extra half-inch,
claims credit for what he does not possess.　In his boots Byron
stood a trifle over five feet eight inches ; but this was the height
of a man standing on his toes, with heels raised by boots of
peculiar make.　His actual height was midway between five
feet seven and five feet eight inches.　And on the nineteenth
anniversary of his birthday this young man of average height
weighed fourteen stone and six pounds ".　Nor was it an ordinary,
all-prevailing fatness—for his shoulders and arms were unusually
broad and thewy, while his legs were undeveloped.　But worst
of all was the effect upon his face.　" It became swollen to unsight-
liness with fleshy tissue."

One is tempted to exclaim, in a parody of Caponsacchi :　" No,
sir, I cannot have the Byron fat ! "　The world could not indeed
have had it ;　and *he* emphatically declined the state.　No
means were neglected :　" violent exercise, much physic, and hot
baths ". . . .　What can the violent exercise have been ?　He
could swim and ride—but these are no exercises for the reduc-
tion of fat.　And " in Byron's days at Trinity, the Cam knew
nothing about eight-oars, and four-oars, and sculling matches ",
which would have been a pleasant way to the desired slenderness.
He could spar with Jackson, and fence with Angelo, but only
for short spurts and at the cost of intense pain.　So the means
were, in sober truth, restricted to starvation, much physic, and
hot baths ;　and all these were unsparingly employed.　Byron
has been scorned for this vigilance ;　I agree with Jeaffreson that
the scorn is unconsidered.　" When a man cannot be natural
without looking like a hog, he does well to be unnatural for the
sake of looking like a man ".　And perhaps it is, more than any-
thing else, the fact that Byron, in being unnatural, achieved not
only the looking like a man, but the looking like an angel, which

has caused him to be derided. If he had emerged an average advertisement of his processes, we may conjecture that much less would have been heard of them.

Moreover, with the thickness of body, he found that there arrived a corresponding thickness of mind ; and when we add to this the further power of dyspepsia to stupefy its victims, we perceive that Byron—to whom his intellectual activity brought the only real happiness he ever knew—had motives more than sufficient for the sacrifices which he made. Gross, stupid, and repulsive ! When we find the man who can accept that destiny without a struggle, we have found one whose destiny is of little importance.

The effect of the austerities was, as I have said, all too enviable. There issued from them a creature of " matchless beauty " —of beauty about which such observers as Walter Scott, Coleridge,[1] Stendhal, were eloquent in later years. " I never in my life saw anything more beautiful or more impressive. Even now, when I think of the expression which a great painter should give to genius, I always have before me that magnificent head ". So Stendhal wrote. And Walter Scott : " The beauty of Byron is one which makes one dream ". Writing of him in 1816, Scott said further that a brother-poet (probably himself) had compared Byron's features to the sculpture of a beautiful alabaster vase, lighted up from within.

I suppose there are few of us who have not believed, and some of us who still believe, that Byron's colouring was dark. On the contrary, his hair was light chestnut in childhood, and " never darkened to the deepest brown of auburn " ; his blue-grey eyes seemed dark only by reason of their black lashes ; and the tone and tint of his complexion were those of transparent fairness. There was scarcely one personal charm that he did not possess. The hair, luxuriant and lustrous, was of feather-like softness—while with our modern revolt from the cult of curly locks in a man, we may console ourselves for *his* ringlets by the knowledge (acquired from Scrope Davies) that they were not natural. Scrope, in the great Dandy-Days of 1813, penetrated into the poet's bedroom one morning before he was up or even awake ; and found him with his hair in curl-papers. " Ha, ha ! the S—S—Sleeping Beauty ! " cried a familiar stammer (Davies had an irresistible stammer) among the dreamings. The Sleeping Beauty awoke. He was very angry at first, but soon saw that there was only one way to take it. " I'm a d—d fool ! " Davies acquiesced : " But I was sure your hair curled naturally ".

---

[1] Coleridge said : " So beautiful a countenance I scarcely ever saw . . . his eyes the open portals of the sun—things of light, and for light " (*Astarte*, pp. 14–15).

" Yes—naturally, every night ; but don't let the cat out of the bag, for I'm as vain of my curls as a girl of sixteen ".[1]

With the burden of fat removed, Byron's form became graceful and buoyant ; he could move with ease and security, though of course only for short distances. To hide his lameness, he would " enter a room quickly, running rather than walking, and stop himself by planting the sound foot on the ground, and resting on it. On the rare occasions when he was seen walking in the streets . . . he moved with a peculiar sliding gait . . . in fact, with the gait of a person walking on the balls and toes of his feet, and doing his best to hide this singular mode of progression ".[2] He never could forget his one defect—the Bad Fairy's bundle. Once he turned on Hobhouse, and said irritably (they were walking together in his garden at Genoa) : " Now I know you're looking at my foot ". " My dear Byron ", said Hobhouse, " nobody ever thinks of or looks at anything but your head ". Perhaps the morbidity was the more natural because he was so richly otherwise endowed. Lips, chin, brow, throat, hands—the slim white hands upon which he prided himself racially no less than personally—all were exquisite ; and as if to sum up in expression the beauty of the whole, he had a voice which made the children of a house he frequented in later years distinguish him from other visitors as " the gentleman who speaks like music ".

But enough ! See Byron we must ; gloat over him we may not. He was preposterously beautiful, and there is no concealing it ; but he was so much more besides that, once stated, his loveliness may be for practical purposes forgotten.

He left Newstead for London on January 19, with the MS. of his Satire in his pocket. There was, besides that, another

---

[1] Gronow, *Reminiscences*, 1st series, p. 209. But this statement of Scrope Davies was flatly denied by Lady Anne Blunt, Byron's granddaughter, from the evidence of locks of Byron's hair in her possession (*Astarte*, p. 321).

[2] Jeaffreson (p. 36), from whom I quote, says the left foot was the comparatively sound one. He gives (p. 22) a decisive statement of the case. " The lameness . . . was due to the contraction of the tendon Achilles of each foot, which, preventing him from putting his heels to the ground, compelled him to walk on the balls and toes of his feet. Both feet may have been equally well formed, save in this sinew, till one of them was subjected to injudicious surgery ; the right, however, being considerably smaller than the left. . . . This foot was also considerably distorted, so as to turn inwards ". But this Jeaffreson attributes to the operations of Lavender, the Nottingham quack. He considers also that such a form of lameness was far more afflicting to the body and vexatious to the spirits than the lameness of an ordinary club-foot like Sir Walter Scott's. " Had Sir Walter been constrained to pick his way through life hopping about like a bird . . . he would certainly have been less happy " than he was " with his club-foot to plant firmly on the ground " (p. 23). (I quote from the standard edition.)

serious matter to be attended to—the taking of his seat in the House of Lords. Byron was under the impression that it was necessary—or at any rate so customary as to seem necessary— for a young peer, on presenting himself, to have some friend's support. He had therefore written to Lord Carlisle to say that he should be of age at the opening of the session. The hint at desire for an introduction was plain, and, despite the glacial nature of their intercourse, he had confidently expected the mere courtesy of an offer to be with him. A note arrived from Carlisle. It acquainted him with the technical etiquette of the occasion—and that was all.

Byron already conceived himself to have reason for resentment against his former guardian. *Hours of Idleness*, in its second edition (with the altered title of *Poems Original and Translated*), had been dedicated to " The Right Honourable Frederick, Earl of Carlisle . . . by his Obliged Ward and Affectionate Kinsman ". Mr. Prothero thinks that Carlisle may never have seen the dedication ; but, however that may be, Carlisle *had* seen and acknowledged a copy of the privately-printed Juvenilia in 1807. He had written before opening the book—a method often recommended for recipients of authors' copies, though its artifice should be transparent for all but the very ingenuous. Byron, of course, had seen through it from the first. No further tribute had come ; and now, in conveying his hope for a friendly face and hand at his first appearance in the Lords, he had felt himself to be giving Carlisle a last chance—though indeed a further test was (unavoidably) to be afforded, and was to be used in the wonted manner. This was concerned with the same business. To enable the sixth Baron Byron to take his seat in the House of Lords, it was essential to procure affidavits of his grandfather's marriage with Miss Sophia Trevanion, which had been celebrated in the private chapel of Carhais in Cornwall. No certificates [1] were to be found, so affidavits became indispensable. There was difficulty in procuring evidence ; and it was thought that Carlisle, whose mother had been Admiral Byron's sister, might be able to give some. Possibly, as Mr. Prothero suggests, he had none to give—but of his refusal (the word is Moore's, as well as Byron's) " to afford any explanation respecting the family ", one cannot help suspecting that the manner left something to be desired. True, he was ailing [2] ; true also that within the last

---

[1] " Before Lord Hardwicke's Marriage Act, the records of . . . regular marriages celebrated in private chapels were kept so carelessly that it was no uncommon thing for people to be without legal evidence of their wedlock " (Jeaffreson, p. 125).

[2] But Mr. Prothero, his apologist, merely says " it is certain that in 1809 he was ill " . . . a vague date !

few years, he had heard little to gratify him of his young cousin, already depreciated in favour by that troublesome mother; but when every point in Carlisle's favour is weighed, there remains a repugnant impression of priggishness—the more repugnant too in him, because his own investiture of virtue had been so tardy.

By March 13, however, the proofs of the marriage were obtained without his aid. On that day, Dallas (who was occupied in seeing the Satire through the press) happened to pass down St. James's Street—Byron's quarters were at No. 8—and saw his " chariot " at the door. Dallas had had no intention of calling, but this induced him to go in, and he found his host somewhat pale and agitated. " I am going to take my seat in the Lords ", said he; " I am glad you happened to come in; perhaps you will go with me ? " " I expressed ", says Dallas, " my readiness to attend him; while at the same time I concealed the shock I felt on thinking that this young man, who by birth, fortune and talent, stood high in life, should have lived so unconnected and neglected by persons of his own rank that there was not a single member of the senate to which he belonged, to whom he could or would apply to introduce him in a manner becoming his birth. I saw that he felt the situation, and I fully partook his indignation ".

They drove down to the House, which was very empty. Lord Eldon, the Lord Chancellor, was going through some ordinary business. Byron looked (thought Dallas, watching him in the sympathy which was so keen yet tactful through all the poignant incident) " even paler than before; and he certainly wore a countenance in which mortification was mingled with, but subdued by, indignation ". After the oaths had been administered, the Lord Chancellor left his seat and went towards the novice with a smile, putting out his hand to welcome him. Byron made a stiff bow, and put the tips of his fingers into the Lord Chancellor's hand. The overture so repulsed was not continued; Eldon went back to his place, and Byron, carelessly seating himself for form's sake, remained but a minute or two in the assembly of which he was now a member. . . . Dallas had not been able to hear anything of what the Lord Chancellor and he had said to one another. What had passed was an apology from the former for the delay caused by legal demands—the certificates, affidavits, and so forth. " These forms are part of my *duty* ", Eldon had murmured. " Pray do not apologise ", the pale and angry-eyed young stranger had replied. " Your Lordship . . . did your *duty*, and you did *no more* ".

On rejoining Dallas, Byron did not speak of this. He merely said, on hearing his friend's regret at the repulsion of Eldon's advance, " If I had shaken hands heartily, he would have set me down for one of his party—but I will have nothing to do with any of them, on either side ". They went back to his rooms. He was terribly dejected. The one prospect that he clung to seemed to be the foreign trip ; even the Satire had for the moment lost interest for him. In a day or two he returned to Newstead—there to remain, in what frame of mind we may conjecture, until the success of *English Bards and Scotch Reviewers* brought him back to town.

His original intention had been to insert a compliment to his guardian.

> " Lords too are Bards : such things at times befall,
> And 'tis some praise in Peers to write at all.
> Yet, did or Taste or Reason sway the times,
> Ah ! who would take their titles with their rhymes ?
> On *one* alone Apollo deigns to smile,
> And crowns a new Roscommon in Carlisle ".

But Dallas had written in a spirit of pure criticism to protest against this. " I agree that there is only *one* among the peers on whom Apollo deigns to smile ; but, believe me, that peer is no *relation* of yours ". Byron acquiesced so far as to alter, but the alteration still was kind. On his twenty-first birthday he received [1] from Carlisle the letter which has been described ; and between the twenty-fifth of the same month and the second week in February, the following lines were written (to be added after, " Ah ! who would take their titles with their rhymes ? ") :

> " Roscommon ! Sheffield ! with your spirits fled
> No future laurels deck a noble head ;
> No Muse will cheer, with renovating smile,
> The paralytic puling of Carlisle.[2]
> The puny schoolboy and his early lay
> Men pardon, if his follies pass away ;
> But who forgives the Senior's ceaseless verse,
> Whose hairs grow hoary as his rhymes grow worse ?
> What heterogeneous honours deck the Peer !
> Lord, rhymester, *petit-maître*, pamphleteer !
> So dull in youth, so drivelling in his age,
> His scenes alone had damned our sinking stage ;
> But Managers for once cried, ' Hold, enough ! '
> Nor drugged their audience with the tragic stuff ".

---

[1] Dallas, *Recollections*, 1824, pp. 16, 17.
[2] Carlisle suffered from a nervous disorder, and Byron was informed that some readers had scented an allusion in the words, " paralytic puling ". " I thank Heaven ", he wrote in his diary, " I did not know it ; and would not, could not, if I had. I must naturally be the last person to be pointed on defects or maladies ".

There was a further allusion later in the poem, and to this Byron appended a prose note :

" It may be asked, why I have censured the Earl of Carlisle, my guardian and relative, to whom I dedicated a volume of puerile poems a few years ago ? The guardianship was nominal, at least as far as I have been able to discover ; the relationship I cannot help, and am very sorry for it ; but as his Lordship seemed to forget it on a very essential occasion to me, I shall not burden my memory with the recollection. . . . I have heard that some persons conceive me to be under obligations to Lord Carlisle ; if so, I shall be most particularly happy to learn what they are, and when conferred, that they may be duly appreciated and publicly acknowledged ".[1]

Such was his revenge. It was a stinging one, and he was to repent of it in later years. " Much too savage . . . the provocation was not sufficient to justify such acerbity." When he wrote that *mea culpa*, he was twenty-eight—but the provocation had been shown to an unfriended, sensitive, and passionate boy of twenty-one. I question if any of us wishes a pang away from Frederick, Earl of Carlisle, as he read, or listened to, the acerbity.[2]

Byron spent a short time in London, at Batt's Hotel, Jermyn Street, collecting the miniatures of his school-friends, and sitting for his own portrait in oils to George Sanders ; then he returned to the Abbey to arrange the second edition [3] of *English Bards* for the press, and to entertain at last a small party of intimates. Charles Skinner Matthews and Hobhouse were the prominent guests ; there were seven or eight altogether, including the " occasional presence of a neighbouring parson ". From the starry youth of Cambridge, we have a diverting description (written to his sister on May 22, 1809) " of the singular place I have lately quitted ". There is first a picture of the Abbey from the architectural standpoint. " Fancy all this surrounded with bleak and barren hills, with scarce a tree to be seen for

---

[1] This note, which appeared in the first edition, was an unmistakable clue to the authorship ; but the anonymity was not meant to be preserved, and indeed never for a moment really existed.

[2] Byron's *amende* in *Childe Harold* (iii. 29–30) is well known. Carlisle's third son, the Hon. Frederick Howard, fell at Waterloo.

> " Yet one I would select from that proud throng,
> Partly because they blend me with his line,
> And *partly that I did his sire some wrong* ".

(See *Poems*, ii. 233, and note at end of canto.)

The third canto of *Childe Harold* was published on November 18, 1816. Lord Carlisle lived until 1825.

[3] He added nearly four hundred lines, and to this edition his name was prefixed.

miles . . . and you will have some idea of Newstead. . . . But
if the place itself appear rather strange to you, the ways of the
inhabitants will not appear much less so. Ascend, then, with
me the hall-steps . . . but have a care how you proceed . . .
for, should you make any blunder—should you go by the right
of the hall-steps, you are laid hold of by a bear ; and should you
go to the left, your case is still worse, for you run full against a
wolf ! Nor, when you have attained the door, is your danger
over ; for the hall being decayed, and therefore standing in need
of repair, a bevy of inmates are very probably banging at one
end of it with their pistols ; so that if you enter without giving
loud notice of your approach, you have only escaped the wolf
and the bear to expire by the pistol-shots of the merry monks
of Newstead ".

The merry monks got up at one o'clock, most of them.
Matthews, appearing between eleven and twelve, was esteemed
a prodigy of early rising. Breakfast finally ended at about half-
past two ; then they would read or fence or play shuttlecock in
the " great room ", or practise with pistols in the hall, or walk,
ride, play cricket, sail on the lake, play with the bear, tease the
wolf. Dinner was between seven and eight, " and our evening
lasted till one, two, or three in the morning. The evening dis-
cussions may be easily conceived ".

At dinner, the famous Skull-Cup was handed round, filled
with Burgundy. This was a skull which the gardener, in digging,
had turned up in the grounds. It was of great size and in a
perfect state of preservation. " A strange fancy ", said Byron
to Medwin, " seized me of having it set and mounted as a drink-
ing-cup. I accordingly sent it to town, and it returned with a
very high polish, and of a mottled colour like tortoiseshell " [1]
Probably the guests drank from the revolting goblet, for their
whims were many and foolish. They took the trouble of dressing
in the costume of the old monks at dinner—Byron posing as the
Abbot ; and one night, passing down the Long Gallery where
stood a stone coffin, Hobhouse heard a hollow groan. He went
nearer ; a cowled figure rose from the coffin and blew out his
candle. " It was Matthews ". . . . But they had more brilliant
moments, and in these we may be sure that Matthews played
the star-part. There was no one like him in Byron's estimation.
Not good-tempered (as Byron himself was not), the prestige of

---

[1] He wrote some " Lines to be inscribed on a cup formed from a
Skull ", which did not appear until the seventh edition of *Childe Harold*,
though they are now included among the Juvenilia. They are dated
" Newstead Abbey, 1808 ".

Soon after Mr. Webb bought Newstead in 1862, the skull-cup was
buried by Mrs. Webb.

Matthews nevertheless made any amount of managing worth while. During the visit, he and Hobhouse quarrelled, and he threatened to throw the latter out of a window. This so offended Hobhouse that he left the house next morning. Evidently he came back, for when the party finally broke up, he and Matthews, who were by that time wholly reconciled, " agreed, for a whim, to *walk together* to town ". They quarrelled again on the way, and walked the latter half of the journey, occasionally passing and re-passing, without once addressing one another.

When, in *Childe Harold*, Byron described the home of that pestilent young man as a monastic dome condemned to uses vile —and added :

> " Where Superstition once had made her den,
> Now Paphian girls were known to sing and smile ",

he was enjoying his favourite game of inverted hypocrisy. Dallas, who always believed him when he was in the mystifying mood, has recorded that on leaving for the Albanian tour, he " broke up his harems ". The truth is (as Moore points out) that Byron could not possibly have afforded any such Oriental luxuries. But what he could, and (by Moore's admission) did, afford in that direction was certainly not more admirable, and was much less picturesque. It could not have added a stanza to the poem —nor, if it could, have added the ever-desired shudder to the effect. For the Paphian girls were the women-servants, and on such enchantresses Society did not deign to frown.

Soon afterwards he started on his Albanian tour. A large sum of money was borrowed, partly by means of a life insurance ; Rochdale, he told Hanson, might be sold in his absence, but never Newstead. " Were my head as grey and defenceless as the Arch of the Priory, I would abide by this resolution ". It was in blackest mood that he made his preparations for the journey. " Allow me to depart from this cursed country, and I promise to turn Mussulman rather than return to it ". He was persuaded that he had drunk the cup of dissipation to the bottom, that there was nothing left for him to see through in the world of pleasure. Yet it is no overstatement of the case to say that he was ignorant of every seduction of the senses save such as have been briefly indicated—the attractions of a vulgar *fille-de-joie*, and of his women-servants. Nothing, however, could have convinced Byron that his experience—merely because it *was* his—was not all-embracing. Read his comment on the early poems and the two first cantos of *Childe Harold*—a comment made when he was thirty-three. " [They] are the thoughts of one at least ten years older than the age at which they were written—I don't mean for their solidity, but their experience ".

And then, let any experienced man (nay, woman) turn to those early poems and those two first cantos, and, reading them with that remark in mind, preserve a serious countenance.

This belief—that he must, by the very nature of his being, run through the gamut of experience, that no one could either outdo him or present a wider compass to the fingers of the Fates —is one of the great simplicities of Byron's character. It is part of his supreme self-consciousness, which, again, is part of his supreme unreserve. We shall find, as we go on, that to keep this in mind, to realise how vitally his vanity was bound up with his sufferings (real or imaginary) will help us at once to forgive him, and to refuse him any extreme of sympathy.

CHAPTER IX

CHILDE HAROLD'S FIRST PILGRIMAGE—1809—1811

Byron's duality—Black moods—Delawarr's desertion—Farewell to Mrs. Byron—Embarkation—*Childe Harold*—The prose aspect of the Pilgrimage—Spanish conquests—*The Girl of Cadiz*—Mrs. Spencer Smith—John Galt, and his book on Byron—Zitza—Visit to Ali Pasha—The Pasha's galliot—Greece—The Maid of Athens—The Swim—Etiquette—Hobhouse goes home—Athens again—Lord Sligo, and *The Giaour*—Return to England

CHILDE HAROLD was called, in the MS. of the first canto, Childe Burun, which was the old Norman rendering of Byron ; yet after the poem was published with the altered name, his creator was strenuous to deny any identity. As Dallas told him, however, " the not identifying yourself with the travelling Childe is a wish not possible to realise ". And, paradoxical as it may sound, the fact that Harold is not an accurate portrait of Byron merely makes the resemblance more complete. One of his most characteristic sequences was the perpetual revelation to the world of his idea of himself, and the annoyance which he never failed to express (and to feel) at that world's credulity—for the idea was of course devoutly hailed as the reality. This sequence grew out of the uncertainty of touch to which I have already alluded. The ambition and the pusillanimity of his vanity were for ever at war with each other—the one driving him, in fancy, to flagrant revolt against convention ; the other bending him, in actual life, meekly before it. There is something tragic in his perpetual battle with this duality, which is the real problem, as I think, of his character. That other duality of gaiety and gloom, which has drawn upon his head the epithet chameleon, needs but an elementary knowledge of human nature to remove it from the region of the abnormal, exaggerated though it was in him—in whom, for that matter, everything was exaggerated. In Byron, not a letter but is, so to speak, in capitals and double capitals : he is so typical as to be almost mythical. And this has always seemed to me the reason for his immense popularity. Every one got something from him. The intellectuals retrieved the puzzle-period of their nonage, and sighed and smiled together in recognition of their " old footsteps meeting them " ; while the general reader, enthralled (like the others) by his passionate vitality, snatched as well the fearful joy of being shocked.

He spent some weeks in London before his departure. Dallas, who was with him almost every day, found him in a mood of bitter discontent. " Resentment, anger, and disgust held full sway over him, and his greatest gratification . . . was over-charging his pen with gall, which flowed in every direction against individuals, his country, the world, the universe, Creation and the Creator ". It was during these dark hours that Lord Dela-warr's desertion (already alluded to [1]) took place. They had had their portraits—probably miniatures by Sanders—painted, framed, and surmounted with their respective coronets, and these were to be exchanged as parting gifts ; but before the transaction was completed, Delawarr began to display that aloofness which was to culminate in the Visit to the Milliner's.

On the day before Byron left London, Dallas called, and found him bursting with indignation. " Will you believe it ? " he cried. " I have just met Delawarr, and asked him to come and sit for an hour with me ; he excused himself ; and what do you think was his excuse ? He was engaged with his mother and some ladies to go shopping ! And he knows I set out to-morrow, to be absent for years, perhaps never to return ! Friendship ! I do not believe I shall leave behind me, yourself and family excepted, and perhaps my mother, a single being who will care what becomes of me ". The remembrance rankled long. In the notes to the second canto of *Childe Harold*, written after his return, he took occasion to compare the English nobleman, greatly to his disadvantage, with an Albanian servant who had wept bitterly at their parting. Could anything be more Byronic ? One can imagine the scorn with which the handsome, frivolous, but quite amiable, Delawarr must have commented—for of course he read *Childe Harold* like the rest of his world—on the parallel. " Did he expect *me* to behave like a savage ? " Certainly, as Harness said, the strain was great ; and Delawarr had from the first honestly accepted, and tried to make his friend accept, his own inadequacy.

Byron said no good-bye to the mother whose solicitude he so oddly—and be it said, for all her faults, so unjustly—doubted. From Falmouth, on the 22nd of June, he wrote her his fare-well. The violent, unhappy woman [2] must have read it with an

---

[1] See Chapter III.

[2] There had been a terrible scene between them when he had last been with her.

aching heart. He was to be absent for years, " perhaps " (as he
said himself) " never to return "—yet these are the words she
had before her :

" I am about to sail in a few days ; probably before this
reaches you. . . . I leave England without regret, and with-
out a wish to revisit anything it contains, except yourself and
your present residence.—Believe me, yours ever sincerely " . . .

He was her only child—the one creature now in all the world
who in any sense belonged to her, and he was setting out upon
a journey in those days highly adventurous. He wrote to her
often from the distant lands ; but at the end, that good-bye
letter must have haunted the soul of each—for Mrs. Byron never
saw her son again.

Augusta was left without a farewell, even by letter ; since
the encounter with Lord Carlisle, she, intimate as she was with
the " proud grandee ", had been cut out of his heart. She was
now married and a mother ;[1] he had not written to her since the
December of 1808, and he did not write to her again until a month
after his return to England in 1811.

But Hobhouse was going with him, and Dallas, *vice* Delawarr,
was the companion of his last day in town. On June 11 he went
down to Falmouth ; and thence, in the days immediately before
he sailed, wrote two letters besides the good-bye to his mother.
One was to Henry Drury, the other to Francis Hodgson. Hodg-
son got the pick of the basket : a list of fellow-passengers, a
burlesque description of Falmouth and its " tway castles, St.
Maws and Pendennis, extremely well calculated for annoying
everybody except an enemy " ; and those verses, " a foretaste
of the true Byron ", as Henley says :

> " Huzza ! Hodgson, we are going,
>   Our embargo's off at last "—

in which Hobhouse figures unforgettably as a sea-sick poet,
equally oppressed by his breakfast and his verses. No more
striking example of the difference between the real and the
self-imagined Byron is to be found than this production, enclosed
as it was in a letter ending with the words : " I am like Adam,
the first convict sentenced to transportation, but I have no Eve,
and have eaten no apple but what was sour as a crab ;—and thus
ends my first chapter ".

The influence of the Albanian tour upon his mind and work
impairs its value, in a measure, as biographical material. Since
he tells all in verse, we well might blush to recapitulate that all in

[1] She married her first cousin, Colonel Leigh, in 1807.

prose. The reading of *Childe Harold* is the accompanying Byron step by step in this the first adventure of his body and soul. The poem is, as Mr. Ernest Coleridge has said, " a rhythmical diorama ". Crammed with faults as it is (and as every first work of genius has ever been ; one hopes, will ever be)—I find it hard to believe that anybody coming to it for the first time can escape an attack of the primal Byron fever. There are things in it that thrill to the heart's core, and seem as if they must discover that heart's core in every one, no matter what his intellectual calibre ; though there is, perhaps, one element which robs it of such universality of appeal. He saw the scenes, the men, the manners, that from childhood [1] he had dreamed of seeing ; and his spirit sang aloud. There is no stronger note in *Childe Harold* than that of this peculiar form of personal exultation : " I—here, at last ! " Not all of us are its thralls ; but when one who is can utter it, the brotherhood hails a king, while those outside discern merely an ingenuous if diverting fellow. So it happens that for one, *Childe Harold* comes bringing treasure not to be sagely reckoned ; while by another the true beauties only are perceived, and nothing missed of what is wise—though something, it may be, of what is heavenly-foolish ! To give the example which best displays this effect : in the midst of a rhapsody upon the Spanish women, he breaks with absolute inconsequence into the great apostrophe to Parnassus. It is all wrong ; yet to many the " sudden glory " flashed on the mind by such spontaneity will turn the critical preoccupation with form into a sudden absurdity. Most true it is that Byron, " Never a great artist, was over and over again a great poet ". He did not so much write great poetry as *be* a great poet ; indeed, one might almost say that one of his functions was to show us what bad poetry a great poet can write. It is like a convulsion of nature —the volcano flinging lava ; out of the course, eccentric, and yet, beyond all cavilling, from the centre.

But there was prose as well as poetry in his travels. The diffidence of which I have spoken may not be wholly indulged, since if we wish to see him as he really was, we must fix our gaze on Byron as well as on the Childe. And so, here follow some of the trivial particulars. To quote a latter-day adventurer : " The way things happen generally turns out to be at least more amusing than the way they were meant to happen " ; [2] and Byron, who had meant to sail for Malta, about which, when he did go

---

[1] " All travels, or histories, or books upon the East I could meet with, I had read . . . before I was *ten years old* " (written by Byron in his copy of d'Israeli's *Literary Character*. Moore, p. 119).

[2] Charles Marriott, *A Spanish Holiday*, chap. i. p. 1, Methuen, 1908.

there, he found nothing worth recording,[1] sailed instead for Portugal, about which he found a great deal. He did not like Lisbon, yet was very happy there, " because I loves oranges, and talks bad Latin to the monks . . . and goes into society . . . and swims in the Tagus all across at once, and I rides on an ass or a mule, and swears Portuguese ". They rode—but not on mules or asses—the nearly five hundred miles to Seville and Cadiz ; and at Seville, where he lingered but three days, adventures in one sort began. To his mother, of all possible correspondents, he recounted the first. It was concerned with locks of hair, and with " an offer, which my *virtue* induced me to decline ". His refusal produced a laugh, and the information that the lady was going to be married to an officer in the Spanish army. " When a woman marries ", he explains in this singular filial confidence, " she throws off all restraint. . . . If you make a proposal which in England would produce a box on the ear from the meekest of virgins, to a Spanish girl, she thanks you for the honour you intend her, and replies, ' Wait till I'm married, and I shall be too happy '. This is literally and strictly true ".

Cadiz, though " a complete Cythera ",[2] produced something more decorous. He went to the opera with Admiral Cordova's family—" an aged wife and a fine daughter . . . very pretty,

[1] Such record as he gave it is in the lines to Mrs. Spencer Smith to which I shall shortly refer, and in the lively doggerel, " Farewell to Malta ", which was written on his return sojourn there in 1811, but not published until 1816 (see *Poems*, iii. 24).

> " [I'll] only stare from out my casement,
> And ask ' for what is such a place meant ? ' "

[2] At Cadiz, or soon after leaving it, he wrote the gay, spirited verses entitled *The Girl of Cadiz*, which were originally inserted after stanza 86, canto i. of *Childe Harold*. In this stanza, the Childe is represented as struggling " 'gainst the Demon's [melancholy's] sway ". It was a singularly successful struggle which resulted in such high-hearted singing ! " The inconsistency was seen in time ", says Mr. Coleridge. *The Girl of Cadiz* was suppressed in favour of the verses *To Inez* which now follow stanza 86. This lyric, with its " settled, ceaseless gloom ", was not written until January 25, 1810. Truly we are behind the scenes to-day, and can watch, with attentive and admiring amusement, the make-up of the Byronic hero.

> " Through many a clime 'tis mine to go,
>> With many a retrospection curst ;
> And all my solace is to know,
>> Whate'er betides, I've known the worst.

> What is that worst ? Nay, do not ask—
>> In pity from the search forbear ;
> Smile on—nor venture to unmask
>> Man's heart, and view the Hell that's there ".

And now, let the reader find *The Girl of Cadiz*, actual production of the moment.

in the Spanish style ". There were also the inevitable little brother, and an aunt or duenna. Señorita Cordova dispossessed this last of her chair in front of the box, and commanded Byron to take it. " She proposed to become my preceptress in the Spanish language " ; and it was either to her or to one of the more enterprising ladies of the place (or of Seville), that, in his own delightful phrase, he " made earnest love with the help of a dictionary ". It can hardly have been Señorita Cordova who set her heart on a ring he wore, and insisted on his giving it to her. That could not be ; he offered anything else, but nothing else would do. Both grew angry, and they angrily parted. The ring, a valuable yellow diamond, went with him to Malta (whither he soon sailed) ; but at Malta left his possession, coveted and demanded there also by a more potent charmer.

This was the Mrs. Spencer Smith—the Florence of *Childe Harold* and of two or three short lyrics—whose adventures with the Marquis de Salvo " form one of the prettiest romances in the Italian language ". She had somehow managed in 1806 to incur the special enmity of Napoleon, and from this distinction had issued the chapter in her life which now captivated Byron's fancy. There was everything in it—imprisonment, tears, platonics, post-chaise, boy's disguise, a rope-ladder ; [1] and, above all, a heroine with golden hair, lissom form (" like the apparition in an exquisite dream ", said the Duchesse d'Abrantès), and lovely short-sighted eyes which gazed on men with bewildered and bewildering vagueness. Plainly the duty of somebody to fall in love ; but should it be Byron or Harold ? It was Byron —and to key up an affair somewhat flattened by its obviousness, he had the really brilliant inspiration of posing the Childe as cold.

> " Fair Florence found, in sooth with some amaze,
> One who, 'twas said, still sighed to all he saw,
> Withstand, unmoved, the lustre of her gaze ".

But she prevailed upon the " marble heart " to the extent at any rate of three lyrics—and the yellow diamond ring. Both Moore and Galt believe in the remoteness ; and indeed the lady was already a laureate in the school of platonics. The Marquis de Salvo had been, before he asked, nobly repulsed : " I must warn you, in our mutual interest, that my principles and my outlook on life are wholly opposed to what you doubtless hope for as your reward ".[2] De Salvo had been, for his part, nobly wounded by her suspicion, and in fact his chivalry was without alloy ;

---

[1] The story is told in detail by the Marquis de Salvo (*Travels in the Year* 1806) and by the Duchesse d'Abrantès (*Mémoires*, xv. 1–74).

[2] Duch. d'Abrantès, *Mémoires*, xv. 13–14.

they parted, when her rescue had been accomplished, as they had set out—the very Knight and Lady of romance.

What Florence [1] may have thought of the *Harold* stanzas is another question. In them her virtue is less insisted on than the Childe's obduracy—a turn of which Byron alone was capable ; while the lines which sum up the episode are unqualifiable in any measured language.

> " 'Tis an old lesson—Time approves it true,
> And those who know it best, deplore it most ;
> *When all is won that all desire to woo,*
> *The paltry prize is hardly worth the cost ".*

The yellow diamond can scarce have seemed a redemption of such a generality, appended as it was to an explicit allusion. Florence must have realised what most women realised : that once " that lovely, harmless [2] thing " entered the story, Byron's baseness, sooner or later, inevitably proclaimed itself. At Athens in 1810 the final word was said :

> " The spell is broke, the charm is flown ! "

—Florence disappeared, and the Maid of Athens took her place.

But before Athens, before even Malta, a delightful personage claims our attention. This is John Galt, author of two novels which still survive. [3] In 1830 he published his *Life of Byron ;* in the eighth chapter of this occurs a passage that should live while the name of its subject lives, for nothing else that has been written of Byron's effect comes anywhere near it in bringing that effect home. I make no apology for quoting : the glee of Galt's every reader is assured.

They had met at Gibraltar, and had embarked together for Sardinia, Cagliari, and Malta. Galt, without knowing who he was, had seen Byron in the garrison library at Gibraltar, and had been particularly impressed by a recurrent frown, which he first thought an affectation " for picturesque effect and energetic expression " ; but afterwards discovered to be " undoubtedly the occasional scowl of some unpleasant reminiscence ". Meeting him next day on board the packet, the frown again intrigued Galt, who by this time knew that its owner was Lord Byron. " I suspected him of pride and irascibility. The impression that evening was not agreeable, but it was interesting ". Hobhouse made himself at home at once ; " but Byron held aloof, and sat on the rail, leaning on the mizzen shrouds, inhaling, as it were,

---

[1] Her actual Christian name was Constance.

[2] It is amusing to note, in the MS., that he was uncertain whether to use this epithet, or its opposite.

[3] *Annals of the Parish* and *The Entail.*

poetical sympathy from the gloomy rock ". He was wayward and petulant : " ill at ease with himself and fretful towards others ". But there was something redeeming in his voice, and Galt was soon convinced that instead of being ill-natured, he was only capricious. About the third day, he " relented from his rapt mood ". They landed at Cagliari in Sardinia, and were invited to dinner by Mr. Hill, the ambassador. " On this occasion, Byron and his Pylades dressed themselves as aides-de-camp—a circumstance which . . . did not tend to improve my estimation of the solidity of the character of either ". And then Galt sums up the transit to Malta. It is here that the unforgettable passage occurs. " If my remembrance is not treacherous, he only spent one evening in the cabin with us . . . for, when the lights were placed, he made himself a man forbid, took his station on the railing . . . and there, for hours, sat in silence, enamoured, it may be, of the moon. All these peculiarities, with his caprices, and something inexplicable in the cast of his metaphysics, while they seemed to awaken interest, contributed little to conciliate esteem. He was often strangely rapt—it may have been from his genius ; and had its grandeur and darkness been then divulged, susceptible of explanation ; but, at the time, it threw around him, as it were, the sackcloth of penitence. Sitting amidst the shrouds and railings, in the tranquillity of the moonlight, churming an inarticulate melody, he seemed almost apparitional, suggesting dim reminiscences of him who shot the albatross. *He was as a mystery in a winding-sheet, crowned with a halo* ".

If Byron had but known that this was the effect he was producing, the passage from Gibraltar to Malta would have been one of the happiest moments of his life. Galt, shrewdly observant and sceptical though he was, showed himself the most sensitive plate for the Byronic image which that image ever found. No wonder that the novels survive : an observer of such keenness, joined to such extraordinary receptivity for the desired impression, must have drawn vital characters.[1]

The whole account of their short journeying together abounds in these illuminating *aperçus*, these ludicrous yet delightful phrases. Byron thanks somebody for his hospitality " with more elocution than was precisely requisite ", and Hobhouse laughs at him. " But Byron really fancied that he had acquitted himself with grace and dignity ", and became petulant. Hobhouse walked on ; the poet, on account of his lameness, took Galt's arm, and appealed for praise. Galt was inclined to agree

---

[1] Byron himself said of the *Annals of the Parish* and *The Entail* that the characters had " an identity that reminded him of Wilkie's pictures " (Lady Blessington's *Conversations*, p. 74).

with the censor (unsympathetic as ever for exuberance !), but
" as his lordship's comfort, at the moment, seemed dependent
on being confirmed in the good opinion he was desirous to entertain
of his own graces ", Galt civilly assented. He was taken into
favour from that night onward ; " and, as [Byron] was always
most agreeable and interesting when familiar, it was worth my
while to advance, but by cautious circumvallation, into his
intimacy ; for his uncertain temper made his favour precarious ".
The next day the " passengers partook of the blessings of peace.
. . . Byron was in the highest spirits ; overflowing with glee,
and sparkling with quaint sentences. The champagne was
uncorked, and in the finest condition ". Hobhouse had been
forgiven and had accepted the situation, for, as he remarked
to Galt, " it was necessary to humour him like a child ".

Byron's impression of the new acquaintance was told, many
years afterwards, to Lady Blessington. " When I knew Galt . . .
I was not in a frame of mind to form an impartial opinion of
him ; his mildness and equanimity struck me even then ; but,
to say the truth, his manner had not deference enough for my
then aristocratical taste, and finding I could not awe him into
a respect sufficiently profound for my sublime self, either as a
peer or an author, I felt a little grudge towards him that has
now completely worn off ".

They parted at Malta, not to meet again until the February
of 1810 in Athens. In the meantime, Byron and Hobhouse
penetrated to the interior of Albania, where Ali Pasha, the
Mahometan Buonaparte, then reigned. They stayed three days
at Yanina, leaving on October 11 to ride through the mountains
to Zitza, that " small but favoured spot of holy ground " on the
way to Tepeleni, whose situation Byron considered to be the
finest without exception in Greece. As they were approaching
the village in the evening Hobhouse and two others rode forward,
leaving Byron to follow with the baggage and servants, among
whom was his English valet Fletcher. Just as the advance-
guard reached Zitza rain began to pour in torrents (they had,
in fact, undertaken their Albanian adventure a month too early
in the year, and suffered from bad weather most of the time) ;
and by seven o'clock the storm had developed into " a fury I
had never before ", says Hobhouse,[1] " and indeed have never
since, seen equalled ". Byron and his party were within three
miles of the village when it began, yet they did not arrive until
two o'clock in the morning. They had lost their way amid the
mountains ; the luggage-horses had fallen ; they had been
exposed to the tempest for nine hours ; the guides had run

[1] J. C. Hobhouse, *A Journey through Albania*, second edition, 1813,
p. 81.

away, the dragoman had fired after them with his pistols, and Fletcher—true to the part of the average English servant in such emergencies—had contributed to the occasion nothing but terrors and tears. " His eyes ", wrote Byron afterwards, " were a little hurt by the lightning, or crying—I don't know which ".

" It was long ", says Hobhouse, " before we ceased to talk of the thunderstorm in the plain of Zitza ". The adventure—really a considerable one—inspired Byron with the *Stanzas composed during a Thunderstorm* (he affirmed that they really were) in which " sweet Florence " was remembered and apostrophised. The lines relating to her alone redeem the effort from something worse than mediocrity.

> " Do thou, amidst the fair white walls,
>   If Cadiz yet be free,
> At times, from out her latticed halls,
>   Look o'er the dark blue sea ;
>
> Then think upon Calypso's isles,
>   Endear'd by days gone by ;
> To others give a thousand smiles,
>   To me a single sigh ".

.   .   .   .

After a nine days' journey they reached Tepeleni, where Ali Pasha then was, and the much-described [1] visit to him took place. Nothing in the event delighted Byron more than a remark of Ali (how often quoted in the letters home !) that " he was sure I was a man of birth, because I had small ears, curling hair, and little white hands ". Twenty times a day did the Pasha send " his son " tribute of almonds, sugared sherbet, fruit, and sweetmeats ; and there were three more meetings between them. " It is singular that the Turks . . . pay so much respect to birth ; for I found my pedigree more regarded than my title ". Thus many vanities were gratified ; nor did Ali forget his visitor, for when a Dr. Howard, travelling in Albania some years later, told the Pasha of *Childe Harold*, " he seemed pleased, and stated his recollections of Lord Byron ".

After a stay at Prevesa, sailing thence to Patras in a galliot of the Pasha, especially provided for them by his orders, they had another ordeal by tempest. The storm was not violent, but their captain was of a peculiar type. First they ran aground in getting out of the harbour ; then, in tacking before a fair

---

[1] *Childe Harold*, ii. 56-64.   Letter to Mrs. Byron, *L. and J.* i. 249-51 ; and Hobhouse's soberer description, *A Journey in Albania*, letter xi. 109-25.

wind, the mizzen-sail split from top to bottom,—whereupon
the captain put the string of beads (called a *comboloio*), with
which he had hitherto been absorbed, into his pocket and wrung
his hands. The breeze was now fresh, they were rolling violently,
nobody knew how to steer, " and when the main-yard snapped
in two, the guns broke loose, and the foresail split "—it is
little wonder that everything was given up for lost. The
ship lay like a log on the water, and as they contrived to keep
her broadside on to the heavy sea, the danger of swamping
was added to all the others. . . . The transit, thus described
in the prim narrative of Hobhouse, reads like one made in a
nightmare.

" The captain, being asked what he could do, said he could
do nothing.

" ' Could he get back to the mainland ? '

" ' If God chooses '.

" ' Could he make Corfu ? '

" ' If God chooses '.

" ' Would he give up the management of the vessel to the
Greeks ? '

" ' He would give it up to anybody ' ".

Fletcher was meanwhile (to turn to Byron's account) " yelling
after his wife, the Greeks were calling on all the saints, and the
Mussulmans on Allah ". Byron undertook Fletcher, and " finding
him incorrigible, wrapped myself up in my Albanian capote
and lay down on deck to wait the worst ". He had tried to be
of service, but his lameness disabled him. Hobhouse often
told Moore of his singular coolness and courage ; for (like Heine
in a similar situation) not only did he lie down on the deck, but
he went fast asleep. . . . And the whole mad hour was wasted ;
for they were driven on the coast of Suli at one o'clock in the
morning, and had to go by land back to Prevesa, whence they
had sailed the day before !

This was on November 11. On November 21 they reached
Missolonghi. Moore makes the obvious reflection, which no
reader can fail to make for himself. They stayed a fortnight at
Patras, and on December 5, on the way to Vostitza, he beheld
Parnassus.

> " Oft have I dreamed of Thee ! whose glorious name,
> Who knows not, knows not man's divinest lore :
> And now I view thee—'tis, alas, with shame
> That I in feeblest accents must adore.
> When I recount thy worshippers of yore
> I tremble, and can only bend the knee ;
> Nor raise my voice, nor vainly dare to soar,
> But gaze beneath thy cloudy canopy,
> In silent joy to think at last I look on thee ! "

Later, going to the Fountain of Delphi, he saw above the mountain a flight of twelve eagles (" Hobhouse said they were vultures ") ; " and I seized the omen. On the day before, I composed the lines to Parnassus, and on beholding the birds, had a hope that Apollo had accepted my homage ". This passage is from the *Detached Thoughts* of 1821 ; but in the Diary of 1813 he recalled the incident in a less romantic vein. Only six eagles, by this account, were seen, and " it was the number, not the species . . . that excited my attention ". Following this quaint discrepancy-in-advance is another reminiscence of the same journey which, in its poignant simplicity of narration no less than in the disposition it reveals, is one of those things which incline our hearts to forget his every failing. " The last bird I ever fired at was an *eaglet*, on the shore of the Gulf of Lepanto, near Vostitza. It was only wounded, and I tried to save it, the eye was so bright ; but it pined, and died in a few days ; and I never did since, and never will, attempt the death of another bird ".

On Christmas Eve, 1809, they arrived at a " most miserable and half-deserted village, called Skourta ", and passed the night " in the worst hovel of which we had ever been inmates. The cows and pigs occupied the lower part of the chamber, where there were racks and mangers and other appurtenances of a stable ".[1] It strikes one as odd that not Byron nor Hobhouse nor any of the biographers should seem to have felt the dramatic significance of passing Christmas Eve in a place so described. They moved on next day, and at half-past two, ' just as we had got to the summit of the mountain overlooking a deep glen, one of our guides called out, ' *Affendi, affendi, to chorio !* ' (Sir, sir, the town !) ". The town was Athens. At half-past eight in the evening of Christmas Day, they entered it.

" Where'er we tread 'tis haunted, holy ground "

—the stanzas[2] need no citation.

At Athens they stayed ten weeks, in the house of Madame Theodora Macri, widow of the late English Vice-Consul. Her daughter, Teresa ("sometimes called Thyrza "), eldest of three lovely girls, was the Maid of Athens whom Byron has immortalised. That lyric, and the following passage in a letter to Henry Drury, are Byron's only references to her. " I almost forgot to tell you that I am dying for love of three Greek girls at Athens, sisters. I lived in the same house. Teresa, Mariana, and Katinka are the names of these divinities—all of them under

---

[1] J. C. Hobhouse, *Travels in Albania*, p. 285.
[2] *Childe Harold*, ii. 87–88.

fifteen ".[1] Moore thought that it was in making love to one
of these girls that Byron adopted a custom frequent in that
country—namely, giving himself a wound across the breast
with his dagger. The lady, whoever she was, " by his own
account, looked on very coldly during the operation, considering
it a fit tribute to her beauty, but in no degree moved to gratitude ".
During this sojourn Hobhouse visited the Negroponte, a trip which
took five days (from February 8 to 13). " Lord Byron was unex-
pectedly detained at Athens "—and this circumstance Mr. Ernest
Coleridge connects, by implication, with the Teresa Macri affair.[2]
Hobhouse's tribute to his companion may appropriately be given
here.   " Any additional defects in the narration of this short tour
must be attributed to the absence of a companion who, to quick-
ness of observation and ingenuity of remark, united that gay
good-humour which keeps alive the attention under the pressure
of fatigue and softens the aspect of every difficulty and danger ".

After their ten weeks' stay they were offered a passage in
an English sloop-of-war, the *Pylades*, to Smyrna.   They accepted
it ; and on March 5 took leave of Athens with many a backward
look, full of the pain of parting.   The sojourn at Smyrna is
memorable chiefly because the two first cantos of *Childe Harold*
were finished there.[3]   Nor was Byron the only scribbler.   Hob-
house's " woundy preparations for a book " (reported by his
friend from Falmouth) had been made in earnest—in such deadly
earnest that one fears he can have enjoyed himself, in any other
way, but half-heartedly.   The book must have obsessed his
every moment.   It is with a singular mixture of feelings that
one turns over the ponderous tomes—they grow steadily more
erudite and more unreadable as the places visited grow more
interesting—and compares the mental processes simultaneously
taking place in the two travellers.   The one notes and describes
the very pebbles of the highway, and we recoil in mingled irritation,
fatigue, and pity ; the other utters merely the emotions that
compelled his spirit, and compels our own to such sharing as

[1] Three later travellers—Hughes, Walsh, and Williams, all authors of
books recording their adventures, and Williams, moreover, an artist of
distinction—speak of these girls as the belles of Athens.   But Teresa's
beauty waned early.   In 1820 Hughes " observed the remains only of that
loveliness which elicited such strains from an impassioned poet ".   Walsh,
in 1821, said that she had " lost all pretensions to beauty, and had a coun-
tenance singularly marked by hopeless sadness ".   Williams, the artist,
was more enthusiastic, but he too noticed the " pensiveness " of the two
elder sisters.   They were dark ; Katinka was fair.   Teresa married an
Englishman named Black, survived her husband, and fell into great
poverty.   She died in 1875, aged eighty.

[2] *Poems*, 1904, ii. note to p. 75.

[3] *Childe Harold* had been begun at Yanina, October 31, 1809, and these
cantos were completed at Smyrna on March 28, 1810.

gives the illusion of actual vision. No sharper antithesis between accuracy and truth could be devised. Byron did not know how profoundly he was criticising his friend when, in his letters to Drury and Hodgson, he begs them jestingly not to believe one word Hobhouse says, but come for the truth to him.

Appropriately enough, as I write these words, I find beneath my hand the first mention of the most tedious fact, to me, in the whole life of Byron. " This morning "—let me set up all the paraphernalia and state that this morning was May 3, 1810— " I *swam* from *Sestos to Abydos* ". He did, and so did Mr. Ekenhead, an officer of the English frigate *Salsette* ; and Byron was one hour and ten minutes in the water, and Ekenhead five minutes less ; and it was more than four miles, and the current was very strong and cold, and they were not fatigued but a little chilled. It was the famous Swim across the Hellespont, and Byron (literally) never after that morning wrote a letter home without describing it. In 1820 one William Turner published a *Journal of a Tour in the Levant*, and the whole question came lumbering up again. Byron sent an interminable letter to John Murray (which occupies five and a half pages of print),[1] and the letter was published in two magazines, and Turner's reply, not printed until after Byron's death (by Turner's own wish), declared that he was still unshaken in his opinion—which was, to put it as shortly as possible, that Byron had performed only half Leander's feat, and that the easier half. And alternatively, as a lawyer would say, that Leander had never performed it. Byron characteristically based his whole case on the fact that Turner had failed to perform either *his* feat or Leander's. . . . I know not if I be blamably feminine in thinking this the dullest of all possible discussions ; but I do think it so, and am incapable of prolonging it any further.

Constantinople was, as the reader will have inferred from the Swim, the next place they visited ; but there is an anecdote (recorded in Hobhouse's Journal, a far more amusing production than his book) to be offered before we proceed. They had stayed at Smyrna in the house of the Consul-General, a Mr. Werry, and " Mrs. Werry actually cut off a lock of Byron's hair on parting with him to-day (April 11) and shed a good many tears. Pretty well for fifty-six, at least ! "[2] They sailed in

[1] *L. and J.* v. 246-51. And Appendix : Turner's answer, 601-3.
[2] Hobhouse, writing to Byron from Malta, July 31, 1810, says : " Mrs. Bruce picked out a pretty plate of a woman in a fashionable dress in Ackerman's *Repository*, and observed it was vastly like Lord Byron. I give you warning of this, for fear you should make another conquest and return to England without a curl upon your head " (*L. and J.* i. 299).

the *Salsette* frigate, which was bound for Constantinople to convey the English Ambassador, Mr. Adair, to England. Galt had reappeared both at Athens and Smyrna, and at Smyrna had found Byron " something changed, and not with improvement ". He was less cordial with Hobhouse, and was altogether " more of a Captain Grand than improved his manners ". A striking instance of this occurred at a dinner on the day after Galt's arrival. Byron and one of the officers of the *Salsette* disagreed over politics, and the naval man prevailed. " Lord Byron . . . became reserved, as if he deemed that sullenness enhanced dignity. I never in the whole course of my acquaintance saw him *kithe* [1] so unfavourably as he did on that occasion ". He got over it before the party broke up (" his austerity began to leaf "); nevertheless Galt saw then what others saw increasingly as time went on—that " the unchecked humour of his temper was, by its caprices, calculated to prevent him from ever gaining that regard to which his talents and freer moods . . . ought to have entitled him. Such men become objects of solicitude, but never of esteem ".

In justice to him—and Galt is careful to consider the point —it should be said, on the testimony of a letter from Smyrna to Mrs. Byron, that the negligence of his lawyer was now becoming a serious matter. He was obliged to consider whether he should be able to proceed at all after Constantinople, or even then to return without remittances. In the event money must have arrived, for he stayed abroad another year ; but just at this time the uncertainty was awkward and humiliating, and Galt thought that the false dignity he assumed, which seemed so like arrogance, might well be .the thing we now call bluff.

A little contretemps marked the stay of two months at Stamboul. Mr. Adair, the Ambassador Extraordinary, now going home, had his farewell audience of the Sultan soon after they arrived, and Byron unluckily got it into his head that he had claims to some sort of precedence. Stratford Canning (afterwards Lord Stratford de Redcliffe) sat near Moore at dinner on May 23, 1819, and in Moore's Journal [2] we read that he " gave a ludicrous account of Lord Byron's insisting on taking precedence of the *corps diplomatique* . . . and, upon Adair's refusing it, limping, with as much swagger as he could muster, up the hall, cocking a foreign military hat on his head. He found, however, he was wrong, and wrote a very frank letter acknowledging it, and offering

---

[1] This unfamiliar Scotch word means " to show one's self ". (Communicated after the publication of my book in 1912.)

[2] Vol. ii. p. 313.

to take his station anywhere ".[1] This jealousy of his rank was nervously awake at Constantinople, says Galt, who considered it one of his greatest weaknesses. That such things should have so morbidly affected his sensibility appeared to this observer almost inconceivable ; " yet they certainly did so, and even to a ridiculous degree. But ", he gloriously continues, " the alloy of such small vanities, his caprice and feline temper, were as vapour compared with the mass of rich and rare ore which constituted the orb and nucleus of his brilliancy ".

An anonymous writer in the *New Monthly Magazine,* quoted by Moore, tells of an encounter at Constantinople which confirms Galt's observations. This traveller was in a pipe-shop, when there entered an Englishman in a scarlet coat richly embroidered with gold, " in the style of an A.D.C.'s uniform ". He had with him a janissary and a cicerone. The traveller was much struck by his beauty—his fine blue eyes, remarkably delicate features, and curly auburn hair. Unforgettable, he calls him. A " very visible " lameness proclaimed his identity, for Lord Byron's arrival in the *Salsette* was already known. He had become a great lover of smoking, and was there to buy some pipes ; but the difficulty of language—for the cicerone spoke Turkish badly—irritated his traffic with the shopkeeper, and so the stranger, coming forward, addressed him in English. He was delighted, shook hands cordially, and when both had finished their bargaining, they roamed about together for the rest of the day. The traveller frequently addressed Byron by name, and this seemed to cause him no surprise, nor did he hint at any desire for the usual reciprocity. They separated thus, after some hours' wandering. During the next week they met at dinner at the English Ambassador's, and our traveller at once begged a secretary for the formal introduction. He was amazed to find himself freezingly received by his new acquaintance. " He immediately turned his back on me." Some days later they met in the street, and Byron greeted the hesitating victim of his caprice with a beautiful smile. " ' I am an enemy ', he explained, ' of English etiquette, especially out of England ; I always make my own acquaintances without awaiting the formality of an introduction ' ". The stranger was conquered by the " irresistible attraction " of his manner, and they spent another pleasant, desultory day together. But one cannot avoid a suspicion that it was precisely the detested English etiquette which had brought about the snubbing—that the traveller, obviously of inferior rank as he was, had sinned against that very fetish in being the first to ask for an introduction.

[1] " It took Byron quite three days to get over the trivial contretemps ", says Hobhouse's Journal.

And the old English Baron had risen in his wrath, while the
mere gentleman, next day resuscitated, had perceived and
redeemed the paltriness.

They left Constantinople on July 14, in the *Salsette*. Hob-
house was going home, and Byron was returning to Athens for
a second stay. He was in an extraordinary state of dejection,
as Mr. Adair noticed.[1] One day, walking on the deck, he saw
a small *yataghan* or Turkish dagger lying on a bench, took it
up, unsheathed it, and said to himself in a low voice (which was
nevertheless overheard) : " I should like to know how a person
feels after committing a murder ". Both Moore and Galt regard
this as a very impressive incident ; I cannot agree with them
—indeed, their awe appears to me a puerility. Such speculations
are the common food of an imaginative mind—silently, it is
true, pursued by most ; but Byron's moods were seldom inarticu-
late when they were so admirably scenic as this one.

He was landed, by his own request, on the island of Zea,
a small port near Athens. Here he said farewell to Hobhouse.
and " in one of his manuscripts " (says Moore) " he has described
the proud, solitary feeling with which he stood to see the ship
sail swiftly away—leaving him there, in a land of strangers,
alone ". Hobhouse's record of the parting is much more human.
" *July* 17, 1810.—Arrived at the port of Zea. . . . Took leave,
non sine lacrymis, of this singular young person on a little stone
terrace at the end of the bay, dividing with him a little nosegay
of flowers, the last, perhaps, that I shall ever divide with him ".
Writing from Malta on July 31, Hobhouse was betrayed into a
postscript and a sentimentality. " I kept the half of your little
nosegay until it withered, and even then I could not bear to throw
it away. I can't account for this, nor can you either, I dare
say ". Byron, answering from Patras on October 4, reveals
even through the medium of pen and ink a very evident embarrass-
ment. " Your last letter closes pathetically with a postscript
about a nose-gay ; I advise you to introduce that into your
sentimental novel. I am sure I did not suspect you of any fine
feelings, and I believe you were laughing, but you are welcome ".
His conscience may have pricked him a little, if he recalled some
of his recent gibes at this suddenly revealed devotee. Just
before the parting at Zea, he had written to Hodgson (Hobhouse
was taking the letter home !) that twelve months of any given
individual was perfect ipecacuanha. Again, to his mother, on
July 25 : " I am woefully sick of travelling-companions, after
a year's experience of Mr. Hobhouse ". Yet it would certainly

---

[1] This depression was noticed at Athens too, by Lady Hester Stan-
hope's companion, Mr. Bruce.

seem from Galt's account that Byron was the difficult one of the two.

He fell in at Athens with an old fellow-collegian, the Marquis of Sligo, who, in company with Lady Hester Stanhope and Michael Bruce (" the Bruce who was to be one of those to contrive the escape of Lavalette from Paris in 1816 "), was one day passing the Piræus when he saw a man jump from the molehead into the sea. He recognised Byron, and called to him to dress and join them. " Thus began ", said Mr. Prothero, " what Byron, in his Memoranda, speaks of as ' the most delightful acquaintance which I found in Greece ' ". Lady Hester Stanhope, niece of the younger Pitt, was then starting on that uncommon adventure which was to stamp her as one of the most notable women of her time.[1] She inherited from her grandfather, the Great Commoner, many picturesque traits—" pride, generosity, courage, fervent heat as well as indomitable will " ; [2] she " ignored the word impossibility ", and, like most real Romantics, had insight and practical sagacity as well. She was on her way at this time to what proved to be her sojourn of twenty-six years among the wild tribes of Lebanon. Moore speaks of the cordial friendship between her and Byron ; but the direct personal testimony of both is against this view of their intercourse. He thought her overbearing and argumentative ; while she is represented in her physician's Memoirs of her travels [3] as saying that Byron was a strange character. " One time he was mopish, and nobody was to speak to him ; another he was for being jocular with everybody. Then he was a sort of Don Quixote, fighting with the police for a woman of the town ; and then he wanted to make himself something great. . . . He had a great deal of vice in his looks—his eyes set close together, and a contracted brow . . . oh, Lord ! I am sure he was not a liberal man, whatever else he might be. The only good thing about his looks was this part (drawing her hand under the cheek, down the front of her neck) and the curl on his forehead ".

Sligo evidently felt the Byronic spell, for when the new arrival said he was going into the Morea he was at once implored to let the Marquis go with him. He acquiesced reluctantly, since he was woefully sick of travelling-companions, but Sligo's ecstasy was inconceivable—so Mrs. Byron heard. Sligo was well enough himself (continued her son), but the swarm of attendants that he carried with him made his society an intolerable annoyance. However, they went as far as Corinth together and there separated, Sligo for Tripolitza, Byron for Patras—the latter very glad to be once more alone, for " my nature leads me to solitude, and

[1] Henley, p. 354.   [2] *L. and J.* i., note to p. 302.
[3] Dr. Meryon, *Memoirs*, 1846, iii. 218-19.

every day adds to this disposition ". " My old seas and mountains ", he adds, " are the only acquaintances I ever found improve upon me ".

He fell very ill at Patras with malarial fever ; five days were spent in bed. There were two doctors, "one of whom trusts to his genius (having never studied)—the other to a campaign of eighteen months against the sick of Otranto, which he made in his youth with great effect ". Byron protested against " both these assassins—but what can a helpless, feverish, toasted-and-watered wretch do ? " His two Albanian servants, however, seeing the doctors incapable, threatened to cut the throat of the more persistent of the two—one Romanelli—if their master was not cured within a given time. This frightened the man away ; and to the threat and a resolute refusal of all Romanelli's prescriptions, Byron attributed his recovery.[1]

He was still thin and weak when he returned to Athens and met Sligo again. The latter told Moore a little tale about this interesting condition. One day, standing before a looking-glass, Byron said, " How pale I look! I should like, I think, to die of a consumption ". His friend wondered why. " Because then the women would all say, 'See that poor Byron—how interesting he looks in dying !' " Moore narrates this with solemn reflections added, and that he should do so—he who knew the speaker so well !—assists one to understand the long misapprehension of Byron. Was *persiflage* ever more patent ? If Sligo reported it seriously, he must have been a dense young man.

Byron was writing regularly to his mother at this time, yet to Sligo it seemed that his feeling for her was little short of aversion. " Some time or another ", he said, " I will tell you why I feel this towards her ". A few days later they were bathing together, and Byron, referring to this promise, pointed

---

[1] Recalling this illness, in a discussion on revealed religion with Francis Hodgson soon after his return to England, during a period of deep sorrow and dejection, he wrote with reference to his disbelief in the immortality of the soul : " I hope I am sincere ; I was so at least on a bed of sickness in a far distant country, when I had neither friend nor comforter nor hope to sustain me. I looked to death as a relief from pain, without a wish for an after-life, but a confidence that the God who punishes in this existence had left that last asylum for the weary ". He added, in the Greek, " *He whom God loves dies young* ". Francis Hodgson's son, who wrote a Memoir of his father, comments thus on the passage quoted : " It is so sadly and strangely prophetic that its only possible answer is a sorrowful and sympathetic silence " (i. 197–98). Patras is within sight almost of Missolonghi, where, fourteen years later, at thirty-six, Byron was to die ; and in view of the confusion of tongues by his death-bed, one cannot help speculating on all that might have been averted if the resourceful guardians of 1810 had but been with him in 1824.

to his naked leg and foot and exclaimed : " Look there ! It is to her false delicacy at my birth that I owe that deformity ; and yet, as long as I can remember, she has never ceased to taunt and reproach me with it. Even a few days before we parted . . . she in one of her fits of passion uttered an imprecation upon me, praying that I might prove as ill-formed in mind as I am in body ". Moore adds on his own account : " His look and manner, in relating this frightful circumstance, can be conceived only by those who have seen him in a similar state of excitement ".

Sligo's intercourse proved useful at a later period, when in 1813 *The Giaour* was published, and " some gentlewomen of our acquaintance " circulated a story which was a little too close to the text. There was *some* foundation on facts, but the " real incident was remote enough from the poetical one " ; and to put himself right with his friends or posterity (says Mr. Coleridge), Byron wrote to Sligo, requesting him to tell what he had heard at Athens about the affair. Sligo wrote a letter which Byron characterised as curious, and which Mr. Coleridge considers inconclusive ; it is markedly confined to " all I heard ", for the actual facts, whatever they were, had happened a day or two before Sligo arrived at Athens. They were matter of common talk when he did arrive—but common talk is commonly untrust-worthy. What the girl had actually done is not detailed, but the governor had ordered her to be sewn up in a sack and thrown into the sea. Byron, coming back from bathing, met the pro-cession on its way to execute the order. He immediately inter-posed,[1] or (as Sligo never fails cautiously to insert) " report said " he did. The men would not obey him ; he threatened them with force, but still they refused. Byron then drew a pistol, and said if the leader did not yield and come back to the Aga's house, he would be shot dead. On this the man surrendered ; they went back ; and partly by threats, partly by bribing and entreaty, Byron procured the girl's pardon, on condition of her leaving Athens. " I was told " (continues Sligo) " that you then con-veyed her in safety to the convent, and dispatched her at night to Thebes, where she found a safe asylum ".

The letter might pass as a very probable clearing-up of the mystery had not Byron, in his Journal of 1813, indulged in some of the many dark hints which that document contains. To Medwin—if we put any faith in Medwin—he told the tale circumstantially, with himself as the Frankish lover. This was contradicted by Hobhouse, and the lover said to have been his Turkish servant. But Hobhouse was in England at the time of the occurrence ; and Byron expressly says in his Journal

---

[1] It is plainly to this incident that Lady Hester Stanhope referred (see *ante*).

of 1813 that " H. doesn't know what I was about the year after
he left the Levant ; nor does any one ". That something sinister
happened we must be certain ; what that something was
must be left to the reader's judgment. Byron said on another
occasion that he had had a great deal of trouble with his servants
in the matter of their intercourse with women in that difficult
land ; and this supports Hobhouse's statement, which seems
to me the most probable solution of the Giaour Mystery.

During this second sojourn in Athens, he did not renew
his acquaintance with Teresa Macri. He took lodgings in a
Franciscan convent, and there wrote the *Hints from Horace*—
" that Satire ", observes Moore, " which, impregnated as it is
with London life from beginning to end, bears the date, ' Athens,
Capuchin Convent, March 12, 1811 ' "—and the even more
unreadable, because more topical, *Curse of Minerva*.

His stay was also marked by one of those ambiguous friendships
with a youth infinitely below him in rank which have already
been seen to recur in his life. This time the protégé was a subject
of France but born in Greece, named Nicolo Giraud. The patron
was supposed to be learning Italian from him ; this made a
pretext for giving him, on their parting at Malta in 1811 (for
so far homewards did the new Edleston accompany him), a
considerable sum of money ; while soon after his return home,
Byron made the fantastic will already alluded to, in which by
no means the least fantastic feature was a legacy to Giraud of
seven thousand pounds.

He set sail for England on June 3, 1811, from Malta, where
he had gone through another severe attack of fever. His letters
on the way home make melancholy reading. A year before
he had written to Hodgson : " I hope you will find me an altered
personage—I do not mean in body, but in manner, for I begin to
find out that nothing but virtue will do in this damned world.
I am tolerably sick of vice . . . and mean, on my return, to
cut all my dissolute acquaintance, leave off wine and carnal
company, and betake myself to politics and decorum. I am
very serious and cynical, and a good deal disposed to moralise ".
He quickly wavered from one of these intentions. " I shall
perhaps essay a speech or *two* in the House . .. but I am not
ambitious of a parliamentary career, which is of all things the
most degrading and unthankful ". As the time drew nearer
for his return, this listlessness increased. The old, sore question
of selling Newstead cropped up again, conveyed through his
mother from the dilatory Hanson ; and he wrote that if the
Abbey must go, so would he. " If I preserve Newstead, I return ;
if I sell it, I stay away ". Hanson himself wrote at last, and

his letter contained the news that Messrs. Brothers, upholsterers of Nottingham, had put in an execution at the Abbey for £1600.[1] It was not encouraging, and to Dallas and Hodgson the returning Pilgrim wrote dismally of his prospects. " Much business must be done with lawyers, colliers, farmers, and creditors. Now this, to a man who hates bustle as he hates a bishop, is a serious concern ". " I am returning home without a hope, and almost without a desire. . . . In short, I am sick and sorry, and when I have a little repaired my irreparable affairs, away I shall march ".

He arrived in England on July 17, 1811, after an absence of two years.

[1] Old Joe Murray was outraged by this occurrence. The sight of the notice of sale, pasted on the Abbey door, was more than he could endure. But he was sufficiently afraid of " the Law " to hesitate at tearing the paper down, and so at last hit upon a compromise. He pasted a large piece of brown paper over it (Moore, p. 121).

CHAPTER X

THE RETURN—1811

Reunions—Dallas discovers *Childe Harold :* Byron's misjudgment—
Hints from Horace—John Murray the Second—Mrs. Byron's death—*The
Scourge*—Death of Charles Skinner Matthews—Byron's grief—The Will
of 1811

BYRON came back with an odd collection of spoils : a
phial of Attic hemlock,[1] four Athenian skulls,[2] four
live tortoises and a greyhound (the last died on the passage)
to say nothing of two " live Greek servants, one an Athenian,
t'other a *Yaniote*, who can speak nothing but Romaic and Italian ".
These were for himself.   There were soberer offerings for others :
a shawl and a quantity of attar of roses for Mrs. Byron, and
marbles for Hobhouse, who was the first of his friends to welcome
him.   He saw Hodgson and Drury also in these early days of
return ; and Hodgson, whose meeting with him had been inter-
rupted, dispatched in the evening of the same day, from Harrow,
a copy of verses.

> " Alone, my Byron, at Harrovian springs—
> Yet not alone—thy joyous Hodgson sings ".

What trait could better exhibit to us the facility with which
the Alexandrine school could turn on the tap !

> " O flow along, all unrestrain'd by art,
> Thou glad effusion of that grateful heart " . . .

But the effusions would have brought about a second deluge if
many young men had been so copious as Hodgson, of whom it
might be truly said, " Touch him ne'er so lightly, into song he
broke ".

Dallas, too, was eager to greet the returned pilgrim.   As
soon as possible after the arrival in London, that admirable
personage appeared at Reddish's Hotel, St. James's Street. . . .
But before enlarging on this interview, so pregnant with destiny
as it was, I must turn aside to notice Galt's comments on the
state of Byron's affairs.   " The embarrassed condition in which

---

[1] At present in Mr. Murray's possession.
[2] Given afterwards to Sir Walter Scott.

he found [them], sufficiently explains the dejection and uneasiness with which he was afflicted during the latter part of his residence in Greece ; and yet it was not such as ought to have affected him so deeply, nor have I ever been able to comprehend wherefore so much stress has been laid on his supposed friendlessness.   In respect both to it, and to his ravelled fortune, a great deal too much has been said ; and the manliness of his character has suffered by the puling ". This is admirably sane. Delawarr the ever-disappointing was done with ; but what other friend had betrayed him, had even neglected him ?   He returned to open arms and hearts—Hobhouse's, Hodgson's, Drury's, Dallas's : which of us can reckon more than four to whom our coming back from absence is an event ?

Dallas thought him looking better than his own account had betokened, nor was he so melancholy as the kindly creature had feared to find him.   He spoke eagerly of his travels ; but " No ! he had never had the least idea of writing them ; satire was his *forte*, and he had written a satire while away.   It was a paraphrase of Horace's *Art of Poetry*, which would make a good finish to *English Bards* ".   He seemed sanguine about it : would his friend see it through the press, as he had done with the earlier one ?   But they were interrupted.   He gave Dallas the MS., and engaged him to breakfast the next morning.

That day Dallas read the paraphrase . . .   Was this the outcome of the romantic adventure—this the fruit that had ripened beneath the cloudless skies of Greece ?   Not that the verse was bad—or so the disconcerted reader forced himself to believe, for " the poem was his, and the affection he had acquired in my heart was undiminished ".   But indeed the verse *was* bad.   The lines were sprawling and inanimate, the satire was thin—little was here of even *English Bards*, and even *English Bards* would have been a poor result of two years' wandering in the wild, of long sojourns in such cities as Stamboul and Athens. . . The adoring man went to next morning's breakfast with a heavy heart.   He said what he could ; then ventured to inquire if *nothing* else had been written ?

His host understood, and spared him as yet *The Curse of Minerva*, twin abortion of the second stay in Athens.   But it was very negligently that he confessed to some short poems and " a great many stanzas in the Spenserian measure, relative to the wanderings ".   They were not worth Dallas's troubling with, but he should have them all if he liked—and Byron took from a small trunk a number of papers.   " Only one person [1]

---

[1] This was thought by Galt to have been Hobhouse, a very natural supposition. But Hobhouse repudiated it. " There is not the slightest foundation for the conjecture ". Elze suggests the Marquis of Sligo.

had read them, and that person had found very little to commend and much to condemn, and he, their perpetrator, bowed to this sentence, and Dallas would be sure to do the same ". Dallas listened, and after a promise to put the *Hints from Horace* in train immediately, went off with the sheaf of papers under his arm. Whatever they might be like, they could hardly prove more disappointing than the paraphrase.

" So came I " (he wrote) " by *Childe Harold's Pilgrimage* ". And so, in a sense, came the world by it.[1]

We move in our chairs as we read the story, and feel again the old envy of that discoverer. Let us figure it to ourselves once more. The enigmatic brilliant boy—only twenty-three !— and his fond anxious relative ; the former day's disappointment, the bundle of papers now so likely to be disappointing also ; the opening of the parcel, possibly upon the lyrics, none of them arresting; and then . . .

That very evening Dallas sat down and wrote, and caught his idol before a flight to Harrow and Henry Drury's. " You have written one of the most delightful poems I have ever read. . . . I have been so fascinated with *Childe Harold* that I have not been able to lay it down. I would almost pledge my life on its advancing the reputation of your poetical powers ".

But to his amazement, on breakfasting soon again with Byron, he found him quite unmoved by this appreciation. The author of *Childe Harold* [2] maintained that it was " anything but

---

[1] Moore thought so, at any rate. His feeling was that if Byron had published then the *Hints from Horace*, his former assailants would have resumed their advantage over him, and he would have flung *Childe Harold* into the fire. " The deuce he would ! " retorted Christopher North. . . . " He would instantly have written another satire . . . and it would have been a red-hot bar of iron. We cannot believe that the power of a mighty poet could have been palsied by a single stumble, however inopportune ". But Moore thought too that at no other time could *Childe Harold* have produced " that explosion of success . . . into which, coming, as it were, fresh from the land of song, he now surprised the world " ; and this, since Destiny has her destined moments, we may well believe.

[2] In a note (p. 122) Moore records the denial given by Hobhouse to the story of Byron's hesitation to publish *Childe Harold*. " [It] is at complete variance with all he repeatedly mentioned to me on the subject ". Moore makes no comment. Dallas's explicit testimony must stand against this mere assertion—for though we know that Byron delighted to mystify him, there would have been nothing to be gained by the game in this instance. The best way out of the difficulty is to recognise (and it is patent) that Dallas and Hobhouse were mutually most jealous of Byron's confidence. Each betrays this frequently ; Dallas, of course, with the greater simplicity, and with the greater hold upon our sympathy because he was, in the end, wholly cast aside by his idol. He was inevitably the one to lose, if either was to lose ; but at *this* moment he had his definite niche in Byron's scheme of things, and it is to him that, on the point of the hesitation to print, our credence should be given.

poetry—it had been condemned by a good critic—had not Dallas
seen the sentences on the margins of the MS. ? " And then he
fondly recurred to the dismal paraphrase. That was to be
given to Cawthorn, that was to be brought forth without delay.
But Dallas was tenacious—and, after all, the great MS. was his.
He reminded Byron. " You gave it to me, and I am so convinced
of its merit that I shall certainly publish it ". This seemed
to impress him at last. But he varied much in his feelings
about it ; said that it was going to get him into a scrape with
his old enemies—finally said that his name must not be put to
it. Dallas merely " entreated him to leave it to me ; I would
answer for this poem silencing all his enemies ". But still,
though Byron acquiesced, he doubted.

What are we to think of this ? It is not alone in literary
history ; authors have frequently preferred their failures to
their triumphs ; but such an extraordinary misjudgment as
Byron's remains inexplicable. For in nearly every other case,
there has been some personal reason to explain the unreason.
The loved inferior has in some way touched the writer's heart,
has been, autobiographically or locally, " his " book. But here
was only paraphrase—and poor paraphrase. And there, half-
torn from Dallas's bravely unfastened hand, was an " accident
of genius ", an original and dazzling creation, a thing by itself.

The quest of Byron's life was originality, as the passion of
it was fame. Originality was here : of design, says Mr. Coleridge,
but, for the age, there was surely another—of expression. The
same things had been thought before (" they were coeval with
reflection "),[1] but they had not been said like that. It was
the message of the Romantic Movement, in short, delivered by
the most romantic creature (in one sense) that has ever lived.
Let us accept for the moment an ancient fallacy, and say that
a boy dreams glorious dreams—a girl, sentimental ones. Byron
dreamed both, and dreamed them to extremity. . . . Well ! he
had caught his long-chased nymph, Originality, and now he did
not recognise her. Or was it rather that she had caught him ?
Not in poetry had he set himself to grasp her ; it was in the
mere external round that he had listened for her slackening
footfall. And the rogue had stolen up behind him in his study,
where he sat and copied Pope and betrayed her with her enemy
Convention ; and, turning round to find her there unbidden,
a perversity of faith had seized him, and Convention was hugged
to his heart, and Originality was handed over to Dallas. In
Dallas she found her knight. Not only by him was she enthroned,
but by him the enemy Convention was imprisoned. . . . Dallas
delayed the paraphrase by artful difficult devices, until the

[1] *Poems*, ii. xiii.

poem was acclaimed ; and by doing so, delayed it to the end. *Hints from Horace* did not see the light until seven years after the death at Missolonghi.[1] We must remember, in partial explanation of Byron, that adverse criticism was (until he found himself to the full in *Juan*) always with him more powerful than praise. " Years after, in the plenitude of his fame, he confessed that ' the depreciation of the lowest of mankind was more painful to him than the applause of the highest was pleasing ' ".[2]

When the publication of *Childe Harold* was at last decided on, Cawthorn was the publisher first thought of by Dallas. He had done well with the early Satire ; it seemed only fair that he should have the greater work. But Byron now declared that Cawthorn was obscure. " I found ", says Dallas with naïve jealousy (he was a very jealous man), " that this had been instilled into Lord Byron's ear since his return . . . probably at Harrow ". All the more reason, in the elder's view, for using him ; it would be good for Byron to make as Pope did (and Dallas must surely have used the potent plea !) " *his* bookseller the most fashionable one ; and this he could easily have done. He thought more modestly of himself "—and the poem was offered to Miller, of Albemarle Street. But Miller was Lord Elgin's publisher, and Lord Elgin was bitterly attacked (it was the period of the Marbles controversy) in *Childe Harold*. Miller declined it. This reawakened all Byron's fears ; there is a letter to the publisher of July 30, 1811, in which he is " perfectly aware of the justice of your remarks ". Here was another vacillation for Dallas to combat. He again prevailed, and promising that Longmans (who had refused *English Bards*) should not be approached, he once more went forth, this time with *carte blanche*. He could follow his heart now, and to his own man he turned.

This was John Murray the Second—that coming publisher who in the February of 1809 had launched the *Quarterly Review* with Gifford as editor, who counted Gifford among his " readers " too, and who had already expressed to Dallas a wish to number the author of *English Bards* among his authors. John Murray's shop at 32 Fleet Street, opposite St. Dunstan's Church,[3] was,

---

[1] Dallas published selections from the paraphrase in his *Recollections* in 1824. He probably transcribed them from his fragmentary proof-sheets, and " it may be inferred " (says Mr. Coleridge) " that the press was stopped at line 272 ". The full text was first published in 1831.

[2] Moore quotes this as " one of the MS. notes in the last edition of Mr. d'Israeli's work on *The Literary Character*, which that gentleman found in a copy of the work that belonged to [Lord Byron] ".

[3] In September 1812, John Murray moved to 50 Albemarle Street, and soon made that as historical a spot as his old quarters had been for long before his time. *Romeo and Juliet* (1609) and *Hamlet* (1611) were published

then, the Mecca of *Childe Harold's* next pilgrimage. "Lord
Byron has put it into my hands", said Dallas, offering the
manuscript. "I expect that you will make a very liberal agree-
ment with me". Murray took some days to consider it ; but
before Dallas visited him at all, events had so crowded into
the life of its author that I must for the moment leave the publisher
with his literary advisers, and follow Byron to Newstead, whither
he had gone on August 2.

On July 23 he had written to his mother from London to
say that law-business was detaining him. "It is with great
reluctance I remain in town". As soon as he could he would go
down, and she was to consider Newstead as her house, and
him only as a visitor.

On the first day of August she died. In the beginning her
indisposition had seemed a trifling one, so he had not been sum-
moned ; but excessive corpulency rendered her a dangerous
subject for illness, and just as this one took a critical turn, the
upholsterers' bills came in, so infuriating her by their amount
that she was seized by one of her unhappy rages, and never
recovered from its effects. . . . Always superstitious, she had
had a haunting fancy, when he left England in 1809, that she
should never see him again. The farewell letter had doubtless
heightened this imagining, and the more because their last
parting had been the scene of one of her most terrible outbursts.
He had returned, safe and well ; yet when he wrote to tell her
so and promise that he would soon be with her, she had said to
her maid, "If I should be dead before Byron comes down, what
a strange thing it would be !"

He came down, and she was dead.[1] On the night after his
arrival, the maid was passing the room where her former mistress
lay, when she heard a heavy sigh from within. She entered.
The room was in darkness, but she could distinguish the young
lord's figure by the bed. She tried to utter some words of com-
fort: "he must not so give way to grief". But his tears came
irresistibly ; she stood beside, embarrassed and distressed, till at
last she heard him articulate amid the sobs, "I had but one friend
in the world, and she is gone". . . . Such a sudden experience
had been this woman's ; and it must have been with amazement

by Southwick, who had his shop "under the Diall"; and in 1653, *The
Compleat Angler* first saw the light in the same bookselling centre, published
by Richard Marriot. John Murray the First had also published from
No. 32 very many famous books : Langhorne's *Plutarch*, Mitford's *Greece*,
Isaac d'Israeli's first *Curiosities*, and Lavater's famous *Physiognomy*
(Henley, p. 376).
[1] He had heard of her serious condition on July 31, and had at once
started for Newstead, but the news of her death reached him on the road.

9

that, on the day of the funeral, she not only saw him refuse to follow the procession to the churchyard and stand watching it from the Abbey door till it was out of sight, but then turn to one of the inferior men-servants and desire him to fetch the sparring-gloves, that they might have their usual morning exercise. He was silent and abstracted all the time ; the man thought his blows were more violent than usual—then, suddenly flinging the gloves away, he left the hall and was unseen for many hours. " Not Shakespere ", said the *Quarterly* in 1831, reviewing Moore, " could have conceived such a scene ".

We may not too closely analyse his emotion. When he wrote, on his way to the Abbey after hearing the news, to his old friend John Pigot of Southwell—who alone among his present acquaintance had known Mrs. Byron—and quoted Gray's " We can only have one mother ", a deeper than the obvious meaning may well have pierced his consciousness. The mother *he* had had—what mingled wretchedness and anger she had stirred in him ! And all had been reciprocal ; what she had called forth from him, he had called forth from her. . . . Such sorrow is the more poignant for its ambiguity. Which, in truth, was he mourning—her death or her life ?

To attribute to her conduct with him his own caprice and violence is to ignore the daily fruits of observation. Courses like hers have more frequently the opposite consequence. They teach their victim meekness—or if not meekness, evasion—or if not evasion, an iron stoicism. Bitter words may now and then be uttered, but for the most part it is by the parade of dumb endurance that revenge is taken. Byron, being who he was (and in what has been urged above, no more than the question of personal influence has been considered), must have been all that he was—wayward, violent, resentful, sad. His mother might assuredly have made his life with her less hateful, but she could not have instilled into his soul one impulse that was not, in germ or in flower, already there.

Doubtless, among the cloud of feelings stirred by her death, a chivalrous anger loomed large. One of his first acts on returning to England had been to buy a copy of a paper named *The Scourge*. In the March number there had appeared an article headed " Lord Byron ". It attacked him savagely, in revenge for *his* attack in *English Bards* on one Hewson Clarke, a journalist, whom he had characterised as

> " A would-be satirist, a hired buffoon,
> A monthly scribbler of some low Lampoon ".

Clarke, who was a sizar at Emanuel College, Cambridge, in

Byron's time, had been abusing him in the *Satirist* for some years, and the lines in *English Bards* had been Byron's answer. Now all was summed up, as it were, in *The Scourge* article. To term it libellous is a mild form of speech. He was called " the illegitimate descendant of a murderer ", " a vulgar debauchee ", " the son of a profligate father and a mother whose days and nights are spent in the delirium of drunkenness " ; he was said to be " hated for malignity of temper and repulsiveness of manners, and shunned by every man who does not want to be considered a profligate without wit, and a trifler without elegance ". He put the case in the hands of Sir Vicary Gibbs, Attorney-General, who gave his opinion against legal proceedings, because a considerable time had elapsed since the publication, and because Byron himself had provoked the attack. The decision must have sorely chafed him. He had written confidently to Pigot and Hanson of the case. To Hanson : " I will have no stain on the memory of my mother ; with a very large portion of foibles and irritability, she was without a *vice* (and in these days that is much). . . . Cost what it may, Gold or blood, I will pursue to the last the cowardly calumniator of an absent man and a defenceless woman ". He wrote this on August 4, amid the preparations for her funeral. But neither blood nor gold was shed.

On August 7, comes his next letter—to Scrope Davies. " MY DEAREST DAVIES,—Some curse hangs over me and mine. My mother lies a corpse in this house ; one of my best friends is drowned in a ditch ". . . .

The friend was the starry youth of Cambridge—his adored Charles Skinner Matthews. On the very day before Matthews' end, he had written to Byron ; and the letter, forwarded from London, reached Newstead on August 5, when he had been three days dead. For it was on August 2 that there took place at Cambridge the terrible scene detailed by Henry Drury in a letter to Hodgson.[1] Matthews had gone to bathe alone in the Cam, at the fork above the mills, and had got entangled in the weeds. " Not fifty of the strongest-bodied men in England ", wrote Drury, who had since visited the spot, " could, without ropes, have given the slightest assistance. . . .There is *literally* a bed of weeds, thick, more than *eight feet deep."* A man named Hart, who was unknown to Matthews, had witnessed in agonised impotence the unspeakable last moments. He had thought to hear a cry for help, and came to the spot. " Nothing was to be seen. . . . Conceive his horror when on a sudden there darted up in the middle of the river a human form half-length

[1] *Memoir of Rev. F. Hodgson*, i. 182–85. A similar account was given by Scrope Davies in a letter to Hobhouse, who sent it to Byron, saying, " I would that he had not been so minute in his horrid details ".

out of the water. He made an excessive struggle. His arms were locked in weeds ; so were his legs and thighs. You never saw such a place ". Hart shouted, " For God's sake, make no more exertions ; try to keep still till a rope is procured ". " In a resistless struggle, Matthews then disentangled the weeds from his arms . . . and threw them from him. This effort was his last ; as if exhausted in it, he fell back. He was under the water in an instant, and no trace was left of him ".[1]

Davies hurried down to Newstead in answer to Byron's cry : " Come to me, Scrope, I am almost desolate, left almost alone in the world ". . . . Indeed we may forgive him his extravagance of sorrow now. What a return ! No sooner alighted in England than he hears of Wingfield's death—no sooner rallied from that than his mother chokes herself out of existence before he can see her—no sooner *that* accepted than his imagination, through the pitiless details of Drury's and Davies's letters, is gripped and strangled as by the very weeds that dragged the worshipped Matthews down to death. " What can I say, or think, or do ? " he cries—that oldest cry, and most unanswerable in its moments of most poignant utterance . . . while as if to add the last drop to the cup, here, in grim grotesquerie, is Dallas writing him almost daily homilies on the immortality of the soul, and enclosing amid the countless sheets a Formal Protest against the sceptical passages in *Childe Harold* ! " Let me hear from you on anything but death ; I am already too familiar with the dead ", he cries—and in his wild and restless misery draws up that fantastic Will of 1811, wherein he desired to be buried beside his dog, " without any ceremony or burial-service whatever, or any inscription, save my name and age ".

---

[1] " Every one who was on the spot highly commends all Hart did. I verily think he nearly killed himself in his endeavours ". For Hart " succeeded in having him got out in twelve minutes ; but all too late " (*Memoir of Rev. F. Hodgson*, i. 185).

CHAPTER XI

NEW LIFE—1811–1812

Thomas Moore—Samuel Rogers—The dinner at Rogers's—Byron's impressions—London life—Religious questions—Murray accepts *Childe Harold*—Gifford's praise, and Byron's anger—" I awoke one morning " . . . —First speech in the Lords—Lord Holland—The Byron Fever

WHILE *Childe Harold* was still unpublished, and Byron still lingered in the country or at Cambridge, there reached him a letter destined to be fruitful in consequences and friendship. To display the incident adequately, I must go back so far as 1806. In that year Thomas Moore, writing as Thomas Little, had published a volume of poetry which was attacked by the *Edinburgh Review*. So savage was the mauling that Moore sent Jeffrey a challenge. They met at Chalk Farm, and according to Henley, " took a fancy to each other on the ground. But the affair had taken wind, and they were arrested. . . . When the pistols were examined at Bow Street, it was found that one had a bullet in it, but the other had not ". Moore's was the other. The newspapers of course got hold of the story, with the result that may be imagined. Moore published a letter stating (which was true) that Jeffrey's second had sworn to seeing both pistols loaded ; but it was no use—for several months he was a target of the wits.[1] Nor did the memory quickly die ; for in 1809, three years after the event, the cruellest of all these wits emerged in the anonymous author of *English Bards and Scotch Reviewers*, who, in an ironic allusion to Jeffrey, recalled

> " That ever glorious, almost fatal fray,
> When Little's leadless pistol met his eye,
> And Bow-Street myrmidons stood laughing by ",

—and added a note which enshrined the original story, since contradicted by Moore.

[1] Medwin gives this version : " . . . The ball is said to have fallen out of one of the pistols and to have been lost ; the seconds, having no other ammunition at hand, there was nothing to be done but to draw the ball from the other pistol. The principals, who knew nothing of this, *fired without bullets* ". They never fired at all.

As soon as Moore saw the second and acknowledged addition of the Satire (which he did not do for some months), he sent Byron a challenge. It is dated January 1, 1810—a date on which we know, though he did not, that Byron was out of England. The letter was placed by the friend to whom Moore entrusted it, in Hodgson's hands; and Hodgson, suspicious of its purport, resolved to keep it back. By the time Byron returned (he thought) Moore's anger would have cooled.

By the time Byron returned, Moore had at any rate married and become a father, two occurrences which modified his views about duelling. But the note to the leadless pistol lines still rankled, and he determined to have it out with the offender. Mrs. Byron's death delayed his purpose, but as soon as might be afterwards—at the end of October 1811—he wrote another letter. He referred to the former one: had it ever reached Lord Byron? In case it had not, he recapitulated it, but frankly avowed his changed intentions. The injured feeling still existed—there was no vindictive sentiment, but "that uneasiness under a charge of falsehood which must haunt a man of any feeling to his grave, unless the insult be retracted or atoned for." He added that if by any satisfactory explanation, Byron could enable him to seek the honour of being included among his acquaintances, it would give him sincere pleasure.

Byron's answer was that he had never received the first letter, nor ever seen Moore's public refutation of the gossip. He asked what Moore wished to have done. " I can neither retract nor apologise for a charge of falsehood which I never advanced." He was ready to do anything, conciliatory or otherwise—and was Moore's obedient, humble servant. Moore was not satisfied. The letter contained all that " the strict *diplomatique* of explanation could require "; but he felt that there was some ambiguity in Byron's allusions to the challenge. He replied with a good deal of hurt feeling, saying that the answer was as satisfactory as he could expect.

Byron had not even yet received from Hodgson the original challenge; and in his reply to Moore's second letter, he said so. But there had been another sore point for Moore in Byron's first answer. This was his having left entirely unnoticed the overture towards acquaintance, and Moore had alluded to the omission with *hauteur*. Byron now said that he had felt himself unable to take the first step towards friendship. Was not Moore the offended person? If Moore was ready, *he* was ready; but with Moore it rested. The Irishman was still dissatisfied. With the sensibility of his race, he detected a rebuff in one saying of Byron's : " until the *principal point* was settled between us " ; and he therefore answered frigidly that " his lordship had made him feel the imprudence he was guilty of in wandering from the point immediately in discussion between them "—adding that their correspondence might, from this moment, cease for ever. He was "satisfied with Byron's explanation."

In a question of graciousness, the Irish instinct may be trusted. Where it finds something lacking, something *is* lacking. Moore had been true to its prompting, and the next day confirmed him in his faith. Byron wrote on October 30, 1811, that "frank and open-hearted" letter which so auspiciously began the closest friendship of his life. Moore (he said) having at last unequivocally declared himself satisfied, the technical quarrel was over ; [1] etiquette was thrown to the winds ; he would be most happy to make acquaintance, when, where, and how Moore pleased. In Moore's comment he attributes any blame there may have been to himself and to the "somewhat national confusion" he had made of the boundaries of hostility and friendship. All credit for the happy issue is awarded to Byron—a trait as national as the earlier confusion. [2]

The immediate result was two new friendships, for Moore at once confided the affair to Samuel Rogers, who was an intimate of his, and Rogers proposed that the meeting should take place at his table. This suggestion was conveyed to Byron, and he (now in London) cordially accepted it. So did he come for the first time into relation with the really notable men of his day, breaking (as he had broken from the Southwell bonds) out of the coterie of mere scribblers like Hodgson, Hobhouse, Dallas, into the van of contemporary intellect—his natural place, and soon to be dominated by this boldest spirit of them all.

Samuel Rogers's house in St. James's Place, overlooking the Green Park, was just then the rival of Holland House as the great social meeting-place for the intellectuals in every sort. "He was that most perfect of all hospitable things, a perfect bachelor host " ; [3] and he made himself that kind of host for almost every one of value whom he met. He knew everybody, was "permanently, as far as any one ever was, in Lady Holland's good books ", and was as famous for his generosity as for his

[1] The original challenge was returned unopened to Moore, at his own suggestion.
[2] Moore tells an amusing anecdote of the dawning days of friendship. He and Byron went on December 14, 1811, to visit Campbell at Sydenham. They drove down in Byron's carriage, and started at midday. As the servant was shutting the door of the *vis-à-vis*, Byron asked him, "Have you put in the pistols ? "—and the man replied that he had. "It was difficult " says Moore—" more especially taking into account the circumstances under which we had just become acquainted—to keep from smiling at this singular noonday precaution " (p. 148).
[3] R. Ellis Roberts, *Samuel Rogers and his Circle*. Methuen, 1910.

caustic wit, which seemed, as Fanny Kemble said, to cut his lips as he uttered it. A small, slender creature, his facial appearance was so lugubrious that one of his friends asked him (in the gracefully personal taste of the age) why he did not set up his hearse, while another, coming out with him at Rome from a visit to the Catacombs, shook hands at the entrance with " Goodbye, Rogers ".

Moore, the sweet singer in a double sense of London, had been intimate with him since 1805. " Though in his society one walks upon roses ", wrote Moore to Lady Donegal, " it is with constant apprehension of the thorns that are among them ". They had their points of acute difference. Naïve, almost attractively naïve, as Moore's snobbery was (the artless glee and pride in dukes for dukes' sakes), there lay beneath it, as there lies beneath all snobbery, a moral flaw. He had begun his literary career with a different ambition—to be the poet of the people of Ireland. Long before thirty-two (his age in 1811) that ambition was, not forgotten, but overgrown. He had become the Princes' Poet, the darling of the high-set drawing-rooms, wherein the cause of Ireland was not a passport to favouritism. Now and again the national note was sounded ; but Irony would seem to bend a disconcerting ear to the singing, and the note would decline to sentimentality. If Irony would have let him alone, he would have sung of The Dark Rosaleen in the London salons, to the half-puzzled and half-patronising and more than half-indignant British ears ; but Irony pursued him in that furtive but relentless way she has, and, susceptible as the artist must ever be, Moore suffered under the haunting, and to escape it sang of other things—until the spirit of patriotism hovered over him again and spurred him to another effort. Perhaps the ghost would have gone ? But the ghost never went. Irony condemned each cry for Erin. Whatever it might sound like now (she whispered to him), it would sound like tinkling cymbals to posterity.

Rogers, immune from any form of snobbery, watched and felt it all. When the gay little man laid down as an axiom that in high life one meets the best society, the caustic little man answered him with a gibe. For Rogers, " never lost his sense of proportion ", and his sense of values was consummate. You took delightful things where you found them, and you found them often in high life. But the " pale head, white, bare, and cold as snow ", and the " large blue eyes, cruel, scornful ",[1] must surely have brooded fastidiously upon the further question (which could not occur to Moore) : " What *is* ' high life ' ? "

---

[1] Carlyle's impression of Rogers, whom he met in 1838.

Early in November 1811 the famous dinner took place. Rogers had never seen Byron before ; neither had Moore, nor Thomas Campbell (already past his zenith, though but thirty-four), who was the only other guest. Rogers arranged with them that he should be alone in the drawing-room when the stranger entered—a trait of delicate consideration for his lameness. Shortly afterwards the other two returned, and Moore saw Byron for the first time. He was in mourning for his mother, and the " pure, spiritual paleness of his features ", enhanced by the dark dress and the " curling, picturesque hair ", made the usual indelible impression. The beautiful voice added its spell to the rest ; and so, among the three small men, one with his keen spectral face, the other two with their round and lively countenances, Byron, Adonis of the Ages, sat down to dinner.

Rogers asked him if he would take soup.

" No ; I never take soup ".

" Some fish ? " as the soup vanished.

" No ; I never take fish ".

Presently the mutton arrived. The same question ; the same answer.

Our perfect host bore up. " A glass of wine ? "

" No ; I never taste wine ".

" It was now necessary ", says Rogers in his account of this far from perfect guest, " to ask what he *did* eat and drink ; and the answer was, ' Nothing but hard biscuits and soda-water '. Unfortunately, neither hard biscuits nor soda-water were at hand ; and he dined then upon potatoes bruised down upon his plate and drenched with vinegar. . . . Some days after, meeting Hobhouse, I said to him, ' How long will Lord Byron persevere in his present diet ? ' He replied, ' Just as long as you continue to notice it ' ". Rogers adds that he came to learn as a fact that Byron, after leaving his house very late, went to a club in St. James's Street and ate a hearty meat supper. That may be true, but it seems unlikely. He was sincere in his austerities, for (as we have seen) the best of reasons.

Thenceforth, despite this beginning, Byron saw a great deal of Rogers, and the latter recorded his impressions in his *Table-Talk*. Byron was not yet emancipated from the family shyness, if indeed he ever was. " He had no readiness of reply in conversation ", says Rogers. " If you happened to let fall any observation which offended him, he would say nothing at the time ; but the offence would lie rankling in his mind, and perhaps a fortnight later, he would suddenly come out with some very cutting remarks upon you, giving them as his deliberate opinions, the result of his experience of your character ". But, as Mr. Ellis Roberts points out, we must remember that Rogers's

recollections of Byron in London were written many years
afterwards, and that in the meantime they had met somewhat
discomfortably in 1821, during the Italian exile. Rogers's
venom came out in his later account of this companionship.
" [Byron and I] travelled some time together ; and if there was
any scenery particularly well worth seeing, he generally con-
trived that we should pass through it in the dark ". Byron's
early impressions were recorded in the Journal of 1813. " Rogers
is silent, and, it is said, severe. When he does talk, he talks
well ; and, on all subjects of taste, his delicacy of expression
is as pure as his poetry. . . . There is not a gem, a coin,
a book thrown aside . . . that does not bespeak an almost
fastidious elegance in the possessor. But this very delicacy
must be the misery of his existence. Oh, the jarrings his dis-
position must have encountered through life ! " The Ravenna
Journal of 1821 (*Detached Thoughts*) strikes a different note.
" Rogers is the reverse of the line :

" ' The *best* good man with the *worst* natured Muse '.

being

" ' The *worst* good man with the *best* natured Muse '.

His Muse being all Sentiment and Sago and Sugar, while he
himself is a venomous talker. I say ' *worst good man* ' because
he is (perhaps) a good man ; at least he does good now and
then, as well he may, to purchase himself a shilling's worth of
Salvation for his slanders. They are so *little*, too—small talk—
and old Womaney, and he is malignant too—and envious—and
—he be damned ! " [1]

For Moore, Byron at once conceived the liking that lasted
all his life. " The epitome of all that is exquisite in poetical
or personal accomplishments ", he wrote to Harness of the Irish
poet ; and the diary of 1813 contained a similar tribute. " More
pleasing than any individual with whom I am acquainted. He
has but one fault—and that one I daily regret—he is not *here* ".
Campbell, too, impressed him pleasantly, though by no means
to the same degree. He thought him a warm-hearted and honest
man, and highly admired his work ; but already at the time
they met, Campbell's great reputation (too easily acquired, said
George Ticknor) was waning, and his exertions to retrieve it
were, in Walter Scott's opinion, ruining his individuality.
    So passed the time before the publication of *Childe Harold*.
There were dark hours now and then, but on the whole life was

[1] And see Chapter XXIV.

more favourably regarded. Byron joined the Alfred Club, in Albemarle Street—the Savile of its age ; but he was not enthusiastic. " It was a decent resource, on a rainy day, or a dearth of parties, or parliament, or in an empty season ". For the rest, there was a vigorously renewed correspondence with William Harness, who was soon with Hodgson to pay him a visit at Newstead ; there were lyrical outbursts—the group of *Thyrza* poems ; there seems to have been no woman ; there were theatres —Kemble in *Coriolanus,* and Romeo Coates (the Amateur of Fashion, laughing-stock of the public) " who performed in a *damned* and damnable manner " ; there was a good deal of intercourse with Galt, who met him one night at the Opera and talked with him in Italian—a friend who was with Galt observing them closely the while. " Who was he ? " asked this friend ; " a foreigner, evidently ? " Galt disabused him ; he then said that " he had never seen a man with such a Cain-like mark on his forehead ".

And there was of course continual traffic with Dallas, in connection not only with *Childe Harold,* but with a question eternally opened up by the persistent elder—the religious one. Already in 1811 this had loomed too large. There had been the interminable letters upon the immortality of the soul which had caused Byron's outcry : " Let me hear from you on anything but death " ; there had been the Formal Protest against the scepticism of *Childe Harold.* No less vast screeds pursued him still, and not only Dallas kept him in harassment. Hodgson had joined in, and he lived through troublous days between them. " I *deny nothing,* but doubt everything ", he cried at last in desperation to the latter. . . . I do not propose, in any part of this book, to discuss Byron's religious opinions. Whatever they were, we have only to concern ourselves with them as he expressed them in his work and in his life. In his work, such expression is lucid enough and often enough afforded ; in his life, the implication is what it is in most lives—of an ideal alternately found and lost. Manners have changed, in that respect, more perhaps than in any. We are not prepared, as were the men of Byron's day, to assign either atheism or Christianity to others. The former word is obsolete ; the latter . . . in process of definition.

Byron, after a short stay at the Abbey, returned to London in the middle of January 1812, and took up his old quarters in St. James's Street. He had no fewer than four works in the press : *Childe Harold* with Murray ; *Hints from Horace, The Curse of Minerva,* and the fifth edition of *English Bards* with Cawthorn. Murray, during the early days of the first stay at

Newstead, had decided to publish *Childe Harold* at his own expense in a handsome quarto edition. Byron grumbled. " A cursed unsaleable size ; but it is pestilent long, and one must obey one's bookseller ". Dallas was to share the profits with Murray, and the agreement for the copyright was to depend on the success. (The copyright, it will be remembered, was Dallas's property.) After much discussion, Byron had consented to let his name appear. Gifford had been shown the MS.—to his adorer's violent indignation. He had pronounced it not only the best thing Byron had written, but equal to any of the present age ; yet even this glory had not mollified the angry author. " I *will* be angry with Murray ", he had written. " It was a bookselling, back-shop, Paternoster-Row, paltry proceeding ". " It is bad enough to be a scribbler, without having recourse to such shifts to extort praise, or deprecate censure. It is anticipating, it is begging, kneeling, adulating—the devil ! the devil ! the devil ! and all without my wish, and contrary to my express desire ". " I have written to [Murray] as he never was written to before by an author, I'll be sworn ".[1] Byron's fear was that Gifford should think it (from so publicly-professed an admirer) a hint to get a favourable review of the poem in the *Quarterly*. His anger seems nowadays out of all proportion to the offence ; but evidently the " reader " was not then a recognised functionary.

Murray's indiscretion had at all events the good effect of bringing Byron to see that Dallas was wise in delaying the *Hints from Horace*. By this time it was generally known that he had a poem in the press, and Galt fancied that the many paragraphs which began to appear were inspired by him. On alluding to one of them, his suspicions were increased by Byron's embarrassment. " I mention this incident ", continues Galt, " not in the spirit of detraction . . . but as a tint of character, indicative of the appetite of distinction by which, about this period, he became so powerfully incited that at last it grew into a diseased crave ". But he adds that at this time only the earliest symptoms were apparent : " the fears, the timidity, the bashfulness of young desire still clung to him, and he was throbbing with doubt if he should be found worthy of the high prize for which he was about to offer himself a candidate ".

He was found worthy. There never has been such a triumph, nor did anybody ever invent an apter phrase to define one.

---

[1] Byron had expressly forbidden Murray to send the MS. to Gifford. " If it must needs be shown, send it to another. . . . He is the last man whose censure (however eager to avoid it) I would deprecate by clandestine means ". But, as we have seen (p. 128), Gifford was one of Murray's " readers ". Byron evidently did not know this.

" *I awoke one morning and found myself famous* ". The morning
was the 10th of March 1812.[1] In three days an edition of five
hundred copies was sold ; and Murray then bought the copyright
for £600.[2]

The book was, in our modern jargon, well-handled. The
right people read the proofs and early copies, and talked about
them in the right way ; and Byron himself provided a brilliant
advertisement. On February 27 he had delivered his maiden
speech in the House of Lords, and it had been a success. Coming
out, elated with many compliments, he encountered Dallas, who
in the emotion of the moment held out his left hand, for his
right clasped an umbrella. " What, give your friend your left
hand on such an occasion !" The umbrella was displayed and
suppressed ; Byron was content, and gleefully assured the
proprietor of *Childe Harold* that the début had been the best
possible advertisement for the poetry.

His speech, not too well delivered—but better delivered than
either of the succeeding ones—reads admirably. The debate
was on the Nottingham Frame-breaking Bill. There was trouble
in Nottingham. Trade was bad, the stocking-weavers had been
losing work, and their discontent was increased by the introduc-
tion of machinery for the manufacture of gaiters and stockings.
Employment, they supposed, would now decrease still further,
and in the November of 1811 there had been serious rioting—
houses broken into, stocking-frames destroyed. The military
had been called out in force ; by January 1812, the town was
swarming with soldiers. A Bill was introduced in the Commons
on February 14, increasing the severity of punishment for frame-
breaking. It passed its third reading on February 20, without
a division. Lord Liverpool then introduced it into the House
of Lords,[3] and it was on the second reading (February 27, 1812)
that Byron spoke against the Bill. He said of his perform-
ance, " I spoke very violent sentences with a sort of modest

---

[1] Moore (p. 157) implies that the date was February 29 ; and Dallas
(*Recollections*, p. 220) says that he obtained a copy on Tuesday, March 3.
But in the *Times* and the *Morning Chronicle* for March 5, " future publica-
tion " is announced ; and advertisements in the *Courier* and the *Morning
Chronicle* on Tuesday, March 10, announce " first appearance " (*Poems*,
ii. xii.).

[2] The whole sum fell to Dallas, who gives this account of the transaction
with Byron. " After speaking of the sale, and settling the new edition, I
said, ' How can I possibly think of this rapid sale, and the profits likely to
ensue, without recollecting——' ' What ? ' ' Think what a sum your
work may produce '. ' I shall be rejoiced, and wish it doubled and trebled ;
but do not talk to me of money. I never will receive money for my
writings ' " (*Recollections*, p. 230).

[3] As introduced into the Lords, it rendered the offence of frame-break-
ing punishable by death.

impudence, abused everything and everybody, and put the Lord Chancellor very much out of humour ".

There is a strong note of modernity in some of the violent sentences. " The police, however useless, were by no means idle : several notorious delinquents had been detected—men, liable to conviction, on the clearest evidence, of the capital crime of poverty, men who had been nefariously guilty of lawfully begetting several children "—that " lawfully " is good ! And in his denunciation of the course adopted in calling out the military, we seem to hear an echo before the time of comments now familiar to our ears. " I cannot see the policy of placing [the military] in situations where they can only be made ridiculous. As the sword is the worst argument that can be used, so it should be the last. In this instance it has been the first ". He went on to compare, to England's disadvantage, the state of England with the state of the most oppressed provinces in Turkey. " And what are your remedies ! After months of inaction, and months of action worse than inactivity, at length comes forth the grand specific. . . . These convulsions must terminate in death. . . . Are there not capital punishments enough in your statutes ? . . . Will the famished wretch who has braved your bayonets be appalled by your gibbets ? When death is a relief, and the only relief it appears that you will afford him, will he be dragooned into tranquillity ? " He begged them to consider longer, not to rush this measure through the Lords as it had been rushed through the Commons. " When a proposal is made to emancipate or relieve, you hesitate, you deliberate for years, you temporise and tamper with the minds of men ; but a death-bill must be passed off-hand ". In peroration he drew a picture of an arrest —of one of the weavers dragged into Court to be tried for this new offence, under this new law ; and cried, " There are two things wanting to condemn him, and these are, in my opinion, twelve butchers for a jury, and a Jeffreys for a judge." [1]

It is not difficult to believe that a Tory Lord Chancellor may have been very much out of humour ; nevertheless, our orator was warmly complimented by " divers persons *ministerial* —yea, *ministerial !* " while, on his own Whig side, Lords Holland and Grenville were enthusiastic. The former said he would beat them all if he persevered ; and the latter, that he was very like Burke.

" My delivery ", he told Hodgson, " [was] loud and fluent enough, perhaps a little theatrical ". He suffered from the Harrow sing-song—" the same chanting tone ", says Moore, " that disfigured his recitation of poetry . . . encroaching just

[1] The Bill passed its third reading on March 5, and became law as 52 George III. c. 16.

enough on the boundaries of song to offend those ears most by which song is best enjoyed and understood." This defect was so marked in his second and third essays [1] as to make them more or less actual failures ; yet it is recorded that Sheridan urged him to take up the career of an orator. " But it never was my turn of inclination to try ", he confesses. Elze attributes this to mental indolence, saying that to become an orator he must have worked hard, while in poetry he could gratify his love of fame with the least expenditure of toil. The reproach refutes itself by the very measure of truth which it possesses. Men inevitably, and fortunately, turn to the thing in which they are so gifted that it comes easily ; otherwise, we should behold a world of comic opera, wherein everybody pursued the aim which fore-doomed him to failure. But indeed the simple explanation of Byron's choice is given by himself in the *Detached Thoughts*. " Just after [my first speech], my poem of *Childe Harold* was published, and nobody ever thought about my prose afterwards, nor indeed did I ".

When Moore and Byron first met, the latter was still in that state of isolation which had long been familiar to him. The coffee-house companions whom he had picked up before his absence from England, were either relinquished or dispersed ; he had but the three or four college-chums, the fussy Dallas, and the precarious Hanson (liable at any moment to annoy him, as men of law must do, by delay or conscientiousness), whom he could call his friends. It is not a tragic picture, as Galt very sanely says ; but it *is* an arresting one. Lordlings are not often solitaries by compulsion ; and Byron, moody and difficult though he was, was never the true solitary by election. He liked, more than most, somebody to whom he might not only say, " How sweet is solitude ! " but " How interesting of me to prefer it to society ! " With the new intimacy—the Moore intimacy—there arrived, true to the law by which neither misfortunes nor joys come single, the opening for another. Rogers was a frequenter of Holland House, and Byron's pro-jected début in the Lords was spoken of by him in that high

---

[1] His second speech (April 21, 1812) was in support of Lord Donough-more's motion for a Committee on the Roman Catholic claims ; his third, in the Debate on Major Cartwright's Petition (June 1, 1813) with respect to circumstances at Huddersfield in January, 1813, in which Major Cartwright was involved. Moore relates that on Byron's return from the House he walked up and down the room, spouting his sentences in a mock-heroic voice. " I told them that it was a flagrant violation of the Constitution ", etc. " But what was this dreadful grievance ? " asked Moore. " The grievance ? " repeated Byron, pausing as if to consider. " Oh, *that* I forget ".

political and literary sphere. The topic interested Lord Holland, for he was then Recorder of Nottingham, and he intended, like Byron, to oppose the Bill. Only one thing stood between them : the offensive lines on him and Lady Holland in *English Bards and Scotch Reviewers*. It would be difficult for one who had written as Byron had of the hospitalities of their table to be offered, or to accept, them. Of that peer whose exquisite temper so affected all who knew him—Brougham, writing of its irresistible charm, said that in his " whole experience of our race, he never saw such a temper, or anything that at all resembled it "— few more characteristic traits are recorded than the manner in which he solved this problem. Lord Holland, a distinguished man of nearly forty, allowed himself to be brought to the lodgings of the then almost wholly obscure youth of twenty-three, and there and thus introduced to him. Dallas was present, and thought it a curious event. His jealousy, always acute and now growing ever acuter, prevented him, one surmises, from seeing or saying that it was something more than that. Byron was " evidently awkward " ; no one else showed any embarrassment at all. And so an intercourse began which was to continue in the same sense—of frequent kindness from Lord Holland, and warm, remorseful gratitude from Byron, culminating in the suppression, then and for ever, so far as the author was concerned, of the fifth (and every previous) edition of *English Bards*. Directly *Childe Harold* appeared, Byron sent a copy to Holland House, and alluded shyly but feelingly to the magnanimity which had been shown him, quoting (the error is, in him, worth recording) a line of Dryden's as one of Pope's. Soon afterwards he became an intimate at the house ; soon afterwards, for that matter, an intimate at any house he chose. " Splendid crowds courted his society "—and no wonder ; for to read a work of genius, see the author, and see him the dazzling, perplexing, fascinating thing that Byron was, might turn steadier heads than those of " that sex, whose weakness it is " (I will not dispute it : let Moore speak for the women of his day) " to be most easily won by those who come recommended by the greatest number of triumphs over others ".

For, of course, the splendid crowds were led by the women, commandeered by the women . . . and is it not an occasion for amused conjecture to remember, for an instant, the other men ? How did *they* like it ?

CHAPTER XII

LADY CAROLINE LAMB

Lady Caroline Ponsonby—The Beautiful Duchess of Devonshire—
Lady Betty Foster—Caroline's girlhood—William Lamb—The marriage of
Caroline—1812, and Byron—Lady Melbourne—Caroline's letter to Medwin
—Lamb's apathy—Byron's letter: Was it a forgery ?—The rupture—
Lady Heathcote's ball—The last scene—Letters in 1816—Lamb's vacilla-
tion—*Glenarvon*—Her share in the rumours of 1816—Her life afterwards :
letters to Godwin—The news from Greece : 1824—The meeting—Bulwer
Lytton—Death of Caroline Lamb

ON June 3, 1805—before Byron had left Harrow—there
took place in the most brilliant and talked-of set in
London a wedding, of which the news in a letter from
his mother drew from one Augustus Foster, Secretary of Lega-
tion at Washington, the following written comments. " I cannot
fancy Lady Caroline married. I cannot be glad of it. How
changed she must be—the delicate Ariel, the little Fairy Queen,
become a wife and soon perhaps a mother ! She is under the
laws of a Man. It is the first death of a woman. They must
die twice, for I am sure all their friends, their male friends at
least, receive a pang when they change character so completely ".
But when his mother [1] wrote again, she was able to console him
to some extent. " You may retract all your sorrow about
Caroline Ponsonby's marriage, for she is the same wild, delicate,
odd, delightful person, unlike everything ". Already she had
been characteristic. She had written to welcome a new sister-
in-law into the family, and had dated the letter from her husband's
country-house, on " heaven knows what day ".

A girl who can inspire such whimsical and fantastic feeling
(for Augustus Foster, though notoriously susceptible, had never
been at all in love with her) seems marked out for an unusual
destiny ; and indeed from her earliest years, Caroline Ponsonby
had known only strangeness in all her surroundings. She was
the one daughter of the third Earl of Bessborough, by his wife

---

[1] She was Lady Elizabeth Foster, daughter of the fourth Earl of Bristol
and Bishop of Derry ; she married first J. Foster, M.P. ; second, the fifth
Duke of Devonshire.

Lady Henrietta Spencer, daughter of the first Earl Spencer and sister of Georgiana, the Beautiful Duchess of Devonshire. When Caroline (born on November 13, 1785) was a baby of three, her mother had a paralytic stroke and was sent to Italy to recover. She took her little daughter with her, but growing worse instead of better, soon returned to England and left the child behind. Not until she was nine years old did Caroline see mother or home again ; and home, when she did see it, meant only England, for " my angel-mother " (as she called Lady Bessborough),[1] was still too ill to undertake her ; and so she was sent to her Aunt Georgiana at Devonshire House, and brought up with her young Cavendish cousins.

The Devonshire marriage had been purely *de convenance* on the Duchess's side. At seventeen Georgiana Spencer had been married, and had soon found that it was to " the personified quintessence of English apathy "—capable, nevertheless, of blazing infidelity. She had been ready for domesticity—carefully trained by a notably pious mother, and in herself most tender, natural, and kind. Witty and lovely—the Juno of the Three Graces [2] who inspired a popular epigram—she was quite unspoiled by the adulation which had from childhood been her daily bread. But she was spirited, too (she, the descendant of Sarah Jennings) ; and pondering on her Duke, she decided that his faithlessness, consolable though it might leave her, absolved her from any extreme devotion to his service. She threw herself into political life ; Devonshire House became the fortress of the Whig Coalition which gathered round the Prince of Wales, and included Charles James Fox and Richard Brinsley Sheridan. That phase culminated in 1784 in the famous Kiss for the Vote. Fox was the candidate for the Long-acre butcher's suffrage. . . . Need the consequence of either sort be recorded ? Fox won ; and the Duchess of Devonshire, so far as her reputation was concerned, lost. Her name was thenceforward inseparably connected with Fox's—and soon not only with his. Her son was said now to be Fox's, now the Prince of Wales's, now not hers at all but Lady Elizabeth Foster's, changed at nurse for a daughter of the Duchess. Some years after the great electioneering campaign, Fanny Burney met her at Bath ; and, though she was despoiled of her beauty and deeply melancholy, said of her that the word charming might have been invented expressly to describe her. She was then accompanied everywhere by her inseparable—that Lady Betty Foster who, when the

---

[1] Byron called Lady Bessborough " Lady Blarney ", and professed a great dislike of her in the troubles later on. See many letters to Lady Melbourne in *Lord Byron's Correspondence*, 1922 (Vol. I).

[2] The others were the Duchesses of Gordon and Rutland.

Duchess died in 1806, was to write of her "unceasing regrets for the angelic, the unequalled qualities of my loved, my adored friend, since whose death I have lived in a sort of stupor"; and was to marry in 1809 the Duke of Devonshire, that friend's widower—of whom she had been for many years the mistress.

Caroline Ponsonby, brought up (if it could be called bringing-up) by her brilliant and then entirely undomesticated Aunt Georgiana, looked back upon her childhood with pure amazement. Never were babies so neglected as the small grandees of Devonshire House, who, served on silver in the morning, would carry their costly plates into the kitchen among the ever-quarrelling servants, to beg for their favourite tit-bits. The Marquis of Hartington, aged fourteen months, had his own house, carriage, servants; all the children believed that horses fed on beef, that bread and butter grew in loaves and pats, that anybody who was not a duke or a marquis must be a beggar, and that dukes and marquises could never spend all their money, no matter how much they spent, for beggars having none, *they* must have all there was. Her grandmother, Lady Spencer, to whose care Lady Bessborough soon removed her, surveyed the product of this training with uneasiness. Something more than the usual childish naughtiness seemed to emerge, and soon the family doctor was sent for to examine her. He ordered her to be taught nothing, and to be kept as far as possible from "seeing people", for the violent passions and caprices that she showed might, if not restrained, lead in the end to madness. The result was that at ten, the little Lady Caroline could not yet read. But when at fifteen she began to learn, she showed extraordinary eagerness. The modern languages were not enough for her; Greek and Latin were voluntarily undertaken, and in her later apotheosis, one of the great distinctions was her recital of the Ode to Anactoria of Sappho. She loved music too, and listened to it with that excessive sensibility which in 1816 led her sparkling cousin, Harriet Cavendish (then Lady Granville) to say of a reading by Benjamin Constant: "I have begged that Caroline may be present, to cry and make sensation for us". She painted, played, caricatured ("never spitefully"); and as she grew up, became noted for unusual and picturesque attire. Disdainful, or more accurately, heedless (for this was a true original) of the mode in dress, she was no less unconventional in her social attitude. To talk of the weather, of how everybody was, of arrangements—why you had or had not gone or come to one place, when and how you were going to the next . . . all this was by Caroline Ponsonby not to be endured. Facts eluded her; once, in asking that a book might be sent to her

brother, she confessed that she forgot the number of his house ;
we have seen already that she could date on "heaven knows
what day " ; and in 1811 there is a letter from her to Lady
Morgan, then Miss Sydney Owenson, apologising for not having
sent her carriage for this new friend as had been arranged. " I
could never have imagined it possible for me to forget your
address " ; but she *had* forgotten it, and had been obliged to
entrust her apology to a vague sketch of a direction, from which
ordeal the Post-Office emerged triumphantly.

Already, as a schoolgirl, this bewildering creature had met,
fascinated, and fallen in love with, her future husband. At
twelve she had read some verses of his and had heard that he
was a friend of Charles James Fox. That was enough ; she
" longed to meet him "—just as, fourteen years later, she was
to read the somewhat more remarkable verses of another young
man, and long to meet him too. . . . With her thirteenth year
came this first encounter. There arrived at Brocket Hall (where
she was visiting with her cousins) the nineteen-yeared William
Lamb, son of Lord Melbourne and of Elizabeth Milbanke, only
daughter of Sir Ralph Milbanke, of Halnaby in Yorkshire—one
of the loveliest, cleverest, and most ambitious women of her day.
. . . As soon as William Lamb beheld his youthful admirer, he said,
" Of all the Devonshire House girls, that is the one for me ! "

Brocket Hall in Hertfordshire was the smaller country-house
of the Melbournes, who were among the *richissimes* of their day.
They possessed, besides, Melbourne Manor in Derbyshire, and
Melbourne House in Whitehall.[1] The second son, William, was
born on March 13, 1779.[2] His elder brother, Peniston, then
nine years old, was his father's darling to such a degree that
Lady Melbourne despaired of ever winning any paternal affection
for William. Her presage proved correct. In Torrens's [3] book
no explanation of this peculiar coldness is given ; in Dunckley's,[4]
on the contrary, so much is hinted that Lord Melbourne's attitude
towards the second son becomes all too explicable. The Prince

---

[1] It occupied the space between the Horse Guards and the Treasury
and was called, familiarly, the Round House ; officially, before the Mel-
bournes had it, York House, for the Duke of York lived there ; he ex-
changed houses with the Melbournes. Theirs was a magnificent mansion
in Piccadilly—now the Albany region.

[2] To the superstitious in numbers it is worth pointing out the domi-
nance of the sinister thirteen in Caroline Lamb's dates. She and William
Lamb were both born on the thirteenth of the month ; she met him at
thirteen ; it was in 1813 that the rupture between her and Byron culmin-
ated in the famous scene at Lady Heathcote's ball.

[3] Torrens, *Memoirs of Viscount Melbourne.* 1878.

[4] H. Dunckley (" Verax "), *Lord Melbourne.* 1890. In The Queen's
Prime Ministers Series, edited by Stuart Reid.

of Wales was a constant guest at Melbourne House; and when
on his attaining his majority and being established at Carlton
House, Lord Melbourne was named his Gentleman of the Bed-
chamber, Dunckley remarks that the qualification for the post
" had best be regarded as inscrutable ". There was Fox too,
and there was the fascinating Lord Egremont, " all of whose
children ", said the Greville Memoirs, " are illegitimate ". Many
years after Lady Melbourne's death, Lord Melbourne (formerly
William Lamb) was showing to Landseer a portrait of Lord
Egremont which hung in one of his houses. With Landseer's
first glance at the face, he wheeled round involuntarily to
examine his host's. " Ah, you're thinking of the old story ",
said Melbourne coolly. " There's nothing in it ".

Whether there was anything in it or not, the first Lord Mel-
bourne as nearly as might be repudiated him. When Peniston
died in 1805, Lady Melbourne tried to obtain for her favourite
the allowance of £5000 a year which the elder son had enjoyed.
All her powers of persuasion failed; she then induced a friend
to remonstrate—but in vain. William must do with £2000,
which was " quite enough for him ". He was then twenty-six,
very handsome, something of a fop, yet with a fine air of care-
lessness which enhanced everything that he did, said, and wore;
" nobody ever *happened* to have coats that fitted better ". He
was a friend of Brummell, but (despite the faultless coats) Brum-
mell's way of life seemed to William Lamb unworthy of an
intelligent being. He had his own affectation, however, as we
all have; and that was a desire to be thought indolent, careless,
haphazard. But in the brilliant countenance, with the large
eyes so unusually well-opened, there was a kind of suppressed
glow which contradicted the drawl and the yawn—though these
were not entirely histrionic. William Lamb *could* be bored, he
was lazy—is not his falling asleep in Queen Victoria's presence
an historical triumph? for she, ordinarily so punctilious, would
suffer no one to disturb her loved and then ageing Minister. . . .
But his boredom was impatience with the unessential, his laziness
was perception of the impossible, or at any rate undesirable,
activity. Once let Lamb perceive the essential, the desirable,
and the great eyes flashed, the face kindled, the famous " Why
can't you leave it alone ? " was as though such eager lips could
never have uttered it. It was this hidden fervour which attracted
to him more and more as they grew up together the ardent
Caroline Ponsonby. Before his prospects grew into brilliancy,
while he was still a budding lawyer not in any degree distinguished,
he proposed to her and she refused, because " I adored him ".
" I knew I was a fury, and I would not marry him "; but that
he might have no doubt of her devotion, she offered to go with

him " anywhere " as his clerk.   Such a rosy clerk would hardly
have advanced his legal career ; but in 1805 that had become a
thing of the past.   He was the future Lord Melbourne now—
and at once he offered himself again.   This time she yielded, and
the wedding took place about which young Augustus Foster
was to write and feel so fantastically.

Caroline was nineteen and a half, and William Lamb twenty-
six.   Already she was the star of the drawing-rooms, the most
talked-of, written-of girl of her period—hung about with pretty
nicknames, of which she was vain enough to make a list in her
commonplace-book.   Sprite, Young Savage, Ariel, Squirrel,
Fairy Queen, Her Lavishship—do they not bring before us the
tiny, eager, slender thing with her fawn-flaxen hair shot with
gold, her great dark eyes, her low, caressing voice (that " beauty
and charm to which she owed the greater part of her fascina-
tion ",[1] according to Lady Morgan), her vivacity, sweetness,
kindness, folly—and fury ?   At her very wedding, she flew into
a rage with the officiating bishop, and tore her exquisite gown
to pieces ; then fainted, and had to be borne out to the carriage
like that !   But though so ill-inaugurated, the honeymoon days
were good : at Brocket Hall we have seen that she had lost
count of time.   " It won't last ".   Did the Cavendish cousins
—Georgiana and the mordant Harriet—whisper that to one
another, knowing their Caroline ?

If they did, they proved true prophets.   Adored by a de-
lightful husband, and rich, young, brilliant, fascinating, one
would have called Caroline Lamb the spoiled child of fortune—
and that is precisely what she was.   Like the spoiled child,
she cried for the moon ; and, more spoiled and more unhappy
than he, was given it. . . .   But though they quarrelled and were
often, as she said, very troublesome to one another, until 1812
there was no scandal.   She had three children, of whom only
one survived—that son, born in 1807, whom the young mother
carried Miss Berry, the famous blue-stocking, up to a room at
the top of a house in Whitehall to see asleep in his cradle.   Next
day he was seized with fits ; it was thought they must be fatal ;
but he survived—unhappily, as it proved, for the godson of the
Prince of Wales, named by him George Augustus Frederick,
never attained to full mental stature.   He remained all his life,
which lasted until he was twenty-nine, what he was at the
beginning—a gentle, sweet-natured, obedient child : " to his
father a grief incurable ".

----

[1] " Despite a certain artificial drawl, habitual to the Devonshire House
set ", said Lord Lytton in his description of her as she was in 1824.   He
adds to her list of attractions one which others have omitted : " exceed-
ingly good teeth " (Life, Letters, etc., of Lord Lytton, 1883, by his son).

Caroline grew ever more wayward; her restlessness and caprice were inordinate. From one moment to another her relatives did not know what they might hear. But the moment was fast approaching in which they were at least to know with whose name everything that they did hear would be connected. It was 1812—the year when " language can hardly exaggerate the folly that prevailed "—the year of the Byron Fever.

To her, whose verdict upon a book was still, despite her eccentricities, the making or unmaking of it no less in the *salons* than in the mere drawing-rooms, Rogers took care to lend his very early copy of *Childe Harold*.

She read it, summoned the lender. " I must see him—I am dying to see him ! "

" He has a club-foot," said Rogers. "And he bites his nails".

" If he is as ugly as Æsop, I must see him ! "

Soon, at Lady Westmorland's,[1] she did see him. Her hostess led her up to be introduced. The Queen of the Drawing-Rooms submitted to that—it gives one the measure of his vogue—but when, coming nearer to the god, she beheld " all the women throwing up their heads at him ", a swift revulsion seized her. She stood at gaze a moment ; then turned on her heel, and walked away.

That night she wrote in her diary the only wise words, perhaps, that she ever used with respect to him—the renowned phrase : *Mad, bad, and dangerous to know.* But another phrase, as renowned, though not confided to paper on the first, triumphant evening, was sounding in her soul ; *That beautiful pale face is my fate.* . . . Two days later, she was calling at Holland House when Lord Byron was announced. He was presented to her, and he said directly : " This offer was made to you the other day— may I ask why you declined it ? " She does not record her answer ; his next move was to ask permission to come and see her. She was then living at Melbourne House (the William Lambs had no separate establishment) which " was the centre of all gaiety, at least in appearance " ; and when Byron arrived on the following morning, he found her with Rogers and Moore.[2]

---

[1] Whom Byron had met at Algeciras, at the beginning of the Pilgrimage, in 1809.

[2] She said in after-years to Lady Morgan : " Rogers and Moore were both my lovers ; I was in the clouds ". Neither was, in any degree of the accepted sense, her lover ; but only a malicious insistence on that one definition can turn this statement into a weapon for those who accuse her of boundless vanity. Every woman of her sensuous intellectual type has the " platonic " lover as well as the real one, distinguishes unerringly between the two, and knows that any understanding friend will understand that she can do so. Lady Morgan assuredly understood. The same thing had been part of her own experience from the first days of girlhood.

In her account of the visit, there emerges strikingly the coarse-
ness of phraseology which then prevailed. She was among the
great *élégantes* of her day ; her speech, semi-Blue though she
might be, was the speech of fashion—and here are the words she
used to describe her condition after the morning's ride. She
had just returned from it : " I was on the sofa, *filthy and heated* " !
Our slangiest modern Diana would shrink from such vernacular
—but that Caroline's eccentricity may be proved to have nothing
to do with it, let me finish the story. " When Lord Byron was
announced, I flew to change my habit. When I came back,
Rogers said, ' Lord Byron, you are a lucky man. Here has
Lady Caroline been *sitting in all her dirt* with us, but as soon as
you were announced, she fled to make herself beautiful. ' "

The *partie carrée* did not satisfy Byron. He intimated
that he would like to come and see her when she was alone,
preferably at dinner. " I said he might. From that moment,
for more than nine months he almost lived at Melbourne House ".

Melbourne House, we must remember, had other attractions
besides hers. One of the most delightful women in, and of,
the world, was its mistress. Lady Melbourne, now sixty-two,
and a good deal withdrawn into herself, nevertheless felt Byron's
spell ; and he felt hers. " The best friend I ever had in my life
and the cleverest of women ", he wrote in the Journal of 1813.
" If she had been a few years younger, what a fool she would
have made of me, had she thought it worth her while—and I
should have lost a most valuable and agreeable *friend* ". She
found him really congenial, and confided to him many matters
which, taught by bitter lessons, she hesitated to confide to
anybody else. . . . Did Lady Melbourne, then, so sagacious,
cynical, experienced as she was, suspect nothing of what was
going on in her son's quarters ?[1] It must have been fairly evi-
dent. Before Byron's advent, the great craze in those quarters
had been waltzing. It had but just been introduced, and the
prejudice it had excited was still in force ; at Devonshire House,
for instance (where the second wife, the Bishop's daughter, now
reigned), it was not allowed. Lord Hartington enjoyed it ;
he " wanted ", wrote Caroline, " to have waltzes and quadrilles
. . . so we had them in the great drawing-room at Whitehall.
All the *bon ton* assembled there continually. There was nothing
so fashionable. But after a time Byron contrived to sweep

---

[1] In 1922, Mr. John Murray published *Lord Byron's Correspondence*
(2 vols.) consisting of hitherto unpublished letters, of which in vol. i.
the great majority are to Lady Melbourne. From these it is made clear
that she was aware from the beginning of his affair with Caroline ; frowned
upon it then and always ; and in the end was the recipient of all his con-
fidences with regard to Caroline's " scenes " and persecutions.

them all away ". That is significant of two things : his egotism, and his influence. Dancing had always irritated the morbid creature who could not join in it ; yet with girlish Mary Chaworth in 1804, he had not prevailed. With married, fashionable Caroline Lamb he prevailed at once. She was unable to refuse him anything ; all that she could sacrifice, indeed, was his before he asked for it. Her first letter to him—it is said to have been delivered by herself, figuring as her own page—contained not only the offer of her love, but of all her jewels if he should ever be in need of money. That was Caroline Lamb all over. She would do anything for the people she liked, but " it was hazardous to refuse the offer." And it was no less hazardous to accept it. She was unacquainted with moderation, with reserve, with patience. Exacting and violent, egotistic (even Lady Morgan, who really cared for her, said that for all her eloquence and graceful, gracious expression, her subject was always herself), impulsive beyond belief . . . such a mistress was foredoomed to disaster with such a lover. He had every fault of hers, in full measure ; and had, for women, none of her chief virtue, generosity.

But when one speaks of happiness with reference to any woman's relations with Byron, one is bringing two irreconcilable things into sharp opposition. The woman did not live, has never lived, who could reconcile them. Obsessed as he was by the idea of woman, at bottom Byron despised her wholly ; and no one can be happy with, or make happy, a creature scorned. Always to tyrannise, humiliate, wound, her he had fascinated, in revenge as it were for the power upon him with which mere sex endowed her, was to him the game of love—for in life, he saw love only as a game. In his poetry, it is true, the passion is exalted, the woman frequently wins—but always, let us perceive, by abnegation of her very being. She is the lovely loving slave, or else she is the tigress ; and his tigress never even in appearance wins. Unless she, so to speak, ceases to be, except as an instrument of passion, she is punished invariably—by remorse, or death, or shame. I hold no brief for the tigress. All that Byron sang of gentleness, devotion, sacrifice, may find an echo in most women's hearts ; but there is a wide distinction between our choice, and man's proclamation of its sole rightness for us.

Caroline Lamb was a good deal both of slave and tigress. Her nature seized instinctively upon the drama of the alternating relations. Since she was untamed, how exciting to submit ; since she had submitted, how exciting to rebel ! It was a perpetual balance between the two extremes. Now she would be kneeling before a man, now (the Charles Kembles saw her do both in Paris with her husband, from their hotel-window which commanded hers) springing up in a fury from that attitude, and dashing the china to the floor. When she did such things with Byron, he would assume the posture which had always so successfully infuriated his mother—standing coolly to watch, and interjecting a gibe at the most theatrical moment. Then would come the tears and the vehement remorse, and the bored, contemptuous forgiveness. . . . But let us trace the incidents of their two-years conflict, wherein she skirmished long after all was decided against her.

One day he came to Melbourne House with a rose and a carnation in his fingers. It was before the season of either —in the early spring of 1812—and presenting them, he said with a half-sarcastic smile, " Your Ladyship, I am told, likes all that is new and rare—for a moment ". A day or two afterwards, she wrote, on blue-bordered paper, embossed at the corners with scallop-shells, one of her " pretty " letters. It is in the third person ; all the vague sentimentality of the time informs it. The Rose had died, " probably from regret at its fallen fortunes ". She was going to Brocket Hall, but would soon be back, and then he was to receive a book with a picture of the Flower she wished most to resemble. It was the sunflower. We can guess, before we read, the reason for choosing it. " Having once beheld in its full lustre the sun that for one moment condescended to shine upon it, never while it exists could it think any lower object worthy of its worship and admiration". And when the " little Page " brings the submissive image, she hopes it will be graciously received without any more Taunts about Love of what is New. As to *that* fault, she does not plead guilty, but if she did, would attempt no excuses. She is full of faults that any one might see on the shortest acquaintance, but " there is not one, though long indulged, that shall not be instantly got rid of if Lord Byron thinks it worth while to name them ".[1]

Little wonder if he believed he had found the lovely loving slave of his imaginings ! But at first all was platonic. He would spend hours at Melbourne House in the mornings, talking gently, gravely, in the incomparabie voice, while he held on his knee caressingly the little boy about whom such apprehensions now hovered. Other devices too were brought into play—the famous Marble Heart, the Byronic remorse and inverted hypocrisy : he would compare himself with her husband—" as much above me as Hyperion above the Satyr " ; and she, listening, felt surer every day that he was hers as she was his. Read her touching letter[2] to Medwin in November 1824, when the

[1] *L. and J.* ii. App. iii. p. 446.   [2] *Ibid.* p. 451.

Conversations with Lord Byron had done its work of ruining her finally. She had been very ill ; she had read—in that unpardonable book—read for the first time the horrible stanzas of "Remember thee ! "[1] " I feel secure the lines were his ", she writes in her anguish. " Let me confide to you at least the truth of the past—you owe it to me—you will not I know refuse me. . . . Byron never never could say I have no heart. He never could say, either, that I had not loved my husband. In his letters to me he is perpetually telling me I love him the best of the two ; and my only charm, believe me, in his eyes was, that I was innocent, affectionate, and enthusiastic. . . . Let me not go down in your book as heartless.[2] Tell the truth ; it is bad enough, but not what is worse. . . . I was not a woman of the world. Had I been one of that sort, why would he have devoted nine entire months almost entirely to my society ; have written perhaps ten times a day ; and lastly have pressed me to leave all and go with him, and this at the very moment when he was made an Idol of, and when, as he and you justly observe, I had few personal attractions. Indeed, indeed, I tell the truth. Byron did not affect—but he loved me as never woman was loved. . . . Besides, he was then very good, to what he grew afterwards ; and, his health being delicate, he liked to read with me and stay with me out of the crowd. Not but what we went about everywhere together, and were at last invited always as if we had been married. It was a strange scene—but it was not vanity misled me. I grew to love him better than virtue, Religion—all prospects here. He broke my heart, and still I love him ".

We read, turning from her indictment of herself, the comments of the time. Rogers's, the Duchess of Devonshire's, Harriet Countess Granville's, Galt's, Dallas's—in all she is condemned. She absolutely besieged him, said Rogers, the friend of both, who firmly believed what no one else did, or does, believe : that there was nothing " criminal " between them. He

---

[1] " Remember thee ! remember thee !
    Till Lethe quench life's burning stream,
    Remorse and shame shall cling to thee,
    And haunt thee like a feverish dream !

Remember thee ! Aye, doubt it not,
    Thy husband too shall think of thee :
By neither shalt thou be forgot,
    Thou *false* to him, thou *fiend* to me ! "

The stanzas were first published by Medwin.

[2] In the New Edition of the *Conversations*, published later in the year 1824, not one word of these confidences from Byron stands ; there is merely a passing reference to *Glenarvon*. The verses, too, are suppressed.

tells of her endless indiscretions and absurdities ; how he, Rogers, would come home late at night, and find her walking about in his garden, waiting for him. " We have had a quarrel, and I want you to reconcile him to me ". If she was not invited to a party where Byron was to be, she would wait in the street for him till it was over. One night, after a great affair at Devonshire House to which she had not been bidden, Rogers saw her—" yes, saw her "—" talking to Byron with half of her body thrust into the carriage which he had just entered ". And all through society ran rumours of her raids upon Byron's rooms, oftenest disguised as a page (she had a veritable mania for pages), but once in the latter days as a common carman, admitted by the valet Fletcher, who did not recognise her. And what was that to her proceeding with the valet himself, when she wrote and asked him to come and see her " some evening at 9, and no one will know of it. . . . I want you to take the little Foreign Page I shall send, in to Lord Byron. . . . *Do not think it is me* ". It was so that the great lady, the wife and mother, wrote to her lover's servant ! Well might Byron say, in one of his earliest letters to her, that all her gifts were " unfortunately coupled with a want of common conduct ".

Did no one try to guide her ? Was this an occasion when William Lamb murmured, " Why can't you leave it alone ? " *She* said it was ; she told Lady Morgan that her husband cared nothing for her morals. " He was privy to my affair with Lord Byron, and laughed at it. His indolence rendered him insensible to everything. When I ride, play, and amuse him, he loves me. In sickness and suffering he deserts me. His violence is as bad as my own ". Let us examine this statement, remembering what she also said in 1823 : " My husband was my guardian angel ". Which are we to believe, for both cannot be true ? We must believe that William Lamb saw, rightly or wrongly, but at any rate sincerely, in this case the case where nothing can be done. All through her wild unhappy book, *Glenarvon*, the cry " Where are you, Avondale ? " resounds.[1] " Be my saviour, Avondale ! " implores Calantha (who stood for herself). " Who knows where this capricious will of mine may lead me ? " Calantha blames her husband for his coldness and indifference ; ambition in him has supplanted love ; she seeks for their lost happiness in " guilty passion ". . . . If Lamb *had* intervened ? We must grant something to his experience of her violence, her self-will ; something also to his pride—it is ill confessing to such jealousies ; something, again, to the insanity of the time about Byron. It was the fashion to be in love with the author of *Childe Harold* ; and Caroline was always, though with a differ-

---

[1] William Lamb was the original of Avondale.

ence, in the fashion. When the mode passed, her love, thought
Lamb, would pass with it. Add to this the scorn that other men
must have begun to feel for the " *hot-pressed* darling of the
drawing-rooms " (as Byron himself described himself at this
period), and we can watch without indignation the shrug, the
glance, of William Lamb at his too-glittering rival, can hear
without contempt the " Why can't you leave it alone ? " by
which he would silence his uneasiness and anger. And moreover,
the morals of the age! Hardly a woman in his sphere whose
name was not coupled with a lover's. Wherever he looked, there
was or had been intrigue. Had he divined, as he grew up,
by his father's attitude, anything of the gossip about his mother ?
Had he heard, again, anything of the monstrous scandal about
Caroline's—not to be characterised as yet ? Small marvel if
William Lamb was cynical, less still if he was apathetic.

Lady Melbourne did not love her fantastic daughter-in-law.
The match had pleased her well enough ; the wife, as time
went on, had not. Caroline had already made herself absurd,
and now she was making herself notorious. If she must fall in
love with Lord Byron—and Lady Melbourne granted him all
his charm—let her at least do it decently ! But that was pre-
cisely what Caroline was incapable of doing. The mother-in-
law did speak ; but she spoke to Byron. He answered at first
with a reminder, in the best manner of *Childe Harold*, of the
Marble Heart. Such an absurdity can never for a moment have
deceived such a woman ; and soon all pretence was dropped
between them. Lady Melbourne knew everything there was to
know, and became Byron's firm adherent in all the distresses
which ensued.

Hobhouse, the serene and lucid, was active on the side of
the angels during the very tumultous days. Lady Bess-
borough, ill, tormented by the scandal, had enlisted him ; and
in his Journal for the summer of 1812, we find three consecu-
tive entries.

" *June* 30.—Found an odd note from Lady Bessborough ".

" *July* 2.—Called on Lady Bessborough—a very curious
scene ".

" *July* 3.—Note from Lady Bessborough. Went to Byron,
who agrees to go out of town ". On July 6 he finds on his table
" most strange letters from Melbourne House " ; ten days
later, goes " by desire to Lady Bessborough's. In midst of
our conversation in comes Lady C. Lamb, who talked of Lady
Bessborough and myself looking guilty. Here's a pass for the
world to come to ! " To fastidious Hobhouse, the gross bad
taste of such an *agaçerie*—and it was in the frequent tone of
Caroline's—would indeed be little short of a portent.

If Byron kept his promise of going out of town at all, he quickly returned, for on the 19th Hobhouse dined with him. Lady Bessborough soon heard that the lovers had gone off together. It was not true, but the rumour was enough to make her fall dangerously ill. " She broke a blood-vessel ", says Caroline in her letter to Medwin. " Byron would not believe it, but it was true. When he was convinced, we parted ". He was convinced in another raid from his mistress, who forced herself into his rooms, and implored him to fly with her. He refused, took her back to Melbourne House, and wrote that letter which all who read must regard as one of the many enigmas of his story. As Rabbe[1] says, " It is difficult to believe it authentic". It is so difficult that there flashes into memory an affair in January 1813, when Caroline forged so skilfully a letter in Byron's name that John Murray, on receiving it, transferred to her a miniature (the one by Sanders) which had been left in his charge. She at once confessed to Byron that she had done this, and he wrote to Murray[2] that the " culprit " had put herself into his hands, adding, *more suo*, very unmistakable indications of who that culprit was. . . . I hesitate to present this as a theory ; rather let me call it a flash of supposition born of the extreme unlikeness of this letter[3] to all of Byron's, and its close likeness to all of hers that we have. The date is uncertain, but we may place it with some confidence—if he wrote it—in the end of July or beginning of August 1812.

" MY DEAREST CAROLINE,—If tears which you saw and know I am not apt to shed—if the agitation in which I parted from you—agitation which you must have perceived through the *whole* of this most *nervous* affair, did not commence until the moment of leaving you approached—if all I have said and done, and am still but too ready to say and do, have not sufficiently proved what my real feelings are, and must ever be towards you, my love, I have no other proof to offer. God knows, I wish you happy, and when I quit you, or rather you, from a sense of duty to your husband and mother, quit me, you shall acknowledge the truth of what I again promise and vow, that no other in word or deed, shall ever hold the place in my affections, which is, and

---

[1] Félix Rabbe, *Les Maîtresses authentiques de Lord Byron.*

[2] *L. and J.* ii. 185. See also *Lord Byron's Correspondence,* 1922. (I., pp. 129–31, where a facsimile of the forged letter is given.)

[3] She sent the letter—the original : she who at another time would part with none of Byron's letters !—to Lady Morgan, enclosed in one of her own. Mr. Prothero prints from the Murray MSS. (*L. and J.* ii. 135). Jeaffreson, who also prints the letter, says that *his* copy was made from the original MS. There are differences between his version and Mr. Prothero's ; I use the latter.

shall be, most sacred to you, until I am nothing. I never knew till *that moment* the *madness* of my dearest and most beloved friend; I cannot express myself; this is no time for words; but I shall have a pride, a melancholy pleasure, in suffering what you yourself can scarcely conceive, for you do not know me. I am about to go out with a heavy heart, because my appearing this evening will stop any absurd story which the event of the day might give rise to. Do you think *now* I am *cold* and *stern* and *artful*? Will even others think so? Will your *mother* even —that mother to whom we must indeed sacrifice more, much more on my part than she shall ever know or can imagine? ' Promise not to love you ! ' ah, Caroline, it is past promising. But I shall attribute all concessions to the proper motive, and never cease to feel all that you have already witnessed, and more than can ever be known but to my own heart—perhaps to yours. May God protect, forgive, and bless you.—Ever, and even more than ever, your most attached, BYRON

" *P.S.*—These taunts which have driven you to this, my dearest Caroline, were it not for your mother and the kindness of your connections, is there anything on earth or heaven that would have made me so happy as to have made you mine long ago? and not less *now* than *then*, but *more* than ever at this time. You know I would with pleasure give up all here and all beyond the grave for you, and in refraining from this, must my motives be misunderstood? I care not who knows this, what use is made of it—it is to *you* and to *you* only that they are *yourself* [*sic*]. I was and am yours freely and most entirely, to obey, to honour, love—and fly with you when, where, and how yourself *might* and *may* determine ".

Idle to discuss this, if Byron wrote it. It does not offer any aspect for reason to consider. He did not love her ; he was not faithful to her even at the height of their intrigue. To say, as some do, that he wrote to gratify, to soothe her, because he had so resolutely refused " to fly " . . . whatever the letter stands for, it does not stand for that. Either it represents his mere madness of a moment, or it represents her dream of what he might have written her, and never did, or could, write her. I said just now that my conjecture was hesitating ; but as I copied, it increased in confidence. The phrases are not those which enter a man's mind—that " obey, honour, love ", for instance, which is, or was, the very cant-phrase of a woman's passion. And then, the postscript. " These taunts which have driven you to this " . . . does not that read like the afterthought of a woman publicly scorned, who shields herself at the vulnerable point ? Does it not read as if people had said, " He doesn't want you " ? They *had* said it, as we see in every letter of the period ; and then, when all was gone by, she wrote to her friend Lady Morgan of the long anguish, and sent the wild disordered missive, where he is " hers to fly when, where, and how she may determine ". With such a message in her heart, would she have consented—reckless and impassioned creature that she was— to be taken to Ireland by her parents, as she was taken at that time ? It is difficult, indeed, to believe it authentic.

Well, letter or no letter, she went to Ireland and remained there (we have only her own authority for it, in the letter to Medwin) three months. " He wrote, every day, long kind entertaining letters " she says ; " it is these he asked Murray to look out[1] . . . but I would not part with them . . . they would only burn them . . . and nothing of his should be burnt ". The Bessboroughs and she returned in a month, if we are to believe the testimony of her cousin Harriet ;[2] in November, if we accept her own date. But the point, though interesting, is not of cardinal importance ; at both dates, Byron was closely *liè* with Lady Oxford, whose coronet and initials adorned the seal of the letter quoted in *Glenarvon*, and who was afterwards said to have dictated it. It was at Dublin, on her way back to England, that Caroline received it. Here it is, as given in *Glenarvon*, sole text for these acknowledged words—for Byron *acknowledged* that what we are now to read had formed at any rate part of the original document.

" Mortanville Priory, *November* 9 [3]

" Lady Avondale,—I am no longer your lover ; and since you oblige me to confess it, by this truly unfeminine persecution . . . learn that I am attached to another, whose name it would be dishonourable to mention. I shall ever remember

[1] *L. and J.* v. 379 ; with a warning as to forgeries. " They treat of more topics than love occasionally ".

[2] " The Bessboroughs ", writes Lady H. Leveson Gower (as Harriet Cavendish then was) from her house in Staffordshire, on September 12, 1812, " have been unpacked about a couple of hours. My aunt looks stout and well, but poor Caroline most terribly the contrary. She is worn to the bone, as pale as death, and her eyes starting out of her head. She seems indeed in a sad way, alternately in tearing spirits and in tears . . . to see her poor careworn face is dismal. . . . She appears to me in a state very little short of insanity, and my aunt describes it as at times having been decidedly so. . . . Caro. has been excessively entertaining at supper. Her spirits, while they last, seem as ungovernable as her grief. . . . Poor Lord Bessborough *me pèse sur le cœur et l'esprit*. William Lamb laughs and eats like a trooper " (*Letters of Harriet, Countess Granville*, i. 40, 41).

[3] This imaginary date corresponds with her own.

with gratitude the many instances I have received of the predilection you have shown in my favour. I shall ever continue your friend, if your ladyship will permit me so to style myself; and, as a first proof of my regard, I offer you this advice : correct your vanity, which is ridiculous ; exert your absurd caprices on others ; and leave me in peace.—Your most obedient servant,

" GLENARVON "

Does it call for comment—rather, is any comment possible ? The thing is simply unspeakable.[1]

More fortunate than the women of to-day, in that age the recipient of such a message could faint off-hand. Caroline fainted. " Then they bled me, and applied leeches " (she told Lady Morgan) ; " and I had to stay a week at the filthy *Dolphin* Inn, at Rock ". She was brought to England a mere wreck, as we have seen : " worn to the bone, as pale as death, her eyes starting out of her head ". So alarmed did Lady Bessborough, even Lady Melbourne, become that they allowed her on reaching London, to see—for she desired to see—Byron.[2] " He asked me to forgive him ; he looked sorry for me ; he cried. I adored him still, but I felt as passionless as the dead may feel. Would I had died then ! "

Would she had died before then, if we are to talk of dyings ! She should never again (adore him as she might) have recognised his existence. " But unhappily we continued occasionally to meet ". Yes : on July 6, 1813, they met at Lady Heathcote's ball. Let us read first her own story (in the letter to Medwin) of this wretched business.

" He had made me swear I was never to waltz. Lady Heathcote said, ' Come, Lady Caroline, you must begin ' ; and I

---

[1] I should like to believe that Lady Oxford did not dictate it. We have only the authority of one C. Lemon, writing in 1816 to Lady H. Frampton, for the supposition that she did. " This letter she really dictated to Lord Byron to send to Lady Caroline Lamb, and is now very much offended that she has treated the matter so lightly as to introduce it into her book " (*Journal of Mary Frampton*, pp. 286, 287).

[2] Lady Melbourne advised that a third person should be present. The witness Byron chose was Lady Oxford ! Lady Melbourne reproached him for this, saying : " Why did you not ask me ? I would have left the room if she was calm ". (*In Whig Society*, by Mabell, Countess of Airlie, 1921, p. 152.) But in the event Lady Oxford declined to be present or to see Lady Caroline ; and this particular interview did not take place. (*Correspondence*, I, 140–1.) Evidently *some* interview between Caroline and Byron did take place, for there is a letter from him to her on April 29, 1813, submitting to her persistence (*Correspondence* I, 152) ; and on May 9 or 21, it would seem from two notes of Byron's to Lady Melbourne that Caroline and he were to meet at a fixed hour and place (*Correspondence*, I, pp. 154–5).

bitterly answered, ' Oh yes ! I am in a merry humour '. I did so—but whispered to Lord Byron, ' I conclude I may waltz *now* ? ' and he answered sarcastically, ' With everybody in turn —you always did it better than any one. I shall have a pleasure in seeing you '. I did so—you may judge with what feelings. After this, feeling ill, I went into a small inner room where supper was prepared ; Lord Byron and Lady Rancliffe[1] entered after ; seeing me, he said, ' I have been admiring your dexterity '. I clasped a knife, not intending anything. ' Do, my dear ', he said. ' But if you mean to act a Roman's part, mind which way you strike with your knife—be it at your own heart, not mine—you have struck there already '. ' Byron ! ' I said, and ran away with the knife. I never stabbed myself. It is false. Lady Rancliffe and Tankerville screamed and said I would ; people pulled to get it from me ; I was terrified ; my hand got cut, and the blood came over my gown. I know not what happened after—but this is the very truth. I never held my head up after—never could. It was in all the papers, and put not truly."

It was indeed in all the papers, and in all the letters, and in all the mouths.[2] The *Satirist* for August 1813 had an article headed Scandalum Magnatum ; and one Francis Jackson, writing to his brother in July, told " what happened after ". " They carried her away, and supposing that she had fainted, brought her a glass of water. She instantly broke the glass, and wounded herself with one of the pieces ". Fanny Kemble says that before this, she had tried to throw herself out of the window ; Galt says that some declared it was an already broken jelly-glass with which she wounded herself ; others, a pair of scissors, and that she tried to cut her throat. He also says that Byron was in another room at the time, when Lord P——, with horror in his face, rushed in to tell him what had happened. He " knitted his scowl and said, with contemptuous indifference, ' It's only a trick ' ".

We may believe as little as we choose of all this ; her own

---

[1] Lady Rancliffe was sister to the beautiful Lady Adelaide Forbes, of whom Byron wrote to Moore at this time that " he was amazingly inclined to be seriously enamoured ".

[2] Lady Melbourne, writing next day to Byron, said that it might have been kept secret " but for Lady O. and Lady H." Lady H. was probably Lady Heathcote. There is an evident error in the name supplied to the initial O. in *In Whig Society*. Both in the text and in the cited letters from Lady Melbourne, the name supplied is Oxford. This is clearly erroneous, for Lady Oxford had sailed from Portsmouth on June 28 (*Correspondence*, I, 161). It is plain from several allusions in Byron's letters to Lady Melbourne that " Lady O." was Lady Ossulstone. For an interesting account in the text of this scene, and for Lady Melbourne's version, see *In Whig Society*, pp. 153–7.

narrative, so far as she was able to carry it, is instinct with truth. *" 'Byron ! ' I said, and ran away with the knife "*. We can see the maddened creature ; and we do not desire, on that miserable night, to see her any longer.

She told Lady Morgan that the Glenarvon letter temporarily deprived her of reason. That danger had always hovered ; and an incident in the December of 1812 certainly points to some degree of insanity. She was down at Brocket Hall—brooding, miserable ; and one day she got together a number of young village-girls, dressed them in white, and burned Byron in effigy, while the girls danced round the pyre. She herself was attired as a page, and spoke, before the bonfire actually began, some doggerel lines of her own composing. Into the fire where the waxen image burned she cast his " book, ring, and chain ", and *copies* (!) of his letters.

> " Ah ! look not thus on me, so grave, so sad ;
> Shake not your heads, and say the lady's mad ".[1]

What else could the puzzled little village-maidens think or say—and what else we ? . . . Then came the forgery for the miniature ; furious letters " threatening my life ", as Byron told Hodgson ; the ball at Lady Heathcote's ; the maddest of all the visits to his rooms—" it *is* true I went to see him as a Carman after all that ". . . . Yes ; and found, or so he told Medwin, another woman with him. Finally, after he had moved into the Albany (which he did on March 28, 1814) came the last scene. " He pressed his lips on mine . . . he said, ' Poor Caro, if every one hates me, you, I see, will never change—no, not with ill usage ! ' And I said, ' Yes, I *am* changed, and shall come near you no more '. For then he showed me letters, and told me things I cannot repeat, and all my attachment went. This was our last parting scene—well I remember it. It had an effect upon me not to be conceived ".

The last scene, but not the last meeting.

" Shortly after he married, once, Lady Melbourne took me to see his wife in Piccadilly. It was a cruel request, but Lord Byron himself made it. . . . Mrs. Leigh, myself, Lady Melbourne, Lady Noel, and Lady Byron, were in the room. I never looked up. Annabella was very cold to me. Lord Byron came in and seemed agitated—his hand was cold, but he seemed kind. This was the last time upon this earth I ever met him " . . . It must have been in the March or April of 1815. His wife was her cousin, Anna Isabella (called Annabella) Milbanke. They had

---

[1] The lines are preserved, and endorsed in Augusta Leigh's handwriting, " December 1812 ".

never liked one another. Miss Milbanke called her Beautiful
Silliness ; Fair-Seeming Foolishness ; and Caroline said, when
she heard of the engagement, that Byron would " never be able
to pull with a woman who went to church *punctually*, understood
statistics, and had a bad figure ".

When, in 1816,[1] her prophecy was proved true, Caroline
wrote twice to Byron, each time urging him to wise action ;
for, as many chroniclers say of her, she was full of common-
sense for everybody except herself. First, she adjures him
to " consent to what is for the peace of both parties "—namely,
to arrange " nobly and generously " a separation. " They tell
me ", she adds, " that you have accused me of having spread
injurious reports about you. Had you the heart to say this ?
I do not greatly believe it. . . . You have often been unkind
to me, but never so unkind as this. . . . Oh, Lord Byron, let
one who has loved you with a devotion almost profane find
favour so far as to incline you to hear her. Sometimes from the
mouth of a sinner advice may be received that a proud heart
disdains to take from those who are upon an equality with them-
selves. . . . God bless and soothe you, and preserve you. . . . I
cannot believe that you will not act generously in this instance.
—Yours, unhappily, as it has proved for me,

" CAROLINE " [2]

And again, referring (it is said) to the publication of *Fare Thee
Well !* in April 1816[3] she cries, " Byron, hear me. . . . I do
implore you for God's sake not to publish them . . . you will
draw ruin on your own head and hers if at this moment you
show these. I know not from what quarter the report originates.
You accused *me*, and falsely ; but if you could hear all that
is said at this moment, you would believe one who, though your
enemy, though for ever alienated from you, though resolved
never more, while she lives, to see or speak to or forgive you,
yet would perhaps die to save you ".[4]

He did not answer. " Lord Byron never once wrote to
me—and always spoke of me with contempt ". When she found
herself so despised, she grew quite ungovernable in her violence.
One of her multitudinous pages was at that time in favour ;
she liked to play ball with him in the dining-room. But he,

---

[1] In the *Correspondence* (1922) two more letters from her appear. In
one of these she offers to swear that she forged any incriminating letter
that may have reached Lady Byron's hands (App. B, II, p. 307).

[2] *L. and J. ii.* App. iii. p. 449.

[3] Or, as seems to me far more likely, indeed certain, the *Stanzas to
Augusta*, then written, but not then published.

[4] *L. and J.* ii. App. iii. p. 450.

" a little *espiègle* " (as she described him), " would throw detonating squibs into the fire. Lord Melbourne always scolded me for this, and I the boy. One day I was playing ball with him ; he threw a squib into the fire. I threw the ball at his head, it hit him on the temple, and he bled. He cried out, ' Oh, my lady, you have killed me '. Out of my senses I rushed into the hall and screamed, ' Oh, God, I have murdered the page ! ' Servants and people in the street caught the sound, and it was soon spread about. William Lamb would live with me no longer. His family insisted on a separation. While instruments were drawing up, in one month I wrote and sent *Glenarvon* to the press. . . . When printed, I sent it to my husband, who was delighted with it, and we became united just as the world thought we were parted for ever ".[1]

Urged by his family, Lamb *had* consented to take the necessary steps for separation. Caroline, in the subdued and pensive mood that often followed her " accidents " (as the Duke of Wellington called them), received the chastisement mildly. All was prepared ; the deed lay, awaiting signature, in the library. Lamb went up to her room for the final interview. But he was away so long that his brother ventured to go to the door and ask for him. He was invited to enter—" and found Lady Caroline seated by her husband's side, feeding him with tiny transparent scraps of bread and butter ". . . . " She had had him to herself for one half-hour ", remarks a chronicler ; and no separation was arranged between Calantha and Avondale until 1825.

If William Lamb was really, as she said, delighted with *Glenarvon*, he is the only one of its readers that ever has been. If it were not for the biographical interest, no one could get through it at all. But of course it had a huge success, and not only in England but on the Continent. In the year of its publication, it was given a forty-page notice in the *Bibliothèque Universelle* ; in 1819 a translation was published in Paris, and a second edition of this was called for in 1824. She said that she wrote it in a month, that when the copyist arrived to prepare it for the press she received him in a page's habit, and that he was incredulous that a boy should have written such a thing. She wrote to Murray, four months after it appeared,[2]

---

[1] In *In Whig Society*, the author states that Caroline herself admitted that when the book came out, William Lamb told her that if she really had published it, he would never see her again. (pp. 183–4).

[2] It was published in May 1816, and her letter to Murray is endorsed (not dated) September 1816. She had had a copy splendidly bound for Byron, with his coronet and initials on the cover, and a key to the characters

" Have you ever heard what *he* said of *Glenarvon*? I burn to know ".[1]

Here are some of the things he said. In July to Murray, from the Villa Diodati at Geneva : " Of *Glenarvon* Mme. de Staël told me (ten days ago, at Coppet) marvellous and grievous things ; but I have seen nothing of it but the Motto, which promises amiably ". He must have seen a copy of the second edition, for it was to that edition that the *Corsair* lines were prefixed :

> " He left a name to all succeeding times,
> Link'd with one virtue and a thousand crimes "—

and his allusion to these lines is explicit.[2] He proceeds : " The generous moment selected for the publication is probably its kindest accompaniment, and, sooth to say, the time was well chosen. I have not even a guess at the contents . . . and I know but one thing which a woman can say to the purpose on such occasions, and that she might as well for her own sake keep to herself ". He quoted to Rogers a filthy line from Pope about " furious Sappho " ; but it was Moore who got the immortal reference. " As for the likeness, the picture can't be good—*I did not sit long enough* ". In August 1917 he was asked to sanction the publication of an Italian version, and informed the Censor that he did not recognise the slightest relation between that book and himself. The translation was accordingly going forward. " You may say this, with my compliments to the author ". Evidently it stung her, for on September 17 he writes to Murray : " I have received your enclosed letter from Lady Caroline Lamb, and am truly sorry (as she will one day be) that she is capable of writing such a letter ; poor thing ! it is a great pity ".

Her whole life was a " great pity ". The most indulgent of us can say no more ; the least indulgent, no less. *Had* she helped to spread the reports about Byron and Mrs. Leigh at the time of the separation—reports which are to make a part of our future reading? She denied it, as we have seen ; but are we able to believe her ? It is the type once more. Some must say everything ; they have the vanity of suffering, as others have the pride. When Caroline Lamb heard whisperings about the man who had been hers, she could not sit and listen—she must whisper too. " Yes : I have heard him say terrible things about such relationships ; I have heard him defend them ". . . . It

in her own handwriting. But it was never sent to him. Glenarvon was of course Byron. Lady Mandeville was Lady Oxford.

[1] When she heard what he had said " she caused a bonfire to be lit which consumed every copy she had " (*In Whig Society*, p. 186).

[2] Moore, p. 309.

is the dramatic instinct—the melodramatic, say! And then, once off the stage, can we not see how that betrayal seems to them a thing incredible? " I did not say it; I could not have said it!" They could not; but they did. So it was with Caroline Lamb; yet when Byron heard that she had "said it" —had gossipped of the confidences of her lover, those strange, undreamed-of confidences that are part of every passion . . . we may not wonder that he condemned her without pity. I do not often defend Byron where a woman is concerned; here I can do nothing else. If she is to be pardoned for the errors that were implicit in her being, so must he be pardoned for those that were so in his.

In 1819 she wrote to a friend, after recovering from a dangerous illness : " I believe, in truth, I died. . . . I seem to have buried my sins, grief, melancholy, and to have come out like a newborn babe . . . and never mean to answer any questions later than the 15th of this month, that being the day of the new Lady Caroline's birth; and I hate the old one ". Her correspondence with William Godwin began in that year; her letters to him are the most touching she ever wrote, except that poignant one to Medwin. " I am like the wreck of a little boat . . . a little gay merry boat which perhaps stranded itself at Vauxhall or London Bridge ". This was in 1821; again in 1823, she wrote to Godwin: " I have been, as you said I might be, calm and perfectly well, and tolerably happy. . . . I want you to tell me how to go on. . . . There is no particular reason why I should exist; it conduces to no one's happiness. . . . Every one as usual is kind to me—I want for nothing this earth can offer but self-control ".

Striving for this, hoping, praying to be calm, she was living down at Brocket in 1824. In March she was taken very ill; two nurses sat up with her. " In the middle of the night, I fancied I saw Lord Byron—I screamed, jumped out of bed, and desired them to save me from him. He looked horrible, and ground his teeth at me; he did not speak. . . . I felt convinced I was to die. . . . I had not dreamed of him since we had parted. . . . I told William, my brother, and Murray at the time. Judge what my horror was, as well as grief, when, long after,[1] the news came of his death. It was conveyed to me in two or three words : ' Caroline, behave properly, I know it will shock you—Lord Byron is dead '. This letter I received when laughing at Brocket Hall ".[2]

[1] Byron died on April 19, 1824. His death was not known of in England until May 14.
[2] *L. and J.* ii. App. iii. p. 454.

She fell ill of a fever, " from which I never yet have recovered " ; [1] but on July 12, she was pronounced to be well enough to go out driving in an open carriage. Her husband rode on before her, and at the turnpike gate he met a funeral procession. " Whose is it ? " he inquired.

They told him, " Lord Byron's ".

It passed her carriage.

" I of course was not told, but as I kept continually asking where and when he was to be buried . . . I heard it too soon, and it made me very ill again ". But not instantly did she succumb, though she heard so soon that she wrote on July 13 to Murray, " Lord Byron's hearse came by our gates *yesterday* ". Then she was struck down again by the illness from which she had barely recovered, and for a time " lay as one who had been stunned ".

I am very sorry I ever said one unkind word against him. So she wrote to Murray on the day after that meeting which has placed her story among those that can never be forgotten. It was the third key-note, as it were, of the sad, wild episode. *Mad, bad, and dangerous to know. That beautiful pale face is my fate. I am very sorry I ever said one unkind word against him*—each as true as it is poignant.

And so, his story being ended, hers might well be thought to have ended too. But there are further pages in the tattered book, and one of these must needs be glanced at here. It is like some child's travesty of a great stage-scene ; and in the very year of his death it happened—that affair of hers with the pseudo-Byron of our literature, the feeble, flashy imitation of the Great Romantic, known at first as Edward Bulwer Lytton ! Nothing in her confused and miserable destiny is more disconcerting than this ludicrous repercussion of the past.

After Byron's death her waywardness reached at length the bounds of even William Lamb's toleration ; and when Medwin's book appeared in the autumn of 1824, the end of their life together soon showed itself as inevitable. She was not at first mischievous nor malicious ; she was simply not be to controlled—nor endured. But soon the habits of insanity began to appear, and her nervous disarray was aggravated by the drinking of brandy mixed with laudanum—a fashionable perversity of the day. It is piteous to read the vivid accounts of her degeneration—the violence, the ugly slovenliness. For a time she was shut up in her rooms at Brocket, under the surveil-

[1] This, and the foregoing extract, are from her letter to Medwin, which was probably written in November 1824.

lance of two female keepers; and one day, in a fit of fury she
tore the doctor's watch from his hands and smashed it.

In January 1828, she died at Melbourne House, London,
in William Lamb's arms.[1]

Since November her life had been despaired of, and the disease
which killed her seems of all diseases the most improbable—
dropsy. The suffering and detestable discomforts of her state
were borne by her with the utmost serenity and sweetness ; she
had reached at last, poor soul, the calm for which she had so
often prayed. " Her letters to her husband ", says Torrens,
" might have been written by one who never knew a troubled
hour ". No repining, only one recurrence to the past. " What
pleased me most of all was your dear letter saying you loved
and forgave me ". As the end approached, her great anxiety
was that he might be with her at the last. He had not realised
the imminent danger—he had delayed in Ireland ; not until
January 23 did he leave Dublin, and she died on January 26.
" Her feeble accents were of the old love only, the first great
triumph of her life, and the last ".

" A kinder or better heart ", wrote her brother to Lady
Morgan, " has never ceased to beat ". " Never perhaps was
there a human being who had less malevolence " : her husband,
writing with his own hand an obituary notice for the *Literary
Gazette*, said that among many other tender things. " All her
errors hurt only herself ". As we read those words, we ask
ourselves : " Which had Caroline Lamb the more deeply injured
—her lover or her husband ? " ; and, with the answer, sound
the depth of Byron's nothingness, where women were concerned,
in love and understanding and generosity.

[1] She left to Lady Morgan a miniature of Byron—" *the original by
Sanders* ". Was it the one that she had obtained by forgery those fifteen
years ago ? After Lady Morgan's death it was sold with other pictures at
Christie's.

CHAPTER XIII

LOVE AND POETRY—1812–1814

Byron's view of Caroline Lamb : the Medwin Conversation—Lady
Oxford—First Sale of Newstead : Mr. Claughton—Restlessness—*The
Giaour*—Lady Adelaide Forbes—Lady Frances Wedderburn Webster—
The Journal of 1813–14—Suspense—*The Bride of Abydos ; The Corsair ;
Lara*—Abatement of the Byron Fever

WHAT was Byron's view of the affair ? We have hints
in the letters, always too communicative on such
subjects ; and we have the Conversation with Medwin
which wrung from Caroline the appeal already given to my
readers. Medwin's response—the complete suppression of the
interview in the next edition of his book—seems to me a proof
of his good faith. Byron knew that he was to be Boswellised ;
and so each talk with Medwin served an alternative purpose
—either to add a further spell to the Legend, or to set the hero
of it in that pose which seemed at the hour most interesting.
But whichever purpose directed his confidence about Caroline
Lamb proved ineffectual. *That* was a stupid as well as a graceless
mistake ; for if he wished to hold her up to contumely, he would
more effectively have achieved it by showing his own behaviour
as redeemed by some sincerity. But he simply did not under-
stand that. To him, it was a *panache* not to have loved at all,
yet to have taken. It was the view of many another man in
his day (in all days, it may be) ; but since to Byron much of
greatness in many things was given, so something of great-
ness in other things is required. Less than the lesser ones can
he be pardoned. For that matter, few of the lesser ones have
needed, in this regard, anything like so much indulgence. Others
have done, but few have spoken and written, as he did—with
so little of dignity, mercy, or comprehension.

Let us read, however, what he said to Medwin in 1821–22
—remembering, that justice may be done, all that had hap-
pened in the meantime to embitter him against her : *Glenarvon*,
and the rumours to which she too probably had contributed.

" About this period " (1812–14) " I became *un homme à
bonnes fortunes*, and had what one calls a serious liaison. The

lady had scarcely any personal attractions. Her figure, though genteel, was too thin to be good, and wanted that roundness which elegance and grace would vainly supply. She was, however, young, and of the first connexions. *Au reste*, she possessed an infinite vivacity of mind, and an imagination heated by novel-reading. She was married, but *de convenance*; no couple could be more fashionably indifferent to, or independent of, one another than she and her husband. It was at this time that we happened to be thrown much together. She had never been in love—at least where the affections are concerned—and was perhaps made without a heart, as many of the sex are; but her head more than supplied the deficiency.

" I was soon congratulated by my friends on the conquest I had made, and did my utmost to show that I was not insensible to the partiality I could not but perceive. I made every effort to be in love, expressed as much ardour as I could muster, and kept feeding the flame with a constant supply of billets-doux and amatory verses. . . . I am easily governed by women ; she acquired an ascendancy from which it was not easy to free myself. I submitted long to the thraldom, for I hate ' scenes ', and am habitually indolent, but I was forced to snap the knot rather rudely at last. Like all lovers, we had had several quarrels before the final rupture. We were reconciled on one occasion in a somewhat singular manner, without a word of verbal explanation. She will not have forgotten it. . . . Even during our intimacy, I was not at all constant to this fair one, and she suspected as much. In order to detect my intrigues, she watched me, and earthed a lady into my lodgings—and came herself, terrier-like, in the disguise of a carman. . . . Imagine the scene ; it was worthy of Faublas !

" Her after-conduct was unaccountable madness—a combination of spite and jealousy." He gives a version (not different from her own) of the Heathcote ball scene, and adds, " Soon after, she promised young X—— . . . if he would call me out. Yet can any one believe that after all this . . . she should call at my rooms ? I was from home ; but, finding *Vathek* on the table, she wrote in the first page ' Remember me ! ' . . . Yes, I had cause to remember her, and in the irritability of the moment, wrote beneath the words the following stanzas ". With the *Remember Thee* stanzas, already given,[1] the conversation ends.

I imagine that, with every allowance made for anger, there can be but one opinion of this confidence.

All Byron's actions at the time correspond with it. In the late summer of 1812—first year of his intrigue with Caroline

[1] See notes, page 155.

—he proposed to, and was rejected by, her cousin by marriage, Anna Isabella Milbanke, whom he afterwards married. In September, after Caroline's departure for Ireland, he left London for Cheltenham. There he saw much of Lady Oxford; and with her he formed, as he told Medwin, " a liaison that continued without interruption for eight months. She told me she was never in love until she was thirty ; and I thought myself so with her when she was forty. I never felt a stronger passion, which she returned with equal ardour ".

It is remarkable that alone of his conquests, Lady Oxford is referred to with gratitude. The Woman of Thirty—who is usually she of forty—may ponder this and exult. " A woman ", he proclaimed to Lady Blessington (who must have listened with amusement), " is only grateful for her *first* and *last* conquest. The first of poor dear Lady Oxford's was achieved before I entered on this world of care ; but the *last*, I do flatter myself, was reserved for me, and a *bonne bouche* it was ". She was the wife of the fifth Earl of Oxford, and the daughter of a clergyman[1]. Married in 1794—" sacrificed ", said Byron, " almost before she was a woman, to one whose body and mind were equally contemptible in the scale of creation "—she was the mother of several children[2] " who were perfect angels . . . and to whom the law gave him " [Lord Oxford] " the right to be called father ". Horne Tooke thought her the most brilliant Englishwoman of her day, and she was a great collector of poets and wits. Shelley was one of those whom she most desired to humanise, as she said ; but he escaped her snares. They were widespread, and not cruel ; " she was full of affectionate kindness to those she loved, whether as friends or as lovers. . . . Her failings ", said Uvedale Price, writing to Rogers just after her death, " were in no small degree the effect of circumstance ; her amiable qualities all her own ". She was unusually lovely, as her picture by Hoppner in the National Portrait Gallery clearly shows. When Byron met her, she " resembled a landscape by Claude Lorraine, with a setting sun, her beauties enhanced by the knowledge that they were shedding their last dying beams, which

---

[1] The Rev. James Scott, Vicar of Itchin, Hants.

[2] In *Astarte*, Lord Lovelace tells us that these were called The Harleian Miscellany. One of them was Lady Charlotte Harley, to whom, under the name of Ianthe, the introductory lines to *Childe Harold* (first published in the seventh edition of February 1814) were written in the autumn of 1812, when she was eleven years old.

" Love's image upon earth, without his wing ".

Her portrait was painted by Westall, at Byron's request. She married in 1820 Captain Anthony Bacon, afterwards Brigadier-General, and died in 1880.

threw a radiance round ". He adds that " the autumn of a beauty like hers is preferable to the spring in others ".

Certainly *he* was among her thralls. " I had great difficulty in breaking with her, even when I knew she was inconstant to me ". Two short poems published in the seventh edition of *Childe Harold* (February 1814), " Thou art not false, but thou art fickle " ; and " On being asked what was the origin of Love ",[1] may be taken as celebrating this affair and her inconstancy—which, by the way, does not chime with his remark to Lady Blessington that he believed he was the last of her conquests. Hobhouse had met her in London before the Cheltenham sojourn ; and the comment in his Journal is illuminating. " Dined at Lord Oxford's. Lady O. most uncommon in her talk, and licentious—uncommonly civil ". We have the profligate, but delightful, great lady there to the life. She next appears in his chronicles on January 12, 1813. " Got a picture of Lady Oxford from Mrs. Mee. Lord Byron's money for it ."

After Byron's stay in Cheltenham, he went on a visit to her and her husband (October 1812) at Eywood, Presteigne, Hereford, and remained until the middle of November. According to the *Glenarvon* date, it was at this time that the insulting letter to Caroline Lamb, sealed with Lady Oxford's coronet and initials, was written ;[2] and it was on a second visit in January 1813 that he told Murray of the forgery for the miniature. In February Hodgson was told that he had taken Kinsham Court (a dower-house of the Harley family), so as to be near the Oxfords ; and an explanation of this plan followed as a matter of course. " I cannot answer for the future, but the past is pretty secure ; and in it I can number the last two months as worthy of the gods in Lucretius ". The classical allusion was mere plagiarism from the lady herself. She had said to him : " Have we not passed our last month like the gods in Lucretius ? " In the Journal of 1813, where he records this, he adds, " And so we had. She is an adept in the text of the original[3] (which I like too) ; and when that booby Bus[4] sent his translating prospectus, she subscribed. But, the devil prompting him to add a specimen, she

---

[1] This was inscribed " To Ianthe ", but the little Lady Charlotte Harley was, we may guess, the merely ostensible object of verses which her mother was sure to read. There is much about the liaison with Lady Oxford in his correspondence with Lady Melbourne. (*Lord Byron's Correspondence*, I.)

[2] But see Chapter XII.

[3] " The passage in Lucretius probably is *De Rerum Naturâ*, i. 57–62 " (*L. and J.* ii. note to p. 325).

[4] Dr. Thomas Busby, musical composer, brought out a translation of Lucretius in 1813.

transmitted him a subsequent answer, saying that, 'after perusing it, her conscience would not permit her to allow her name to remain on the list of subscribblers' ''. We perceive that Lady Oxford was a Blue, as indeed were nearly all Byron's reputable loves. He who railed perpetually against learning in women, was only once attracted by an ignoramus. That is of a piece with his uncertainty of pose in other social matters, the pusillanimity which made Caroline Lamb say that he was ashamed to be in love with her because she was not beautiful—" an expression ", remarks Galt, " at once curious and just, evincing a shrewd perception of the springs of his Lordship's conduct ".

His life at this period was a sad mixture of Olympian blisses and very mundane financial embarrassments. In the early autumn of 1812 he had found himself obliged to put up Newstead Abbey for auction. Only £90,000 was bid, and the property was withdrawn ; but in September a private purchaser appeared in the person of a Mr. Claughton, who agreed to the price of £140,000. On September 28 Byron wrote to William Bankes of this piece of luck—for it was that melancholy kind of luck to which necessity is sole sponsor ; he hinted at Rochdale hopes as well. But by October 18 apprehension was again hovering. " Is not Claughton's delay very strange ? " he inquires of Hanson ; and " What is to be done with Dearden ? "—the lessee of the Rochdale coal-pits. It was the interest on his minority loans which was crippling him, as it continued to do until 1817 ; for in the event, it was found for the hundredth time that nothing could be done with Dearden, and Claughton gradually emerged in his true character as a too-sanguine acquirer of great estates for which he could not find the purchase-money. Not till many months afterwards, not indeed until late in 1814, was the final arrangement made—Claughton, unable to complete purchase, forfeited £25,000 on the contract.

" It cost me more than words to part with it ", Byron wrote in the November of 1813, thinking still that he *had* parted with it. The dual trouble was depressing in the extreme ; his Journal at this time is black with every word of gloom. For long he had been desperately restless. To leave England for ever (it was always for ever, until it *was* for ever, and then only did he not believe it was) had become the sole desire of his mind ; and in the early days of resolve, of his heart as well, for at first it was with Lady Oxford that he planned to go. But that project fell through, resolutely though it was conceived, and over and over again announced. " My intention cannot be altered " ; " I cannot act otherwise . . . with or without [money] I must go " ; " I must be ready in April at whatever risk, whatever loss " ; " Here no power on earth shall make me remain six weeks longer " (on March 6, 1813). Debts and passion were equal factors. " Everything I have done to extricate myself has been useless "—and he was really economising ; he had sold his books and horses, dismissed his groom. April had to be abandoned ; June became the fixed month. But when June arrived he was still in England—either in London or at Salthill, near Maidenhead, probably with Lady Oxford, for the Post Office at Salthill was his only address ; but " still as determined as I have been for the last six months " on going abroad " at all hazards, all losses ". As far as going with the enchantress was concerned, hope died ere June was far advanced. He went to Portsmouth with her, to see her off, on June 13 ; and on July 8 wrote to Moore from Bennet Street, St. James's (his London rooms), to say, " The Oxfords have sailed almost a fortnight ". So ended the Lucretian blisses.

Still he wanted to get away. Everything was tried, a companion was found in Mr. Dudley Ward (afterwards fourth Earl of Dudley), one of the most delightful men of his time ; but obstacles of every kind interposed, and, in a word, Byron never left England even for a day until in 1816 he left it for ever.

How had the poesy progressed ? Until 1813 he did nothing worth speaking of. At Cheltenham he wrote the entirely worthless *Waltz*, which was published anonymously in the spring of 1813 ; and the still more uninteresting Address for the Opening of Drury Lane Theatre on October 10, 1812, after the fire of 1809. The latter task was undertaken at Lord Holland's special request. A prize of twenty guineas had been offered for an address ; one hundred and twelve aspirants had entered, but no effort was considered worthy of the prize.[1] Lord Holland, who was one of the Committee of Selection, then asked Byron to write an address. He had not competed, though at first he had meant to do so ; he agreed to write one now, and spent an infinity of pains and enthusiasm on the thing. From Cheltenham there came to Lord Holland no fewer than thirteen letters, sometimes two in a day, and all filled with corrections and alternative readings. " I am almost ashamed ", wrote the kindly peer to Rogers, " of having induced Lord Byron to write on so ungrateful a theme. He took so much pains, corrected so

---

[1] This competition and its abortive result produced the famous *Rejected Addresses* by James and Horace Smith—a volume of brilliant parodies of all the notable poets of the day. That on Byron, called " Cui Bono ? " was the source of infinite delight to him : he said that the second and third stanzas were just what he could have wished to write on a similar subject.

good-humouredly. . . . You cannot imagine how I grew to like Lord Byron in my critical intercourse with him." The Address, spoken by Elliston (Charles Lamb's " joyousest of once embodied spirits "), was a failure, and the circumstances in which it was written produced much irritation among the unsuccessful competitors.

In the earliest days of the Cheltenham sojourn, Byron had written to Murray : " What will you give *me* or *mine* for a poem of six cantos (*when* complete—*no* rhyme, *no* recompense) as like the last two as I can make them ? I have some ideas which one day may be embodied, and till winter I shall have much leisure ". His leisure was eaten up until October by the troublesome Address ; moreover, the love-affair with Lady Oxford idled him a good deal. But at last he spurred himself to effort ; and in May sent Murray " a corrected, and, I hope, amended copy of the lines for the ' fragment ' already sent this evening ". The fragment was the first draft of *The Giaour*. In the Journal for that year he affirmed that it was a week's work ; but it is only to these first four hundred lines that that can be said to apply. The poem, either in the course of printing or in the successive editions, expanded from 407 to 1334 lines.

Byron's feeling about it was mingled pride and annoyance. He was amazed at his facility, but somewhat irritated by its fragmentary form. " I have, but with some difficulty, *not* added any more to this snake of a poem, which has been lengthening its rattles every month ". In sending Moore a copy of the fifth edition he wrote : " I send you . . . that awful pamphlet, *The Giaour* . . . you will perceive that I have added much in quantity ". He had added close on two hundred lines. Nor was that the end, for on September 29, in preparation for the seventh edition (which presented the poem in its final shape) there is a note to Murray : " Pray suspend the *proofs*, for I am bitten again, and have quantities for other parts of *The Giaour* ".

These technical details would be better omitted if they were not so highly characteristic of Byron's method. On the passage beginning

" Clime of the unforgotten brave ! "

and consisting of 138 lines, there is a note, quoted by Mr. Ernest Coleridge, from the edition of 1837.[1] " From hence to the conclusion of the paragraph, the MS. is written in a hurried and almost illegible hand, as if these splendid lines had been poured forth in one continuous burst of poetic feeling, which would hardly allow time for the pen to follow the imagination ".

[1] This was a Collected Edition of the *Poems*, " with all the notes by Sir Walter Scott ".

The idea of a poem in fragments had been suggested to
Byron by Rogers's *Columbus*, which appeared in 1812; and the
method certainly indulged to the full his impatience of " those
mechanical difficulties which, in a regular narrative, embarrass,
if not chill, the poet, leaving it to the imagination of his readers
to fill up the intervals between those abrupt bursts of passion
in which his chief power lay ".[1] He could dash off a purple
passage, and dispatch it to Murray with a note : " I have not
yet fixed the place of insertion for the following lines, but will
when I see you—as I have no copy ". But as with Balzac, it
was when the proofs came that his serious work began. He
would touch and retouch, finding fresher epithets, more musical
lines, a sharper emphasis—and finding also, to his infinite anger
and our infinite amusement, those unbelievable blunders of the
printer over which every writer has in his turn blinked and
fulminated. " There is an ingenuity in his blunders peculiar
to himself ", wrote Byron, convinced like each new sufferer
that the ingenuity of his peculiar printer *was* peculiar. It was
with *The Giaour* that he first passed the ordeal by proof-sheets ;
for Dallas had seen the Satire and *Childe Harold* through the
press. He bore it worse than most of us. Galley-proofs were
a surprise, almost an insult : " a mile-long, ballad-singing sheet.
. . . I can't read them distinctly ". And soon another spectre
barred his path. " Do you know anybody who can stop—I
mean *point*—commas, and so forth ; for I am, I hear, a sad
hand at your punctuation ". Hodgson came to the rescue ;
but the novelty of the terror had left traces on Byron's nerves.
In another letter enclosing revise, he added a postscript : "Do
attend to the punctuation ; I can't, for I don't know a comma
—at least, where to place one ".
     The anguish temporarily ceased on June 5, 1813, when *The
Giaour* made its first appearance—a fragment of no more than
685 lines. It pleased sufficiently in this guise for a second
edition to be demanded before the end of the month. This was
swelled by 131 lines, among them perhaps the most renowned
of all Byron's purple passages :

" He who hath bent him o'er the dead "—

that strange, slipshod loveliness, where He never fulfills his
destiny as the subject of the opening phrase. Bent o'er the
dead he remains immovable to the end of time. It is another
instance of the Spell—that transfixed form, who for so long
was never seen to be transfixed ! As an instance of his retouching

---

[1] Moore, p. 178.

none seems to me more striking—though Moore chooses a long passage [1]—than the single line :

> " Such moment *pours* the grief of years,"

which in the two first editions had the variants :

> " Such moment *holds a thousand years* "—

and

> " Such moment *proves* the grief of years "—

both entirely uninteresting, while the final rendering is made, by a single word, one of the most striking of his isolated beauties. In the seventh edition there stood for the first time the quatrain :

> " She was a form of life and light,
> That, seen, became a part of sight,
> And rose, where'er I turned mine eye,
> The Morning-Star of Memory ! "

These lines, and the long passage beginning :

> " Yes, Love indeed is light from heaven "

—the hundred and twenty-six lines which " Hodgson liked ", and which the world followed him in liking—were, it has been supposed, the expression of his love for Lady Frances Wedderburn Webster.[2]

> " My good, my guilt, my weal, my woe,
> My hope on high, my all below.
> Earth holds no other like to thee,
> Or, if it doth, in vain for me . . ."

How many a lover has murmured those syllables to " the cherished madness of his heart ", and how many an one will still murmur them, whether he be a reader of Byron or not ! For they are, like so much else that he wrote, the instinctive language of humanity ; and in deep emotion, that is the language which humanity uses. How natural, for example, is the *arrière-pensée* " Or, if it doth, in vain for me "—that anti-climax which, to a lover's brooding soul, will seem the very climax of his answer to the woman's eternal question.

The tragic narrative of this poem became of course a theme for gossip. We have seen, in Chapter IX., that Byron called Lord Sligo to his rescue. The letter thus obtained left the

---

[1] That beginning " Fair clime ! where every season smiles "—lines 7 to 20 (*Poems*, ii. 86).

[2] But he did not meet her till the September of 1813. And when he did, these lines would be a highly idealized expression of his feeling for her, as detailed in his letters to Lady Melbourne !

mystery unsolved ; but it is clear from an entry in Byron's
Journal of 1813 that some poignant memory had informed
the poem. " 12, *midnight.*—Here are two confounded proofs
from the printer. I have looked at the one, but for the soul
of me, I can't look over that *Giaour* again—at least just now
and at this hour—and yet there is no moon ". In Chapter IX.,
I have put the various theories together ; we shall get no further
by any cudgelling of the brains or of the Journal.

His success was beyond doubt. Edition crowded on edition,
and the great Reviews were kind ; the *Edinburgh's* article upon
it came second in the summer number. " So very mild and
sentimental ", said Byron, " that it must be written by Jeffrey
in love ' .[1]

All this time a sort of correspondence with Caroline Lamb
was kept up. She was mentioned to Murray as one of those
to whom the earliest copies of *The Giaour* were to be sent ; but
there was no longer any pretence at love on Byron's side. Even
Lady Oxford was hardly gone before a new charmer began to
figure in the letters to Moore. This time it was from a matrimonial
point of view. On July 13 : " Do you know, Moore, I am
amazingly inclined—remember I say but *inclined*—to be seriously
enamoured of Lady Adelaide Forbes ". Lady Adelaide's father
was the sixth Earl of Granard, and her mother a daughter of
the first Earl of Moira. Lord Moira was Moore's patron, and
political sympathies brought the Irish poet into close relation
with Lord Granard as well. The daughter was a noted beauty.
When in 1817 Byron visited Rome, he wrote to Moore : " The
Apollo Belvedere is the image of Lady Adelaide Forbes—I think
I never saw such a likeness ". Moore, whom Byron treated as
the match-maker in this very transient affair, was reluctant to
assume the part. He confesses that he smiled upon his friend's
suit—such as it was—but adds, " If the lady could have con-
sented to undertake the perilous—but still possible and glorious
—achievement of attracting Byron to virtue, I own that,
sanguinely as in theory I might have looked to the result, I
should have seen not without trembling the happiness of one
whom I had known and valued from her childhood risked in the
experiment ".

In a fortnight Byron perceived that he was making no way.
" I am not well-versed enough in the ways of single woman to
make much matrimonial progress ". It was directly after the
scene with Caroline at Lady Heathcote's ball that he had

---

[1] It was written by Jeffrey, and Jeffrey *was* in love ; he had just " gone
to America to marry some fair one ", with whom he had long been " *éper-
dûment amoureux* ".

begun the wooing ; and though Moore affirms that Lady Adelaide herself never suspected Byron of any serious purpose, it is evident that her sister, Lady Rancliffe, saw and disapproved. " Had Lady [Rancliffe ?] appeared to wish it—or even *not* to oppose it—I would," wrote Byron on May 31, 1814, " have gone on, and very possibly married (that is, *if* the other had been equally accordant) with the indifference which has ' frozen over ' the Black Sea of almost all my passions. It is that very indifference which makes me so uncertain and apparently capricious. . . . In almost all cases, opposition is a stimulus. In mine, it is not ; if a straw were in my way, I could not stoop to pick it up ".

Yet in the interval between his first announcement of admiration for Lady Adelaide [1] and this new setting of the Marble Heart theme, there had run the whole course of his romantic passion for Lady Frances Wedderburn Webster. In that business there were obstacles enough ; and the evidence of his Journal and of his letters to Lady Melbourne is convincing proof that he was not too indifferent to remove them. [2]

Lady Frances Annesley was a daughter of the first Earl of Mountnorris and eighth Viscount Valentia ; and Byron had long been intimate with her husband, whom she married in 1810—from the schoolroom, it would seem, for in 1819 she was only twenty-six. [3] Byron did not make her acquaintance until September 1813. There is a note, not to her but to her husband, in August, consenting to be godfather to an expected baby. It was to be called after him if a boy. " If it is a *girl*, why not also ? Georgina, or even *Byron*, will make a classical name for a spinster ". [4] From September 15 to 24 he stayed for the first time with the Websters at Aston Hall, Rotherham, Yorkshire. In a letter to Moore after he had left, he refers to the visit in his own peculiar manner. " I was a visitor in the

---

[1] Lady Adelaide, who in 1813 was twenty-four, never married. She died at Dresden, in 1858.

[2] In 1821, giving Murray a hint or two about collecting his letters, he says : " As to those to other correspondents (female, etc.), there are plenty scattered about in the world . . . most of them have kept them—I hear at least that L*y*. O. and F. W. W. have kept theirs ; but these letters are of course inaccessible (and perhaps not desirable) ". Elsewhere, he refers to Lady F. W. W. as one of " my loves "—all of whom " make a point of calling on " Augusta Leigh (*L. and J.* v. 379 ; 371).

[3] Moore met her at a county ball in that year, and they spoke much of Byron. He adds : " She must have been very pretty when she had more of the freshness of youth, though she is still but five or six and twenty, but she looks faded already " (*Journals*, etc. ii. 249).

[4] It was a boy—the eldest son—and was christened Byron Wedderburn. He died young ; and when Byron was told, he " almost chuckled with joy or irony ", and said, " Well, I cautioned you, and told you that my name would damn almost any thing or creature " (MS. note by Wedderburn Webster, cited in *L. and J.* ii. 259).

same house which came to my sire as a residence with Lady
Carmarthen (with whom he adulterated before his majority—
by the by, remember *she* was not my mamma)—and they thrust
me into an old room with a nauseous picture over the chimney
. . . which, inheriting the family taste, I looked upon with great
satisfaction. I stayed a week with the family and behaved
very well—though the lady of the house [1] is young, and religious,
and pretty, and the master is my particular friend. I felt no
wish for anything but a poodle-dog, which they kindly gave me.
Now for a man of my courses not even to have *coveted* is a sign
of great amendment ".

Moore may have smiled at the familiar pleasantries, but how
much broader must his smile have become when from the pages
there slipped a copy of verses ! " Here's an impromptu for you
by a person of quality, written last week, on being reproached
for low spirits ".

> " When, from the heart where Sorrow sits,
>   Her dusky shadow mounts too high,
>   And o'er the changing aspect flits,
>   And clouds the brow, or fills the eye ;
>   Heed not that gloom, which soon shall sink :
>   My Thoughts their dungeons know too well ;
>   Back to my breast the Wanderers shrink,
>   And *droop* within their silent cell ".

On September 30 he wrote to Webster, promising to return
to Aston. Lady Frances had invited Augusta to stay at the
same time, but Augusta did not go ; and on November 8 she
received a note from Byron to say that his silence had been
occasioned by a thousand things, with which *she* was not con-
cerned. " It is not L^y. C. nor O. ; but perhaps you may *guess*,
and if you do, do not tell. You do not know what mischief
your being with me might have prevented . . . in the meantime
don't be alarmed. I am in *no immediate* peril ".[2] These words
and two or three other allusions point unmistakably to the
fancied risk of a duel. On November 30 he wrote Moore a
mysterious letter. " We were once very near neighbours [3] this
autumn ; and a good and bad neighbourhood it has proved to
me. Suffice it to say, that your French quotation [4] was con-

---

[1] In the summer of 1815, Caroline Lamb met Lady Frances in Brussels ;
and wrote to Lady Melbourne that she was " too ridiculous ", " most
affected ", and that a certain Mr. Bradshaw had said that he felt ill for two
hours after seeing her. (*In Whig Society*, p. 172.)

[2] *L. and J.* ii. 277.

[3] Moore was at this time living at Mayfield Cottage, Ashbourne, Derby-
shire.

[4] Moore had written : " I should say with old Fontenelle, *Si je recom-
mençais ma carrière, je ferais tout ce que j'ai fait* ".

foundedly to the purpose—though very unexpectedly pertinent, as you may imagine by what I *said* before, and by my silence since. However, ' Richard's himself again ', and except all night and some part of the morning, I don't think very much about the matter ". In the Journal for the same month (November) we find complaints of not hearing from " ** ". " Not a *word* from **. Have they set out from ** ? or has my last precious epistle fallen into the lion's jaws ? If so—and this silence looks suspicious—I must clap on my ' musty morion ', and ' hold out my iron '. I am out of practice—but I won't begin again at Manton's [1] now. Besides, I would not return his shot ". The suspense lasted until January 1814, for there is a letter to Moore on the 6th : " I have a confidence for you—a perplexing one to me, and, just at present, in a state of abeyance in itself ". Here follow many asterisks,[2] and the text resumes with, " However, we shall see. In the meantime, you may amuse yourself with my suspense, and put all the justices of the peace in requisition, in case I come into your county with ' hackbut bent '. Seriously, whether I am to hear from her or him, it is a *pause* which I shall fill up with as few thoughts of my own as I can borrow from other people. Anything is better than stagnation ; and now, in the interregnum of my autumn and a strange summer adventure which I don't like to think of . . . the antithetical state of my lucubrations makes me alive. . . . *P.S.*—Of course you will keep my secret, and don't even talk in your sleep of it. Happen what may, your dedication [3] is ensured, being already written ; and I shall copy it out fair to-night." But by the 8th the danger had vanished. " The devil, who ought to be civil on such occasions, proved so, and took my letter to the right place ".

There is no doubt that many of the references in the letters and the Journal are to Lady Frances. The lines :

> " Remember him, whom Passion's power
> Severely—deeply—vainly proved :
> Remember thou that dangerous hour,
> When neither fell—though both were loved ".[4]

—are the raw material, as it were, of the two sonnets *To Genevra*, which unquestionably she inspired, if we can use the word inspired

---

[1] Joe Manton, the renowned gunsmith, had a shooting-gallery in Davies Street, to which the Dandies, and especially Byron, much resorted. Byron boasted to Manton that he considered himself the best shot in London. Manton differed from him.

[2] Moore, with his maddening discretion, omits even the asterisks.

[3] The dedication of *The Corsair* to Moore.

[4] They were first published with the seventh edition of *Childe Harold* in 1814.

of such very dismal failures. He scorned the form. " I will
never write another. They are the most puling, petrifying,
stupidly platonic compositions ". Certainly his are ; they must
be among the worst in any language. . . . That Genevra stands
for Lady Frances—blue-eyed, dark-lashed, fair-haired, pale, " the
soul of melancholy Gentleness "—is certain from the earlier
names in the *The Corsair.* The heroine was called first Francesca,
then Genevra—finally Medora.

She was clearly, despite the duel-alarm, what he had at
first declared her to be—" religious ". If she yielded to him
(in whatever degree) she was quickly seized with remorse ; over
the whole episode, indeed, there hangs a mist of melancholy.
At the time it influenced, to the extent of actually altering, his
work ; for in *The Bride of Abydos* (which is its immediate flower,
so to speak)[1] he strove for a wan ethereal pathos very different
in quality from the genuine Byronic gloom. In a measure he
achieved it ; the long rhapsody of the White Rose is charged
with the hesitant faint fragrance, lit with the " lonely lustre,
meek and pale ", which we may take to have been the atmo-
sphere of Lady Frances. Precisely this note was struck at no
other time ; nor is it, in reality, his note. He knew this, and
said to Moore, " Tenderness is not my forte ". Moore said the
same thing in different words : " To aim at vigour and strong
feeling after *you* is hopeless—that region was made for Cæsar ".

The Bride of Abydos was published on November 29 or 30,
1813. " My first *entire* composition of any length, (except the
Satire, and be damned to it), for *The Giaour* is but a string of
passages, and *Childe Harold* is, and I rather think always will
be, unconcluded ". I care for it very little. The passages
describing Zuleika, and the White Rose rhapsody, are the sole
abodes of beauty ; here and there a striking phrase emerges,
though the best known of them all is a mere translation from
Tacitus : [2]
" He makes a solitude, and calls it—peace ! "

Among the others, I choose two examples of his keen,
authentic observation—the passage where, after the murder
of Selim, he speaks of the trampled beach where one might see
" *dashed* into the sand, The print of many a struggling hand " ;
and again, when Selim's body floats upon the water :

[1] I retain this opinion even against the revelations of *Astarte* with
respect to that poem—to be alluded to later. In a letter to Lady Melbourne,
to whom he detailed the affair almost hour by hour, he says that he is
prepared " to go all lengths ", including divorce : and that he loves Lady
Frances, " and much too ".
[2] " *Solitudinem faciunt—pacem appellant* " (*Agricola*, cap. 30).

" ' That hand, whose motion is not life,
Yet feebly seems to menace strife,
Flung by the tossing tide on high,
Then levelled with the wave ' " . . .

the reminiscence of a scene actually beheld by him in the Darda-
nelles during the Albanian tour.[1]

For the rest, this seems to me the least successful of the
Oriental tales. When narrative turns to dialogue we are
frequently reduced to laughter, as, for example, when the
tyrannical Pasha says to Selim :

" If thus Zuleika oft takes wing—
Thou see'st yon bow—it hath a string ! "

—which could hardly be beaten for absurdity in a Surreyside
theatre. In the dialogue between Selim and Zuleika (canto ii.)
there are many passages of similar calibre.

But *The Bride* quickly ran through ten editions, and within
a month of its appearance six thousand copies had been sold.
Murray offered him for this, *The Giaour*, and some shorter poems,
the sum of one thousand guineas ; but Byron refused (the offer
was made before *The Bride* was published) to allow anything
to be formally arranged until Easter 1814, when Murray would
" know whether he could afford it ". When he did accept the
money, he used it for a friend.

It will be convenient to discuss in this chapter two of the
four remaining Eastern tales—namely, *The Corsair* and *Lara*,
both published in 1814. In less than three months after the
Bride had blushed upon the reading public, Byron, vividly in vein
as he was, had begun " a devil of a long story . . . in the regular
heroic measure ". It was on December 18 that he sat down
to the composition ; by December 31 the fair copy of the first
draft was ready—and on this occasion he was more definitely
the improvisatore than ever before. For not only was *The
Corsair* written in three weeks, but it was hardly at all corrected
or retouched. He composed it at the rate of two hundred lines
a day. Together with the sixth edition of *The Bride of Abydos*,
the seventh of *Childe Harold*, and the ninth of *The Giaour*, it
was issued on February 1, 1814.

In two days there came from Murray (who had bitterly
offended Byron by issuing a warning against over-writing—
and very nearly lost *The Corsair* for his pains) a letter of panting
exultation, which presents, says Mr. Ernest Coleridge, a vivid
picture of a great literary triumph.

" My Lord,—I have been unwilling to write until I had
something to say. . . . I am most happy to tell you that your

---

[1] Galt, p. 144.

last poem *is*—what Mr. Southey's is *called*—a *Carmen Triumphale*. Never in my recollection has any work . . . excited such a ferment. . . . *I sold on the day of publication*—a thing perfectly unprecedented—*10,000 copies*. . . . You have no notion of the sensation which the publication has occasioned ; and my only regret is that you were not present to witness it ".

Byron was at Newstead—which was still dangling between him and the elusive Claughton—snowbound with Augusta [1] Leigh, who was paying her first visit to the ancestral home. He was gratified by the news, " not the less so because it was unexpected " ; and while thanking Murray for wishing him in town, thought that success is most felt at a distance. " I enjoy my solitary self-importance in an agreeable sulky way of my own ".

The Corsair was one of the many last appearances. He had announced this with a flourish in the dedicatory letter to Moore ; [2] and he now developed the theme for Murray's benefit. " Our Finale has pleased and the Curtain drops gracefully. . . . I *was* and *am* quite in earnest in my prefatory promise not to intrude any more. . . . My rhyming propensity is quite gone, and I feel much as I did at Patras on recovering from my fever— weak, but in health, and only afraid of relapse. I do most fervently hope I never shall ". (This is perhaps the most amusing place to record that by April 10 he *had* relapsed. " I have written an Ode on the Fall of Napoleon, which, if you like, I will copy out, and make you a present of. . . . You may show it to Mr. Gifford, and print it or not, as you please—it is of no consequence ". If Murray did print it, it was to be anonymous ; " but you may *say* as openly as you like that it is mine, and I can inscribe it to Mr. Hobhouse [3] from the *author*, which will mark it sufficiently ").

The blazing success of *The Corsair* was due not entirely to its excellence. There were two contributory causes besides. One of these will presently be detailed ; the other was the

---

[1] On a tree with a double stem Byron in this year cut the two names, " Byron " and " Augusta ". The English translator of Elze's Life tells us that the stem bearing the names (being threatened with decay) was re-moved by Mr. Webb, who bought the estate in 1862 at the death of Colonel Wildman. That portion of the tree-trunk is preserved in a glass case at Newstead. The date cut by Byron is September 20, 1814. At Mr. Webb's death, Newstead passed to his daughter, Lady Chermside, who died in 1910. The place then passed to Mr. Webb's third daughter, Mrs. Fraser, to whom (1924) it still belongs.

[2] *The Giaour* had been dedicated to Rogers, and *The Bride of Abydos* to Lord Holland.

[3] He did not inscribe it ; and Hobhouse, in his Journal, has the de-lightful comment : " This I got off ". A first edition of the Ode was issued on April 16, 1814 ; a second followed immediately. It was published anonymously, but there was no secret about the authorship.

unmistakable self-portraiture in the hero Conrad, who, with his development, Lara, is the very quintessence of Byronism. To say, as people of course did say, that Byron had really done the things which Conrad did, is actually to destroy the illusion. Again, as we saw a little differently with *Childe Harold*, the value of the self-portraiture consists in the fact that he was *not* his hero's facsimile. . . . This is to me an amazement in the writings about Byron. What does it mean to be a poet, if that poet must use the chapter and verse of mere fact for everything he describes ? The reference of creative artists is precisely not to that, but to the chapter and verse of the transfiguring imagination. Thus, to make acquaintance with these two melancholy personages is to know and see Byron as we could never have known and seen him otherwise. The traits which he assigns to them are those traits which set him dreaming. So, in such cases, he would have desired to act and be—and so, in such cases, he for the most part did not act nor be. The reticence of Conrad and Lara, for example—and the communicativeness of Byron ! It is the same with even the externalities. We may well suppose that to the Byronic imagination, Byron's fairness of colouring seemed a defect, even a disaster—and so, Conrad and Lara have " sable locks ". There are accuracies, of course ; each has some feature unaltered from the apparent life.

> " Sunburnt his cheek, his forehead high and pale
> The sable curls in wild profusion veil ;
> And oft perforce his rising lip reveals
> The haughtier thought it curbs, but scarce conceals.
>
> . . . .
> His features' deepening lines and varying hue
> At times attracted, yet perplexed the view ;
> As if within that murkiness of mind
> Worked feelings fearful, and yet undefined.
>
> . . . .
> There was a laughing Devil in his sneer . . ."

It would be an amusing exercise to verify the authentic features in this Portrait of a Gentleman, Byronic Period. To a woman who knew him well, Byron wrote the report of his identity with *The Corsair* ; [1] and he records in his Journal that " she says she don't wonder, since ' Conrad is so like '. It is odd that one who knows me so thoroughly should tell me this to my face. However, if she don't know, nobody can ".

Despite the Spell, we now find Conrad tedious. He is agreeable to look at, but there our liking for him ends. We feel that when he comes back from the last expedition—the disguise as a Dervish, the burning of the city of Seyd, the dread adventure

---

[1] Almost certainly, Augusta Leigh.

with " Gulnare, the Homicide "—it is no more than he deserves to find Medora dead. And when he disappears :

> " His death yet dubious, deeds too widely known ",

leaving

> " . . . a Corsair's name to other times,
> Link'd with one virtue, and a thousand crimes "—

we are momentarily converted to the dictum of Ninon de Lenclos : " Love is a passion, not a virtue ; and a passion does not turn into a virtue because it happens to last—it merely becomes a longer passion ".

Lara was finished on June 14 in the same year (1814). There was long hesitation about publishing. Byron felt shy at the thought of " trespassing on public patience " again after the protestations in the letter to Moore. But Rogers on June 27 sent him the MS. of a poem [1] to read ; Byron " paid him in kind, or rather *un*kind ", with " two cantos of darkness and dismay " —namely, the two cantos of which *Lara* consisted ; and this exchange of unpublished works suggested a happy compromise. " Rogers and I ", he wrote to Moore on July 8, " have almost coalesced into a joint invasion of the Public ".[2] Rogers, after the first plunge, began to vacillate ; and though Murray advertised the Coalition on August 3, Byron told Moore that both authors were " still demurring and delaying and in a fuss ". Murray, as Mr. Coleridge says, knew his man ; and sure enough on August 5 came the ostensibly reluctant word of command : " Out with *Lara*, since it must be ". *How* well the publisher knew his man is shown by the fact that the coalition-volume had sold to the number of six thousand on August 6 ! Murray had done every-thing but actually deliver the copies before the magic word was spoken. A week after publication Byron wrote to Moore : " Murray talks of divorcing Larry and Jacky. . . . Seriously, I don't care a cigar about it, and I don't see why Sam should ". The divorce was quickly made, and at least four separate editions of *Lara* were published during the autumn of 1814.

Lara's identity with Conrad was admitted by the author. Kaled, the mysterious page, stands for Gulnare, the Homicide. (Caroline Lamb, reading the poem, may well have seen in the episode a reminiscence of her many escapades in this sort.) But Lara, though yielding nothing to Conrad in gloom, contrives to

---

[1] *Jacqueline.*
[2] " Lord Byron afterwards proposed that I should make a third in this publication ; but the honour was a perilous one, and I begged leave to decline it " (Moore, p. 257, note 2).

be much more interesting.   Doubtless the change of scene from
the East to England has something to do with this nearer
appeal; the gloomy Lara pacing an ancestral English hall, comes
home to us in a way that the far less ridiculous Conrad never
does.   But I think the real reason is that the peculiar absurdity
of *Lara* has been for every one of us, at some time in our lives,
our own absurdity.   We laugh—and justly laugh—at the total
lack of irony with which Lara is presented; yet in the last
resort this adds a pang to the realisation of our kinship with
him.   Take stanza 18 in canto i.; [1] take the immortal " Lord
of himself—that heritage of woe "; take the passage in stanza
19 of the same canto :

> " He had (if 'twere not nature's boon) an art
> Of fixing memory on another's heart . . .
> But they who saw him did not see in vain,
> And once beheld—would ask of him again.
> .   .   .   .   .
> None knew nor how, nor why, but he entwined
> Himself perforce around the hearer's mind ;
> There he was stamped, in liking, or in hate,
> If greeted once ; . . .
> You could not penetrate his soul, but found,
> Despite your wonder, to your own he wound ;
> His presence haunted still, and from the breast
> He forced an all unwilling interest :
> Vain was the struggle in that mental net—
> His spirit seemed to dare you to forget ! "

Are there many of us to whom that dream has not seemed
realisable—if once the ideal conditions could be found!   For
Byron it *was* realised; and in a degree which, arrogant as
he was, seemed to him incredible.   This is one of the great
paradoxes of his career, and of his character.   He set the world
ablaze and knew that he had set it so—yet was convinced both
that his vocation was not poetry, and that the world did not
at all appreciate or understand him.   Certainly it did not
understand him ; yet, with the woman who said that Conrad

---

[1] " There was in him a vital scorn of all :
As if the worst had fallen which could befall,
He stood a stranger in this breathing world,
An erring Spirit from another hurled ;
A thing of dark imaginings . . .
.   .   .   .   .   .
With more capacity for love than Earth
Bestows on most of mortal mould and birth,
His early dreams of good outstripped the truth,
And troubled Manhood followed baffled Youth . . .
.   .   .   .   .   .
But haughty still, and loth himself to blame,
He called on Nature's self to share the shame ".

was so like, it eagerly accepted him on his own terms. He
spent the resources of his genius in vilifying himself, and
then wondered that people frowned. Such a psychological
problem as we find in *Lara* might well perplex the drawing-
rooms :

" Too high for common selfishness, he could
At times resign his own for others' good,
But not in pity—not because he ought,
But in some strange perversity of thought,
That swayed him onward with a secret pride
To do what few or none would do beside ;
And this same impulse would, in tempting time,
Mislead his spirit equally to crime ;
So much he soared beyond, or sunk beneath,
The men with whom he felt condemned to breathe ". [1]

It was true, and it was not true. [2] To those who met him
in society, and found his liveliness and unreserve confronting
them, instead of the gloom and almost inhuman reticence of
his heroes (who yet were immutably identified with him), the
puzzle may well have been given up as insoluble. Moore found,
when they met in town during the spring of 1813, that already
the Byron Fever was abated. Those who saw him often were
learning the lesson ; only strangers or casual acquaintances now
believed that " the fierce gloom and sternness of his imaginary
characters " was reflected from his own. And yet, despite
Moore's testimony to the external truth that it was not so reflected,
the deeper, the essential truth is that it *was*. Somewhere in
Byron, melancholy reigned supreme. Neither the gaiety nor
the gloom was histrionic ; one did not mask the other—both
were frankly what they called themselves. There never was a
more spontaneous poser—using pose in its true sense of poise.
His spontaneity in this amounted to simplicity : that is why
he puzzled and continues to puzzle the world. " The causes ",
he said (disingenuously), of his separation from his wife, " were
too simple to be easily found out ". We might use the remark
to cover the whole of Byronism ; and, so doing, impart to it a
veracity which it does not, in the actual connection, possess.

[1] Canto i. stanza 18.
[2] In one of Lady Byron's Narratives (*Astarte*), she says that he said
of *Lara*, " ' There's more in *that* than any of them,' shuddering and avoiding
my eye. I said it had a stranger mysterious effect than any, and was ' like
the darkness in which one fears to behold spectres '. The remark struck
him . . . at least I presume so from his singular commendation of it with
the usual mysterious manner. He often said that *Lara* was the most meta-
physical of his works " (pp. 20–21).

CHAPTER XIV

THE MAN'S MAN—1812–1814

Social glories—Presentation to the Prince Regent—Sir Walter Scott—
Byron's beauty—*Venetia*—Affectations—His relation to the world—
The Man's Man : his letters—Lack of literary jealousy—*Don Juan*—
Hodgson and Webster contrasted—Mrs. Mule—The Prince Regent :
Fracas at Carlton House—*Lines to a Lady Weeping*—Hysterics of the
Press—The gloom of Byron's Journal—Byron as lover—His engage-
ment.

THROUGH his friendship with Moore, and the consequent
widening of his social relations, Byron first became
in the lesser but not wholly ignoble sense of the word,
civilised. It was odd that he should enter his natural spheres,
both intellectual and social, by favour of the son of an obscure
Irish tradesman—the old English Baron chaperoned, as it were,
by little Tommy Moore ; and his earlier friends regarded the
paradoxical development with differing sensations. " This ",
writes the jealous and exacting Dallas, " was the trying moment
of virtue, and no wonder it was shaken ". " For some time ",
says Galt, " after the publication of *Childe Harold*, the noble
author appeared to more advantage than I ever afterwards saw
him ". William Bankes, remote and touchy, continually nagged
him in letters which Byron answered with extraordinary patience
and gentleness ; Hodgson and Hobhouse, more genial and more
worldly, accepted the new state of things with amusement and
interest. Hobhouse, for that matter, belonged to the same set,
though his place in it was naturally less conspicuous. There
was no one whom they did not meet ; and for all whom they
met, no matter how eagerly those were courted, Byron was the
cynosure. " Glory darted thick upon him from all sides ",
continues Dallas ; " . . . he was the wonder of greybeards, and
the show of fashionable parties ".

One of these, in the June of 1812, was so fashionable that the
Prince Regent was among the earliest guests, and, noticing Byron,
asked who he was. On being told, he at once desired that Lord
Byron should be presented to him. In connection with this social
triumph—His Royal Highness was very gracious—a striking
instance of how delightful Byron could be with men (for with men

he *was* delightful) shows forth. The illustrious dialogue naturally turned upon poetry, and " after some sayings peculiarly pleasing from royal lips, as to my own attempts ", the Prince referred to Walter Scott. About him he was so enthusiastic that a day or two afterwards, Byron called upon John Murray, " merely ", wrote Murray to Scott, " to let off the raptures of the Prince concerning you, thinking, as he said, that . . . it might not be ungrateful to you to hear of his praises ". This at once produced a letter from Scott to Byron, wherein he thanked him very warmly for his flattering communication, and added a kindly reference to the measure of praise and blame which had been awarded him in *English Bards*. He had been praised for his poetry, but blamed for writing *Marmion* " on contract for a sum of money ". Scott showed, with equal dignity and gentleness, that he had not done this. Byron's answer was worthy of the explanation, and a firm friendship thus began between the great poetic rivals of the age. But the rivalry was entirely vicarious—a device of the reviewers and debating-societies to add savour to their articles and discussions ; [1] for Scott and Byron could not be brought to regard one another with any sort of jealousy. Jealousy in literary matters was indeed a thing that never troubled Byron from first to last. He knew this. " I really have *no* literary envy ", he wrote to Moore in 1814.

His interview with the Regent turned his thoughts for a moment towards Court-circles. Soon afterwards Dallas found him, " with his fine black [*sic*] hair in powder, which by no means suited his countenance ", ready, in full dress, to attend a levee at Carlton House. But the levee was put off, and he never again donned the livery of the courtier—partly from genuine disinclination, partly because an incident of his literary life (soon to be detailed) made it impossible to present himself.

Among the most interesting notes upon him at this time of lionising is one by Jane Porter, author of *The Scottish Chiefs*, a novel which to a period within our own memories enjoyed a sentimental vogue. She met him at the house of William Sotheby, a man of letters and of fortune, whom in 1818 Byron was to immortalise (in *Beppo*) as Botherby, the " solemn, antique gentleman of rhyme ". Miss Porter made the following note of Byron's appearance, and after his death sent it to Augusta Leigh. " I was not aware of his being in the room, or even that he had been invited, when I was arrested from listening to the person conversing with me by the Sounds of the most melodious Speaking Voice I had ever heard. . . . I turned round . . . and

---

[1] " At the time when they were the two lions of London, Hookham Frere observed, ' Great poets formerly (Homer and Milton) were blind ; now they are lame ' " (*Table-Talk of Samuel Rogers*).

saw a Gentleman in black, of an elegant form (for nothing of his lameness could be discovered), and with a face I shall never forget. . . . The Eye deep set, but mildly lustrous; and the Complexion . . . a sort of moonlight paleness. It was so pale, yet with all so Softly brilliant ".

" How very pale you are ! " wrote Caroline Lamb to him at the same period. " . . . *E la beltà della morte*. . . . I never see you without wishing to cry ". Upon other women of the Devonshire House set he made a less terribly sentimental impression. Elizabeth, Duchess of Devonshire, thought his face sickly but handsome, and his figure bad ; Harriet Cavendish (then Lady H. Leveson-Gower) found him agreeable, but wished for nothing further than mere acquaintance. " His countenance is fine when it is in repose ; but the moment it is in play, suspicious, malignant, and consequently repulsive. His manner is either remarkably gracious and conciliatory, with a tinge of affectation, or irritable and impetuous, and then, I am afraid, perfectly natural ".

He must often, in this hour of electric triumph, have found it difficult to be natural in any way. Round him at each gathering there was always to be seen a circle of star-gazers. Lord Beaconsfield, in his *Venetia*, inimitably presents to us the " new poet, Cadurcis ", as he appeared at the evening parties of 1812.

" ' Watch Cadurcis ', said Mr. Horace Pole to a fine lady. ' Does not he look sublime ? . . . Alone in a crowd, as he says in his last poem. Very interesting ! '

" ' Wonderful creature ! ' exclaimed the dame.

" ' Charming ! ' said Mr. Pole. ' Perhaps you will be fortunate enough to be handed in to dinner by him. . . . You must take care, however, not to eat ; he cannot endure a woman who eats.'

" ' I never do ', said the lady simply ; ' at least, at dinner ' ".

.   .   .   .

" ' He must be a man of genius ', said Mr. Pole ; ' he is so unlike everybody ; the very tie of his cravat proves it. And his hair, so savage and dishevelled ; none but a man of genius would not wear powder. Watch him to-day, and you will observe that he will not condescend to perform the slightest act like an ordinary mortal '.

" ' Dear me ! ' said the lady. ' I am delighted to see him ; and yet I hope that I shall not sit by him at dinner ' ".

She did sit by him, and he was the most entertaining member of the party. " Lady Monteagle " was the hostess—she stands, in *Venetia*, for Caroline Lamb ; and Lady Monteagle was quite delighted, for now " everybody would circulate throughout the

world that it was only at *her* house that Lord Cadurcis conde-
scended to be amusing ".

Mr. Horace Pole's sardonic comments were not unjustified.
Moore describes Byron's demeanour as " that of one whose better
thoughts were elsewhere, and who looked with melancholy
abstraction on the gay crowd around him ". He attributes it
in part to shyness ; but admits that a love of effect may also
have contributed. In the Diary for 1813 Byron records a
criticism made by Mme de Staël. " She told Lewis . . . that
I was affected, in the first place ; and that in the next place,
I committed the heinous offence of sitting at dinner with my
eyes shut, or half-shut. I wonder if I really have this trick.
I must cure myself of it, if true. One insensibly acquires
awkward habits, which should be broken in time. If this is
one, I wish I had been told of it before ". Thus we see that
an apparent affectation of a peculiarly irritating kind was quite
unconscious. The truth is, I think, that the Byronic poise
suffered from an excess of the qualities both of poises and poses.
It was at once too sincere and too effective. Precisely as Byron
looked, he felt—alone in a crowd ; but then self-consciousness
arrived to show him how sublime he appeared in this betrayal
of his feeling, and thenceforth, though sincerity survived, it
was sincerity under the limelight—hardly, like a good actor in
a similar plight, to be recognised for the thing it was.

" Nothing ", says Moore, " could be more amusing and delight-
ful than the contrast which his manners afterwards when we
were alone, presented to his proud reserve in the brilliant circle
we had just left. It was like the bursting gaiety of a boy let
loose from school, and seemed as if there was no extent of fun
or tricks of which he was not capable. Finding him thus in-
variably lively when we were together, I often rallied him on
the gloomy tone of his poetry, as assumed ; but his constant
answer was (and I soon ceased to doubt of its truth) that, though
thus merry and full of laughter with those he liked, he was, at
heart, one of the most melancholy wretches in existence ".

" Most of his life ", observes Mr. Arthur Symons [1] in a pene-
trating analysis of his mind, " he was a personality looking out
for its own formula. . . . Byron was at once the victim and
the master of the world . . . [he] and the world seem to touch
at all points, and to maintain a kind of equilibrium by the equality
of their strength. . . . Never, in English verse, has a man been
seen who was so much a man and so much an Englishman. It
is not man in the elemental sense, so much as the man of the
world, whom we find reflected . . . in this poet for whom (like

---

[1] Arthur Symons, *The Romantic Movement in English Poetry*. Con-
stable, 1909.

13

the novelists, and unlike all other poets) society exists as well as human nature ".

Beside that profound explanation of him, a shallower one may blush to place itself ; but this has its small excuse for existence. There is an everyday side to everything—even to Byron. When he got away with Moore or another intimate, he turned into a merry, happy boy ; and the reason for it was that he was a man's man. Where women ruled he was a blighted being—in a meaning different from the usual meaning of that phrase. Everything that was delightful, even (one might go so far as to say) everything that was good in him, emerged for men alone. A woman, perceiving this, becomes aware of a stirring of envy. He would have been so well worth loving like that ; but like that no woman, of all those in his life, ever knew him. We are more fortunate nowadays. Men show us the man's side sometimes ; and hence it is that one often finds the modern woman in love with Byron's ghost. She is persuaded—and not without justification—that if Byron had lived to-day, he would have liked women better; and that women, liking *him* better, would more wisely and more happily have loved him. However that may be, it is the man's side to which in this chapter I wish to draw attention.

His letters are its best exposition. By this time they had become incomparable, in their kind, with any but his own later ones. Vivid, witty—with a sort of unconscious wit that comes of their amazing gusto—spontaneous, human, they vibrate with the sound of him as his first reckonable verse does, but far more than that does—for, as he was to find later, this natural prose way of telling things was the way for him in verse as well as in life. Since his day, we have had our gifts from great letter-writers—Edward FitzGerald, Robert Louis Stevenson, T. E. Brown, to mention only a few ; in my opinion, Byron surpasses them all. His range is wider, his diapason richer ; his voice has a thrilling quality, a boldness and freedom in the launching, which makes the other voices seem like those of brilliant amateurs beside a great singer's. He has the audacity of Casanova (though he yields him a good deal in *gauloiserie*) ; the wit of Voltaire ; the intensity of Rousseau—and, beyond and away from all this cosmopolitan brotherhood, he has the peculiar " salt " of the Englishman. None of the names above cited stands for such almost visible delight in the wielding of the word as Byron's does. So soon as the early days in Southwell, this emerged. As I then pointed out, the lamentations over his wretched family-life broke down almost in laughter ; his pen, as he describes, seems to shake its sides. This—a part of the generic literary spirit, it is true, in one way of regarding it—seems to me a peculiar attribute of the English and Irish mind.   No other men (*cæteris paribus*) get the *fun* out of their tribulations that Englishmen and Irishmen get.   Soldiers' and explorers' letters are curious instances of this.   Behind the most spirited from any who are not either English or Irish, there lurks always the phantom of self-pity ;   in theirs, self-pity seems forgotten in the sheer absurdity of finding one's self in such a plight.   So it was with Byron, once he began to narrate his woes ;   and when we remember the self-consciousness of his verse, and rejoice in the spontaneity of his letters, we cease to wonder at his persistent cry that poetry was not his vocation.   Until he found the form that really liberated his genius, poetry *was*, in a sense, a prison-house for his mind.   With *Beppo* came the first awakening ;   with *Don Juan* his verse became, as Mr. Arthur Symons says, " for the first time as good as his prose ".

To give instances were to give nearly every letter he wrote, except almost any that he wrote to women.[1]   Of those there are comparatively few.   It was to his men-friends, and especially to Moore and Murray, that he sent his masterpieces.

But besides the letters there are other proofs of Byron's generosity, in both kinds, towards men ;   and of his delightful enthusiasm for the traits in them which appealed to his imagination.   Of Sheridan he never wearied to sing the praises ;   of Curran he wrote to Moore and in his Journal with an ardour which leaves us mourning (with Rogers) that so little of Curran's brilliant table-talk has been preserved ;   of and to Moore he spoke and wrote in terms so admiring and affectionate that our hearts warm as we read.   Moore had moods of depression, and these were possibly intensified by the arrival of so dazzling a competitor in his own field of Eastern poetry.   Byron never flagged in encouraging and praising him.   " My dear Moore, you strangely underrate yourself.   I should conceive it an affectation in any other.. . .   But you are laughing at me . . .and if you are not laughing, you deserve to be laughed at.   Seriously, what on earth can you, or have you, to dread from any poetical flesh breathing ?
. . I know *you* will believe me when I say that I am as anxious for your success as one human being can be for another's—as much as if I had never scribbled a line ".

This complete absence of jealousy is the more endearing because Byron regarded his own glory as very precarious.   One side of him was sincerely indifferent to this ;   the other— what we may call the publisher's side, for publishers play an important part in creating it—drove him to that watching of

[1] This does not apply to the letters written to Lady Melbourne, which are in the authentic Byron manner; but these had not been published when my book first appeared in 1912.

the public taste which too often wrecks a writer's individuality. That Byron escaped this disaster we might almost attribute to the other which he did not escape. It was exile from England which produced *Don Juan*, the sole masterpiece of English poetry that has no parallel in English literature. The form, as in the instance of *Childe Harold* also, was not his own invention ; but the matter for which he used the form (again as with *Harold*) was an invention of the first order ; and, oddly enough, he has never been imitated in the later combination. *Don Juan* stands alone—a thing done with mastery so complete as to make it, so to speak, its own last word.

To Francis Hodgson, in 1813, Byron's generosity showed itself in a very practical shape. Hodgson had become engaged, and was anxious, before he married, to clear off his father's liabilities. Byron gave him altogether £1500 for the purpose. And here, in addition to the generosity, we find him displaying a beautiful delicacy of feeling. Hodgson had been unable to keep from talking of his friend's kindness, and in December 1813 Byron came to know of this. He wrote : " Now . . . you, or Drury, must have told this, for upon my own honour, not even to Scrope, nor to one soul (Drury knew it before) have I said one syllable of the matter. So don't be out of humour with me about it, but you can't be more so than I am. I am, however, glad of one thing ; if you ever conceived it to be in the least an obligation, this disclosure most fairly and fully releases you from it. . . . And so there's an end of the matter ". In his Journal he wrote : " I wish there had been more convenience and less gratification to my self-love in it, for then there had been more merit ". It was about the same time that he lent James Wedderburn Webster £1000 ; but this transaction, on the beneficiary's side, falls short of the grace which distinguishes that with Francis Hodgson. " I lent him ", wrote Byron (only then repaid) from Genoa in 1822, " a thousand pounds on condition that he would not go to the Jews ; he took the moneys, and went to the Jews ". Webster, with his black wig, and his mistresses, and his easy sense of honour, was in 1822 on the eve of a separation from his wife—a moral separation he called it, but that, one imagines, must always have existed. Byron tried, in 1823, to bring about a reconciliation. It remains uncertain if he, or any one, succeeded in doing so—Lady Frances showed at any rate no sign of yielding to the intervention of him who, ten years before, had played so different a part.

But let me give an instance [1] of Byron's generosity to a woman.

[1] At Ravenna, in 1821, there was a similar episode. He gave an old woman of ninety-five a weekly pension for the rest of her life.

In March 1814 he moved into The Albany from lodgings in Bennet Street, St. James's. He had been attended at these lodgings during one of his transient illnesses by an ancient housemaid, one Mrs. Mule, " of whose gaunt and witch-like appearance ", says Moore, " it would be impossible to convey any idea but by the pencil ". For a whole season she had been the perpetual scarecrow of his visitors, and when he took chambers in The Albany, they all rejoiced in the thought that she would be left behind. " But no ! there she was again ; he had actually brought her with him from Bennet Street ". When he married in 1815 and took a house in Piccadilly Terrace, it " was concluded, rashly, that the witch had vanished ". But one of the friends who had her most in horror happened to call one day when the men-servants were off duty, and the door was opened to him by Mrs. Mule, greatly improved in dress, " with a new peruke ". He asked Byron how he came to carry such a guy about with him ; and " Byron's only answer was, ' The poor old devil was so kind to me ' ". He had actually honoured her with an entry in his diary during the Bennet Street days—and in the oddest of connections. " There is something very softening to me ", he wrote, " in the presence of a woman—some strange influence, even if one is not in love with them—which I cannot at all account for, having no very high opinion of the sex. But yet—I always feel in better humour with myself and everything else, if there is a woman within ken. Even Mrs. Mule, my firelighter—the most ancient and withered of her kind—and (except to myself) not the best-tempered, always makes me laugh ". He sincerely believed that this account of himself was true ; but, as Moore has shown us, it was not.

Through 1813 his pre-eminence in the drawing-rooms endured ; but with the early months of 1814, though in them his greatest literary triumph (in the sense of sales) occurred, an incident connected with it, and indeed part of the reason for the later sales, brought about the first real abatement of the Byron Fever. When in 1810 King George III had first shown symptoms of insanity, a Regency had been proclaimed ; and the Tories, still smarting from the scandal of Mary Anne Clarke and the Duke of York in 1809,[1] were for stringent restrictions on the power of the Prince. The Whigs, always the Prince's friends, were

---

[1] This was the inquiry into the charges made by Colonel Wardle against the Duke of York and his mistress, Mrs. Clarke, of traffic in high posts in the Army. The Commons acquitted the Duke of " connivance and corruption " on March 17 ; he resigned his post of Commander-in-Chief on March 20. The Regent, as one of his acts of power, reappointed his brother in 1811.

opposed to these restrictions. They were made, but early in 1812 they expired; and the Whigs, who for twenty-five years had been out of favour at Court, now naturally expected to be called to power. Lords Grenville and Grey were invited to form a Coalition. As a condition, they demanded the right to nominate afresh all offices in the Household. The Regent peremptorily refused; and at Carlton House on February 22, 1812, expressed surprise and mortification at their attitude. Lord Lauderdale ("shrill, Scotch, and acute", as Byron described him) who was present, said with rare courage that the reply of Grey and Grenville expressed not only *their* opinion, but that of every other Whig. The Prince, who had drunk immoderately, was profoundly affected by this answer, and broke into violent abuse of the Whigs. Princess Charlotte of Wales (his daughter) " dropt her head and burst into tears ". Miss Mercer [1] was at the banquet, and gave Hobhouse an account of the scene. " In spite of pushing round the dessert, Princess Charlotte's emotion became sensible, so that the Prince said, ' You had better retire ', with which all the ladies rose ". The Prince then, laying hold of Miss Mercer's arm, dragged her into an inner room, and sat there for half an hour. " In consequence, Miss Mercer was forbidden for eight months the entrée to Warwick House—the residence of Princess Charlotte ".

On March 7 there appeared anonymously in the *Morning Chronicle* two four-lined stanzas, entitled *Lines to a Lady Weeping*. Their drift remained inexplicable to the general public until March 10, when the *Courier* ventured to insert an account of " The Fracas at Carlton House on the 22nd ult ". The Prince was profoundly hurt and angered by the lines, which were indeed sufficiently insulting; they were universally attributed to Moore, whose *Twopenny Post-Bag* was then convulsing the town. They were, in fact, written by Byron. As we have seen, the Regent, still unknowing of this prank, caused him to be presented privately in June 1812; and Byron dressed for the levee at Carlton House soon afterwards. That he should have done this, knowing himself the unsuspected author of the so deeply-resented verses, is one proof among many of that strange lack of delicacy which continually emerges in his actions; and indeed this very incident was to offer a second and more remarkable instance of the same thing. On February 1, 1814—two years after the scene—*The Corsair* was published; and to the second edition, which immediately was called for, there were appended six short pieces. Among these stood the *Lines to a*

---

[1] Supposed to be the original of Miss Edgeworth's Miss Broadhurst; called the " fops' despair " ; not handsome, but with fine eyes, attractive, sensible, and not at all shy (Hobhouse's Journal).

Lady Weeping—thus wantonly acknowledged, long after they and the tears which produced them had been forgotten by all the world ! What his motive was remains a mystery. Jeaffreson suggests that it may have been a generous sympathy with Leigh Hunt, who had also libelled the Regent, and had been imprisoned for it in Horsemonger Lane Gaol. Byron had met Hunt in the summer of 1812, through Moore's introduction, and had been greatly attracted. If it *were* sympathy, it was of a very foolish kind. The avowal of the lines could not possibly serve Hunt in any way, and was sure to make their author many enemies.

Murray tried to save the situation. For the second edition he could do nothing ; but, Byron being out of town, he " omitted the Tears " from the third, and drew down upon himself hot anger and insulting letters from the author. There are three scathing notes—one of February 12, the other two both of February 14 ; and in the fourth edition Murray was forced to restore the verses. The turmoil in the Press was inconceivable. Abuse was poured upon Byron every day ; all that he had ever done or been or said or written was raked up against him, and the writers did not spare even his physical defect. In short, as he said himself, they were in hysterics. The Prince, it was reported, had shed tears on learning that the lines were by Byron ; and this did disturb him. " I feel a little compunctious as to the Regent's *regret* :—would he had been only angry ! but I fear him not ". He professed himself otherwise indifferent ; but that he was not entirely so is proved by a MS. fragment, not printed, but plainly intended as a reply to the *Courier*, which had led the attack from the first.

His friends were furious. Dallas rushed into the fray ; Mackintosh wrote a defensive article in the *Morning Chronicle* ; Wedderburn Webster, too, longed to engage, but Byron stringently forbade him. His own letters at the time were so melancholy that Moore grew uneasy, and offered to come to town that they might laugh it off together. But Byron, though admitting the depression, repudiated any notion of its being the doing of the newspapers. No : he had much to ponder on of the most gloomy description, but it arose from other causes. " Some day or other, when we are *veterans*, I may tell you a tale of present and past times ; and it is not from want of confidence that I do not now—but—but—always a *but* to the end of the chapter. There is nothing, however, upon the *spot* either to love or hate ; but I certainly have subjects for both at no very great distance, and am besides embarrassed between *three* whom I know, and one (whose name at least)[1] I do not know. All this

[1] This was probably Claire Clairmont. See Chapter XVIII.

would be very well if I had no heart ; but unluckily I have
found that there is such a thing still about me . . . and also
that it has a habit of attaching itself to *one* whether I will or no ".

All through the Journal at this time run the same mysterious
references.[1] On March 10, the entry is obscure to a degree.
" I shall have letters of importance to-morrow. Which, **, **,
or ** ?   Heigho ! ** is in my heart, ** in my head, ** in my eye,
and the *single* one, Heaven knows where. All write, and will
be answered ".

In the chambers of the West End, I wonder how many
another attractive bachelor might make an identical entry in
his (improbably existent) diary !   Byron, like most men of his
day, was never out of intrigue, and never in love. Not to be
in love is nearly as uncomfortable a thing as to be in it.   Diaries
darken for both states.   Byron's, at the time of Lady Frances
Wedderburn Webster's reign, was no more gloomy than at
the period when three were claimants, and the single one Heaven
knew where.   It cannot be too sedulously borne in mind that,
for love in all its phases and disguises, he was the sentimentalist
to an extent so great as to absolve us from sympathy, not to
say serious interest.

In this respect, Moore was a bad friend for Byron.   Thomas
Little had done much to drag love down to the level at which
Byron actually, though not consciously, regarded it ; and
the spirit of the age was with them both.   But the difference
between them was that Moore, lesser as he was in all things,
could sing in one way and live in another.   With his Bessy,
there was no happier husband than Anacreon—and the
domesticated Anacreon still sang the Cynthias of the moment.
That kind of duality was impossible for Byron.   " He is
fundamentally sincere ", says Mr. Arthur Symons.   " In his
work, truth lies at the root of rhetoric . . . Not to have
been sincere . . . would have been, for Byron, to have lost
all hold on our sympathy, all command of our admiration ".
And so, while the one could prattle of lust and live cleanly,
the other went through life as the Don Juan of the ideal, never
finding the " *single* one " ; incapable (as I think) of recognising
her if he had found her, so distorted was his actual vision of
woman—and made restless from beginning to end of his days
by the quest.

By the end of 1814, he was engaged.   Marriage was his
grand convulsive effort to end the quest. He could not bear it
and its consequences any longer.   The mistake he made is made

---

[1] The publication of *Astarte* made these references very much less
enigmatic.

over and over again by men and women. Just *because* they
have not ended the quest—they end it, or think to end it. That
they fail in doing so is everyday's news. Byron failed more
inevitably and more ruinously than most—more inevitably,
because he was so emphasised a creature ; more ruinously,
because he gave the girl he married so much more to bear than
" her duty to God and man " permitted her to bear. Most
women would have found him hard to live with ; most women
would have been dismayed by such a speech as his on the night
of his marriage. Waking from his first sleep, he found himself
in a red world. " A taper which burned in the room was casting
a ruddy glare through the crimson curtains of the bed. He
exclaimed in so loud a voice that he wakened Lady Byron,
' Good God, I am surely in hell ! ' " . . . Annabella Milbanke
—a woman incapable of humour—heard that speech. She
who could, after the first pain, have laughed at it, would assuredly
have been made of coarser stuff, but she would have had a better
chance with Byron. Not to be able to understand the vein
in him which created such a moment was to be foredoomed
to failure ; and not only to failure, but to more and more of
the same pain—for he was like a boy in that, as he was in so
much else. The more he found he could shock, the more he tried
to shock ; and malignity entered the game when he found that
each attempt was silently resented. What finally separated
Lord and Lady Byron we now know ; what made it impossible
for them to live together we have always known—those of us
who have any instinct for incompatibilities.[1]

[1] Before Byron approached her matrimonially through Lady Mel-
bourne, Annabella had given her aunt a description of what she desired in a
husband, admitting that she herself had an irritable temper. (Her
description is given in *In Whig Society*, pp. 136–40.) Lady Melbourne then
told her that Byron had been in her mind when she asked Annabella for
this confidence. At this time, Annabella rejected his proposal. Byron
said of the description, which Lady Melbourne sent him to read, that he
did not understand it, would rather have seen Lady Melbourne's answer,
and that Annabella would probably find what she wanted, " and then
discover that it is much more dignified than entertaining " (*Corre-
spondence* I, 177–8.)

CHAPTER XV

MARRIAGE AND SEPARATION—1815–1816

Annabella Milbanke—Thoughts of marriage—The two proposals—An
entry in his diary—Engaged—Married—*The Dream*—Honeymooning
at Halnaby—Discrepant accounts—Seaham—Restlessness and dejection—
Life in London—Money matters—Drury Lane—Annabella and Augusta—
Bitter words—Birth of Ada—Departure of Lady Byron—Madness ?—
Letters from Kirkby Mallory—The separation

ANNA ISABELLA (ANNABELLA) MILBANKE was the daughter
and only child of Sir Ralph Milbanke of Halnaby,
Darlington, Yorks, and Seaham House, in the county
of Durham. He had married the Hon. Judith Noel, eldest
daughter of Viscount Wentworth, and this one child was born to
them in May 1792. Sir Ralph was brother to Lady Melbourne,
and it was at Melbourne House that Miss Milbanke and Byron
became acquainted—meeting at the very height of the Byron
Fever, and of the intrigue with Caroline Lamb, who was Anna-
bella's cousin by marriage.

Byron's first mention of the name which was to shadow his
own so darkly occurs in a letter to Caroline of May 1, 1812.
She had sent him some verses of her cousin's composition for
his criticism ; and he wrote in much praise of them, and in
more, yet less, praise of their author. " She certainly is an
extraordinary girl; who would imagine so much strength and
variety of thought under that placid countenance ? . . . I
have no desire to be better acquainted with Miss Milbanke ;
she is too good for a fallen spirit to know, and I should like her
more if she were less perfect ".[1]

She made this impression on others besides Byron. That
susceptible young man Augustus Foster (who had been so
disconcerted by Caroline Ponsonby's marriage) was one of Miss
Milbanke's serious suitors. Away in Washington, he would
eagerly read reports from his mother about this " odd girl ",
as the Duchess of Devonshire,[2] so different in temperament,
could not but find her. " Good, amiable, and sensible "—those

---

[1] *L. and J.* ii. 118.
[2] She had been, by her first marriage, Lady Elizabeth (Betty) Foster.

blighting eulogies !—" but cold, prudent, and reflecting ". And
the Duchess, writing on May 4, 1812 (three days after Byron's
letter to Caroline), adds something which proves her to have
been almost uncannily sharp-sighted. " Lord Byron makes
up to her a little, but she don't seem to admire him except as
a poet, nor he her, *except as a wife* ". That was a hit indeed—
more palpable than she can at all have supposed ; for, adored
by Caroline Lamb, run after by the half of feminine society,
already marked for approval by the irresistible and unresisted
Lady Oxford, Byron nevertheless had approached Miss Milbanke
as a suitor before the autumn of 1812 was over—and had been
repulsed.

At the end of August 1813, she wrote and told him the reason
for her refusal of the year before. His advances had not been
made in person : Lady Melbourne had undertaken to ascertain
how far he might hope, and had been given to understand, by
the girl's mother, that he might not hope at all. Annabella
now, a year later, told him that she cared for some one else,
but that her love was not returned. He answered by saying
that his offer to her had been the first approach ever made on
his part to a permanent union with any woman, and in all
probability would be the last ; and went on, " I must be candid
with you on the score of friendship. It is a feeling towards you
with which I cannot trust myself. I doubt whether I could
help loving you ".[1] His first mention of the correspondence
occurs in his Journal on November 26. " Two letters ; one
from [Annabella],[2] the other from Lady Melbourne . . . [Anna-
bella's] contained also a very pretty lyric on ' concealed griefs ' ;
if not her own, yet very like her. Why did she not say that the
stanzas were, or were not, of her own composition ? " An
irresistibly amusing entry ! We see that Byron could be
naïve ; we see also that he was not a coxcomb. She wrote again
three days later : " A very pretty letter . . . which I answered.
What an odd situation and friendship is ours !—without one
spark of love on either side, and produced by circumstances
which in general lead to coldness on one side and aversion on
the other ". (Here again I cannot refrain from pointing out
that Byron could be naïve.) " She is a very superior woman,
and very little spoiled, which is strange in an heiress—a girl of
twenty—a peeress that is to be, in her own right—an only child,
and a *savante*, who has always had her own way. She is a poetess
—a mathematician—a metaphysician, and yet, withal, very
kind, generous, and gentle, with very little pretension. Any

[1] *L. and J.* iii. App. iii. pp. 398 and 399.
[2] According to Jeaffreson (p. 161). He alone gives the name ; other
editors employ asterisks.

other head would be turned with half her acquisitions, and a tenth of her advantages ".

At this time he was thinking half-seriously of wooing Lady Frances Webster's younger sister, Lady Catherine Annesley ; and his Journal contains a characteristic passage on matrimony. Lady Catherine " is young, beautiful, and, I think, a fool. But I have not seen enough to judge ; besides, I hate an *esprit* in petticoats. That she won't love me is very probable, nor shall I love her. But on my system, and the modern system in general, that don't signify. . . . She would have her own way ; I am good-humoured to women, and docile ; and, if I did not fall in love with her, which I should try to prevent, we should be a very comfortable couple. . . . If I love, I shall be jealous ; and for that reason, I will not be in love. Though, after all, I doubt my temper, and fear I should not be so patient as becomes the *bienséance* of a married man in my station. Divorce ruins the poor *femme*, and damages are a paltry compensation. . . . So ' I'll none o't ', but e'en remain single and solitary—though I should like to have some one now and then to yawn with ".

Beyond doubt his thoughts were tending marriagewards,[1] but another girl was to intervene before Annabella's spell worked again. On March 21, 1814, he saw at a party Lady Charlotte Leveson-Gower,[2] eldest daughter of the then Countess of Stafford (later Duchess of Sutherland). " They say she is *not* pretty. I don't know—everything is pretty that pleases ; but there is an air of *soul* about her—and her colour changes—and there is that shyness of the antelope (which I delight in) in her manner so much that I . . . only looked at anything else when I thought she might perceive and be embarrassed by my scrutiny ".[3] This evidently exquisite girl was a friend of Augusta, and was also closely connected with the Carlisles. It is significant that at this time he was anxious to make it up with Lord Carlisle, and told Rogers that he felt disposed to do anything reasonable or unreasonable to effect it.

Was Lady Charlotte the " other lady " to whom he proposed by letter, in the same hour that he proposed, also by letter, for the second time to Annabella Milbanke ?[4] Moore

---

[1] In 1814 Byron proposed to Miss Mercer Elphinstone, *suo jure* Baroness Keith. She married in 1817 Auguste Charles Joseph, Comte de Flahault de la Billarderie, subsequently Ambassador to Vienna, Berlin, and (1860) London. With Lady Jersey, Miss Elphinstone stood by Byron in the storm of public opinion against him in April 1816. She was a great heiress, and became in 1837 *suo jure* Baroness Nairne.

[2] Afterwards Countess of Surrey.

[3] Journal for March 22, 1814.

[4] The correspondence with Lady Melbourne shows that she was ; and that " the friend " was Augusta.

gives the extraordinary story only so far as he could trust his recollection of Byron's Memoranda. " A person who had for some time stood high in his affection and confidence "—it was Augusta : Hobhouse says that he wrote his letter of proposal to Miss Milbanke from her house [1]—". . . advised him strenuously to marry ; and, after much discussion, he consented. The next point . . . was—who was to be the object of his choice ; and while his friend mentioned one lady, he himself named Miss Milbanke ". But his adviser strongly objected. Miss Milbanke had at present no fortune, and he must not marry without one ; moreover, she was a learned lady, and that would not suit him. He then agreed that his friend should write a proposal for him to the other lady named, which was accordingly done ; and an answer containing a refusal arrived while they were sitting together. " ' You see ', said Byron, ' that after all Miss Milbanke is to be the person ; I will write to her '. He accordingly wrote on the moment, and . . . his friend, remonstrating still strongly against his choice, took up the letter, but, on reading it over, observed, ' Well, really, this is a very pretty letter ; it is a pity it should not go—I never read a prettier one '. ' Then it *shall* go ', said Lord Byron ; and in so saying sealed and sent off, on the instant, this fiat of his fate ".

" Nothing ", said Christopher North, commenting on this part of Moore's book, " in the lowest farce was ever lower " ; but though we can scarcely restrain a smile as we read in Hobhouse that Miss Milbanke not only answered by return of post, but sent a duplicate of her letter to London, in case that directed to the country should miss him—the comedy seems to turn to something very like tragedy in the narrative of Mrs. Beecher Stowe's interview with Lady Byron in 1856.[2] " At last " (and the phrase is significant) ". . . he sent her a very beautiful letter, offering himself again. ' I thought ', she added, ' that it was sincere, and that I might now show him all I felt. I wrote just what was in my heart. Afterwards, I found in one of his journals this notice of my letter : ' A letter from Bell—it never rains but it pours ' '".

" There was through her habitual calm ", says Mrs. Stowe, " a shade of womanly indignation as she spoke these words. . . . I said, ' And did he not love you then ? ' She answered, ' No, my dear ; he did not love me ' '".

---

[1] *Recollections of a Long Life*, ii. 193. But in the *Letters and Journals*, letters of this period—see particularly two of September 15 to Moore—are dated from Newstead. And a letter to Lady Melbourne proves that it was not from Augusta's house that he wrote.

[2] For the history of the Beecher Stowe revelations, see Appendix I : " Mrs. Beecher Stowe ".

All this happened between September 15 and 18. He wrote
to Moore on the 15th to say that a circumstance of importance
was likely to occur and change his plans. If it did not, he was
off for Italy next month. If it did, " I can't well go abroad at
present ". He was " in three or four perplexities, which he
did not see his way through, but a few days, perhaps a day,
would determine one of them ". On the 18th he wrote to tell
Hanson that he was engaged to Miss Milbanke. " I have this
day received her acceptance, and an invitation from Sir R.
to join them in the country ". Moore tells us that the day her
letter of acceptance arrived, he was at dinner when the gardener
came in and gave him his mother's wedding-ring, which she
had lost many years before, and which the gardener had just
found in digging. Almost at the same instant, Annabella's
letter was handed to him, and he exclaimed, " If it contains a
consent, I will be married with this very ring ". Strange, that
the superstitious Byron should have chosen so ominous a token
—just as the original wearer had chosen the unpropitious 13th
of May for her own wedding.

Shortly afterwards, he went to Sir Ralph's in the character
of betrothed ; and here I turn again to the narrative of Mrs.
Stowe. " The visit was to her full of disappointment. His
appearance was so strange, moody and unaccountable, and
his treatment of her so peculiar that she came to the conclusion
that he did not love her, and sought an opportunity to converse
with him alone. She told him that she saw from his manner
that their engagement did not give him pleasure ; that she should
never blame him if he wished to dissolve it . . . and if, on a
nearer view of the situation, he shrank from it, she would release
him and remain no less than ever his friend. ' Upon this ', she
said, ' he fainted entirely away '. She stopped a moment, and
then, as if speaking with great effort, added, ' Then I was *sure*
he must love me ' ".

Hodgson met him by chance at Cambridge,[1] on his way to
Seaham, and wrote a gushing account to his *fiancée*, Miss Tayler.
There were confidences relating to money affairs, and the good
fellow adds : " He is sacrificing a great deal too much. . . .

---

[1] It was at this time that Byron went to Cambridge to vote for Dr.
Clark, who was a candidate for the Professorship of Anatomy. When he
appeared in the Senate House on November 23, 1814, to give his vote, " the
young men burst out into the most rapturous applause ". Hobhouse was
present, and makes the comment : " This, they tell me, is unique. He
looked as red as fire." But Hodgson, who met him coming away, was
struck by his extreme paleness and agitation. He asked Hodgson to write
and tell Miss Milbanke, which Hodgson did, and received from her a note
in the manner which was peculiarly hers—a kind of graceful stiffness,
more like an elderly great lady's than a girl's.

Her parents (although B. speaks of them with the most *beautiful* respect) certainly appear to me to be royally selfish persons. Her fortune is *not* large at present, but he settles £60,000 upon her. This he cannot do *without selling Newstead again* ; [1] and with a look and manner that I cannot easily forget, he said, ' You know we must think of these things as little as possible. . . . Bless her ! she has nothing to do with it ' ".

Now this evidence against Miss Milbanke's parents, written spontaneously before the troubles, seems to me more weighty than even the detailed account by Hobhouse of their arrangements with Byron, whereby the pecuniary advantages were entirely theirs. The marriage-settlements gave him £1000 a year at present with his wife, but out of this he was to pay her £300 a year as pin-money—so that his actual gain in marrying was £700 a year. In return for this addition to his income, he settled on her £60,000 on the Newstead estate. She was heiress to Lord Wentworth's £7000 a year, but would not come in for it until after her mother's death. The parents considered this contingency as a set-off against Lord Byron's settlement, for they made no proposal of securing any part of Sir Ralph's estate to his Lordship ; and although Hanson informed him that he might fairly demand it, " Lord Byron positively refused ". When Hobhouse and Jeaffreson indignantly refute the theory that Byron married for money, they are justified of their indignation ; and Hobhouse, later on, was to have such proof of Lady Milbanke's (Noel's) rapacity as to draw from him the epithet " indecent ".

On December 24, 1814, at twelve o'clock, Byron and Hobhouse, who was to be groomsman, left London on the wedding-journey to Seaham. They parted company for a day on the road ; [2] on the 26th they set out again, and Hobhouse, in his Journal, makes the significant comment, " Never was lover less in haste ". Next day he amplifies it : " The bridegroom more and more *less* impatient ". Further, in his statement of 1816 about the separation, he says : " Lord Byron frankly confessed that he was not in love with his intended bride ; but at the same time he said that he felt for her that regard which was the surest guarantee of continued affection and matrimonial felicity ". Byron told him too that he (Byron) had suggested waiting a year or so—he considering himself as an engaged man—before marrying. His affairs were again involved, and he thought it fair to

---

[1] By this time Mr. Claughton had paid his forfeiture of £25,000.

[2] Byron went to stay with Augusta at Six Mile Bottom, Newmarket (*Astarte*, p. 360, App. K). And see also his own letter to Lady Melbourne (*Correspondence* I, 286).

give Annabella and her family every opportunity of delay. His suggestion had been declined.

They arrived at Seaham on December 30, at eight o'clock in the evening. Hobhouse's first impression was not flattering. " Miss Milbanke rather dowdy-looking, and wears a long and high dress (as Byron had observed) though she has excellent feet and ankles. . . . The lower part of her face is bad, the upper expressive, but not handsome, yet she gains by inspection ". Here is Byron's own description of her to Medwin. " There was something piquant and what we term pretty about Miss Milbanke. Her features were small and feminine, though not regular. She had the fairest skin imaginable. Her figure was perfect for her height ; and there was a simplicity, a retired modesty about her which was very characteristic ". The round-ness of her face suggested to him the nickname of Pippin, by which she liked to call herself during the happy period of their intercourse.

There was some feeling at Seaham about the long delay on the road, and Annabella, on greeting Byron, burst into tears— " but not before us ", says Hobhouse, meaning himself and Sir Ralph, who had " tottered in " to receive them. Lady Milbanke had gone to her room before they arrived. An inauspicious beginning ; but " of my friend, Miss Milbanke seemed dotingly fond, gazing with delight on his bold and animated face. . . . Byron appears to love her personally when in her company " ; but Hobhouse thought that she inspired an interest which it was easy to mistake for love. " Sir Ralph ", he continues, " is an honest, red-faced spirit, a little prosy,[1] but by no means devoid of humour. My lady, who has been a dasher in her day, and has ridden the grey mare, is pettish and tiresome, but clever. Both are dotingly fond of Miss Milbanke."

January 2, 1815, was the wedding-day. The ceremony took place in the drawing-room at Seaham, the Rector of Kirkby Mallory [2] officiating. Miss Milbanke, " dressed in a muslin gown trimmed with lace at the bottom, with a white muslin curricle jacket, very plain indeed, with nothing on her head ", was quite composed, and " during the whole ceremony, looked steadily at Byron ". " Byron . . . when he came to the words, ' with all my worldly goods I thee endow ', looked at me with a half smile ".

This amusing and unmistakably veracious detail of Byron's demeanour accords badly with the familiar passage in *The*

---

[1] The Duchess of Devonshire called him " old twaddle Ralph ".

[2] Kirkby Mallory was the Leicestershire estate of Viscount Wentworth, to which Lady Milbanke (Noel) succeeded later in the same year.

Dream, where he describes his feelings and behaviour at his wedding.[1]

> " . . . as he stood
> Even at the altar, o'er his brow there came
> The self-same aspect, and the quivering shock
> That in the antique Oratory shook
> His bosom in its solitude ; and then—
> As in that hour—a moment o'er his face
> The tablet of unutterable thoughts
> Was traced—and then it faded as it came,
> And he stood calm and quiet, and he spoke
> The fitting vows, but heard not his own words,
> And all things reeled around him ; he could see
>
> .   .   .   .
>
> The day, the hour, the sunshine, and the shade,
> All things pertaining to that place and hour
> And her who was his destiny, came back
> And thrust themselves between him and the light :
> What business had they there at such a time ? "

Moore says that this agrees closely with Byron's own account, in his destroyed Memoirs, of the wedding. He woke (says that account) in the morning " with the most melancholy reflections, on seeing his wedding-suit spread out before him " ; and, still melancholy, wandered about the grounds alone till summoned for the ceremony—then joining, for the first time that day, his bride and her parents. " He knelt down, he repeated the words after the clergyman ; but a mist was before his eyes—his thoughts were elsewhere ; and he was but awakened by the congratulations . . . to find that he was—married ". Jeaffreson's comment on this passage is (especially when taken with Hobhouse's little detail) a refreshing draught of common-sense. He reduces the melancholy to the sanctioned low-spiritedness of bridegrooms ; and Byron's surprise at finding himself married " may be said of fifty out of every hundred of them ". The really striking point that Jeaffreson makes, however, is that in this account of Byron's own, no mention is made of any memories of Annesley. " It does not appear that Byron, either before or at the ceremony, had a single thought of Mary Chaworth on his wedding-day ".

We must not forget—and I have pointed this out before— the time at which *The Dream* was written : July 1816, just after the separation. But I do not go so far as to call the publication an act of revenge, which is Jeaffreson's view. A dream of Mary may well have visited Byron at this (or for that matter, any) epoch ; and if it visited him then, we must be unversed indeed in the literary spirit if we call the poem false, because he had not

---

[1] And see also his account of the " hard cushions " on which they knelt, in *Correspondence*, I, 292–3.

felt just like that at just the right moment. To feel like that at *some* moment was enough, in the artistic sense, for veracity.

Now that the marriage-ceremony is over, we enter without delay the region of the Byron Separation Mystery. From the moment of leaving the house on the honeymoon-trip to Halnaby, discrepancies begin—all fervently attested by the makers of them. He himself, as might have been expected, was one of these makers, and of course Medwin was the hearer. " I was surprised ", Byron is reported to have said to him, " at the arrangements for the journey, and somewhat out of humour to find a lady's-maid stuck between me and my bride. It was rather too early to assume the husband, so I was forced to submit, but it was not with a very good grace. . . . I have been accused of saying, on getting into the carriage, that I had married Lady Byron out of spite, and because she had refused me twice. Though I was for a moment vexed at her prudery, or whatever you may choose to call it, if I had made so uncavalier, not to say brutal, a speech, I am convinced Lady Byron would instantly have left the carriage ".

When Hobhouse, in 1824, read this, he " exclaimed fiercely that Medwin was an infamous impostor. He had himself handed Lady Byron into the carriage, and could swear there was no maid in it ".[1] In his Journal we have an account of the going away. " Lady Byron came down in her travelling-dress, a slate-coloured satin pelisse trimmed with white fur. . . . Byron was calm and as usual. I felt as if I had buried a friend. . . . At a little before twelve, I handed Lady Byron downstairs and into her carriage. When I wished her many years of happiness, she said, ' If I am not happy it will be my own fault ' ".

His testimony must be accepted, for no one else could know so well ; and we are aware that Byron told Medwin anything that happened to come into his head. But in a letter to Moore of March 8, on the eve of their departure from Seaham (whither they had returned after the honeymoon at Halnaby), there is a remark which is not without significance. " By this time to-morrow I shall be stuck in the chariot with my chin on a bandbox. I have prepared another carriage for the abigail, however ".

Possibly there is truth in both stories. The maid may have been called into the carriage on the way ; and in this connection it will be well to examine the account given, after Lady Byron's death, by Lord Lindsay. His testimony was based entirely on a written passage by Lady Anne Barnard,[2] who had known

---

[1] Jeaffreson, p. 178.

[2] Lady Anne Barnard was sister to Lady Margaret Bland Burges ; they were both born Lindsay. Sir James Bland Burges was the second

Annabella from infancy. During the early days of the separation scandal she wrote and asked Lady Byron to come and see her, if sympathy or counsel would be any help. " She came ; but what a tale was unfolded by this interesting young creature. . . . They had not been an hour in the carriage which conveyed them from the church [sic] when, breaking into a malignant sneer : ' Oh, what a dupe you have been to your imagination ! How is it possible a woman of your sense could form the wild hope of reforming *me* ? . . . It is enough for me that you are my wife for me to hate you. If you were the wife of any other man, I own you might have charms '. . . . I who listened " (says Lady Anne) " was astonished : ' How could you go on after this, my dear ? ' I said ; ' why did you not return to your father's ? ' ' Because I had not a conception that he was in earnest. . . . He laughed it over when he saw me appear hurt.' "

In Mrs. Stowe's account of her interview with Lady Byron, his words are differently given. " ' You *might* have saved me once, madam ! You had all in your own power when I offered myself to you first. Then you might have made me what you pleased ; but now you will find that you have married a devil ' ".

Both these reports claim to have been taken down from the wife's own lips : there must be some truth in them. We may take it that the point of the maid's presence is thus cleared up. Almost certainly she was summoned to the carriage, at their first resting-place,[1] by her terrified young mistress. Girls were older at twenty-three in those days than they now are, but they were still too young to be capable of dealing with such a companion.

For the arrival at Halnaby we have the same conflict of tongues. Miss Martineau—a friend of Lady Byron's later years—says that the bride " alighted from her carriage with a face and attitude of despair. . . . The bridegroom jumped out . . . and walked away. . . . [She] came up the steps alone with a countenance and frame agonised and listless ".[2] Directly contrary to this is the testimony of Mrs. Minns, the maid, who declared to a northern newspaper (*The Newcastle Chronicle*), in 1869,[3] that

husband of Lady Margaret, who was his third wife. He had married first the Hon. Elizabeth Noel, sister of Lady Milbanke. Lady Anne Barnard was the author of *Auld Robin Gray*; Sir James Bland Burges was the Jamie of that poem. Lady Margaret was, before she married him, Lady Margaret Fordyce. Lady Anne Barnard died in 1825.

[1] She was, according to her own testimony, present at the wedding-ceremony, and therefore cannot have " preceded them " (as she also affirmed) by very far.

[2] Harriet Martineau, *Biographical Sketches*, " Lady Noel Byron ", p. 316 (second edition, 1869).

[3] Cited in *Quarterly Review*, October 1869.

she saw the bride descend " buoyant and happy as a bride should be ".

To judge from Byron's letters to his friends, during the three weeks at Halnaby,[1] their honeymoon—treaclemoon, as he called it with his wonted ribaldry—survived this inauguration. But Mrs. Minns gives an account which shows that, whatever *he* may have felt, the bride was far from happy. " The irregularities of Lord Byron occasioned her the greatest distress, and she even contemplated returning to her father. Mrs. Minns was her constant companion and confidant through this painful period, and she does not believe that her ladyship concealed a thought from her ". But the lady's-maid absolutely refused to disclose the particulars of Lord Byron's conduct at this time ; " she had given Lady Byron a solemn promise not to do so ". So alarming did she consider his behaviour that she advised the bride to tell all to her father. At one time Lady Byron had resolved to do this ; but when, after the three weeks at Halnaby, they returned to Seaham Hall, Mrs. Minns was told that she had changed her mind and that not a word was to be said on the subject.

Byron was considerably bored at Seaham, where they stayed six weeks, arriving on January 21. He wrote to Moore on February 2 : " The treaclemoon is over, and I am awake and find myself married. My spouse and I agree to—and in—admiration. . . . I still think one ought to marry upon *lease* ; but am very sure I should renew mine at the expiration, though next term were for ninety-and-nine years. . . . I must go to tea— damn tea ". On February 10 : " By the way, don't engage yourself in any travelling expedition, as I have a plan of travel into Italy. . . . If I take my wife, you can take yours ; and if I leave mine, you may do the same ". But a fortnight later, " So you *won't* go abroad, then, with *me*—but alone. I fully purpose starting much about the time you mention, *and alone, too* ". This significant announcement is followed by asterisks ; and it is in the same letter that he alludes in such bitter dejection to the death of the Duke of Dorset : [2] " There was a time when this event would have broken my heart, and all I can say for it now is that—it is not worth breaking. Adieu—it is all a farce ".

On March 9 they left Seaham, and on their way to London stopped with Augusta at Six Mile Bottom, Newmarket, until the 28th. Augusta wrote much to Hodgson of their bliss, though she found Byron's nerves and spirits " very

---

[1] In Hobhouse's statement (*Recollections*, ii. 281) we find the admission that " her ladyship appeared always dismayed when she spoke of her residence at Halnaby ".

[2] See Chapter III.

far from what she wished ". She attributed this to the uncomfortable state of his affairs ; for in her view, he had found a paragon in Annabella. " I think I never saw or heard or read of a more perfect being in mortal mould than she appears to be ".[1]

On the 28th the bride and bridegroom left for London, where Hobhouse had taken for them *Thirteen* Piccadilly Terrace (now 139), from the Duchess of Devonshire, at a rent of £700 a year. Again the omen ! Yet Byron was among the most superstitious of men. Hobhouse saw him on the day of arrival. " [Byron] advises me not to marry, though he has the best of wives ". This friend then went over to Paris—it was the Hundred Days, and he wished to see his other idol, Napoleon—and did not return until July 23. On the 27th he saw the Byrons, and heard that Newstead was again in the market. It was put up at Garraway's on the 28th, but had to be bought in at £95,000. " Called on Lady Noel,[2] who wants Byron to sell hugely ". Henceforth that invaluable weather-glass, the Journal of Hobhouse, shows a steady-gathering storm.

" *July* 31.—Byron confesses he sometimes thinks that nothing is left for it but to follow Whitbread's example.[3] Byron is not more happy than before marriage ".

" *August* 4.—B. tells me he and she have begun a little snubbing on money-matters. Marry not, says he ".

" *November* 25.—Called on B. In that quarter things do not go well. Strong advice against marriage. Talked of going abroad ".

Now let us look at Lady Byron's side.

They lived very quietly in Piccadilly Terrace, for two reasons. " Lady Byron ", wrote her husband to Moore on June 12, 1815, " is better than three months advanced in her progress to maternity. . . . We have been out very little this season, as I wish to keep her as quiet as possible ". The other reason was want of means. Lord Wentworth's death in April had enriched only Lady Milbanke (Noel). Its result for Byron was to bring down creditors upon him with loud demands for a payment which, mistaking the circumstances, they believed that he was

---

[1] *Memoir of Francis Hodgson*, ii. pp. 13, 14, 16.

[2] Lord Wentworth had died in April, leaving the bulk of his property to his sister, Lady Milbanke, who was to assume the name and arms of Noel only.

[3] Samuel Whitbread, the son of a wealthy brewer, was a well-known public man. He was M.P. for Bedford. At the time of Byron's connection with Drury Lane Theatre in 1815, Whitbread was manager. He killed himself on July 6, 1815.

now in a position to make. All he had gained from his marriage, as we have seen, was £700 a year—the mere rent of his abode as a married man. Newstead was again in the market, but the purchaser had not appeared, and did not appear until 1817. In short, money-matters were in the hopeless state familiar to all Byrons. Before January 15, 1816, there were nine executions in the house. Byron's health and temper suffered seriously. He told Hobhouse that his embarrassments were such as to drive him half-mad. " No man should marry ", he said ; " it doubles all his misfortunes and diminishes all his comforts. My wife is perfection itself—the best creature breathing ; but mind what I say, *don't marry* ".

Other more trifling matters contributed to Lady Byron's discomfort. Her husband's frequent visits to Melbourne House caused her uneasiness. This feeling was on account of Caroline Lamb, for Lady Melbourne had always been a firm adherent of Annabella. Caroline, in her letter to Medwin, says that Lady Melbourne took her to Piccadilly Terrace shortly after the marriage ; it was then that she saw Byron for " the last time upon this earth ". Byron's story of the visit occurs in the Medwin book. " It so happened that three married women were on a wedding visit to my wife (and in the same room at the same time) whom I had known to be all birds of the same nest ". By Caroline's account " Mrs. Leigh, myself, Lady Melbourne, Lady Noel, and Lady Byron were in the room ". Annabella's version is entirely at variance with these, and very interestingly so. " [Caroline] has never called on me, and when I made her a vis— [*sic*] with my mother, was very dignified. I never told you of it, nor of my meeting with Mrs. Musters there. She asked after B. Such a wicked-looking cat I never saw. Somebody else looked quite virtuous by the side of her ".[1] But it is idle to linger over these dubieties. If any one's story is veracious, it is Lady Byron's. She was remarkable for her truthfulness and accuracy. That could not be said, in even a modified degree, of either Byron or Caroline Lamb.

Byron's position on the Committee of Management of Drury Lane Theatre was another thorn. Augusta Leigh, who stayed at Piccadilly Terrace from April to June, wrote to Hobhouse : " At first it struck me as a good thing, employment being desirable, but as in other good things, one may discover objections ". It was one of the great subjects of scandal in later days.

In August, Annabella wrote to tell Augusta how lovingly Byron had been talking of her, and how he had made a will in her and her children's favour. She also spoke with pleasure of his consideration for Lady Noel. " He said he meant to have

[1] Jeaffreson, Letter to Augusta, Appendix, p. 474.

her at Seaham (not that I should like it) during my accouchement, because she would be so anxious at a distance " ; and concluded : " I am as apt to fancy that the sort of things which please me are to be traced more or less to you, as that those which pain me come from another quarter—and I always feel as if I had more *reasons* to love you than I can exactly know ".[1]

Thus, to go by their own letters and the observations of their friends, did matters stand in August 1815. The marriage, so far, seems no unhappier than many. If he was difficult, she was patient ; if she was jealous and a little censorious, she seemed content to display both demerits to her sister-in-law alone. He was at work. *The Siege of Corinth* and *Parisina* were sent to Murray in November and December, both MSS. being in Lady Byron's writing. Their financial position was discomfortable, and his temper suffered sadly, but many a marriage has rallied from such blows. . . . Between August and October, though, a dire change declared itself. Annabella entered his study one day during that period, and found him standing before the fire musing on his troubles.

" Byron, am I in your way ? " she asked.

" Damnably ", he answered. He told Medwin that he was sorry afterwards—but did he tell her ? Jeaffreson admits that he said many things " far more brutal and inexcusable than this " ; at other times, " sulking and scowling . . . he maintained an insulting and exasperating taciturnity . . . for days together ". One day in a fit of wrath, he threw a favourite watch on the hearth and smashed it to pieces with the poker. This and other ebullitions are accounted for by Jeaffreson in these words : " Byron was at this time . . . a laudanum-drinker ". He *was*, as is clear from one of Lady Byron's letters to Augusta at the time of the separation ; but not all laudanum-drinkers behave like that. Another reason given by Jeaffreson for his " maniacal conduct " was the coming-on of an attack of jaundice. He was assuredly in bitter mental and physical distress ; but it is not wonderful that the young wife—suffering in her own way, be it remembered—should have attributed such outbursts to incipient mania. And apart from these active cruelties, there was the vaguer one of utter neglect—by no means the least painful to a woman. Possibly there is none which has murdered so much wifely affection. Every one knows of his ridiculous whim that he could not bear to see a woman eat. It is easy for us to laugh at it ; but his wife, who breakfasted, lunched, and dined alone, in her inevitably depressed condition, can scarcely have found it amusing. Day after day she spent like this—or if he did come in, he never looked at

---

[1] Jeaffreson, Appendix, p. 475.

her, far less cheered her by any pleasant talk. " Small things ",
say Harness and Hobhouse ; but of such small things hell may
be made—a woman's hell nearly always is made.

On December 10, 1815, the baby was born—a daughter.
She was christened ¹ Augusta Ada—" the second ", wrote Byron
to Moore, " a very antique family name ; I believe not used
since the reign of King John ". The first was in honour of
Mrs. Leigh, who was with Lady Byron during her confinement.
That took place at 13 Piccadilly Terrace, not at Seaham, as had
been at first planned. It was three days after the anniversary
of his marriage that Byron wrote to Moore announcing " my
papa-ship ". He was in very low spirits. " Just at present,
I am absorbed in 500 contradictory contemplations, though with
but one object in view—which will probably end in nothing, as
most things we wish do. But never mind—as somebody says,
' for the blue sky bends over all '.² I only could be glad if it
bent over me where it is a little bluer ".

Moore was struck by the melancholy tone and the longing
for blue sky, which he had found to be an invariable sign of that
" restless and roving spirit which unhappiness or impatience
always called up ". He answered in this sense, and added, " I
long to be near you that I might know how you really look and
feel. . . . But only do tell me you are happier than that letter
has led me to fear, and I shall be satisfied ".

That letter was written on January 5, 1816. Bailiffs were
in the house at Piccadilly Terrace, and other claims were pouring
in by every post. The next day, January 6, Byron sent a note
—a very unpleasing note ³—to his wife, requesting her to leave
home with her child as soon as it was possible for her to do so,
and go to her parents at Kirkby Mallory. She was to fix the
date herself, but it had better be soon, for he wished to break
up his establishment. " He did not conceal ", says Hobhouse,[4]
" from himself or friends that her ladyship had been much offended
by this note ". She replied in writing on January 7 : " I shall
obey your wishes, and fix the earliest day that circumstances

¹ Lord Lovelace states that Ada was not *christened* until November 1,
1816. The names of Augusta Ada were given at the baptismal registration,
which took place while Lady Byron was still confined to her room. The
christening, in those days, was often deferred till long after the baptismal
registration. Augusta was to have been godmother ; but at the ceremony
Lady Noel and Lady Tamworth were the godmothers. The change was
not announced to Augusta, but she heard of it and wrote to inquire.
Lady Byron apparently did not answer (*Astarte*, p. 67).
² Coleridge, *Christabel.*
³ See *Astarte*, p. 39.
⁴ Lord Broughton, *Recollections of a Long Life,* ii. 215.

will admit for leaving London " ; but on some other day, " an altercation ensued of very short duration ". In the end, she declared herself satisfied, fixed the date of her departure, and they lived on conjugal terms up to the last moment.[1]

But it is evident, from Lady Byron's other actions on receiving her husband's note, that his discourteous treatment had rankled more deeply than Hobhouse gives us to understand. She consulted Dr. Baillie on January 8 on the question of Byron's sanity, and on the 9th requested John Hanson to see her at twelve that morning. The brutality which had long been Byron's habitual manner towards her had (as she told Lady Anne Barnard) persisted and even increased during the hours of her confinement. He had caused her to be told, directly it was over, that her mother was dead ; he had asked her, in the first instant of seeing her after the event, if the child was not born dead ; [2] and when he first looked at the baby in the cradle, had exclaimed, " Oh, what an implement of torture have I received in thee ! " . . . That she refused to see him after these incidents may have been (despite Hobhouse) the reason for his writing to ask her to leave his house ; but even if we so far hold her accountable, it does not provide Byron with a very sympathetic excuse.

Dr. Baillie, consulted on the 8th, thought that her absence might be advisable as an experiment ; but he had not seen Byron, and could only assume the fact of mental derangement. Lady Byron, he said, was to avoid all but light and soothing topics in her correspondence with her husband after she left London. On January 15, 1816, she departed for Kirkby Mallory. The day after, Byron received from Woburn an affectionate note; and after her arrival at Kirkby she wrote the famous letter beginning " Dearest Duck ". It is dated January 16,[3] and contains the following passage : " If I were not always looking about for B——, I should be a great deal better already for country air . . .—Ever thy most loving

" PIPPIN . . . PIP . . . IP "

The next direct communication received by Byron from Kirkby was, on February 2, a letter from Sir Ralph Milbanke

[1] Broughton, *Recollections*, pp. 215–16.
[2] When Byron's friends asked him if this horrible tale were true, he answered, " *She* will not say so, though, God knows, poor thing ! it seems now she would say anything ; but no—she would not say that " (Broughton, ii. 280).
[3] Broughton, *Recollections*, ii. 202–3.

informing him that Lady Byron's parents could not feel them-
selves justified in permitting her return to his house.   He was
called upon to provide a professional friend to confer with " a
person of the same description provided by me, that they may
discuss and settle such terms of separation as may be mutually
approved ".   Byron was confounded.   He turned to the letter
of January 16—the Dearest Duck letter.   He had not answered
it—Augusta had been his channel of communication with Kirkby
Mallory—but his silence could scarcely be the reason for this
resolve.   Yet nothing had passed between him and Annabella
since that affectionate note was written.   What, then, had
been happening at Kirkby ? [1]

Annabella had arrived on the night of the 16th, and her
looks had shocked her parents.   Pale and thin, harassed, dejected
. . . Sir Ralph and Lady Noel could not conceal their distress ;
and before she went to bed that night, she had been induced
by their anxiety to lay before them—*not*, as Jeaffreson affirms,
" all without a single reserve ", but the particular question of
her husband's sanity.   That night too she wrote not only the
Dearest Duck letter, but also a long one to Augusta, in which
she says that she has made " the most explicit statement to
my father and mother, and nothing can exceed their tender
anxiety to do everything for the sufferer. . . . [They] agree
that in every point of view it would be best for B. to come here.
They say he shall be considered in everything, and that it will
be impossible for him to offend or disconcert them after the
knowledge of this unhappy cause. . . . Has Le Mann [2] advised
the country ?   *It will be by means of the heir that it can be effected* ".
In conclusion :   " My Mother suggests what would be more
expedient about the Laudanum bottle than taking away.   To
fill it with three-quarters of water, which won't make any observ-
able difference, or, if it should, the brown might easily be made
deeper coloured " [3]

On the 17th Lady Noel wrote cordially to Byron, inviting
him to Kirkby.   He had promised to stay there before he went
abroad—" the promise ", says Jeaffreson, " being accompanied
with a very remarkable and important statement of the poet's

---

[1] So soon as February 5, Lady Melbourne wrote to tell Byron that
report said that he and Annabella were separated,   She did not then credit
it : but on the 14th a letter from her seems to show that she was no longer
out of his counsels.   This is the last letter known to have been exchanged
between her and Byron.   She died on May 6, 1818, aged 66.

[2] Mr. Le Mann was the medical man who had attended Lady Byron
during her confinement, and whom she was now employing to investigate
her husband's mental condition, under pretext of attending him for his
chronic disease of the liver.

[3] Jeaffreson, App. 475–6.

main purpose in determining to join his wife in Leicestershire, and to stay with her there for some weeks ". The purpose was, in plain words—and plainly stated in Lady Byron's letters to Augusta from Kirkby—to remain with her until she should be in the first stage of another progress to maternity ; for the birth of a daughter had of course been a disappointment.

But on the morning of January 18, what news arrived at Kirkby Mallory from London—news that " troubled Annabella " ? [1] It was the news (probably from Le Mann) that her husband was *not* to be considered insane.

Here seems the best place to insert her *Remarks on Mr. Moore's Life of Lord Byron*, with Moore's comment : " While these sheets " (of volume ii. ; volume i. ended with the account of the separation) " were passing through the press, a printed statement has been transmitted to me by Lady Noel Byron ".[2]

" I have disregarded various publications in which facts within my own knowledge have been grossly misrepresented ; but I am called upon to notice some of the erroneous statements proceeding from one who claims to be considered as Lord Byron's confidential and authorised friend. Domestic details ought not to be intruded on the public attention : if, however, they *are* so intruded, the persons affected by them have a right to refute injurious charges. Mr. Moore has promulgated his own impressions of private events in which I was most nearly concerned, as if he possessed a competent knowledge of the subject. Having survived Lord Byron, I feel increased reluctance to advert to any circumstances connected with the period of my marriage ; nor is it now my intention to disclose them, further than may be indispensably requisite for the end I have in view.

" Self-vindication is not the motive which actuates me to make this appeal, and the spirit of accusation is unmingled with it ; but when the conduct of my parents is brought forward in a disgraceful light, by the passages selected from Lord Byron's letters, and by the remarks of his biographer, I feel bound to justify their characters from imputations which I *know* to be false. The passages from Lord Byron's letters, to which I refer, are the aspersion on my mother's character : [3]—' My child is very well, and flourishing, I hear ; but I must see also. I feel no disposition to resign it to the *contagion of its grandmother's society* '. The assertion of her dishonourable conduct in employ-

---

[1] Jeaffreson, p. 199.

[2] Moore, p. 461. Moore inserted Lady Byron's Remarks as an appendix. It was also privately circulated by her, printed as a pamphlet of fifteen pages. This was in 1830.

[3] In each quotation, she gave the page-reference ; but this is useless here since I have used a different edition of Moore.

ing a spy, ' a Mrs. C. (now a kind of housekeeper and *spy of Lady N.'s*), who, in her better days, was a washerwoman, is supposed to be—by the learned—very much the occult cause of our domestic discrepancies '. The seeming exculpation of myself with the words immediately following it,—' Her nearest relatives are a ——; ' where the blank clearly implies something too offensive for publication. These passages tend to throw suspicion on my parents, and give reason to ascribe the separation either to their direct agency, or to that of ' officious spies ' employed by them.

" From the following part of the narrative, it must also be inferred that an undue influence was exercised by them for the accomplishment of this purpose. . . . ' [Lady Byron] had left London at the latter end of January, on a visit to her father's house, in Leicestershire, and Lord Byron was in a short time to follow her. They had parted in the utmost kindness,—she wrote him a letter full of playfulness and affection, on the road ; and immediately on her arrival at Kirkby Mallory, her father wrote to acquaint Lord Byron that she would return to him no more '. In my observations upon this statement, I shall, as far as possible, avoid touching on any matters relating personally to Lord Byron and myself.[1]

. . . .

" It has been argued, that I parted from Lord Byron in perfect harmony ; that feelings, incompatible with any deep sense of injury, had dictated the letter which I addressed to him ; and that my sentiments must have been changed by persuasion and interference, when I was under the roof of my parents. These assertions and inferences are wholly destitute of foundation. When I arrived at Kirkby Mallory, my parents were unacquainted with the existence of any causes likely to destroy my prospects of happiness ; and when I communicated to them the opinion which had been formed concerning Lord Byron's state of mind, they were most anxious to promote his restoration by every means in their power. They assured those relations who were with him in London, that ' they would devote their whole care and attention to the alleviation of his malady ', and hoped to make the best arrangements for his comfort, if he could be induced to visit them. With these intentions, my mother wrote on the 17th to Lord Byron, inviting him to Kirkby Mallory. She had always treated him with an affectionate consideration and indulgence, which extended to every little peculiarity of his feelings. Never did an irritating word escape her lips in her whole intercourse with him.

" The accounts given me after I left Lord Byron by the

[1] An omission here consists of matter already stated in my text.

persons in constant intercourse with him, added to those doubts
which had before transiently occurred to my mind, as to the
reality of the alleged disease, and the reports of his medical at-
tendant, were far from establishing the existence of anything like
lunacy. Under this uncertainty, I deemed it right to communicate
to my parents, that if I were to consider Lord Byron's past
conduct as that of a person of sound mind, nothing could induce
me to return to him. It therefore appeared expedient, both
to them and myself, to consult the ablest advisers. For that
object, and also to obtain still further information respecting
the appearances which seemed to indicate mental derangement,
my mother determined to go to London. She was empowered
by me to take legal opinions on a written statement of mine,
though I had then reasons for reserving a part of the case from
the knowledge even of my father and mother.

" Being convinced by the result of these inquiries, and by
the tenor of Lord Byron's proceedings, that the notion of insanity
was an illusion, I no longer hesitated to authorise such measures
as were necessary, in order to secure me from being ever again
placed in his power. Conformably with this resolution, my
father wrote to him on the 2nd of February, to propose an amicable
separation. Lord Byron at first rejected this proposal ; but when
it was distinctly notified to him, that if he persisted in his refusal,
recourse must be had to legal measures, he agreed to sign a
deed of separation. Upon applying to Dr. Lushington, who was
intimately acquainted with all the circumstances, to state in
writing what he recollected upon this subject, I received from
him the following letter, by which it will be manifest that my
mother cannot have been actuated by any hostile or ungenerous
motives towards Lord Byron :—

" ' MY DEAR LADY BYRON,—I can rely upon the accuracy
of my memory for the following statement. I was originally
consulted by Lady Noel on your behalf, whilst you were in the
country ; the circumstances detailed by her were such as justified
a separation, but they were not of that aggravated description
as to render such a measure indispensable. On Lady Noel's
representation, I deemed a reconciliation with Lord Byron
practicable, and felt most sincerely a wish to aid in effecting it.
There was not on Lady Noel's part any exaggeration of the
facts ; nor, so far as I could perceive, any determination to prevent
a return to Lord Byron : certainly none was expressed when I
spoke of a reconciliation. When you came to town in about a
fortnight,[1] or perhaps more, after my first interview with Lady
Noel, I was, for the first time, informed by you of facts utterly

---

[1] Lady Byron's interview with Lushington took place on February 22.

unknown, as I have no doubt, to Sir Ralph and Lady Noel. On receiving this additional information, my opinion was entirely changed : I considered a reconciliation impossible. I declared my opinion, and added, that if such an idea should be entertained, I could not, either professionally or otherwise, take any part towards effecting it.—Believe me, very faithfully yours,

" ' STEPH. LUSHINGTON

" ' GREAT GEORGE-STREET, *Jan.* 31, 1830 '

" I have only to observe, that if the statements on which my legal advisers (the late Sir Samuel Romilly and Dr. Lushington) formed their opinions were false, the responsibility and the odium should rest with *me only.* I trust that the facts which I have here briefly recapitulated will absolve my father and mother from all accusations with regard to the part they took in the separation between Lord Byron and myself. They neither originated, instigated, nor advised that separation ; and they cannot be condemned for having afforded to their daughter the assistance and protection which she claimed. There is no other near relative to vindicate their memory from insult. I am therefore compelled to break the silence which I had hoped always to observe, and to solicit from the readers of Lord Byron's Life an impartial consideration of the testimony extorted from me.

" A. I. NOEL BYRON

" HANGER HILL, *Feb.* 19, 1830 "

Immediately on receipt of Sir Ralph's letter of February 2, Byron directed Augusta to write to Annabella and ask if it had been sent by her desire. Augusta had known since January 25 that such a step was to be taken, but had been strictly enjoined by Annabella to say nothing of it, " as it would be prejudicial to me and mine ". She had also had interviews with Lady Noel during the visit to London, and had said that announcing a separation to her brother might induce him, she believed, to put an end to his existence. To this Lady Noel had answered, " So much the better ; it is not fit such men should live ".[1] . . . The sister now wrote as Byron directed, and was answered on February 3.[2]

[1] Broughton, *Recollections*, ii. 207.
[2] The following letter is cited in full by Jeaffreson (p. 216), and was published in 1869 by the *Quarterly Review*.

" MY DEAREST AUGUSTA,—You are desired by your brother to ask if my father has my concurrence in proposing a separation. He has. It cannot be supposed that in my present distressing situation, I am capable of stating in a detailed manner the reasons which will not only justify this measure, but compel me to take it. . . . I will only recall to Lord Byron's mind his avowed and insurmountable aversion to the married state, and the desire and determination he has expressed ever since the commencement to free himself from that bondage, as finding it quite insupportable. . . . He has too painfully convinced me that all [my] attempts to contribute to his happiness were wholly useless, and most unwelcome to him. I enclose this letter to my father " (Sir Ralph was in London, at Mivart's Hotel), " wishing it to receive his sanction ".

While Augusta was writing to Annabella, Byron was writing to Sir Ralph. His letter was, as Hobhouse says—and Hobhouse gives the full text [1]—" firm, though temperate ; . . . fearless, but moderate " ; and no one who reads it can deny it any of these attributes. He declined to take any further step until he had his wife's express sanction of Sir Ralph's proceedings.

On the 3rd, before seeing this sanction in the letter to Augusta, he wrote himself to Annabella, " asking in affectionate terms for an explanation of Sir Ralph's conduct ".[2] No answer came to him ; but Augusta heard next day. " I hope, my dear A., that you would on no account withhold from your brother the letter which I sent yesterday . . . particularly as one which I have received from himself to-day renders it still more important that he should know the contents of that addressed to you. I am, in haste, and not very well, etc.".[3] But evidently Augusta did withhold it ; for on February 5 after a meeting with Hobhouse, who found him in an agitation which scarcely allowed him to speak, Byron wrote to his wife the following note :—

" DEAREST BELL,—No answer from you yet ; but perhaps it is as well ; only do recollect that all is at stake, the present, the future, and even the colouring of the past. My errors, or by whatever harsher name you choose to call them, you know ; but I loved you, and will not part from you without your express and expressed refusal to return to, or receive me. Only say the word that you are still mine in your heart, and

" ' Kate, I will buckler thee against a million ' ".

Hobhouse too sent a note, begging that he might be permitted

---

[1] *Recollections*, ii. 211-13.   [2] *Ibid*, ii. 216.
[3] *L. and J.* iii. App. to chap. xii. p. 303.

to see her—an error in tact, but pardonable from him who had heard that speech as she drove away from Seaham on the wedding-day : *If I am not happy, it will be my own fault.* He recalled this to her ; and later in the same day wrote a prolix letter of remonstrance. This was—unnoticed otherwise—sent to Dr. Lushington, and the note was answered freezingly. His offered visit, and all discussion, were declined.

On the same day—February 7—Byron's letter too was answered. Here is the most pregnant passage : " After seriously and dispassionately reviewing the misery that I have experienced almost without an interval from the day of my marriage, I have finally determined on the measure of a sepa-ration. . . . It is unhappily your disposition to consider what you *have* as worthless—what you have *lost* as invaluable. But remember that you believed yourself most miserable when I was yours.

" Every expression of feeling, sincerely as it might be made, would here be misplaced.

" Anne Isabella Byron "

To make a long story short, her determination remained, so far as he was permitted directly to know, inflexible. Indirectly, he had reason for supposing her to be—as he afterwards declared she was—influenced, to the extent of being actually driven, by her parents and their satellite, Mrs. Clermont. Her maid was now Mrs. Fletcher, the wife of Byron's valet. From Mrs. Fletcher had come to her husband a letter saying that Lady Byron was in distress and agony ; that " she was rolling on the floor in a paroxysm of grief at having *promised* to separate from Lord Byron " . . . and (to sum up in Hobhouse's words) that " her mind was perpetually in the balance between an adherence to what she had said, and a feeling for that which she really wished to do ". This testimony was thought so important that it was reduced to a legal form, and Mrs. Fletcher made affidavit of the substance of what she had written to Fletcher.[1]

On February 11 and 13, Byron heard from his wife. He had written on the 8th, imploring her to see him " when and where you please—in whose presence you please. The interview shall pledge you to nothing, and I will say and do nothing to agitate either. It is torture to correspond thus ". Her answer of the 11th declined to see him. For all response to his more personal expressions, she said, " I have determined, *if possible*, not to indulge the language of feeling in addressing you, as it could only be injurious in our present relative situations. I wish that you had spared *me* by a similar conduct ". On re-reading

[1] See *L. and J.* iii. App. to chap. xii. p. 320.

his letter, she however found " some allusions which she would not leave to be answered by others, because the explanation might be less disagreeable to him from herself ". She wrote then again, on February 13, to explain (as we saw on p. 217) her affectionate letters on the way to Kirkby. She concluded : " If for these reasons . . . I did not remonstrate at the time of leaving your house, you cannot forget that I had before warned you, earnestly and affectionately, of the unhappy and irreparable consequences which must ensue from your conduct, both to yourself and me. That to those representations you had replied by a determination to be wicked, though it should break my heart. What, then, had I to expect ? I cannot attribute your state of mind to any cause so much as to that total dereliction of principle, which *since* our marriage, you have professed and gloried in. . . . I have *consistently* fulfilled my duty as your wife ; it was too dear to be resigned until it became hopeless. Now my resolution cannot be changed.

" A. I. BYRON " [1]

Two days later, writing cordially—in a very different tone from what she used with Hobhouse—to Francis Hodgson who, on his side, had approached her with far greater tact and delicacy,[2] she made this statement : " I may give you a general idea of what I have experienced by saying that he married me with the deepest determination of revenge, avowed on the day of my marriage, and executed with systematic and increasing cruelty which no affection could change. . . . My security depended on the total abandonment of every moral and religious principle, against which . . . his hatred and endeavours were uniformly directed. The circumstances, which are of too convincing a nature, shall not be generally known while Lord B. allows me to spare him. . . . He *does* know—too well—what he affects to inquire. I must add that Lord Byron had been fully, earnestly, and affectionately warned of the unhappy consequences of his conduct ".[3]

Hodgson wrote again (his second letter has been lost), and she again answered, " I believe the nature of Lord B.'s *mind* to be most benevolent ; but there may have been circumstances . . . which would render an original tenderness of conscience the motive of desperation, even guilt, when self-esteem had been forfeited too far. . . . I entrust this to you under the most absolute secrecy ".[4]

---

[1] Published in *Athenæum*, 1883, and by Jeaffreson.
[2] See his letter in *Memoir of Rev. F. Hodgson*, ii. 24–27.
[3] *Memoir of Rev. F. Hodgson*, ii. 28–30.
[4] *Memoir of Rev. F. Hodgson*, ii. 30–33.

15

Byron persistently refused to assent to an amicable separation, and maintained that he had not been told with what he was charged. " In the meantime ", he wrote to her, " I hope your ears are gratified by the general rumours ". Hanson, his solicitor, calling on Sir Ralph and on Dr. Lushington, was refused explanation. " Oh ", said Lushington, " we are not going to let you into the forte of our case ". . . . Byron then altered his attitude. Indignant, and apparently resolute, he demanded the publicity with which Sir Ralph Noel had originally threatened *him*. On February 21 Hanson communicated to Sir Ralph his client's positive refusal to separate by consent. " From that moment ", says Hobhouse's statement (written, though not until comparatively recently published, in 1816), " every effort was made to conciliate him into acquiescence in an amicable arrangement ". Lord Holland was induced to intervene, and Byron consented to see him. His mission was not only verbal : he was entrusted with a written proposition of specific terms of separation. The document is given in full in *Letters and Journals*, iii. 319 ; but Hobhouse's *précis* is sufficient for our purpose. It will be remembered that Miss Milbanke came to Byron with a fortune of £1000 per annum, of which he resigned her £300 as pin-money, retaining £700 for himself. It was now proposed that out of this thousand a year, five hundred should be resigned to her and that he should sign an instrument giving up half the Wentworth property (to which Annabella succeeded on her mother's death) to his wife. But unfortunately the proposal was thus drawn up :

" Under this arrangement Lord B. will claim immediately a pecuniary profit of £500 per an. in consequence of his marriage with Lady B. and be relieved of all expense of maintaining her.

" At the death of Lady Noel he will be benefited to the extent of from £3500 to £4000 per an."

Byron was overwhelmed with anger at the wording of these clauses. Beyond question they are insulting in effect, though they were not in intention. He rejected the terms at once ; but he was to learn that his wife had herself drawn up the proposal. In her letter to him, acknowledging this (she was " not less surprised than hurt " that he was not satisfied), she urges her personal desire for the separation. " After your repeated assertions that when convinced my conduct has not been influenced by others, you should not oppose my wishes, I am yet disposed to hope that these assertions will be realised ".

To make, again, a long narrative as short as may be, let it be stated that after legal and personal *tracasseries* of every kind ; after every friend—Hobhouse, Hodgson, Lord Holland, Lady Melbourne—had in vain interceded ; and after Lady Byron had, under pressure, signed a disavowal (which disappeared, and was never repeated, after the breakdown at one attempt at intervention) of the worst reasons that rumour had assigned for her resolution, Byron—who could, by bringing a suit for restitution of conjugal rights, have extorted the specific charge which he complained of never having been able to extort—yielded ; and on Sunday, April 21, 1816, signed the deed of amicable separation, husband and wife having not once met during the whole course of the proceedings.

CHAPTER XVI

" ASTARTE "

Mystery—*Astarte*—The Lushington document—Augusta's confession—A letter to Augusta—Disagreement with Lady Byron—Byron's Memoirs—" I speak not "—1813–1814—Mrs. Beecher Stowe—Lady Byron and Augusta—Annabella's love for Byron—Her martyrdom—Augusta Leigh—Last interview with Annabella —Death of Augusta—The end of conjecture—The Magic Voice

FOR long the Byron Separation remained a mystery. Rumour swelled and died and swelled again ; writers of every class exhausted themselves in conjecture, or maintained that they had access to irrefutable and decisive information. Serious books, frivolous books ; Mrs. Beecher Stowe's revelations, followed by *Quarterly* and *Edinburgh* and *Blackwood* articles ; commentaries on the poems, loading every line with a narrow personal significance ; pamphlets virtuous and vicious ; little filthy contraband *brochures* that purported to be " Letters from Lord to Lady Byron ", and told of things unspeakable in villainous alexandrines . . . such a rank growth of printed matter crowded about a problem with which the public had all along been made too familiar, and in the end left that problem precisely where the Separation Proceedings had found it.

And there, for that matter, we find it to-day. Conjecture, indeed, is at an end—if we hear not Lord Lovelace and *Astarte*,[1] neither will we be persuaded though one rose from the dead ; but what Lord Lovelace proves in *Astarte* is precisely what rumour was murmuring, in the town alive with rumour and with rancour, all through the spring and summer of 1816.

Lord Lovelace, grandson of the poet, was the son of Ada Byron, who in 1835, aged twenty, married William, eighth Baron King—created in 1838 Earl of Lovelace. Ada's mother, dying in 1860, eight years after her daughter's death, and nine after the death of Augusta Leigh, left a mass of manuscript referring to the separation. By a paper signed in February 1850 and confirmed in her will ten years later, she consigned to friends

---

[1] First edition 1905 ; re-issued 1921. See Preface. The page references throughout are to the 1921 edition of *Astarte*.

and trustees a box holding these MSS., and mentioned 1880 as the earliest possible date for a " discretionary disclosure ".

But 1880 came and passed, and still her friends hesitated. There was great reluctance to corroborate the tale " so wickedly sprung on the world " by Mrs. Beecher Stowe in 1869 ;[1] there was " want of union between executors, trustees, descendants, friends " (including the future author of *Astarte*) ; and not until 1905, when the last of the trustees had died and the sole responsibility rested with Lord Lovelace, did *Astarte*, " for limited circulation only ", make its appearance.[2] It was compiled from the documents entrusted by Lady Byron to her friends and trustees in 1850.

Since 1830 the vital question had been : What was the communication made by Lady Byron to Dr. Lushington in February 1816, which caused him to change entirely the opinion he had till then held of the case ? " I considered a reconciliation impossible. . . . If such an idea should be entertained, I could not, professionally or otherwise, take any part towards effecting it ". Ever since the circulation of Lady Byron's Remarks, in 1830, conjecture had raged round this point. The Remarks had proved that Lady Byron was *not* unduly influenced by her parents or Mrs. Clermont. They had proved, too, that Byron's epigram : " The causes [of the separation] were too simple to be easily found out ", must be, at least, disingenuous. Something very grave the young wife must have had to tell her lawyer.

On March 14, 1816, soon after his decisive opinion against reconciliation had been pronounced, Dr. Lushington again saw Lady Byron ; and on that day he, and her friends Mr. Robert Wilmot[3] and Colonel Doyle[4], induced her to draw up a document, the text of which was given for the first time to the world in Lord Lovelace's book.

This document stated that during the time that Lady Byron lived under Byron's roof there had been incidents and suggestions which caused her to suspect that a criminal relation had once existed, and might still exist, between Lord Byron and " Mrs. L——".[5] But the incidents and suggestions were not sufficient for proof, and Lady Byron did not hold herself justified in acting upon them by at once leaving Lord Byron's house. For this she gave, in the document, the following reasons.

---

[1] See Appendix I : " Mrs. Beecher Stowe ".

[2] Lord Lovelace died the next year—1906—and was succeeded by his half-brother, son of the first Earl by a second marriage.

[3] Afterwards Sir Robert Wilmot Horton (he married an heiress). He was Byron's second cousin.

[4] Afterwards Sir Francis Hastings Doyle.

[5] Only the initial given in document.

1. The causes of suspicion did not amount to proof, though they impressed her forcibly ; and she held that while there was a possibility of innocence, all duty forbade her to act as if guilt existed, since even a hint at so great an offence must strike at Mrs. Leigh's reputation and well-being.

2. Lady Byron could take no *via media* ; she was totally unable to sequestrate Mrs. Leigh from Lord Byron, or to keep her out of his house, unless she definitely charged her with the offence in question.

3. Mrs. Leigh had always been most kind and attentive to Lady Byron, and had tried, so far as she could, to alleviate Lord Byron's violence and cruelty to his wife.

4. Mrs. Leigh had at times shown symptoms of profound compunction ; or at any rate Lady Byron had thus read her conduct and expressions, though Lady Byron did not, by saying this, intend to declare that these were marks of compunction for the particular offence to which Lady Byron referred, or any offence so dire.

5. Lady Byron thought it conceivable that the offence, if ever perpetrated, might be profoundly regretted, and might never have been committed since Lord Byron's marriage.

These (continuing my paraphrase of the document) were the reasons why Lady Byron, while she remained under Lord Byron's roof, had never hinted at her suspicions.[1] Since her departure from London, rumour of such a relation had sprung up ; but such rumour was not set in motion, nor was it ratified, by Lady Byron. Mrs. Leigh's reputation had in some degree suffered. Lady Byron was unable to clear her own mind of the suspicions ; but she was keenly desirous to avoid all possibility of harming Mrs. Leigh, and by nothing *she* did to involve Mrs. Leigh in suspicion. She had been told that nothing could so well shield Mrs. Leigh as a resumption of friendly relations with herself (Lady Byron), and therefore she consented to that resumption.

[1] In 1920, Mary, Countess of Lovelace, published a biographical sketch of the author of *Astarte*. It is entitled *Ralph, Earl of Lovelace ;* and it contains some letters not displayed in either edition of *Astarte*. One of these, written in 1869 to Lady Anne Blunt (then Noel King) by Lord Lovelace, relates that a member of the Noel family had been " much startled " to learn that Lady Byron had ever wavered in her belief in Augusta's " continuance in the same course for the whole time " ; for he had heard that she (Lady Byron) was witness of a scene " which could *hardly* receive any other interpretation " ; that this immediately preceded, if it did not cause, the departure; and that it was (so Lord Lovelace understood his relative to say) " what gave rise to the resolution not to come back ". (*Ralph, Earl of Lovelace*, p. 23.)

" Now this Statement is made in order to justify Lady B.
in the line of conduct she has now determined to adopt, and
in order to prevent all misconstruction of her motives in case
Mrs. L. should be proved hereafter to be guilty, and if any cir-
cumstances should compel or render it necessary for Lady B.
to prefer the charge, in order that Lady B. may be at full liberty so
to do without being prejudiced by her present conduct " (*Astarte*,
pp. 46–48).

It was pointed out that the document did not give, or set
out to give, any of the causes which produced the suspicion
which had arisen, and which still persisted, in Lady Byron's
mind.

Mr. Robert Wilmot, Colonel Doyle, and Dr. Lushington
subscribed the paper, and stated that, in all the circumstances
given therein, and from their acquaintance with the actions
of every one alluded to, their opinion was that Lady Byron's
decision was strictly right and honourable, and fair to Mrs.
Leigh, and that no matter what might happen in the future,
Lady Byron ought not to be prejudiced by that decision.

The document was dated March 14, 1816, and headed " STATE-
MENT—A. L.". In case of Lady Byron's death, it was to be
given to Colonel Doyle. It is shown in facsimile in the 1905
edition of *Astarte*.[1]

Thus the field of widest and wildest conjecture is closed.
One fact is established, and that the vital fact. And if the
mystery is replaced but by a wider, deeper problem—that of
human character—this can at least henceforth be investigated
by the light of knowledge.

It will have been noticed that in the document only
suspicion was affirmed. Lord Lovelace states that after the
Separation-deed had been signed, Lady Byron wrote and told
Mrs. Leigh what she believed. Augusta made no attempt
to deny it, and in fact admitted everything in her letters of
June, July, and August, 1816. Moreover, she made a verbal con-
fession to Lady Byron in the early days of September in the same
year. I quote from *Astarte*, p. 65, where the citation is from
one of Lady Byron's Narratives. " [Augusta] had never felt
any suspicions of my suspicions at the time in the Summer
of 1815 when I evidently wished she would leave us, but she
had often told him he said such things before me as would have
led *any other* woman to suspect. He reassured her when these
doubts occurred, and she seems to have acted on the principle
that what could be concealed from me was no injury. She
denied that during the business of the separation he had ever

---

[1] Not in the 1921 edition.

addressed any criminal proposals to her. [She] told me that she had never seen remorse for his guilt towards her in him but once—the night before they last parted, previous to his going abroad."

Lord Lovelace did not consider it necessary to produce Augusta's letters in *Astarte*[1] " because " (he said) " their contents were confirmed and made sufficiently clear by the correspondence of 1819 "—which comprises a letter from Byron to Augusta of May 17, letters from Augusta to Lady Byron in June, and Lady Byron's answers to those letters. Byron's is, in fact a vehement love-letter. Beginning " My dearest love," its strongest note is that of reproach for her change of conduct towards him since his marriage.

Speaking of his separation from her, he says : " Dante is more humane in his ' Hell ', for he places his unfortunate lovers (Francesca of Rimini and Paolo, whose case fell a good deal short of *ours*, though sufficiently naughty) in company—and though they suffer, it is at least together. If ever I return to England it will be to see you, and recollect that in all time and place and feelings, I have never ceased to be the same to you in heart. Circumstances may have ruffled my manner and hardened my spirit ; you may have seen me harsh and exasperated with all things around me ; grieved and tortured with your *new resolution*, and the soon after persecution of that infamous fiend who drove me from my Country and conspired against my life by endeavouring to deprive me of all that could render it precious—but remember that even then *you* were the sole object that cost me a tear—and *what tears !* do you remember our parting ? "[2]

---

[1] Sir Leslie Stephen said " it made him quite uncomfortable " to read Augusta's letters of humiliation dated in 1816 (*Astarte*, p. 58). Sir Leslie Stephen had written the article on Byron in the *Dictionary of National Biography ;* he authorised a statement in *Astarte*, after accurate knowledge had been given him in 1887, that he " had long rejected the hypothesis of illusion on Lady Byron's part to which he gave some support in that article " ; but, dying as he did before the next edition of the *D.N.B.* was published in 1908, his article remained unchanged. He gave Lord Lovelace a summary of the best way of stating the case, and in 1900 wrote that *he was convinced by the documents, i.e.* the Lushington paper, Byron's letters to Augusta, and Augusta's other correspondence in 1819. It was by his advice that her " letters of humiliation " were not displayed. Lord Lovelace, following it, kept back much of Mrs. Leigh's correspondence with Lady Byron, and also the whole of Lady Byron's with Mrs. Villiers ; and thus left some opening for disbelief. This, after the 1921 edition—displaying, as it does, both these correspondences in full together with several letters from Byron to Augusta—can scarcely now exist in any impartial mind. See also the letters to Lady Melbourne in *Lord Byron's Correspondence* (2 vols., Murray 1922).

[2] *Astarte*, p. 82.

Augusta, enclosing this letter to Lady Byron—who all along was assigned the part of guardian angel [1]—wrote on June 25, 1819, to ask advice in answering it. Lady Byron advised her either to say that she felt it her duty to break off all communication, or to take no notice whatever of *this* letter, and continue her correspondence in the same cautious style which had driven Byron to make such an appeal. She felt sure that he would never cease until he had ruined Augusta, and that Augusta could do little more, by any line of conduct, than postpone this evil day.

Augusta answered on June 28. She was divided between the two courses, and wrote in her worst and most ambiguous manner of " d——d crinkum-crankum ", as Byron used to call it. It does not appear how she actually did answer the letter ; but in December there came another from him, announcing his speedy return to England ; [2] and at once she dispatched this to Lady Byron, with the comment that she did not die easily, or she thought this would about kill her.

Hitherto, Augusta had been submissive to all her protector's counsels ; but now, on the question of her attitude towards Byron should he re-appear in England, a difference of opinion arose. Lady Byron's urgent advice was not to receive him, and it was the only advice that any one could have given to a woman whose standing in society had already been threatened by such rumours as Mrs. Leigh, by Lady Byron's help, had lived down. But the sister had searchings of heart—how should she explain her brother's exclusion from her house to relations, friends, husband ? Hopes of that brother's reformation, too, had begun to spring, and she found it hard to relinquish the fond prospect of making some impression on his better feelings. But she added that she scarcely ever trusted to her own view of a case. Lady Byron answered decisively and convincingly. Similar hopes of reformation had been indulged before, and had been deceived. She laid no compulsion on Mrs. Leigh ; but if Byron was received by her, Annabella must give her up. Augusta had been made acquainted with the wife's unhappy knowledge as a measure of kindness—that of befriending her ; but

---

[1] Augusta, writing to Lady Byron on September 17, 1816, after her verbal confession, and her first ensuing meeting with Mrs. Villiers, said that Mrs. Villiers called Lady Byron her (Augusta's) guardian angel, " and I am sure you are so ". Mrs. Villiers, to whom also Augusta confessed, regarded her rather as a victim than a sinner, and said to her that for Byron (Mrs. Villiers's) " horror, detestation, and execration exceeded all expression ". Mrs. Villiers had been Augusta's friend from childhood.

[2] He wrote to Murray about the same time (on December 4, 1819) : " I think of setting out for England . . . in a few days, so that I could wish you to direct your next letter to Calais " (Moore, p. 429).

also as a measure of precaution, for Lady Byron had hoped to influence her in precisely the sense which was now under discussion. Augusta persisted, however, in thinking that she must consent to receive her brother ; though she trusted she might be spared this, to her, almost the sharpest imaginable trial. She *was* spared it, for Byron did not return ; but the episode had greatly altered Lady Byron's feeling towards her. Lady Byron was " much dissatisfied ", and wrote to Mrs. Villiers (with whom she had been in constant correspondence since the spring of 1816) to say that, while reluctant to give her own impressions, she would like to hear Mrs. Villiers's opinion, on her learning the facts. After this period there was much less concert between Lady Byron and Augusta, though they had no open quarrel until 1829, when Mrs. Leigh wanted a new trustee to the Byron Marriage-Settlement (in which she had a contingent interest) after Douglas Kinnaird resigned his trust.

Byron wrote to his wife on December 31, 1819, from Ravenna, offering her the perusal of his Memoirs,[1] and adding : " The part you occupy is long and minute ". In the original draft of her first answer, which by Dr. Lushington's advice was not sent, she expressed surprise that *he* should wish to disclose their private relations ; and added that she would endure some injustice from the world for the sake of others, but that there was a line to be drawn, and that it *was* drawn, definitely drawn, in her feeling. In this unsent letter, and in that which was sent, she firmly declined to read the Memoirs, for she considered " the publication or circulation of such a composition as prejudicial to Ada's future happiness ". " For my own sake ", she added, " I have no reason to shrink from publication ; but, notwithstanding the injuries I have suffered, I should lament some of the *consequences* ".[2]

Later in this year (1820) Byron wrote several times, now pleadingly, now angrily, to request her to be " kind to Augusta " ; and, compassionate though inflexible, she answered in December that the past should not deter her from acting as a friend to Mrs. Leigh and her children whenever events should require it of her. She gave her word for this, and added that Augusta was in ignorance of her promise.[3]

He answered from Ravenna on December 28, 1820, and his

[1] See Appendix II. : " The Memoirs ".

[2] Her letter was published in 1853, in Moore's Diary (*Memoirs*, etc., iii. 114), without her sanction ; but Ada was then dead, and Lady Byron " did not regret that her reason . . . should become known ". (See *Astarte*, p. 108.)

[3] The letter is given in facsimile in the Appendix to the 1905 edition of *Astarte*.

letter contained a significant passage referring to Augusta. He pointed out that Lady Byron had never had cause to complain of Mrs. Leigh, let her be what she might ; that she did not, indeed, know how deeply she was indebted to her (Augusta) ; and added : " Her life and mine, and yours and mine, were two things perfectly distinct from each other. When one ceased, the other began—and now both are closed ".[1]

Certainly those words are clear ; and they prove, among other things, that though he professed ignorance of his wife's charge against him, he was entirely aware of what it was. At the time of the separation he could, by use of his right of citation, have brought the Noel side into court ; and that a man about whom such rumours were current, should *not* take the necessary steps to disprove them (if it could be done), was a tacit confession of knowledge, if not of guilt, of the " specific charge " with which he afterwards complained that he had never been furnished. Hobhouse, both in 1869 and in the *Recollections of a Long Life*,[2] maintained that Byron was willing to go into court ; but anybody reading his account together with *Astarte* must see that each side was playing as it were a game of bluff with the other, and that " Byron who could have extorted a charge, allowed instead an amicable arrangement for separation to be extorted from him ".[3] Observe too that he never, in direct words, *wrote* that he did not know his wife's *reason*.[3] He only said that he had had no " specific charge "—knowing that no such charge in tangible shape would be made, unless all other means of separation failed. His *Blackwood* manifesto, written on March 15, 1820—a splendid piece of prose—was not published till after his death, and he himself commanded Murray not to publish it.[4]

From other documents in his possession—" Lady Byron's Narratives ", numbered by the letters of the alphabet—Lord Lovelace tells us that in 1817 Augusta confessed to Lady Byron that the lines " I speak not, I trace not ", were written to her. Byron sent them to Moore in a letter dated May 4, 1814.[5]

---

[1] The letter is given in facsimile in the Appendix to the 1905 edition of *Astarte*.

[2] Vol. ii. Hobhouse's Statement was written in May 1816, but not published till after his death.

[3] *A Vindication of Lady Byron*, published anonymously by Bentley in 1871, from articles in *Temple Bar*, 1869-70.

[4] *L. and J.* v. 17. " Keep them by you as documents ".

[5] In the original MS. (erased but legible), stanza 5 begins thus :—

> " And thine is the love which I will not forego,
> Though the price which I pay be Eternity's woe ".

(*Poems*, iii. 415 [note].) The lyric was first published in Moore's book, 1830.

" I speak not, I trace not, I breathe not thy name,
There is grief in the sound, there is guilt in the fame :
But the tear which now burns on my cheek may impart
The deep thoughts that dwell in that silence of heart.

Too brief for our passion, too long for our peace,
Were those hours—can their joy or their bitterness cease ?
We repent, we abjure, we will break from our chain—
We will part, we will fly to—unite it again !

Oh ! thine be the gladness, and mine be the guilt !
Forgive me, adored one ! —forsake, if thou wilt ;—
But the heart which is thine shall expire undebased
And man shall not break it—whatever *thou* may'st.

And stern to the haughty, but humble to thee,
This soul, in its bitterest blackness, shall be :
And our days seem as swift, and our moments more sweet,
With thee by my side, than with worlds at our feet.

One sigh of thy sorrow, one look of thy love,
Shall turn me or fix, shall reward or reprove ;
And the heartless may wonder at all I resign—
Thy lip shall reply not to them, but to *mine* ".

It is in 1813–14 that Lord Lovelace places the intercourse
with Mrs. Leigh.

She sent Byron from Six Mile Bottom in 1813 a lock of dark-
brown hair. Inside the paper of the packet and underneath
the lock of hair is written in autograph : " Augusta " ; and
there is this inscription :—" Partager tous vos sentimens (*sic*)
ne voir que par vos yeux n'agir que par vos conseils, ne vivre
que par vous, voila (*sic*) mes vœux, mes projets, et le seul
destin qui peut me rendre heureuse——"

The seal bore " Augusta ".

Byron wrote on the outside of the paper containing the hair :
" La Chevelure of the *One* whom I most loved X ". (*Astarte*
p. 263.) On p. 63 of *Astarte* we are told that the symbol X was
used by Byron and others for Augusta.

There was a money-crisis at Six Mile Bottom in 1813 ; and
Augusta—miserably married to her first cousin, Colonel George
Leigh, a selfish and troublesome spendthrift—came to Byron
for an indefinite stay. He had just given up his project of
going with Lady Oxford to Sicily, and now thought of taking
Augusta there instead. But Lady Melbourne, who was fully
in his confidence, dissuaded him, saying that it was a " crime
for which there was no salvation in this world, whatever there
might be in the next ". He followed her advice so far as stay-
ing at home went, and she tried still to rescue him from this
irremediable offence by encouraging him to inaugurate a fresh

intrigue, giving, indeed, detailed hints towards the seduction of
another woman.[1] He advanced wild arguments in public at
Melbourne House with respect to the relations of brothers and
sisters ; and Caroline Lamb said that when she made him her
last scene at the Albany,[2] " he showed me letters and told me
things I cannot repeat, and all my attachment went . . .
It had an effect upon me not to be conceived ".[3] (We have
already seen that Caroline was held, by him and others, to be
responsible for the rumours of 1816.) Among other things
he told her that a woman he adored was pregnant by him, and that
if a girl were born it was to be named Medora.[4] Caroline also
asserted that he showed her a letter which contained these words :
" Oh ! B——, if we loved one another as we did in childhood—
then it was innocent ". And before *Glenarvon* was published
in May 1816, Caroline met Lady Byron. " What she then
said to me I *may not repeat.* . . She accused me of knowing
everything, and reproached me for not having stopped the mar-
riage. How could I ! "[5]
But to what end does one multiply and decipher hints ?
While this was but an hypothesis, as for so many years it re-
mained, the fitting of the pieces was worth the infinite trouble
that many writers gave themselves. Now it is superfluous.
We can read with interest such ingenious guessing ;[6] but the
present page is from knowledge. It remains for us to essay
the reading of the enigma of character which each actor presents
—and that we may the better do so, let us eliminate once for
all the books, the articles, which exalt any of the three to the
skies, as we eliminate also those which drag down Byron or
his wife to the mud. There were plenty of both. Mrs. Beecher
Stowe's book is by this procedure put out of court. The central
fact which she so disingenuously displayed was true, but never
had truth so poor an advocate. It all belongs to the obsolete
—that course of invective and sanctification which she began,
and many others prolonged.

The salient problem is that of Lady Byron's attitude to-
wards Mrs. Leigh, whom she suspected of such guilt, yet left

[1] *Astarte*, p. 34.
[2] He moved there on March 28, 1914.
[3] *L. and J.* ii., App. iii. p. 453.
[4] On April 15, 1814, a daughter was born by Augusta Leigh, and was
named Elizabeth Medora. For this see Appendix III. : " Medora Leigh ".
[5] *L. and J.* ii. App. iii. pp. 453–54.
[6] As for instance the articles, already twice referred to, entitled *A
Vindication of Lady Byron*. The first of the series was published before
Mrs. Beecher Stowe's articles appeared. They were by Mr. John Fox.
(*Astarte*, p. 338.)

behind at Piccadilly Terrace, and addressed in written terms of deepest affection for many days after her own departure. The evident explanation is that she was fighting hard against the ideas which had been put into her mind so soon as during the " dismaying " honeymoon at Halnaby. There, the day after their marriage, Byron received a letter from his half-sister, wherein she addressed him as " Dearest, first, and best of human beings ".[1] The effect on him was " a kind of fierce and exulting transport " ; he repeated the words of love to his wife, and asked her eagerly what she thought of them. A few days afterwards, Lady Byron, reading a play by Dryden[2] which deals with such relations, spoke of the topic. It had a notable effect ; Byron broke out in singular and overwhelming anger, and she was much alarmed. Care in avoiding the subject was of no avail ; *he* brought it up frequently, as if to trick or surprise her in some way, while she, young and inexperienced, walked as it were in the dark—fearful of being thought inquisitive, yet never sure of where the pitfalls lay.[3]

Augusta's first stay at Piccadilly Terrace was from April to the end of June, 1815. During this period suspicion was forced on Annabella ; allusions unmistakable were frequent from Byron ; but the wife, once released from the immediate pain of his sayings, would scourge herself mentally for harbouring such thoughts. (Let me recall here in passing what we are strangely apt to forget—that she was only twenty-three.) Nevertheless, as these moments recurred, the young hostess showed increasing aloofness, which at last conveyed to Mrs. Leigh that she was desired to go ; and Lady Byron, during the twenty weeks of her absence, could again convince herself that her fears were a sick delusion. Statements of 1816–17 describe Annabella's misery and perplexity during the whole short period of her life with Byron, for Mrs. Leigh's real kindness and gentleness, and wish to protect her from the paroxysms of rage with which he visited them both equally,[4] made her long

---

[1] *Astarte*, p. 63. These Narratives were written by Lady Byron about 1854, after the death of Ada, Countess of Lovelace (in 1852). In a kind of preface, she wrote : " And now, after the lapse of forty years, I look back on the past as a calm spectator, and *at last* can speak of it. I see what was, what *might* have been, had there been one person less amongst the living when I married. Then I might have had duties, however steeped in sorrow, more congenial with my nature than those I was compelled to adopt. Then my life would not have been the concealment of a Truth, whilst my conduct was in harmony with it " (*Astarte*, p. 140).

[2] *Don Sebastian*. [3] See *Astarte*, p. 54.

[4] Here is a letter from her to Augusta in the end of 1815 : " B. speaks to me only to upbraid me with having married him when he wished not, and says he is therefore acquitted of all principle toward me, and I must

to believe in " Dearest Augusta ". She did believe in her for many years—and was right in so believing—as having been honestly desirous of promoting their married happiness ; it was this desire, not to be mistaken, which sharpened the anguish of Annabella's struggle.

Augusta returned to Piccadilly Terrace on November 15, 1815. Byron seemed cold to her, absorbed in women of the theatre. During December and the first fortnight of January (as we have seen) he appeared hardly responsible ; and Augusta was more earnest than any one else to pronounce him temporarily deranged. The young new-made mother now really believed he might be mad ; and after a violent scene in her room on January 3 (when he boasted of his relations with " women of the theatre ", seeming to aim more at Augusta in his desire to wound than at his wife [1]) and the curt note of dismissal on January 6, she left London on the 15th, resolute to believe in Augusta and crush the ever-reviving, ever-sharpening suspicions.

Almost every day, the distracted girl at Kirkby Mallory wrote to and heard from the distracted woman [2] left behind at Piccadilly Terrace— a measure declared by Augusta to be necessary to prevent suicide . . . Was ever such a situation ? and as we read Annabella's letters, we feel our pity gradually lose the disbelief with which at first it is mingled, and turn to a genuine aching of the heart. " No ; if all the World had told me you were doing me an injury, I *ought not* to have believed it. . . . I *have* wronged you, and you have never wronged me ". " My dearest A., it is my great comfort that you are in Piccadilly ". On January 20 : " Indeed I don't think you do know what I am feeling, nor all the causes I have to feel ; and it makes me sicker still to write about them . . . [I] am growing altogether a little rebellious. Oh, that I were in London, if in the coal-hold. . . . *P.S.* A little more crazy still. Nothing but conscience to comfort me, and just now it is a Job's comforter ". On January 23 : " You have been ever since I knew you my best

consider myself only to be answerable for the vicious courses to which his despair will drive or is driving him . . . Oh, Augusta, will it ever change for me ? . . . It seemed impossible to tell whether his feelings towards you or me were most completely reversed ; for, as I have told you, he loves or hates us together. . . . During the paroxysm you became ' Mrs. Leigh ', and I expected you would soon be ' The Hon ! ' " (given in an article in the *Quarterly Review*, January 1870). The writer of the *Temple Bar* articles conjectures that Byron's anger arose from the " sincere and earnest repentance " of Mrs. Leigh, and Lady Byron's support of her in this attitude.

[1] See *Astarte*, pp. 38–9.

[2] Augusta was thirty-two at this time. She was born in 1874, according to Lord Lovelace.

comforter, and will so remain, unless you grow tired of the office, which may well be. You cannot think how severe my father is —much more than my mother ".[1] For she did waver, and often repented the putting into words of those cruelties which had justly enraged her parents. On January 25 she wrote : " I have neither forgotten considerations of *justice* or charity—and for the latter I have done much since I saw you. My own mind has been more shaken than I thought, and is sometimes in a useless state for hours ". And again (the second letter on the same day) : " Shall I still be your sister ? I must resign my *right* to be so considered. . . . [The] struggle is now past ; I will not renew your anxiety in the same way ". On January 28 : " I dare not *feel* anything now " ; and then, on February 3, the letter to Augusta, declaring that her father had acted by her desire in writing to her husband.

On February 19 she wrote to Mrs. Leigh much more coldly, about the reports which had already begun to circulate. " If they allude to anything I know to be false I will bear testimony of its falsehood " ; and on the 21st : " I must desire that you will *explicitly* state to me everything that you allude to as suppressed ". Her next letter[2] is undated, and declines, by Lushington's orders, an offered interview, " since we might both be called upon to answer for words uttered in the *most private* conversation ". At the end of March,[3] she however prayed Augusta to grant her what she had refused. " I scarcely know if I am justified in requiring your attention to so unwelcome a subject of conversation. I cannot give you pain without feeling yet more myself.—Dearest Augusta, yours ever,

A. I. BYRON "

Almost at the same time, she wrote to Mrs. George Lamb :[4] " I am glad that you think of *her* with the feelings of pity which

---

[1] At this time Sir Ralph and Lady Noel were unacquainted with Lady Byron's suspicions of Augusta, except apparently through a few incoherent words to Lady Noel, when telling her that Byron had threatened to take Ada away from her, and commit the child to Augusta's charge (*Astarte*, pp. 40–41.

[2] These quotations from Lady Byron's letters are taken, some from *Letters and Journals*, iii., Appendix to chapter xii., and some from the Appendix to Jeaffreson's book.

[3] Augusta remained until March 16 at Piccadilly Terrace—that is, for three months after Lady Byron's departure. She then went to her rooms at St. James's Palace.

[4] The Hon. Mrs. George Lamb was wife of the third son of Lord Melbourne, and sister-in-law of Lady Caroline. Her maiden name was St. Jules, and she was the adopted daughter of Elizabeth, Duchess of Devonshire. Lady Airlie (in *In Whig Society*) speaks of her as this Duchess of Devonshire's daughter.

prevail in my mind, and surely if in *mine* there must be some cause for them ". Mrs. George Lamb, at Melbourne House, was at the very centre of the scandal said to have been originated by Lady Caroline.

Turning for a moment from the strange relations between the wife and the sister-in-law, do not the tormented letters from Kirkby display beyond all doubt Annabella's love for Byron? They add a poignancy to the reproach she made him : " I have *consistently* fulfilled my duty as your wife. It was too dear to be resigned till it became hopeless " ; and sharpen the truth of what she wrote to Lady Anne Barnard : "It is not necessary to speak ill of his heart in general ; it is sufficient that to me it was hard and impenetrable—that my own must have been broken before his could have been touched. . . . So long as I live, my chief struggle will probably be not to remember him too kindly ". She was not yet twenty-four—and she felt that her life was over. Augusta had met her in the March of that agonising spring, and had written to one of Byron's friends that it was like meeting one from the grave, and that the memory would never leave her.

Lord Lovelace, in his brilliant analysis of her, tells us that she had the very fanaticism of self-sacrifice ; she dreamed of miracles, of helping—she the only one who could—to the purification from sin of the woman who had injured her. Her letters during the two crises which arose—that of Byron's letter of May 17 1819, and the return-scare in the end of the year—are admirable. They are wholly free from the moral arrogance of which accredited guardian angels are too often guilty. Augusta is to take the line which her own feeling suggests ; she must do nothing of whose rightness she is not herself persuaded, for otherwise she would not act in a consistent manner ; Annabella, freely giving her requested advice and reasons, has nevertheless no desire to enforce them. But the " sick and hunted deer of the herd, a separated wife "[1] had her moments of lapse from sacrifice and pure reason. Not always could she look with selfless eyes upon the ruin of her life ; now and again she must speak out to one or another, and most of all when in 1830 Moore's book appeared, with its load of blame for the woman, and of insult for the girl whose crime had been to make the worst of all mistakes about Byron—the mistake of marrying him. Her Remarks were then printed and circulated ; and the result was to draw upon her head more censure. " Why did she not speak out ? why did she not bravely accuse her husband ? " So they

[1] Mrs. Norton's memorable phrase, when reviewing (anonymously) the Countess Guiccioli's book about Byron in *The Times*, February 13, 1869.

had clamoured in 1825 ; so again they clamoured in 1830.[1] She ought to speak out—and, in the same article, she ought not to have printed her Remarks ! For the first time now we can cordially admire Mrs. Beecher Stowe, who, commenting on the *Noctes* for May 1830, exclaims : " Here is what John Stuart Mill calls the literature of slavery for Women in length and breadth ". Lady Byron might not defend even her parents against the husband who had outraged *her* a hundred times in prose and verse since 1816 ! But it was foolish work to rate her thus ; for every one had heard the rumours, and every one could guess the motive for her obstinate silence. There were the destinies of two women at stake : Augusta's now, and the daughter Ada's (fifteen in 1830) in the future. . . . Let us have done with this attack upon the sick and hunted deer of the herd —it was, as Mrs. Stowe declares, public persecution. " The direct implication was that she had no feelings to be hurt, no heart to be broken, and was not worthy even of the consideration which in ordinary life is to be accorded to a widow ".[2] The only one who defended her was Thomas Campbell,[3] and he but made matters worse. Expressing himself so ambiguously as

---

[1] See the *Noctes Ambrosianæ* of Christopher North (John Wilson) in *Blackwood*, November 1825, and May 1830.

[2] *Lady Byron Vindicated : A History of the Byron Controversy from its Beginning in* 1816 *to the Present Time.* By Harriet Beecher Stowe, 1870.

[3] *New Monthly Magazine*, 1830. Lord Lovelace says : " It is right to state most distinctly that the separation papers leave no possible place for other charges besides the two common-places of adultery and cruelty, and that connected with Mrs. Leigh ". Campbell was, at the time of his article, said to be the recipient of Lady Byron's confidence, though he expressly repudiated this, and displayed a letter from her in which she refused to give him any information. Here it is, as shown by him : " DEAR MR. CAMPBELL,—In taking up my pen to point out for your private information those passages in Mr. Moore's representation of my part of the story which were open to contradiction, I find them of still greater extent than I had supposed ; and to deny an assertion *here and there* would virtually admit the truth of the rest. If, on the contrary, I were to enter into a full exposure of the falsehood of the views taken by Mr. Moore, I must detail various matters which, consistently with my principles and feelings, I cannot under the existing circumstances disclose. I may, perhaps, convince you better of the difficulty of the case by an example : It is not true that pecuniary embarrassments were the cause of the disturbed state of Lord Byron's mind, or formed the chief reason for the arrangements made by him at that time. But is it reasonable for me to expect that you or any one else should believe this, unless I show you what were the causes in question ? and this I cannot do.—I am, etc.,

A. I. NOEL BYRON "

Campbell, publishing this, added a note : " I had not time to ask Lady Byron's permission to print this private letter ; but it seemed to me important, and I have published it, *meo periculo* ".

to convey the impression of knowledge quite different from that
of which the world had long whispered, he dragged her name
into an infamy which is embodied in the filthy *brochure* already
alluded to—and, in the end, protesting that such insinuations
had never been in his mind at all, he excused himself for his
disastrous action by saying that " he did not know what he was
about when he published the paper ".

From 1830 then to 1860, Lady Byron was, says Lord Love-
lace, outlawed by public opinion ; and in 1869, when she was
dead, a writer in *Blackwood*[1] thus expressed himself : " The
most degraded of street-walkers in the Haymarket was a worthier
character than Lady Byron "—if she had known what she had
known and acted as she had acted. Do we too think so, after
the evidence of her grandson's book ? *He* thought she was
mistaken in her mode of action, that it would have been better
to let things take their course—which, in his view, would have
meant the open revolt of the half-brother and sister. Augusta's
salvation was, he thought, an unmixed evil to the wife. " If
Augusta had fled to Byron in exile . . . the victory remained
with Lady Byron, solid and single ". I imagine that most of us
applaud her for rejecting such a victory. We may not love
Annabella Byron, but we must respect her. To her husband, we
may feel that she might have spoken out ; we may even wonder
that she did not ; yet the wonder is but hesitant, knowing, as
we now know, the brutality with which his speech and pen
could treat not only her, but the sister who had given him so
terrible a secret to hint at—nay, openly to betray.[2] Another
type of woman might have found a kindlier manner of keeping
silence ; but character is unalterable, and Annabella Milbanke's
had always been, as her mother wrote to her on March 3, 1816,
" like *Proof Spirits*—not fit for common use ". On the day that
Byron left England for ever—April 25, 1816—his wife went
down into the country to break her heart. So Rogers said, and
said truly. Thenceforth she secluded herself ; she made her
life a " sanctuary of renunciation ". Writing to Augusta on
February 14, 1816, she had said, " Happiness no longer enters
into my views ; it can never be restored " ;[3] and she acted on
the words. Mirth had left her for ever. George Ticknor, the
American, met her for the second time in 1835. In 1815 had come
their first meeting, and he had been greatly struck by her talent

---

[1] This article, with others, was afterwards (1874) published in a volume
—*Paradoxes and Puzzles*. They were by a barrister named Paget.

[2] He had betrayed her " completely, even in writing, to two or three
women " (Hon. Mrs. Villiers to Lady Byron, May 18, 1816).

[3] Jeaffreson, p. 479.

—" all grace and delicacy "—and the ingenuousness of her face.
Now he found the upper part still fresh and young, while the
lower bore strong marks of suffering and sorrow. " Once or
twice she was amused, and laughed, but it was plain that she
has little tendency to gaiety ". Châteaubriand saw her in 1840,
and said she looked " as if she did not dream enough " ; but
Fanny Kemble thought her " capable of profound and fervid
enthusiasm, with a mind of rather a romantic and visionary
order ". She held at any rate fervidly the theory of the unreality
of evil. Everybody was innately good ; evil was an illusion—
much the doctrine which is preached to-day by the Christian
Scientists. And if she had calamitous deficiencies—the inversions
of virtues, Lord Lovelace[1] calls them—if she was too severe
on young people, boys especially, if she lost sense of proportion
in her vivid realisation of the harm that those vices which were
at the same time but illusions could work, she had too her great
faiths, her great beliefs in human nature ; and her best side
showed itself to those in grief, for her feelings were profound,
and her self-command supreme. She quarrelled with the first
Lord Lovelace after Ada's death (he was father of the author of
Astarte), and he wrote to her that in most great qualities she had
not her equal in the world, but added that for all her mildness,
she lacked sympathy for those who did not feel precisely as she
felt. . . . Putting this together with the story of her life as we
already knew it, she takes shape as a woman whom all must
have respected, a few have ardently loved, and many have poig-
nantly disliked. She made herself the Martyr of Duty. Few can
love the man or woman to whom that title belongs. But that
title, and a clear perception of the part which·moral vanity—the
snare of all martyrs—played in her attitude, must not rob her
of our pity and respect. Her life was first one short, and
then one long, heart-break. When Fletcher came to her in
1824 with the unintelligible last message from Missolonghi,
she walked about the room, her whole frame shaken by her
sobs, imploring the servant to " remember " the words he had
never heard.

Of Augusta Leigh, let us not forget that she was the daughter
of Mad Jack Byron by his adulterous marriage with the March-
ioness of Carmarthen. Vague, irresponsible, optimistic, childish,
affectionate, arch ; ever ready to laugh, to talk nonsense, grace-
fully and harmlessly malicious—such is the sum of the vivid
sketch of her by Lord Lovelace, who is concerned to show,

---

[1] He says of Annabella : " She was the one person involved in that
tragic story who was innocent of wrong, true in word and deed, generous,
resourceful, courageous amidst crushing difficulties, and so she remained
to the end of her life " (*Astarte*, p. 136).

by a charming miniature,[1] that she was " very attractive, though
not a regular beauty ". When the Beecher Stowe war was begun
in 1869, the defence of Mrs. Leigh was based upon Lady Byron's
early letters to her from Kirkby, and her own personal unat-
tractiveness. Lord Stanhope, in a private letter at the time,
described her as " extremely unprepossessing . . . more like a
nun than anything ; [she] can never have had the least preten-
sion to beauty " ; and Lady Shelley, who as a young fashionable
girl had at one time been a good deal with her, stated in a letter
to *The Times* that she was like a mother to Byron, and not at
all attractive. Somewhere else the same authority spoke or
wrote of her as " a Dowdy-Goody ". Lord Lovelace points
out that she was only four years older than her half-brother,
and therefore only twenty-nine in 1813 ; and that none of her
friends and acquaintances at the time—not Lady Melbourne,
nor Caroline Lamb, nor Mrs. Villiers—ever said that she was
plain.

She was a member of the innermost Court-circle—a waiting-
woman to the Queen ; outside the Court, she belonged to a
brilliant set and was there delighted in. Abominably married,
as we have already seen, for ever in financial turmoil and for
ever longing to escape from the remembrance of it—like all
Byrons—Augusta was the product of her birth and class and
time. So long as no one was unhappy, all was well in her view ;
and though Lady Byron summarised this into " a kind of moral
idiocy ", Augusta's friend, Mrs. Villiers, made a more indulgent
analysis : " I think I am justified in saying *very* confidently
that her mind *was* purity and innocence itself ". But (says
Lord Lovelace) her moral ideas were much confused. This is
indeed strikingly apparent in the letters to Lady Byron, given
in the 1921 *Astarte*. Religious in a way, " spurious yet not
hypocritical ", the giver of Bibles and Prayer-books to all and
sundry, with many lovable and some good qualities, yet incessantly
infuriating others by her sophistries and expedients and sub-
terfuges ; huffy and voluble, evasive yet leaky, overdoing grat-
itude as she overdid resentment . . . do we not all know the
type ? She had a language of her own, half-fact, half-fiction,
an ambiguous mist of hints, parentheses, innuendoes, dashes
and italics. She seems, from the little we directly know of her,
to have been the Goose which Byron called her affectionately when
the trio was assembled and " he loved or hated us together ".

---

[1] The miniature is by Holmes (who did one of Byron also, " shortly
before I left your country "). Byron said of Holmes that he did inveterate
likenesses. The drawing by Hayter, reproduced in this book, seems to
show her as several years younger than in Holmes's miniature, where the
dress evidently belongs to a later period—1825–1830.

In his unfailing manner, he said to others that Augusta was a fool ; but that no one loved him as she did, or understood so well how to make him happy. Lord Lovelace says that she charmed him from all else, whether good or evil ; and probably the childishness and levity were the chief attractions. He had not been entirely mistaken in himself when he said he hated an *esprit* in petticoats. Certainly no other woman ever got from him (so far as we have any evidence) the kind of letters which Augusta got from Italy. Lord Lovelace gives many fragments (all that remain) of these ; but there are specimens, also given by him, which depart from the attitude of longing affection shown in most.[1] He wrote to her bitterly àpropos *Don Juan* (which she would not continue reading) that he was delighted to see *her* grown so moral. On *Manfred* he was silent for long, and then wrote to ask her if it had not caused " a pucker ". She had suffered much from the comment which *Manfred* inevitably aroused, and the reference wounded her in precisely the way that all women who had to do with Byron were wounded sooner or later.[2] Of the poems to her from abroad, she wrote to Annabella on November 6, 1816 : " I heartily wish the verses in the *Red Sea* ". The Epistle was to be published only if she permitted, and she did not permit until 1830. Her first impulse had been to withhold the Stanzas also, but on second thoughts she wrote to Murray that the least objectionable line would be to let them appear. " I am so afraid of *his* being hurt "— that was her first reason. A week later she wrote more frankly : " He might be provoked to something worse . . . and in short I hope I decide for the best ". But already for so long rumour had whispered her name ! Lord Lovelace declares that when the *Bride of Abydos* was published in 1813, even schoolboys knew that it was supposed to refer to her. I retain, nevertheless, my opinion that Lady Frances Webster was the Zuleika of that poem. Byron's admission to Galt that the first part of the story(which hovers round forbidden relations : Selim and Zuleika believe themselves to be brother and sister) was " from observation ", may be given its full weight, without necessarily dismissing the ethereal Lady Frances from the poet's dreams.

[1] In a letter to Augusta dated August 19, 1820, he says : " I have always loved you better than any earthly existence, and I always shall, unless I go mad ". (*Astarte*, p. 300.)

[2] In the notes to *Astarte*, Lord Lovelace says that Napoleon and Byron " inspired the like imperishable resentment in women who had known what it was to be in their power ". Lady Byron, for instance, said of Byron that " his character was a labyrinth, but the clue to his *heart* could be found by none " ; and Mme. de Staël used almost the same words of Napoleon : " *C'est un labyrinthe, mais un labyrinthe qui a un fil : l'égoïsme* ".

When Augusta wrote to Hodgson in June 1816, " None can know *how much* I have suffered from this unhappy business —and indeed I have never known a moment's peace and begin to despair for the future ",[1] she wrote no more than all her friends could clearly see. The rumours were then at their worst. Some of her acquaintance had dropped her definitely, and her desperation was so great that it very nearly drove her to follow Byron abroad. Mrs. Villiers believed she would, and felt that the one way to cure the infatuation was to prove to her how completely he had betrayed her both in speaking and writing to other women. This was done, and Augusta was completely broken-hearted ; on August 5 she wrote to Annabella that she had long felt that Byron had not been her friend, and would never see him again—in the old way ;[2] but that she " saw difficulties " in saying that she would *never* see him again.

On September 17, 1816, Byron wrote and urged her to join him ; and it was in September too that he wrote the *Lines on Hearing that Lady Byron was Ill*, which were not published until 1832. It has been generally supposed that they were inspired by resentment at the failure of Mme. de Staël's efforts towards a reconciliation ; but Mr. Coleridge thinks that it was the echoes through Shelley, from whom he heard in that September, of the still persistent rumours which provoked him to fury. He wrote at the same time the Incantation now incorporated with *Manfred*, but originally published alone in the *Prisoner of Chillon* volume.

> " Though thy slumber may be deep,
> Yet thy Spirit shall not sleep :
> .   .   .   .   .
> By a Power to thee unknown,
> Thou canst never be alone ;
> Thou art wrapt as with a shroud,
> Thou art gathered in a cloud ;
> And for ever shalt thou dwell
> In the spirit of this spell.
> Though thou seest me not pass by,
> Thou shalt feel me with thine eye
> As a thing that, though unseen,
> Must be near thee, and hath been ;
> And when in that secret dread
> Thou hast turned around thy head,
> Thou shalt marvel I am not
> As thy shadow on the spot ".

---

[1] It is worth recording, on Lord Lovelace's authority, that in the *Memoir of Francis Hodgson* (who died in 1852) the latter half of this passage was omitted, but was brought to light at the auction of the original letter in 1885 (*Astarte*, note to p. 61).

[2] *Astarte*. Letter of August 5, 1816 ; pp. 249–50.

His summons to Augusta was answered on October 13, very
frigidly, by Lady Byron's direction. Byron, though he knew
nothing of Augusta's confession, at once suspected his wife's
influence. In June 1817 he spoke of her as "that infernal fiend",
and said that he had signed the Separation-deed for Augusta's
sake alone ; then for nearly nine months he did not write, and
when he did, it was to tell Augusta that his silence had been
because she had annoyed him in many ways. In this letter he
asked the outrageous question about *Manfred*. We have seen
his letter to her of May 1819,[1] and her irresolution with regard
to his threatened return in the same year . . . Apart from their
secret correspondence, she remained to the last his medium of
information about Ada ; there are two letters to her from Greece—
that dated Missolonghi, February 23, 1824, being found, unfin-
ished, on his writing-table after his death.[2]

Augusta died on October 12, 1851. In the April of that year
she had had her last interview with Annabella. They had been
more or less estranged since 1829-30 ; but in the February of 1851
Lady Byron wrote, suggesting a meeting. They arranged one
at Reigate. Augusta had heard that Lady Byron now said
of her that hers was the influence which prevented Byron from
coming to just and kindly views about his wife.[3] She wished
to hear this gossip denied, or to disabuse Lady Byron's mind
of its import. She was very ill, she knew indeed that she could
not have long to live, and the misconception—for it *was* one—
she longed to remove. She came alone from London ; but Anna-
bella, coming from Brighton, brought a witness, the Rev. Fred-
erick Robertson. The interview was painful, and ended in bitter-
ness. No better comment on its futility can be given than Lady
Byron's letter to her of April 12, 1851.

"Your letter of the 10th affords the last proof that during our
interview, trying and painful as it was to me, I did not for a
moment forget the consideration I was bound to observe by your
having trusted me *unconditionally*. As I have received the
communication which you have so long and anxiously desired
to make—and upon which I offered no comment except ' Is
that all ? '—I have done all in my power to contribute to your
peace of mind. But I remain under the afflicting persuasion
that it is not attained by such means as you have taken. Fare-
well ".[4] In this letter we can perceive the self-righteousness of

---

[1] At this time his relation with the Countess Guiccioli had begun.
Lord Lovelace tells us that he taunted Augusta bitterly about this
" ignominious fan-carrying bondage ", and accused her of having driven
him to it.
[2] See Chapter XXVI.   [3] Jeaffreson, p. 457.
[4] *Ibid*, Appendix, p. 493.

which she has often been accused. It had developed with the years; but we must remember that since their estrangement in 1829, there had come Moore's book and the publication of the *Epistle to Augusta* :

" My sister ! my sweet sister " . . .

Those verses made hard reading for the wife, and all the more because she had been shown (by Moore) that they were written at the same time with the *Lines on Hearing that Lady Byron was Ill.*

Augusta's answer was vehement. " I had not, and never implied that I had, anything to reveal to you with which you were not previously acquainted. . . . Nor can I at all express to you the regret I have felt ever since those words escaped you, showing that you imagined I had ' encouraged a bitterness in feeling in Lord Byron towards you.' I can as solemnly declare to you as if I were on my oath, or on my death-bed, that I never did so in any one instance, but that I invariably did the contrary ".[1] Six months later, she *was* on her death-bed. She died of heart-disease and dropsy, with her hands in those of her youngest daughter, Emily. Her financial ruin was complete. For years before her death she had been painfully anxious and miserable ; she looked " a sunk and aged person ", and " her heart seemed frozen ". A week before the end, Lady Byron wrote to Emily Leigh, and asked her to whisper to her mother the old word of affection : *Dearest Augusta.* The dying woman's answer could hardly be heard . . . " my greatest consolation " . . . So much was distinguished ; but the rest, as on the death-bed at Missolonghi, was inarticulate murmuring.

Augusta dead, and Ada dead in the year following, Lady Byron " *at last* " could speak. Even then, by her desire, the public were still to wait for thirty years. Mrs. Beecher Stowe, to whom she confided her story in 1856, betrayed her long before that time ; but few believed the truth that was so untruthfully told. In 1905 came *Astarte,* and the end of conjecture.

We look on one of the great problems of human relationship as we look on the three at 13 Piccadilly Terrace in December 1815. The young tormented wife and mother ; the guilty, now remorseful, sister—and he, " loving and hating them together ", violent and sullen by turns, outraging both with his talk about women of the theatre, smashing his watch on the hearthstone, coming in drunk from Sheridan and Kinnaird dinners, and then calling himself a monster and throwing himself in agony at his wife's feet. " Astonished at the return of virtue, my tears, I believe,

[1] Jeaffreson, Appendix, p. 493.

flowed over my face, and I said, ' Byron, all is forgotten ; never, never shall you hear of it more '. He started up, and folding his arms while he looked at me, burst into laughter. ' What do you mean ? ' said I. ' Only a philosophical experiment ; that's all ', said he. ' I wished to ascertain the value of your resolutions ' ".[1]

Only pity will avail for understanding of this household ; and we need but know the future of all three for pity to constrain our hearts. The two women's we have seen ; his I have to show. Let us feel *now* the anger we should feel against him—now while still, in this book, his Word is unspoken. His spell as poet and as man will then be upon us. The imprecation of *Harold* shall peal through the Colosseum :

" Dost thou not hear my heart ?—Awake, thou shalt, and must " . . .

Manfred's pang shall find a voice ; in Tasso, Dante, the old Doge of Venice, Cain, there shall be found the likeness to his own dark destiny which ever was his inspiration—and all our knowledge of the truth shall vainly fight against the magic voice and verse, for

" There is that within me that shall tire
Torture and Time, and breathe when I expire ".

---

[1] Lady Byron's letter to Lady Anne Barnard, written in 1816 (Lord Lovelace so corrects Lord Lindsay, who gave 1818 as the date). Cited in Lord Lindsay's letter to *The Times*, September 3, 1869.

CHAPTER XVII

THE DEPARTURE

Farewell messages—The ostracism—Byron's lack of reticence—The *Farewell* Verses—Turmoil in the Press—The *Sketch*—*Stanzas to Augusta* —Byron's state of mind—Dr. Polidori—Dover, and *Churchill's Grave*— Curiosity about Byron—Review of Work since *Lara : Hebrew Melodies* and Lyrics of 1814–16 ; the Napoleon Poems ; *The Siege of Corinth*, and Coleridge's influence ; *Parisina*

O N Wednesday, April 24, 1816, Byron left London. To his wife he had sent a farewell letter ; the whole import of it was " Be kind to Augusta ". He wrote it immediately after parting from Mrs. Leigh—" almost the last being you have left me to part with "—and after showing, as we learnt from her confession, the only signs of remorse she had ever seen in him. With it he sent for Ada a ring containing the hair of one of the Scottish kings from whom Mrs. Byron had claimed descent. . . . His last word from England was for his sister. Only a portion of it remains, and that is entirely colourless.

Moore, absent in Dorsetshire, was not forgotten. The opening stanza of " My boat is on the shore " was written in April 1816.

> " My boat is on the shore
> And my bark is on the sea ;
> But before I go, Tom Moore,
> Here's a double health to thee !
>
> Here's a sigh to those who love me,
> And a smile to those who hate ;
> And whatever sky's above me,
> Here's a heart for every fate ". [1]

A smile to those who hate—there were many such. In London he had not ventured to appear at the theatres ; even in the streets he was insulted. In the second week of April Lady Jersey, one of the great social leaders, had given a party expressly

---

[1] He sent the whole to Moore on July 10, 1817, from Venice, adding, " This should have been written fifteen months ago—the first stanza was " (Moore, p. 362).

for him. She hoped to reinstate him, to silence scandal : he and Augusta both appeared. It was a horrible fiasco. Mrs. George Lamb cut Augusta ; every one, except Miss Mercer Elphinstone,[1] cut Byron. " It was done by Countesses and ladies of fashion leaving each room in crowds as he entered it ".

" We know no spectacle ", wrote Macaulay in 1831, reviewing Moore's book,[2] " so ridiculous as the British public in one of its periodical fits of morality. . . . Once in six or seven years our virtue becomes outrageous. We cannot suffer the laws of religion and decency to be violated. Accordingly some unfortunate man . . . is singled out as an expiatory sacrifice . . . He is cut by the higher orders, and hissed by the lower. . . . At length our anger is satiated. Our victim is ruined and heart-broken. And our virtue goes quietly to sleep for seven years more. It is clear ", he continues, " that those vices which destroy domestic happiness ought to be as much as possible repressed. . . . It is good that a certain portion of disgrace should constantly attend on certain bad actions. But it is not good that the offenders should merely have to stand the risks of a lottery of infamy. . . . The obloquy which Byron had to endure was such as might well have shaken a more constant mind. . . . All those creeping things that rot in the decay of nobler natures hastened to their repast ; and they were right ; they did after their kind. It is not every day that the savage envy of aspiring dunces is gratified by the agonies of such a spirit and the degradation of such a name. . . . The howl of contumely followed him across the sea, up the Rhine, over the Alps ; it gradually waxed fainter ; it died away. . . . His poetry became more popular than it had ever been ; and his complaints were read with tears by thousands and tens of thousands who had never seen his face ".

Macaulay said there the last word on the subject of Byron's ostracism. Let us remember that forbidden relationships were in the air of the French Revolution—that upheaval of all accepted ideas. In 1789 Lord Bolingbroke had eloped with his half-sister ; of Napoleon such rumours had long been prevalent ; to make a closer juxtaposition, Caroline Lamb's mother, Lady Bessborough, had been the subject of similar whisperings. In *René*, Châteaubriand had long anticipated *Manfred*.[3] Byron,

---

[1] He sent her a little parcel from Dover by Scrope Davies, saying : " Tell her that had I been fortunate enough to marry a woman like her, I should not now be obliged to exile myself from my country ".

[2] *Edinburgh Review*, June 1831.

[3] " In intimate circles, [Châteaubriand] often recurred to the similarity between his nature and Lord Byron's, and to the affinity between their Muses. This caused him to regret the more vividly that there was not a single mention of his name (even in a casual allusion in *Don Juan*, where so many

always in actual conduct the mere creature of his age, became in truth (to quote Macaulay again) " a sort of whipping-boy, by whose vicarious agonies all the other transgressors of the same class are, it is supposed, sufficiently chastised ".

On October 25 of that year, Goethe, conversing with George Ticknor, said of the Separation-drama that " it was so poetical in its circumstances . . . that if Byron had invented it, he could hardly have had a more fortunate subject for his genius ". In *Marino Faliero*, the Doge, speaking of himself, is made to say—

> " . . . There was that in my spirit ever
> Which shaped out for itself some great reverse " ;

and despite the cynicism implied in such a comment, we may almost say that with this calamity Byron for the first time found himself. All through his work, from the earliest days, this (as it were) longing for remorse declares itself. He was like a boy in that, as he was in so much else ; he wanted to terrify mankind, and make them see, as in *Manfred*—

> " . . . A dusk and awful figure rise
> Like an infernal god from out the earth ".

It is worth observing that not until remorse *had* entered his soul did he ever think of keeping a Journal. On November 14, 1813, he began one. Nobody can read it and escape the conviction that its dark hintings at some extreme error were (though veracious) written for posterity—or at any rate for his friends to see and marvel at. Almost directly after he ceased to keep it, he gave it to Moore. He had made to the same friend half-confidences by the score about the " strange summer adventure which I don't like to think of ".[1] . . . " The thought ", he wrote

others are inscribed) in the works of the British poet who had been so evidently inspired by *René* " (De Marcellus, *Châteaubriand et son Temps*, p. 117). M. Edmond Estève (*Byron et le Romantisme français*, 1907) says that Châteaubriand's amour-propre suffered sensibly from this neglect. He declared that, on the appearance of *Atala*, he had received a letter from Cambridge, signed " G. Gordon. Lord Byron " (*sic*) and had replied to it. M. Estève points out that Byron did twice mention his name : in a note to *The Bride of Abydos*, and in a stanza of *The Age of Bronze* (*Byron et le Romantisme français*, p. 22 ; and see *Poems*, vols. iii. and v.).

[1] He ceased to keep this Journal on April 19, 1814. On June 14, he wrote to Moore : " Keep the Journal . . . if it has amused you, I am glad that I kept it ". For his half-confidences to Moore, see his letters in 1813 of August 22 and 28, November 30, December 8 ; and in 1814, those of January 6, March 3 and 12, and August 3. It is clear from the letter in January that something else besides the summer adventure was weighing on his mind—this is the period of the apprehension about a duel with Webster which he expressly differentiates.

in the Journal, "always runs through, through—yes, through ";
but it was not the thought alone which so persisted. On the
point of his pen the betrayal trembles incessantly. We have
seen what rumours were current of *The Bride of Abydos*, and have
seen that he said to Galt—and not Galt alone but others—that
it was written "from observation". Such sayings, with the talk
then rife, must have set in motion many tongues that else
might have been silent—for vanity is peculiarly vulnerable in
the matter of gossip. When others assert their knowledge, it
is hard to conceal our own ; and Byron, most talked-of man of his
time, had friends and acquaintances in the two most scandalous,
perhaps, of all circles—the ultra-fashionable and the literary.
His communicativeness was swiftly punished. Had it not been
for that, his wife's departure from his side might have passed
comparatively unnoticed ; but where everything was already
hinted at, such an action was at once interpreted in the sense
of scandal. The injury she did him by refusing to return was
incalculable—so far he might justly name her his " moral Clytem-
nestra " ; but it was his own speech and pen which had given
the signal for the outlawry that ensued.

Speech and pen were no less active now. Already on March
17, the famous *Farewell* verses were written.

> " Fare thee well ! and if for ever,
>   Still for ever, fare *thee well* :
> Even though unforgiving, never
>   'Gainst thee shall my heart rebel.
>
> Would that breast were bared before thee
>   Where thy head so oft hath lain,
> While that placid sleep came o'er thee
>   Which thou ne'er canst know again :
>
> Would that breast, by thee glanc'd over,
>   Every inmost thought could show !
> Then thou wouldst at last discover
>   'Twas not well to spurn it so.
>
> Though the world for this commend thee,
>   Though it smile upon the blow,
> Even its praises must offend thee
>   Founded on another's woe :
>
> Though my many faults defaced me,
>   Could no other arm be found
> Than the one which once embraced me
>   To inflict a cureless wound ?
>
> Yet, oh yet, thyself deceive not—
>   Love may sink by slow decay,
> But by sudden wrench, believe not,
>   Hearts can thus be torn away :

Still thine own its life retaineth—
Still must mine, tho' bleeding, beat ;
And the undying thought which paineth
Is—that we no more may meet.

There are words of deeper sorrow
Than the wail above the dead ;
Both shall live—but every morrow
Wake us from a widowed bed.

And when thou wouldst solace gather—
When our child's first accents flow—
Wilt thou teach her to say—' Father, '
Though his care she must forego ?

When her little hands shall press thee—
When her lip to thine is pressed—
Think of him whose prayer shall bless thee—
Think of him thy *love had* blessed !

Should her lineaments resemble
Those thou never more mayst see,
Then thy heart will softly tremble
With a pulse yet true to me.

All my faults perchance thou knowest—
All my madness—none can know ;
All my hopes—where'er thou goest—
Wither—yet with *thee* they go.

Every feeling hath been shaken ;
Pride—which not a world could bow—
Bows to thee—by thee forsaken,
Even my soul forsakes me now.

But 'tis done—all words are idle—
Words from me are vainer still ;
But the thoughts we cannot bridle
Force their way without the will.

Fare thee well ! thus disunited—
Torn from every nearer tie—
Seared in heart—and lone—and blighted—
More than this I scarce can die."

Tears, he said, fell fast over the paper as he wrote. Moore saw the MS. and confirms this : " It is blotted all over with the marks of tears ".[1] . . . He had not definitely meant to publish these verses. They were for the Initiated, as was also

[1] Mr. E. H. Coleridge (*Poems*, iii. 537) observes that there are no tear-marks on the first draft, which was sold at Sotheby's on April 11, 1885. He thinks that Moore must have seen a fair copy. Tears would be far more likely to fall on a fair copy, as most authors can testify. In the glow of composition there is no time for self-pity ; nor can the whole effect be perceived, amid the alterations and additions. With the fair copy, and the " emotion recollected in tranquillity ", and the clear view of the composition, tears, if they are germane to the matter, will for the first time fall.

A Sketch, written twelve days later ; but Murray was commissioned to print both " *for privute distribution* " ; and through somebody's indiscretion both found their way into the public press. They were published on April 14 by the *Champion*, a Tory paper ; and the other journals, " on the plea that the mischief was out, one after the other took up the cry ". The *Courier* at first refused to print *A Sketch*, but two days later found itself compelled, " in the interest of its readers ", to follow suit. The turmoil was almost as hysterical as over the Weeping lines in 1814 ; and Wordsworth, to whom the editor of the *Champion* sent an earliest copy, was more rampantly virtuous than even the Tory journalists—for the controversy was conducted all along on party lines. He said that the man was insane ; that the *Sketch* was the Billingsgate of Bedlam, and the *Farewell*, " wretched doggerel, disgusting in sentiment, and in execution contemptible ". Madame de Staël, on the other hand, said of the *Farewell* that if her husband had written such verses to her, she must at once have run to his arms and been reconciled : " *Je n'aurais pu m'y tenir un instant* ". But even his fervents differed. Moore thought the *Sketch* was justly condemned ; and of the *Farewell* he says, " I could not help regarding the sentiment that could, at such a moment, indulge in such verses " as suspicious, and the taste that prompted or sanctioned their publication appeared to him still more questionable. The publication was generally thought to be owing to the injudicious zeal of a friend. There is no proof of Byron's real intention, or feeling after the event, to confirm or contradict this theory.

The *Sketch* is best forgotten, except for the tribute to his wife's high soul that " panted for the truth it could not hear ".[1] The influence of Mrs. Clermont—subject of the lines—was by Byron exaggerated beyond all reason ; we may take her to have been the ordinary confidential woman, no worse and no better than the rest, of a hundred conjugal catastrophes. The *Stanzas to Augusta*—first of the three poems addressed to her— were also of this period, and were the last verses he wrote in England. They did not appear until after he had gone. It is to them that Caroline Lamb's letter of remonstrance—" You will draw ruin on your own head and hers if at this moment you show these "—must be thought to refer. He wrote to Murray on April 15 : " I wished to have seen you to scold you. Really you must not send anything of mine to Lady *C. L.* I have often sufficiently warned you on the topic—you do not know what mischief you

---

[1] He wrote in it of Lady Byron this also :

" Serenely purest of her sex that live ;
But wanting one sweet weakness—to forgive ".

do by this ". But her appeal had had its effect, for he adds : " Of the copies of things written by me—I wish more particularly the *last* not to be circulated, at present. (You know which I mean, those to A.) "

His letters to friends during the troubled period from February to April 1816 are interesting in their revelation of a variously harassed man, " contending with the slings and arrows of outrageous Fortune, some of which have struck at me from a quarter whence I did not indeed expect them ". Opinions of the two poems of this period—*The Siege of Corinth* and *Parisina*—were not all favourable. He was accused of carelessness and roughness ; and Moore seems to have accused him, as well, of overwriting himself. He wrote to Murray of these matters and added : " Excuse all this damned nonsense and egotism. The fact is, that I am rather trying to think on the subject of this note, than really thinking on it ". And in a postscript : " You need not be in any apprehension or grief on my account : were I to be beaten down by the world and its inheritors, I should have succumbed to many things—years ago. You must not mistake my *not* bullying for dejection ; nor imagine that because I feel, I am to faint ".

To Moore he wrote on February 29 : " I don't know that in the course of a hair-breadth existence I was ever, at home or abroad, in a situation so completely uprooting of present pleasure or rational hope for the future, as this same. I say this, because I think so, and feel it. But I shall not sink under it. . . . I have made up my mind. . . . I had a few weeks ago some things to say that would have made you laugh ; but they tell me now that I must not laugh, and so I have been very serious —and am . . . In all this business, I am the sorriest for Sir Ralph. He and I are equally punished . . . I shall be separated from my wife ; he will retain his ". Later he wrote again to Moore : " I do not believe—and I must say it, in the very dregs of all this bitter business—that there ever was a better, a kinder, or a more amiable and agreeable being than Lady B. I never had, nor can have, any reproach to make her while with me. Where there is blame, it belongs to myself, and, if I cannot redeem, I must bear it ". (It was in this letter that the passages about Sir Ralph and Lady Noel occurred which were part of the reason for Lady Byron's Remarks in 1830.) Referring to the new poems, he says : " I agree with you . . . that I have written too much. With those countries . . . all my really poetical feelings begin and end. Were I to try, I could make nothing of any other subject, and that I have apparently exhausted ".

17

Thus, with that dreariest judgment of having over-written himself, and a distraint for half a year's rent at 13 Piccadilly Terrace added to all the rest, he sailed on April 25,[1] having once more, and not yet for the last time, set England by the ears.

Hobhouse and Scrope Davies accompanied him as far as Dover. He had with him three sevants, including Fletcher, and a travelling physician. This was John William Polidori, M.D., a youth of twenty who had taken his doctor's degree at the early age—"I believe almost unexampled," says Mr. W. M. Rossetti [2]—of nineteen. He had been recommended to Byron by Sir Henry Halford, and proved a troublesome satellite : touchy, vain, and sentimental—a bad parody of his employer.

Thursday was spent at Dover, seeing the carriage packed up. This was a curiosity : a huge coach, copied from the celebrated one of Napoleon. Besides a bed, it contained a library, a plate-chest, and every apparatus for dining.[3] They visited Churchill's grave :

> " I stood beside the grave of him who blazed
> The Comet of a Season " . . .

The name of Charles Churchill now conveys nothing to the mind ; in 1816 his repute—he died in 1764—was still considerable. The visitors found his grave neglected, and Byron asked the sexton if he knew why so many came to see this undistinguished resting-place.

> " And thus he answered—' Well, I do not know
> Why frequent travellers turn to pilgrims so ;
> He died before my day of Sextonship,
> And I had not the digging of his grave ".[4]

The train of thought was inevitable at such a moment :

[1] Hobhouse went to stay with him on April 3 at Piccadilly Terrace, where he was then alone. Scrope Davies and Leigh Hunt dined there during his stay. Rogers came to take leave of him on April 22.

[2] *The Diary of Dr. John William Polidori*, 1816, relating to Byron, Shelley, etc. Edited and Elucidated by W. M. Rossetti. 1911. John William Polidori was the son of Gaetano Polidori, a Tuscan man of letters who, after being secretary to Alfieri, had settled in London as a teacher of Italian. He married a Miss Pierce. Mr. W. M. Rossetti was the nephew of Byron's Polidori. Polidori's portrait is in the National Portrait Gallery.

[3] Pryse Gordon, *Personal Memoirs*, ii. 328.

[4] The lines were not written until three months later. Byron openly said they were in imitation of Wordsworth.

" . . . . I did well
With a deep thought and with a softened eye
On that old sexton's natural homily,
In which there was obscurity and fame—
The Glory and the Nothing of a name ".

The early part of that evening—his last in England—was spent in laughing at a play written by Polidori, who had delivered it into their hands. The author's spirit was ruffled, and somebody was touched, took up the pages again, and read the better passages aloud with due solemnity. Polidori does not say which of the party this was ; but it is like Byron, and unlike either Hobhouse or Scrope Davies. . . . At nine o'clock Byron embarked for Ostend. He had walked to the boat through a lane of spectators ; indeed, the curiosity at Dover was so great that many ladies had dressed themselves as chambermaids, and stood about the passages and doorways at his inn. Hobhouse and Davies saw him off—the former recording the departure in his Journal with this moving comment : " God bless him for a gallant spirit and a kind one ! " His destination was Geneva. The journey thither was to be through Flanders and up the Rhine to the Lake of Geneva—or Leman, as he always preferred to call it.

While he rides the waves, let us review the work done by him since *Lara* in 1814.

After his engagement in the September of that year, he spent the autumn and winter at his chambers in the Albany ; and it was probably in the late autumn that he began the *Hebrew Melodies,* so called because they were set to Hebrew airs by Isaac Nathan. Byron's friend Douglas Kinnaird [1] brought them together, and Nathan became one of Byron's favourites. [2] Despite this liking, Moore's chaff on the subject of the Hebrew airs

---

[1] Douglas Kinnaird, a son of the seventh Baron Kinnaird, was a partner in the bank of Ransom and Morland, and a member of the committee of management of Drury Lane. In 1829 he resigned his trusteeship for Lady Byron's marriage-settlement, thus bringing about her estrangement from Mrs. Leigh.

[2] Isaac Nathan was " musical historian to George iv.", and instructor in music to the Princess Charlotte. He wrote in 1829 *Fugitive Pieces and Reminiscences of Lord Byron,* with notes of conversations and three letters from the poet. A section is also devoted to Lady Caroline Lamb, who had been very friendly with him. Nathan was with Byron " the best part of the three last days before he left London, to quit England " (*Fugitive Pieces*, p. 87). Byron gave him a fifty-pound note ; and Nathan, knowing that he was particularly fond of biscuits, sent him some Passover cakes to " accompany him on his pilgrimage ", and added a blessing. Byron wrote to thank him—one of the last letters from England.

(which he did not admire) caused Nathan to be cursed and " sunburned " during their arrangement. "Have I not told you it was all Kinnaird's doing, and my own exquisite facility of temper ? . . . All I have got by it was ' a speech ', and a receipt for stewed oysters ".

The title, *Hebrew Melodies*, is misleading, for the collection opens with " She walks in Beauty, like the night "—which is an English love-song pure and simple, and was written in June 1814.[1] Another as alien in spirit was " Oh! snatched away in Beauty's bloom "—of which Nathan, in submitting his music, asked in what manner the lines referred to any scriptural subject. " He appeared for a moment affected—at last replied, ' Every mind must make its own references ; there is scarcely one of us who could not imagine that the affliction belongs to himself ; to me it certainly belongs ' ". The first and third stanzas are of great beauty : the second is one of those lapses into utter artificiality which so confound our judgment of his verse. About " My Soul is Dark " Nathan tells a droll tale. Rumours of Byron's madness were already current, and at this time the gossip amused him. " ' I'll try how a *Madman* can write, Nathan ! ' and seizing the pen, he fixed his eyes in majestic wildness on vacancy ; then, like a flash of inspiration, without erasing a single word ", he wrote the verses named. They are not among his best—or worst. The real Hebrew songs are uninteresting, and were written mostly at Seaham. Our schooldays were brightened by " The Assyrian came down like the wolf on the fold " ; but it is wise to leave the pleasant memory in peace.

Many of the best-known lyrics were written between 1814 and 1816. " Farewell! if ever fondest prayer " belongs to the former year ; "When we two parted "—by many reckoned the finest short poem he ever wrote—to the latter. Both are believed by Lord Lovelace to have been addressed to Mrs. Leigh ; but it is worth remarking that in February 1816 James Wedderburn Webster brought an action against one Baldwin for a libel charging Lady Frances and the Duke of Wellington with adultery. Webster obtained £2000 ; and on February 16 there is an ironic letter from Byron to Murray : " I thank you for the account of Mr. and Lady F. W.'s triumph ; you see by it the exceeding advantage of unimpeachable virtue and uniform correctness of

---

[1] At a party with Wedderburn Webster, Byron saw for the first time his cousin, the beautiful Mrs. Wilmot, who was in mourning with spangles in her dress. When he and Webster returned to the Albany, Byron ordered Fletcher " to give him a tumbler of brandy, which he drank at once to Mrs. Wilmot's health ". Next day he wrote " She walks in Beauty ", admittedly inspired by her. She was the wife of Mr. Robert Wilmot, who was one of Lady Byron's advisers during the separation proceedings. See p. 229 (*note*).

conduct, etc. etc.". It is quite legitimate (with the knowledge
of his reference to the love-letters from him that Lady Frances
had) to conjecture that the lines of " When we two parted "
were inspired by this incident.

Three Napoleon poems mark this period. *Napoleon's Fare-
well* ; " Must thou go, my glorious Chief ? " and " We do not
curse thee, Waterloo ! " All were feigned to be from the French.[1]
Byron's feeling for Napoleon ranged from extreme sympathy to
angry disdain. All the world knows that he received the news of
Waterloo with the exclamation, " Well, I'm d——d sorry for
it ".[2] He covered him with scornful or pitying epithets ; but
liked to think that he and Napoleon signed with the same initials,
N. B. (after Byron's taking of the Noel name in 1822). He had
fought for a bust at Harrow against the boys, who designed to
smash it ; and the Journal of 1813–14 abounds in allusions to
the Napoleonic doings and undoings. Many a thrilling line in
his verse is similarly inspired ; indeed, Byron and Napoleon
might in itself be the subject of a book.

The two long works of this period are *The Siege of Corinth*
and *Parisina*. The *Siege* was begun in January 1815, and more
than half written before the summer. The MS. was sent to
Murray at the beginning of November. Byron at first intended
to publish it " quietly " in Murray's forthcoming Collected
Edition ; but Gifford, in whose hands the MS. had at once been
placed, expressed great delight, and Murray offered a thousand
guineas for it and *Parisina*—which, begun before the *Siege*, was
sent him at the beginning of December. (Lady Byron transcribed
both MSS.) Byron at first declined the money. " I cannot
consent to this separate publication. I do not like to risk any
fame (whether merited or not) which I have been favoured with,
upon compositions which I do not feel to be at all equal to my
own notions of what they should be ".[3] Rogers and Sir James
Mackintosh then suggested to him that he might accept the sum
and use it for another—William Godwin.[4] To this he yielded,

[1] The *Morning Chronicle* of March 15, 1816, said : " The original [of
" We do not curse thee "] is circulating in Paris, and . . . is ascribed to
the Muse of M. de Châteaubriand ". The verses were first published on
that day in that paper. (*Poems*, iii. 431.)

[2] George Ticknor, *Life*, i. 60. This attitude towards Napoleon was a
Whig convention at that period.

[3] In a P.S. he added : " I have inclosed your draft *torn*, for fear of
accidents by the way. I wish you would not throw temptation in mine.
It is not from a disdain of the universal idol, nor from a present superfluity
of his treasures, I assure you, that I refuse to worship him ; but what is
right is right, and must not yield to circumstances ".

[4] The soon-to-be father-in-law of Shelley, and a philosopher and
novelist of renown ; renowned also for his financial troubles and his

proposing to give £600 to Godwin, and divide the remainder between two other needy geniuses. Murray strongly protested, and Byron was very angry. " What was the difference ", he demanded, " between Godwin and Dallas ? " There was much difference, as Godwin's victims well knew ; but Byron's further point was that it was no business of any one's how he used the money once he had accepted it. " The things ", he concluded, " shall not be published at all. . . . You will oblige me by returning the Manuscripts by the bearer immediately ". The letters give us no further information ; but plainly the difference was arranged, for Byron, hard pressed by creditors, took the sum offered and used it to pay some of his debts. The two poems, in a single volume, *were* published separately on February 7, 1816.

The influence of Coleridge's *Christabel*—" that wild and singularly original and beautiful poem ", as Byron described it—upon *The Siege of Corinth* is unmistakable. Byron felt this so strongly that, while the *Siege* was unfinished, he sent Coleridge the passage where it is most marked ; and to the stanza itself appended a note.[1] *Christabel* was not published until May 1816. On the day in 1815 that Byron wrote he had for the first time seen the MS., " by the kindness of Mr. Coleridge himself ". Coleridge had begun the poem in 1797, and in 1801 a friend who had read the MS. repeated the lines to Walter Scott. He in his turn recited them to Byron in the June of 1815 (when they saw one another almost daily in Murray's parlour)—fourteen years after he had first heard them. They influenced *him* to the irregular versification of *The Lay of the Last Minstrel* ; and now their haunting music was echoed by Byron too. So strong was the resemblance that Byron himself proposed to Coleridge to cancel the passage, although he had written it before he had even heard *Christabel* recited by Walter Scott ! Mr. E. H. Coleridge thinks that as the MS. had a pretty general circulation in the literary world [2] long before the summer of 1815, Byron may have heard, without heeding, this or other passages quoted by privileged readers ; or may have caught its lilt at second-hand from the published works of Southey, or of Scott himself. Whatever the explanation, this is well-nigh the most extraordinary instance of literary coincidence that exists.

To catch the Coleridge lilt could leave no poetical intonation unglorified, and accordingly *The Siege of Corinth* is incomparable,

---

various ingenious methods of evading them. At the time of Shelley's ostracism, Godwin accepted from him a cheque for a large sum, but desired that it should not be made out in his name—their relative positions making *that* undesirable.

[1] *Poems*, iii. 471. Stanza xix, lines 521–532.
[2] Medwin, *Conversations*, 1824, p. 261.

among Byron's narrative poems, for music. But the reviewers
were disconcerted ; he was indicted for carelessness. That fault
was conspicuous in the historical and grammatical fields ; but as
Murray, defending him in a letter to Blackwood, observed,
" Many can write polished lines who will never reach the name
of poet ".[1] The opening lines (1 to 45) did not appear until the
edition of 1832. He had " forgotten them " ; and in his odd
uncertainty about his work, said when he did send them that
he was not sure that they had not better be left out now. Murray
or " his Synod " was to determine. It sheds a strange light on
both that they should have determined as they did ; for the
lines are among the most delightful that he ever wrote. To
read the poem without them is like beginning a task with no
sort of exhilaration ; add these lines—and we are refreshed as
by a draught of bright water.

> " In the year since Jesus died for men,
> Eighteen hundred years and ten,[2]
> We were a gallant company,
> Riding o'er land, and sailing o'er sea.
> Oh ! but we went merrily !
> We forded the river, and clomb the high hill.
> Never our steeds for a day stood still ;
> Whether we lay in the cave or the shed,
> Our sleep fell soft on the hardest bed ;
> Whether we couch'd in our rough capote,
> On the rougher plank of our gliding boat,
> Or stretch'd on the beach, or our saddles spread
> As a pillow beneath the resting head,
> Fresh we woke upon the morrow :
>   All our thoughts and words had scope,
>   We had health, and we had hope,
> Toil and travel, but no sorrow.
> We were of all tongues and creeds ;—
> Some were those who counted beads,
> Some of mosque, and some of church,
> And some, or I mis-say, of neither ;
> Yet through the wide world might ye search
>   Nor find a motlier crew nor blither.
>
> But some are dead, and some are gone,
> And some are scatter'd and alone,
> And some are rebels on the hills
>   That look along Epirus' valleys
>   Where Freedom still at moments rallies,
> And pays in blood Oppression's ills ;

---

[1] The *Siege* was dedicated to Hobhouse, and there is an amusing entry
in his Journal : " I should have liked it better if he had not dedicated
Parisina to Scrope Davies. I told him this ".

[2] The date is miscalculated from the death instead of the birth of
Christ.—E. H. COLERIDGE.

> And some are in a far countree,
> And some all restlessly at home ;
> But never more, oh ! never, we
> Shall meet to revel and to roam.
> But those hardy days flew cheerily !
> And when they now fall drearily,
> My thoughts, like swallows, skim the main,
> And bear my spirit back again
> Over the earth, and through the air,
> A wild bird, and a wanderer.
> 'Tis this that ever wakes my strain,
> And oft, too oft, implores again
> The few who may endure my lay,
> To follow me so far away.
>
> Stranger—wilt thou follow now,
> And sit with me on Acro-Corinth's brow ? "

Gifford wrote some critical notes on pages torn from the first edition of the poem, probably with a view to an emended version in the Collected Works ; but at no time were his suggestions incorporated in the text. " What vulgarism is this ! " he exclaims at the use of *downs* as a transitive verb ; on the phrase *human hecatombs* he comments, " There can be no such thing ; but the whole of this is poor, and spun out ". " Despicable stuff ! " he cries of lines 1030–56 ; draws a pen (his one error) through the fine description of the dogs devouring the dead ; and in the high altar passage in stanza xxxii. erases the line :

> " Oh, but it made a glorious show ! "

and appends three marks of exclamation.

Parisina deals with the love of a bastard son for his father's wife. This brought down the critics : " too disgusting to be rendered pleasing by any display of genius ". Byron's mind was now fixed on forbidden relations,[1] but he " was aware that the delicacy or fastidiousness of the reader might deem such subjects unfit for the purposes of poetry ". " The Greek dramatists ", he continued, " and some of the best of our old English writers, were of a different opinion ; as Alfieri and Schiller have also been more recently on the Continent ". Gifford was enthusiastic over *Parisina*, and Mr. E. H. Coleridge speaks highly of it. I, on reading it again for the first time since my schooldays, was much disappointed. It seems to me inferior to any of the former narratives—more equal, it is true (or more

---

[1] It is worth pointing out, nevertheless, that the lines, " It is not to list to the waterfall " (15–18) were written before *Lara*, and that the name Francesca, rejected from *The Corsair*, was originally used here also. These lines were set to music by Nathan.

equable) but wholly lacking the authentic " Byronism ", without which Byron sinks to the level of Scott in poetry.

The two poems passed (for works of his) comparatively unnoticed. They appeared at a time when public curiosity was more delightfully engaged with his private affairs, and were soon forgotten in the turmoil over *Fare Thee Well* and *A Sketch*. When this had died away, the new canto of *Childe Harold* and *The Prisoner of Chillon*, " with its brilliant and noticeable companion poems ", arrived to eclipse decisively *The Siege of Corinth* and *Parisina*.

CHAPTER XVIII

THE OUTLAW—1816

The Childe goes forth again—The Low Countries—Pictures—Water-
loo—Arrival at Geneva—Claire Clairmont—Friendship with Shelley—The
Rousseau, Gibbon, and Voltaire Regions—*Frankenstein*—Departure of
the Shelley Party—Visitors from England—The Bernese Alps—Southey—
The Vision of Judgment—Dismissal of Polidori—Madame de Staël—
Attempt at Reconciliation with Lady Byron—Failure

" ONCE more upon the waters ! yet once more !
     And the waves bound beneath me as a steed
     That knows his rider. Welcome to their roar !
Swift be their guidance, wheresoe'er it lead !
Though the strained mast should quiver as a reed,
And the rent canvas fluttering strew the gale,
Still must I on ; for I am as a weed,
Flung from the rock, on Ocean's foam, to sail
Where'er the surge may sweep, the tempest's breath prevail.

In my youth's summer I did sing of One
The wandering outlaw of his own dark mind ;
Again I seize the theme, then but begun,
And bear it with me, as the rushing wind
Bears the cloud onwards " . . .

So, frankly at last identified with his creator, did the Childe go
forth again,

" With nought of Hope left—but with less of gloom " ; [1]

while, in a travesty of the old dualism, it was neither Harold
nor Byron, but Polidori, who watched the stars during the
sixteen-houred passage " with the wind completely in our teeth ".

From Ostend they passed through Bruges, Ghent, Antwerp,
and Mechlin to Brussels. The Low Countries made little im-
pression : [2] " not a rise from Ostend to Antwerp—a molehill

---

[1] Compare with this : " It is odd, but agitation or contest of any kind
gives a rebound to my spirit and sets me up for the time " (Letter to Moore,
March 8, 1816) ; and the " rage and resistance and redress " in 1809, which
produced *English Bards and Scotch Reviewers.*

[2] Polidori has an apt phrase or two for their ennui : " The country is
tiresomely beautiful.   Fine avenues which make us yawn with admiration
. . . sometimes terminated by a church or a house—the church very ugly,
and both very tiresome, as they always prove much farther off than is at
first expected " (*The Diary of Polidori*, pp. 44–45).

would make the inhabitants think that the Alps had come on a visit ". Churches and pictures he had stared at till his brains were like a guide-book (as he told Augusta in a letter of May 1, from Brussels) and he was far from enthusiastic. The pictures in especial left him cold—or rather, hot. " The Flemish School, such as I saw it in Flanders, I utterly detested, despised, and abhorred ". And a year later, to Murray from Venice : " I never was so disgusted in my life as with Rubens and his eternal wives and infernal glare of colour [1]. . . . You must recollect however that I know nothing of painting and that I detest it ". This was one of his favourite attitudes, and was, like most of them, entirely sincere. Byron was too violent and too self-absorbed to care for the arts. Only in his rare moods of tranquillity could he suffer these abiding methods of expression. We shall see that in Florence and Rome, where he was almost really at rest, he for the first and last time wrote eagerly and passionately in praise of painting and sculpture. In the life which to him was normal—the hours of great distresses or greater dejections—his imagination, fiercely self-disdainful, fastened upon the men of action as the only beings worth consideration. The impulse towards poetry (in dark hours always at its most urgent) added what for him was a kind of infamy to the other tortures. Hamlet, unpacking his heart with words which by their vehemence lash the fury in him for his impotence in other things, is like Byron when the goad first pricked him. Once submissive to it, he found relief, and only so could find it ; but that was the core of the humiliation. " [Poetry] is the lava of the imagination, whose eruption prevents an earthquake. . . . I prefer the talents of action ". So he wrote of his own art. " The lava of the imagination . . . is precisely ", says Mr. Arthur Symons, " what poetry was to Byron ; and it is characteristic of him that he cannot look beyond himself even for the sake of a generalisation ".

In this mood of rage and resistance and redress he visited the field of Waterloo, having come out of his way to the Rhine on purpose. [2]

" Stop !—for thy tread is on an Empire's dust ! "

But his deep intellectual sincerity quickly triumphed over the rhapsodical vein, and he became one of the obstinate questioners of the Day.

---

[1] Polidori's description of one passage in Rubens's *Crucifixion* at Antwerp is worth quoting : " A woman rising from the dead—surely a woman large as Guy Warwick's giant's wife . . . most hellish egregious breasts, which a child refuses with horror in its face " (p. 52).

[2] It was not yet, I may remind my readers, a year since the battle.

" Oh, bloody and most bootless Waterloo !

.   .   .   .   .   .

Won half by blunder, half by treachery ".[1]

That terse summary was not attained till 1822. Wearied in 1816 by the effort to dupe himself into flamboyance, Byron's imagination fastened on the hours before the battle, apt theme for the poet " for whom, unlike all other poets, society exists as well as human nature ".

Polidori's Diary tells us that they rode over the field, " myself silent, my companion singing a Turkish riding-tune " ; and in a letter to Murray, written from Ouchy in June, Byron says : " I shall be glad to hear you have received certain helms and swords, sent from Waterloo, which I rode over with pain and pleasure ". A further entry in Polidori's Diary on that day, states : " My friend has written twenty-six stanzas—some on Waterloo ". This, if it refers to the first twenty-six stanzas of the third canto, would leave Byron on that evening with one of his most famous lines in his brain :

" Or whispering with white lips—' The foe !   They come ! they come ! ' " [2]

From Brussels they reached the Rhine through Liège and Aix-la-Chapelle. On May 11, leaving Bonn, they passed the Drachenfels ; and that day were written, on the Rhine bank, the lines addressed to Augusta which were among those she wished in the Red Sea.

" The castled crag of Drachenfels
Frowns o'er the wide and winding Rhine " . . .

He sent her with them (for they were at once sent to her) a bunch of lilies which a girl on the road had offered him. At Morat, in Switzerland, he brought away from the pyramid of bones on the battle-field " as much as may have made a quarter of a hero " ; [3] and thus, and in such moods, he came to Sécheron, a suburb of Geneva. They arrived on May 25—just a month after leaving England ; and alighted at Dejean's Hôtel d'Angleterre, where Byron put his age down as 100. There they found, installed ten days before, Shelley and his wife-to-be, Mary Godwin, with their travelling companion and relative, variously called Jane, Claire, and Clara Clairmont. It was Byron's first meeting with his brother-poet ; it may have been his first meeting with Mary

---

[1] *The Age of Bronze*, v. 223. *Poems*, v. 535.

[2] He wrote on May 5 or 6, in Mrs. Pryse Gordon's album, stanzas 17 and 18 (Pryse Lockhart Gordon, *Personal Memoirs*, ii. 325).

[3] Mr. Murray has still in his possession the parcel of bones which Byron sent home.

Godwin ; it was not his first meeting with Miss Clairmont, for she was already the expectant mother of his child.

Jane Clairmont was William Godwin's step-daughter through his second wife, Mrs. Clairmont, of whom Charles Lamb reported that she was a truly disgusting woman, and wore green spectacles. Jane (for in her schooldays she was contented with the homely-name) was about the same age as her sister-by-affinity, Mary Godwin, whose birth had cost the life of her mother, Mary Wollstonecraft, Godwin's first wife. Mary Wollstonecraft had left two daughters, this Mary, and the offspring of an earlier illicit union, Fanny Imlay. The three girls, thus brought up together, were all to have unusual destinies. Fanny, melancholy and sentimental, was later in 1816 to put an end to her existence ; Mary was living with Shelley in the bonds of love, for Harriet Westbrook was still alive ; and Miss Clairmont was at present the mistress, quickly to be discarded, of Byron.

It was in July 1814 that Shelley had eloped with Mary Godwin, a girl of sixteen. Harriet's day as queen of his heart was over ; and, in his view, the fact that she was his legal wife must exercise no restraining influence on his love for another woman. This is not the place to discuss Shelley's relations with Harriet and Mary ; I am glad to restrict myself to recording facts. . . . When in 1814 Mary and he fled to the Continent, they took Jane Clairmont with them—on the pretext, somewhat ambiguously reported by her, of her better acquaintance with French. She was nothing loth to go, for in the girlish trio at Skinner Street [1] she represented the adventurous type. Fanny was the Senti-mentalist ; Mary, the Practical-Romantic ; Jane, the Dare-devil and Dreamer. Tall, with a lovely lissom figure, with masses of rich black hair, dark eyes that flashed or brooded, a fine sensitive mouth, and a singing voice which her master, Corri, likened to a string of pearls, she was one of those women who " if not pretty, are worse " ; and her character and temperament were expressed in her brilliant and eager externality. She was all for love and liberty and emancipation ; disdainful of those who bowed down in the Temple of Rimmon, disdainful above all of marriage— " I can never resist the temptation of throwing a pebble at it as I pass by " ; disdainful too of masculine usurpation, yet with moments of stormy and ecstatic submission to it. The very girl, in short, to fall in love with the ardent visitor to Skinner Street, who for his part had fallen in love with quiet, piquante Mary. The affection of Claire (I shall henceforth call her by the name which most belongs to her) for Shelley has been, like most things Shelleyan, the subject of keen debate. She, in her old

[1] The abode of William Godwin.

age,[1] declared that he was the only man she had ever loved,
and that she had loved him with all her heart and soul ; but
of her statements it is usually wise to believe but half. Of this
one, we may believe that she loved Shelley's memory with all
her heart and soul, and saw clearly that he was the man most
worthy of a woman's affection whom she had ever known ; but
it is difficult to believe that she loved him in the sense which
she attached to the word, during the time at any rate of her
relation with Byron. For it was not Byron who wooed, but
she : she offered him all herself before she ever exchanged a
single word with him.

When Shelley and Mary returned from Switzerland in the
September of 1814, Claire returned with them, but not to Godwin's
house. Her mother refused to receive her there, for she had
been greatly angered by Claire's refusal to come back when Mrs.
Godwin followed the lovers to Calais (in July) and demanded at
least her own daughter's restoration. The triple ménage, for
Claire stayed with the Shelleys, proved the failure that it always
proves. Mary was jealous, Shelley angelically tactless, Claire
difficult and capricious. She would spend days without opening
her lips ; she was hypochondriacal, " filled with chimerical
terrors "—one day gentle and cheerful, the next a detestable
creature without feeling of any sort. Mary, now *enceinte*, was
difficult too ; the situation soon became unbearable. But Mrs. God-
win, though in November she consented to receive her daughter
for a night or two, would not again undertake her as an inmate ;
and the question of what to do with Claire became acute. At
last a solution was found. Claire was sent to Lynmouth in
Devonshire, to live with a Mrs. Bicknall, who was Mrs. Godwin's
friend. On the day of her departure, in Mary's Diary we find
the entry :

" Clara goes. . . . I begin a new journal with our regenera-
tion ". And the outcast wrote immediately to Fanny Imlay :
" After so much discontent, such violent scenes, such a turmoil
of passion and hatred, you will hardly believe how enraptured
I am with this dear little quiet spot. . . . It is in solitude that
the powers concentre round the soul, and teach it the calm
determined path of virtue and wisdom."

" But Quiet to quick bosoms is a Hell ".

Though Byron's line was not yet written, Claire might have
quoted it by intelligent anticipation. At what date she left
Lynmouth and returned to Shelley's abode is uncertain ; it is

---

[1] William Graham, *Last Links with Byron, Shelley, Keats.* She lived
to be eighty, and died unmarried.

uncertain too when her intrigue with Byron began. Several letters from her to him are printed [1] in Mr. Prothero's edition of the *Letters and Journals*, vol. iii, Appendix vii. The first is in the feigned name of E. Trefusis ; he is asked to answer to an address in Marylebone. (The Shelleys were at this time living in a furnished house at Bishopsgate, the eastern entrance of Windsor Park.) The letter is throughout in the third person.

" An utter stranger takes the liberty of addressing you. . . . It may seem a strange assertion, but it is not the less true that I place my happiness in your hands. . . . If a woman, whose reputation has yet remained unstained, if without either guardian or husband to control her, she should throw herself upon your mercy, if with a beating heart she should confess the love she had borne you many years, if she should secure to you secrecy and safety, if she should return your kindness with fond affection and unbounded devotion, could you betray her, or would you be silent as the grave ? "

The probability is that Byron did not answer this letter ; he had had many of its kind before. Her second attempt was made under the initials G. C. B.

" Lord Byron is requested to state whether seven o'clock this Evening will be convenient to him to receive a lady to communicate with him on business of peculiar importance. She desires to be admitted alone and with the utmost privacy ". He answered this, to say that he was unaware of any importance which could be attached by any person to an interview with him ; but he would be at home at the hour mentioned. Mr. Prothero seems to think that the appointment was not kept, for he says, in referring to a later letter from Claire, that Byron and she were still strangers ; but either there is a lacuna in the Claire letters as printed by him, or else they must have met before her next communication (which is signed with her real name), for she says, " Remember that I have confided to you the most important secrets. I have withheld nothing ".

This was the period of Byron's connection with the management of Drury Lane Theatre. [2] Claire in this letter says that she is desirous of entering upon a stage-career, and asks him to tell her what are the first steps to be taken. The result of her appeal was a reference from Byron to Douglas Kinnaird (also on the Sub-Committee) of which she made no use, alleging as her reason that she was " considering ", for she might not appear on the stage under her own name, and she dared not apply to Mr. Kinnaird before she received Byron's approbation

---

[1] The originals are among the Murray MSS.
[2] He was on the Sub-Committee of Management. Samuel Whitbread was the manager.

to this change. It is not much wonder that Byron began to be suspicious of so vacillating an applicant, and the more, because in this letter a new ambition is disclosed. " I have written half of a novel or tale . . . I am now wavering between the adoption of a literary life or a theatrical career. Perhaps for neither am I fitted ". By this time Byron knew of her connection with Shelley. She speaks much of him and his works, and says that he is now turned three-and-twenty, which sets the possible date of this letter in August.[1] " One thing I am afraid of ", she proceeds ; "—you rather dislike me. . . . I am often quite surprised at your gentleness and kindness ". Nothing could be clearer than Byron's reluctance, from beginning to end of this correspondence. The two next letters from Claire complain of no answer. But he answered before Number Eight, for in it she says, " You bid me write short to you, and I have much to say ". She was indeed distressingly prolix ; but in this eighth, though still far from laconic, she is unmistakably direct. " I do not expect you to love me ; I am not worthy of your love . . . yet much to my surprise, more to my happiness, you betrayed passions I had believed no longer alive in your bosom. . . . I do assure you, your future will shall be mine, and everything you say or do, I shall not question. Have you then any objection to the following plan ? On Thursday evening we may go out of town together by some stage or mail about the distance of ten or twelve miles ? There we shall be free and unknown ; we can return early the following morning. . . . Will you admit me for two moments to settle with you *where* ? Indeed I will not stay an instant after you tell me to go ".

In the last of the series, she alludes to his departure for Italy ; she is to go " God knows where ". We have seen that she went to Geneva, where he too went ; but assuredly with no desire to meet her, whether they arranged to meet or not. This concluding letter makes it clear that he was already tired of an intrigue to which he had never more than half-heartedly assented. " Do not delay our meeting after Saturday—I cannot endure the suspense. . . . When I am alone and left to my own thoughts, I become the most miserable and nervous of beings. . . . You call me ' a little fiend '. I thought it so criminal to doubt anything you said that I was much impressed

---

[1] " Shelley had not turned three and twenty till August 4, 1815 ", says Mr. Prothero, assigning the date ; but Claire's accuracy is at no time remarkable, and the phrase is always a tolerably vague one. I feel sure from the internal evidence of this letter that Claire and Byron were *not* strangers at the time it was written. She uses the word stranger, but I read it in the sense that she had no claim of old friendship, or even old acquaintance, to justify her appeal to him.

by this appellation "—and she adds a certificate of character from Shelley and thinks it " an honourable testimony of that part of my character you have accused, that the man whom I have loved, and for whom I have suffered much, should report this of me ". Love was a word much used in the Shelley circle. We may easily assign too much significance to its appearance here ; for whether Claire loved Shelley un-platonically or not, it is quite certain that only platonically did he love her. . . . A postscript requests that her letters be brought to be " committed to the flames ". They were not (or at any rate not all) brought, as we have now learned.

The Shelleys had in any case intended to leave England at this time. Shelley's health was far from good—or he thought so, for he was something of a hypochondriac ; his money affairs were discomfortable ; and his position as the " husband " of both a wedded and unwedded wife made social intercourse for Mary precarious. After the " turmoil of passion and hatred " at Bishopsgate, it seems odd that Mary should have consented to Claire's accompanying them on the Continent ; but too much may be made, and has been made, of this inconsistency. At Bishopsgate, Mary was in a state of health which places its victim at the mercy of unreasoned angers and apprehensions ; and she, the sanest of women at other times, probably recognised this as soon as she was restored to her normal condition. There were to be quarrels between them in the future. Claire was a creature with whom nor man nor woman could live tranquilly ; but there was not again any such "turmoil ", though the Shelleys had to endure obloquy and the loss of friendship for her sake, after she became the mother of Byron's child.

It was not until May 3, 1816, that the caravan—comprising Mary, Shelley, Claire, and Mary's " little Blue-eyes ", William [1] —left Dover for the Continent ; but going by the Paris route, they reached Geneva at least ten days before Byron. " On Saturday, May 25 ", says Professor Dowden, " . . . there was bustle at Dejean's, and Clara's heart must have moved quick, for Byron had entered the hotel ".

Byron's account of the re-union is, as usual, stripped of all ornament. It occurs in a letter to Augusta of September 8, after the Shelley party had returned to England. " Now don't scold ; but what could I do ? A foolish girl, in spite of all I could say or do, would come after me, or rather went before —for I found her here—and I have had all the plague possible to persuade her to go back again ; but at last she went. Now, dearest, I do most truly tell thee that I could not help this,

---

[1] Mary's second child (the first died after a few days of life), born during the Bishopsgate sojourn.

18

that I did all I could to prevent it, and have at last put an end to it. I was not in love, nor have any love left for any ; but I could not exactly play the Stoic with a woman who had scrambled eight hundred miles to unphilosophise me. . . . And, now you know all that I know of that matter, and it's over '.[1] We have seen that this crude version is substantially true ; yet Claire must have charmed him for her hour, for I think there can be little doubt that one of his lyrics was inspired by the same voice which drew a lovelier one from Shelley—that *To Constantia singing*. Byron's was :

> " There be none of Beauty's daughters
> 	With a magic like thee ;
> And like music on the waters
> 	Is thy sweet voice to me :
> When, as if its sound were causing
> The charméd ocean's pausing,
> The waves lie still and gleaming,
> And the lulled winds seem dreaming :
> And the midnight moon is weaving
> 	Her bright chain o'er the deep ;
> Whose breast is gently heaving
> 	As an infant's asleep :
> So the spirit bows before thee
> To listen and adore thee ;
> With a soft but full emotion,
> Like the swell of Summer's ocean ".

The verses are dated March 28, 1816.

At the end of May the Shelleys moved to the Maison Montalègre, on the southern shore of the Lake (Sécheron is on the northern shore) ; and Byron followed them on June 10, taking the Villa Diodati, within a few minutes' walk. Shelley had long desired to make acquaintance with Byron. In 1813 he had sent him one of the privately printed copies of *Queen Mab*, together with an explanatory letter. The letter had miscarried, but Byron had admired *Queen Mab* ; and now that they were both exiles, and that his relation with a member of Shelley's party [2] drew them naturally together, intercourse became a part of the daily routine. It is singular that no mention of Shelley occurs in Byron's letters until the eve of the former's return to England at the end of August ; but Shelley wrote to Peacock [3] in July : " Lord Byron is an exceedingly interesting

---

[1] First published in Sharpe's *London Magazine*, N.S. vol. xxxiv. p. 236.
[2] It remains uncertain whether the Shelleys knew anything of Claire's relation with Byron, before leaving England.
[3] Thomas Love Peacock, poet and novelist, was a close friend of Shelley. He was long connected with the East India Company ; in 1816, became Chief-Examiner of Indian correspondence—a post in which he was

person ; and as such, is it not to be regretted that he is a slave
to the vilest and most vulgar prejudices, and as mad as the
winds ? " This referred to Byron's private character only. As
a poet he excited the unmeasured enthusiasm to which Shelley
was so prone. This gift for admiration was too facile to be
greatly valuable. Over minds of quite mediocre quality, Shelley
could rave as he had raved over that of the Miss Hitchener who,
later on, became The Brown Demon—" an artful, superficial,
ugly, hermaphroditical beast of a woman . . . of desperate
views and dreadful passions, but of cool and undeviating
revenge ".[1] It was not surprising, therefore, that the outlawed
and obscure Shelley should bow his head to the outlawed and
dazzling Byron. The contrast as well as the likeness between
their careers must have struck the younger man ; but it struck
him to humility, not envy, in the Genevan days. Later he was
to say in bitter mood : " I do not write. I have lived too long
near Lord Byron, and the sun has extinguished the glow-worm " ;
but that was in the period of estrangement produced by many
disillusions. Despite this early humility, there is no doubt that
Shelley, during the Swiss sojourn, strongly influenced Byron ;
as indeed he influenced, unconsciously, every one with whom
he came in contact. I say unconsciously, because when he con-
sciously sought to sway others, he nearly always failed to do
so. It was not his preaching, but his practising, that prevailed.
When he preached, it was volubly and tediously and in a high
screeching voice ; when he practised, it was with a sweet eager-
ness, a radiant spontaneity, that captured the heart and imagina-
tion of any one who possessed either. " I always go on till I
am stopped, and I never am stopped ". The will in the frail
bending body was stupendous. He shot like an arrow from the
bow of impulse—as impossible to hinder, once launched ; and
often, alas ! as mistakenly launched as any bungler's shaft.
Two men more different than Shelley and Byron can hardly be
imagined. Shelley all such impulse and such activity, Byron
with hardly any impulse at all in daily life, the well-nigh perfect
type of drifter ; Shelley with his eyes fixed on the peaks of heaven,
Byron intent on the world he could see ; Shelley loving humanity
yet bearing its decree of banishment with tranquillity, Byron
scornful of all yet goaded by *their* scorn to a too-conscious defiance
—here are the very images of the Angel and the Man. And
in the far greater personal spell of Byron, we find as it were the

succeeded, on his retirement in 1856, by John Stuart Mill. His novels are
delightful—the best-known being *Crotchet Castle* and *Gryll Grange*. He
wrote some very interesting memoirs of Shelley in *Fraser's Magazine*.
    [1] " She was, of course ", says the late Mr. Clutton-Brock in his admir-
able *Shelley : the Man and the Poet,* " nothing of the sort " (p. 68).

secret of fascination; for Shelley, rare and attaching as he was, was yet too single-minded to display that sensitive quiver between extremes which, in human beings, we watch with the same eager delight as in the compass.

The poets, both inordinately fond of boating, made the tour of the Lake together, starting on June 23 and visiting, with the emotions of the age, the Rousseau region. Mrs. Byron, long ago, " *would* have it " that her son was like Rousseau ; and he was at pains in one of his future diaries to prove the comparison an unjust one, basing his argument, very characteristically, altogether on externalities. If he had looked within, he could have found a more essential point of difference ; for not of Rousseau could it ever be said, as Swinburne said of Byron, that the power of his personality lay in " the splendid and imperishable excellence which covers all his offences and outweighs all his defects : the excellence of sincerity and strength ".[1] Lausanne and Ferney, in their turn, called up the forms of Gibbon and Voltaire ; and in the Gibbon stanza of *Childe Harold* occur two of the most famous lines of Byron :

> " Sapping a solemn creed with solemn sneer ;
> The lord of irony—that master-spell ".

They visited his house, and found the garden neglected; but Byron gathered a sprig of Gibbon's acacia and some rose-leaves, and sent them to Murray in a letter dated June 27, from Ouchy near Lausanne. Three days before they had been nearly wrecked by a squall off Meillerie ; and Shelley, describing it to Peacock, said : " My feelings would have been less ·painful had I been alone ; but I knew that my companion would have attempted to save me, and I was overcome with humiliation when I thought that his life might have been risked to preserve mine ". Moore tells us that Shelley seated himself on a locker, and " grasping the rings at each end firmly in his hands, declared his determination to go down in that position without a struggle ". The wind had been high enough to tear up some huge trees from the Alps above them.

They visited also the Prison of Chillon—scene of the poem, begun and finished in two days at Ouchy, where they were detained by the weather. On July 1 they were back at Montalègre and Diodati. The routine began again : evening after

---

[1] Estève, in his *Byron et le Romantisme français*, draws an elaborate parallel between Byron and Rousseau ; and Mr. Ernest Coleridge, in the Notes to Canto III. of *Childe Harold*, says that " there was a resemblance, and consequently an affinity " between them, quoting Coleridge, in *The Friend*, as his authority. " The Teacher " (said Coleridge of Rousseau) " of stoic pride in his principles, yet the victim of morbid vanity in his feelings and conduct ".

evening they would embark upon the lake with Mary, Claire, and Polidori. Byron, one evening, sang them an Albanian song. " Now, be sentimental and give me all your attention ". " It was a strange wild howl that he gave forth ", says Mary ; " . . . laughing the while at our disappointment, who had expected a wild Eastern melody ". After this experience the Shelleys, much addicted to *petits noms*, gave him that of Albé, by which Mary usually mentions him in her diary and letters. On other evenings (for it was a very wet inclement summer) they would talk until, as Polidori says, " the ladies' brains whizzed with giddiness ". Not only the ladies'. For it was at Geneva, before the tour round the lake, that the strange horror suddenly seized on Shelley which was the origin of the ghost-stories scheme, whence issued Mary Shelley's renowned *Frankenstein*. On a night in June the Shelleys were with Byron at Diodati ; they had been reading and talking of ghosts and spectres, and Byron repeated the lines from *Christabel* describing the witch Geraldine's bosom. " When silence ensued ", says Polidori, in his diary for June 18, " Shelley, suddenly shrieking and putting his hands to his head, ran out of the room with a candle. Threw water in his face and after gave him ether. He was looking at Mrs. Shelley, and suddenly thought of a woman he had heard of who had eyes instead of nipples, which, taking hold of his mind, horrified him ". When the spasm passed and calm was restored : " We will each write a ghost-story ", said Byron, and with a universal promise to try, they separated for the night. They all did try—the result being Byron's fragment of *The Vampire* ; [1] Polidori's complete story on the same foundation ; and Mary's *Frankenstein*. Shelley and Claire began stories, but never did anything with them. On more tranquil evenings, Shelley and Byron would " maintain the nightly debate " ; and Mary, soon after her husband's death, made the following entry in her diary : " I do not think that any person's voice has the same power of awakening melancholy in me as Albé's. . . . When Albé ceases to speak, I expect to hear *that other voice*. . . . Since my incapacity and timidity always prevented my mingling in the nightly conversations at Diodati, they were, as it were, entirely tête-à-tête between my Shelley and Albé ; and thus, as I have said, when Albé speaks and Shelley does not answer, it is as thunder without rain—the form of the sun without heat or light —as any familiar object might be, shorn of its best attributes ; and

---

[1] Byron sent his fragment to Murray, on the appearance of Polidori's complete story in 1819, and it is inserted in his works. Polidori was not to blame for the false attribution of his story to Byron ; he wrote to the editor of *The New Monthly Magazine* explaining the circumstances. (*Diary of Polidori*. Introduction, pp. 11–23.)

I listen with an unspeakable melancholy that yet is not all pain ".

Claire, then, was silent like Mary. What were her relations with Byron at this time ? There is said to be in existence a letter from her declaring that they were never alone together at Geneva. She transcribed the third canto of *Childe Harold*, *The Prisoner of Chillon*, and the *Monody on the Death of Sheridan*, which were among the poems written there. It is scarcely likely that they were not alone together while this work was in progress. Moreover, there were urgent matters to be arranged between them which could not—in the earliest stages, at any rate—be discussed in the presence of a third person. " Before we parted at Geneva ", Claire wrote afterwards in a notebook, " he talked over with me our situation ; he proposed to put the child when born in Mrs. Leigh's care ". Claire objected. " He yielded and . . . promised, faithfully promised, never to give it until seven years of age into a stranger's care ; I was to be called the child's aunt, and in that character I could see it and watch over it without injury to any one's reputation ". On August 2 there is an entry in Mary's diary : " Shelley and Claire go up to Diodati ; I do not, for Lord Byron did not seem to wish it ". That is almost conclusive evidence that Shelley was then acquainted with the state of affairs : the interview must have been one for discussion and confirmation of the arrangements already made with Claire. . . . Having come to know Byron better, it was doubtless with a heavy heart that she left Geneva with the Shelleys on August 29, for England.

Byron had had visitors from home. In August, Matthew Gregory Lewis [1]—better known as Monk Lewis, from his most famous work—arrived for a stay at Diodati. They had met much in London, and Byron had liked him in an impatient, condescending fashion. " Lewis was a good man—a clever man, but a bore—a damned bore, one may say. My only revenge or consolation used to be setting him by the ears with some vivacious person who hated bores especially—Mme de Staël or Hobhouse, for example. But I liked Lewis ". At Diodati they quarrelled about Sheridan, who had died in July ; and on whom Byron, at Douglas Kinnaird's request, had written on July 17 the Monody of which he said to Lady Blessington in after years that every word came direct from his heart. Lewis, in return for his bread and salt (as Byron said) translated Goethe's

---

[1] Lewis published *Ambrosio, or the Monk*, in 1795. It at once secured his fame, and thenceforth he devoted himself to a literary career. The book was severely criticised on the score of immorality. Lewis wrote also many songs and ballads which became very popular, and two successful plays. He died in 1818.

Faust to him by word of mouth; and Mr. Ernest Coleridge thinks that there can be no doubt whatever that the primary conception of the character of Manfred is to be traced to the ' Monk's ' oral rendering. Byron was laconic on the point. " The devil may take both the Faustuses " (for Marlowe's was also mentioned), " German and English—I have taken neither ". . . . After Lewis came Hobhouse and Scrope Davies. Byron went with them and Polidori to Chamounix.

The Shelley party had made the same tour in July, and it was then that Shelley made the famous " atheist " entry in the hotel-album at Montanvert. Hobhouse said that Byron, showing him the words, observed : " Do you not think I shall do Shelley a service by scratching this out ? "—and forthwith defaced the entry; but evidently not with sufficient care, for in 1817 a second poet saw it at Montanvert. This was Robert Southey, Poet Laureate ; and Southey thought it worth while to " transcribe the names, the avowal, and the comment " (he says nothing of any defacement), and to speak of the circumstance on his return. Byron heard of this, and heard too that Southey had said that he (Byron) and Shelley were, during the Genevan sojourn, living in " promiscuous intercourse with two sisters ".

To anticipate a little, in the interest of coherence :—

" He is a burning liar ! " wrote Byron at once to Murray, and enclosed in a parcel of MS. the Dedication to Southey of the first canto of *Don Juan*. Shelley, who was then living in Italy, had heard Byron read this piece, and described it in a letter to Peacock as more like a mixture of wormwood and verdigrease [*sic*] than satire. It did not appear when *Don Juan* was published on July 15, 1819. " As the Poem is to be published anonymously, *omit* the Dedication. I won't attack the dog in the dark ". Southey, who had had absolutely nothing to do with spreading the incest slander,[1] heard of the Dedication and its character ; and when King George III died in January 1820, and he as Laureate sat down to his task of composing a funeral ode, he seized the occasion to compose a preface also, in which he " repaid some of his obligations to Lord Byron by a few comments on *Don Juan* ". Southey's *Vision of Judgment* was published on April 11, 1821, with its preface ; therein the Laureate described Byron and his followers as men of diseased hearts and depraved imaginations, and launched his notorious phrase, The Satanic School. Byron answered the challenge by a note in the Appendix to *The Two Foscari*, published December 11, 1821. He accused the Laureate of scattering abroad calumnies, knowing them to be such, on his return from Switzerland in 1817.

[1] This was afterwards generally attributed to Brougham's malignity against Byron.

Southey answered in *The Courier* for January 6, 1822, giving
" *a direct and positive denial* " to the charge of slander ; and in
doing so expressed himself very caustically. He had " made
no inquiry concerning Byron when he was abroad, because he
felt no curiosity. . . . He had sought for no staler subject than
Saint Ursula ". As regarded the entry in the hotel-album,
" the gentleman in question would not have thought himself
slandered by having that recorded of him which he has so often
recorded of himself ". He then pointed out that these were
side-issues ; and that *his* charges of impiety, lewdness, and so
forth, in *Don Juan*, had not been answered, and were unanswer-
able.[1] Lord Byron had called him a scribbler of all work. " I
will tell Lord Byron what I have *not* scribbled, what kind of
work I have *not* done "—and it must be allowed that Southey
scores heavily in this enumeration. He turned next to the
work he *had* done, and in this sort pointed with exultation to
the phrase Satanic School. " I have sent a stone from my sling
which has smitten their Goliath in the forehead. I have fastened
his name upon the gibbet for reproach and ignominy as long as
it shall endure. Take it down who can ! "

Medwin, in the Conversations, describes the effect of reading
this on Byron. " He looked perfectly awful ; his colour changed
almost prismatically ; his lips were as pale as death. He said
not a word. He threw down the paper, and asked me if I thought
there was anything of a personal nature . . . that demanded
satisfaction ; as if there was, he would instantly set off for
England, and call Southey to account. . . . I said that as to
personality, his own expressions [2] were much stronger than
any in the letter before me. He paused a moment, and said,
' Perhaps you are right ; but I will consider of it.[3] You have
not seen *MY Vision of Judgment*. I wish I had a copy to show
you ; but the only one I have is in London. I had almost decided
not to publish it, but it shall now go forth to the world ' ".

It went forth to the world in the first number of *The Liberal*,
issued on October 15, 1822 ; and the world will be for ever grateful
to Southey. Byron hardly deserved to win, but he did win.
The undelivered challenge would have been a poor revenge, had
the issue even been fatal for Southey, compared with those
immortal slings and arrows. The Laureate took no public notice
of the rival *Vision*—not even when, after Byron's death and in
answer to Medwin's Conversations, he reopened the Satanic
School controversy in the *Courier* for December 9, 1824. He
was wise in keeping silence ; there was nothing to be said.

[1] E. H. Coleridge, *Poems*, iv. p. 477.
[2] In the Appendix to *The Two Foscari*.
[3] He sent a challenge through Douglas Kinnaird, who never delivered it.

Byron had other and genuine reasons for contemning Southey ; these are summed up in the epithets turncoat and renegade with which he made such play. . . . But (returning on our steps) we cannot doubt that the cause of his exceeding bitterness was the imputed slander about the Genevan sojourn—slander of which Southey was wholly guiltless, but slander which was current, and moreover stamped with that "staleness" which afforded Byron's opponent so much too palpable a hit. Incest, of all crimes, must have been the most abhorrent to be again charged with, for a man who had but now incurred its punishment of social outlawry. He had indeed from the earliest days at Diodati endured that blazing notoriety which seemed part of his ineludible destiny. He said to Medwin in later years : " I never led so moral a life as during my residence in Switzerland, but I gained no credit by it. . . . On the contrary, there is no story so absurd that they did not invent at my cost. I was watched by glasses on the opposite side of the Lake. . . . I was waylaid in my evening walks . . . and once [Mme de Staël] invited me to a family dinner, and I found the room full of strangers, who had come to stare at me as at some outlandish beast. . . . One of the ladies fainted ". This was a Mrs. Hervey, aged sixty-five, the author of several romances, and a sister of Beckford.[1] Polidori says that " she thought proper to faint out of the house, though her curiosity brought her back to speak with Lord Byron ".

Hobhouse on September 9 wrote to Augusta of the " telescopes of some inquisitive moralists ", which were said to have " discerned certain robes and flounces on his Lordship's balcony " —but by that time the Shelley caravan had departed, and he could assure her that her brother had given no cause for scandal. He alludes to the women at Mont Alègre with some lack of consideration ; but scorn was the tone of the time with respect to Shelley, and his womenkind suffered with him. Byron never forgot or forgave the attitude of the English at Geneva. From Venice in 1817 he wrote to Murray : " If I met with any of the race in the most beautiful parts of Switzerland, the most distant glimpse or aspect of them poisoned the whole scene. . . . This feeling may be probably owing to recent events . . . but

---

[1] William Beckford, author of *Vathek*, succeeded at the age of eleven to a million of ready money, and £100,000 a year. He wrote *Vathek* (published in 1787) in three days and two nights, as he said ; but evidence exists to prove that this is untrue. His house at Fonthill was renowned for its magnificence, and for the more than dubious way of life pursued there by its master. Beckford died in embarrassed circumstances (Fonthill and its contents had been sold) in 1844 at Bath—where he built the tower on Lansdown Hill.

it does not exist the less, and while it exists, I shall conceal it
as little as any other ".

Scrope Davies [1] quickly returned to England. Hobhouse
remained, and he and Byron made that tour through the Bernese
Alps which was the theme of the Journal for Augusta, and the
real inspiration of *Manfred*. The day before they started Byron
had dismissed Polidori, who had been very troublesome to him
during the sojourn. Their mutual discomfort had been so great
that Polidori, jealous and touchy, had once been on the point
of taking poison—the way in which he did actually end his
tormented and tormenting young life in 1821. Byron wrote
of him to Murray in 1817 : " He understands his profession well,
and has no want of general talents ; his faults are the faults of
a pardonable vanity, and youth. His remaining with us was out
of the question ; I have enough to do to manage my own scrapes
. . . . but I know no great harm of him, and some good ". In
this letter he strongly recommended Polidori to Murray's kindness;
and that although he had encountered the young man, free of
his service, at Milan, and had had an unpleasant tussle with the
authorities on his account. But in a later note he spoke less
mildly : " I never was much more disgusted with any human
production than with the eternal nonsense, and *tracasseries*,
and emptiness, and ill-humour, and vanity of that young person ";
and Moore tells an anecdote which is Polidori's condemnation
as a social creature. At Clarens, when Byron and Shelley were
walking together through the vineyards which had once been
the Bosquet de Julie, Byron exclaimed, " Thank God, Polidori is
not here ! " That his absence should have been thus suddenly
and ardently reckoned among the sources of joy, is a summary
of his effect which no detail of grievances could rival in cogency.
On September 17 Byron and Hobhouse set off on their Bernese
tour. They visited the places which Byron had already seen
with Shelley, and their effect upon him was unimpaired : he
again found the whole region beautiful as a dream. Then,
passing over the Dent de Jaman towards Thun, they arrived at
a lake in the very " nipple of the bosom of the mountain " and
" came to some snow in patches, upon which my forehead's
perspiration fell like rain, making the same dints as in a sieve ".
They heard the Swiss Boy playing on his pipe, and the music
of the cow-bells—it "realised all that I ever heard or imagined
of pastoral existence," and he enshrined the experience in
Manfred, the entire scene of which is set in this Alpine world.

[1] Davies and Hobhouse did not arrive until after the Shelley party had
left for England on August 29. Davies was on his way home, and stayed
only a few days.

They saw " a torrent *nine hundred feet* in height of visible descent"
(the Staubbach), and " heard the avalanches falling every five
minutes nearly—as if God was pelting the Devil down from
Heaven with snow-balls ". The two incidents were recorded
both in *Manfred* and *Childe Harold,* the torrent inspiring the
famous image of Death on the Pale Horse, " as told in the
Apocalypse ", in the former poem. At Grindelwald they saw
their first glacier, " like a *frozen hurricane* ", and " passed whole
woods of withered *pines, all withered.* . . . Their appearance
reminded me of me and my family ". Once out of the mountain
region, his interest flagged : it was insipid civilisation. They
regained Diodati on September 29, and he summed up the tour
and its emotions in the last day's entry. " But in all this—the
recollections of bitterness, and more especially of recent and
home desolation, which must accompany me through life, have
preyed upon me here ; and neither the music of the shepherd,
the crashing of the Avalanche, nor the torrent, the mountain,
the Glacier, the Forest nor the Cloud, have for one moment
lightened the weight on my heart, nor enabled me to lose my
own wretched identity in the majesty, and the power, and the
Glory, around, above, and beneath me.
[1] " I am past reproaches ; and there is a time for all things.
I am past the wish of vengeance, and I know of none like for
what I have suffered ; but the hour will come when what I feel
must be felt, and the—but enough. *To* you, dearest Augusta,
and *for* you I have kept this record of what I have seen and felt.
Love me as you are beloved by me ".

During the Genevan sojourn he had seen a great deal of
Mme de Staël, who was then living at Coppet. They had often
met in London ; but though he admired her works, he had never
then enjoyed her society or conversation—" all snow and
sophistry ", he said. She, as we have seen, had been deeply
moved by the *Farewell* in April ; now at Coppet she " took him
to task upon his matrimonial conduct—but in a way that won
upon his mind, and disposed him to yield to her solicitations ".
He was persuaded to write to a friend in England, and he sent
her the letter to do what she would with, saying : " My letter
is at your disposal, but it will be useless ; it contains however
the truth of my wishes and my feelings on that subject, and as
they have been doubted I am willing to put them to the proof ".[2]

---

[1] This paragraph was omitted by Moore. It appears in *Letters and
Journals,* iii. 365.
[2] The original of this note to Mme de Staël is in the possession of
Professor Kölbing (*Letters and Journals,* iii. 343). We have not Byron's
enclosed appeal to the friend in England.

The date of the note is August 25. The effort proved fruitless ; and to its failure has been attributed the writing of *The Dream*, and of the Incantation in the first act of *Manfred*.[1] This is not true of *The Dream*, for it was written in July ; it may be true of the Incantation, of which he desired it to be thought (on its first publication) that it formed part of " A Witch Drama, begun some years ago " ; it *is* true of the *Lines on Hearing that Lady Byron was Ill*, which, however, though written in September (immediately after Mme de Staël's failure) were not published until 1832. He heard too, about the same time, from Shelley that the rumour of his relations with Augusta was still alive in England ; and this inspired the famous phrase (in the *Lines*) of " the significant eye which learns to lie with silence ". In that piece, too, he first launched the parallel which became almost a synonym for Lady Byron with him :

" The moral Clytemnestra of thy lord "—

the phrase to which for so long his wife submitted in " silence ".

[1] The Incantation was first published separately from *Manfred* in *The Prisoner of Chillon and other Poems*, 1816.

CHAPTER XIX

VENICE—1816–1819

Third canto of *Childe Harold*—Ada, Countess of Lovelace—*The Prisoner of Chillon* volume—Italy: Milan—Stendhal—Verona and Venice—More domestic troubles; Ada a ward in Chancery—Letter to Lady Byron—Marianna Segati —Margarita Cogni—His depravation at Venice—His letters—Venetian " Blues "—Florence and Rome—*Manfred* —Fourth canto of *Childe Harold*

BEFORE leaving Switzerland, word came from Murray of Gifford's good opinion of the MSS. which Shelley had taken to England. These were the third canto of *Childe Harold*, *The Prisoner of Chillon* and its attendant poems—*The Dream, Churchill's Grave, Prometheus*, the *Manfred* Incantation, and two pieces to Augusta.

" I was thrilled with delight yesterday ", wrote Murray on September 12, " by the announcement of Mr. Shelley with the MS. of *Childe Harold*.[1] I had no sooner got the quiet possession of it than, trembling with auspicious hope, I carried it to Mr. Gifford. He says that what you have hitherto published is nothing to this effort ". " I like it myself ", wrote Byron in answer; " but that must go for nothing. The feelings with which much of it was written need not be envied me ". It was published on November 18; and Murray wrote on December 13 to say that at a dinner at the Albion Tavern he had sold to the assembled booksellers seven thousand of it, and of its companion volume, *The Prisoner of Chillon and other Poems*, which was published on December 5. Walter Scott reviewed both volumes in the *Quarterly* for October 1816. Byron wrote of the notice, before he knew its author, that it had given him as much gratification as any composition of that nature could give, and more than any other had ever given. When he learnt the authorship, he said, " It cannot add to my good opinion of him, but it adds to that of myself ".[2]

---

[1] Murray paid for this canto at a rate of more than 28*s*. a line (Jeaffreson, p. 235).

[2] In 1822, from Pisa, he wrote to Walter Scott of this article : " You went out of your way in 1817 to do me a service, when it required not

285

The third canto opens with the apostrophe to " Ada ! sole daughter of my house and heart " (usually misquoted " home "), which is so familiar to every ear ; and ends on the same note :

> " My daughter ! with thy name this song begun !
> My daughter ! with thy name thus much shall end ! "

In the concluding stanzas he made the prediction which was so strangely and completely fulfilled :

> " Yet though dull hate as duty should be taught,
> I know that thou wilt love me : though my name
> Should be shut from thee, as a spell still fraught
> With desolation, and a broken claim :
> Though the grave closed between us—'twere the same,
> I know that thou wilt love me—" . . .

Lady Byron wrote of these stanzas to Lady Anne Barnard : " It is said that hatred of him will be taught as a lesson to his child. I might appeal to all who have ever heard me speak of him, and still more to my own heart, to witness that there has been no moment when I have remembered injury otherwise than affectionately and sorrowfully. . . . So long as I live my chief struggle will probably be not to remember him too kindly ". But Annabella's was not the only influence ; Lady Noel, violent and imperious, was also to be reckoned with. By her directions Ada, during childhood, was kept in entire ignorance of her father ; by the terms of her will, Ada was not to see his portrait until she had attained her twenty-first year. When, on Lady Noel's death in 1822, Byron heard of this interdiction, the stanza of *Childe Harold* can hardly have failed to recall itself—so sadly triumphant a prophecy had it proved.

Ada Byron married in 1835 William King, eighth Baron King, created Earl of Lovelace in 1838.[1] She was an unusually talented

merely kindness, but courage, to do so. . . . There could not be *two* who *could* and *would* have done this at the time. . . . The very tardiness of this acknowledgment will show, at least, that I have not forgotten the obligation ". And then, referring to his treatment of Scott in *English Bards*, he says : " So you see you have been heaping ' coals of fire ', etc., in the true gospel manner, and I can assure you that they have burnt down to my very heart ".

[1] There were three children of the marriage : (1) Viscount Ockham, who died in 1862 (that strange young nobleman who served as a common seaman, and then worked at Millwall Docks as a ship-carpenter) ; (2) Anna Isabella Noel, who in 1869 married Mr. Wilfred Scawen Blunt ; * (3) Ralph Gordon Noel Milbanke, second Earl of Lovelace, the author of *Astarte*, who died in 1906. This Lord Lovelace was an eccentric man, with a strain of the authentic family violence. In *Astarte* most of those portions which are from his own pen display this vehemence plainly. But his documents are irrefutable, and it is with those that Byron's biographers are chiefly concerned.

---

* She died in November, 1917.

and original woman. " Her genius ," said a writer of an obituary notice in 1852—" for genius she possessed—was not poetic, but metaphysical and mathematical ". She translated and annotated Menabrea's *Notices sur la machine analytique de Mr. Babbage* (1842)—a defence of the famous calculating-machine. She was not yet twenty-eight when she achieved that feat ; but she was no pedant. " Her manners, tastes, accomplishments . . . were feminine in the nicest sense of the word ". Unlike her father in features, she " inherited his mental vigour and intensity of purpose ". There are indications that towards the end of her life she was for a while estranged from her mother. Teresa Guiccioli, in her book about Byron,[1] told the following incredible tale of Ada's " discovery " of her father. She was staying at Newstead with Colonel Wildman *about a year before her death in 1852* ! One day in the library he quoted to her a passage of verse with whose beauty she was enchanted, and she asked the author's name. Her host pointed to the portrait of her father by Phillips, which hung in the room. She was overwhelmed ; and from that moment a change took place in her feelings. " She shut herself up in the rooms he had occupied, and eagerly studied his works ". On her departure from the Abbey, she became seriously ill, and died not long afterwards (November 27, 1852). . . . By her own request her coffin was placed beside Byron's in the vault at Hucknall Torkard.

All we have from Lady Byron with respect to this is in two letters (published by Jeaffreson) after Ada's death. They are both to Mrs. George Lamb. " Many falsehoods concerning Ada's last days are circulated. Pray enable me to contradict any you may hear. Some are most wicked ".[2] . . . *What is*

---

[1] *Lord Byron jugé par les Témoins de sa Vie* (1868) ; translated in 1869, under the title of *My Recollections of Lord Byron*. From whom she heard this tale of Ada and the portrait remains unknown ; it is plainly apocryphal.

[2] In Mrs. Stowe's narrative (as originally published in *The Atlantic Monthly*) the following allusion to Ada occurs : " The daughter inherited from the father not only brilliant talents, but a restlessness and morbid sensibility which might be too surely traced to the storms and agitation of the period in which she was born. It was necessary to bring her up in ignorance of the true history of her mother's life ; and the consequence was that she could not fully understand that mother. During her early girlhood her career was a source of more anxiety than comfort. She married a man of fashion, ran a brilliant course as a gay woman of fashion,* and died

---

* Mary, Countess of Lovelace, strongly dissents from this phrase. " Lord and Lady Lovelace ", she says, " no doubt lived in the best society of their day, but neither can ever have been of fashion. They spent the greater part of their time in the country . . . Lady Lovelace took but little interest in ordinary society . . . Lady Byron blamed Lord Lovelace for having at first encouraged his wife's taste for racing . . . but from his letters it appears to me that he was never more than passively acquiescent ". (*Ralph, Earl of Lovelace*, App. pp. 165–6.)

truth ? said jesting Pilate. But if Annabella Byron made it into her Juggernaut car, she crushed herself, no less than others, beneath it.[1]

The third canto differs from the former two in being at its best when what Byron called metaphysical. In the earlier work, Harold's causeless gloom was merely tedious ; we turned with relief from it to the dioramic stanzas. Here, though the diorama passes no less vividly before our eyes, it is the traveller that we follow with our interest and sympathy. Sympathy—for the magic voice has now the word. " Making a public show of a very genuine misery ",[2] he swept across Europe, in Matthew Arnold's renowned phrase, " the pageant of his bleeding heart " ; and it is vain to recapitulate, as we turn the page, our knowledge of the truth. Reading him now, we are his thralls. He captures and he holds our hearts at every moment that his pang finds a voice.

> " Yet must I think less wildly ; I *have* thought
> Too long and darkly, till my brain became
> In its own eddy boiling and o'erwrought,
> A whirling gulf of phantasy and flame :
> And thus, untaught in youth my heart to tame,
> My springs of life were poisoned " . . .

> " Where rose the mountains, there to him were friends ;
> Where rolled the ocean, thereon was his home ;
> He had the passion and the power to roam ;
> The desert, forest, cavern, breakers' foam,
> Were unto him companionship ; they spake
> A mutual language " . . .

And the great stanzas 42 to 44 :

early of a painful and lingering disease. In the silence and shaded retire-ment of the sick-room, the daughter came wholly back to her mother's arms and heart. . . . To the children left by her daughter, [Lady Byron] ministered with the faithfulness of a guardian angel " (*History of the Byron Controversy*, p. 298). This last is one of Mrs. Stowe's few indubitably truthful statements.

In a newspaper cutting (I have no means of tracing its source) I find an interesting anecdote of Ada's childhood. When she saw the sea for the first time at Brighton—that sea which her father loved—she exclaimed, " I don't like it. It is so like my governess ".

[1] The second Earl of Lovelace in 1861 (after Lady Byron's death) exchanged the surname King for Milbanke, and shortly afterwards became Lord Wentworth. His father, the first Earl, had added the Noel to his own surname of King, on inheriting Lady Byron's estates. The name King *only* was chosen by the third Earl in 1906, and confirmed by licence in 1908. This Earl bears no relationship to Byron, being the child of the first Earl's (Ada's husband's) *second* marriage.

[2] Arthur Symons, *The Romantic Movement.*

" But Quiet to quick bosoms is a Hell—
. . . . . .
Their breath is agitation, and their life
A storm whereon they ride, to sink at last ".

The intellectual influences of Wordsworth and Shelley were at work in this third canto. Stanza 72 is Wordsworthian even in language :

" I live not in myself, but I become
Portion of that around me ; and to me
High mountains are a feeling, but the hum
Of human cities torture " . . .

No influence, however, could long impose itself on that spirit. As Mr. Coleridge points out, " The secret of Wordsworth is acquiescence ; Byron . . . is in revolt. To him Nature and Humanity are antagonists, and he cleaves to the one, yea, he would take her by violence, to mark his alienation and severance from the other ".

" And thus I am absorbed, and this is life ;—
I look upon the peopled desert past,
As on a place of agony and strife,
Where, for some Sin, to sorrow I was cast,
To act and suffer, but remount at last
With a fresh pinion " . . . [1]

In stanza 92 occurs the description of the storm, with its renowned *onomatopeia* :

" . . . Far along
From peak to peak, the rattling crags among
Leaps the live thunder ! "

He had been in this tempest at midnight on June 13, 1816. " I have seen several more terrible, but none more beautiful " ; and it gave him, besides the lines above, a definition of his own ideal of poetry.

" Could I embody and unbosom now
That which is most within me—could I wreak
My thoughts upon expression, and thus throw
Soul—heart—mind—passions—feelings—strong or weak—
All that I would have sought and all I seek,
Bear, know, feel—and yet breathe—into one word,
And that one word were Lightning, I would speak ".

---

[1] Moore points out the note of Shelley's Pantheism of Love in the stanzas on the Rousseau region. It was through Shelley, moreover, that Byron was first to read with any sort of patience the works of Wordsworth. Hitherto he had vehemently disliked the " Lakers " (as he called them) with the exception of Coleridge in *Christabel*, which, as we have seen, he admired and proclaimed from the first hearing.

" And so indeed ", says Mr. Arthur Symons, " at his best he did speak, condensing the indignation of his soul, or the wrath of Europe, into one word, and that word lightning ".[1]

Our familiarity with the opening lines of *The Prisoner of Chillon* [2] disturbs our serious consideration of the poem. The critics of 1816 were insistent on the Wordsworthian strain. " Lord Byron has evidently become a tardy convert " ; and no doubt the charming episodes of the bird—

> " A lovely bird with azure wings,
> And song that said a thousand things,
> And seemed to say them all for me ! "

—and the fish that swam by the castle wall,

> " And they seemed joyous each and all ",

—are reminiscent both in matter and manner. But, however we may value Wordsworth, it is Byron that we want from Byron. Nor could he have retained this stamp. His nature was rhetorical, and in rhetoric alone, at this period, could truly express itself.[3] Later he was to find a more perfect means of self-utterance ; and that was as far removed from the Wordsworthian manner as the earth is from the skies.

Prometheus was a subject that, sooner or later, he was certain to attempt ; from boyhood he had loved it, and now it struck the peculiar personal note.

> " All that the proud can feel of pain,
> The agony they do not show,
> The suffocating sense of woe,

---

[1] Mr. Arthur Symons cites, as examples of Byron's " unparalleled justness of expression. . . perfect hitting of the mark ", some phrases (among others) from the fourth canto of *Childe Harold*. Those where Napoleon is seen

> " With a deaf heart that never seemed to be
> A listener to itself " ;

where

> " France got drunk with blood to vomit crime " ;

and where Cromwell

> " Hewed the throne down to a block ".

" There is, in these vivid and unforgettable phrases, a heat of truth which has kindled speech into a really imaginative fervour ".

[2] Byron carved his name on the southern side of the third column ; the Prisoner's place of durance was the fifth. " Much has been written ", says Mr. Coleridge, " for and against the authenticity of this inscription ". It was, as Mr. Edgcumbe has pointed out, *in situ* as early as August 22, 1820 (*Notes and Queries*, v. xi. 487. *Poems*, iv. note to p. 15).

[3] " In his work, truth lies at the root of rhetoric . . . lifting it into a kind of powerful, naked, and undeniable poetic existence " (Arthur Symons).

Which speaks but in its loneliness,
And then is jealous lest the sky
Should have a listener, nor will sigh
Unless its voice is echoless "—

that portrayal of himself, the Never-Silent, which yet had some-
where its mysterious fidelity to truth! The Stanzas to Augusta
were parodied by Hobhouse, and indeed lend themselves
generously to travesty—though Byron thought well of them as
a composition. Mrs. Leigh at first desired to suppress these
as well as the Epistle, but " after reflecting on every possibility
and probability, *did* think the *least objectionable* line would
be to *let them be published* ".[1] She wrote to Byron to say
that the Epistle must be withheld, and it did not see the light
until Moore's book appeared in 1830. It is among the best of
his shorter pieces. " There is nothing, perhaps ", said the
Quarterly, reviewing Moore, " more mournfully and desolately
beautiful in the whole range of his poetry ".

Leaving Diodati on October 6, Hobhouse and Byron went
by the Simplon and Lago Maggiore route to Milan. They stayed
there until the first week of November, visiting the Ambrosian
Library, where Byron fell in love with a lock of Lucrezia Borgia's
hair, and took a single hair of it as a relic. Stendhal, who had
been through the Russian campaign of 1812, met him here and
recorded his impressions. " I idolised Napoleon, and . . . sub-
sequently discovered that Lord Byron was at once enthusiastic
in [his] favour, and jealous of his fame ". The young French-
man's feeling was at first decidedly unfavourable : Byron struck
him as vain, snobbish, and affected. " When his personal
attractions were not the subject of his consideration, his noble
birth was uppermost in his thoughts ". But when neither was
in the ascendant, " he again became the sublime poet and the
man of sense. Never, after the example of Mme de Staël, did he
indulge in the childish vanity of ' turning a phrase ' ". Stendhal
proceeds, after alluding to the poet's remorse for some mysterious
crime, to say, " It must be admitted that during nearly a third
of the time we passed in the noble poet's society, he appeared
to us like one labouring under an access of folly, approaching to
madness ". A caustic observer of all things and creatures,
this critic was yet to be spellbound by Byron's personal beauty.
" It was the supreme look of genius and power. . . . Internally
I made a vow that I never would of my own accord sadden a
spirit so noble ".[2]

[1] Letter to Murray (*L. and J*. iii. note to pp. 366–67).
[2] This version of Stendhal's account is translated by Galt from *The
Foreign Literary Gazette* (*Life of Byron*, p. 347).

Byron met some old and dear friends at Milan—the Jerseys ; and Polidori, who reappeared, got himself (and as a consequence Byron and a party of friends) into a ridiculous row at the Scala Theatre. He had found his view of the stage impeded by the fur cap of an Austrian officer on guard, and had rather impolitely called upon him to remove it. This caused fiery indignation ; Polidori only just escaped, by the intervention of Byron and some Milanese noblemen, from being shut up for the night in the guard-house. Next morning he received an order to quit Milan within twenty-four hours. " I left . . ." (on October 30) he records in his Diary, " with rage and grief so struggling in my breast that tears often started to my eyes ".

From Milan Byron and Hobhouse went by Verona to Venice. They stayed a day or two in Verona, " to gape at the usual marvels . . . that time-tax of travel " ; but despite this *blasé* attitude, Byron was much affected by the sight of Juliet's tomb, of whose authenticity the Veronese were tenacious to a degree ; [1] and he brought away a few pieces of the granite for Augusta " and the babes (at least the female part of them) and for Ada, and her mother, if she will accept it from you ".[2] He had written to Lady Byron from Milan. " I feel so miserable ", he explained to Augusta, " that I must write to her, however useless. . . . I have seen a good deal of Milanese society, but nothing to make me forget others, or forgive myself ". But from Venice he again wrote to Augusta on December 19. " My letter to my moral Clytemnestra " (this phrase was already in working-order, and was henceforth kept incessantly at work) " required no answer, and I would rather have none. I was wretched enough when I wrote it, and had been so for many a long day and month ; at present I am less so, for reasons expressed in my late letter (a few days ago) ; and as I never pretend to be what I am not, you may tell her if you please that I am recovering, and the reason also if you like it ". We shall shortly learn the reason, which, as Augusta wrote to Hodgson, was only one among a million of melancholy anticipations of hers.

They reached Venice before November 11. His first letter thence deals with a new grievance against the Noel family. Somebody a little while before had written, with no intention of making mischief, that it was said that Lady Byron intended to pass the winter abroad. Instantly Byron had dashed off and

---

[1] Mr. Prothero, in a note (*L. and J.* iii. 382), states that the authentic tomb has long been destroyed ; " its substitute, said to have been originally a washing-trough, is shown in a chapel of a suppressed Franciscan monastery, in the Via Cappuccini ".

[2] This, and the immediately following quotations, are from *Letters and Journals*, iv., early pages.

entrusted to Augusta, " to be despatched with all speed ",[1] a
letter to the Noel family insisting upon a promise that the child
should never leave England. The answer received by Augusta
was that Lady Byron had never had any intention of quitting
England. This had not satisfied Byron, and he now wrote to
John Hanson, desiring him to take immediately the proper
steps to prevent the possibility of such an occurrence. " My
daughter and only legitimate child ",[2] he said, " shall not leave
England with my consent. In the present state of the Continent,
I would not have my child rambling over it for millions ". He
was much worried by this apprehension, and equivocal replies
from the other side prolonged the strain until the end of January
1817, when Hanson succeeded in extracting the following docu-
ment :

" KIRKBY MALLORY, *January* 30, 1817

" There never has existed, nor does there exist, the remotest
intention of removing Miss Byron out of the Kingdom.

ANNE ISABELLA BYRON
RALPH NOEL "

But under Sir Ralph's signature, some pregnant words were
added : " *Without the leave of the Chancellor* ". This was the
first intimation given, either to Byron or Hanson, that Ada had
been made a ward in Chancery. He was furiously angered.
The bill in Chancery had been filed against him in the midst
of the Separation proceedings of April 1816, and no hint
whatever had been afforded him. He wrote to his wife on
March 5[3]—directly after hearing from Hanson—a proud bitter
reproof.

" Throughout the whole of this unhappy business, I have done
my best to avoid the bitterness which, however, is yet amongst
us ; and it would be as well if even you at times recollected
that the man who has been sacrificed in fame, in feelings,
in everything, to the convenience of your family, was he whom
you once loved, and who—whatever you may imagine to the
contrary—loved you. If you conceive that I could be actuated
by revenge against you, you are mistaken : I am not humble

---

[1] See Augusta's letter to Hodgson of March 4, 1817 (*Letters and Jour-
nals*, iv. 23–24). We have not Byron's letter.

[2] Claire's child was not yet born. And see p. 375.

[3] *L. and J.* iv. 66–68. Printed from draft in Murray MSS. But we
must remember that the Noel family had reason to fear that, if left to any
degree in Byron's power, the child might even still be transferred to
Augusta's charge ; and this, for many motives, they strongly deprecated.

enough to be vindictive.[1] Irritated I may have been, and may be—is it a wonder ?—but upon such irritation, beyond its momentary expression, I have not acted from the hour that you quitted me to that in which I am made aware that our daughter is to be the entail of our discussion, the inheritor of our bitterness. If you think to reconcile yourself to yourself by accumulating harshness against me, you are again mistaken ; you are not happy, nor even tranquil, nor will you ever be so. . . . Time and Nemesis will do that which I would not, were it in my power remote or immediate. You will smile at this piece of prophecy—do so, but recollect it : it is justified by all human experience. No one was ever even the involuntary cause of great evils to others, without a requital : I have paid and am paying for mine—so will you ".

> " The child of Love ! though born in bitterness,
> And nurtured in Convulsion ! "—

those words and the words of the letter above and many, many others, must have sounded in the mother's heart in 1852. There have been few more striking examples of the second-sight of poets.

He had not yet been dealt this blow when he sent the defiant message to Augusta, stating that he was no longer wretched and that his wife might be told the reason. Our earliest information about it is in a letter to Moore, dated November 17. " I have fallen in love. . . . Marianna (that is her name) is in her appearance altogether like an antelope. She has the large black oriental eyes. . . . I cannot describe the effect of this kind of eye—at least upon me ". The woman was Marianna Segati, wife of a draper in the Frezzeria (a side-street of Venice), in whose house Byron was lodging.[2] His liaison with her certainly lasted until the winter of 1817, and may have lasted longer. During part of its course, it ran concurrently with an affair with Margarita Cogni (La Fornarina) wife of a baker, and Marianna's equal if not superior in vice. About *her* he wrote, in August 1819, a letter of nine printed pages to Murray. Both women shared

---

[1] Her view of him, inspired by her advisers, is indicated by a letter from her of April 1, 1816, to Mrs. George Lamb : " In regard to the child, it appears to my advisers most advantageous that it should not be made a subject of discussion at present . . . because it is highly improbable that he would resign the power *in a formal manner ;* and, by not making any particular provision for it, if he goes abroad, he will virtually, to a certain extent, acknowledge my guardianship. *To let him know these reasons would be to defeat them* ".

[2] In a MS. note to Moore's life, Rawden Brown stated that " Marianna was a demon of avarice and libidinousness, who intrigued with every resident in the house, and every guest who visited it ".

in his sojourns at the villa of La Mira, which he used as his place of *villeggiatura* in the summer ; and both ruled, at different periods, in that palace on the Grand Canal where he kept an establishment which it would be gross flattery to call a harem. The just word for his arrangements there is best left unprinted. On this wretched period I do not propose to linger. Moore, for the decenter episodes in his career so reticent, printed all his letters about these two women; and despite the vivacity of Byron's narrative, they make sad reading. Here Jeaffreson shall speak, for he speaks more frankly and more justly than any other of the biographers. " Less harm would have come to him from these creatures . . . had he possessed the cynical hardness and spiritual grossness to think of them as animals, differing from the brutes only in shape and speech. But the softness of his nature prevented him from taking so disdainful a view. . . . However dissolute she might be, the woman he regarded with passion became for a moment the object of an affection that was no less tender than transient. To call it love would be a profanation ; but no less sacred word would adequately describe the fleeting sentiment of perverted sympathy and debasing admiration with which he cherished these miserable beings. . . . Hence his almost appalling delight in their exhibitions of caprice and jealousy, in the humour of their sorry jests, and in the piquancy of their vulgar persiflage. In the whole story of our literature, few things can be found more painfully humiliating ".

Shelley's letter to Peacock, after meeting Byron again in 1818, is arresting. He found him deeply melancholy, filled with a dull distaste for life. " I remonstrated with him in vain on the tone of mind from which such a view of things arises. . . . The fact is that, first, the Italian women with whom he associates are perhaps the most contemptible of all who exist under the moon. . . .[He] is familiar with the lowest sort of these women, the people his *gondolieri* pick up in the streets. He associates with wretches who seem almost to have lost the gait and physiognomy of man, and who do not scruple to avow practices which are not only not named, but I believe seldom even conceived, in England. He says he disapproves, but he endures. He is heartily and deeply discontented with himself. . . . No, I do not doubt, and for his sake I ought to hope, that his present career must end soon in some violent circumstance ".[1]

---

[1] Lord Lovelace says : " There was no foundation for the crass and egregious suggestions of Shelley " ; and declares that " trustworthy contemporary information . . . disposes completely of the most repulsive abominations " (*Astarte*, p. 124). He attributes Shelley's belief to the inventions of Claire Clairmont.

No more cogent proof of Byron's own sense of degradation could be given than his subsequent bitter hatred for the Venice which at first he had declared to be the greenest island of his imagination : " As much as I expected, and I expected much. It is one of those places which I know before I see them ".

> " I loved her from my boyhood—she to me
>   Was as a fairy city of the heart " ;

and though he had found her in her decadence, she was

> " Perchance even dearer in her day of woe,
>   Than when she was a boast, a marvel, and a show ".

That feeling belonged to the summer of 1817, when he began and finished the fourth canto of *Childe Harold*. Something of it lingered still a year later (when the *Ode to Venice* was composed), though already the prophetic note of despair for the " sea Cybele " was sounding. Two more years, and he had left the place for ever—and at Ravenna had begun his tragedy of *Marino Faliero*. That was finished in July 1820 ; and in the dying imprecation of the discrowned Doge, we hear the last word of Byron's rage against the scene of his infamy.

> " Thou den of drunkards with the blood of Princes !
>   Gehenna of the waters ! thou Sea-Sodom !
>   Thus I devote thee to the Infernal Gods !
>   Thee and thy serpent seed ! "

During this period his letters attain their highest excellence. Of the hundred and twenty-two from Venice, seventy-two are to Murray. The others are divided between Moore, Augusta, the Hansons father and son (on matters of business), and Richard Belgrave Hoppner, the British Consul at Venice, with whom he became very intimate. Hobhouse, Rogers, Hodgson,[1] Wedderburn Webster heard once or twice. Murray got the masterpieces. It was known to Byron that these would be handed round to the Synod, as he called the club in Murray's back-parlour at Albemarle Street, and they were written with an eye on posterity as well. But no one ever more successfully concealed his art. As the *Edinburgh* said in 1831, reviewing Moore, " If the epistolary style of Lord Byron was artificial, it was a rare and admirable instance of that highest art which cannot be distinguished from nature ". And he wrote incessantly. It is pathetic to see, amid all his abandonment to the Venetian licence, how constantly his heart was fixed on the England which

---

[1] Now, according to Byron, " a little too much japanned by preferment in the church and the tuition of youth, as well as inoculated with the disease of domestic felicity . . . but otherwise a very worthy man " (Letter to Moore, December 5, 1817).

he rarely failed to vituperate, yet to which, in these earlier days
of exile, he over and over again dreamed of returning. It is
evident that he was restlessly unhappy, for he " found that his
mind wanted something craggy to break upon " ; [1] and the
crag he chose was a curious repetition of an episode in the earlier
Harold tour. In 1810 he had taken quarters in the Franciscan
monastery at Athens, and studied the modern Greek ; now, in
1817, he studied daily at an Armenian monastery the Armenian
language. He did this with the same zest and energy that he
had shown in the earlier adventure. The Armenian was " a
Waterloo of an Alphabet ", but he persevered. In January he
sent home some sheets of an English-Armenian grammar com-
piled by his teacher, Father Aucher, and made eager inquiries
as to the existence of Armenian type in England ; and in January–
February 1817, he did into English some passages from the
Armenian version of St. Paul's Epistle to the Corinthians, together
with an Armenian prose-poem, entitled *The Pleasure-Houses of
Byzantium.*

He frequented some of the private *salons*, notably those of
the two Venetian Blues, the Countesses Albrizzi and Benzoni.
The Albrizzi secured him first. She was known as the de Staël
of Venice ; the most distinguished men of the day were her
friends—Pindemonte, Alfieri, Foscolo, Canova ; it was for her
that Canova executed in 1814 his bust of Helen, which drew so
enthusiastic a tribute from Byron when he saw it in her drawing-
room. " [It] is, without exception, to my mind the most perfectly
beautiful of human conceptions, and far beyond my ideas of
human execution ". He wrote a terrible versicle about it :

> " In this beloved marble view
> Above the works and thoughts of Man,
> What Nature *could*, but *would not*, do,
> And Beauty and Canova *can* ! "

When Moore, visiting Venice in 1819, went to one of the
Countess's assemblies, he thought it " much worse than one of
Lydia White's ; " [2] but Byron endured them for some time.

[1] He was thinking, in saying this, of the advice given by the King of
Prussia to d'Alembert, after the death of Julie de l'Espinasse, to study
quelque problème bien difficile à résoudre. This advice Byron had adopted
as a motto to the third canto of *Childe Harold.* " To think of something
else ! " comments Mr. Symons. " The mockery of a remedy, and yet the
only one ".

[2] Miss Lydia White, the Miss Diddle of Byron's *Blues*, was a wealthy
Irishwoman, well known for her hospitality in all the capitals of Europe.
It was to her that Sydney Smith, during a time of crisis in the Whig party,
made the famous remark (she was the one Tory at her own dinner-table) :
" We had better sacrifice a Tory Virgin ". Miss White answered, " Oh, the
Whigs would do anything to raise the wind ". She died, after many years
of ill-health, in February 1827.

They were a little absurd. The women sat in a semi-circle round the hostess, the men stood in a semi-circle opposite ; rum-punch and ices were the refreshments, for the Albrizzi was an Anglo-maniac.[1] She scribbled a good deal herself (her work on Canova passed through three editions in Byron's lifetime) ; sketched and wrote Portraits of her famous friends, in the high-sentimental manner of the period. Byron was done, but he declined to read the MS., and curtly advised her to burn. She did not burn ; but neither did she publish until 1826, so the original never saw it. If he *had* seen it, he would certainly have burned it himself. This was the kind of thing : " What varied expression in his eyes ! They were of the azure colour of the heavens from which they seemed to derive their origin. . . . His teeth resembled pearls ; but his cheeks were too delicately tinged with the hue of the pale rose ". As if with a suspicion of these horrors, Byron quarrelled with the Countess towards the end, withdrew a good deal from her circle, and joined that of her rival, the Countess Marina Benzoni, less starched, as he said—and this must have been a mild manner of describing the lady who in 1818 took La Fornarina under her protection. Moore, attending her salon in 1819 with Byron, found the evening more enjoyable than the Albrizzi one. " Thoroughly profligate. . . . Her manners very pleasant and easy ". There were many English in the Benzoni circle also, and to these Byron " repeatedly refused to be intro-duced—of a thousand such presentations pressed upon me, I accepted two, and both were to Irish women ".

The Carnival of 1817 had not ended before he was sickening for an attack of the type of fever that had struck him down during the Albanian tour of 1809–11. It was due in no small degree to nervous prostration resulting from the dissipations of the mumming ; and to the frantic scenes which he (who hated scenes more cordially even than other men) had suffered from Marianna Segati and a sister-in-law who designed to supplant her. There had been screams, boxes on the ear, torn hair, hats, and handkerchiefs, faints, smelling-bottles, and Signor Segati. But with Lent came " invalid regimen . . . abstinence, and sacred music ". The varied influences produced—he scribbled it in a letter to Moore on February 28—the most beautiful short poem he ever wrote : one of those things which seem to have been blown into the world like April showers.

> " So we'll go no more a-roving,
>   So late into the night,

---

[1] Byron wrote of this : " *Punch*, by my palate ! and this they think *English*. I would not disabuse them of so agreeable an error—' no, not for Venice ' ".

Though the heart be still as loving,
And the moon be still as bright.

For the sword outwears its sheath,
And the soul wears out the breast,
And the heart must pause to breathe,
And Love itself have rest.

Though the night was made for loving,
And the day returns too soon,
Yet we'll go no more a-roving
By the light of the moon ".

The last line, shortened as though a sudden sob had caught the breath, is exquisite in poignancy : an example of that identification of sound and sense which makes the undying utterances of the world. This lyric seems as if it must always have been there : it comes to us like the air about us. If Byron had written nothing else, his name must have survived through this.

In the same letter he said of himself : " If I live ten years longer, you will see, however, that it is not over with me—I don't mean in literature, for that is nothing ; and it may seem odd enough to say so, I do not think it my vocation. But you will see that I shall do something or other ". He had England in his head. " I intend for England this spring " ; but when the malarial fever [1] at last left him, he wrote to Murray on April 9 : " In a few days I set off for Rome : such is my purpose. I shall change it very often before Monday next. . . . I never know what I shall do till it is done. . . . You tell me to ' take care of myself '—faith, and I will. I won't be posthumous yet, if I can help it. Notwithstanding, only think what a ' Life and Adventures', while I am in full scandal, would be worth. . . . Be assured that I *would live* for two reasons, or more ; there are one or two people whom I have to put out of the world, and as many into it, before I can ' depart in peace '. . . . Besides, when I turn thirty, I will turn devout ; I feel a great vocation that way in Catholic churches, and when I hear the organ ".[2]

He went to Rome by Ferrara instead of Mantua, because " I would rather see the cell where they caged Tasso than the birthplace of that harmonious plagiary and miserable flatterer " —Virgil—" whose cursed hexameters were drilled into me at Harrow. . . . I go *alone*—but *alone*, because I mean to return here. I only want to see Rome. I have not the least curiosity

[1] There is a characteristic remark upon this illness : " Mine was a fever of my own, and had nothing in common with the low vulgar typhus which is at this moment decimating Venice " (Letter to Moore, March 31, 1817).

[2] Walter Scott had said to him in 1815 that he would look to see him (Byron) retreat upon the Catholic faith, and distinguish himself by the austerity of his penances. " He smiled gravely, and seemed to allow I might be right ".

about Florence, though I must see it for the sake of the Venus,
etc. etc. ". But already he was more in the mood for works
of art. Immediately before his departure from Venice he visited
the Manfrini Palace, and wrote of the Titian Ariosto : " It is the
poetry of portrait, and the portrait of poetry. There was also
one of some learned lady. . . . I never saw greater beauty, or
sweetness, or wisdom ; it is the kind of face to go mad for,
because it can't walk out of its frame ". Giorgione's portrait
of his wife inspired a stanza in *Beppo* later on.[1] Nevertheless,
he still stoutly maintained his attitude towards painting.
" Depend upon it, of all the arts, it is the most artificial and
unnatural. . . . I never yet saw the picture—or the statue—
which came within a league of my conception or experience ;
but I have seen many mountains and seas and rivers and views,
and two or three women who went as far beyond it—besides
some horses, and a lion in the Morea, and a tiger at supper at
Exeter 'Change ".[2]

In the middle of April he left Venice, and on the 26th wrote
to Murray from Foligno. He had spent but a day at Florence,
and had there written the *Lament of Tasso* ; he despatched it to
England on April 23. The Florentine Galleries completed the
conquest half-begun at Venice. He had " returned from them
drunk with beauty. The Venus [de' Medici] is more for admira-
ion than love ". But the stanzas of *Childe Harold* are more
like love than admiration.

> " We gaze and turn away, and know not where,
> Dazzled and drunk with Beauty, till the heart
> Reels with its fulness.
>
> .   .   .   .   .   .
>
> The unruffled mirror of the loveliest dream
> That ever left the sky on the deep soul to beam ".

At Rome, reached on April 29, he rejoined Hobhouse, with
whom he had parted company in December. " As a whole,
ancient and modern, it beats . . . everything—at least that I
have ever seen. But I can't describe, because my first impres-
sions are always strong and confused, and my *memory selects* and

---

[1] The Manfrini collection was partly dispersed in 1856 ; but some of the
pictures are in the Accademia delle Belle Arti. Titian's Ariosto is now the
property of the Earl of Rosebery. According to Vasari, Giorgione was not
married.

[2] In his Journal of 1813–14 there occurs, on November 14, 1813, the
following : " Two nights ago, I saw the tigers sup at Exeter 'Change. . . .
Such a conversazione ! There was a hippopotamus, like Lord Liverpool in
the face ; and the Ursine Sloth had the very voice and manner of my valet
—but the tiger talked too much. The handsomest animal on earth is one
of the panthers ; but the poor antelopes were dead. I should hate to see
one *here* ; the sight of the camel made me pine again for Asia Minor ".

BYRON

FROM THE ORIGINAL MODEL FOR THE STATUE ERECTED AT THE GRAMMAR SCHOOL,
ABERDEEN, 1923, BY PITTENDRIGH MACGILLIVRAY, LL.D., R.S.A., SCULPTOR ROYAL
FOR SCOTLAND

reduces them to order. . . . There must be a sense or two more than we have as mortals ". He studied it on horseback, " as I did Constantinople. But Rome is the elder sister and the finer ". The day before he left he saw three robbers guillotined, and wrote Murray a minute and gruesome description. " The first ", he added, " turned me quite hot and thirsty, and made me shake so that I could hardly hold the opera-glasses (I was close, but determined to see as we should see everything, once, with attention) ; the second and third . . . I am ashamed to say, had no effect on me as a horror, though I would have saved them if I could ". While in Rome he permitted Hobhouse to write to Thorwaldsen, asking whether and when Byron could sit to him for a bust. Thorwaldsen, who was a very indolent letter-writer, probably delayed to answer, and Byron went to him without ceremony. " He placed himself opposite me " (so Thorwaldsen told Andersen), " but at once began to put on a quite different expression from that usual to him. ' Will you not sit still ? ' I said to him ; ' you need not assume that look '. ' That is my expression ', said Byron. ' Indeed ? ' said I, and I then represented him as I wished. When the bust was finished, it was universally admitted to be an excellent likeness. Byron, when he saw it, said ' It is not at all like me ; my expression is more unhappy '. ' He intensely desired to be so exceedingly miserable ', added Thorwaldsen with a humorous expression ".[1]

Byron had meant to stay in Rome till June ; but his eagerness to return to Marianna was so great that he left on May 26, and by his request she travelled half-way to meet him. He was back in Venice on the 28th, and soon went to the villa La Mira, on the Brenta, about seven miles inland and close to the city. " I have determined on another year ", he wrote to Murray on June 4, " and *many years* of residence if I can compass them. Marianna is with me ". Hobhouse joined him early in July ; Monk Lewis arrived in Venice about the same time, and stayed until the middle of August. His visit is memorable for the La Mira Separation Document. Lewis, during his stay, reported one of Brougham's indiscretions ; and Hobhouse, writing to Augusta in 1818, told her how he had found Byron and the Monk together, and a paper [2] just written and sealed. Augusta

---

[1] This account is taken from Karl Elze's *Life of Lord Byron* (English translation, 1872, p. 221) ; and there is a note to the page, pointing out that Thorwaldsen's impression agrees with that of the American painter William Edward West, who later painted Byron at Leghorn. " He assumed a countenance that did not belong to him, as if he were thinking of a frontispiece for *Childe Harold* ". The bust, which was done for Hobhouse, is now in the possession of the Right Hon. Henry Hobhouse. The head of Thorwaldsen's statue in Trinity College, Cambridge, is a repetition of this bust (*L. and J.* iv. 130).   [2] *Astarte*, p. 349. (App. I and J.)

wrote to Lady Byron, reporting this, and how Byron " called
upon Hobhouse to prove that he had done everything to induce
you to *come into court!* " (The italics and exclamation are in
the original letter from Augusta, and go far to prove that this
statement was regarded by her, and would be regarded by her
correspondent, as surprising and ludicrous.) " Hobhouse ", she
continues, " tried *Heaven and Earth* to persuade him not to give
it to Monk Lewis . . . *in vain* . . . and only the hour after it
was *gone*, B. expressed regret he had written and given it ".[1]
The document was found among Lewis's papers after his death
in 1818, and was first published in *The Academy* for October 9,
1869. The gist of it is that Byron had called repeatedly and in
vain for a statement of the charges against him. He added a
postscript to say that he was utterly ignorant of the allegations,
charges, or whatever name they had assumed. It may again
be noted that he speaks all through of charges. He knew the
reason ; the charges he could have extorted, as we have seen.
This very paper " shows his consciousness that he ought to have
done so, if his case had been producible " ; [2] and Lewis's sup-
pression of it from even private circulation shows that he too
recognised this. In *A Vindication of Lady Byron*, the writer
says : " He boasts that he stood at bay in Venice : he should
have stood at bay in London. . . . No man of the world,
conscious of a common offence only, and suffering under such
imputations, would have allowed his adversaries to keep back
any part of the charge ". But for Augusta's sake, as we now
know, he could not take action.

He had written to Murray on January 2, 1817—the anniversary
of his wedding-day, or funeral,[3] as he called it—to say : " I
have not done a stitch of poetry since I left Switzerland, and
have not at present the *estro* upon me. . . . [My poesy] is the
dream of my sleeping passions ; when they are awake, I cannot
speak their language, only in their Somnambulism, and just
now they are not dormant ". But the great success and the
many praises from friends of the Third *Harold* and the *Prisoner
of Chillon* soon awakened the desire to be forthcoming again.
On the 28th he wrote to Moore : " I am glad you like [the new
Childe Harold]. It is a fine indistinct piece of poetic desolation,
and my favourite. I was half mad during the time of its composi-
tion between metaphysics, mountains, lakes, love unextinguish-

---

[1] *Astarte*, p. 349.
[2] *Dict. Nat. Biog.*, article " Byron " (L. S.).
[3] " You talk of ' marriage '—ever since my own funeral, the word makes
me giddy, and throws me into a cold sweat. Pray, don't repeat it " (Letter
to Murray, April 2, 1817).

able, thoughts unutterable, and the nightmare of my own delinquencies ".

On February 15, he gave Murray the first hint of *Manfred*. " I have no great opinion of this piece of phantasy " he said ; " I have not even copied it off, and feel too lazy at present ". But he forwarded some pages of extracts under the same cover. He then applied himself in earnest to the third act, and on March 9 sent the MS. to Murray. " I have really and truly no notion whether it is good or bad. . . . It is too much in my old style. . . . I certainly am a devil of a mannerist, and must leave off ". To Moore, while awaiting Gifford's verdict, he called it a Bedlam tragedy ; and again to Murray, at the same time demanding three hundred guineas, he said, " You may put it in the fire if you like, and Gifford *don't* like ". On March 20 Murray wrote to say that Gifford, with a delighted countenance, had pronounced the first act wonderfully poetical ; but on March 28 came a further report. Gifford did not by any means like the third act. Byron answered at once : " The third act is certainly damned bad, and . . . has the dregs of my fever, during which it was written. It must on *no account* be published in its present state ". But he added that the impulse was gone, and he had no chance of making anything out of it. Perplexedly he wondered what the devil possessed him ; he would try again, perhaps, but " recollect *not* to publish, upon pain of I know not what ".

Meanwhile he wrote his *Lament of Tasso*. In this poem he used again the fine phrase : " I am not humble enough to be vindictive ", which stands in his letter to Lady Byron of March 5.[1] There is another of great beauty (little known) where, addressing Leonora d' Este, Tasso is made to say :

" I know not how—thy genius mastered mine—
My Star stood still before thee ".

In stanza ix., we find the self-portraiture which, whatever the subject, alone called forth the full range of the magic voice. " Every line he writes is a reminiscence, the reminiscence of a place or a passion. His mind was a cracked mirror, in which everything reflected itself directly, but as if scarred ".[2]

At Rome he " had at " the third act of *Manfred* and sent it home on May 5, having begun it later than April 26.[3] The

<hr>

[1] " No—still too proud to be vindictive—I
Have pardoned Princes' insults, and would die ".
(*Lament of Tasso*, line 105.)

[2] Arthur Symons, *The Romantic Movement*.

[3] Letter to Murray, April 26 : " I have done nothing at *Manfred's* third act ". This re-casting is the only example of a second attempt in all Byron's work. He wrote to Murray of *Don Juan :* " I am like the tiger ; if I miss my first spring, I go grumbling back to my jungle. . . . I can't correct ; I

drama was published on June 16, 1817, before *The Lament of Tasso*, which did not see the light until July.

From *Manfred*, Lord Lovelace's book derives its title of *Astarte*. The Nemesis in Act II bears that name, and is the dead whom Manfred would question.

> " Astarte ! my beloved ! speak to me :
> I have so much endured—so much endure—
> . . . Thou lovedst me
> Too much, as I loved thee ; we were not made
> To torture thus each other—though it were
> The deadliest sin to love as we have loved ".

The scene is laid throughout in that Alpine world which formed the theme of the Journal for Augusta. " It was the Staubbach, and the Jungfrau, and *something else* " which inspired him ; and though the literary influences assigned by the critics were manifold, we need but read the drama to acknowledge the authentic Byron. It is worth pointing out, too, that the Germanism of *Manfred* is accounted for by the fact that now, for the first time, he had been subjected to the influence of German landscape. He had seen the Rhine and the great Rhenish cities ; in the Bernese Alpine tour, had passed through German Switzerland, so different in feeling from the French region of Lausanne. No mind was ever so receptive as his for the spirit of place, as externally expressed. The character of the scenes he saw, in every country, coloured his imagination through and through. Nothing in Byron is more remarkable than his extreme sensibility to such influence, and the inveterate victory of his Self over it all. In this trait alone do I partially accept the hard-worked epithet of chameleon, as applied to him. He adapted himself to the scenic—and only to the scenic— environment like a chameleon ; but from the very adaptation he emerged more triumphantly the same than before. His personality dominated even the Alps ! Thus, in *Manfred*, we see Galt's " mystery in a winding-sheet, crowned with a halo " stalking from peak to peak ; as in the early narrative pieces we saw the glorified pirate of the salad-days stride Eastern sands and hills and plains, and become an old English Baron of repellent mien as soon as he was transferred, mysteriously, to Lara's broad domain.

The motive of *Manfred* is remorse for an inexpiable crime. This had been long the spell for Byron's imagination ; now, with the real remorse, he wrote it out of him. " I am certainly a devil of a mannerist and must leave off ", he had said in send-

can't and I won't. Nobody ever succeeds in it, great or small " (Moore, p. 464.)

ing home the drama ; and I do not think it has before been pointed out that with this work he *did* leave off. " My pang shall find a voice "—that cry of *Manfred* is the word of his poetic life till then. *Then* he did know the pang, then uttered it—and for the last time. Not again does the Byronic hero take the stage. He turned to historical and metaphysical drama, and to the Pulcian *Beppo, Vision of Judgment, Don Juan* : in a word, he left off, and was no more a devil of a mannerist. Hence *Manfred* is of supreme importance in a review of his work. To speak for the moment as a fatalist, I feel that Byron was forced by character, which is the only destiny, to do as he had done. Remorse he *had* to know ; and only by some such error of the heart could he have known it. To do spiritual murder—that was, to speak cynically, the formula for his development. Physical murder would have left him where it found him ; he would have felt too well the scenic value of a Cain. In such " murder " as he had done, there was no scenic value—only remorse and shame. The pang had all its bitterness, and thus could find a voice so poignant that the final word was said ; and he could feel his imagination emancipated at last by the measure of its knowledge and its suffering.

> " She had the same lone thoughts and wanderings,
>
> . . . .
> Pity and smiles and tears—which I had not ;
> And tenderness—but that I had for her ;
> Humility—and that I never had.
> Her faults were mine—her virtues were her own—
> I loved her and destroyed her.
>
> . . . .
> Not with my hand, but heart, which broke her heart ;
> It gazed on mine, and withered. I have shed
> Blood, but not hers—and yet her blood was shed ;
> I saw—and could not stanch it ".[1]

" Conclusions most forbidden "—only those would serve.

> " Because my nature was averse from life,
> And yet not cruel ".

***

Already with the Fourth Harold, his emancipation is apparent. It is from an altered standpoint that he sees himself. Remorse is done with. Seated by the tomb of Cecilia Metella on the Appian Way, he dreams of a little bark of hope, wonders whither he should steer his rude boat if he had it, and concludes :

> " There woos no home, nor hope, nor life, save what is here ".

But the tone is manlier.

---

[1] This passage is immeasurably the best he ever wrote in blank verse.

20

" The thorns which I have reaped are of the tree
I planted—they have torn me—and I bleed :
I should have known what fruit would spring from such a seed ".

. . . .

" All suffering doth destroy, or is destroyed
Even by the sufferer—and, in each event,
Ends " . . . .

—the maxim of Epicurus, which Montaigne adapted : " *Tu ne
la sentiras guère longtemps, si tu la sens trop ; elle mettra fin à soy
ou à toy* ".
The feeling may return .

" . . . It may be a sound—
A tone of music—summer's eve—or spring—
A flower—the wind—the ocean—which shall wound,
Striking the electric chain with which we are darkly bound "

but we shall " demand our souls back " . . . and he, demanding
his, now for the first time swept the full chords of his intellect.
Here are such phrases as Mr. Symons cites ; and let me point
out that no phrase thus cited is of earlier date than this fourth
canto.

Not that the past is forgotten. It will colour his life and
work to the end. But he has found another way to use it ;
" the ineradicable soul " learns a new word. He stands in the
Colosseum, and appeals to Nemesis—the great imprecation
breaks forth.

" . . . Let me not have worn
This iron in my soul in vain—shall *they* not mourn ?

. . . .

. . . A far hour shall wreak
The deep prophetic fulness of this verse,
And pile on human heads the mountain of my curse !

. . . .

That curse shall be Forgiveness.—Have I not—
Hear me, my mother Earth ! behold it, Heaven !—
Have I not had to wrestle with my lot ?
Have I not suffered things to be forgiven ?
Have I not had my brain seared, my heart riven,
Hopes sapped, name blighted, Life's life hid away ?

. . . .

But there is that within me which shall tire
Torture and Time, and breathe when I expire ".

***

In was on July 1—having made a beginning on June 26—
that he sent to Murray in a letter the opening stanza of the
fourth canto. " There ! there's a brick of your new Babel for
you ! and now, sirrah, what say you to the sample ? " On the
15th : " The stanzas of Canto Fourth have jumped to *one*

hundred and four; and such stanzas! By St. Anthony . . .
some of them are the right thing!"

He had had in June a lively encounter with "my Murray"
about the payments for *Manfred* and *The Lament of Tasso*.
For each he had demanded three hundred guineas. But Murray
had demurred, and he had threatened to desert to Paternoster
Row. "If you come over with me your pitiful-hearted speeches
about 'can' and 'not', of which, if you are not ashamed, you
ought to be".

Murray gave the six hundred guineas.

This was the first payment which Byron used for his own
benefit. Henceforth, he announces, he means to be as mercenary
as possible; he tells Murray fairly that it will be a convenience
to him to be paid as soon as may be, and desires that a price
be named for the fourth canto. "If you don't, *I* will, so I advise
you in time".

Murray offered fifteen hundred guineas.

"I won't take it. I ask two thousand five hundred guineas
for it, which you will either give or not as you think proper. . . .
If we do not agree, recollect that you have had the refusal".
In a later letter, before hearing, he says: "I look upon *Childe
Harold* as my best; and as I begun, I think of concluding with
it "; but remembers the similar intention with the *Corsair*, and
makes no resolutions. "However, I fear I shall never do better.
. . . God grant me some judgment! . . . for I doubt my own
exceedingly".

It was the period of transition. In this letter occurs the
famous pronouncement: "Depend upon it, it is all Horace
then "—alluding to the age of Pope—" and Claudian now,
among us; and if I had to begin again, I would model myself
accordingly". His admiration for Pope altered only from that
to worship; we shall find him, later, speaking of that cult as the
Christianity of poetry; and most of his prose writings are con-
cerned with "the little Queen Anne's man" beyond the verge
of tediousness. He always regarded himself as a prodigal son
from the Alexandrine mansions. "No one has done more
through negligence to corrupt the language". "We are all
wrong, except Rogers, Crabbe, and Campbell ", he again laments
—and at the very time, was writing *Beppo*! . . . He put a
sketch of the Fourth Harold into Hobhouse's hands at La Mira,
and Hobhouse "made a list of objects which [Byron] had not
noticed, and which he afterwards described in several magnificent
stanzas ". The extended work was not finished until December
1817. On January 7 Hobhouse left Venice for England,[1] carry-

---

[1] On January 27 Byron wrote to Murray: "Mr. Hobhouse is, or
ought to be, swimming with my Commentaries and his own Coat of Mail

ing with him the whole of the MSS.—including *Beppo*. *Harold* was published on April 28; *Beppo*, two months earlier—the latter anonymously at first, but a second edition was soon called for, and this bore Byron's name.

in his teeth and right hand, in a cork jacket, between Calais and Dover ". In this passage, how like the manner is to that of Dickens in *his* letters ! There is no other such example, though, in all Byron's prose writings.

CHAPTER XX

REALISATION OF EXILE—1817-1819

Birth of Allegra—Allegra is brought to him at Venice—The Hoppners—
Visit from John Hanson—Newstead Abbey sold—Ennui and depravation
—Affection for Moore—Begins *Don Juan*—Sir Samuel Romilly—Friends
advise suppression of *Don Juan*—Byron's confidence in its worth—His
powerful letter

MEANWHILE at Bath, on January 12, 1817, Claire
Clairmont's baby had been born—a daughter, called
before her baptism Alba ; but when the ceremony took
place on March 9, Clara Allegra. Both names were reminiscent of
the Genevan days. Alba was the feminine, as it were, of Byron's
petit nom of Albé ; Allegra was derived from the Villa Mont
Alègre.

Claire had remained with Shelley and Mary after the return
to England, passing at Bath as Mrs. Clairmont. She was cheer-
ful in the early days of home-coming—reading the Chaworth
Duel trial, and finding the Wicked Lord's behaviour truly Albeian.
" He seemed to have the family complaint of suspicion and
defence where any reasonable man would have taken no offence ".
But soon such trouble fell upon the household as stopped all
smiles together. First they heard of Fanny Imlay's suicide—
then of Harriet's. Claire fell into low spirits—wretched, irritable
brooding, and Mary felt again the strain and ennui of such
society. She wrote to Shelley, away on his constant occupation
of house-hunting : " Give me a garden, and *absentia* Claire, and
I will thank my love for many favours ". She was not yet her
Sweet Elf's wife, but on December 30 in the same year she
became so ; and in the last week of February 1818, the Shelley
household—now consisting of husband and wife and their little
William, with Claire and her Alba—moved to Albion House,
Marlow. Claire resumed the style of *Miss* Clairmont, the baby
passing as the child of a friend, Mrs. Auburn, who lived in London,
and had sent her to the country for her health. But there was
little hope of this fiction's gaining credence, for Claire (as she
wrote to Byron in 1820) nursed Allegra day and night during
the first year of her infancy.

In September the desirability of again leaving England became acute. Shelley's health was poor ; but a more cogent reason was the embarrassment which had inevitably arisen about Alba. Already in 1816, the party had suffered under similar scandal ; and in this July of 1818, Shelley had proposed to Byron that the child should be boarded out at Marlow. No answer had been vouchsafed. If they now went to Italy, there would be an opportunity of placing Alba in her father's hands ; and Mary was unfeignedly desirous that this should be done as soon as possible. " Indeed, my love ", she wrote to Shelley, " Alba's departure must not be delayed. I do not see how she is to get there unless we take her. Claire talks about promises . . . but promises with Albé ! The first thing that engaged his attention would put them all out of his head. . . . Why, it is the labour of several months to get any kind of answer ".

At last the Italian sojourn was decided on. The caravan left England on March 11, 1818—Shelley looking for the last time, as it was to prove, on English fields and skies. Claire was with them—Claire and her " darling ", the pretty baby whom they called the little bright-eyed Commodore. Two days earlier she, with the two Shelley children, had been baptized ; and thenceforth she was Allegra—for the first name, Clara, was entirely ignored.

They went first to Milan. From Lyons, on their way, Shelley had written to Byron (who had refused to correspond with Claire) telling him that Allegra was so far on the road ; he wrote again from Milan, and there came on April 21 (as Claire entered in her Journal) " a letter from Albé : nothing but discomfort ". Shortly afterwards Shelley met a Venetian at Milan Post-Office ; and this chance acquaintance gave him such tidings of Byron's manner of life as made the project of sending Allegra seem ill-advised. But Claire was resolved. Nothing ought to stand in the way of her child's acknowledgment by " an English nobleman, the most illustrious poet of Europe ". Accordingly on April 28, Elise, the Swiss nurse who had been with the baby from the first, started with her for Venice. " I sent my little darling " wrote the mother in a note-book in after years. " She was the only thing I had to love . . . and I had never parted from her from her birth, not for an hour even ". Shelley pointed out the risk she was running. " Remember, Claire ", he wrote to her four years later, " when you rejected my earnest advice, and checked me with that contempt which I have not merited from you, at Milan, and how vain now is your regret ! " Still, the mother felt that she " ought not, for the sake of gratifying my own affections, to deprive [the child] of a brilliant position in life ".

Byron's first mention of the new element occurs in a letter to Augusta of May 27, 1817, while the Shelleys were still in England. " By the way, it seems that I have got another [child]—a *daughter* by that same lady, whom you will recognise . . . I mean *her* who returned to England to become a Mamma incog., and whom I pray the Gods to keep there.   I am a little puzzled how to dispose of this new production, but shall probably send for and place it in a Venetian convent, to become a good Catholic and (it may be) a Nun, being a character somewhat wanted in our family.   They tell me it is very pretty, with blue eyes and dark hair ; and, although I never was attached nor pretended attachment to the mother, still, in case of the eternal war and alienation which I foresee about my legitimate daughter, Ada, it may be as well to have something to repose a hope upon ".

When the new production arrived, he had left the Segati lodgings in the Frezzeria, and was oscillating between La Mira and the Palazzo Mocenigo on the Grand Canal—Marianna Segati and Margarita Cogni sharing the honours of *maîtresse-en-titre*.   Mrs. Hoppner, wife of the English Consul-General at Venice (who was now the closest intimate Byron had there), seeing the forlorn condition of the child and the difficulties for Elise in doing anything for her (the Mocenigo household consisted only of men-servants), soon proposed to Byron to take charge of her.   He had already sent Augusta a report : " Very pretty, remarkably intelligent . . . but what is remarkable, much more like Lady Byron than her mother—so much so as to stupefy the learned Fletcher and astonish me. . . . She has very blue eyes, and that singular forehead, fair curly hair, and a devil of a spirit —but that is Papa's ".

Letters from Elise decided Claire to set out from Bagni di Lucca—where the caravan now was—with Shelley as her companion, and entreat through him for some brief intercourse with her child.   On August 19 they started.   Claire had at first resolved not to go so far as Venice, but remain at a little distance, " so as not to irritate Albé by entering the same city ".   But at Padua she changed her mind : she would go on to Venice, but would not do more than write to Byron.   Shelley was to go to him, and she would wait at the Hoppners'.   Arrived at Venice, their very gondolier told them unedifying tales of Byron ; the Hoppners' account was in essence the same ; and on discussion, it was resolved that Claire's presence should be kept a secret, for Hoppner confessed that Byron had said he should instantly leave the place if she appeared in it.

Shelley saw Byron at three o'clock, and found him good-humoured.   He did not wish to part with Allegra for any length of time, but offered to let Claire have her for a week at Padua.

" In fact ", he added, " after all I have no right over the child. If Claire likes to take it, let her take it. I do not say what most people would in such a situation, that I will refuse to provide for it, or abandon it, if she does this ; but she must surely be aware herself how very imprudent such a measure would be ".

Shelley was the more inclined to agree to the Paduan plan because he had greatly liked the Hoppners—" the most amiable people I ever knew . . . Mrs. Hoppner [1] has hazel eyes, and sweet looks—rather Maryish ", he wrote to Mary. And Byron's good-humour lasted ; he took Shelley for a ride on the Lido, where they talked of many things besides Allegra. Back at the Mocenigo, he developed the Paduan plan *en prince*. He had rented from Hoppner a villa—I Cappuccini—on the Euganean Hills, near Este and within a few miles of Arquà, where Petrarch loved and died. He had not yet inhabited it himself,[2] though he had taken it for two years ; now he offered to lend it to Shelley and his family, and send Allegra thither to be with Claire for a while.

Accordingly Mary hastened from Lucca to Este. One of her babies was taken dangerously ill on the road, and after many vicissitudes of travel, died at Venice on September 24. Claire was then at the Cappuccini Villa with little William and Allegra. Mary and Shelley stayed at Venice until the 29th with the Hoppners—seeing Byron each day. On October 12, leaving Claire at Este, they came again to Venice. Mary was much with the Hoppners, her husband with Byron. It was now, with calmer vision, that Shelley could gauge the ruin working in Albé's character. He had written, in the summer-house at the Cappuccini Villa, the opening lines of *Julian and Maddalo*, in which he draws portraits of himself and Byron. In the Introduction, Count Maddalo—Byron—is depicted as " a person of the most consummate genius. . . . But it is his weakness to be proud. . . . I say that Maddalo is proud, because I can find no other word to express the concentrated and impatient feelings which consume him ; but it is on his own hopes and affections only that he seems to trample, for in social life no human being can be more gentle, patient and unassuming. . . . His more serious conversation is a sort of intoxication ". The poem opens with a description of the ride on the Lido, and of a sunset at Venice ; then comes the famous picture of Allegra.

---

[1] Mrs. Hoppner was of Swiss birth. Byron, writing to her husband in 1819, says : " Pray make my respects to Mrs. Hoppner, and assure her of my unalterable reverence for the singular goodness of her disposition ".

[2] He never did inhabit it.

"A lovelier toy sweet Nature never made ;
A serious, subtle, wild, yet gentle being ;
Graceful without design, and unforeseeing ;
With eyes—Oh ! speak not of her eyes ! which seem
Twin mirrors of Italian heaven, yet gleam
With such deep meaning as we never see
But in the human countenance. . . ."

On October 29 the sojourn at Byron's villa ended. Shelley took Allegra to Venice, yielded her back into the Hoppners' care, and on November 5 the caravan set off again—this time for Rome.

This—and for long previously—was the time of Byron's daily rides along the Lido with Hoppner,[1] of which the latter gave Moore an account for the Life. Byron needed a friend, for his English correspondents cruelly neglected him ; during the summer of 1818 his letters are full of reproaches on this score. " When I tell you ", he wrote to Murray on June 18, " that I have not heard a word from England since very early in May, I have made the eulogium of my friends, or the persons who call themselves so, since I have written so often and in the greatest anxiety. Thank God, the longer I am absent, the less cause I see for regretting the Country or its living contents. . . Tell Mr. Hobhouse that . . . I will never forgive him (or any-body) the atrocity of their late neglect and silence at a time when I wished particularly to hear (for every reason) from my friends ".[2]

Newstead had been sold for £94,500 to Colonel Wildman in 1817, and Byron had at once begun to make arrangements for the liquidation of his debts. The Rochdale business was in full swing again, but the Hansons, father and son, were as of old exasperating him with delays. They and Hobhouse urged upon him a return to England—or if this were too decided a step, at least to come as far as Geneva to meet and discuss proceedings. He had written in April most positively to refuse : " Every step nearer to England would be to me disgusting ". Hanson or his messenger must come to Venice. "I won't stir ". He was particularly hurt with Hobhouse for joining in the persuasion : " Hobhouse's wish is, if possible, to force me back to England : he will not succeed ; and if he did, I would not stay. I hate the country and like this ; and all foolish opposition, of course,

---

[1] Richard Belgrave Hoppner was the second son of John Hoppner, R.A., and had inherited some of his father's talent. He was appointed English Consul at Venice in 1814. Byron said of him to Lady Blessington : " He was a good listener, and his remarks were acute and original ; he is besides a thoroughly good man ". Hoppner lived until 1872.

[2] The words from " Tell Mr. Hobhouse " were omitted by Moore. I quote from L. and J. iv. 243.

merely adds to the feeling ". Hobhouse's wish was natural ;
but Byron's friends seem certainly to have treated him with a
surprising lack of consideration. Apparently he *had* been half-
persuaded to go to Geneva after all ; for in July he wrote to
Murray to say that he was still waiting for Hanson's clerk,
" but luckily not at Geneva. All my good friends wrote to
me to hasten there to meet him, but not one had the good
sense or good-nature to write afterwards to tell me that it
would be time and a journey thrown away, as he could
not set off for some months after the period appointed. If I
had taken the journey . . . I never would have spoken to one
of you as long as I existed ".

At last John Hanson, his son Newton, and the solicitor for
Colonel Wildman left England on October 12,[1] and reached
Venice a month later. Newton Hanson's account of the visit
is entertaining. His father was to have brought some packages
from Murray—three large bales. " But he would only take
one of them. Unfortunately, the one he selected did not contain
a single book, only a few different-sized kaleidoscopes, tooth-
brushes, tooth-powders, etc.[2] At this Lord Byron was greatly
annoyed, and would not be pacified for some hours ". At first
meeting the youth observed " a nervous sensitiveness in his
lordship, which produced a silence for some minutes. It was
broken by his observing, ' Well, Hanson ! I never expected
you would have ventured so far '. . . . His eyes were suffused
with tears. . . . Lord Byron could not have been more than
thirty, but he looked forty. His face had become pale, bloated,
and sallow. He had grown very fat, his shoulders broad and
round, and the knuckles of his hands were lost in fat ".

This was the period of Byron's deepest depravation, not only
morally but physically. If it had not been for the daily gallops
on the Lido, he would probably have sunk under the malaria
of the canals and the enervation of his own debauchery. It
was at Venice that he first realised the bitterness of banishment.

---

[1] They had expected to meet Byron at Sécheron, which they reached
on October 21, but a letter from him awaited them : " The season . . .
being so far advanced, I cannot possibly cross the Simplon now ". Evi-
dently the persuasion had gone further than one could have supposed
from his earlier letters.

[2] The tooth-powder ought to have pleased Byron. His requests for
" Waite's red tooth-powders " were incessant and urgent : " by the Lord,
send them ! " Soda-powders were as often needed ; he told Murray that he
would rather have them than any " poeshies ". The kaleidoscopes remain
unaccounted for. He wrote to Murray of Hanson's chosen parcel : " ' For
what we have received, the Lord make us thankful '—for without his
aid I shall not be so. . . . You may imagine his [Hanson's] reception ".
Newton Hanson's account of the visit is quoted from *L. and J.* iv, 266–67.

In Switzerland the Shelleys and Hobhouse had been his companions and fellow-voyagers ; Hobhouse too had spent many months of 1817 with him at La Mira or the Mocenigo. But with the dawning of 1818, the exile found himself indeed an exile. We have read Shelley's view of his Venetian companions ; outside that circle there lay indeed the Albrizzi and Benzoni salons, but to him, even at the best impatient of Blues, these gatherings must have seemed provincial indeed compared with Holland and Melbourne Houses, and the drawing-rooms of Rogers, Lady Jersey, the Humphry Davys, and a score of others. Moreover, in those rooms he had been the idol to whom great ladies were submissively led for presentation ; here, though run after, it was in a different spirit—and in a foreign speech. When he became more familiar with the Venetian language, he too soon discovered all the shallowness and ignorance which " that soft bastard Latin " covered. . . . And in this isolation and ennui, his English friends forgot him. Alone and sick at heart, he wrote oftener than they wanted ; soon, with a piercing pathos, we find him—not ironically—apologising for his frequent letters. There, in London, amid all the familiar bustle and talk and pre-occupations, they " meant to write " (like Rogers and many another,[1] and ourselves to our own exiles) ; and here, in Venice, almost daily he dashed off a brilliant eager appeal—so gay for all the reproaches, so full of spirit, gusto, and affection, that even

---

[1] He did hear from Augusta, but her style was at no time exhilarating. He told Murray in July 1817 that he heard from nobody who did not tell him something as disagreeable as possible ; and again, in November, " I hear nothing . . . except in a few unintelligible words from an unintelligible woman ". Again, in 1821 (àpropos documents for his Memoirs) he told Murray that Augusta might let him have the Swiss Journal ; " but her nerves have been in such a state since 1815, that there is no knowing. Lady Byron's people, and Lady Caroline Lamb's people, and a parcel of that set, got about her and frightened her with all sorts of hints and menaces, so that she has never since been able to write *me* a *clear common letter*, and is so full of mysteries and miseries that I can only sympathise without always understanding her. All my loves, too, make a point of calling on her . . . the year before last, I think, Lady F. W. W. marched in upon her, and Lady O., a few years ago, spoke to her at a party ; and these and such-like calamities have made her afraid of her shadow. It is a very odd fancy that they all take to her ; it was only six months ago that I had some difficulty in preventing the Countess G. from invading her with an Italian letter " (*L. and J.* v. 371). This is plainly—almost confessedly—written for posterity ; but Lord Lovelace gives a letter to Augusta on June 3, 1817, which bears out the description of her communications. " For the life of me I can't make out whether your disorder is a broken heart or ear-ache—or whether it is *you* that have been ill or the children—or what your melancholy and mysterious apprehensions tend to, or refer to—whether to Caroline Lamb's novels—Mrs. Clermont's evidence—Lady Byron's magnanimity, or any other piece of imposture " (*Astarte*, p. 285).

to-day, as we read, our anger burns against the hearts that could wait so long to throb into an answering word.

Chafing and fretting thus, in the pain of unacknowledged home-sickness, he fell deeper and deeper into the state we have seen. " He had grown very fat ". To grow fat was, paradoxically, the mark of Byron's despair. He might not eat like other men—it was excess for him ; at Venice in this period, he did eat like other men, and (never so abstemious with wine as with food) he drank much more than most of them. Soon he became gross in form and visage (Jeaffreson, from whom this account is largely taken, is always vivid and convincing on these external matters) ; and, far worse than in the days at Cambridge, " his flesh was pasty and flaccid, and the pallor of his countenance had the faint yellow tinge . . . of the sufferer from liver ". He suffered tortures from dyspepsia—maddening torment, sleepless nights and wretched days ; his temper grew more violent and more sullen ; his voice lost the music which had made children turn from play to hear it ; his hair thinned and whitened —" anxiety was discernible in the resoluteness of his blue eyes, whilst his countenance wore a peculiar look of apprehension and distress ".

To Moore, who alone seems to have felt and shown the sympathy he needed (and Moore had hitherto been a bad correspondent), he wrote in the early part of 1818 : " I don't much care what the wretches of the world think of me—all that's past. But I care a good deal what *you* think of me, and so say what you like. You *know* that I am not sullen ; and as to being *savage*, such things depend on circumstances. . . . Throughout life, your loss must be my loss, and your gain my gain ; and though my heart may ebb, there will be always a drop for you among the dregs ". It is always in the letters to Moore that Byron as the man's man most lovably emerges. Murray got the brilliant *tours de force* ; Moore, the warm heart's voice. Both got the *chronique scandaleuse* of the English milord at Venice; both, those searching analyses of Italian morality which it so fascinated him to indite—him, for whom, " unlike all other poets, society exists as well as human nature ". But if we knew Byron only through the letters, and knew not those to Moore, we should miss him at his best. Of the appearance of *Lalla Rookh*, he wrote : " Really and truly I want you to make a great hit, if only out of self-love because we happen to be old cronies ; and I have no doubt you will—I am sure you *can*. But you are, I'll be sworn, in a devil of a pucker ; and *I* am *not* at your elbow, and Rogers *is*. I envy him." Again : " To *you*, Fortune is a good deal in arrear, and she will come round —mind if she don't. . . . What you can do for yourself, you have done and will do ; and surely there are some others in the world who would not be sorry to be of use, if you would allow them to be useful ". But even Moore delayed sometimes to answer. " Death and fiends ! why don't you tell me where you are, what you are, and how you are ? . . . If you think of coming out for a summer or so, tell me, that I may be on the hover for you ".

Moore did not visit Venice until 1819, when Byron's life had taken a different turn—one which, in the Irishman's eyes, gave no promise of lasting happiness. But before this change he had at least modified his courses. A reform was urgent, and after the Carnival of 1819 he definitely entered upon it. Disgust with his excesses had already driven him more than once to escape from his infamous house, and spend whole nights on the water in his gondola. Hoppner too had made many a remonstrance ; but a more powerful influence than Hoppner's or any man's or woman's was at work. He had begun *Don Juan*.[1] In July 1818 occurs the earliest allusion : " Two stories, one serious and one ludicrous (à la *Beppo*) ". But energy was lacking. He had heard little from England of his last publications ; Murray's silence had, indeed, been so prolonged that Byron had written to warn him that he meant to turn to Messrs. Longman with his next productions. Over and over again he begged for news of the reception of *Manfred*,[2] *The Lament of Tasso, Beppo*. " I should then know how and in what manner to proceed. I should not like to give them " (the public) " too much, which may possibly have been the case already. I once wrote from the fulness of my mind and the love of fame (not as an *end*, but a *means*, to obtain that influence over men's minds which is power in itself and in its consequences), and now from habit and from avarice ; so that the effect may probably be as different as the inspiration. I have the same facility, and indeed necessity, of composition, to avoid idleness (though idleness in a hot country is a pleasure), but a much greater indifference to what is to become of it, after it has served my immediate purpose ".

---

[1] Mr. Coleridge points out in the Introduction to *Don Juan*, that " the composition of Byron's two great poems was all but co-extensive with his poetical life. He began the first canto of *Childe Harold* in the autumn of 1809, and he did not complete the fourth canto till the spring of 1818. He began the first canto of *Don Juan* in the autumn of 1818, and he was still at work on a seventeenth canto in the spring of 1823 ".

[2] In *A Vindication of Lady Byron*, the author says : " Lord Byron was eager to learn, and Mr. Murray as eager to conceal, what the publisher thought and what the world said of *Manfred*. . . . [Lord Byron] suspected a cause for the silence, and concluded his part of the correspondence by the assurance that he was prepared to hear, ' not of the mere paltry disappointments of an author, but things more serious ' " (p. 350).

He spurred himself to work, however, and in September announced to Moore : " It is called *Don Juan*, and is meant to be a little quietly facetious about everything ". He added : " The bore of copying it out is intolerable ; and if I had an amanuensis he would be of no use, as my writing is so difficult to decipher ". Perhaps in this dilemma, he remembered the vituperated Blues—Annabella and Claire—who had been so eager and so skilful in his service ; perhaps this, and the other troubles, helped to urge him towards the renaissance of January 1819. Not yet, though, was he ready for the *vita nuova*. In this letter to Moore we find another rhapsody on Margarita Cogni. " I like this kind of animal, and am sure that I should have preferred Medea to any woman that ever breathed ". And instantly there flashes forth a memory of his wife. " You may perhaps wonder that I don't in that case "—a long line of asterisks is all that Moore here vouchsafed to posterity ; but the allusion is evident from the sequel. " I could have forgiven the dagger or the bowl—anything but the deliberate desolation piled upon me, when I stood alone upon my hearth with my household gods shivered around me.[1] . . . Do you suppose I have forgotten it ? It has comparatively swallowed up in me every other feeling, and I am only a spectator upon earth, till a tenfold opportunity offers. It may come yet. There are others more to be blamed than ***, and it is on these that my eyes are fixed unceasingly ". Soon tidings came from England to indulge this dream of Nemesis. On November 18 he heard of the suicide of Sir Samuel Romilly, who, on October 29, had " cut his throat for the loss of his wife ".[2] At once he sat down and wrote to Lady Byron—a pæan of savage triumph. And why ? Because Sir Samuel, who had a general retainer from Byron, had either (as he himself alleged) forgotten it and so allowed himself to be retained for the other side in 1816, or (as Jeaffreson distinctly states) had " returned the fee [3] by which Byron had retained him, on the ground that Lady Byron had a right to the privileges of separation ". Not only to his wife did Byron write of this. It

---

[1] Here is an interesting instance of Byron's repetition of phrases. This of the household gods appears in *Don Juan*, canto i. stanza 36, and—more remarkably still—in *Marino Faliero*, the Venetian tragedy of 1820.

[2] Sir Samuel Romilly had been Solicitor-General in 1806–7. He was distinguished for his probity, independence, humanity, and liberality. " His moral character ", said Sir James Mackintosh in 1810, " stands higher than that of any conspicuous Englishman now alive ". Lord Lansdowne told Moore that Lady Romilly " was the only person in the world to whom Romilly wholly unbent and unbosomed himself ; when he lost her, therefore, the very vent of his heart was stopped up ".

[3] " A long and general retainer " is the way in which Byron described the arrangement.

is horrible to read his words to Murray on the same topic.[1]
" Could not the dotard wait till his drivelling did it ? ". (Sir
Samuel was only sixty-four at the time of his death.) " It may
be very fine to forgive—but I would not have forgiven him
living, and I will not affect to pity him dead ". In a later letter :
" I still loathe him—as much as we can hate dust " ; and again,
on Murray's remonstrance : " You ask me to spare Romilly—
ask the worms. . . . You may talk to the wind . . . but *not*
to me on the subject of a Villain who wronged me ".

At this time his constitution was so racked by excesses that
everything infuriated him. It is the time of the Dedication of
Don Juan to Southey ; of the ineffably tedious abuse of Sotheby,[2]
an inoffensive old gentleman of letters whom he suspected of
having sent him an anonymous criticsm of the *Prisoner of Chillon*
volume ; of the long sulking with Hanson and his son ; of the
averted breach with Murray. But almost as soon as he and his
publisher were friends again, they were to be plunged into the
Don Juan turmoil. Quickly came the news from Murray that a
committee of Byron's friends—Hobhouse, Kinnaird, Scrope
Davies, Moore, and Hookham Frere—were unanimous in advising
the suppression of the poem. He acquiesced at first. " But I
protest . . . I write in a passion and a sirocco ".[3] For once—
for the first time—he was sure of himself. Hitherto all adverse
criticism had shaken him ; now he wrote with increasing confi-
dence, as the feeling across the water grew stronger against the
design of publishing even anonymously. Already by February 1,
he was changing his mind about acquiescence in suppression.
He wrote to Murray, who had volunteered a great price [4] for
the poem : " We will circumvent your cursed puritanical com-
mittee on that point in the end. . . . If they had told me the
poetry was bad, I would have acquiesced ; but they say the
contrary, and then talk to me about morality. . . . I maintain
that it is the most moral of poems ; but if people won't discern
the moral, that is their fault, not mine ". So far, though, he
still half-consented to suppression : " in any case, you will
print fifty for private distribution ". But by February 22 :
" It is very probable that I shall decide on publication ".

---

[1] In the first edition of his book, Moore retained the passages in letters
to Murray relating to Sir Samuel Romilly, " though aware of the erroneous
impression under which they were written ". But it was represented to
him that such an attack upon such a man ought not to be left on record,
and in the second edition the passages were expunged, though a note
(p. 399) alluded to them with some explicitness.

[2] Sotheby was attacked in *Beppo*.

[3] " I have not been in bed till seven or eight in the morning these
ten days past ".

[4] *Letters of Joseph Jekyll*, p. 75.

In the end of January he had at last fallen seriously ill. On April 6—after finishing the second *Juan* canto—he wrote to Murray : " About the beginning of the year, I was in a state of great exhaustion . . . and I was obliged to reform my ' way of life '. . . . I am better in health and morals, and very much yours ever—B ".

This is the concluding paragraph of the letter. Murray thus answered the whole on April 27 : " Your stomach may be weak, but, upon my soul, the Intellects are in full vigour, for I never read a more powerful letter in my life than the last with which you favoured me ".

Here it is, that we may end on the same note of admiration for the exile with whom our hearts have ached till now.

" You shan't make *canticles* of my cantos. The poem will please, if it is lively ; if it is stupid, it will fail ; but I will have none of your damned cutting and slashing. If you please, you may publish *anonymously* ; it will perhaps be better ; but I will battle my way against them all, like a porcupine.

" So you and Mr. Foscolo, etc., want me to undertake what you call a ' great work ' ? an Epic Poem, I suppose, or some such pyramid. I'll try no such thing ; I hate tasks. And then ' seven or eight years ' ! God send us all well this day three months, let alone years. If one's years can't be better employed than in sweating poesy, a man had better be a ditcher. And works, too !—is *Childe Harold* nothing ? You have so many ' *divine* ' poems, is it nothing to have written a *human* one ? without any of your worn-out machinery. Why, man, I could have spun the thoughts of the four cantos of that poem into twenty, had I wanted to book-make, and its passion into as many modern tragedies. Since you want *length*, you shall have enough of *Juan*, for I'll make fifty cantos.

" Besides, I mean to write my best work in *Italian*, and it will take me nine years more thoroughly to master the language ; and then if my fancy exist, and I exist too, I will try what I *can* do *really*. As to the estimation of the English which you talk of, let them calculate what it is worth, before they insult me with their insolent condescension.

" I have not written for their pleasure. If they are pleased, it is that they chose to be so ; I have never flattered their opinions, nor their pride ; nor will I. Neither will I make ' Ladies' books ' ' al dilettar le femine e la plebe '. I have written from the fulness of my mind, from passion, from impulse, from many motives, but not for their ' sweet voices .'

" I know the precise worth of popular applause, for few scribblers have had more of it ; and if I chose to swerve into their paths, I could retain it, or resume it. But I neither love ye, nor fear ye ; and though I buy with ye and sell with ye, and talk with ye, I will neither eat with ye, drink with ye, nor pray with ye. They made me, without my search, a species of popular idol ; they, without reason or judgment, beyond the caprice of their good pleasure, threw down the image from its pedestal ; it was not broken with the fall, and they would, it seems, again replace it—but they shall not ".

He had his compensations, as he had had in the long-ago South-well days—as genius always has.

CHAPTER XXI

TERESA GUICCIOLI—1819

The Countess Guiccioli—Letters to Hoppner and Murray—Departure for Ravenna—Byron's licence in letters—His cruelty to women—Life at Ravenna—The Guicciolis leave for Bologna—*Cavalier' serventism*—*Don Juan*—Harassments—The Corinne letter—Establishment with Teresa at La Mira—Moore arrives—Count Guiccioli intervenes—" I am for England "—The summons to Ravenna—Byron goes

WITH Byron's restoration to health in the spring of 1819, he began a definite reform in his way of living. The women of the Mocenigo had been banished during his illness and convalescence ; and none of them ever returned. This was partly owing to Hoppner's influence. That wise friend had told him, not that Venice was shocked, but that Venice was contemptuously amused, by his courses. It was sufficient now, as it had been in the milder Newstead days, to disgust him with his Paphian girls ; and now as then he marked the change of mind and life by a return to society. He began again to frequent the salons, which he had for the last year seldom visited ; and in April 1819 he met at the Countess Benzoni's the young bride of an elderly nobleman—Teresa, daughter of Count Gamba of Ravenna, and wife to Count Guiccioli, aged sixty, one of the richest landowners in the Romagna.

Byron and she had been together at the Countess Albrizzi's in the autumn of 1818, three days after Teresa's marriage ; but they had not been introduced. Now, at Madame Benzoni's, they were presented to one another. Neither desired the introduction. She was tired, had " come with great repugnance to this party, purely in obedience to Count Guiccioli " ; Byron, as we know, refused most new acquaintances. The Countess threw over this attitude, in her special case, a good deal of romantic glamour. " When I entered the room I saw what appeared to be a beautiful apparition reclining on a sofa. . . . Asked if he would be presented to me, Byron answered, ' No. I cannot know her—she is too beautiful '. . . . From that evening, during the whole of my subsequent stay at Venice, we met every day ".

Teresa Gamba, born in 1802, was educated in a convent till she was fifteen, and at sixteen was married as his third wife to the rich, sexagenarian Count Guiccioli. Her husband was, in fact, older than her father. She was very pretty— much prettier than the Fornarina, Byron was later on to tell Murray. Later still, in asking Murray to propose to Holmes the miniature painter (who had done both him and Augusta in 1815) [1] that he should come out to Ravenna and paint Allegra and the Countess, Byron says of Teresa : " Mme G. is very handsome . . . completely blonde and fair—very uncommon in Italy ; yet not an *English* fairness, but more like a Swede or Norwegian. Her figure, too, particularly the bust, is uncommonly good ". Jeaffreson, describing her, uses the terrible epithet of chumpy. " Too massive everywhere for grace, she possessed . . . the proportions and development of an almost matronly attractiveness ". She had, in his list of her charms, large languishing blue eyes, singularly long brown lashes, ample white eyelids, arched eyebrows, wickedly pretty teeth, and hair " so absolutely golden that if a guinea-golden fillet of the deepest yellowness ever seen in gold, had been put about her head, the tresses and the ornament would have been precisely the same hue and quality of colour ". " The prevailing air of her intelligent face was peculiarly expressive of simplicity, good-humour, and good-breeding ".

" That shyness of the antelope which I delight in "[2] was lacking here, and so was the dark colouring which was Byron's ideal —though of his loves only Mary Chaworth, Augusta Leigh, and Claire Clairmont possessed it. Caroline Lamb, Lady Frances Webster, Annabella Milbanke [3]—all were fair women. Teresa Guiccioli, in her turn, proved to have charms sufficient without that dark eye of which his verse is so eloquent—for at this first meeting he made up his mind to enslave her, and as he learned that the Guicciolis were leaving Venice in a fortnight, there was little time to lose. " At parting ", she relates, " Lord Byron wrote something on a scrap of paper, and handed it to me ". Thenceforth, they saw one another every day.

Byron's earliest allusion is in a letter to Murray of May 6 —reticent as yet, but soon to be greatly the reverse. " About the 20th, I leave Venice, to take a journey into Romagna ; but shall probably return in a month ". The Guicciolis had gone in the end of April to visit the Count's Romagnese estates. He had several houses on the road from Venice to Ravenna (their ultimate destination), and from each of the halting-places Teresa

---

[1] Holmes did not accept the offer to go to Italy, and Byron, much offended, called him to Murray, " one rascal more ". This is not the Holmes miniature of Augusta which appears in *Astarte*.
[2] Journal of 1813-14. See Chapter XV.
[3] Though of fair complexion, Lady Byron had brown hair and brown eyes, as had also her daughter and grandchildren.

wrote to Byron. " The thousand enchantments that surrounded him ", the difference between him and the other men she knew—all had at once made such an impression upon the bride as more than satisfied the farthest-reaching desires of the English Milord. Before she left Venice, they were lovers in the most extended sense of the term. This is painfully proved by Byron's letter to Hoppner when he did, more than a month after Teresa's departure, set forth to retrieve her. He wrote, having got as far as Padua on the way : " La G's instructions are rather calculated to produce an *éclat*—and perhaps a scene—than any decent iniquity. . . . The Charmer forgets that a man may be whistled anywhere *before*, but that *after*—a journey in an Italian June is a conscription, and therefore she should have been less liberal in Venice, or less exigent at Ravenna. If I were not the most constant of men, I should now be swimming from the Lido, instead of smoking in the dust of Padua ".

The Countess had fainted three times on the first day's journey; and when she reached Ravenna was half-dead. Though even then she managed to write, her illness was no fanciful or sentimental one, as we learn (again by a letter to Hoppner) after Byron's own arrival. " Her miscarriage has made her a good deal thinner ". . . . *He*, on the way, had stopped two days at Ferrara and greatly enjoyed himself, going to a conversazione of which he gives this odd report to Hoppner : " Far superior to anything of the kind at Venice—the women almost all young —several pretty—and the men courteous and cleanly ". " Whenever I meet ", he adds, " with anything agreeable in this world, it surprises me so much and pleases me so much . . . that I go on wondering for a week to come ".

He visited the Certosa Cemetery there, and found " such a pretty epitaph, or rather two ; one was,

> ' MARTINI LUIGI
> *implora pace* ' ;

the other,

> ' LUCREZIA PICINI
> *implora eterna quiete* '.

That was all ; but it appears to me that those two and three words comprise and compress all that can be said on the subject —and then, in Italian, they are absolute music. They contain doubt, hope, and humility. . . . They have had enough of life—they want nothing but rest—they implore it, and *eterna quiete*. . . . Pray, if I am shovelled into the Lido churchyard in your time, let me have the *implora pace*, and nothing else, for my epitaph. I never met with any, ancient or modern, that pleased

me a tenth part so much ". Writing to Murray from Bologna—
where he next spent a few days—he adds to this : " I trust they
won't think of ' pickling, and bringing me home '. . . . I am sure
my bones would not rest in an English grave, or my clay mix
with the earth of that country. I believe the thought would
drive me mad on my death-bed, could I suppose that any of
my friends would be base enough to convey my carcase back to
your soil. I would not even feed your worms, if I could help it ".

From Bologna he wrote to Hoppner that he should return
thence to Venice ; but two days later, dispatching the letter,
he scribbled on the outside cover : " I am just setting off for
Ravenna. I changed my mind this morning, and decided to
go on ". When at last he arrived, Count Guiccioli instantly called
and asked him to the Palazzo. It would distract the Countess
in her illness, said the husband. Byron went next day and
found Teresa in bed, with a cough and spitting of blood, " all
of which " (a few days later) " have subsided, and something
else has recommenced. . . . *She* manages very well " (here is
a row of asterisks), " but if I come away with a stiletto in my
gizzard some fine afternoon I shall not be astonished "—for
the Count passed as the most jealous of husbands, and was said
to have had two lovers of his two former wives assassinated.

During Teresa's absence from Venice, Byron had written
to Murray a letter describing his intrigue with an unmarried
girl (" the daughter of one of their nobles "). It is the famous
one which caused Moore, on being shown it, to enter in his diary,
" This is really too gross ". In it, he announced his imminent
departure for Ravenna. . . . One knows not how to regard this
trait in him. Vanity was a factor ; yet vanity is a foible from
which most of us suffer, and there are no other extant letters
quite like his. He had always been too free on such matters,
but the degree of licence which he gives himself here is rare even
with him.

His freedom, as we see above, could disgust the far from
prudish Moore ; what Hoppner can have thought of the letters
he soon received from Ravenna, it is difficult to imagine. The
Italian institution of the *cicisbeat* was so accepted that there
was a set code of rules and regulations for it ; and that would
seem to make a decent reticence part of the official attitude.
Where everything was taken for granted, what need to detail
arrangements ? But Byron, from the letter of June 2, where he
is " going to cuckold a Papal Count ", to the end of the earlier
stage of this liaison, detailed them without stint—and to a man
who had met the Countess Guiccioli socially, and knew the
whole of what *cavalier' serventism* implied.

On the way to Ravenna, perceiving that his " conscription "

was picturesque enough, he wrote the long sentimental poem:

> " River, that rollest by the ancient walls
> Where dwells the Lady of my Love " . . .

which was first published by Medwin in 1824. The verses are entitled *Stanzas to the Po* ; but the Po does not run by the ancient walls of Ravenna. We must yield the point and conclude that Byron thought it did, for the piece is dated June 1819, when he was on his way to join Teresa there.

> " A stranger loves the Lady of the land,
>   Born far beyond the mountains ; but his blood
> Is all meridian, as if never fanned
>   By the bleak wind that chills the Polar flood.
>
> My blood is all meridian ; were it not
>   I had not left my clime, nor should I be,
> In spite of tortures, ne'er to be forgot,
>   A slave again of love—at least of thee.
>
> 'Tis vain to struggle—let me perish young—
>   Live as I lived, and love as I have loved " . . .

It was precisely as he had loved that he was now to love— impatiently, half-heartedly. This poem was written at the same time as the letters to Hoppner. If he was, as he said, always flippant in prose, he might have said too that he was always flippant in love. Long ago; there had been his cry : " It is the plague of these women that we cannot live with them, or without them." " *Besoin impérieux de la femme, et mépris de la femme* " : so the incisive Frenchman, Félix Rabbe, has summed up Byron's relation to women. It is the key to that enigma in his story—the constant preoccupation with intrigue, the lack of all real feeling in it, and the void which he for ever felt because his heart was for ever empty. Were she worthy or unworthy of him, Byron would have been happier if he could have loved a woman. His nature was not cruel, as he truly said ; yet in the perversity of his disdain for the creature con- quered, he was always cruel in the event. The Medeas of the Mocenigo, indeed, had enthralled him by their very infamy. Such screaming, scratching, howling furies left him the amused contemptuous master of the miserable situation ; yet even *they* had suffered in their sort. Marianna Segati had found a sister-in-law installed ; Margarita Cogni had nearly drowned herself. . . .So, too, had Caroline Lamb, had Augusta, had Annabella, been tortured ; while for Claire Clairmont the worst of all woman's sorrows was soon to come. Sad as future days were to be for Teresa Guiccioli also, she had a saving grace of stupidity which upbore her through the evil hours. No other

woman held him so long, and no other woman enshrined his
memory as that of an angel.

These early days at Ravenna were happy for her. " During
my illness, he was for ever near me . . . It is impossible to describe
the anxiety he showed—the delicate attentions that he paid me.
For a long time he had perpetually medical books in his hands ;
and not trusting my physicians, he obtained permission from
Count Guiccioli to send for . . . a friend of his ". This was
Aglietti, the renowned Venetian doctor, who came and ordered
a continuance of the treatment. It consisted, apparently, in
Byron's visits. " The inexpressible happiness which I experi-
enced in Lord Byron's society had so good an effect on my health
that only two months afterwards I was able to accompany my
husband in a tour he was obliged to make ".

" I find my situation very agreeable ", wrote Byron ; " I can
fix no time for my return to Venice—it may be soon or late—or
not at all. . . . My coming—going—and everything depends
on *her* entirely, just as Mrs. Hoppner said, in the true spirit of
female prophecy. . . . I can't make *him* out at all—he visits
me frequently, and takes me out . . . in a coach and six horses.
The fact appears to be that he is completely *governed* by her
—for that matter, so am I.[1] The people here don't know what
to make of us ; as he had the character of jealousy with all his
wives—this is the third ". But Hoppner, already acquainted
with the details, soon became insufficient as a confidant. It
was judged to be full time for the Albemarle Street parlour to
enjoy them. On June 29, then (with many editorial asterisks):
" I have been here these four weeks. . . . I came to see my
Amica, the Countess Guiccioli. . . . She bears up most *gallantly*
in every sense of the word. . . . All this " (the content, no
doubt, of the suppressed passages) " will appear strange to you;
who do not understand the Meridian morality. . . . You would
find it much the same in these parts. At Faenza there is Lord
Kinnaird with an opera-girl ; and at the inn at the same town
is a Neapolitan Prince, who serves the wife of the Gonfaloniere
of that city. I am on duty here—so you see ' Cosi fan tut*te*
e tut*ti* " '.

He had his horses sent from Venice, and rode or drove every
day in the renowned Pineta ; he composed *The Prophecy of Dante*
at Teresa's request ; saw her every day, " at the proper (or
improper) hours "—but that Albemarle Street might be reminded

---

[1] Here may be appropriately quoted the valet Fletcher's famous saying,
" It is very odd, but I never yet knew a lady that could not manage my
Lord, *except* my Lady ". Jeaffreson contemns this, observing that a valet's
opinion is not worth a rush. More cogently, one may point to the lack of
all evidence for, say, Caroline Lamb's successful management !

of the Byronic melancholy, he now began to feel seriously uneasy about her health. " In losing her ", he wrote to Murray, " I should lose a being who has run great risks on my account, and whom I have every reason to love. . . . I do not know what I *should* do if she died, but I ought to blow my brains out—and I hope that I should. Her husband is a very polite personage, but I wish he would not carry me out in his coach and six, like Whittington and his Cat ".

We must applaud the sincerity of this. " I ought to blow my brains out—and I hope that I should ". Very assuredly he would not have blown his brains out, but that was by no means so clear to him as it is to us. The intrigue with Teresa Guiccioli was another of the many into which, indubitably, he was more or less forced. When, later in the year, he wrote to Hoppner, " I should like to know *who* has been carried off—except poor dear *me*. I have been more ravished myself than anybody since the Trojan war "—he wrote only a very little more than the truth. In a sense, Byron was perfectly consistent in his attitude. He recognised depravation, and he recognised marriage ; the illicit great passion he did not recognise. A woman was either virtuous or vicious. If she was virtuous, she would yield to no man whom she could not marry ; if she was vicious, she would yield to any, and make her profit from it. Such was the—largely unconscious—persuasion of the man. The poet might write of lovely lawless love, such as Haidee's in *Don Juan*, Medora's in the *Corsair*, even Astarte's in *Manfred* . . . but when real life and the circumstances of real life presented themselves, Byron could not believe in romance. Such passions belonged to desert islands, rocky promontories, solitary Alpine heights. If a woman of the drawing-rooms or the cities yielded to her feelings, she must be an abandoned or a venal creature : only Nature's child might hear the voice of Nature. Many another man holds, as unconsciously, the same opinion.

In all Byron's affairs we can trace this blindness to the image of " Free Love " as seen by its genuine devotees, such as Shelley, for example. The innocent boy-passion for Mary Chaworth was real, and the boy dreamed only of marriage with the girl. Then came the intrigues with Caroline Lamb and Lady Oxford. The latter was frankly profligate : from her, therefore, he could accept the oft-given gift with grace. Caroline Lamb, innocent until she came within his orbit, offered herself impetuously to him alone—and no rigour was too harsh for the woman by that sufficiently condemned. During the whole course of these two affairs, his mind was fixed with matrimonial intentions on the woman he later married—and the only one, except Mary Chaworth, whom he ever had to woo. Of Claire Clairmont we have seen the shameless persistency : she had still to learn the hardest lesson of all. Now, with Teresa Guiccioli, the same story was begun. He had made up his mind to enslave her : yes, but only for the little while that she abode in Venice, and, even so, plainly not in the degree which so soon ensued. If she had left the city without being " so liberal ", he would have forgotten her at once, and was ready to forget her even as it was, as the letter from Bologna testifies. " Your Blackwood ", he wrote to Murray at the end of this year, " accuses me of treating women harshly : it may be so, but I have been their martyr. My whole life has been sacrificed to them and by them ". That is true. Scarcely in one of his affairs is any trace of real love to be found ; yet almost the whole course of his life was swayed by women. It was their sex's revenge, perhaps ! He who despised them was thwarted by them.

The month of August was inaugurated by the famous letter to Murray—of nine printed pages—about La Fornarina. It concludes with a postscript : " The Countess Guiccioli is much better than she was ". She was so much better that by the ninth she had resumed, with her husband, the tour of his estates. They went to Bologna ; and the prospect of follow-ing her there as *cavalier' servente* was detestable to Byron. He greatly liked Ravenna ; he hated moving—" If I stay six days in a place, I require six months to get out of it "—and, more than all, the institution of the *cicisbeat* revolted him. After he was established in it some months later, he wrote to Hobhouse : " I can't say that I don't feel the degradation. Better be an unskilful planter, an awkward settler—better be a hunter, or anything, than a flatterer of fiddlers and fan-carrier of a woman. I like women—God he knows—but the more their system here develops upon me, the worse it seems, after Turkey too ; here the polygamy is all on the female side. . . . And now I am a Cavalier' Servente—by the holy ! it is a strange sensation ".

The allusion to an unskilful planter is explained by the project unfolded in this letter. He had been reading newspaper puffs of " Bolivar's country "—the Venezuela territory, and had already (we have not the letter) spoken of wishing to go and settle there, to both Hobhouse and Murray. The desire had fastened on him as he endured longer " the degradation ". On August 10 he had left Ravenna for Bologna. Before doing so, he had, in his distaste for the prospect he saw before him, actually implored Teresa to elope with him openly. But this was to her unthinkable. " To an Italian wife ", says Chiarini, an Italian writer on Byron, " everything is forgiven but the actual leaving

of her husband. . . . In Italy, it alone *is* the error, and from
its rarity seems no less monstrous than odious ". She, in her
horror at such a proposal, had made an alternative one. She
would represent herself as dead, like Juliet, and allow herself
to be committed to the shroud and vault, thence to escape
secretly to his arms, and thus save the honour of the houses of
Gamba and Guiccioli !

" I hate a theatrical *mise-en-scène* ". It was to the man
who had said that, that this project was suggested. It is humorous
only to think of Byron's face as he read—for the plan was sketched
in a letter. Of course it was rejected, and he wretchedly resigned
himself to the sole alternative. On August 12 we find him in
the best hotel at Bologna, writing to Murray : " I am not very
well to-day. Last night I went to the representation of Alfieri's
Mirra,[1] the two last acts of which threw me into convulsions . . .
the agony of reluctant tears and the choaking shudder which I
do not often undergo for fiction. . . . The worst was that the
dama in whose box I was went off in the same way ".

Thus, with a tactlessness surely unparalleled in the annals
of woman, did Teresa Guiccioli initiate her definite reign. His
description of the next morning is droll enough. " We are all
languid and pathetic, with great expenditure of Sal volatile " ;
but he was in reality almost beside himself at this time with
nervous strain. Ill, enervated as he had been—to a degree
which had permanently undermined his constitution—he was
not, and never again was to be, fit to encounter the excitements
and vexations of life. The *Don Juan* worry was in full blast.
The first and second cantos had been published, without author's
or publisher's name, on July 15. " You seem in a fright ", he
had said to Murray in May ; " remember you need not publish,
unless you like it. . . . Why, man, it will be nuts to all of them ;
they never had such an opportunity of being terrible ; but don't
you be out of sorts. I never vex you wilfully . . . but you
sometimes touch a jarring string . . . and although I think you
a little spoilt by . . . wits, persons of honour about town,
authors, fashionables, together with your ' I am just going to
call at Carlton House : are you walking that way ? ' . . . you
deserve and possess the esteem of those whose esteem is worth
having and of none more (however useless it may be) than yours
very truly—B ".

[1] *Mirra* deals with those forbidden relations on which Byron's mind had
long been fixed. It was but lately emancipated, and doubtless the recall to
such broodings had something to do with his seizure. Mirra, in the play, is
the victim of a passion for her father. Matthews, in the *Diary of an In-
valid*, says : " I have seldom seen a tragedy where the distress is more
affecting ".

But though with Murray he could be patient, Hobhouse's apprehensions and his comments on the proof-sheets put Byron almost beside himself. " Mr. Hobhouse is at it again about in-delicacy. There is *no* indelicacy. . . .¹ For my part, I think you are all crazed ". But Hobhouse, in hesitating at the Donna Inez stanzas, was certainly not crazed. " This is so very pointed ", he pleads, of the famous lines about her duty both to man and God. " *Carissimo,* do review the whole scene, and think what you would say of it as written by another "—such is the engaging manner of his protest against the bedroom episode of the first canto. In vain ; he succeeded in getting one Damn omitted —that was all. " I am already sick of your remarks ", wrote Byron to his two censors ; " to which I think not the least attention ought to be paid ". Finally : " I trust you have not waited for further alterations—I will make none. . . . Think *you* of the sale, and leave me to pluck the porcupines who may point their quills at you. . . . You ask me if I mean to continue *D.J.,* etc. How should I know ? what encouragement do you give me with your nonsensical prudery ? Publish the two Cantos, and then you will see ". And a fortnight after *Don Juan* had burst upon the world : " You will see me defend myself gaily—that is, if I happen to be in spirits. . . . You may perhaps see some good tossing and goring. But I must be in the right cue first, and I doubt I am almost too far off to be in a sufficient fury for the purpose ; and then I have effeminated and enervated myself with love and the summer in these last two months. . . . Come what may, I never will flatter the millions' canting in any shape. . . . I will not sit ' on a degraded throne ' ; so pray put Messrs. Southey, or Sotheby, or Tom Moore, or Horace Twiss upon it—they will all of them be trans-ported with their coronation ". This letter is remarkable as the only one in which he permits himself a gibe at Moore.²

He had heard nothing of the effect on August 9. " You chicken-hearted, silver-paper Stationer, you ! . . . I never saw such a set of fellows as you are : and then the pains taken to exculpate the modest publisher—he had remonstrated, forsooth !

¹ Yet five days later he writes : " You talk of ' approximations to indelicacy ' ; this reminds me of George Lamb's quarrel at Cambridge with Scrope Davies. ' Sir ', said George, ' he hinted at my illegitimacy '. ' Yes ', said Scrope, ' I called him a damned adulterous bastard ' " (*L. and J.* iv. 304–5).
² " The only one, as far as I can learn, that ever fell from [his] pen during our intimacy ". Moore relates that he " made the . . . harmless little sneer a subject of raillery " with Byron when they shortly afterwards met at Venice ; " but he declared boldly that he had no recollection of ever having written such words, and that if they existed, ' he must have been half-asleep when he wrote them ' " (Moore, p. 403).

. . . I will cut you all up (and *you* in particular) like Gourds . . .
you have no more . . . blood than a water-melon! And I
see there hath been asterisks and . . . ' demned cutting and
slashing '. But never mind ".

When he wrote that, he was setting out for his slavery at
Bologna ; and in the letter describing the seizure at the theatre,
he says : " You are right, Gifford is right, Hobhouse is right—
you are all right, and I am all wrong ; but do pray let me have
that pleasure. Cut me up root and branch . . . make me, if
you will, a spectacle to men and angels ; but don't ask me to
alter, for I can't ; I am obstinate and lazy—and there's the
truth ". There follows a defence of the quick succession of fun
and gravity, in answer to one of his critics [1]—too long for quota-
tion, but to be read by all who care for brilliant controversy.
And then : " You ask me for the plan of Donny Johnny : I
have no plan—I *had* no plan . . . but if continued, it must be
in my own way. . . . Why, Man, the soul of such writing is
its licence ".

Soon he was to suffer from the public condemnation. " The
cry is up ", he wrote, " and cant is up ". He was indicted for
obscenity, blasphemy, studious lewdness, laboured impiety—
his work was a pestilent poem, and he himself was called " this
miserable man (for miserable he is, as having a soul of which
he cannot get rid) ". . . . That notice, which appeared in the *British
Review*, is a mild sample of the sort of thing which reached him.
Ere long he wrote to Murray : " Keep the anonymous. It
helps what fun there may be ; but if the matter grows serious
about *Juan* . . . *own that I am the author.* I will never *shrink.*
. . . I wish that I had been in better spirits, but I am out of
sorts, out of nerves, and now and then (I begin to fear) out of
my senses.[2] All this Italy has done for me, and not England ;
I defy all of you and your climate to boot, to make me mad ".

The Guicciolis had now left Bologna on another tour of
the estates. Byron remained behind, in a sort of distraction—
infinitely harassed about *Juan*, about his present situation, about
Allegra. There had been difficulty in the beginning of July,
while he was still at Ravenna. The Hoppners were about to
travel in Switzerland ; and Mrs. Hoppner desired, before depart-
ing, to make adequate arrangements for the little girl. She had
for some time thought it unwise in Claire to insist on Allegra's

---

[1] Francis Cohen, afterwards (on assuming his mother's maiden name)
Francis Palgrave, knighted in 1832. The passage occurs in a letter of
August 12, 1819 (*L. and J.* iv. 341–42).

[2] Byron had always been addicted to saying he was mad. Scrope
Davies (as Byron loved to relate) used to answer : " More like s-silliness
than m-madness ". Scrope had an irresistible stutter.

remaining in Venice. Nor did Mrs. Hoppner believe that Byron would ever restore her to the mother. The Shelley household at Leghorn became terribly uneasy. Then an English lady, Mrs. Vavassour, a widow with no children of her own, offered to adopt and provide for Allegra, if Lord Byron would consent to renounce all claim to her. Such entire surrender he would not agree to ; and when the Hoppners started on their Swiss trip, Allegra was at first, with a maid of Mrs. Hoppner's choosing, left in the house of one of the men-servants' wives. But as soon as Byron settled down at Bologna he sent for her, and she was with him there when the Guicciolis departed on August 21. " I feel alone and unhappy ", he wrote to Murray on August 24. Next day he wandered up to Teresa's empty house, had her rooms opened, and sat turning over her books and writing in them. With her copy of *Corinne* he descended to the garden, and there, " as he stood looking, in a state of unconscious reverie, into one of those fountains so common in the gardens of Italy, there came suddenly into his mind such desolate fancies, such bodings of the misery he might bring on her he loved . . . that overwhelmed with his own thoughts, he burst into an agony of tears ".[1] This fantastic mood of depression produced the great *Don Juan* [2] stanza :

" Oh Love ! what is it in this world of ours
Which makes it fatal to be loved ? " . . .

—and the famous love-letter to Teresa, written in English (which she could not read) on the fly-leaf of *Corinne.*

" MY DEAREST TERESA,—I have read this book in your garden ;—my love, you were absent, or else I could not have read it. It is a favourite book of yours, and the writer was a friend of mine. You will not understand these English words, and *others* will not understand them—which is the reason I have not scrawled them in Italian. But you will recognise the hand-writing of him who passionately loved you, and you will divine that, over a book which was yours, he could only think of love. In that word, beautiful in all languages, but most so in yours— *Amor mio*—is comprised my existence here and hereafter. I feel I exist here, and I fear that I shall exist hereafter,—to *what* purpose you will decide ; my destiny rests with you, and you are a woman, seventeen years of age, and two out of a convent. I wish that you had stayed there, with all my heart,—or, at least, that I had never met you in your married state.

" But all this is too late. I love you, and you love me,—at least, you *say so*, and *act* as if you *did* so, which last is a great

[1] Moore, p. 407.   [2] Canto iii. stanza 2.

consolation in all events. But *I* more than love you, and cannot cease to love you.

"Think of me sometimes, when the Alps and the ocean divide us,—but they never will, unless you *wish* it.

;"BYRON

"BOLOGNA, *August* 25, 1819 "

In later years, Teresa quoted the final words, and added in a note : " *On ne le voulait pas ; donc ne se fut pas* ". This was the very week in which he wrote to England of the South American project. Soon afterwards Hobhouse was to have the confession : " I can't say that I don't feel the degradation ". He continued, " You must not talk to me of England, that is out of the question. I had a house and lands, and a wife and child, and a name there —once—but all these things are transmuted or sequestered. . . . Of the last, and best, ten years of my life, six have been passed out of it. . . . Yet I want a country and a home, and—if possible —a free one. I am not yet thirty-two years of age. I might still be a decent citizen and found a house and a family as good— or better—than the former. . . . Do not laugh at me ; you will, but I assure you I am quite in earnest if the thing be practicable ". He meant to take Allegra with him.

When he wrote thus to Hobhouse on October 3, he was back at La Mira, and Teresa was with him—definitely established there as his mistress. The Guicciolis had returned to Bologna in September ; but the Count soon afterwards left again for Ravenna; and this time he did not take his wife. The consequences were immediate and remarkable. On September 18 she and Byron left Bologna for Venice. But even then it was not an elopement. A reason was given—the state of the Countess's health ; and the Count " consented that Lord Byron should be the companion of my journey ". " When I arrived at Venice ", writes Teresa, " the physicians ordered that I should try the country air, and Lord Byron, having a villa at La Mira, gave it up to me, and came to reside there with me ". The situation could not be more exquisitely delineated : comment would be profanation. Byron's first word from the villa is to Murray : " You must not mind me when I say I am ill ; it merely means low spirits— and folly ". The next is the letter to Hobhouse.

Moore arrived on October 7, and at once went to La Mira. He reached it at two o'clock. " Byron was but just up and in his bath ; he soon came down to me ; first time we have met these five years ; grown fat. . . . Found him in wild spirits and full of his usual frolicsome gaiety ". That is the entry in the diary. The book enlarges : " The addition of whiskers . . . from hearing that some one had said he had a *faccia di musica,* as well as the

length to which his hair grew down on his neck, and the rather
foreign air of his coat and cap—all combined to produce a dis-
similarity to his former self. He was still, however, eminently
handsome ". They set off at once on an expedition to Venice
(where Moore was to inhabit the Mocenigo Palace), but before
they left, the visitor was presented to the Countess. " She is a
blonde and young ; married only about a year, but not very
pretty ". On the 11th he saw her again : " Looked prettier than
she did the first time ". Byron, reporting on the stay to Murray
when it was over, said, " Moore and I did nothing but laugh ",
and Moore confirms this. " Our course was, I am almost ashamed
to say, one of uninterrupted merriment and laughter. . . . All
that had ever happened, of gay or ridiculous, during our London
life together . . . was passed rapidly in review between us, with
a flow of humour and hilarity on his side ". They spent nearly
all their time together ; the *cicisbeo* was given a holiday, and
rejoiced a little too frankly in his liberty. " He was obliged to
return to La Mira in the evenings, but he made it a point to come
to Venice every day and dine with me ". At the *salons*, whither
Moore went with Byron's friend Alexander Scott, the traveller
came in for Madame Benzoni's opinion of the state of affairs
at La Mira. Madame Albrizzi had already refused to receive
the Countess Guiccioli ; the Benzoni, less rigid (as we have
seen), nevertheless pointed out to Moore that Italian views of
morality were outraged. " You must really scold your friend ",
she said ; " till this unfortunate affair, he had behaved so
perfectly."

On October 9 there came a letter from Count Guiccioli.
The Countess had been expecting it, and with some apprehension,
for the La Mira arrangement can scarcely have been nominated
in the bond. But so far from expressing any censure of her
conduct, what the husband wrote about was to ask her to induce
Lord Byron to lend him £1000—on loan, of course, at five per
cent. interest ; any other course would be degrading, an
avvilimento. Byron showed the letter to Moore that evening ;
and Moore, though disgusted, strongly advised the loan, for he
thought it would "materially" facilitate the retracing of the
imprudent step which had been taken. But Byron disagreed.
He had lately taken up with " the good old-gentlemanly vice "
of avarice ; he kept a hoarding-box, and had collected about
300 sequins, greatly delighting in the contemplation of his
store. He now declared that he could not pay so high as £1000
for his frolic, and laid a wager with Alexander Scott (who
accepted it) that he would manage to save the money and the
lady too.

Moore left on the 11th, going on to Rome. He had been

much disconcerted to find that Byron was seriously thinking of coming with him. It had been suggested between them before Moore knew anything of the situation at La Mira ; now the cruelty and insult of such a step were evident, and the Irishman was horrified that his friend should still intend it. " You cannot leave the Countess in such a position ; it would be most humiliating to her ", he urged—and Byron sighed and acquiesced. He pleaded for at least an expedition to Arquà ; but Moore, tied to time and anxious to reach Rome and if possible Naples, was not to be drawn aside ; and so, a little way from Venice, they said good-bye to one another—never to meet again.

On October 29 there is a letter to Hoppner, now back in Venice after the Swiss tour.[1] " I should like to know who has been carried off except poor dear *me* "—that cry begins the epistle. Further on we read : " Count G. comes to Venice next week, and I am requested to consign his wife to him, which shall be done. . . . What you say of the long evenings at La Mira, or Venice, reminds me of what Curran said to Moore—' so I hear you have married a pretty woman, and a very good creature too—an excellent creature ; pray—um—*how do you pass your evenings ?* ' It is a devil of a question that, and perhaps as easy to answer with a wife as with a mistress. . . . I wish you had been here when Moore was here (at Venice, I mean, not the Mira) ; we were very merry and tipsy ".

Count Guiccioli arrived in the first week of November, and demanded his wife. " They are in high discussion " wrote Byron to Murray on the 8th. " I am expressly excluded in his paper of conditions which he insists on her accepting and she persists in refusing ". Byron himself was slowly recovering from a bad attack of tertian fever, at the crisis of which he had been when the Count first arrived. He was delirious through a whole night, " and on my senses coming back, found Fletcher sobbing on one side of the bed, and La Contessa Guiccioli on the other ". During the delirium he composed a good many verses (so the Countess told Moore) " and ordered his servant to write them down from his dictation. . . . He preserved them for some time after he got well, and then burned them ". He was also haunted by the idea of his mother-in-law (so Moore was informed), taking every one that came near him for her, and reproaching those about him for allowing her to enter the room.

[1] Hoppner, before his departure, had written to urge Byron (then at Ravenna) to leave the place while he had a whole skin, and also to consider the " safety of a person he appeared so sincerely attached to ". Byron had frankly told him that this warning displeased him very much. " Upon that subject we will (if you like) be silent ". Byron was silent only till the letter in the text of October 29.

Thus he did not take an ardent part in the discussion. "As I tell you", he wrote to Murray, "that the Guiccioli business is on the eve of exploding in one way or the other, I will just add that without attempting to influence the decision of the Countess, a good deal depends upon it. If she and her husband make it up, you will, perhaps, see me in England sooner than you expect; if not, I shall retire with her to France or America, change my name, and lead a quiet provincial life. All this may seem odd, but I have got the poor girl into a scrape, and as neither her birth, nor her rank, nor her connections by birth or marriage are inferior to my own, I am in honour bound to support her through; besides, she is a very pretty woman—ask Moore —and not yet one-and-twenty. If she gets over this, and I get over my tertian, I will, perhaps, look in at Albemarle Street some of these days, *en passant* to Bolivar".

The discussions lasted till the end of the month. The Countess wept and pleaded : but in the end she had to go, and to give a promise that all intercourse of any kind should cease between her and Byron. He left La Mira and returned to the Mocenigo Palace, very much out of spirits, as Hoppner told Moore, and out of humour with everybody and everything about him. They resumed their rides on the Lido, and his return to England was much discussed. But the promise not to correspond with the Countess was soon broken—plainly first by her. Byron answered on November 25, in Italian ; the translation is Moore's.

"You are, and ever will be, my first thought. But, at this moment, I am in a state most dreadful, not knowing which way to decide ;—on the one hand, fearing that I should compromise you for ever, by my return to Ravenna and the consequences of such a step, and, on the other, dreading that I shall lose both you and myself, and all that I have ever known or tasted of happiness, by never seeing you more. I pray of you, I implore you, to be comforted, and to believe that I cannot cease to love you but with my life. . . . I go to save you, and leave a country insupportable to me without you. Your letters to F * * and myself do wrong to my motives—but you will yet see your injustice. It is not enough that I must leave you—from motives of which ere long you will be convinced—it is not enough that I must fly from Italy, with a heart deeply wounded, after having passed all my days in solitude since your departure, sick both in body and mind—but I must also have to endure your reproaches without answering and without deserving them. Farewell! in that one word is comprised the death of my happiness ".

On December 4 this is how he wrote to Murray : "I have had a tertian ague ; my daughter Allegra has been ill also, and

22

I have been almost obliged to run away with a married woman.
But with some difficulty, and many internal struggles, I reconciled
the lady with her lord, and cured the fever of the child with bark,
and my own with cold water. I think of setting out for England
by the Tyrol in a few days, so that I could wish you to direct
your next letter to Calais.[1] . . . My present determination to
quit Italy was unlooked for ; but I have explained the reasons
in letters to my sister and Douglas K. a week or two ago ". He
had arranged everything, the very day for departure was fixed,
when he heard alarming accounts from Ravenna of Teresa's
health. She was fretting and pining ; the threatened consump-
tion was again brought into play ;[2] her father and uncle grew
alarmed ; they withdrew all opposition to her wishes, and obtained
the husband's sanction for renewed intercourse with Byron, who
was to be invited to Ravenna. A letter detailing these plans
was written by Count Gamba ; and at the time it was written,
this was what was happening in Venice : " He was ready dressed
for the journey [to England], his gloves and cap on, and even
his little cane in his hand. Nothing was now waited for but his
coming downstairs—his boxes being already on board the gondola.
At this moment, my Lord, by way of pretext, declares that if
it should strike one o'clock before everything was in order (his
arms being the one thing not ready) he would not go that day.
The hour strikes—and he remains ! " This account is from a
letter written to Teresa by a friend, who adds : " It is evident
he had not the heart to go ". . . .

The next day came the summons to Ravenna. Byron wrote
to Teresa, in Italian :

" F * * * will already have told you, *with her accustomed
sublimity*, that Love has gained the victory. I could not summon
up resolution enough to leave the country where you are, without,
at least, once more seeing you. On *yourself*, perhaps, it will
depend, whether I ever again shall leave you. Of the rest we
shall speak when we meet. You ought, by this time, to know
which is most conducive to your welfare, my presence or my
absence. For myself, I am a citizen of the world—all countries
are alike to me. You have ever been, since our first acquaintance,
the sole object of my thoughts. My opinion was, that the best
course I could adopt, both for your peace and that of all your
family, would have been to depart and go far, *far* away from you ;
—since to have been near and not approach you would have
been, for me, impossible. You have however decided that I

---

[1] This was the time of the Return Scare in England, which we have
seen, from that side, in Chapter XVI.
[2] She lived until 1873.

am to return to Ravenna. I shall accordingly return—and shall *do*—and *be* all that you wish. I cannot say more."

Then, on December 10 to Murray, the famous words : " Your Blackwood accuses me of treating women harshly : it may be so, but I have been their martyr. My whole life has been sacrificed *to* them and *by* them ". Yet still the dream of a return to England persisted. " Perhaps I may take a journey to you in the spring ; but I *have* been ill, and *am* indolent and indecisive, because few things interest me ". There is a P.S. : " Pray let my sister be informed that I am not coming as I intended : I have not the courage to tell her so myself, at least as yet ; but I will soon, *with the reasons* ". On December 23 from Bologna, on his way to Ravenna, he did tell her ; but (in the letter we are shown) without the reasons. We have seen how she regarded the prospect of his return : " Luckily, or *un*luckily perhaps, I do not die easily, or I think this stroke would about finish me " ; seen that her resolution to receive him, if he did return, was nevertheless unalterable, " though I trust I may be spared the trial—I scarcely know of any greater that could befall me " ; and seen, too, that this resolution was the cause of a much-lessened intercourse between her and Lady Byron.

He reached Ravenna on December 24, 1819. Venice was done with for ever—Venice, " that now empty oyster-shell ", as he wrote to Hoppner ; Venice, the Gehenna of the waters, the Sea-Sodom, of *Marino Faliero*. " I hate the place and all that it inherits ".

CHAPTER XXII

RAVENNA—1820–1821

Letters to Hoppner and Moore—Installed at the Palazzo Guiccioli—
"Drilling very hard"—*Mazeppa* and *The Prophecy of Dante*—Third
Canto of *Don Juan*—Translations—*Blackwood* manifesto—Allegra—A
breeze with Hobhouse—Dissatisfaction—Carbonarist troubles, and separa-
tion of Count and Countess Guiccioli—Teresa leaves the City—Byron
remains at the Palace—Carbonarist movement collapses—Teresa flies to
Florence—Byron remains behind

THE first letter from Ravenna was to Hoppner, on De-
cember 31, 1819.

"I have been here this week, and was obliged to
put on my armour and go the night after my arrival to the
Marquis Cavalli's, where there were between two and three
hundred of the best company I have seen in Italy. . . . The G.'s
object appeared to be to parade her foreign lover as much as
possible, and, faith, if she seemed to glory in the scandal, it was
not for me to be ashamed of it. Nobody seemed surprised ;
—all the women, on the contrary, were, as it were, delighted
with the excellent example. The vice-legate, and all the other
vices, were as polite as could be ;—and I, who had acted on the
reserve, was fairly obliged to take the lady under my arm, and
look as much like a cicisbeo as I could on so short a notice,—to say
nothing of the embarrassment of a cocked hat and sword, much
more formidable to me than ever it will be to the enemy.

"I can understand nothing of all this ; but it seems as if
the G. had been presumed to be *planted*, and was determined
to show that she was not,—*plantation*, in this hemisphere, being
the greatest moral misfortune. But this is mere conjecture, for
I know nothing about it—except that everybody are very kind
to her, and not discourteous to me. Fathers, and all relations,
quite agreeable ".

On January 2 of the New Year, anniversary of his wedding-
day five years before, he wrote to Moore, leading off with a
rhymed epigram.

> " Here's a happy new year ! but with reason,
> I beg you'll permit me to say—
> Wish me *many* returns of the season,
> But as *few* as you please of the *day* ".

A shower of similar *jeux d'esprit* followed—on Lord Castle-
reagh, Pitt, Tom Paine ; and then Moore got the naked truth
about the situation.
" For my own part, I had a sad scene since you went. Count
Gu. came for his wife, and *none* of those consequences which
Scott prophesied ensued. There was no damages, as in England,
and so Scott lost his wager. But there was a great scene, for
she would not, at first, go back with him—at least, she *did* go
back with him ; but he insisted, reasonably enough, that all com-
munication should be broken off between her and me. So,
finding Italy very dull, and having a fever tertian, I packed up
my valise, and prepared to cross the Alps ; but my daughter
fell ill, and detained me.
" After her arrival at Ravenna, the Guiccioli fell ill again
too ; and at last, her father (who had, all along, opposed the liaison
most violently till now) wrote to me to say that she was in such
a state that *he* begged me to come and see her,—and that her
husband had acquiesced, in consequence of her relapse, and that
he (her father) would guarantee all this, and that there would
be no further scenes in consequence between them, and that I
should not be compromised in any way. I set out soon after,
and have been here ever since. I found her a good deal altered,
but getting better :—*all* this comes of reading Corinna ".
In the early days he put up at an hotel ; but the Count,
resolute to make his profit out of the English Milord's infatua-
tion, if not in one way then in another, arranged that he should
hire a suite of apartments in the Palazzo Guiccioli itself. Here
are some extracts from letters to Hoppner at this time.

" RAVENNA, *January* 20, 1820
" I have not decided anything about remaining at Ravenna.
I may stay a day, a week, a year, all my life ; but all this
depends upon what I can neither see nor foresee. I came because
I was called, and will go the moment that I perceive what may
render my departure proper. My attachment has neither the
blindness of the beginning, nor the microscopic accuracy of the
close to such liaisons ; but ' time and the hour ' must decide
upon what I do ".

Towards the end : " Perhaps we may meet in the spring yet, if
you are for England " ; but he was gradually being tamed.
" I am drilling very hard to learn how to double a shawl,
and should succeed to admiration if I did not always double
it the wrong side out ; and then I sometimes confuse and bring
away two, so as to put all the Serventi out, besides keeping their
Servite in the cold till everybody can get back their property.

But it is a dreadfully moral place, for you must not look at any-
body's wife except your neighbour's,—if you go to the next
door but one, you are scolded, and presumed to be perfidious.
And then a *relazione* or an *amicizia* seems to be a regular affair
of from five to fifteen years, at which period, if there occur a widow-
hood, it finishes by a *sposalizio* ; and in the meantime it has so
many rules of its own, that it is not much better. A man ac-
tually becomes a piece of female property,—they won't let their
Serventi marry until there is a vacancy for themselves ".

Mazeppa had been published on June 28, 1819, with the
Ode on Venice and *A Fragment*—that is, the fragment of his
Vampire story.¹ The volume was reviewed by *Blackwood*, and
the *Monthly* and *Eclectic* Reviews ; but on the whole it may
be said to have fallen quite flat. Thus, with the outcry against
Don Juan, he was, as he confessed to Murray, hurt. " I have not
written *con amore* this time ", he adds of the Third *Juan* ; " very
decent I believe, but do not know ". By February 1820 he did
know, or thought he did. " It is very decent and as dull ".
It is decent but by no means dull, for it contains the scene which
Coleridge compared to Nicolas Poussin's pictures—the return
of Lambro to the island ; and the undying " Isles of Greece "
—an interpolated lyric giving us the lovely stanza on Marathon.

> " The mountains look on Marathon,
>   And Marathon looks on the sea :
> And musing there an hour alone,
>   I dream'd that Greece might still be free ;
> For, standing on the Persian's grave,
>   I could not deem myself a slave ".²

---

¹ Of this scrap, Byron said : " I began it in an old account-book of Miss
Milbanke's, which I kept because it contains the word ' Household ' written
by her twice on the inside blank page of the cover ; being the only two
scraps I have in the world of her writing, except her name to the Deed of
Separation ". He wrote the same thing to her in an unsent letter of
November 17, 1821, acknowledging a lock of Ada's hair. This letter he
enclosed in a note to Lady Blessington on May 6, 1823, and it is printed by
Moore. Mr. Prothero thinks that possibly the date was 1822. Byron
wrote his wife many letters which he did not send.

² The Third Canto of Byron's letters is the third and fourth cantos
of the poem. " I have copied, and cut the third canto of *Don Juan into
two*, because it was too long " ; and he confessed this *coram publico* in
stanza 111 of canto iii.

> " I feel this tediousness will never do—
> 'Tis being *too* epic, and I must cut down
> (In copying) this long canto into two :
>   They'll never find it out, unless I own
> The fact . . ."

Canto iv. contains the death of Haidee, the departure of Juan from the
island, and his meeting with the Italian Opera troupe. " I told you long

The Prophecy of Dante, begun during his first stay at Ravenna, was sent home on March 14, 1820. It was dedicated to the Countess Guiccioli, at whose suggestion it had been begun. But Murray delayed to publish, despite protests from the author. " You are losing (like a goose) the best time for publishing Dante and the Tragedy ". The tragedy was *Marino Faliero*. Both were at last issued in a single volume on April 21, 1821.[1] The poem is in the *terza rima* of Dante. The personal note, as usual, sounds in the finest passages. These are the description of the exile's doom, with their allusion to " that fatal She . . . . the cold partner who had brought Destruction for a dowry " ; the closing lines of the third canto ; and again in the last canto, where contemplation of the outlaw sounds, as remorse had done in earlier days, the now recurrent note of his serious work.

He occupied himself, in these early days of domestication, with a mechanical task—the translation" into *cramp* English " of the first canto of Pulci's *Morgante Maggiore*. This had been begun at Venice, and now served as the desired something craggy for his mind to break on. *Beppo, Don Juan* and *The Vision of Judgment* owe their existence to Pulci ; and so intense was Byron's gratitude that he actually brought himself to regard the translation as his masterpiece. But he never succeeded in getting Murray to publish it ; and after it had been more than two years in " my Admiral's " hands, Byron transferred it to Leigh Hunt's brother and it appeared in the fourth and last number of *The Liberal*. The translation adds nothing to Byron's reputation or our delight. One moment of amusement it does afford—when he rhymes laurels with Charles.

It was now that Byron wrote the *Observations upon an Article in Blackwood's Magazine*—ostensibly a letter addressed to J. D. Israeli, Esq. ; but in reality a personal manifesto. " I am framing an answer (in prose) to the *Blackwood* article of last August ; it will set the kiln in a low. . . .I must now put myself in a passion to continue [it] ". By his own orders on mature consideration, and also partly because of Murray's delays, this was not published during his lifetime. The passage beginning " The man who is exiled by a faction " [2] is magnificent ; not even in

ago ", wrote Byron to Murray, " that the new cantos were *not* good. . . . You may suppress them, if you like, but I can alter nothing ".

[1] Murray paid £1000 for the tragedy and the poem.

[2] " The man who is exiled by a faction has the consolation of thinking that he is a martyr ; he is upheld by hope and the dignity of his cause, real or imaginary ; he who withdraws from the pressure of debt may indulge in the thought that time and prudence will retrieve his circumstances ; he who is condemned by the law has a term to his banishment, or a dream of its abbreviation ; or, it may be, the knowledge or the belief of some injustice of the law, or of its administration in his own particular ; but he who is

his finest verse does the rage and resistance and redress flame
forth into more consuming heat. That is the true climax. The
letter then degenerates into personal attacks on Wordsworth
and the Lakers, and ends in the tedious vindication of " the great
little Queen Anne's man ", which was the King Charles's head of
his critical writings.

Allegra was with him at Ravenna, and there came in the
beginning of May an impassioned appeal from Claire to be allowed
to see her. An application had first been made through the
Hoppners, answered by Byron in a letter which Claire char-
acterised in her Journal as " concerning green fruit and God ".[1]

outlawed by general opinion, without the intervention of hostile politics,
illegal judgment, or embarrassed circumstances, whether he be innocent or
guilty, must undergo all the bitterness of exile, without hope, without pride,
without alleviation. This case was mine. Upon what grounds the public
founded their opinion, I am not aware ; but it was general, and it was
decisive. Of me or of mine they knew little, except that I had written
what is called poetry, was a nobleman, had married, become a father, and
was involved in differences with my wife and her relatives, no one knew
why, because the persons complaining refused to state their grievances.
The fashionable world was divided into parties, mine consisting of a very
small minority ; the reasonable world was naturally on the stronger side,
which happened to be the lady's, as was most proper and polite. . . . I was
accused of every monstrous vice by public rumour and private rancour ;
my name, which had been a knightly or a noble one since my fathers
helped to conquer the kingdom for William the Norman, was tainted. I
felt that, if what was whispered, and muttered, and murmured, was true, I
was unfit for England ; if false, England was unfit for me. I withdrew ;
but this was not enough. In other countries, in Switzerland, in the shadow
of the Alps, and by the blue depths of the lakes, I was pursued and breathed
upon by the same blight. I crossed the mountains, but it was the same :
so I went a little farther, and settled myself by the waves of the Adriatic,
like the stag at bay, who betakes him to the waters. . . . I have heard of,
and believe, that there are human beings so constituted as to be insensible
to injuries ; but I believe that the best mode to avoid taking vengeance is
to get out of the way of temptation. . . . I do not in this allude to the
party, who might be right or wrong ; but to many who made her cause the
pretext of their own bitterness. She, indeed, must long have avenged me in
her own feelings, for whatever her reasons may have been (and she never
adduced them, to me at least), she probably neither contemplated nor con-
ceived to what she became the means of conducting the father of her child,
and the husband of her choice ".

The article in *Blackwood* was on the first and second cantos of *Don Juan*.

[1] Byron had said : " I so totally disapprove of the mode of children's
treatment in [the Shelley] family that I should look upon the child as going
into a hospital . . . I shall either send her to England, or put her in a
convent for education. . . . But [she] shall not quit me again to perish
of starvation and green fruit, or be taught to believe there is no Deity.
Whenever there is convenience of vicinity and access, her mother can
always have her with her ; otherwise no. It was so stipulated from the
beginning ".

It contained the first hint of sending the child to a convent, and this terribly alarmed Claire. " You will inflict the greatest of all evils on my child . . . she will be equally divided from us both "—and she recalled the Bible story of Solomon's judgment. Byron answered not to her but to Shelley, who wrote condemning his harsh tone, though admitting that Claire's letters might too probably be vexatious. We know no more until August 25, when Byron again wrote, declining all correspondence with Claire. Shelley answered on September 17, saying now that any of her letters which he had seen he had thought extremely childish and absurd. " I wonder, however ", he added, " at your being provoked at what Claire writes. . . . The weak and the foolish are in this respect like kings—they can do no wrong ". There the matter ends for that year. Byron sent Hoppner a report of the child : " obstinate as a mule . . . she thinks herself handsome, and will do as she pleases ". In truth, Allegra was (as Hoppner told Moore) by no means a lovable child, despite her great beauty.

In the spring of 1820 there was a little breeze with Hobhouse, who had, as Byron said, foamed into a reformer and subsided into Newgate.[1] This incited Byron to a very dull squib, which Murray showed to Hobhouse and many others. The victim was keenly hurt, and his anger lasted—but it was nobly shown ;[2] and the saddened entries in his Journal are convincing evidence that his deep affection was more wounded than his vanity. But Byron was annoyed by the feeling which his prank had stirred ; and later, finding that the strain still lasted, made through Murray what may almost be called an attack upon the friend of so many years.

The truth is that he was so profoundly dissatisfied with his way of life at this time that all the natural sweetness of his temper was soured—for though vehement and irritable sometimes, he was normally sweet-tempered, with men at any rate. Such feeling as he had ever had for Teresa Guiccioli had faded, and left him in a temper towards her—first of apathy, and then of such impatience as could not easily be endured. Already in May 1820, Moore could make this entry in his diary : " Davy [Sir Humphrey] went to Ravenna to see Lord Byron, who is now living domesticated with the Guiccioli and her husband after all. He was rather anxious to get off with Davy to

---

[1] In 1819, Hobhouse had published a pamphlet which was voted a breach of privilege ; he was committed to Newgate, and remained there until the dissolution of Parliament in February 1820. At the ensuing election, he was chosen as one of the representatives for Westminster.

[2] He wrote Murray an admirable letter (*L. and J.* App. xi.).

Bologna, professedly for the purpose of seeing Lady Davy, but I have no doubt with a wish to give his *Contessa* the slip ". In Byron's diary for January 23, 1821, he sums up the past year.

" The year 1820 was not a fortunate one for the individual me. . . . I lost a lawsuit,[1] after two decisions in my favour. The project of lending money on an Irish mortgage was finally rejected by my wife's trustee after a year's hope and trouble. The Rochdale lawsuit had endured fifteen years, and always prospered till I married ; since which, everything has gone wrong —with me, at least. In the same year, 1820, the Countess T. G., in spite of all I said and did to prevent it, *would* separate from her husband. . . . The other little petty vexations of the year— overturns in carriages—the murder of people before one's door, and dying in one's beds—the cramp in swimming—colics—indigestions and bilious attacks, etc. etc. etc.

" Many small articles make up a sum,
And hey-ho for Caleb Quotem, oh ! "

The stirring of the revolutionary movement of 1820–21 in Italy brought in its train the Carbonari troubles—and, incidentally, the separation of Teresa from her husband. Byron wrote to Murray in April : " There is THAT brewing in Italy which will speedily cut off all liberty of communication, and set all your Anglo-travellers flying in all directions. . . . The Spanish and French affairs[2] have set the Italians in a ferment, and no wonder : they have been too long trampled on ". He was of course on the side of the insurgents against Austria, and Teresa's father and brother were of the same persuasion. But the Count Guiccioli was not—and Byron happened to be lodging under his roof. The Palace soon became the head-quarters of insurrection, for Byron was at the head of the " American " division of the Carbonari in Romagna. " The police ", he wrote in April 1821, " is all on the alert, and the Cardinal glares pale through all his purple ". While these matters were still in embryo, the Count Guiccioli made a move. He requested his wife to dismiss her admirer. She refused. He replied by threatening her with a decree of separation. She laughed in his face, and her family and the public (as Byron wrote) were on her side. " I have given her ", wrote Byron to Moore at the end of May, " the best advice, viz. :

---

[1] Over the Rochdale coal-mines.

[2] After the fall of Decazes and the assassination of the Duc de Berri in 1820, the Government of France became reactionary. There were sporadic insurrections, which were suppressed. In Spain the movement was more successful, and Ferdinand III was forced to take the oath of fidelity to the free Constitution.

to stay with him, pointing out the state of a separated woman . . .
and making the most exquisite moral reflections—but to no pur-
pose. She says, " I will stay with him, if he will let you remain
with me. It is hard that I should be the only woman in Romagna
who is not to have her *Amico* '. . . . You know how females
reason on such occasions. He says he has let it go on till he
can do so no longer. But he wants her to stay, and dismiss
me ; for he doesn't like to pay back her dowry and to make an
alimony. Her relations are rather for the separation, as they
detest him,—indeed, so does everybody. . . . I should have
retreated, but honour, and an erysipelas which has attacked her,
prevent me,—to say nothing of love, for I love her most entirely,
though not enough to persuade her to sacrifice everything to a
frenzy ".

On June 1, a further report to Moore :

" The separation business still continues, and all the world
are implicated, including priests and cardinals. . . He has been
trying at evidence, but can get none *sufficient* ; for what would
make fifty divorces in England won't do here—there must be
the *most decided* proofs.

" All her relations are furious against him. The father has
challenged him—a superfluous valour, for he don't fight, though
suspected of two assassinations—one of the famous Monzoni of
Forli. Warning was given me not to take such long rides in
the Pine Forest without being on my guard ; so I take my stiletto
and a pair of pistols in my pocket during my daily rides.

" I won't stir from this place till the matter is settled one
way or the other. She is as femininely firm as possible ; and
the opinion is so much against him, that the *advocates* decline
to undertake his cause, because they say that he is either a fool
or a rogue—fool, if he did not discover the liaison till now ; and
rogue, if he did know it, and waited for some bad end, to divulge
it. In short, there has been nothing like it since the days of
Guido di Polenta's family, in these parts.

" If the man has me taken off, like Polonius ' say he made a
good end ',—for a melodrame. The principal security is, that
he has not the courage to spend twenty scudi—the average price
of a clean-handed bravo—otherwise there is no want of oppor-
tunity, for I ride about the woods every evening, with one servant,
and sometimes an acquaintance, who latterly looks a little queer
in solitary bits of bushes ".

The final news was sent to the same correspondent on July 13.

" The Pope has pronounced *their separation*. The decree
came yesterday from Babylon,—it was *she* and *her friends* who
demanded it, on the grounds of her husband's (the noble Count
Cavalier's) extraordinary usage. *He* opposed it with all his might

because of the alimony, which has been assigned with all her
goods, chattels, carriage, etc, to be restored by him. In Italy,
they can't divorce. He insisted on her giving me up, and he
would forgive everything—even the adultery, which he swears
he can prove . . . . But, in this country, the very courts hold
such proofs in abhorrence, the Italians being as much more
delicate in public than the English, as they are more passionate
in private.

. . . .

" It is but to let the women alone, in the way of conflict,
for they are sure to win against the field. She returns to her
father's house, and I can only see her under great restrictions
—such is the custom of the country. The relations behave very
well :—I offered any settlement, but they refused to accept it,[1]
and swear she *shan't* live with G. (as he has tried to prove her faith-
less), but that he shall maintain her ; and, in fact, a judgment
to this effect came yesterday. I am, of course, in an awkward
situation enough ".

Decidedly, Count Guiccioli had not managed well. How
little sincerity there had been in the citation of Byron's traffic
with the Carbonari as a cause of offence, is shown by the fact
that the English Milord remained at the Palazzo Guiccioli all
through the movement (which came to its abortive end early
in 1821), and for many months afterwards.

The decree was published at Ravenna in the middle of July.
Teresa left the city at once, and withdrew to her father's villa,
fifteen miles outside. Byron's arrangements were not altered.
He remained at the Guiccioli Palace until October 29, 1821.
While Teresa was still at her father's villa, he visited her—about
once or twice, perhaps, in a month, says Moore ; but Byron's diary
records visits much more frequent. The odd life suited him not
too ill ; but for the woman who had given up riches—her alimony
from the Count was only £200 a year, and the Gambas were very
needy—social standing, pleasant and cultured surroundings,
for love of him, it must have been a mournful period. And worse
was to come. The revolutionary movement collapsed in February
–March 1821. By July, all activity was at an end. The country
was in a state of proscription, and all Byron's friends were exiled
or arrested. The Gambas went to Florence—that is, Count
Gamba, Teresa, and Pietro Gamba, her brother.[2]

---

[1] And refused to the end, as did the Countess herself. She even
declined to allow Byron to include her name in his will.

[2] Byron had become very intimate with Teresa's brother, Count Pietro
Gamba, who had been hand-in-glove with him in all the Carbonari doings.
They were together in Greece, and the Count was by the sick-bed at
Missolonghi.

At this time, Teresa heard that her husband was in Rome, petitioning the authorities to insist upon her either returning to him or going into retreat. Her terror and despair were extreme. She instantly wrote to Byron (in Italian) these moving and significant words :

" Help me, my dear Byron, for I am in a situation most terrible ; and without you, I can resolve upon nothing. . . . I must not speak of this to any one,—I must escape by night ; for, if my project should be discovered, it will be impeded, and my passport (which the goodness of Heaven has permitted me, I know not how, to obtain) will be taken from me. Byron ! I am in despair !—If I must leave you here without knowing when I shall see you again, if it is your will that I should suffer so cruelly, I am resolved to remain. They may put me in a convent ; I shall die,—but—but then you cannot aid me, and I cannot reproach you. I know not what they tell me, for my agitation overwhelms me ;—and why ? Not because I fear my present danger, but solely, I call Heaven to witness, solely because I must leave you ".

All her pleading, at that period, failed. He did not go to her. She left for Florence in the end of July, while he remained in the husband's Palace at Ravenna. He wrote to her on her way—once or twice.

The matter of the heaven-sent passport was easily and soon explained. There was no danger of her being forced into a convent, for the object of the authorities in banishing the Gamba family was to draw the dangerous English Milord after them. It was earnestly desired to get him out of Ravenna, where his benevolence among the poorer classes had made him immensely popular ; moreover, he had provided money and arms for the Movement. The Countess explains : " Not daring to exact [his departure] by any direct measure, they were in hopes of being able indirectly to force him into the step ". And, sure enough, the woman in the end prevailed. On October 29 he left Ravenna and joined her at Pisa, writing to Moore, more than a month before he actually set off : " I am in all the sweat, dust, and blasphemy of an universal packing. . . . As I could not say, with Hamlet, ' Get thee to a nunnery ', I am preparing to follow. It is awful work, this love, and prevents all a man's projects of good or glory. I wanted to go to Greece lately . . . with her brother, who is a very fine, brave fellow . . . and wild about liberty. But the tears of a woman who has left her husband for a man, and the weakness of one's own heart, are paramount to these projects, and I can hardly indulge them ".

To her he wrote : " I set out most unwillingly, foreseeing the most evil results for all of you, and principally for yourself ".

And again : " I leave Ravenna so unwillingly, and with such a persuasion in my mind that my departure will lead from one misery to another, each greater than the former, that I have not the heart to utter another word on the subject ".

She, publishing these letters in after-years, commented : " How entirely were those presentiments fulfilled by the event ! " This assists us to understand the length of Byron's relation with her, and his impatience during most of its four years. A woman at once so insensitive and so sentimental was, perhaps, the only one who could have held him to her ; or for that matter have endured him herself. For she had the art of self-deception. The event—his death in Greece—which she describes as the fulfilment of his " presentiment " was brought about in no way by his rejoining her ; and the presentiment was not presentiment at all, but simply ill-temper at having to set off. Indeed, her comment is so evidently stupid that it is worth recording only as a trait of character which helps to solve the puzzle of Byron's long slavery. She was so obtuse that he could not shake her off.

CHAPTER XXIII

RAVENNA: LITERARY WORK

BYRON'S industry during the Ravenna period—December 1819 to the end of October 1821—was stupendous. Besides the works already considered, he wrote *Marino Faliero*, *Sardanapalus*,[1] *The Two Foscari, Cain, Heaven and Earth*, the fifth canto of *Don Juan, The Vision of Judgment, The Blues* and *The Irish Avatar*—a squib on George IV's visit to Ireland in 1821. This is a vast record of manual labour alone, and there were the diaries and many letters as well. The story of *Marino Faliero*—first of the dramas over which he was to waste many months of energy—had struck his imagination so long ago as the spring of 1817 ; but the project slumbered until 1820. He spent three months in composition, and the final draft was sent to England in September or October. He had again been infuriated by Murray's delays and he again threatened to desert to Paternoster Row. " You must not treat a blood-horse as you do your hacks, otherwise he'll bolt out of the course. . . . Now you have spoken out, are you any the worse for it ? " We discover from a letter to Moore directly afterwards, what Murray had said. " He almost insinuated that my last productions are *dull*. Dull, sir !—damme, dull ! I believe he is right ".

---

[1] *Sardanapalus, The Two Foscari*, and *Cain* were published in a single volume on December 19, 1821 ; *Heaven and Earth* was not published by Murray, but by John Hunt in the second number of *The Liberal* on January 1, 1823 ; the fifth canto of *Don Juan* (Murray) appeared with cantos iii. and iv. on August 8, 1821 ; *The Vision of Judgment* in the first number of *The Liberal*, October 15, 1822 ; *The Blues* in the third number, April 26, 1823. *The Irish Avatar* was first published in Paris, under Moore's supervision (he was then living there), on September 19, 1821. Murray did not publish it in any collected edition until 1831.

"I don't know", he wrote to Murray, in the midst of the loathed task of copying, "what your parlour-boarders will think of it. . . . You'll write now, because you will want to keep me in a good humour, till you can see what the tragedy is fit for. I know your ways, my Admiral".[1] The whole was sent to England, with the adjuration : "None of your *damned proofs*, now *recollect*. Print, paste, plaster, and destroy—but don't let me have any of your cursed printers' trash to pore over. For the rest, I neither know nor care". Again : "I have put my *soul* into the tragedy (as you *if* it) ; but you know that there are damned souls as well as tragedies". The report of the first act was favourable. "What Gifford says is very consolatory . . . 'English—sterling *genuine* English'. I am glad that I have got so much left. I hear none but from my valet, and I *see* none but in your new publications, and theirs is no language at all, but jargon. Even your 'New Jerusalem' is terribly stilted and affected, with '*very, very*'—so soft and pamby.

"Oh! if ever I *do* come amongst you again, I will give you such a 'Baviad and Mæviad'! not *as* good as the old, but even *better merited*. There never was such a *set* as your *ragamuffins* (I mean *not* yours only, but everybody's). What with the Cockneys, and the Lakers, and the *followers* of Scott, and Moore, and Byron, you are in the very uttermost decline and degradation of literature. I can't think of it without all the remorse of a murderer. I wish that Johnson were alive again to crush them!"

After more delay—"What! not a line? Well, have it your own way"—came further encouragement. "Gifford says it is good 'sterling genuine English', and Foscolo says that the characters are right Venetian. Shakespeare and Otway had a million of advantages over me, besides the incalculable one of being *dead* for from one to two centuries, and having been both born blackguards (which ARE such attractions to the gentle living reader) : let me then preserve the only one which I could possibly have—that of having been at Venice, and entered more into the local spirit of it. I claim no more".

The suspense—he had been in great suspense about this new venture—was over ; but there was something still more agonising to come. Byron had been from the first urgent in declaring his tragedy not an acting play. "It is too regular, and too simple, and of too remote an interest" ; and "I will not be exposed to the insolences of an audience without a remonstrance".

---

[1] Murray was publisher to the Board of Admiralty. This letter, much mutilated by Moore, is one of the most amusing that Byron wrote to Murray, particularly at the close, where a contemporary poetaster is criticised. See *L. and J.* v. 55.

" Do not let me be sacrificed in such a manner ", he pleaded. He even drew up and sent a protest for the newspapers, in case the play was piratically produced. On Saturday April 21, Murray published *Marino*.[1] On Wednesday April 25, the play was represented by Elliston, at Drury Lane Theatre. " The drama, sheet by sheet from the compositors' hands, was taken from the printing-office to the theatre, and the whole play, in fact, studied before publication ". Half an hour after Elliston received the formal licence from the Lord Chamberlain, he was served with a writ from Murray's solicitor, announcing that the Lord Chancellor had granted an injunction against the acting of *Marino Faliero*, and that the play must be immediately withdrawn. Byron had been almost beside himself at the prospect, which so early as January was known to him.

RAVENNA, *January* 20, 1821

" If Harris or Elliston persist, after the remonstrance which I desired you and Mr. Kinnaird to make on my behalf, and which I hope will be sufficient—but *if*, I say, they *do persist*, then I pray you to *present in person* the enclosed letter to the Lord Chamberlain : I have said *in person*, because otherwise I shall have neither answer nor knowledge that it has reached its address, owing to ' the insolence of office '.

" I wish you would speak to Lord Holland, and to all my friends and yours, to interest themselves in preventing this cursed attempt at representation.

" God help me ! at this distance, I am treated like a corpse or a fool by the few people that I thought I could rely upon ; and I *was* a fool to think any better of them than of the rest of mankind.

" Pray write.—Yours, &c.

" P.S.—I have nothing more at heart (that is, in literature) than to prevent this drama from going upon the stage : in short, rather than permit it, it must be *suppressed altogether*, and only *forty copies struck off privately* for presents to my friends. What curst fools those speculating buffoons must be *not* to see that it is unfit for their fair—or their booth ! "

Elliston succeeded in getting the Lord Chancellor (Eldon) to suspend the injunction for April 25. Murray, hearing this, issued a handbill declaring the state of affairs. The play was acted that night, and fell flat. Proceedings then took place

---

[1] " The Doge is longer than I expected ", wrote Byron on June 14 ; " pray why did you print the face of Margarita Cogni by way of frontispiece ? It has almost caused a row between the Countess G. and myself " (*L. and J.* v. 308).
Murray had in 1819 bought Harlow's drawings of Margarita Cogni.

23

before the Chancellor, " but no counsel appearing on the part of the plaintiff, the case was struck out ". *Marino Faliero* was acted again on April 30, and on five dates in May ; but no enthusiasm was ever excited, and the greatest receipt was £160.[1]

Byron's anger was supreme—his anguish too. He saw paragraphs in the Italian papers, stating that *he* had brought forward the play. It was galling enough to make him appeal to Hoppner for a statement in the Venetian and Milanese papers saying that he had opposed the representation, and that the play was not hissed, as had also been said. It is pathetic to follow his distress. To Murray, on May 19 : [2] " Now I should be glad to know what compensation Mr. Elliston would make me, not only for dragging my writings on the stage in *five* days, but for being the cause that I was kept for *four* days (from Sunday to Thursday morning, the only post-days) in the *belief* that the tragedy had been acted and ' unanimously hissed ' ; and this with the addition that *I* ' had brought it upon the stage ', and consequently that none of my friends had attended to my request to the contrary. Suppose that I had burst a blood-vessel, like John Keats, or blown my brains out in a fit of rage,—neither of which would have been unlikely a few years ago. At present I am, luckily, calmer than I used to be, and yet I would not pass those four days over again for—I know not what.

" I wrote to you to keep up your spirits, for reproach is useless always, and irritating—but my feelings were very much hurt, to be dragged like a gladiator to the fate of a gladiator by that ' *retiarius*,' Mr. Elliston. As to his defence and offers of compensation, what is all this to the purpose ? I would have flung it into the fire rather than have had it represented ".

Marino Faliero was dedicated to Goethe in a lengthy letter, but the packet containing this was delayed in transit to England. A similar fate strangely awaited the second attempt at homage in *Sardanapalus* ; and it was not until *Werner* appeared in 1823 that Byron succeeded in his purpose of tribute. Since 1816, Goethe had been interested in him. In October 1817 he had received from a young American a copy of *Manfred*, which he at once read and re-read. " It seized upon him with singular force ", says Mr. E. H. Coleridge. No doubt the kinship with his own *Faust* attracted him, vague though it was ; Goethe indeed explicitly repudiated the idea of imitation—and no less warmly than Byron himself. Byron first heard of his interest

---

[1] *Memoirs of R. W. Elliston*, p. 271.

[2] He had by this time written nearly three acts of *Sardanapalus*, but this, with *The Two Foscari* and *Cain*—also begun and finished at Ravenna—was not published until after he had settled down at Pisa. Murray paid for these three £2710.

in May 1820, when somebody sent him some German newspapers.
He did not know a word of the language,[1] and begged Hoppner
to translate for him some remarks " which appear to be Goethe's
on *Manfred* ". He had made out the word *hypocondrisch*, and
judged that the notice was unfavourable. The alarming adjective
proved not to be significant ; for the article (which was Goethe's
review of *Manfred* in his own magazine, *Kunst und Alterthum*)
was enthusiastic. We smile to-day at some of the sage's *obiter
dicta*, such as " Hamlet's soliloquy appears improved on here " ;
but at that time Goethe reigned supreme in European criticism.
And Byron's elation at his praise was unbounded. He sent the
original article, Hoppner's translation, and an Italian one, to
Murray. " The opinion of *the* greatest man of Germany—
perhaps of Europe—upon one of the great men of your advertise-
ments—in short, a critique of Goethe's upon *Manfred*. . . .
Keep them all in your archives ".

The German Jove read *Marino Faliero* too ; and said that
in this piece " one quite forgets that Lord Byron or even an
Englishman wrote it. We live entirely in Venice, and entirely
in the time in which the actions took place. . . . The personages
have none of the subjective feelings, thoughts, or opinions of
the poet ". Byron himself, however, declared that the play
was so far subjective in treatment that he was convinced he
would have done precisely what the Doge did on similar provoca-
tions ; and it is clear that the analogy of Faliero's fate with his
own was the attraction of the subject. Faliero was crowned
and afterwards decapitated on the Giant's Staircase (as Byron
believed, though history contradicts him) of the Doge's Palace
in Venice. The symbolism could hardly have been closer for
the homage of 1812 and the ostracism of 1816, on the Giant's
Staircase of fame in London. Accordingly, the great moments
ring with the personal note, as it now sounded—always for the
downfall of the worshipped and powerful, and their brooding
on the things that were and are. Striking examples are the line,

" Deep Vengeance is the daughter of deep silence "—

the True-Untrue ; and, later, the prophetic cry which first had
sounded in the new *Harold*. The decree goes forth from the
infamous tribunal that the place for this Doge's portrait shall be
left vacant, with a black veil hung over it ; and Faliero exclaims :

" The veil which blackens o'er this blighted name,
And hides, or seems to hide, these lineaments,

---

[1] " Except oaths learned from postillions and officers in a squabble . . .
I like, however, their women (I was once *so desperately* in love with a
German woman, Constance) ".—(Ravenna Diary.)

> Shall draw more gazers than the thousand portraits
> Which glitter round it in their pictured trappings ".

All through the closing scenes Byron's own story emerges
from the legend, his own character from that of the Doge :

> " I had only one fount of quiet left,
> And *that* they poisoned ! My pure household gods
> Were shivered on my hearth, and o'er their shrine
> Sate grinning Ribaldry, and sneering Scorn "

—an almost literal paraphrase of words in a letter of 1817. In
the Doge's final interview with his wife, there occurs this analysis
of Byron's self :

> " . . . there was that in my spirit ever
> Which shaped out for itself some great reverse " ;

and again :

> " . . . in one hour
> I have uprooted all my former life,
> And outlived everything ".

The play closes with the imprecation on Venice already quoted.
He said of it : " I never wrote nor copied an *entire scene of
that play* without being obliged to *break* off—to *break* a command-
ment, to obey a woman's, and to forget God's. . .. The lady
always apologised for the interruption ; but you know the answer
a man must make when and while he can. It happened to be
the only hour I had in the four-and-twenty for composition or
reading, and I was obliged to divide even it. Such are the
defined duties of a *Cavalier' servente, or Cavalier' schiavo* ".
Nevertheless, *Marino Faliero* is the best of the dramas. The
other three share in all its defects, but in few or none of its beauties.
Those are energy and pathos. Its defects of flatness (Byron's
conversational blank verse must be some of the worst ever
written) and monotony are intensified a hundredfold in *Sardana-
palus, The Two Foscari*, and above all, *Werner*, in which I find
nothing whatever to repay perusal. Yet strangely (or not
strangely), *Werner* was the only one of his dramas to attain
anything like success on the stage.[1]

With the extraordinary blindness to his true characteristics
which marked Byron in every self-criticism except that of *Don
Juan*, he was persuaded, and he earnestly sought to persuade
Murray, that in the tragedies he was doing his immortal works.
Murray never was persuaded, and the opinion of posterity is

---

[1] It was acted many times from 1826 to 1860, and was revived in our
own day, for one performance (1887) by [Sir] Henry Irving. Macready was
very successful in the part of Werner : the famous " Macready *burst* "
being finely displayed in Act ii. sc. 2, and Act v. sc. 1 (*Poems*, v. 324).

on his side. Mr. E. H. Coleridge bravely breaks a lance in their defence ; but though most of them, it is true (except *Werner*), contain " hidden treasures ", they are on the whole so terribly defective that when Mr. Arthur Symons dismisses them as " the lamentable attempts of the dramas ", we feel no inclination to dispute his verdict.

The fifth canto of *Don Juan* was begun on October 16, 1820. The two which had been originally the third canto were still in Murray's hands. He had written to say that half the poem (as far as it then went) was good, and here is Byron's spirited reply. " You say that *one half* is very good : you are *wrong* ; for, if it were, it would be the finest poem in existence. *Where* is the poetry of which *one half* is good ? is it the *Æneid* ? is it *Milton's* ? is it *Dryden's* ? is it anyone's except *Pope's* and Goldsmith's, of which *all* is good ? and yet these two last are the poets your pond poets would explode. But if *one half* of the two new cantos be good in your opinion, what the devil would you have more ? No—no ; no poetry is *generally* good—only by fits and starts—and you are lucky to get a sparkle here and there. You might as well want a midnight *all stars* as rhyme all perfect ".

Nevertheless he was discouraged, and had written on October 12 : " I don't feel inclined to care further about *Don Juan*. What do you think a very pretty Italian lady said to me the other day ? She had read it in the French, and paid me some compliments, with due DRAWBACKS, upon it. I answered that what she said was true, but that I suspected it would live longer than *Childe Harold*. ' Ah, but (said she) *I would rather have the fame of Childe Harold for three years than an* IMMORTALITY *of Don Juan !* ' The truth is that *it is* TOO TRUE, and the women hate everything which strips off the tinsel of *sentiment* ; and they are right, as it would rob them of their weapons. I never knew a woman who did not hate *De Grammont's Memoirs* for the same reason : even Lady Oxford used to abuse them ".

By December he had finished. " So prepare ! " But he was nervous about Murray's decision—twice he wrote : " I want to know what the Devil you mean to do ? " Murray was hesitant. It seems to have been a question of money ; for in February there is this from Byron : " I agree to your request of leaving in abeyance the terms . . . till you can ascertain the effect of publication ". He gives then a sketch of his plan.

" The fifth is so far from being the last of *Don Juan*, that it is hardly the beginning. I meant to take him the tour of Europe, with a proper mixture of siege, battle, and adventure, and to make him finish as *Anacharsis Cloots* in the French Revolution. To how many cantos this may extend, I know not, nor whether

(even if I live) I shall complete it ; but this was my notion :
I meant to have made him a cavalier' servente in Italy, and a
cause for a divorce in England, and a sentimental ' Werter-faced
man ' in Germany, so as to show the different ridicules of the
society in each of those countries, and to have displayed him
gradually *gâté* and *blasé* as he grew older, as is natural. But I
had not quite fixed whether to make him end in hell, or in an
unhappy marriage, not knowing which would be the severest :
the Spanish tradition says hell : but it is probably only an allegory
of the other state. You are now in possession of my notions on
the subject ".

But before the existent new cantos were published, the woman
had intervened.[1] Byron told Murray in a letter concerning the
fifth canto : " At the particular request of the Countess G., I
have promised *not* to continue *Don Juan.* You will therefore
look upon these three cantos as the last of the poem ".[2] It is
evident from the further context that La Guiccioli was the very
pretty Italian lady of October 12, before the fifth canto was
begun.

The three were published together in August, without the
name of author or publisher. " The booksellers' messengers
filled the street in front of the house in Albemarle Street, and the
parcels of books were given out of the window in answer to their
obstreperous demands ".[3] Byron, on getting *his* parcel, wrote to
Murray.

" I have received the Juans, which are printed so *carelessly*,
especially the fifth canto, as to be disgraceful to me, and not
creditable to you. It really must be *gone over again* with the
manuscript, the errors are so gross ;—words added—changed—so
as to make cacophony and nonsense. You have been careless
of this poem because some of your squad don't approve of it ;
but I tell you that it will be long before you see anything half
so good as poetry or writing.

"If you have no feeling for your own reputation, pray have
some little for mine. I have read over the poem carefully, and

---

[1] The Countess Guiccioli had not at this time (July 1821) left the
neighbourhood of Ravenna ; she was still living either at her father's villa,
fifteen miles outside, or else in Count Gamba's house in the close vicinity
of the Palazzo Guiccioli (*Shelley and his Friends in Italy*, Mrs. Rossetti
Angeli, 1911).

[2] Moore has the following :

" In this note, so highly honourable to the fair writer, she says, ' Re-
member, my Byron, the promise you have made me. Never shall I be
able to tell you the satisfaction I feel from it, so great are the sentiments
of pleasure and confidence with which the sacrifice you have made has
inspired me '. In a postscript to the note she adds, ' I am only sorry that
Don Juan was not left in the infernal regions ' ".

[3] *Memoir of John Murray*, i. 413.

I tell you, *it is poetry*. Your little envious knot of parson-poets may say what they please : time will show that I am not in this instance mistaken.

" Desire my friend Hobhouse to correct the press, especially of the last canto, from the manuscript as it is. It is enough to drive one out of one's senses to see the infernal torture of words from the original. . . .

" No wonder the poem should fail (which, however, it won't, you will see) with such things allowed to creep about it. Replace what is omitted, and correct what is so shamefully misprinted, and let the poem have fair play ; and I fear nothing ".

He added, in a P.S., " As for *you*, you have no opinion of your own and never had, but are blown about by the last thing said to you, no matter by whom ". But in the envelope :

" The enclosed letter is written in bad humour, but not without provocation. However, let it (that is, the bad humour) go for little ; but I must request your serious attention to the abuses of the printer, which ought never to have been permitted. You forget that all the fools in London (the chief purchasers of your publications) will condemn in me the stupidity of your printer. For instance, in the notes to Canto fifth, ' the *Adriatic* shore of the Bosphorus', instead of the *Asiatic ! !* All this may seem little to you—so fine a gentleman with your ministerial connections,—but it is serious to me, who am thousands of miles off, and have no opportunity of not proving myself the fool your printer makes me, except your pleasure and leisure, forsooth.

" The gods prosper you, and forgive you, for I can't ".

By September his wrath had subsided into sullenness. He had read over the new cantos—" which are excellent. . . . I regret that I do not go on with it ". But in a final blaze of wrath, he adds : " You are so grand, and sublime, and occupied that one would think, instead of publishing for the ' Board of Longitude ', that you were trying to discover it ".

CHAPTER XXIV

THE DEATHS OF ALLEGRA AND SHELLEY—
1821-1822

Allegra sent to the Convent of Bagna Cavallo—Trouble with Claire—
The Hoppner affair: scandal about Shelley in 1821—Mary's letter—
Byron's baseness—Shelley at Ravenna—The move to Pisa—Ailegra left
behind—Meetings with Lord Clare and Rogers—Pisa: the Lanfranchi
Palace—Anxiety of Claire: letters and interviews—Death of Allegra—
Burial at Harrow—Lady Noel's will—Ada—*Cain* published: the
outcry—Other works—Ennui and dejection—Quarrels with Murray—
Leigh Hunt, and *The Liberal*—Banishment of the Gambas and Teresa
Guiccioli—Death of Shelley—Byron's tributes

CLAIRE CLAIRMONT, now living at Florence as governess
in the family of Professor Bojti, and just beginning to
recover hope and spirits, received on March 15, 1821—a
rainy day, as she wrote in her journal—letters from Shelley and
Mary, " with enclosures from Ravenna. The child in the Convent
of Bagna Cavallo ".

Byron had *sent* Allegra there (though it was only twelve
miles outside Ravenna), by a Ravennese named Ghigi.[1] He
told Hoppner that as she was now " four years old complete "
and quite beyond the control of the servants, he had no resource
but to place her there for a time, " at a high pension too ".
He added that he had never intended to give her an English
education, for, being a natural child, it would make " her after-
settlement doubly difficult. Abroad, with a fair foreign education
and a portion of 5 or £6000, she might and may marry very
respectably ". Moreover, he wished her to be a Roman Catholic,
" which I look upon as the best religion ".

Claire, on March 24, wrote him a long and angry letter—a
letter to infuriate him or any one. Deeply as one feels with
her in a bitter grief, there is no doubt that she made her miseries
worse than they need have been by the unbridled sarcasm poured
upon him who had her and her child in his power. She had
the folly to refer to Lady Byron, and by implication to Teresa

---

[1] *La Figlia di Lord Byron*, Emilio Biondi (Faenza, 1899). (I take title
and information from Mr. Prothero's note in *L. and J.* v. 279.)

Guiccioli—the latter suffering nothing less than contumely at her hands. She implored Byron to allow her to place Allegra at her own expense (which would, of course, have been Shelley's) in one of the very best English boarding-schools ; it should be chosen by his own friends. " I will see her only so often as they decide. . . . I entreat you earnestly not to be obdurate on this point. Believe me, in putting Allegra into a convent to ease yourself of the trouble, and to hurt me in my affection for her, you have done almost a greater injury to yourself than to me or her. So blind is hatred ! "

Shelley, though sympathising with Claire, defended Byron's action ; but his championship did not save him from perfidy on Albé's part. The incident which is to develop in this connection is the worst thing we are told of Byron. In all the rest there has been some saving clause ; we have been able to pity, though we were obliged to condemn.

Sending Claire's unhappy letter to Hoppner, he wrote across the top : " The moral part of the letter upon the Italians comes with an excellent grace from the writer now living with a *man* and his *wife* [1]—and having planted a child in the Fl—Foundling, etc.".

This referred to a calumny against Shelley which had come to Hoppner's ears in the spring of 1820 through a pair of servants —Elise the Swiss nurse, and one Paolo Foggi, who, after having betrayed her, had been induced to marry her. Paolo was soon afterwards dismissed from Shelley's service for misconduct ; and out of revenge, began to spread scandals. Byron had at first half-heartedly defended his friend, against whom Hoppner's feeling had wholly turned ; but soon he wrote : " The story is true, no doubt, though Elise is but Queen's evidence. . . . Of the facts, however, there can be little doubt ; it is just like them ".

Writing to Mary from Ravenna in August 1821 (he was there as Byron's guest), Shelley gave her an epitome. " Elise says that Claire was my mistress. . . . She then proceeds to say that Claire was with child by me ; that I gave her the most violent medicines to procure abortion ; that this not succeeding she was brought to bed, and that I immediately tore the child from her and sent it to the Foundling Hospital. . . . In addition, she says that both I and Claire treated *you* in the most shameful manner ; that I neglected and beat you, and that Claire never let a day pass without offering you insults of the most violent kind, in which she was abetted by me ". The Hoppners had declined all intercourse ; Shelley and Mary had wondered—here was the explanation. Already they had known of Paolo's

[1] Claire, as we have seen, was not living with the Shelleys at this time.

schemes ; there had been an attempt at blackmail, but the matter had at once been placed in a lawyer's hands, and they had believed it over. " Imagine my despair of good ! " cried Shelley now ; and he begged Mary to write at once to the Hoppners. She at once did so. Professor Dowden well describes her letter : " the clear flame of a woman's indignant love ". It is moving in the highest degree. She had tried to copy from Shelley's letter the actual accusations. . . . " Upon my word, I solemnly assure you that I cannot write the words " ; [1] and she enclosed Shelley's original letter instead. She sent her own to him first. " I wish also that Lord Byron may see it ; he gave no credit to the tale "—for Byron had represented himself in this light, when telling Shelley the reason for the Hoppners' withdrawal. He had promised Mr. Hoppner in the spring that the accusations should be concealed from Shelley ; but on the first night of their meeting at Ravenna, he had told all—and now, by the letter from Mary, Hoppner would learn that he had broken his word.

Shelley handed it to him, in utter trust for the future as for the past. Byron " engaged to send it, with his own comments, to the Hoppners ". So Shelley told Mary on August 16. Albé had confessed that he had broken his word to Hoppner ; and Shelley accepted this as a good reason for his wishing to send the letter, with his own comments, himself.

The letter was found among Byron's papers after his death.[2]

Mr. Prothero thinks it not impossible that it was sent and at Byron's request returned. " As the answer to a charge closely affecting the mother of Allegra, it would be natural that he should wish to keep the document ". He also refers to a subsequent conversation of Mary Shelley's with the Hoppners as being among Lady Shelley's recollections ; but seems to cite

---

[1] " I think I could as soon have died ", she wrote to her husband.

[2] In *Lord Byron's Correspondence* (1922) it was first publicly made known that the letter was found *with a broken seal*. The seal was Shelley's, in red wax ; and " at the top of the seal there was a drop of black sealing-wax, with a scrap of paper attached to it." (*Corr.* II, 192). Mary's envelope had borne no address, so that if the letter reached its destination, " it must have been conveyed under a separate cover " (*Ibid.*). Mr. Edgcumbe, in the *Correspondence*, pertinently inquires : Who broke Shelley's seal ? (Byron had already read the letter.) He is convinced that it cannot have been Hobhouse, as executor, and therefore takes it as certain that the seal was already broken. He thinks, with Lord Ernle, that the letter was sent by Byron and at his request returned to him. (*L. and J.* v. 74.) I think we may indulge the hope, indubitably pointed to by the broken seal and the adherent scrap of paper, that Byron did send the letter. Nevertheless, I leave my text as it stands, for we are still confronted by the facts that Mary received no answer, and that she cut Mrs. Hoppner " completely " in 1843. Mr. Edgcumbe hopes that the Hoppner papers may some day come to light, and reveal more than we now possess of the truth of this vexed question.

Professor Dowden [1] as an authority for this. I can find no such reference in the edition—that of 1886—before me as I write.[2] I do not attach much weight to the argument that Byron would naturally wish to keep the document, since it affected the mother of Allegra. Had not he himself been eager to underline the charge against Claire to the Hoppners? In Byron, too, the phrase " It is just like them "—of whom nothing could be more unlike—borrows a peculiar shade of baseness. It was not for him, of all men, thus to speak. Mrs. Angeli alludes to his own sufficiently loose morals, and thinks that he might for this reason have thought not too severely of the alleged intrigue. But " It is just like them " robs him of that shield. We must accept it as best we can : nothing in his life so blots his memory as this incident.

In August he had written urgently, inviting Shelley to Ravenna. This was just after the banishment of the Gamba family from the Romagna. Byron had at first determined to go to Switzerland, where they should join him later. " I shall bring Allegra with me ", he told Hoppner. He had gone so far as to write to Hentsch, the Genevan banker, desiring him to engage a house. But again the vague hope of freedom revived. He wrote to Moore (still in Paris) on August 2 : " If you went to England, I would do so still ".[3] It was on the same day that he sent his summons to Shelley ; he wished to talk over plans with that universal counsellor and mediator.[4] Shelley left the Baths of Pisa, where he and Mary then were, on August 3, paid a flying visit to Claire at Leghorn (she had gone there for her holiday) and consulted with her about Allegra ; on the night of August 6 he reached

---

[1] *Life of Shelley*, ii. 429.

[2] In *Shelley and his Friends in Italy*, by Mrs. Rossetti Angeli (1911), I find the following : " Indeed the fact that Mary never received the letter of restored confidence which she demanded as her right from the Hoppners tends to prove that Byron . . . never sent [her letter]. Many years later, in February 1843, Mary Shelley was in Florence. ' The Hoppners are here ', she then wrote to Claire. ' Mrs. and Miss go to the balls. I cut her completely '. This also suggests that the Hoppners remained in ignorance of the truth regarding the Shelley scandal. There yet remains, however, the *possibility* that Byron did send the letter and that it was returned to him ". But Mrs. Angeli (the daughter of the late Mr. W. M. Rossetti) thinks this explanation not very convincing in view of the Hoppners' silence (p. 220).

[3] Already, in December 1820, he had proposed to Moore that they should " get to London again " in the spring of 1821 ; and " set up jointly a *newspaper* . . . take an office—our names *not* announced, but suspected ". In 1812 Moore had made the same proposal to Byron.

[4] " It seems destined ", said Shelley of himself, " that I am always to have an active part in everybody's affairs whom I approach ".

the Palazzo Guiccioli at ten o'clock, and they sat up talking until
five in the morning. Shelley thought Byron greatly improved
in every respect—in genius, in temper, in moral views, in health,
in happiness. His rooms in the Palace were splendid ; he had
many servants, ten horses, eight enormous dogs, three monkeys,
five cats, an eagle, a crow, and a falcon. That was the first list ;
in a postscript Shelley added : " I have just met, on the grand
staircase, five peacocks, two guinea hens, and an Egyptian crane ".[1]
They talked much. " Sit up gossipping until six in the morning "
is part of Shelley's epitome of the daily life. Literature was
their chief topic—Byron silent as to *Adonais*, loud in praise of
Prometheus, and in censure of *The Cenci* ; Shelley cool towards
Marino Faliero, but enthusiastic over *Don Juan*. The fifth canto
he thought transcendently fine. " Every word has the stamp
of immortality. I despair of rivalling Lord Byron . . . and
there is no other with whom it is worth contending ". *Don Juan*,
he said, was something wholly new and relative to the age, and
yet surpassingly beautiful. But the domineering force of Byron's
genius depressed him. " I write nothing ", he told Peacock,
" and shall probably write no more ". To Mary he said, " The
demon of mistrust and pride lurks between two persons in our
situation, poisoning the freedom of our intercourse. . . . I
think the fault is not on my side " ; and to Leigh Hunt he spoke
of the " canker of aristocracy " which, among many generous and
exalted qualities, lurked in Byron's spirit. They considered the
Swiss sojourn ; Shelley's counsel was strongly against it. He
thought the place little fitted for Byron ; the English côterie,
with its gossip, had rendered it odious to him before, and would
so render it again. Byron was convinced. He decided to stay
in Italy, if the Countess Guiccioli and the Gambas would stay
too. Shelley was induced, true to his destiny, to intervene ;
he wrote to Teresa and convinced her also. She added at the
end of her letter to him, that his goodness had emboldened her to
ask a favour : " *Non partite da Ravenna senza Milord* ". She
was then at Florence, whither, on account of the large English
colony there, Byron did not desire to go. He inclined towards
Pisa, where Mary then was, though the Shelleys had thought of
wintering in Florence. The pros and cons were long balanced.
Finally Pisa was decided on for all.

Shelley saw Allegra at Bagna Cavallo, and sent Mary a long

---

[1] Byron's Ravenna diary is full of references to this menagerie—the
oddest little details. " Gave the falcon some water " ; " played with my
mastiff—gave him his supper " ; " crow lame of a leg . . . falcon pretty
brisk " ; " beat the crow for stealing the falcon's victuals ". His small
beer is indeed of the smallest : " Bought a blanket " ; " did *not* eat two
apples " ; " tore a button in my new coat ", etc. etc.

and reassuring report. Though still excessively vivacious, she was more obedient and serious. She seemed, he said, a thing of a higher and finer order than the other children there. Nevertheless, he considered that Byron should take her with him wherever he went. But there would be difficulties ; and Shelley wondered if they, among their friends in Tuscany, could find any one to undertake her. The immediate urgency, however, was to get some person less odious and unfit to take care of her, if she *were* brought to Pisa, " than an Italian woman whom Byron seems to have fallen upon ".

Shelley did not think it incumbent on him to obey the Countess Guiccioli's request. He left Ravenna on August 17, *senza Milord*, who had urgently implored him to remain. Before the end of the month Teresa and her father were in Pisa, and the Shelleys had made the acquaintance of Byron's *dama*. " A very pretty, sentimental, innocent Italian ", wrote Shelley in October to his friend Mr. Gisborne ; " who has sacrificed an immense fortune for the sake of Lord Byron, and who, if I know anything of my friend, of her, and of human nature, will hereafter have plenty of opportunity to repent her rashness ". He had left Ravenna under the impression that when Byron joined them in Pisa— where, soon after Shelley's return, the Palazzo Lanfranchi, " the stateliest on the Lung' Arno ", had been taken for Albé— Allegra was not to be left behind, alone and friendless, in the convent of Bagna Cavallo. Claire, passionately longing for her little daughter, lingered in the neighbourhood ; for they all hoped that an arrangement would be made by which she might have her, for a time at any rate, again.

Byron left Ravenna on October 29. On November 1 Claire was on her way back to Florence from Pugnano, where she had been on a visit, and " just before she entered the narrow streets of Empoli, Byron with his travelling train passed her on the road, as he drove forward to take possession of the Lanfranchi Palace ".[1] For months her diary had been filled with wonderings about her Allegra ; she had dreamed of death one night, of happy reunion the next. Now the hour was near, and her heart almost stood still.

He arrived at Pisa, and Allegra was not with him.

A few days before he broke up house, Byron had written in his Ravenna journal a passage referring to the " earliest and dearest " friend, Lord Clare.[2] On his way across Italy, between Imola and Bologna, they met—to Byron's surprise, for he had not known that Clare was in the country. He movingly recorded the meeting in the same journal; and in 1822 Clare

[1] Dowden, *Life of Shelley*, ii. 445.   [2] See Chap. III.

visited him at Leghorn, to his great delight. " I have a presenti-
ment I shall never see him more ", he then said, and his eyes
filled with tears as they parted. One of the very last letters from
Missolonghi was to My dearest Clare (in the old Harrow formula,
whose omission used to cause such heartburnings). " I hope
you do not forget that I always regard you as my dearest friend,
and love you as when we were Harrow boys together ; and if I
do not repeat this so often as I ought, it is that I may not tire
you with what you so well know ".

That must have been a poignant message, sad yet sweet, for
Clare to receive in April (it was written on March 31) 1824—
probably not until after the fatal 19th.

At Bologna another friend from England was awaiting him.
This was Rogers ; but the meeting, unlike that with Clare, proved
disappointing. Already in 1818 Byron had conceived himself
to have cause of offence against Rogers, the " black drop of
whose liver had oozed through too palpably to be overlooked ".
His annoyance crystallised into the savage lines now known as
Question ; Answer. They were first published in 1833, but Byron
sent them home for private circulation in 1820. Murray wrote
that the side of his talent displayed in them might prove a national
service. If vulgar personal abuse be a form of national service,
Murray was right. The lines are horrible. Mr. E. H. Coleridge
well says : " By far the best comment on satire and satirist is
to be found in the noble lines in Rogers's *Italy* ".[1] These were
left unaltered by him after he had seen, in 1833, the lampoon
which Lady Blessington declared would kill him.

> " . . . Yes, Byron, thou art gone ;
> Gone like a star that through the firmament
> Shot and was lost, in its eccentric course
> Dazzling, perplexing. Yet thy heart, methinks,
> Was generous, noble—noble in its scorn
> Of all things low or little ; nothing there
> Sordid or servile. If imagined wrongs
> Pursued thee, urging thee sometimes to do
> Things long regretted, oft, as many know,
> None more than I, thy gratitude would build
> On slight foundations . . .
> . . . Who among us all
> .   .   .   .
> Tried as thou wert, and with thy soul of flame—
> Pleasure, while yet the down was on thy cheek

---

[1] *Italy* was first published in 1828. In 1830 appeared the great
Turner edition ; in 1839, to another issue, Rogers prefixed the *Selbstpor-
trät* which contains some of the most familiar of his lines :

> " . . . Nature denied him much,
> But gave him at his birth what most he values " . .

> Uplifting, pressing, and to lips like thine,
> Her charméd cup—ah, who among us all,
> Could say he had not erred as much, and more ! "

The lines that Rogers read in 1833 in *Fraser's Magazine*—where they were first published—were a string of couplets containing gross personal insults. His corpse-like aspect was a common jest among his acquaintance ; these verses were concerned not only with that, but with his well-known propensity to talk scandal. Here are the most offensive passages—the *jeu d'esprit* is in the form of a question from an imaginary person, whom another answers.

> " Mouth that marks the envious Scorner,
> With a Scorpion in each corner
> Curling up his tail to sting you
> In the place that most may wring you ;
> Eyes of lead-like hue and gummy,
> Carcase stolen from some mummy . . .
> Is't a Corpse stuck up for show . . .
> Vampire, Ghost, or Goul (*sic*), what is it ?
> I would walk ten miles to miss it ".

The answerer says that it is " the Bard, and Beau, and Banker ".

> " Yet if you could bring about
> Just to turn him inside out,
> Satan's self would seem less sooty,
> And his present aspect—Beauty . . .
> You're his foe—for that he fears you,
> And in absence blasts and sears you :
> You're his friend—for that he hates you,
> First obliges, and then baits you . . .
> He's the Cancer of his Species,
> And will eat himself to pieces ".

Other epithets are rotten, sodden, bilious, devil ; and, with a startling and ludicrous flavour of slangy modernity—blighter !

They spent a day at Bologna, and together crossed the Apennines to Florence ; it was about this trip that Rogers made the gibe already quoted.[1] On October 31 Byron pushed on for Pisa, and Rogers wrote home : " I wish you had seen him set off— every window of the inn was open to see him ". Whether this was due to his many-sided fame, or to the travelling equipage described by Medwin, may be questioned. " Seven servants, five carriages, nine horses, a monkey, a bull-dog and a mastiff, two cats, three pet fowls, and some hens ". Another incident of the flitting was the composition, on the road from Florence to Pisa, of the lines,

> " Oh, talk not to me of a name great in story ;
> The days of our Youth are the days of our Glory ".

---

[1] See Chap. XI.

The concluding stanza, with its renowned last line :

" I knew it was love, and I felt it was glory "

—was added at Pisa on November 6, in the early days of reunion with Teresa. The Palazzo Lanfranchi was a fine sixteenth-century building with a façade attributed to Michael Angelo. Byron called it a famous old feudal palace. There were dank underground rooms which he loved to think of as dungeons and cells ; and an old servant of his used to relate that the English Milord would descend to these basement dens—below the level of the river—on stormy nights, and order cushions to be brought down that he might sleep there. The Shelleys were installed nearly opposite in the Tre Palazzi di Chiesa—a far less sumptuous abode. The Gambas and Teresa Guiccioli had become part of the Shelley circle ; Mary described her as a nice pretty girl, without pretensions, good-hearted, and amiable. They drove together in the afternoons, and Teresa and the young Count spent many evenings at the Shelleys' flat. There they met Edward and Jane Williams (the Jane who plays so prominent a part in the later Shelley story), Medwin (Jeaffreson's " perplexing simpleton "), and the egregious Count Taaffe, an Irishman with a craze for Dante.

Byron's advent set Pisa by the ears. He came with this blazon : " He was said to be of royal birth ; a man of great wealth, of sanguinary temperament and savage customs ; a past master in all gentlemanly accomplishments ; a genius of evil, but of more than human intellect ".[1] One hopes he was aware of this repute—it is hard to say which item would have pleased him most.

No sooner was he arrived than trouble with Claire Clairmont began. She was by that time back in Florence ; but her distress on finding that Allegra had been left behind was so great that Mr. Tighe, a member of the Shelley circle, had gone to Bagna Cavallo to obtain information about the child's surroundings. He sent an alarming report. In the marshes of Romagna there was a form of fever which had ere now ravaged the district ; the food at the convent was meagre ; there were no fires. " What pangs of anguish I suffered in the winter of 1821," wrote Claire in after years, " when I saw a bright fire . . . and knew my darling never saw or felt a cheerful blaze ". With Tighe's report to nerve her, she wrote again to Byron, this time using (as she afterwards declared) not one word of reproach. If he would place Allegra with some respectable family in Pisa, Florence, Lucca, she would consent never to go near her ; nor should even Shelley or Mary visit the child without his consent. No answer

[1] Helen Rossetti Angeli, *Shelley and his Friends in Italy*, p. 234.

was returned. She wrote again after a month had passed—again there was no answer. In February she had some idea of going to Vienna, where her brother was ; and she longed to see Allegra before she went. Byron had just received the news of Lady Noel's death, which made him possessor of a considerable property ; [1] Claire hoped that it might be a propitious moment for pleading. On February 18, then, she wrote again.[2] It was an appeal of utter despair ; there is not (as we are shown it) one word that could offend or even irritate. "I assure you I can no longer resist the internal inexplicable feeling which haunts me that I shall never see her any more. I entreat you to destroy this feeling by allowing me to see her ". Again no answer ; and, almost distraught, Claire hurried to Pisa to consult her friends. Mr. Tighe and Lady Mountcashell (the separated wife of Earl Mountcashell, living in Italy as the wife of Mr. George Tighe—they passed as Mr. and Mrs. Mason) were in favour of decisive measures ; the Shelleys, though now convinced that Allegra ought to be taken out of Byron's hands, thought it better to temporise. With nothing decided, Claire returned to Florence on February 25 ; and Shelley then made an appeal to Byron's mercy on her behalf. "His only reply ", says she in her later account of the proceedings, " was a shrug of impatience and the exclamation that women could not live without making scenes. He never had seen the convent ; yet he confessed he had not made the smallest inquiry as to whether what I had stated was true or no ". There is an account, in a copy by Claire (and therefore to be taken with caution) of a letter from a Miss Elizabeth Parker,[3] of Shelley's interview with Byron. " I never saw Shelley in a passion before. . . . He declared that he could with pleasure have knocked Lord Byron down " ; for when he mentioned Claire's alarm and distraction and declining health, " he saw a gleam of malicious satisfaction pass over Lord Byron's countenance. ' I saw his look ', said Shelley ; ' I understood its meaning ; I despised him, and I came away '. After-

---

[1] Lady Noel died at Kirkby Mallory on January 22 (Byron's birthday), 1822. He inherited the whole property by right of his wife ; but one of the terms of the separation provided that it should be divided by arbitrators. Lord Dacre was arbitrator for Lady Byron ; Sir F. Burdett for Byron. Half the income was allotted to the wife, and half to the husband. Lady Byron already had the £60,000 settled on her at their marriage (*L. and J.* vi. 18–19).

[2] Professor Dowden (ii. 484) prints the letter in full " from a copy in Claire's writing ". In other such copies Claire suppressed much that had appeared in the original ; it is impossible to say whether it is so with this, for no original has survived.

[3] She was an orphan girl sent by Mrs. Godwin to live with Lady Mountcashell, and a firm friend of Claire.

24

wards he said, ' It is foolish of me to be angry with him ; he can no more help being what he is than the door can help being a door ' ".

Mr. Tighe was less philosophical and more human. He said, " You are quite wrong in your fatalism. If I were to horsewhip that door, it would still remain a door ; but if Lord Byron were well horsewhipped, my opinion is he would become as humane as he is now inhumane. It is the feeble character or the sub-serviency of his friends that makes him the insolent tyrant he is ".

Claire soon began to nurse wild dreams of carrying her child off by force. Albé had long since lost all glamour in the eyes of The Snake, as Byron called Shelley, declaring that he was like a serpent, walking about on the tip of its tail [1]; and Shelley wrote now to Claire : " It is of vital importance to me and to yourself, to Allegra even, that I should put a period to my intimacy with Lord Byron, and that without *éclat*. . . . But for your immediate feelings, I would suddenly and irrevocably leave the country which he inhabits, nor ever enter it except as an enemy to determine our differences *without words* ". Nevertheless, he was shocked at the thoughtless vehemence of Claire's designs. " Lord Byron is inflexible and you are in his power. Remember, Claire, when you rejected my earnest advice . . . and how vain is now your regret ! This is the second of my sibylline volumes ; if you wait for the third, it may be sold at a still higher price ". He invited her to come to Pisa, and join them in their *villeggia-tura* ; she arrived on April 15, and on the 23rd started, with Mr. and Mrs. Williams, on a search for houses at Spezzia. They had not been gone many hours when the Shelleys received from Byron the news of Allegra's death.

The fever *had* broken out in the convent ; she had at once fallen a victim ; Byron had been informed of her illness, but apparently had informed no one else. " A short [2] interval of silence led him to hope that she had recovered ". It was a matter in which it saved trouble of more than one kind to be sanguine. On April 22 an express arrived to tell him that she had died on the 20th.[3] " You know Italians ", wrote Mary Shelley to a friend ; " if half of the convent had died of the plague they would never have written to have them removed ; and so the poor child fell a sacrifice. Lord Byron " (this was written on June 2) " felt the loss at first bitterly ; he also felt remorse, for he felt that he had acted against everybody's counsels and wishes,

---

[1] Trelawny (*Records*, i. 85) says : " His bright eyes, slim figure, and noiseless movements strengthened, if they did not suggest, the comparison".

[2] H. R. Angeli, *Shelley and his Friends*, p. 267. Byron in his letter to Shelley says " the *long* interval ".

[3] Some authorities say the 19th.

and death had stamped with truth the many and often-urged prophecies of Claire ".

The search-party returned to Pisa on April 25, bringing news of only one small unfurnished house, the Casa Magni on the Bay of Spezzia between Lerici and San Terenzo. " Met Shelley ", wrote Williams in his journal ; " his face bespoke his feelings ". But Shelley set himself to conceal these as far as he could, for he had resolved that Claire should not be told while she was still in Byron's near neighbourhood. She and Mary must instantly leave Pisa, and try to obtain possession of the Casa Magni. There the news should be broken to her. Trelawny [1] should be their escort. " Like a torrent hurrying in its course ", as Mary wrote, he carried all before him ; and on the 26th Mary, Claire, and Trelawny started for Lerici. By May 1 the whole party, including Mr. and Mrs. Williams, was installed. Next day " the wind rose, and the waves began to cry and knell about the rocks ". Claire, seeing the inadequacy of space, insisted that she must return to Florence ; and the others, now brought to the moment of avowal, retired to talk over their best plan. While they were sitting together Claire entered, saw that this had caused their talk to be broken off—and in an instant divined the truth. " You may judge ", wrote Mary to a friend, " of what was her first burst of grief and despair ". She wrote at once to Byron, who sent the letter to Shelley. Whatever she said (and it is clear, from Shelley's letter to Byron of May 8, [2] that she said what was in her heart), we cannot but be glad that Byron had to read it. His cruelty to her is not to be forgiven, whatever his declared consciousness of having acted for the

[1] Edward John Trelawny, who joined the Shelley circle at Pisa on January 14, 1822, had lived a tumultuous life. Tradition (contradicted by Mr. Garnett) says that he served in the Royal Navy from 1805 to 1811, when, aged nineteen, he thrashed his lieutenant and deserted his ship. In his *Adventures of a Younger Son* (1831) he described his achievements with a wonderful and mysterious person, whom he names De Ruyter, " a cross between paladin and privateer ". Trelawny's veracity is highly questionable, but the book has been pronounced by good critics to be superior to R. L. Stevenson's romances in the same vein. From 1813, when he returned to England, literature loses sight of him until 1820, when his autobiographical writings begin again with the *Recollections of the Last Days of Shelley and Byron*, published in 1858. His acquaintance with Shelley was confined to the last six months of the poet's life, but during that time " Tre " was daily in his company, and in that of Byron. " He is six feet high ", wrote Mary ; " raven black hair which curls like a Moor's, dark gray expressive eyes, overhanging brows, upturned lips . . . a kind of half-Arab Englishman . . . *un giovane stravagante* ".
A further note on Trelawny will be found in Chapter XXVI.

[2] I had no idea ", he wrote, " that her letter was written in that temper " ; and added that he and Mary would not have allowed it to be sent if they had suspected its contents.

best as regarded her child. It was a best that had cost him
very little trouble : he had never once visited the convent.[1]
He wrote to Shelley on April 23 : " The blow was stunning
and unexpected ; for I thought the danger over, by the long
interval between her stated amelioration and the arrival of the
express. But I have borne up against it as I best can, and so
far successfully, that I can go about the usual business of life
with the same appearance of composure, and even greater. There
is nothing to prevent your coming to-morrow ; but, perhaps,
to-day, and yester-evening, it was better not to have met. I
do not know that I have anything to reproach in my conduct,
and certainly nothing in my feelings and intentions towards
the dead. But it is a moment when we are apt to think that,
if this or that had been done, such events might have been
prevented,—though every day and hour shows us that they are
the most natural and inevitable. I suppose that Time will do
his usual work—Death has done his ".

The Countess Guiccioli gives a description, in her own peculiar
manner, of his grief. She saw in it the excess of paternal kindness.
It had been her lot to tell him the news. " A mortal paleness
spread itself over his face, his strength failed him, and he sank
into a seat. His look was fixed, and the expression such that
I feared for his reason ; he did not shed a tear ; and his coun-
tenance manifested so hopeless, so profound, so sublime a sorrow
that at the moment he appeared a being of a nature superior
to humanity. He remained immovable in the same attitude
for an hour . . . I found him on the following morning
tranquillised, and with an expression of religious resignation
on his features. ' She is more fortunate than we are ', he said :
' besides, her position in the world would scarcely have allowed
her to be happy. It is God's will—let us mention it no more '.
And from that day he would never pronounce her name ".[2]

On the day he heard the news, he wrote to Murray of his
intention to send the body home for burial in Harrow Church.
It was to be embalmed, and would be embarked from Leghorn.
He had been willing to let Claire's wishes regulate the funeral

---

[1] There is a legend, so characteristic of the Sentimentalist that it must
be true, that, under an assumed name, he did visit it after Allegra's death.
The date was probably August 1822 (*Letters and Journals*, vi. note to p.
279).

[2] Moore noted in his diary for June 21, 1822 : " A long letter from Lord
Byron to-day ; he has lost his little natural daughter . . . and seems to
feel it a good deal. When I was at Venice, he said, in showing me this
child, ' I suppose you have some notion of what they call the parental feel-
ing, but I confess I have not ; this little thing amuses me, but that's all '.
This, however, was evidently all affected ; he feels much more naturally
than he will allow ".

—but she, her ironic spirit savouring the full bitterness of this concession, had left the matter to him, asking merely for a lock of hair and a portrait. Through Shelley both were granted her; the miniature remained with her to the day of her death.[1] . . . On May 21 she returned to Florence; and never again did Byron see her or hear from her. She lived until 1879 and never married, though, among many others, the picturesque Trelawny made violent love to her. But it was not the memory of her intrigue with Byron—forced upon him by her importunity, it is true, yet resulting in a way which should have won for her some show of kindness . . . it was not that wretched memory which kept Claire Clairmont single. To the end she ardently maintained that Shelley was the only man she had ever loved; and when we think of his sweet patience, his active tenderness for her, the most difficult of women in the most nerve-wrecking of situations, we do not wonder that she enshrined him as the idol of her life.[2]

Allegra's body was embarked on May 26. " I know not in what ship ", wrote Byron characteristically. " I could not enter into details ". The Countess Guiccioli had given all the necessary orders. " I wish it to be buried ", he continued, " in Harrow Church; there is a spot in the churchyard, near the footpath, on the brow of the hill looking towards Windsor, and a tomb under a large tree . . . where I used . . . to sit for hours and hours when a boy : this was my favourite spot ; but as I wish to erect a tablet to her memory, the body had better be deposited in the church. Near the door, on the left hand as you enter, there is a monument with a tablet [3] containing these words :—

> " ' When Sorrow weeps o'er Virtue's sacred dust,
> Our tears become us, and our grief is just ;
> Such were the tears she shed, who grateful pays
> This last sad tribute of her love and praise '.

I recollect them (after seventeen years), not from anything remarkable in them, but because from my seat in the gallery

---

[1] This must be the portrait to which Mrs. Angeli refers. " [It] represents the little girl at the age of about four, standing by a table with a basket of flowers. This portrait does not show Allegra to have been as pretty as I should have expected . . . but bright and vivacious, and remarkably like Lady Byron in the miniature painted by Charles Hayter in 1812 " (*Shelley and his Friends*, p. 28). The lock of hair is in the possession of Mr. T. J. Wise.

[2] Trelawny said that Claire died a fervent and bigoted Roman Catholic; and this is evident from William Graham's book, *Last Links with Byron, Shelley, Keats*.

[3] This tablet, on entering the church, is on the right-hand side of the south door. It is " sacred to the memory of Thomas Ryves, F.R.S.".

I had generally my eyes turned towards that monument. As near it as convenient I could wish Allegra to be buried, and on the wall a marble tablet placed, with these words :—

" In memory of
Allegra,
Daughter of G. G. Lord Byron,
who died at Bagna Cavallo,
in Italy, April 20th, 1822,
aged five years and three months.
' I shall go to her, but she shall not return to me '.
2d Samuel, xii. 23.

" The funeral I wish to be as private as is consistent with decency ; and I could hope that Henry Drury will, perhaps, read the service over her."

Byron's wishes were not carried out. The vicar hesitated to sanction the proposed inscription. He wrote to Murray in protest, and suggested a tablet with merely the child's name, " thus leaving Lord Byron to reflect upon the character of the inscription he may wish to be added ". This letter was quickly followed by a second. The churchwardens had been urged, by " several leading and influential persons, laymen ", to issue their prohibition against *any* tablet ; and for ex-parishioners the churchwardens' consent was as necessary as the vicar's. Allegra was therefore buried at the entrance to the church, but no tablet or memorial was erected.[1] . . . Byron was unable to understand what the objection to his inscription could be ; and revenged himself by an allusion to the Vicar of Harrow which editors convey to us in a five-lined paragraph of asterisks.

Mr. Coleridge, in a note to *The Age of Bronze*, contrasts Byron with Alexander I of Russia (whom Byron called the Coxcomb Czar), and says that " in one respect their destiny was alike. The greatest sorrow of their lives was the death of a natural daughter ". That seems to me a great exaggeration of the truth. Byron's love for Allegra is a doubtful quantity. Despite Moore's disclaimer, the remark that she " amused him : that was all " is probably an accurate statement of his feeling. The proprietary instinct of parenthood was strongly marked in him, it is true ; but we may hesitate in identifying that with love. An affection

---

[1] On December 22, 1822, Byron wrote to Murray, referring to " the calumnies you have allowed to circulate in the papers on the subject of Allegra's funeral ". " And you also knew, or might have known, that I had not the most distant idea that Lady B. was a frequenter of Harrow Church, and to say the truth . . . I should have thought it the last place she should have frequented. . . . Had I known it, the infant would not have been buried there, nor would I myself . . . now rest in my grave if I thought this woman was to trample on it. It is enough that she has partly dug it " (*L. and J.* vi. 152).

which consigns an infant to the care of strangers, however admirable, without even a formal visit of inspection or supervision, is hardly one that will cause the greatest sorrow of a life. Moreover, there is no room for doubt that the greatest sorrow of Byron's life was his outlawry. The letters from Italy prove beyond question that *that* gnawed at his spirit like the vulture at the heart of his long-loved Prometheus. Through all the six years of exile the same note sounds : " I am shortly for England "—a thousand times, it is true, angrily recanted, but in the recantation confirmed as the now most authentic Byronic cry. And the more because with Allegra's death, his parenthood, his instinct of the Mine, was now left with only that object[1] of whom he had heard, just before the news from Bagna Cavallo, that her grandmother's will forbade her to be shown his portrait

---

[1] In the early volume of poems there were some verses *To my Son*. Moore has the following, on p. 51 :—

" Whether the verses are, in any degree, founded on fact, I have no accurate means of determining. Fond as he was of recording every particular of his youth, such an event, or rather era, as is here commemorated, would have been, of all others, the least likely to pass unmentioned by him ; —and yet neither in conversation nor in any of his writings do I remember even an allusion to it.* On the other hand, so entirely was all that he wrote—making allowance for the embellishments of fancy—the transcript of his actual life and feeling, that it is not easy to suppose a poem, so full of natural tenderness, to have been indebted for its origin to imagination alone ".

A stanza in *Don Juan* refers to having paid parish fees in youth ; and, by the context, unmistakably points to illicit parenthood. He told Lady Byron that he had two natural children, whom he should provide for. One was Medora Leigh, his daughter by Augusta. Among the works cited by Mr. Prothero as sources of the text for *L. and J.* is (for three letters to J. Wedderburn Webster) *The Inedited Works of Lord Byron* . . . [by] his son, Major George Gordon Byron. " Two parts of this work appeared in New York in 1849. It was then discontinued, and the manuscripts of which Major Byron was possessed became the property of Mr. Murray " (*L. and J.* vi. p. 460).

---

* " The only circumstance I know, that bears even remotely on the subject of this poem, is the following. About a year or two before the date affixed to it, he wrote to his mother, from Harrow, (as I have been told by a person to whom Mrs. Byron herself communicated the circumstance), to say, that he had lately had a good deal of uneasiness on account of a young woman, whom he knew to have been a favourite of his late friend Curzon, and who, finding herself, after his death, in a state of progress towards maternity, had declared Lord Byron was the father of her child. This, he positively assured his mother, was not the case ; but, believing as he did firmly, that the child belonged to Curzon, it was his wish that it should be brought up with all possible care, and he, therefore, entreated that his mother would have the kindness to take charge of it. Though such a request might well (as my informant expresses it) have discomposed a temper more mild than Mrs. Byron's, she notwithstanding answered her son in the kindest terms, saying that she would willingly receive the child as soon as it was born, and bring it up in whatever manner he desired. Happily, however, the infant died almost immediately, and was thus spared the being a tax on the good-nature of anybody ".—[But see *Don Juan*, c. xvi. st. 61.]

until she was twenty-one—" and should Lady Byron be then living, it is not to be so delivered until after her decease, unless with her Ladyship's assent ".

Riding with Medwin on December 10, 1821, soon after he had settled down at Pisa, Byron was silent and melancholy. " He declined his usual amusement of pistol-shooting, without assigning a cause . . . There was a sacredness in his melancholy ", relates Medwin, " that I dared not interrupt. At length he said, ' This is Ada's birthday, and might have been the happiest day of my life : as it is——!' . . . It lasted till we came within a mile of the Argive Gate. There our silence was all at once interrupted by shrieks that seemed to come from a cottage by the road. We pulled our horses up to inquire of a *contadino*. . . . He told us that a widow had just lost her only child . . . Lord Byron was much affected. . . ' I shall not be happy ', said he, ' till I hear that my daughter is well. I have a great horror of anniversaries ' ". He wrote to Murray on the same day :[1] " I wonder when I shall see her again, or if ever I shall see her at all ". In this letter he asked for a miniature ; one was evidently sent, for Medwin, speaking of Byron's study in the Lanfranchi, mentions among the pictures on the wall a miniature of Ada.

Directly after his arrival at Pisa began correspondence with Murray about *Cain*. It had been sent home on September 10. " I think that it contains some poetry "—and he wished it to be dedicated to Walter Scott. Two days later came a purple passage of three lines : " There's as pretty a piece of imprecation for you as you may wish to meet with in the course of your business ". This was the concluding lines of Eve's curse of Cain in the last act. " Don't forget [them] ; they are clinchers to Eve's speech ". He was confident of the piece—" it is in my gay metaphysical style " ; and was moreover much elated by his own facility and variety. " But no doubt you will avoid saying any good of it, for fear I should raise the price on you : that's right—stick to business ! Let me know what your other ragamuffins are writing, for I suppose you don't like starting too many of your vagabonds at once ". The customary delay ensued on Murray's part—the customary invective on Byron's. Before the report on *Cain* arrived, *The Vision of Judgment* had been sent home with the gibe : " It may happen that you will be afraid to publish this ". By November he had heard of

---

[1] Not without a gibe at the mother of Allegra. In speaking of the tendency in his family to only childism, he says : " My natural daughter (so far at least as I am concerned) [is an only child "].

Cain at last. It had not wholly pleased; but Murray was told that the small talk between Cain and Lucifer (as Byron called it in a letter to Moore) must remain as it was—" the passages cannot be altered without making Lucifer talk like the Bishop of Lincoln ". Moreover, if it was nonsense—" so much the better, because then it can do no harm, and the sillier Satan is made the better for everybody ". Meanwhile he had had praise from Moore, who saw the first proofs. " It is wonderful—terrible—never to be forgotten. . . . Talk of Æschylus and his Prometheus ! " But Hobhouse, already in some disfavour, now fell far by reason of " a most violent invective upon the subject of *Cain* (not on a religious account at all, as he says) [1] and in such terms as make the grossest review in any publication that ever I read . . . moderate in comparison ".

Thus incendiary already, while still in cold proof, *Cain* was to " set the kiln in a low " when on December 19, 1821, it was published with *Sardanapalus* and *The Two Foscari*. It had been announced by a separate advertisement in the *Morning Chronicle*, so as to excite greater curiosity, and was no sooner published than it was pirated by Benbow,[2] of the notorious Byron Head. " One of those preparatory schools ", said Southey, " for the brothel and the gallows, where obscenity, sedition, and blasphemy are retailed in drams for the vulgar ". " *Cain* ". wrote Moore in February " has made a sensation " ; but long before February society was ecstatically shuddering at the newest Byron sin. " Tell dear George ", wrote Lady Granville to her sister on New Year's Day, " that I think *Cain* most wicked, but not without feeling or passion. Parts of it are magnificent, and the effect of Granville reading it out loud to me was ˏthat I roared until I could neither hear nor see ". Roared seems to mean that the lady wept : it must have been exciting to assist at that reading of the poem which now, for all its energy, leaves us shudderless and tearless. " Why, the yellow fever is not half as mischievous ", wrote Mrs. Piozzi ; Crabb Robinson came home early to read *Cain* ; " the parsons preached at it from Kentish Town to Pisa ", as Byron told Moore, and it was literally true ;[3] the King—His Majesty King George IV— expressed his disapprobation of the blasphemy and licentiousness

---

[1] The remonstrance was probably against the dialogue between Lucifer and Cain's sister Adah in Act I, where once more that forbidden relationship is the theme.

[2] Murray, who had paid £2710 for the three tragedies, applied for an injunction, which Lord Eldon at first refused on the ground that a jury might decide that *Cain* was blasphemous, and therefore void of copyright. The injunction was eventually granted.

[3] The Rev. Johnstone Grant at Kentish Town ; Dr. Nott, the English Chaplain, at Pisa.

of Lord Byron's writings ; and Byron himself, in the eleventh canto of *Don Juan*, reckoned *Cain* among the great disasters of his career :

> " But Juan was my Moscow, and Faliero
> My Leipsic, and my Mont Saint Jean seems Cain ".

The praise, however, was as unmeasured as the censure. From Shelley, always in extremes : " *Cain* is apocalyptic—a revelation not before communicated to man "—is hardly amazing ; but similar extravagances from Goethe and Walter Scott do lift the eyebrows. Sir Walter, eagerly accepting the dedication, wrote to Murray, of the " very grand and tremendous drama of *Cain* ", that Byron had certainly matched Milton on his own ground. Goethe considered that in *Cain* he had found his vocation . . . to dramatise the Old Testament. " Its beauty ', he said, " is such as we shall not see a second time in this world ". We of to-day know how different was Byron's vocation ; but *Cain*, though not now to be thus wildly condemned or praised, is doubtless one of the greatly characteristic works of its author. It has his energy, his sincerity—" his splendid and imperishable excellence of sincerity and strength ". All other souls in comparison with his seem inert, as Taine said. With its thousand errors of taste—that barbarian insensibility, as Matthew Arnold (too convincingly citing instances) called his lack of " the true artist's fine passion for the correct use and consummate arrangement of words " [1]—with all this terrible welter of slovenliness and tunelessness, *Cain* is nevertheless a work which abides in the memory as a notable expression of the Byronic spirit ; and the Byronic spirit is a phenomenon of importance in life, whatever modern criticism may deny it of importance in art. Very emphatically it *counts*—the daring, dash, and grandiosity, as Goethe said, of that personality of Byron, which (as Goethe also said) is formative ," because everything great is formative, so soon as we apprehend it.".

Cain, moreover, has this of interest—that, except the remaining eleven cantos of *Don Juan*, it is the last work of any value done by him. *Sardanapalus* and *The Two Foscari*, which appeared with it, may be dismissed with a word of acknowledgment for two or three passages in the former, and one in the latter—Jacopo Foscari's rhapsody on the joy of swimming. *Heaven and Earth*, the mystery-play of the same period—which Murray never could be brought to publish—is not to be considered seriously. Goethe said it might have been written by a bishop ;

---

[1] The Arnoldian rendering of Scott's immortal phrase : " Managing his (Byron's) pen with the careless and negligent ease of a man of quality ",

and Crabb Robinson, to whom he said it, thought it sounded almost like satire. It is regrettable that Goethe did not so intend it.[1] For *Werner*, begun directly after settling down at Pisa and finished in January, there is, as I think, absolutely nothing to be said. Its authorship has been disputed. The Hon. F. Leveson-Gower undertook, in the *Nineteenth Century* for August 1899, to prove that not Byron wrote it, but Georgiana, Duchess of Devonshire, and that through Caroline Lamb it came into Byron's hands. There is something to allure in any theory which goes to prove that this, so incomparably the worst of even the dramas, was not by him.[2]

The Deformed Transformed, written probably between April and July 1822, has the personal interest of being a drama of natural disability. Arnold, the hero, is lame and has a cruel mother. An incident of childhood forms the opening scene of the drama :

> " *Bertha* : Out, hunchback !
> *Arnold* : I was born so, mother ! "

Moore quotes, in connection with these lines, a passage from Byron's Memoranda where he describes the feeling of horror and humiliation that came over him when his mother, in one of her fits of passion, called him a lame brat. " It may be questioned ", says Moore, " whether that whole drama was not indebted for its origin to that single recollection ". Mary Shelley wrote on the fly-leaf of her copy : " No action of Lord Byron's

---

[1] In considering Goethe's sayings we should, as Matthew Arnold points out, remember that they were " uttered at the height of Byron's vogue, when that puissant and splendid personality was exercising its full power of attraction. . . . Goethe, speaking of Byron at that moment, was not and could not be quite the same cool critic as Goethe speaking of Dante, or Molière, or Milton ".

[2] Mr. Leveson-Gower appealed to both external and internal evidence. The former does not take us very far. It establishes the fact that the Duchess of Devonshire dramatised the same tale, by Harriet Lee, which Byron dramatised ; but that is all. In 1815 he had already tried his hand at the subject ; in 1821 he asked for this draft from England ; it was not then forthcoming, but did in the end emerge, and is published in *Poems*, vol. v. The internal evidence is stronger, in my view. The inferiority to which Mr. Leveson-Gower made appeal, does, in spite of Mr. E. H. Coleridge's loyal denial (" There is no such inferiority "), very markedly appear. In *Werner* there is not a line that the most tenacious memory can even dimly retain. But far more weighty than any other evidence is that of Byron's whole character. Nobody—and certainly not he—ever did a thing so unlike. For Byron to *copy*, to say nothing of publishing, another creature's work is so unthinkable that it needs merely the statement to convince us (reluctantly, in my case) that *Werner* is his own fault ! . . . And in 1922 the publication of *Lord Byron's Correspondence* (1922) afforded in a letter from Byron to Hobhouse, a complete refutation of the Leveson-Gower story. (*Corr.* II. 226.)

life—scarce a line he has written—but was influenced by his personal defect ". That statement has all the Shelleyan fervour. The truth lies somewhere between it and as flat a contradiction. *The Deformed Transformed*, condemned by Shelley as a bad imitation of *Faust*, depends for its interest on this personal note and on the fact that it produced from a reviewer in the *London Magazine* for March 1824, this exquisite gem of humility. " Lord Byron ", says the author, " may write below himself, but he can never write below us ".

The Age of Bronze, composed at Genoa " in my early *English Bards* style, but a little more stilted ", has many fine passages of satire, a noble tribute to Napoleon[1], a prophetic rhapsody on Greece and Liberty, and the great *tour de force* on the " *un*country gentleman " of England, where " rent " is seven times rhymed, each time with increasing scorn in the application. This is by far the most notable of his inferior works.[2]

He finished the first canto of *The Island*, his last complete poem, on the same day that he finished *The Age of Bronze*. It is a narrative of the mutiny on board H.M.S. *Bounty* in 1789, and serves as framework for a description of the Friendly Islands, of which he had been delightedly reading in Mariner's report.[3] He felt that he was in danger of running foul of his own *Corsair* ; but hoped (in a letter to Leigh Hunt of January 1823) that it would at least be " above the usual run of periodical poesy ".[4] It is on the whole a terribly dull piece. The passage on the Highlands contains the well-known couplet :

> " The infant rapture still survived the boy,
> And Loch-na-gar with Ida looked o'er Troy ".

There is an interesting line here and there ; but it would be sad if we had to accept in this the last word from Byron. Fortunately that is not the truth. He wrote the fifteenth and sixteenth cantos of *Don Juan* after *The Island* was finished.

To my thinking, the dullness of these Pisan and Genoese labours is reflected from the life he led in the two places. True, that his social circle was at Pisa more interesting than it had lately been, including as it did the Shelleys and Trelawny, and for comedy Tom Medwin and the absurd Count Taaffe. But the ennui of which in his Ravenna Journal he had complained :

[1] Napoleon died on May 5, 1821.
[2] It was written between December 1822 and January 1823.
[3] *An account of the Natives of the Tonga Islands*, compiled and arranged from . . . Mr. William Mariner, by John Martin, 1817.
[4] It was designed for *The Liberal ;* but John Hunt published it separately in June 1823.

" What is the reason that I have been, all my lifetime, more
or less *ennuyé* ? "—had now settled down into a " moping in
quietness " very different from the passionate and dramatic
revolt of the earlier Byronism.   It is as if his spirit had lost power
to soar above the monotonous day-by-day preoccupations—
rides, pistol-shooting, work, " going out to make love ".   The
dyer's hand was subdued to what it worked in.   Gifford, writing
to Murray in the early days of the drama-making, had longed
that Lord Byron should resume his majestic march.   " I *have*
resumed my majestic march ", wrote Byron—most pathetically
when we realise that the announcement was made in sending home
Sardanapalus.   But after the death of Allegra, either as a solace
for his grief or a measure of precaution against his growing
restlessness, he obtained permission from Teresa to continue
Don Juan.   " I have been as decent as need be ", he wrote to
Moore, when four new cantos were done.   In the tenth canto
Juan comes to England :

" Bold Britons, we are now on Shooter's Hill ! "

He warned Murray of the step.   " How do you like that ?
I have no wish to break off our connection, but if you are to be
blown about with every wind, what can I do ? [1]   You are wrong,
for there will be a *reaction*—you will see that by and bye ".
But Murray had suffered much by the dramas ; and the Hunt
connection, which had now begun, was not calculated to add to
his confidence in the future.   Incessant sarcasms from the
author henceforth embittered the relations between Byron and
Murray.   It is saddening to read the angry letters from Pisa,
Leghorn, and Genoa—to realise the apprehension that Murray
could not but feel in risking anything on works which were
almost unreadable, or when not unreadable, actionable ; [2] and
at the same time to realise so acutely as any knowledge of Byron
must enable us to do, how bitter to his proud soul was the loss
of that vogue which, easily disdained, is by no means easily
foregone.   All was lost—and this with the rest.   To me the
Pisan period is the most utterly saddening of his career.
There is nothing to struggle with, nothing to resign.   Weariness
is really come at last—and now that, long-sung in fancy, it *is*
come, he finds it in drear truth unsingable.   It has " folded
such pinions on the heart as will not fly away ".   Only by
flying himself will he dislodge it ; and we know—and our hearts

---

[1] Cantos vi. to xvi. of *Don Juan* were published not by Murray, but
by John Hunt.
[2] E.g. *The Vision of Judgment*, for the publication of which John Hunt
was fined £100 in 1824—after Byron's death.   The first number of *The
Liberal*, which contained the *Vision*, was published on October 15, 1822.

ache beforehand with the knowing—how, in that dislodging, he was to " outsoar the shadows of our night ".

In his letters to Murray during the *Cain* outcry we retrieve the generous, quick-hearted Man's Man, to whose word our hearts beat faster. " I can only say, *Me, me, adsum qui feci* ; . . . *I* alone occasioned it, and I alone am the person who, either legally or otherwise, should bear the burthen. If they prosecute I will come to England. . . . Let me know ; you shan't suffer for me, if I can help it. . . . You will now perceive that it was as well for you that I have decided upon changing my publisher ; though that was not my motive, but dis-satisfaction at one or two things in your conduct, of no great moment perhaps even then. But now, all such things disappear in my regret. . . . They may do what they like with me, so that I can get you out of it ; but cheer up. . . . I write to you about all this row of bad passions and absurdities with the *summer* moon (for here our winter is clearer than your dog-days) lighting the winding Arno, with all her buildings and bridges—so quiet and still— What nothings are we before the least of these stars ! "

It was at this time that the connection with Leigh Hunt and his brother John began to take shape. Leigh Hunt had fallen on evil days. In 1820 he had had a serious illness, and had been obliged to give up his work on *The Examiner*. His wife had next year written to Mary Shelley, entreating that the whole family should be transplanted to Italy : " Ask Mr. Shelley to *urge it to him* ". Shelley had written in July, but Hunt had refused ; then at Ravenna, in August, Byron had himself proposed that he should come to Italy. Shelley wrote, after his return to Pisa, to tell Hunt of this plan. " He proposes that you should come and go shares with him and me in a periodical work to be conducted here : in which each of the contracting parties should publish all their original compositions, and share the profits ". Shelley frankly said that he was not joining the coalition. " Nothing would induce me to share in the profits, and still less in the borrowed splendour, of such a partnership ".

Byron and Leigh Hunt had met in 1813, and had been mutually attracted. Hunt was indeed at that time completely fascinated. Their acquaintance began in his famous *picciol' orto* at the Surrey Gaol—it was the period of his imprisonment for libelling the Prince Regent—and he tells, in his unfortunate Byron Recollections [1], how his Lordship would " enter with a couple of quartos under his arm, and give you to understand that he was prouder of being a friend and a man of letters than a lord. It was thus ", continues Hunt, in one of those confessions which

---

[1] *Lord Byron and some of his Contemporaries*, 1828.

make his autobiographical writings so absurdly engaging, "that by flattering one's vanity, he persuaded me of his own freedom from it; for he could see very well that I had more value for lords than I supposed". They had seen much of one another just after the troubles of 1816; and Hunt's sympathy was with Byron, although he thought him incapable of real love for a woman. Nevertheless at that time he seemed "a generous nature. . . candid, sensitive, extremely to be pitied and if a woman knew how . . . extremely to be loved". They had lost touch with one another after the exile, and Hunt was surprised to find that Byron remembered him so warmly as this proposal seemed to indicate. It indicated perhaps a little more than the truth. Already in 1818 Byron's good opinion was modified. Writing to Moore in that year, he spoke of Hunt's vulgar coxcombry. " He is a good man, but spoilt by the Christchurch Hospital and a Sunday newspaper—to say nothing of the Surrey gaol, which conceited him into a martyr. . . . He is an honest charlatan, who has persuaded himself into a belief of his own impostures, and talks Punch in pure simplicity of heart. . . . But a good man, and a good father . . . a good husband . . . a good friend . . . and a great coxcomb and a very vulgar person in everything about him. But that is not his fault, but of circumstances ". His Journal of 1813 had given a higher form of praise to Hunt. " He reminds me of the Pym and Hampden times—much talent, great independence of spirit . . . a man worth knowing. . . . I don't think him deeply versed in life—he is the bigot of virtue . . . withal, a valuable man, and less vain than success and even the consciousness of preferring ' the right to the expedient ' might excuse ". To put these appreciations together is to obtain both an illuminating stereoscopic view of the perplexing, charming, irritating creature who was to be immortalised in *Bleak House*— and a perception of the reasons favourable to Byron for the utter disaster of their intercourse in Italy.

Moreover, if there had been nothing else, the facts that Moore exerted all his influence against Hunt, and that the Hunt family contained seven children,[1] would be sufficient to account for the personal failure; while the disastrous career of *The Liberal* aggravated all other grievances. Hunt's earlier book— *Lord Byron and some of his Contemporaries*—is a deplorable revelation of his own worst side; the *Autobiography* of later years gives a better impression of both antagonists. There were grave faults in Byron's treatment, and they showed at

---

[1] Little blackguards . . . Dirtier and more mischievous than Yahoos. . . . Was there ever such a *kraal* out of the Hottentot country ? " wrote Byron at various times of the Hunt children.

their worst by contrast with the exquisite conduct of Shelley. *He*, whose death one might almost assign to the fact of Hunt's arrival, had, for the few days that he survived it, proved himself the beautiful and (*pace* Matthew Arnold) *effectual* angel that he always did prove himself in everybody's affairs but his own.

Hunt's transit to Italy is one of the tragi-comedies of literary history ; and, in my view, one of the most delightful morsels of autobiography in the world. It was unimaginably discomfortable, and his manner of recounting it is at once so simple, so gay, and so affecting that we know not whether to laugh or cry.

On June 13 they at last sailed up the Gulf of Genoa ; and after a stay there, set sail for Leghorn on June 28. In Leghorn harbour they found Trelawny, standing on board Byron's brand-new yacht, the *Bolivar*, "with his knight-errant aspect, dark, handsome and mustachio'd ". Byron had told Trelawny that he would find Leigh Hunt a gentleman in dress and address. " I found him ", says Trelawny,[1] " that, and something more. . . . He was in high spirits, and disposed to be pleased with others. . . . But alas ! all those things which seemed so certain,

> '. . . Those juggling fiends
> That keep the word of promise to our ear,
> And break it to our hope ',

so kept—and so broke—it with Leigh Hunt ".

In a day or two, Hunt went out to Byron's country villa at Montenero, a suburb of Leghorn. The day was very hot ; the road was very hot; and when he got there, he found the hottest-looking house he had ever seen. It was a staring salmon-colour. His reception was as fiery as the house. He came right into the middle of a characteristic Byronic row. " I found myself pitched " (a very Huntesque word, by the bye) " into one of the scenes in *The Mysteries of Udolpho*. . . . Everything was new, foreign, and violent ".

There had been a quarrel among the servants, and young Gamba had been stabbed ; one insurgent was lying in wait for the next person that should issue forth, with the avowed intention of stabbing *him* also. " I looked out of window ", says Hunt, " and met his eye, glaring upward, like a tiger ". Byron, grown so fat that Hunt hardly knew him, was in a " loose riding coat of mazarin blue and a velvet cap . . . trying to damp all this fire with his cool tones, and air of voluptuous indolence ". The Countess Guiccioli was earnestly entreating him to keep

---

[1] *Recollections*, p. 71 (1906). First published in 1858. In 1878, there appeared an issue in enlarged form and with an altered title : *Records of Shelley, Byron, and the Author*. (Preface to *Recollections*, 1906, by Edward Dowden.)

back, and Pietro Gamba, wounded and threatening, was angrily holding forth. They all squeezed to the door, each anxious to be the boldest, when a sudden end was put to the tragedy by the servant's throwing himself down and bursting into tears. " This blessed figure . . . more squalid and miserable than an Englishman would think it possible to find in such an establishment . . . reclined weeping and wailing, and asking pardon for his offence, and to crown all, he requested Lord Byron to kiss him ". At this Byron demurred ; but he permitted the man to kiss his hand—and soon Pietro Gamba was warmly shaking the culprit's, and Teresa was looking " in relenting sort, as if the pitying state of excitement would be just as good as the other ".[1]

This absurd affray had immediate and troublesome consequences. It was the cause of the Gambas' final banishment from Tuscany. They were only on sufferance there—having already, as we have seen, been expelled from their native region, Romagna. The Austrian Government had given Byron to understand that they, and he, might reside in Tuscany, provided as little was heard of them as possible. But at the Villa Dupuy, according to an account furnished to Mrs. Rossetti Angeli from the Historical Archives of Leghorn,[2] disputes and domestic disturbances were continually occurring. (Byron managed always to acquire turbulent servants.) Nor was this the sum of his offences. His pistol-shooting caused alarm to the inhabitants around ; he had made inconvenient requests in connection with the *Bolivar* ; and its crew wore the name on bands round their caps, which, being contrary to the custom for private boats, was regarded by the authorities as dangerous and defiant.[3] Above all, there was the memory of an affray at Pisa on March 24 —the notorious Masi row, when a sergeant-major of the dragoons had been wounded by one of Byron's ragamuffin tribe of servants ; mortally, as was at first supposed. It was not mortally ; nevertheless Masi had been rendered incapable of further military service. Many pages are devoted to this shindy in most of the Byron and Shelley books, but it seems to me unimportant ; its interest resides only in the fact that the Gambas were *then*—in the early spring—informed that their presence in Pisa was disagreeable to the Government. As a result, the Villa Dupuy had been hired for the summer season of 1822. There, on the day

---

[1] The servant was dismissed ; and, leaving the region, " called in his way on Mr. Shelley, who gave him some money out of his own disgust, for he thought nobody would help such a fellow if he did not ". (*Lord Byron and some of his Contemporaries*, i. 19. Galignani, Paris, 1828.)
[2] *Shelley and his Friends in Italy*, p. 291.
[3] *Ibid*, p. 300.

of Leigh Hunt's visit, the scuffle between the servants broke
out, and was the cause of the second and definite decree
of banishment from Tuscany. The Gambas were ordered
to leave within three days; but Byron obtained for them a
respite. The two Counts went early in July; not until the
end of September did Teresa follow them. She remained at
the Lanfranchi—whither the party removed on July 2nd or
3rd—with Byron; she was there on the 13th, when Mary Shelley
and Jane Williams arrived from Lerici on that most terrible
quest in history. All unconscious, she came smiling amid her
golden curls to encounter Mary's gasping cry: " *Sapete alcuna
cosa di Shelley ?* "

*   *   *   *   *

" . . . If you can't swim
Beware of Providence ! "

So, in 1819, Shelley's Count Maddalo, who stood for Byron,
had mockingly warned the serious Julian, who stood for Shelley.
" Did no unearthly *dixisti* sound in his ears as he wrote it ? "
asks Francis Thompson in the great essay. " But a brief while,
and Shelley, who could not swim, was weltering in the waters of
Lerici ".

He had come to Pisa to welcome the Hunts. Thornton
Hunt remembered after many years the cry with which Shelley
rushed into his father's arms : " I am inexpressibly delighted ;
you cannot think how inexpressibly happy it makes me ". That
was on July 2, 1822. The days until the 7th were spent in
settling the new-comers in their ground-floor rooms at the Lan-
franchi ; in cheering Leigh Hunt, who had been told by the
renowned Italian surgeon, Vaccà, that his wife could not live
a year ; [1] and in striving to bring Byron to a happier view of the
projected co-operation in journalism. Byron's purpose was
wavering. Moore and Murray had been at work, and to the
indecision produced by their urgent arguments was now added
the anger and suspicion inevitably aroused by the state of
Hunt's personal affairs. Byron has been censured for his
attitude in this crisis ; but few of his biographers seem to have
even tried to realise in what a vexatious position he was. In-
stead of arriving in Italy as the editor of a journal—*The Examiner*
—renowned for its independence, probity, and brilliancy, Leigh
Hunt arrived as an " out-of-work ". *The Examiner* editorship
had passed from his hands ; he had made no arrangements of
any kind for work in England. In short, he arrived avowedly
—and, be it remembered, not until *then* avowedly—as the

[1] Mrs. Hunt lived until 1857.

pensioner of Byron and Shelley. Byron had been counting on the aid of *The Examiner* to float *The Liberal* ; with that, he saw much hope for the new and striking idea of a journal edited from overseas and supported by such names as his, Leigh Hunt's, and Shelley's—the last controversial indeed, but destined, as no one could fail to see, to break through prejudice to high renown. He greeted instead a frank hanger-on, with an ailing wife who was profoundly hostile to himself, and seven intractable children. Even Shelley was dismayed when he learnt from Hunt's lips what ought to have been told before the family left England. But, characteristically, *he* kept faith and courage ; and, as so often before, achieved his end. This was to keep the disconcerted Byron in something approaching good humour and good heart. Shelley obtained from him the promise of the *Vision of Judgment* copyright for the first number of *The Liberal* —and that before July 6. It was to be published serially or separately, as John Hunt [1] thought best. " This offer ", wrote Shelley to Mary, " is *more* than enough to set up the journal ".

With such a triumph his spirits rose ; and on Sunday, July 7, his work done, he took Leigh Hunt to see the sights of Pisa. " We talked of a thousand things ; we anticipated a thousand pleasures ". But though he looked unusually well, Hunt thought that he had " less hope " than in the old days in London. " If I die to-morrow ", he said to Mrs. Hunt, " I have lived to be older than my father ; I am ninety years of age ". Almost their last words to him were a prayer to remain on shore if the weather were violent next day. He borrowed, for reading on the transit, Keats's newest publication, which contained *Hyperion.* " Keep it till you give it to me with your own hands ", said Hunt.

There had been a long drought—Monday dawned in leaden heat. But soon clouds gathered and the rain, much hoped and prayed for, began to fall. Nevertheless Shelley and Williams set off from Leghorn in the *Ariel.* Trelawny, for some technical omission forbidden to accompany them into the offing, watched them from the deck of the *Bolivar.* Ere long a sea-fog enveloped the boat ; " we saw nothing more of her ". Then came great gusts of wind, oily drops of rain, " rebounding [from the surface of the sea] as if they could not penetrate it " ; and suddenly " the crashing voice of the thunder-squall " that burst right over the *Bolivar* in Leghorn harbour. Its fury lasted only twenty minutes ; but in that twenty minutes the *Ariel* went down with all on board.

---

[1] John Hunt, Leigh's brother, was printer, publisher, and part proprietor of *The Liberal.*

For days nothing was known. On the morning of the 11th Trelawny rode to the Lanfranchi, and spoke to Byron and Hunt of his fears. " When I told [Byron], his lip quivered and his voice faltered as he questioned me ".[1] At Casa Magni in the desolate house, amid the beauty that from the first had made her weep and shudder, Mary, not yet wholly recovered from the miscarriage (on June 16) wherein Shelley had saved her life by his promptitude and decision—Mary and Jane Williams passed the fatal Monday in tranquillity of mind. " We did not at all suppose that they could have put to sea ". Gradually apprehension dawned. . . . But our imagination refuses to consider the hours and days from Wednesday, July 10, when a felucca from Leghorn brought word that they had sailed on Monday. In the following month Mary recounted that experience. One word shall suffice. In her recounting, she, though writing with a minuteness which she believed to be exact to every hour, *erred by an entire week*. She had lost sense of time. It is enough ; and we, reading now the awful narrative, lose sense of larger time, and push the book aside with a shudder that might belong to anguish heard to-day of near and dear.

Williams's body was washed ashore on July 16 or 17 ; Shelley's on the 18th. Hunt's copy of Keats, doubled back (it has been stated) at *The Eve of St. Agnes*, was found in one pocket ; a volume of Sophocles in another.[2] It was not till August 16 that Trelawny, with Byron and Leigh Hunt and some officials, burned the body, throwing on it frankincense, salt, and wine, as they had done for Williams's the day before. " Even Byron ", says Trelawny, " was silent and thoughtful ". Yesterday, in watching the disburial and destruction of Williams's body : " Don't repeat this with me ", he had cried. " Let my body rot where it falls ". To-day, he could not face the scene ; he withdrew, and swam off to the *Bolivar*. Leigh Hunt remained in the carriage which had brought them from Pisa. " Byron ", says Trelawny, " asked me to preserve the skull for him ; but remembering that he had formerly used one as a drinking-cup, I was determined Shelley's should not be thus profaned ". The heart would not burn ; Trelawny is said to have plunged his hand into the fiery furnace and snatched it out. He then collected the ashes into a box, and took them on board the

---

[1] There are no letters from Byron between July 12 and August 3—an unusually long silence for him. We may conclude that, like the rest, he could think of nothing else, do nothing else but think, and wildly search, conjecture, inquire.

[2] The Keats, of which only the binding remained after the burial of the body, was burned on the funeral pyre ; the Sophocles is preserved in the Bodleian Library.

Bolivar. (These ashes are now in the possession of Mr. T. J. Wise.)
The day was one of autumnal tranquillity and beauty—" the
Mediterranean ", says Leigh Hunt, " kissed the shore as if to
make peace with it ". He tells an anecdote of the return to
Pisa. He and Byron went together. " The barouche drove
rapidly through the forest. . . . We sang, we laughed, we
shouted. I even felt a gaiety the more shocking because it was
real and a relief. . . . I wish to have no such waking dream again.
It was worthy of a German ballad ".[1]

" Shelley's dying ", says Francis Thompson, " seems a myth,
a figure of his living ; the material shipwreck a figure of the
immaterial. . . . Mighty meat for little guests, when the heart
of Shelley was laid in the cemetery of Caius Cestius ! Beauty,
music, sweetness, tears—the mouth of the worm has fed of
them all ".

Byron's tributes to that exquisite nature are familiar. He
wrote to Murray on August 3 : " You were all brutally mistaken
about Shelley, who was without exception the *best* and least
selfish man I ever knew. I never knew one that was not a
beast in comparision ". And to Moore, on the 8th : " There is
another man gone about whom the world was ill-naturedly, and
ignorantly, and brutally mistaken. It will perhaps do him justice
now, when he can be no more better for it ". Again, to Murray
in December : " You are all mistaken about Shelley. You do
not know how mild, how tolerant, how good he was in Society ;
and as perfect a gentleman as ever crossed a drawing-room,
when he liked and where he liked ". That last certificate was
one which Byron, the whilom Dandy, would have reckoned an
important one.

To Lady Blessington at Genoa in 1823, he spoke still more
feelingly. " He was the most gentle, most amiable, and
least worldly-minded person I ever met ; full of delicacy, dis-
interested beyond all other men, and possessing a degree of
genius, joined to a simplicity, as rare as it is admirable. He
had formed to himself a *beau idéal* of all that is fine, high-minded,
and noble, and he acted up to this ideal even to the very letter.
. . . I have seen nothing like him, and never shall again, I am
certain ".

[1] Shelley's ashes were buried by Trelawny in the Protestant Cemetery
at Rome. Leigh Hunt suggested the words " Cor Cordium " which appear
below the name. It was Trelawny who added the lines from *The Tempest*
which come below the dates of birth and death :

> " Nothing of him that doth fade
> But doth suffer a sea-change
> Into something rich and strange ".

But Trelawny, citing Byron's written tributes, has something to add. " What Byron says of the world . . . is far more applicable to himself. If the world erred, they did so in ignorance ; Shelley was a myth to them. Byron had no such plea to offer, but he was neither just nor generous, and never drew his weapon to redress any wrongs but his own ". He is alluding to a hint from himself that Byron might do Shelley a great service by a friendly word or two in his next work.

" Assuming a knowing look, [Byron] said, ' If we puffed the Snake ' (as he called Shelley) ' it might not turn out a profitable investment. . . . If we introduced Shelley to our readers, they might draw comparisons, and they are *odorous* ' ".

Byron, on his side, said of Trelawny that to save his life he could not tell the truth. We may then allow ourselves to hope that the cited remarks were never made.

CHAPTER XXV

RESTLESSNESS

The Hunt family : Byron as patron—The Shelley circle degenerates :
days at Genoa—*The Liberal*—Tom Medwin—Restless again—Portraits
and painters—American and European tributes—*The Vision of Judgment*
—Quarrel and reconciliation with Murray—Lady Blessington—Byroniana
—Fresh efforts at renewal of intercourse with Lady Byron—Teresa and
Byron—Greek adventure in the air—The Blessingtons leave Genoa

LEIGH HUNT, now indeed at Byron's mercy, felt his
heart die within him. " Lord Byron requested me to
look upon him as standing in Mr. Shelley's place, and
said that I should find him the same friend as the other had
been. . . . I made the proper acknowledgment ; but I knew
what he meant, and I more than ever doubted whether even in
that, the most trivial part of friendship, he could resemble Mr.
Shelley even if he would ". He continues : " I had reason to
fear : I was compelled to try ; and things turned out as I dreaded.
The public have been given to understand that Lord Byron's
purse was at my command, and that I used it according to the
spirit with which it was offered. *I did so* ".

Byron gave him—exclusive of £200 for which he held Shelley's
bond—£300. He paid for the " good and respectable " furniture
which Shelley bought for the family ; gave Hunt £70 at Pisa ;
defrayed the expenses of the move from Pisa to Genoa, and
supplied another £30 for the move from Genoa to Florence in
the summer of 1823. " The sum ", says Jeaffreson, " probably
did not altogether exceed £500 ". Besides this, he gave John
Hunt the copyright of *The Vision of Judgment*; surrendered his
share of the profits in *The Liberal* until the brothers were in
comfortable circumstances again ; gave them the MSS. of the
Pulci translation (which he fervently believed in himself as not
only the best thing he ever did, but " the best translation that
ever was or will be ") and *Heaven and Earth* ; [1] and gave John
Hunt for publication, retaining the copyrights, *The Age of Bronze*,
The Island, and nine cantos of *Don Juan*. " In these publications

---

[1] The Pulci was published in the fourth and last, *Heaven and Earth* in
the second, number of *The Liberal*.

he asked for no share in the profits."[1] And when John Hunt was first prosecuted for publishing *The Vision of Judgment*, Byron paid for his defence.

Thus there can be no question of his generosity—unlavish but unniggardly. Hunt's cool acceptance of money obligations in which he was always the beneficiary made him a difficult man to deal with prudently. A prudent patron was at once condemned. We get in the *Recollections* an indignant accusation of Byron's manner of giving. " During our residence at Pisa I had from him, or rather from his steward, to whom he always sent me for the money, and who doled it out to me as if my disgraces were being counted, the sum of £70 ". Certainly it would have been kinder in Byron to pay over the money himself ; but Hunt was too perfect a specimen of the sponge who will have it both ways. On one page he proclaims his peculiar notions on the subject of money—he has not " that horror of receiving obligations ", *et cetera* ; on the next, his " disgraces are doled out ". Evidently the attitude was agreeable to him only when all the generosity was on one side. Despite his charm as man and writer, Leigh Hunt comes much worse out of this affair than Byron does.

The patron's personal demeanour towards the " kraal " is perhaps more blameworthy ; but here again we should remember that Mrs. Hunt and he had been from the first antipathetic. Nine years before in London, she had spied out all his faults, and his faults only—and had been solicitous to direct her husband's attention on them. Even from that husband's pages she emerges, towards Byron, as a type of the Equalitarian who can never for a moment forget inequalities. But his accost of her at the Lanfranchi infuriated Williams. " She came into his house sick and exhausted, and he scarcely deigned to notice her ; was silent, and scarcely bowed. This conduct cut Hunt to the soul. " He said to his big bull-dog, in Trelawny's hearing, before the Hunts had been forty-eight hours in the house : " Don't let the Cockneys pass our way ! "—and turning to Trelawny, added gloomily, " I offered *you* those rooms. Why did you not take them ? " The children he frankly loathed. After the Pisan circle was broken up, he wrote to Mary Shelley of a sofa which had been in her husband's room : " I have a particular dislike to anything of Shelley's being within the same walls as Mrs. Hunt's children. . . . What they can't destroy with their filth, they will with their fingers ". His dislike of the mother pierces plainly there. We can hardly wonder when we read Hunt's admiring description of her *agaçeries*. She adopted from the first a British Matron attitude towards Teresa Guiccioli. They met in silence—that was not strange, for neither could speak a word of the other's language ;

[1] *L. and J.* vi., note to p. 123.

but it is plain even from Hunt's rather hypocritical statement
that the connection was made a pretext for unpleasantness from
Mrs. Hunt. Her husband's excuse is that it was clear there was
no real love on either side. But that was no business of theirs.
Nothing could be less convincing than Hunt's defence of his wife's
attitude, as offered in the *Recollections* ; and this was made the
more intolerable by her impertinence to Byron. He seldom
visited the Hunt's quarters; and, as we read, we find that not
surprising. He said to " Marianne " one day (it is Leigh who
narrates) : " What do you think, Mrs. Hunt ? Trelawny has
been speaking against my morals ! What do you think of
that ? "

" It is the first time," said Mrs. Hunt, " that I ever heard
of them ".

Byron received the answer in silence. For this, Leigh Hunt
acclaims his wife as triumphant. Such obtuseness is almost
the justification for Byron's epithet of vulgar coxcomb. A man
who could thus interpret so well-merited a rebuke shows himself
incapable of association with a class in any degree removed from
his own ; for Mrs. Hunt's speech, coming from a woman who
was not affectionately intimate, was an impertinence. But her
husband learned nothing from the incident. Some time after-
wards he asked Byron if he knew what Mrs. Hunt had said of
his picture by Harlow to the Shelleys ? Byron expressed curiosity,
whereupon he was told how Marianne had observed that it
resembled a great school-boy who had had a plain bun given
him instead of a plum one. Hunt adds that he did not tell
Byron that the Shelleys shook with laughter over this sally,
because it was " so like ". That is almost the one thing we know
of the Shelleys which gives us a poor opinion of their intelligence.
The portrait is certainly a little amusing in its scorn, but as
certainly Mrs. Hunt's wit leaves us unshaken with laughter.

Not much wonder that Byron mildly described her as " no
great things ". We smile irresistibly at the comicality of this
patron, of all patrons, with such hangers-on ; but what is fun
to us must have been very irksome to him—with his impatience,
his caprice, his moods, his worries ; above all, his vanity. A
too-independent dependent, and a dowdy disagreeable woman,
and a kraal—was this what the Childe, Manfred, Juan, had come
to ? Insolence from Marianne, noise and dirt from the seven
children—and from the author of *Rimini* [1] (now cured for ever
of " My dear Byron ") such My Lording as drove the victim to
begin a letter " Dear Lord Hunt " . . . . Byron was not a
Shelley (and even Shelley's radiancy might have been dimmed

[1] Hunt had, some years before, dedicated *Rimini* to Byron in a fulsome
letter beginning, " My dear Byron ".

by these cloudlets) ;   he was very human ;   probably he *was*
detestable to the Hunts.   Let us put ourselves in his place, and
speculate on our own potential demeanour during two years of
such patronship.

It was all part of the life that now he wearily detested.   Hunt
saw that his affection for Teresa Guiccioli was gone ;   he saw
too that she did not in the least know how to manage him when
things went wrong.   There was jealousy to reckon with, for at
the farm outside Pisa where Byron's pistol-club was established,
there lived a pretty peasant-girl who enjoys the distinction of
being his " last recorded flame ".[1]   Teresa, according to Hunt,
was very anxious about her, but could get no information ;   and
she now began to " indulge in vehement complaints of [Byron]
to his acquaintances ".   Hunt neither much liked nor at all
admired her.   " Madame Guiccioli was a kind of buxom parlour-
boarder, compressing herself artificially into dignity and elegance,
and fancying she walked, in the eyes of the whole world, a heroine
by the side of a poet. . . .   She could both smile very sweetly
and look intelligently, when Lord Byron said something kind
to her ".   That last phrase, so carelessly thrown off, is significant.
When Hunt first saw her at Montenero, she had really something
of the heroine look.   " At that time also she looked no older
than she really was ;   in which respect a rapid and very singular
change took place, to the surprise of everybody.   In the course
of a few months she seemed to have lived as many years.   It
was most likely that in that interval she discovered that she
had no real hold on the affection of her companion ".

It was in the days of Genoa that this alteration began.   After
Shelley's death the Pisan circle broke up, and all that was left
of it established themselves at Albaro, a suburb of Genoa.   " The
fine spirit ", says Trelawny, " that had animated and held us
together was gone.   Left to ourselves we degenerated apace.
Shelley's solidity had checked Byron's flippancy, and induced
him occasionally to act justly and talk seriously ;   now he seemed
more sordid and selfish than ever.   He behaved shabbily to Mrs.
Shelley :   I might use a harsher epithet ".   That, alas ! seems to
be an instance in which Trelawny told the truth.   After Shelley's
death, Byron made frequent offers of money to his widow.   In
June, wishing to return to England, she for the first time did
ask him for help.[2]   " But ", she wrote to Trelawny, " he gave

---

[1] A sketch of this girl, Maria Castinelli, is preserved in Pisa ; it was made
in 1822 by a relative of hers, Paolo Folini (*Shelley and his Friends*, p. 247).

[2] In this connection, see many letters from Mary to Byron in the
Correspondence, II, 265–72, from which it would certainly seem that either
Trelawny was again untruthful, or that Mary could be extremely insincere.

such an air of unwillingness and sense of the obligation he con-
ferred " that she refused his aid, and obtained the sum she
needed from Trelawny. " He regretted this when too late ",
records Trelawny ; " for in our voyage to Genoa he alluded to
Shelley, saying, ' Tre, you did what I should have done ; let us
square accounts to-morrow ; I must pay my debts ' ". Trelawny
put the subject by, and heard no more about it from Byron.
For it was true that Byron had, as he said jestingly of himself
in *Juan*, temporarily taken up with the good old-gentlemanly
vice of avarice. Parsimony had been growing upon him ever
since the early days of reform at Venice ; he would at that time
lose his temper " once every seven days " over his weekly bills.
The kraal aggravated this new susceptibility ; and moreover
(to find him an excuse) he did, for his Greek dreams now
dawning, need all the money that he had, or could save, or could
procure.

   The Liberal was from the first hopeless. Its initial number
was issued on October 15, 1822, and the fourth and last on July
30, 1823. Byron's early patience under this disappointment
was admirable. Let us read a letter to Moore in February 1823,
when the failure was seen to be imminent. Moore had again, as
from the beginning, besought him to " emerge out of *The Liberal* " ;
and Byron answered : " You forget how it would humiliate
[Hunt]. . . . Think a moment—he is perhaps the vainest man
on earth . . . If he were in other circumstances I might be
tempted to take him down a peg ; but not now—it would be
cruel. It is a cursed business ; but neither the motive nor the
means rest on my conscience, and it happens that he and his
brother *have* been so far benefited by the publication in a pecuniary
point of view ". But by March his attitude had changed. He
told John Hunt plainly that he craved permission to withdraw.
" I am not at all sure ", he added, " that this failure does not
spring much more from *me* than any other connection of the
work. I am at this moment the most unpopular man in England,
and if a whistle would call me to the utmost pinnacle of English
fame, I would not utter it . . . . However this may be, I
am willing to do anything I can for your brother or any member
of his family ". He added that no secession should take place
on his part without serious consideration with Leigh Hunt.
Again, a week later, he wrote urging his own idea of himself
as a Jonah. " It is not so much against *you* as against me that
the hatred is directed ; and, I confess, I would rather stand
alone, and grapple with it as I may. . . . Every publication
of mine has latterly failed ; I am not discouraged by this, because
writing and composition are habits of my mind, with which
Success and Publication are objects of remoter reference—not

causes but *effects*, like those of any other pursuit. . . . I continue to compose for the same reason that I ride, or read, or bathe, or travel—it is a habit ". To Mary Shelley he wrote in the same strain,[1] less veraciously, it is true, for he represents himself as having entered upon *The Liberal* scheme chiefly for Hunt's sake. Shelley *had*, at Ravenna, depicted forcibly the distressed condition of Hunt, and doubtless this influenced Byron in some degree ; but it was certainly not his only or even his principal reason for becoming a proprietor. Already in 1817 he had suggested a similar arrangement—except that he was to return to England—for himself and Moore.

I cannot see what blame attaches to Byron in this matter of *The Liberal*. Why should he have done what no one does ? Why should he, more than another man, persist in a ruinous adventure ? In April he told Moore : " I take it that I am as low in popularity and book-selling as any writer can be. . . . This [my friends] attribute to Hunt ; but they are wrong—it must be, partly at least, owing to myself ; be it so. As to Hunt, I prefer *not* having turned him to starve in the streets to any personal honour which might have accrued from some genuine philanthropy. I really act upon principle in this matter, for we have nothing much in common ; and I cannot describe to you the despairing sensation of trying to do something for a man who seems incapable or unwilling to do anything further for himself—at least, to the purpose. It is like pulling a man out of a river who directly throws himself in again ".

Hunt saw the matter differently. " Lord Byron was alarmed for his credit among his fashionable friends. . . . This man wrote to him, and that wrote, and another came. Mr. Hobhouse rushed over the Alps, not knowing which was the more awful, the mountains or the magazine. Mr. Murray wondered, Mr. Gifford smiled (a lofty symptom !), and Mr. Moore . . . said that *The Liberal* had a ' taint ' in it ". He then adds, as if it were a reproach, that Byron expected very large returns from *The Liberal*. It passes comprehension to imagine for what other reason he should have entered upon the scheme. He had never been a coterie-writer ; he was out for resounding fame, or nothing. Quite sincerely he told himself and his friends that he had never *written* for popularity. No ; but he had published for it, and he had obtained it. As sincerely he could now let it go ; but preferred, as he told John Hunt, to grapple with the change " *alone* ". Few more characteristic words were ever written, even by him. Alone : it might be in a crowd, or on

[1] In an undated letter, not certainly, but very probably, addressed to her.

the sea, or on Alpine heights, or amid the whole wide world of
men—but alone he had ever dreamed himself. As well blame
Byron for breathing as for this. Friends were with him or
ready to be with him in all the crises of his life, and he summoned
or accepted them ; nevertheless, with his instinct for the lime-
light, he must be *seen* alone, like the hero at the crisis of a melo-
drama. For life was to him just that—a melodrama. He must
be haloed (in scarlet or in gold), the audience must gape and
wonder, the curtain go up and down, claps and hisses contend
in the theatre. . . . Not the dream of a lofty nature—no ;
but we did not make him, and we want to see him. We
cannot change the play on the boards—and as he, watching
it himself, might have exclaimed : " By the gods, it is a fine
entertainment ! "

The Hunts did not live under his roof at Albaro. Mary,
true to the Shelleyan tradition of being everybody's house-
agent, had preceded the rest of the Pisan circle to Genoa, and
had there taken for Byron the Casa Saluzzi ; for herself and the
Hunts, Casa Negroto at a little distance. Trelawny stayed in
the city of Genoa until December, when he made a cruise into the
interior. Tom Medwin—Jeaffreson's " well-mannered noodle ",
" amiable absurdity ", " perplexing simpleton " ; Mary Shelley's
seccatura, which is the Italian term for a paralysing bore—Tom
Medwin, with his notes of Byron's conversations "when tipsy "
(by Mary's account), had long ago left Pisa. He had returned
at the time of Shelley's death ; [1] on the 28th of August he left
again, parting from Byron " with a sadness that looked like
presentiment ".
It was at the end of September that Byron and Teresa
Guiccioli moved from Pisa. Byron's *déménagement* was a
troublous business, of which Trelawny gives a vivid account.
" If the Lanfranchi had been on fire at midnight, it would not
have been worse ". Trelawny escaped to Leghorn. At Lerici
the Hunts, Byron, Teresa Guiccioli, and he met again. Byron
was taken ill after a swim, and Trelawny went to see him. " I
am always bedevilled for a week after moving ", said he. " No
wonder ", answered the other, " if you always make such dire
commotion before it. . . . How do you feel ? "
" Feel ! " and he vividly compared himself to " that damned
obstreperous fellow ", Prometheus. " Luckily ", adds Trelawny,

---

[1] Medwin in his *Conversations* represented himself as having been
present at the cremation of Shelley, but it seems certain that he was
not. See the late Mr. Buxton Forman's Introduction to his new edition
of Medwin's *Life of Shelley* (1914).

" the medico of Lerici was absent, so in two or three days the patient was well ".

It is generally stated that during his stay at Genoa, which lasted about ten months, Byron was more tranquil and happy than at any other period of his life. " He appeared to . . . his occasional visitors, who knew him in London, to have become more agreeable and manly ".[1] His discontent was increasing, nevertheless. He was tired of Italy. Twice already he had seriously thought and written of emigrating to " Bolivar's country " ; in 1822 he had contemplated taking up residence at Nice ; now, in this autumn of the same year, an old and darling dream began again. From Ravenna he had written to Moore, àpropos the earliest outbreak of the Greek Revolution : " The Greeks ! What think you ? They are my old acquaintances ". And from Pisa in August, just before the move to Genoa, he wrote to the same correspondent that he was fluctuating between South America and Greece. " I should have gone long ago to one of them but for my liaison with the Countess G. . . . *She* would be delighted to go too, but I do not choose to expose her to a long voyage and a residence in an unsettled country ".

The American artist, West, who painted him at the request of some transatlantic Byronians for the Academy of Fine Arts at New York, perceived this restlessness. It was during the Leghorn sojourn that his two or three reluctant sittings from Byron were secured. Byron had been, earlier in the year, mortified by the result of another portrait. This was a bust for which he had sat, at the sculptor's own request, to the fashionable Bertolini of Pisa. " It may be like ", he wrote to Murray, " for aught I know, as it exactly resembles a superannuated Jesuit. . . . I assure you [it] is dreadful, though my mind misgives me that it is hideously like. If it is, I cannot be long for this world, for it overlooks seventy ". West's painting is, according to Teresa Guiccioli, a frightful caricature, the worst portrait of Byron that was ever done—and she was dissatisfied with them all, except Thorwaldsen's bust.[2] But if the American artist failed to represent Byron on canvas, he made one observation of him which strikes me as among the most arresting we have.

" I was by this time sufficiently intimate with him to answer

---

[1] Galt, p. 268.

[2] She says that Sanders represents him with thick lips, whereas his lips " were harmoniously perfect " ; Holmes (whose picture Byron preferred to all others) gives him too large a head ; Phillips, an expression of haughtiness and affected dignity, which was not true to life. Sir Walter Scott said : " No picture is like him ".

his question as to what I thought of him before I had seen him. He laughed much at the idea which I had formed of him, and said, ' Well, you find me like other people, do you not ? ' He often afterwards repeated, ' And so you thought me a finer fellow, did you ? ' I remember once telling him, that notwithstanding his vivacity, I thought myself correct in at least one estimate which I had made of him, for I still conceived that he was not a happy man. He inquired earnestly what reason I had for thinking so ; and I asked him if he had never observed in little children, after a paroxysm of grief, that they had at intervals a convulsive or tremulous manner of drawing in a long breath. Wherever I had observed this, in persons of whatever age, I had always found that it came from sorrow ".

West's commission was the climax of a series of American honours. On Ravenna in 1821 there had fallen from the skies a young Mr. Coolidge of Boston—" a very pretty lad, only somewhat too full of poesy and ' entusymusy ' ". This ardent boy announced that he had bought a copy of Thorwaldsen's bust at Rome to send to America ; and Byron wrote in his journal : " I confess I was more flattered by this . . . than if they had decreed me a statue in the Paris Pantheon . . . because it was *single, unpolitical,* and without motive or ostentation—the pure and warm feeling of a boy for the poet he admired. . . . *I* would not pay the price of a Thorwaldsen bust for any human head and shoulders, except Napoleon's, or my children's, or some ' *absurd womankind's* ', . . . or my sister's. . . . A *picture* is a different matter—everybody sits for their picture ; but a bust looks like putting up pretensions to permanency ".[1]

He told Moore that he feared young Coolidge was disappointed in him in the same way as West had been—thinking him a finer fellow. " I can never get people to understand that poetry is the expression of *excited passion,* and that there is no such thing as a life of passion any more than a continuous earthquake. . . . Besides, who would ever *shave* themselves in such a state ? " Continuing, he recounts other evidences of immortality. That day (July 5, 1821) had come a letter from a dying girl in England, who " could not go out of the world without thanking me for the delight which my poesy for several years, etc.". She begged him to burn her letter, " which . . . I can *not* do, as I look upon such a letter in such circumstances as better than a diploma from Göttingen ". Then, alluding to a similar tribute from Norway which had come in 1819, he adds : " These are the things which make one at times believe one's self a poet ".

He mused on these things in his journal.

" What a strange thing is life and man ! Were I to present

[1] He had sat for the Thorwaldsen bust only at the request of Hobhouse.

myself at the door of the house where my daughter now is, the door would be shut in my face—unless (as is not impossible) I knocked down the porter ; and if I had gone in that year (and perhaps now) to Drontheim (the furthest town in Norway), or into Holstein,[1] I should have been received with open arms into the mansion of strangers and foreigners, attached to me by no tie but that of mind and rumour.

" As far as *fame* goes, I have had my share : it has indeed been leavened by other human contingencies, and this in a greater degree than has occurred to most literary men of a *decent* rank in life ; but, on the whole, I take it that such equipoise is the condition of humanity ".

But it was the homage of America which peculiarly charmed his imagination. In 1813, we have seen that an American edition of *English Bards* had given him " a kind of posthumous feel " ; now the same glamour played round transatlantic visitors. " They make me feel as if talking with Posterity on the other side of the Styx ". Germany too told a flattering tale. Goethe was now " my professed patron and protector . . . he and the Germans are particularly fond of *Don Juan*, which they judge of as a work of art ". And at the Leipsic University, the highest prize had in 1822 been offered for a translation of two cantos of *Childe Harold*. A travelling American, George Bancroft (afterwards the historian of the United States), had told him this—so the Styx was bridged indeed. " All this ", he wrote to Murray, " is some compensation for your English native brutality ".

When the first *Liberal* was issued on October 15, and the notices began to come in, such compensation was badly needed. He suffered then perhaps the most violent of all the brutalities. Read this from *The Courier* of October 26 : " With a brain from heaven and a heart from hell—with a pen that can write as angels speak and yet that riots in thoughts that fiends might envy . . . this compound of rottenness and beauty—this unsexed Circe, who gems the poisoned cup he offers us . . . while the soul sickens at the draught within—seems to have lived only that the world might learn from his example how worthless and how pernicious a thing is genius, when divorced from religion, from morals, and from humanity ".

Prodigious ! " Who would have thought that the old man had so much blood in him ? "—the old man of hypocrisy. For it was at the *Vision of Judgment* that our friend thus shuddered and sputtered—the *Vision of Judgment*, which one refuses to believe that any human being can read without delight.

---

[1] He had received an invitation to Holstein from a gentleman of Hamburg whom he had never seen.

In January 1823 there was another European tribute. A young Swiss, Monsieur J.-J. Coulmann, arrived in Genoa and requested an interview. They met ; and in July of the same year, Coulmann sent him the autographed volumes of several French writers, and Pichot's *Essai sur le génie et le caractère de Lord Byron*, which had been added to the fourth edition of a translation of Byron's works. Àpropos some errors of fact and deduction which this essay contained, Byron wrote Coulmann a long and renowned letter, making, among other things, the defence of his father which I have alluded to in an early chapter. He begged Coulmann to have these errors publicly rectified : " I cannot bear to have [my father] unjustly spoken of ".[1] Such homage cheered him ; he could now write to Murray (more vacillating than ever), " I care but little for the opinions of the English, as I have long had Europe and America for a Public ". His relations with " my Admiral " continued to be stormy. In October 1822 there had been a very angry letter ; but one from Murray crossed it, " and as I am a ' pitiful-hearted negro ', and can't keep resentment, it hath melted my flint ". The diatribe went, all the same. Ere long it was reinforced by one still fiercer, and supplemented by a line to John Hunt, assigning or transferring to him all unprinted MSS.—the six new cantos of *Don Juan*, *Werner*, and *Heaven and Earth*. But again in November, Murray melted him ; and though " I shall withdraw from you as a publisher, on every account, even your own ", Murray in the event obtained permission to keep and publish *Werner*, which accordingly was issued from Albemarle Street at the end of the month—the last of Byron's works to bear that imprint on its first edition. Alas ! this—" our concluding transaction "—led to renewed displeasure. *Werner* was " so full of gross misprints that a publisher might be ashamed of himself ", and the inscription to Goethe was omitted. As that had already occurred with the earlier dedication to him of *Sardanapalus*, Byron was incensed. " Is this courteous ? is it even politic ? I repeat to you that no publisher has a right to be negligent upon subjects. . . . Do not force me to do disagreeable things. But in case of your non-attention I must not only write to Goethe —but publish a statement of what has passed between us on such subjects ". And delightfully he adds, àpropos the Bertolini busts of himself and Teresa, which he had promised to present to Murray : " The busts are finished : are you worthy of them ? "

---

[1] Byron's German biographer, Dr. Elze, regards this letter as self-delusion, or deliberate falsehood, with respect particularly to Byron's statements about the Wicked Lord, his grand-uncle. See my chapters I and II (Note on the Chaworth Duel, p. 22).

26

On April 1, 1823, he met the last woman in his life—
Lady Blessington. She and the Earl, with Count Alfred
d'Orsay, reached Genoa on March 31. In her diary for that
day she wrote : " And am I indeed in the same town with Byron ?
To-morrow I may perhaps behold him. I never before felt the
same impatient longing to see anyone known to me only by his
own works. I hope he may not be as fat as Moore described him ".
He was like a skeleton, as he told Hoppner at this time—so one
disillusion was spared her when, the very next day, she *did*
behold him, at his own house. Her diary for April 1 contained
the entry : " Saw Lord Byron for the first time.

" The impression of the first few minutes disappointed me, as
I had, both from the portraits and descriptions given, conceived
a different idea of him. I had fancied him taller, with a more
dignified and commanding air ; and I looked in vain for the
hero-looking sort of person, with whom I had so long identified
him in imagination. His appearance is, however, highly prepos-
sessing. His head is finely shaped, and his forehead open,
high, and noble ; his eyes are grey and full of expression, but one
is visibly larger than the other. The nose is large and well
shaped, but, from being a little *too thick*, it looks better in profile
than in front-face ; his mouth is the most remarkable feature
in his face, the upper lip of Grecian shortness, and the corners
descending ; the lips full, and finely cut.

" In speaking, he shows his teeth very much, and they are
white and even ; but I observed that even in his smile—and he
smiles frequently—there is something of a scornful expression
in his mouth, that is evidently natural, and not, as many suppose,
affected. This particularly struck me. His chin is large and
well shaped, and finishes well the oval of his face. He is extremely
thin—indeed, so much so that his figure has almost a boyish air.
His face is peculiarly pale, but not the paleness of ill-health,
as its character is that of fairness, the fairness of a dark-haired
person ; and his hair (which is getting rapidly grey) is of a very
dark brown, and curls naturally : he uses a good deal of oil in
it, which makes it look still darker. His countenance is full of
expression, and changes with the subject of conversation ; it
gains on the beholder the more it is seen, and leaves an agreeable
impression. . . . His whole appearance is remarkably gentleman-
like, and he owes nothing of this to his toilet, as his coat appears
to have been many years made, is much too large—and all his
garments convey the idea of having been purchased ready-made,
so ill do they fit him. There is a *gaucherie* in his movements,
which evidently proceeds from the perpetual consciousness of
his lameness, that appears to haunt him ; for he tries to conceal
his foot when seated, and when walking has a nervous rapidity

in his manner. He is very slightly lame, and the deformity of his foot is so little remarkable, that I am not now aware which foot it is.

" His voice and accent are peculiarly agreeable, but effeminate—clear, harmonious, and so distinct, that though his general tone in speaking is rather low than high, not a word is lost. His manners are as unlike my preconceived notions of them as is his appearance. I had expected to find him a dignified, cold, reserved, and haughty person, but nothing can be more different ; for were I to point out the prominent defect of Lord Byron, I should say it was flippancy, and a total want of that natural self-possession and dignity, which ought to characterise a man of birth and education ".

That quotation gives an idea of her quality. There is no comparison between her book,[1] so far as it goes, and any other except Galt's for the early days. Taking these two together, we get a convincing impression which the longer biographies scarcely do more than impair. This impression is not wholly favourable, as it is in Moore's quasi-caricature of one of the most *ondoyant et divers* of human beings ; nor does it, like Jeaffreson's hard unpleasant photograph, betray by its very fidelity to mere externals. Jeaffreson's book is like the work of the camera. Only in *one* light did Byron look like that—and there were so many lights ! Lady Blessington and Galt alone perceived that he was both more, and less, than met the eye.

For the two months from April 1 to June 3 (when the Blessingtons left Genoa), Byron and they met almost daily. They rode together ; he and she exchanged keepsakes and verses, talked of everything and afterwards, and parted in tears. One of the most delightful women that have ever lived, and just one year and a half younger than himself—yet with a sad and varied experience, ever since her sixteenth summer,[2] to make her,

---

[1] *Journal of the Conversations with Lord Byron*, published in volume form, 1834.
[2] Marguerite Power, daughter of a small Irish landowner of Co. Waterford, was forcibly married in 1804 to a Captain Farmer, whom she left at the end of three months, returning to her father's house. From 1807 to 1813 she lived under the protection of a Captain Jenkins at Stidmanton, in Hampshire. There she met Lord Mountjoy, created in 1816 first Earl of Blessington. Captain Farmer died from a fall out of window when drunk, in 1817, and four months later (February 16, 1818) Mrs. Farmer married the Earl of Blessington. She became one of the most renowned of London hostesses : the Most Gorgeous Lady Blessington. After the Earl's death in 1829 she and Count d'Orsay, who had devoted his life to her since 1822, entertained with " lavish splendour ", at Seamore Place, and Gore House, Kensington. In 1849 financial ruin overtook them ; and in June of that year, in Paris, Lady Blessington died. Count d'Orsay died in 1852, and is buried beside her at Chambourcy. He was

in everything but freshness of feeling, many years older—Byron opened his heart to her, as he did for that matter to all and sundry ; but she, unlike the rest, saw deep into his true nature, and exercised a charm upon him which must, had he lived and their friendship prospered, have helped him to a kind of happiness that he had never known before. To quote all her admirable *aperçus* of him would be to quote nearly her whole book. Let me give the most epigrammatic, which indeed sums up her impression : " *He never did himself justice* ". She is guilty of the overworked epithet chameleon, which, in my view, has no pertinence ; for to me all Byron is implied in each manifestation. She dwells much in this connection upon his swervings from sentiment to sarcasm. " He had both sentiment and romance in his nature ; but, from the love of displaying his wit and astonishing his hearers, he affected to despise and ridicule them ". Surely neither sentiment nor romance need exclude from a nature vanity or wit. Indeed, the too fiercely serious romantic is often no true romantic, but a sentimentalist. Byron, on one side, was of the authentic brand—a sentimentalist about women, he was a romantic about almost everything else. Shelley, it is true, could be serious without alleviation, and still be the real thing ; but how rare is Shelley ! He stands almost alone in his seraphic gravity. Byron, on the contrary, touched humanity at every point ; everything in him answered to that magnet— and this was, as I have said before, the secret of his vast popularity. Again, the chameleon takes protectively the colour of its surroundings. When did Byron do that ? He took, not their colour on himself to hide himself, but *from* their colour all that he needed to display himself.

It is not, then, that obsession which makes Lady Blessington so admirable ; but her abounding sympathy with him amid all the psychological perplexities that he made for her. She was, as compared with most of the other women in his life, in an immensely advantageous position ; for she was not at all in love with him, yet was aware that, had she willed it, he could at any moment have been deeply in love with her. And she had experience behind her ; love of both kinds—marital and lover-like—beside her ; while within her was a fund of that light-hearted gaiety and " innocence " which, in some natures, survives the most complicated set of circumstances. So fortunately dowered a woman is every man's potential conqueror ; and the more s o when the man is what Byron was—*ennuyé* yet curious,

married in 1827 to Lord Blessington's daughter by his first wife ; but owing to his conduct, the marriage ended in a separation. Lady Blessington was much blamed for this union ; it was said that she promoted it in order to obtain the daughter's dowry for her lover, d'Orsay.

vain yet enthralled by others' charm, cynical yet idealistic,
solitary yet warmly affectionate. . . . In the *Conversations*,
there are sayings of his which wonderfully reveal the man beneath
and above the poet; for to Lady Blessington he spoke with
more sincerity, and more aphoristically, than was his wont.
A collection of Byroniana might be made from her book alone ;
I shall set down a few at random.

" It is as though I had the faculty of discovering error,
without the power of avoiding it."

" Society and genius are incompatible. . . . If I have any
genius, all I can say is that I have always found it fade away,
like snow before the sun, when I have been living long in the
world ".

" I can so well understand the lover leaving his mistress to
write to her ! I should leave mine, not to write to, but to think
of, her ".

" I am of opinion that poets do not require great beauty in
the objects of their affection ".

" Clever men make a great mistake in selecting wives who
are destitute of abilites. . . . My *beau idéal* would be a woman
with talent enough to be able to understand and value mine,
but not sufficient to be able to shine herself. All men with
pretensions desire this ; though few, if any, have courage to
avow it ".

" I wonder that no one has thought of writing ' Pleasures of
Fear '. It surely is a poetical subject. . . . Cowardice is,
I believe, the only charge that has not yet been brought
against me ".

" I have always found more difficulty in hitting on a subject
than in filling it up . . . and I have remarked that I never could
make much of a subject suggested to me by another ".

" After a season in London, one doubted one's own identity ".

" *Au fond*, I have no malice ".[1]

" No man dislikes being lectured by a woman, provided she
be not his wife, sister, mother, or mistress ".

" How different do the same people appear in London and
in the country ! They are hardly to be recognised ".

" Vanity is the prime mover in most, if not all, of us. *None*
will own to this passion, yet it influences *all* ".

" The English are very envious; they are, *au fond*, conscious
that they are dreadfully dull ".

" Nothing so completely serves to demoralise a man as the

---

[1] Lady Blessington comments : " Never was there a more true obser-
vation ".

certainty that he has lost the sympathy of his fellow creatures ".

" Mathews's [1] imitation of Curran can hardly be so called : it is a *continuation* ".

" Cleverness and cunning are incompatible—I never saw them united ".[2]

" I have not quite made up my mind that women have souls ".

" A successful work makes a man a wretch for life ".

" You see, I am modest in my desires with regard to women : I only wish for perfection ".

" Experience, that dull monitress, who always comes too late ! "

" It is my respect for morals that makes me so indignant against its vile substitute, cant ; with this I wage war, and this the good-natured world chooses to consider as a sign of my wickedness ".

" There are some natures that have a predisposition to grief, as others have to disease ; and such was my case. The causes that have made me wretched would not have discomposed, or, at least, more than discomposed, another ".

" My besetting sin is a want of that self-respect which Lady Byron has in *excess* ; and that want has produced much unhappiness to us both ".

" He who has known vice can never truly describe woman as she ought to be described ".

" I maintain that more than half our maladies are produced by accustoming ourselves to more sustenance than is required for the support of nature ".

" When I recommend solitude . . . I mean a regular retirement with a woman that one loves, and interrupted only by correspondence with a man that one esteems. . . . We are all better in solitude ; we grow better, because we believe ourselves better ".

" I am of a jealous nature, and should wish to call slumbering sentiment into life in the woman I love, instead of finding that I was chosen, from its excess and activity rendering a partner in the firm indispensable ".

" I flatter myself I shall have more than one biographer ".

" If I know myself, I have no character at all ".

" I do not recollect ", says Lady Blessington, " ever having met him that he did not, in some way, introduce the subject of Lady Byron. The impression left upon my mind was that she

---

[1] Charles Mathews, the actor.
[2] This is a striking example of the gradual debasement of the word clever. We could not say the same thing in the same words to-day.

continually occupied his thoughts, and that he most anxiously
desired a reconciliation with her ". Elsewhere she reflects :
" Whatever may be the sufferings of Lady Byron, they are more
than avenged by what her husband feels ". Early in their
acquaintance, Byron learned that a friend of the Blessingtons
who had arrived in Genoa, was also a friend of Lady Byron,
and that his sister was an intimate. He asked Lady Blessington
to use her influence with this Colonel Montgomery to make his
sister write to Lady Byron for her portrait, which he had long
wished to possess. Colonel Montgomery desired that Byron
should specify on paper his exact wishes. Accordingly he wrote :

May 3, 1823

" DEAR LADY BLESSINGTON,—My request would be for a
copy of the miniature of Lady B. which I have seen in possession
of the late Lady Noel, as I have no picture, or indeed memorial
of any kind of Lady B., as all her letters were in her own possession
before I left England, and we have had no correspondence since
—at least on her part.

" My message, with regard to the infant, is simply to this
effect—that in the event of any accident occurring to the mother,
and my remaining the survivor, it would be my wish to have
her plans carried into effect, both with regard to the education
of the child, and the person or persons under whose care Lady B.
might be desirous that she should be placed. It is not my inten-
tion to interfere with her in any way on the subject during her
life ; and I presume that it would be some consolation to her
to know (if she is in ill-health, as I am given to understand)
that in *no* case would anything be done, as far as I am concerned,
but in strict conformity with Lady B.'s own wishes and intentions
—left in what manner she thought proper ".

He confessed to her that he was in the habit of writing to
his wife. " Some of these letters I have sent, and others I did
not, simply because I despaired of their being any good ". In
a day or two, he sent Lady Blessington one of these withheld
letters—that already referred to, written in 1821 or 1822, where
he had acknowledged the receipt of a lock of Ada's hair, and
had spoken of having kept his wife's old household account-
book. He had continued in the same letter :

" The time which has elapsed since the separation has been
considerably more than the whole brief period of our union,
and the not much longer one of our prior acquaintance. We
both made a bitter mistake ; but now it is over, and irrevocably
so. For, at thirty-three on my part, and a few years less on

yours, though it is no very extended period of life, still it is one when the habits and thought are generally so formed as to admit of no modification ; and as we could not agree when younger, we should with difficulty do so now.

" I say all this, because I own to you, that, notwithstanding everything, I considered our reunion as not impossible for more than a year after the separation ;—but then I gave up the hope entirely and for ever. But this very impossibility of reunion seems to me at least a reason why, on all the few points of discussion which can arise between us, we should preserve the courtesies of life, and as much of its kindness as people who are never to meet may preserve perhaps more easily than nearer connections. For my own part, I am violent, but not malignant ; for only fresh provocations can awaken my resentments. To you, who are colder and more concentrated, I would just hint, that you may sometimes mistake the depth of a cold anger for dignity, and a worse feeling for duty. I assure you that I bear you *now* (whatever I may have done) no resentment whatever. Remember, that *if you have injured me* in aught, this forgiveness is something ; and that, if I have *injured you*, it is something more still, if it be true, as the moralists say, that the most offending are the least forgiving.

" Whether the offence has been solely on my side, or reciprocal, or on yours chiefly, I have ceased to reflect upon any but two things—namely, that you are the mother of my child, and that we shall never meet again. I think if you also consider the two corresponding points with reference to myself, it will be better for all three.—Yours ever,

NOEL BYRON " [1]

If anything resulted from Colonel Montgomery's negotiation, or if it was ever attempted, none of the biographies informs us.

It does not appear from her book that Lady Blessington met Teresa Guiccioli at this time ; but their later correspondence seems to prove that they had known and liked one another at some period of the Blessingtons' stay in Italy, which lasted for several years. Byron spoke much of her, confessing that he was not happy, but admitting that it was his own fault. Teresa had, he said, all the qualities to render a reasonable being happy. Lady Blessington, *en revanche*, observed that she feared the Countess Guiccioli had little reason to be satisfied with her lot. He answered, " Perhaps you are right ; yet she must know that I am sincerely attached to her. But the truth is my habits are not those requisite to form the happiness of any woman. I am worn out in feelings. . . . I like solitude . . . am fond of

shutting myself up for hours, and, when with the person I like,
am often *distrait* and gloomy ". He added on another occasion
that if he and Teresa were married, they would, he was sure,
be cited as an example of conjugal happiness. How much irony
there may have been in this, it is difficult to guess ; Leigh Hunt's
story leads us to believe that there was some. But Byron
spoke tenderly, if remotely, of the girl who had given him all
she had to give. " Of the Guiccioli I could not, if I would,
speak ill ; her conduct towards me has been faultless, and there
are few examples of such complete and disinterested affection
as she has shown me all through our attachment ".[1]

It is significant that Teresa was eager to affirm that Byron
saw Lady Blessington only five or six times in two months, and
that his feelings of friendship towards her were not of an ardent
nature. That she deluded herself, or desired to delude posterity,
in this respect, is evident from Byron's notes to the Blessingtons
during their Genoese sojourn : from them we gather that he saw
the Earl and Countess nearly every day.

Before they left, the Greek adventure was almost decided
on ; but Lady Blessington thought it " extraordinary to see a
man engage in a chivalrous . . . undertaking, for which his
habits peculiarly unfit him, without any indication of enthusiasm ".
She found his mockery on this subject disheartening : " the
action loses all its charms ". He declared that as the moment
approached for undertaking it, he almost wished he had never
thought of it. " This ", he said, " is one of the many scrapes
into which my poetical temperament has led me. . . . It
appears now only fit for a travesty. . . . Well, *if I do* . . .
outlive the campaign, I shall write two poems on the subject—
one an epic, and the other a burlesque in which none shall be
spared, and myself least of all ".

The Blessingtons left Genoa on June 3. Byron was with
them on the evening before their departure—in very low spirits.
" I have a sort of boding that we see each other for the last
time ; something tells me I shall never return from Greece ".
He then leaned his head on the arm of the sofa where he and
Lady Blessington were seated, and broke into uncontrollable
tears. On his recovery he tried to turn off attention by some
ironical remark, spoken with a sort of hysterical laugh, upon the
effects of nervousness. He begged Lady Blessington to give
him some trifle that she had worn, as a keepsake ; she gave

---

[1] Her disinterestedness is fully attested. When Byron went to Greece
he gave his banker, Mr. Barry, orders to advance her money ; but she never
would consent to receive any. He had also intended to bequeath £10,000
to her, but she had dissuaded him from fulfilling this purpose. Moore,
Hobhouse, and Barry all testify to her refusal of any settlement.

him one of her rings, and he took a pin from his breast containing
a small cameo of Napoleon which he said he had worn for long,
and presented it to her.   But next morning she received a note
saying that he was superstitious, and had recollected that
memorials " with a point " are of evil augury.   He therefore
begged her to accept instead a chain which he enclosed, and
which had been worn oftener and longer than the other.

CHAPTER XXVI

GREECE : THE END

The Greek Revolution—Greek Committee formed in London : Byron elected a member—Teresa Guiccioli—The departure—Dr. Bruno—A letter from Goethe—The transit—Cephalonia—Illness—Byron's tactics—Arrival of Stanhope—Disappointments—Dr. Kennedy—Missolonghi—Despair—Last verses—A seizure—Hatadjé—Ada—Last words to Teresa—Her subsequent history—Ambitions in Greece—Suicidal abstinence—Troubles increase—Last Days—The Confusion of Tongues—Incompetence of doctors—Fletcher, and the message to Lady Byron—Byron's death—Funeral honours—Trelawny's betrayal—Byron's body embarked for England—Hobhouse—Burial in the Abbey refused—The funeral—Hucknall Torkard, and the grave—Lady Byron's last word—Summing-up

IN 1821, during the Italian insurrectionary movement, Byron had written in the Ravenna Journal : " It is a grand object —the very *poetry* of politics. Only think—a free Italy ! " It would be almost true to say that from the time of the Carbonarist fiasco, Italy became distasteful to him. Not long after the movement had collapsed, his attention fixed itself on Greece, where a revolution had broken out at about the same time. One of its first stages ended with the defeat of Hypsilantes in Wallachia on June 19, 1821. In the Morea the insurgents were more successful, and soon the movement spread over the country south of Thermopylæ and Actium. Military successes against the Turks were frequent ; but political affairs fell into a state of anarchy. There was no real leader ; all parties pursued their own interests alone. At the end of 1822 Odysseus (whom Byron called Ulysses) was undisputed master of Eastern Hellas ; in the Peloponnesus, Kolokotronis was the star ; in Western Hellas, Mavrocordato, long since foremost in fame but discredited by his political action during the war, was now regaining prestige by his defence of Missolonghi against the Turkish forces. The siege was raised on January 12, 1823 ; and the Senate of the National Assembly—constituted in January of the year before—elected Mavrocordato their President. But he, in fear of his life from Kolokotronis—the popular leader, " a brigand by lineage and profession, and a cattle-dealer by trade "—did not dare to take office. The Senate summoned him, threatened him, and forced him to accept ; he, too prudent in matters of personal safety, more of the ambitious statesman than of the soldier, eventually fled to Hydra. That was in August 1823, the time of Byron's arrival at Cephalonia ; and thenceforth the state of parties in Greece grew ever more complicated. " Every corner of the peninsula was torn to pieces by obscure civil contests ".[1]

In January 1823 one Andreas Luriottis had arrived in England to plead the cause of the Greeks. A Greek Committee was formed, and was joined by many distinguished men, among whom were Sir J Mackintosh (whom Byron had known and greatly liked), Jeremy Bentham, and Hobhouse. At the first meeting, Edward Blaquiere, author of several books on Spain, offered to return with Luriottis to Greece and collect information. He saw Byron on the way at about the beginning of April, and Byron then learnt for the first time that in March he had been unanimously elected a member of the Committee, and that " his name was a tower of strength ". This had been brought about by Trelawny, who had written to Blaquiere, mentioning Byron's interest in the cause. " The proposition ", says the Cornishman, " came at the right moment : the Pilgrim [2] was dissatisfied with himself and his position. Greece and its memories warmed him, a new career opened before him. His first impulses were always ardent, but if not acted on instantly, they cooled. . . . The negotiations with the Committee occupied some months before Byron, perplexed in the extreme, finally committed himself ". Trelawny was away at this time ; but he heard from Captain Roberts [3] and Mary Shelley of Byron's vacillations. " ' Well, Captain ', said the Pilgrim, ' if we do not go to Greece, I am determined to go somewhere . . . as I am tired of this place, the shore, and all the people on it ' ". But already in May Mrs. Shelley had perceived the reason for these vacillations. " The G—— is an obstacle, and certainly her situation is rather a difficult one. But he does not seem disposed to make a mountain of her resistance, and he is far more able to take a decided than a petty step in contradiction to the wishes of those about him ".

Jeaffreson points out that Byron could well have taken Teresa to the Ionian Islands (then under the protection of Eng-

---

[1] Gordon, *History of the Greek Revolution*, ii. 72.

[2] Byron was thus designated by the Shelley circle after the stanza in *Adonais*, where he is called " the Pilgrim of Eternity ".

[3] Captain Daniel Roberts, R.N., was a friend of Trelawny and Edward Williams. Byron had seen much of him during the Pisan sojourn, and Roberts had superintended the building of Shelley's *Ariel* and Byron's *Bolivar*.

land), whither he intended first to go, had not his passion com-
pletely burnt itself out. " He wished " (knowing that his every
movement would be chronicled in the English newspapers) " to
figure in the way that might dispose Lady Byron to send him
the miniature he had so recently solicited ". Jeaffreson's insistent
harshness in all allusions to the Countess Guiccioli must be re-
membered in considering his view. It is evident, indeed, that
not only in this matter but in all others, the ruling idea of Byron's
mind—once the Greek expedition was decided on—was to clean
the slate. But it is evident too that, whatever safety and ease
might be reckoned on at Zante or Cephalonia, the moment for
departure to the mainland would be greatly embarrassed by the
presence of a woman. If Byron was to go at all, Teresa must
be left behind. He saw that clearly, and in May had written
to John Bowring, Hon. Secretary to the Greek Committee :
" To this project the only objection is of a domestic nature, and
I shall try to get over it ; if I fail in this, I must do what I can
where I am ".

There was no poesy on hand. The fifteenth and sixteenth
cantos of *Don Juan* had been sent home in the spring.[1] He had
made another definite effort to approach his wife ; he had set
the Hunts on their feet by the abandonment of his share in *The
Liberal* and by the gift of his latter works, and had arranged for
the expenses of their removal to Florence ; Teresa Guiccioli,
Byron once departed, would rejoin her father at Bologna, whither
the old Count had gone some little time ago. . . . It was
precisely the situation to inspire him ; and so soon as he
really escaped from Italy, it did inspire him. Like a child he
regarded his clean slate—resolute, like the child, to write on it
this time only what should gain him credit. And the credit was
to arrive through and for Greece : " the only place I was ever
contented in ".

No wonder he could disregard the omens ! He, who would
do nothing even of the most trivial on a Friday, started on
Friday the 13th. And when the fabled day asserted itself, and
first they could not sail for the calm, and next had to put back
for the storm, he, of all men the most apprehensively superstitious,
appeared thoughtful only for a moment, and then remarked
that he considered a bad beginning a favourable omen. But he
had strange forewarnings. Already we have heard him say to
the Blessingtons : " I shall never return from Greece ". Now,

---

[1] Trelawny tells us, on Murray's authority, that on reading the later
cantos of *Juan,* Gifford said : " Upon my word, I do not know where to
place Byron. I think we can't find a niche for him unless we go back and
place him after Shakespere and Milton . . . there is no other place for
him " (*Recollections*, p. 106).

while waiting to re-embark, he said to young Pietro Gamba, " Where shall we be in a year ? " Gamba comments : " On the same day of the same month in the next year, he was carried to the tomb of his ancestors ".

In the evening of that day, July 16, 1823, they finally set sail. Their ship was the *Hercules*, chartered by Byron at the end of June without expert advice. On June 15 he had written to Trelawny in Rome : "You must have heard that I am going to Greece—why do you not come to me ? I want your aid, and I am exceedingly anxious to see you. Pray, come, for I am at last determined to go to Greece :—it is the only place I was ever contented in. I am serious : and did not write before, as I might have given you a journey for nothing. They all say I can be of use to Greece ; I do not know how—nor do they ; but, at all events, let us go ".

Trelawny comments : " Knowing him, I took no heed nor made any preparations until he wrote that he had chartered a vessel ". But this—the *Hercules*—was in Trelawny's view most unsatisfactory. " A collier-built tub of 120 tons, round-bottomed, bluff-bowed, and of course a dull sailer ". He expressed his disgust. " Why, then," Byron retorted, " did you not come here sooner ? I had no one to help me ".

" You had Captain Roberts, the very man. . . . We might as well have built a raft, and chanced it ".

But Byron smiled. " They say I have got her on very easy terms ".

He had in another matter practised the same bad economy. A travelling physician was necessary to such an adventure, and Byron had engaged " an unfledged medical student ", Dr. Bruno.[1] He proved as bad a choice, though for different reasons, as Polidori had been ; and Trelawny again protested. " If he knows little ", answered Byron, " I pay little, and we will find him plenty of work ".

Thus equipped, he embarked on a Friday the 13th with Pietro Gamba and Trelawny ; Fletcher, Tita, and six other servants attended the party. They re-landed on the 14th in a dead calm ; weighed anchor on the 15th and were towed out to

---

[1] Bruno afterwards confessed that for the first fortnight of the voyage he lived in perpetual terror, having been told that if he committed the slightest fault Lord Byron would have him torn to pieces by his dogs, which he kept for that purpose. Count Gamba tells this tale in his Narrative. It gives us the measure of Bruno's intelligence. But he attended Byron devotedly to the best of his ability ; went to England with the body, and was present at the funeral service at Hucknall Torkard. He refused to accept from the executors any fee for his services, " and thereafter disappears into the unknown " (*Byron : The Last Journey*, by Harold Nicolson, 1924).

the offing by some American ship's boats, sent in compliment
to Byron ; that night were forced, by a gale which frightened
the horses (there were four of Byron's, one of Trelawny's) and
caused them to kick down their badly-built boxes, to put into
port again—and finally started on the Monday evening. The
passage to Leghorn took five days ; " Byron unusually quiet
and serious ". There they took on board two Greeks, who were
said (by friends attending them) to be Russian and Turkish spies.
Trelawny received this confidence, and imparted it as a sample
of the morality of the modern Greeks. But on that score Byron
had no illusions whatever. All along, it was in the abstract
cause of freedom that he sang and worked for Greece. Since
the first *Harold*, he had known and judged the people ; he now
went there better prepared to deal with them than any of the
" practical " men who were sent out in other capacities.

At Leghorn on July 24, he received a letter from Goethe—
the first and only one he ever had from him—enclosing some
lines[1] composed by the great man himself. Moore's comment
is interesting.

" It would have been the wish of Lord Byron, in the new
path he had now marked out for himself, to disconnect from his
name, if possible, all those poetical associations which, by throw-
ing a character of romance over the step he was now taking,
might have a tendency, as he feared, to impair its practical
utility ; and it is, perhaps, hardly saying too much for his sincere
zeal in the cause to assert that he would willingly at this moment
have sacrificed his whole fame, as poet, for even the prospect
of an equivalent renown, as philanthropist and liberator. How
vain, however, was the thought that he could thus supersede
his own glory, or cause the fame of the lyre to be forgotten in
that of the sword, was made manifest to him by a mark of homage
which reached him, while at Leghorn, from the hands of one
of the only two men of the age who could contend with him in
the universality of his literary fame ".

There joined them at Leghorn, besides the suspect Greek
gentlemen, Mr. Hamilton Browne, a Scotchman who " knew a
good deal of the Greeks ", and who induced the party to change
their original intention of going to Zante. He recommended
Cephalonia instead, because Colonel Napier, the English Resi-

---

[1] These lines :

" Ein freundlich Wort kommt eines nach dem andern " :

are translated in the appreciation of Byron which Goethe contributed to
Medwin's Conversations. Byron wrote at once in acknowledgment, and
Goethe preserved the letter " among my most precious papers ", in the
famous red portfolio, and cut a small cardboard box to protect the seal
with its motto : *Crede Biron.*

dent there, was a known Philhellene. Thus at last, all was
in train; they put to sea in perfect weather, and Byron said
to Trelawny: "I am better now than I have been for years".
"I never was", says this keen critic of the Pilgrim, "on ship-
board with a better companion. He was generally cheerful,
gave no trouble, assumed no authority, uttered no complaints.
When appealed to, he always answered, 'Do as you like'".

Passing Stromboli, Byron sat up all night, hoping for an
eruption. As he went down to his cabin at daybreak, he said,
"If I live another year, you will see this scene in a fifth canto
of *Childe Harold*". Such a speech contrasts interestingly with
his avowed—and perfectly genuine—impatience at being re-
garded in this expedition as in any sense a literary pilgrim.
Somebody proposed to him, during a visit to Ithaca, the inspec-
tion of some of the Homeric localities. "He turned peevishly
away, saying to [Trelawny], 'Do I look like one of those emas-
culated fogies? Let's have a swim. I detest antiquarian
twaddle. Do people think I have no lucid intervals, that I came
to Greece to scribble more nonsense? I will show them I can
do something better: I wish I had never written a line, to have
it cast in my teeth at every turn". Hardly a writer in the world
but will sympathise with this ebullition. Byron subconsciously
knew that he was accumulating material; but, like all creative
artists, he was at the moment absorbed in the outward event
alone. Even Moore, on this subject, suffered rebuke. Very
late in the adventure, Byron wrote to him (March 4, 1824): "I
have not been 'quiet' in an Ionian Island" (this was in defence
of his sojourn in Cephalonia) . . . "neither have I continued
Don Juan[1] nor any other poem. You go, I suppose, by some
newspaper report or another". Moore comments:

"It is amusing to observe that, while thus anxious, and from
a highly noble motive, to throw his authorship into the shade
while engaged in so much more serious pursuits, it was yet an
author's mode of revenge that always occurred to him, when
under the influence of any of these passing resentments. Thus,
when a little angry with Colonel Stanhope one day, he exclaimed,
'I will libel you in your own Chronicle'; and in this brief burst
of humour I was myself the means of provoking in him, I have
been told, on the authority of Count Gamba, that he swore to
'write a satire' upon me.

"Though [his] letter shows how momentary was any little

---

[1] The seventeenth canto is unfinished. On May 8, 1823, Byron began
it, and took the MS. with him to Greece. Trelawny said he found 15
stanzas in the room at Missolonghi. The fourteen (not fifteen) were
printed and published for the first time in Mr. Coleridge's edition of the
Poems.

spleen he may have felt, there not unfrequently, I own, comes over me a short pang of regret to think that a feeling of displeasure, however slight, should have been among the latest I awakened in him ".

His spirits, as the ship progressed towards Cephalonia, grew higher and higher. He and Trelawny swam every day at noon ; he practised with his pistols ; he played a practical joke on their captain, one Scott, who, when he wished to be very ceremonious, wore a bright scarlet waistcoat. Scott was immensely stout ; and Byron, curious to know if the sacred garment would not button round both himself and Trelawny, one day persuaded the cabin-boy to bring it up to them during the captain's siesta. " Now ", he cried, standing on the gangway with one arm in the waistcoat, " put your arm in, Tre ; we'll jump overboard and take the shine out of it ". And so they did, to the great anger of Scott, who accused them of inciting the crew to mutiny. Fletcher, hero of the thunder-storm at Zitza those many years ago, had preserved all his old character. " My master can't be right in his mind ", he confided to Trelawny. " Why, sir, there is nothing to eat in Greece, or to drink ; there is nothing but rocks, robbers, and vermin. I defy my Lord to deny it ". Byron, unexpectedly arriving, overheard. " I don't deny it ", said he. " What he says is quite true to those who take a hog's eye view of things. But this I know, I have never been so happy as I was there ". On August 2 Cephalonia and Zante were in sight, and pointing out the line of the Morea, he said : " I don't know why it is, but I feel as if the eleven long years I have passed through since I was there, were taken off my shoulders ".[1]

Next day they anchored in the harbour of Argostoli, chief town of Cephalonia. It was here that the first of the long series of vexations occurred. Byron heard from the Secretary that Edward Blaquiere, who was to have awaited his arrival, was on his way back to England, and had left no message of any kind for him. He at once declared to Trelawny that he saw he had been used merely as a decoy by the Greek Committee in London. " Now they have got me thus far, they think I must go on. . . . They are deceived ; I won't budge a foot farther till I see my way. We will stay here ". But his anger quickly vanished before the sensation that his presence in Argostoli excited. He was " greeted with a welcome so cordial and respectful as not only surprised and flattered him " (accustomed as he now was to accept himself as an outlaw in his countrymen's

[1] All through the voyage, as they passed hills and sheltered coves, he would point to some serene nook, and exclaim : " There I could be happy ! " (Trelawny, *Records*, p. 126).

eyes), " but, it was evident, sensibly touched him ".   His health
was drunk at the mess, and he made a short speech.   " He was
much pleased when he had delivered it, and frequently asked
the Colonel if he had acquitted himself properly, as he was so
little in practice ".   Serious business, however, was not for-
gotten.   Directly he heard of Blaquiere's departure, he sent a
message after him to Corfu ; the messenger could nowhere fall
in with him, nor even at Corfu had he left any message for Byron.
Another envoy was sent to Marco Bozzaris at Missolonghi.
Bozzaris, a Suliot chief, was fighting on the Greek side, and was
then endeavouring to check the Turkish advance on Anatolikon.
He received Byron's letter on August 18, and answered without
delay : " Your Excellency is exactly the person of whom we
stand in need.   Let nothing prevent you from coming into
this part of Greece. . . . Do not delay ".   Within a few hours
after signing this, he was killed in battle.   " Thus ", comments
Mr. Prothero, " of the two Greek leaders to whom Byron had
been recommended, one was dead, and the other, Mavrocordato,
was a fugitive ".   Before long, too, he heard from the default-
ing Blaquiere, " requesting me (contrary to his former opinion)
not to proceed to Greece *yet* ".   For the first month after his
arrival he remained on board the *Hercules* ; then he paid off
the vessel, and took a house for himself, Gamba, and Bruno
at Metaxata, a pleasant village about four miles and a half
from Argostoli.   There he remained until December 28, when
he embarked for Missolonghi.

The stay at Argostoli and Metaxata was marked by many
incidents, all of which have been recorded at length by various
writers.   The most engaging of these narratives is that by an
Englishman, one Mr. S—— (later to be connected closely with
the miserable Medora Leigh[1] scandal), who was completely
fascinated by him.   They met on the island of Ithaca, which
Byron visited directly after his arrival with Gamba, Bruno,
Trelawny, and Hamilton Browne.   Mr. S—— had much talk
with him, and found him so delightfully different from what
he had heard that " my faculties were visibly affected by my
amazement ".   He spoke freely of literature—Pope and Walter
Scott[2] (whom he called Watty) being the principal themes ; and

[1] See Appendix, Medora Leigh.   Mr. S——'s narrative was first
published in Mackay's *Medora Leigh*, 1869.

[2] Byron's delight in the Waverley Novels was so great that he never
travelled without his copies of them, and *Quentin Durward* was one of the
last books he read.   Dr. Henry Muir, a resident of Cephalonia, happened to
receive a copy, and at once lent it to Byron, knowing that he had not read
it.   He immediately shut himself in his room, refused dinner, and " merely
came out once or twice to say how much he was entertained, returning to his
room with a plate of figs in his hand ".   This was the day before he left for
Missolonghi; and, not having finished the book, he took it with him.

of his hopes and fears for the cause. " I find but one opinion . . .
that no good is to be done for these rascally Greeks, that I am
sure to be deceived, disgusted, and all the rest of it. It may
be so ; but it is chiefly to satisfy myself upon these points that
I am going. I go prepared for anything, expecting a deal of
roguery and imposition, but hoping to do some good ". He
then led the conversation to his private affairs, and especially the
separation, ending with : " I dare say it will turn out that I
have been terribly in the wrong, but I always want to know
what I did ". Mr. S—— had not courage to touch on this
delicate topic ; and the incident must have come back to him,
with even increased amazement, when in process of time he en-
gaged himself in the interests of the girl who was so tragically
fathered and mothered.

Next morning, when Mr. S—— again beheld Byron :
" I never saw and could not conceive the possibility of such
a change in the appearance of a human being as had taken
place since the previous night. He looked like a man under
sentence of death, or returning from the funeral of all that he
held dear on earth. His person seemed shrunk, his face was
pale, and his eyes languid and fixed on the ground. He was
leaning upon a stick, and had changed his dark camlet-caped
surtout of the preceding evening for a nankeen jacket em-
broidered like a hussar's—an attempt at dandyism, or dash, to
which the look and demeanour of the wearer formed a sad con-
trast ".

He recovered looks and spirits ; they all went on an excursion
to the Fountain of Arethusa—but this, the first indication of
his shattered state, is a note which recurs twice in a narrative
comprising the events of one week only. His suicidal impru-
dence is here also deeply marked. When counselled not to eat
fresh-gathered grapes, as not having had the first rain, he de-
liberately chose them in preference to the riper figs and nectarines
—" in order to accustom myself to any and all things that a man
may be compelled to take where I am going ". He drank twice
in one afternoon of " gin-swizzle ", and then of various Greek
wines. Next morning Bruno reported that he had spent many
hours at Byron's bedside during the night, and when his em-
ployer appeared after bathing and boating, the young doctor
wrung his hands and tore his hair with alarm and vexation.
That same afternoon, at Saint Euphemia, Byron ate largely
at a luxurious feast given to the party by the English Resident.
" Verily ", he said, " I cannot abstain ". They slept at a monas-
tery on the hill of Samos, across the bay. Almost directly they
reached it, Byron retired ; in a few minutes the rest were alarmed
by the entrance of Bruno, again wringing his hands and tearing

his hair—" a practice much too frequent with him ", mildly re-
marks Mr. S—— of this incompetent young man. He announced
that Byron had been seized with violent spasms, and that his
brain was excited to " dangerous excess, so that he would not
tolerate the presence of any person in his room. He refused
all medicine, and stamped and tore all his clothes and bedding
like a maniac. We could hear him rattling and ejaculating.
Poor Dr. Bruno . . . implored one or more of the company to
go to his lordship and induce him, if possible, to save his life
by taking the necessary medicine. Trelawny at once proceeded
to the room, but soon returned, saying that it would require ten
such as he to hold his lordship for a minute, adding that Lord
Byron would not leave an unbroken article in the room. The
doctor again essayed an entrance, but without success. The
monks were becoming alarmed, and so, in truth, were all present.
The doctor asked me to try to bring his lordship to reason ;
' he will thank you when he is well ', he said, ' but get him to
take this one pill, and he will be safe '. It seemed a very easy
undertaking, and I went. There being no lock on the door,
entry was obtained in spite of a barricade of chairs and a table
within. His lordship was half-undressed, standing in a far
corner like a hunted animal at bay. As I looked determined to
advance in spite of his imprecations of ' Back ! out, out of my
sight ! fiends, can I have no peace, no relief from this hell !
Leave me, I say ! ' he lifted the chair nearest to him and hurled
it direct at my head ; I escaped as I best could, and returned to
the *sala*. . . . Mr. Hamilton Browne, one of our party, now volun-
teered an attempt, and the silence that succeeded his entrance
augured well for his success. He returned much sooner than
expected, telling the doctor that he might go to sleep ; Lord Byron
had taken both the pills, and had lain down on my mattress and
bedding, prepared for him by my servant, the only regular bed
in the company, the others being trunks and portable tressels,
with such softening as might be procured for the occasion ".
    Trelawny gives an account of some very strange behaviour
from Byron during this stay, to which Mr. S—— does not allude.
The Abbot had been told of their coming, and he prepared a
great reception for the English nobleman. Monks were ranged
along the terrace, " chanting a hymn of glorification and wel-
come " ; the Abbot, clad in sacerdotal robes, received him at
the porch. A vast hall was illuminated ; boys swung censers
under the poet's nose; and then the Abbot proceeded to intone
a turgid and interminable eulogium in a polyglot of tongues.
" Byron had not spoken a word since we entered. . . . Suddenly
he burst into a paroxysm of rage . . . a torrent of Italian exe-
crations . . . then, turning to us with flashing eyes, he vehem-

ently exclaimed : ' Will no one release me from the presence
of these pestilential idiots ? they drive me mad '. Seizing a
lamp, he left the room ". The Abbot was struck to stone for
some moments ; then, in a low tremulous voice he said " *Eccolo,
é matto, poveretto !* " (Poor fellow, he is mad). Byron did not
reappear. Next morning they left. " However we might
have doubted ", says Trelawny, " the sincerity of their ovation
on receiving us, we did not question the relief they felt, and
expressed by their looks, on our departure ".

It is worth pointing out that while Mr. S—— does not mention
this episode, Trelawny does not mention that of the attack of
illness. I imagine that the Cornishman, who "could not tell the
truth to save his life ", is here guilty of embroidery, and that the
far more credible story of momentary dementia is the true one.
Byron had brought on himself a veritable crisis of dyspepsia.
The next night, back at Argostoli and on board the *Hercules*,
he had a terrible nightmare from which Trelawny waked him. He
stared wildly at his visitor : " I have had such a dream ! I am
not fit to go to Greece. I am trembling with fear. If you had
come to strangle me, I could have done nothing ". " Who
could, against a nightmare ? " was Trelawny's sage answer.

But Trelawny soon grew irritated by what he calls Byron's
" old routine of dawdling habits, plotting, planning, shilly-shally-
ing, and doing nothing ". He and Hamilton Browne resolved to
start at once for the Morea and ascertain the real state of affairs,
for the daily-conflicting accounts distracted them all. They
accordingly left Cephalonia on September 29, with letters to the
Greek Government at Tripolitza. But this lingering of Byron's
at Cephalonia had its well-chosen reason. Trelawny was the
adventurer pure and simple—the somewhat obvious firebrand
and swashbuckler ; Byron, not naturally any more cautious,
yet showed himself now to be admirably restrained and far-
sighted. By this time he had settled himself at Metaxata, having
refused Colonel Napier's invitation to take up quarters with him.
His reason was the fear of embroiling the British authorities with
their Government ; and in every arrangement at this time he
practised the same prudent reserve. From every side came
letters urging him to attach himself to one or other of the fac-
tions. He replied in the same sense to all : " Make up your
differences. . . . I have come to help none of you as a partisan,
but all of you as a common friend ".

News now arrived : it was hoped that the Greek Loan would
immediately be floated in London. In November Hamilton
Browne returned with letters from the Greek Government,
asking Byron to advance £6000 for the payment of the fleet.
Byron had carried with him from Italy 10,000 Spanish dollars

in ready money, with bills of exchange for 40,000 more ; and he
now advanced to the Greek Government £4000—the first of
the large sums of money he devoted to the cause. At about
the same time, Colonel the Hon. Leicester Stanhope (afterwards
fifth Earl of Harrington) arrived at Cephalonia, having been
deputed by the London Committee to act with Byron.

From this time onward nothing but disappointment awaited
him. Soon after his instalment, he had taken into his pay a
body-guard of forty Suliots,[1] had almost at once learned his
error, given them two months' pay, and sent them to Missolonghi.
He soon wrote, in the diary he kept for a short time : " One should
not despair, though all the foreigners that I have hitherto met
with . . . are going or gone back disgusted. . . . The worst
of [the Greeks] is, they are such damned liars, ... but they
may be mended by and by ". Writing to Colonel Napier, he
said : " I can hardly be disappointed, for I believed myself on
a fool's errand from the outset. . . . But I like the Cause at least,
and will stick by it ".

Colonel Stanhope had been much hoped for, but proved
an acute disillusion. He was the perfect type of *doctrinaire* ;
Byron said of him to Parry (who arrived in February 1824),
" He is a mere schemer and talker, more of a saint than a soldier ;
and, with a great deal of pretended plainness, a mere politician,
and no patriot. . . . [He] begins at the wrong end . . . and
like all political jobbers, mistakes the accessories of civilisation
for its cause. . . . I thought, being a soldier, [he] would have
shown himself differently ". Stanhope's plan for establishing
newspapers was the grand absurdity of his scheme for Greece.
Byron and he pulled well at first ; but the newspaper project,
and Stanhope's idolisation of Jeremy Bentham, soon caused
a breach. Moreover Stanhope, as a Benthamite, of course
advocated a republican form of Government ; while Byron saw
that in the then degraded state of the country, a republic was
out of the question. Though they thus differed, however, each
respected the other ; and Stanhope, in his book,[2] paid many
a generous tribute to Byron—while Byron, though he spoke
bitterly to and of the *doctrinaire*, nevertheless bore with him in
extraordinarily good-humoured fashion.

It was at Metaxata that the renowned conversations with
Dr. Kennedy took place. This was a Scottish medical man,
Methodistically inclined, who undertook to convert Byron.
Mr. S—— speaks disdainfully of him. " He was very weak in

---

[1] The Suliots were a military caste of orthodox Christian Albanians,
fighting on the Greek side. They were a turbulent and mercenary race.
Byron had learned something of them during the first *Harold* tour.

[2] *Greece*, 1823–1824.

mind and body, ignorant of the most common controversial arguments even on his own side. He was a shallow and ill-informed man. His book showed the results, but it did not, and could not, show the quizzing that he excited in the garrison ". The conversations often lasted five or six hours, and Byron told Parry[1] that, " even though unprepared, I had very often the best of the argument. . . . He was not a very skilful disputant ". The knowledge of the Bible displayed by his sceptic perplexed the Methodistical doctor. Byron had always been, and still was, a student of it (" I read a chapter every day ", he told Parry) ; so that with his prodigious memory for all reading, he must have made a formidable adversary.

In December the call to Missolonghi became urgent. Màvrocordato was there ; he and Stanhope (who had gone in November) wrote to beg Byron to come as soon as possible. " It is right and necessary to tell you ", said Stanhope, " that a great deal is expected of you, both in the way of counsel and money. . . . All are eager to see you. . . . Your further delay . . . will be attended with serious consequences ". On December 28, 1823, Byron embarked. After many adventures—with the weather and with the Turkish fleet—he arrived at Missolonghi on January 5, 1824, and was received with military honours[2] and popular applause. " I cannot describe the emotion ", wrote Pietro Gamba. " Hope and content were pictured on every countenance ". Thus did he land from his last voyage on earth ; thus, " greeted as a Messiah ", did he set foot in the poisonous place that killed him.

To recapitulate the long mental and physical torture of Missolonghi would make sad writing and reading. From the day of his arrival it began, with Gamba's foolish overstepping of a commission entrusted to him for red cloth and oilskin. " The whole ", wrote Byron, " could not have amounted to 50 dollars. The account is 645 ! " He had a superstition about the young Italian—that he was one of those ill-starred people with whom everything goes wrong. Speaking of Stanhope's newspaper to Parry, he said : " I have subscribed to it to get rid of importunity, and, it may be, to keep Gamba out of mischief. At any rate, he can mar nothing that is of less importance ". He was very angry over this matter of the exceeded commission ; and told Stanhope, with customary exaggeration, that " he never would, to the last moment of his existence, forgive Gamba for

---

[1] *Last Days of Lord Byron,* p. 209.
[2] He landed in a British uniform, borrowed from Colonel Duffie, of the garrison at Cephalonia.

having squandered away what would have maintained an excellent corps of ragamuffins with arms in their hands ".

But that was only the beginning of the vexations. The incompetence, indolence, and rapacity all around soon reduced him to rage and despair. When Parry—one-time firemaster in the Royal Navy, and now clerk in the Ordnance Department at Woolwich—arrived as " artificer " from the London Committee in February 1824, and showed himself to be a really practical man, he was at once entrusted with an extraordinary degree of confidence by Byron, who took to him from the first. Here is Parry's impression of *him*. " He seemed almost to despair of success, but said he would see the contest out. . . . I have since thought that his fate was sealed before my arrival . . . and that even then he was, so to speak, on his death-bed. . . . . There was a restlessness about him . . . he seemed weary of himself and others. . . . It was evident to me, from the very commencement of our acquaintance, that he felt himself deceived and abandoned—I had almost said betrayed. . . . He might put a good face upon it to others . . . he might even be, as in fact he sometimes was, the first to laugh at his own difficulties . . . but in his heart he felt that he was forlorn and forsaken."

All through Parry's book the same note sounds, and his impression is borne out by the facts. There was no kind of trouble that did not overwhelm Byron. First, the place was most unhealthy, scarcely above the level of the waters ; the soil consisted of decomposed seaweed and dried mud. It was insanitary to a revolting degree ; his own dwelling was on the verge of a dismal swamp, " which might be called the belt of death ". The weather was bad ; he could seldom get the horse-back exercise that was so necessary to him, and he was pursuing, in that miasmic region, the debilitating starvation system of so many years. Fresh vexations came with every day that dawned. The English mechanics who had come out with Parry grumbled, finally deserted ; so did the German officers who had been sent from England to assist. Parry's appointment by Byron to be Major of the Artillery Brigade—his one foolish action in the adventure—brought about this latter trouble. " From the day Parry was appointed ", say Millingen,[1] " all the hopes which the rapid progress of that corps had excited were at an end. The best officers gave in resignations ". " The result was not surprising ", comments Mr. Prothero, " as Parry drilled his men in an apron, with a hammer in his hand ".[2]

[1] *Memoirs*, p. 94.
[2] Trelawny speaks severely of Parry. " A rough, burly fellow, never quite sober, but he was no fool. He was three months in Greece, returned

Disagreement with Stanhope increased. He and Trelawny (who had left Missolonghi) inclined to the Odysseus party ; Byron thought Mavrocordato the one hope of Greece—" an honest man, and a man of talent " ; though somewhat lacking in energy and industry, with a disposition to make too many promises.[1] But Mavrocordato, like every one else, was pressing him for money. The Greek Loan was not yet floated in London. Byron now had the £34,000 for which, late in 1823, Rochdale had at last been sold, and he devoted this entire sum to the cause ; but even so, he felt that his resources were not to be regarded as inexhaustible. Some time before this the Suliots in Missolonghi, among whom were Byron's former body-guard of forty, had turned mutinous again. It had been agreed that 600 of them should be taken into his pay, and act under his orders. His expenses amounted (according to Parry, whom he made his paymaster and steward) to two thousand dollars a week in rations alone. Moreover, there was difficulty in obtaining money ; bills could not be cashed on any terms ; and now that he had a small army to maintain, Parry saw that he was "fretted and teased" beyond endurance. Soon it was made clear to all that Parry had seen aright.

Byron had been twice disappointed of actual military work. In January there had been great hopes of an expedition against Lepanto, an important Turkish fortress. It was then that he took the 600 Suliots into his pay ; and, in Stanhope's words, " he burns with military ardour and chivalry, and will proceed to Lepanto ". But ere long these projects were seen to be doomed ; the mutiny among the Suliots, and the disaffection caused by Parry's peculiar methods of drilling, deferred indefinitely all hopes of an expedition. Again in the same month, however, the military ardour burned. The Turks blockaded Missolonghi on the 21st, and the only chance against them seemed to be a night-attack in boats manned by the European volunteers. Byron took the matter in hand, and insisted on joining personally in the expedition. From this he was dissuaded by Mavrocordato and others, who thought his life too valuable to be risked in such an adventure ; and in the end the Turks suddenly abandoned the blockade. This was on the day before his birthday, January 22 ; he had hoped, no doubt, to celebrate it by wearing one of the famous helmets of which Moore tells us : " Among other preparations for his expedition, he ordered three splendid helmets to be made, —with his never forgotten crest engraved upon them,—for

to England, talked the Committee out of £400 for his services, and drank himself into a madhouse ". Parry did die in the asylum at Hanwell.

[1] Parry called him " an old gentlewoman ".

himself and the two friends[1] who were to accompany him. In this little circumstance, which in England (where the ridiculous is so much better understood than the heroic) excited some sneers at the time, we have one of the many instances that occur amusingly through his life, to confirm the quaint, but, as applied to him, true observation, that ' the child is father to the man ' ; —the characteristics of these two periods of life being in him so anomalously transposed, that while the passions and ripened views of the man developed themselves in his boyhood, so the easily pleased fancies and vanities of the boy were for ever breaking out among the most serious moments of his manhood. The same schoolboy whom we found, at the beginning of this volume, boasting of his intention to raise, at some future time, a troop of horse in black armour, to be called Byron's Blacks, was now seen trying on with delight his fine crested helmet, and anticipating the deeds of glory he was to achieve under its plumes ". . . . Instead, he composed those verses, the last he was to write,[2] which he read to Stanhope and other friends on the evening of his thirty-sixth birthday. The concluding stanza runs :

" Seek out—less often sought than found—
    A soldier's grave, for thee the best ;
Then look around, and choose thy ground,
    And take thy rest ".

He said to Tita at this time : " No, Tita, I shall never go back from Greece—either the Turks, or the Greeks, or the climate, will prevent that ".

A period of dreadful weather ensued ; for days he could not get out at all. On February 15 he felt ill, but in the evening seemed to regain spirits and " laughed and joked with Parry and the Colonel ".[3] Parry then takes up the tale, Gamba and Stanhope having left the room.

" Lord Byron began joking with me about Colonel Stanhope's occupations, and said he thought the author would have his brigade of artillery ready before the soldier got his printing-

---

[1] Trelawny and Pietro Gamba.

[2] It is not certain whether these birthday verses were composed before or after another poem which was found among his papers at Missolonghi. This was of six stanzas, and was a lyric of ardent love. It retraces, stanza by stanza, the principal events which had taken place since his arrival in Greece : the mutiny of the Suliots, the adventurous passage to Missolonghi, a fever which had fallen on someone of those with him in the expedition, the earthquake, and a convulsive seizure of his own. To whom they were addressed remains unknown. Mr. Edgcumbe, indeed, insists that it was Mary Chaworth ; but his annotations in this sense are even less convincing than elsewhere.

[3] Gamba's *Narrative*.

press fixed. There was evidently a constrained manner about Lord Byron, and he complained of thirst. He ordered his servant to bring him some cider, which I entreated him not to drink in that state. . . . He had scarcely drunk the cider, when he complained of a strange sensation, and I noticed a great change in his countenance. He rose from his seat, but could not walk, staggered a step or two, and fell into my arms.

" I had no other stimulant than brandy at hand, and having before seen it administered in similar cases with considerable benefit, I succeeded in making him swallow a small quantity. In another minute his teeth were closed, his speech and senses gone, and he was in strong convulsions. I laid him down on the settee, and with the assistance of his servant kept him quiet.

" When he fell into my arms, his countenance was very much distorted, his mouth being drawn on one side. After a short time his medical attendant came, and he speedily recovered his senses and his speech ".

He had scarcely done so when word was brought to him that the Suliots had risen, and were about to attack the Arsenal. This was not true ; but the mutineers did break into his room, brandishing their arms and loudly demanding their " rights ". Stanhope, relating this, says : " Lord Byron, electrified by this act, seemed to recover from his sickness ; and the more the Suliots raged, the more his calm courage triumphed. The scene was truly sublime ".

Next day he was better, but very pale and weak; and he complained of a weight on the forepart of his head. Bruno applied eight leeches to his temples ; " the blood flowed copiously, but when the leeches were removed, the doctor was so unskilful that he could not stop the blood ". The temples bled so as almost to bring on syncope ; they sent for Millingen,[1] who applied lunar caustic, and this was efficacious. Byron writing to Murray on the 25th, said amusingly, " They had gone too near the temporal artery for my temporal safety " ; but this light allusion concealed a very serious view of his case. He wrote in an interrupted diary : " Had it lasted a minute longer, it must have extinguished my mortality " ; and on hearing from the doctors that the attack had a strong appearance of epilepsy, he fell into a state of melancholy from which, says Millingen, " none of our arguments could relieve him ". In Millingen's opinion, he was never the same man again : a change took place in his bodily and mental functions. " Would to Heaven ", he said to this narrator,

---

[1] Julius Millingen opened a dispensary at Missolonghi in January 1824. He attended Byron in his last illness. In 1831 he published his *Memoirs*. Trelawny spoke of him very scornfully (*Letters*, edited by H. Buxton Forman. 1910).

"the day were arrived on which, rushing sword in hand on a body of Turks, and fighting like one weary of existence, I shall meet immediate, painless death—the object of my wishes!" His great dread was that he should lose his senses : "end my days like Swift—a grinning idiot". But he rallied to some extent ; went out in boats or on horseback every day, and lived " as temperately as can be, without any liquid but water, and without any animal food ". This régime, advised by Bruno, was in Parry's opinion a great contributing cause of his death.

Worries began again on the 19th, when he was barely recovered. Lieutenant Sass, a Swedish officer, was murdered by a Suliot chief at the Arsenal ; the English mechanics finally demanded their passage home, and were sent by Byron to Zante, where, during their quarantine, he advanced them " *not more than a dollar a day* . . . to purchase some little extras as comforts ". To crown all, an alarm of plague spread through the filthy town, and on February 20 they had a " very smart earthquake ", the second since his arrival in Greece.[1] It was at this time that he procured the release of twenty-four Turkish women and children, who were to have been dispersed as slaves among the Greek householders. One woman, the wife of Hussein Aga, with her daughter, Hatadjé, implored English help. The Greeks had murdered all her relatives ; she had seen the brains of her youngest boy dashed out against the walls of the dispensary. (When she applied to Millingen the marks still remained on the wall.) Little Hatadjé, nine years old, had alone been spared. She was a lovely child : " her large, beautiful eyes . . . looked at me now and then, hardly daring to implore pity ". Millingen spoke of this incident to Byron, and he asked to see the mother and daughter, who were now under Millingen's roof. Hatadjé's beauty and spirit struck him so deeply that he decided on adopting her. He arranged for the rest of the Turkish prisoners to be sent to Prevesa, while she and her mother were to be placed under Dr. Kennedy's care at Cephalonia, unless Byron could induce Lady Byron (through Augusta) to let her go to England as a companion for Ada. He wrote to Augusta of this matter and others on February 23 ; but the unfinished letter was found on his table after his death.[2] Hatadjé was never sent to Cephalonia. She and her mother remained at Missolonghi until Byron's death ; then they went in the *Florida*, his funeral-ship, to Zante. Thither came an application from Usouff Pasha to give them up ; the little

---

[1] The first was in Cephalonia, in October 1823.
[2] It is endorsed, in Augusta's writing, with the words, " His last letter ". It was his last to her ; but there are several of later date to other correspondents.

girl was consulted, and said that now his lordship was dead, she preferred to go back to her country. Her mother agreed, and they were sent to Patras.

The letter to Augusta of February 23 is in answer to one from her, containing a " minute mental and physical account " of Ada, inscribed by Lady Byron. It was addressed to Augusta, but written for him ; and, together with the fact that it contained a profile of Ada, may be regarded as the one sign of relenting towards him that his wife ever showed. It may have been the result of the overtures through Lady Blessington's friends ; at any rate, it must have served to lessen for her some of the pain she was so soon to know.[1]

What of Teresa Guiccioli ? The only words we have from him to her are three extracts from letters in October from Cephalonia. She herself provided Moore with these.

Let us read them ; they are highly significant, as having been chosen from the rest for publication.

" October 7

" Pietro has told you all the gossip of the island,—our earthquakes, our politics, and present abode in a pretty village. As his opinions and mine on the Greeks are nearly similar, I need say little on that subject. I was a fool to come here ; but, being here, I must see what is to be done ".

" October —

" We are still in Cephalonia, waiting for news of a more accurate description ; for all is contradiction and division in the reports of the state of the Greeks. I shall fulfil the object of my mission from the Committee, and then return into Italy ; for it does not seem likely that, as an individual, I can be of use to them ;—at least no other foreigner has yet appeared to be so, nor does it seem likely that any will be at present.

" Pray be as cheerful and tranquil as you can ; and be assured that there is nothing here that can excite anything but a wish to be with you again,—though we are very kindly treated by the English here of all descriptions. Of the Greeks, I can't say much good hitherto, and I do not like to speak ill of them, though they do of one another ".

" October 29

" You may be sure that the moment I can join you again,

---

[1] Lady Byron's letter was dated " Hastings, December 1823 ", and was in answer to one from him to Augusta (we have not the letter) of December 8, from Metaxata.

will be as welcome to me as at any period of our recollection. There is nothing very attractive here to divide my attention ; but I must attend to the Greek cause, both from honour and inclination. Messrs. B. and T. are both in the Morea, where they have been very well received, and both of them write in good spirits and hopes. I am anxious to hear how the Spanish cause will be arranged, as I think it may have an influence on the Greek contest. I wish that both were fairly and favourably settled, that I might return to Italy, and talk over with you *our*, or rather Pietro's adventures, some of which are rather amusing, as also some of the incidents of our voyages and travels. But I reserve them, in the hope that we may laugh over them together at no very distant period ".

The wonder is that she should ever have permitted the world to know that he could address her in such unloverlike fashion. Moreover, such as they were, they (and all his other letters to her) were written in English, which she could not read without the help of a dictionary.[1] Now and then he would put a few words into Gamba's letters to her.[2] There is a tradition, which

[1] Mr. Prothero tells us that Morandi, a friend of Pietro Gamba, told Maxime du Camp that Byron wrote to her in English, and that she replied in Italian, " writing her answers in red ink between the lines in his letters " —an inexplicable arrangement. Pietro Gamba died in Morandi's arms in Metana, a small peninsula in the Morea, in 1827, from the effects of a chill. On his death-bed he gave Morandi a packet to deliver to Teresa ; it contained about forty letters, some in Italian, some in English, a few in French, and two or three in a mixture of all three languages. Morandi lost the packet, and it was never recovered (*L. and J.* vi. 276).

[2] The subsequent history of Teresa Guiccioli was as follows. After Byron's death, she is said to have returned to her husband's protection. Byron's immediate successor—in both senses of the word immediate— was the Hon. Henry Edward Fox, who met her first in the year of Byron's death. (*Journal of H. E. Fox.* First published in 1924.) Lord Malmesbury met her at a ball in Rome in 1829 ; " she showed " (he says) " splendid teeth when she laughed, which she was doing heartily at the time I remarked her ". He became friends with her and found her full of fun. She came to England in 1832–33. [" With Pietro Gamba " : *sic* in Mr. Prothero's note upon her in vol. iv. of *Letters and Journals*, pp. 289–94 ; but in the note quoted *ante* from vol. vi. pp. 275–76, he says that Pietro Gamba died in 1827.] There she saw and corresponded much with Lady Blessington ; among her letters is one expressing reluctance to " publish *now* any of Lord Byron's letters to me ". [She had a brother with her. Byron in 1821 spoke of the " whole Gamba family ", and enumerated only the old Count, Count Pietro, and Teresa ; in 1835 there is a letter from Lady Blessington, condoling with her on the death of this brother.] She dined with the Drurys at Harrow on one of her visits to England, and spent a day with Augusta Leigh, " speaking always of Lord Byron ". In 1851 (but the date is uncertain)* she married as her second husband

* Given in *Dict. Nat. Biog.* as above.

rests on Gamba's evidence alone and is not mentioned by those who were present, that among the broken utterances of the last hours was this in Italian : *" Io lascio qualche cosa di caro nel mondo "* (I leave something dear in the world). Gamba was not at the death-bed ; he was so overcome by emotion that he was unable to revisit the room when Byron awoke after his last sleep. " I wished to go to him ", he said, " but I had not the heart." Thus the last authentic records we have of Byron's feeling for Teresa Guiccioli are the letters from Cephalonia, and a phrase which occurs in a curious confession to Barry, his Genoese banker, in September 1823. He is writing of the possible intrigues of the Greek Government. " If these gentlemen *have* any undue interest, and discover my weak side, viz. a propensity to be governed, and were to set a pretty woman, or a clever woman, about me . . . why, they would make a fool of me. . . . But if I can keep passion, or at least that passion, out of the question (which may be the more easy, as I left my heart in Italy), they will not weather me with quite so much facility ".

In March he was offered by the Greek Government the post of Governor-General of Greece—" that is ", says Moore, " of the enfranchised part of the continent, with the exception of the Morea and the Islands ". He answered that he was first going to the Congress at Salona, and that afterwards he would be at their commands. This is the place to speak of the ambitions attributed to him in Greece. Trelawny says distinctly that if he had lived to reach the Congress of Salona, " the dispenser of a million silver crowns would have been offered a golden one ". He says too that Byron spoke of the possibility to him, during the voyage from Leghorn. The two Greek passengers —suspected of being Turkish and Russian spies—had declared that the Greeks favoured monarchical government ; and he, already summoned so urgently, already told that his name was a tower of strength, now heard that the country needed and wished

another elderly nobleman, the Marquis Hilaire de Boissy, of the new nobility of France. He was very rich, and highly eccentric. Byron's portrait hung in her salon at Paris ; and it is generally said that the Marquis always introduced her as " Madame la Marquise de Boissy, ma femme, ci-devant maîtresse de Lord Byron ". After his death in 1866 she returned to Florence ; in 1868 published her book on Byron (translated into English by Hubert Jerningham in 1869), and died in March 1873.

> " Ah, Love, what is it, in this world of ours,
> Which makes it fatal to be loved ? " . . .

Byron need not have wept, with foreboding for her fate, by the garden-fountain at Ravenna in 1819.

for a king. In Parry's book we find an anecdote which almost
definitely states that overtures had been made to him. " I
have had offers that would surprise you . . . and which would
turn the head of any man less satiated than I am ". Parry
insists that they *were* made (they could of course have had
no high validity, in the divided state of parties) and rejected.
" He never wished to possess political power in Greece " ; " he
might have been the head man of the country, had he chosen to
oppose the Government ".

Long since, in 1813, he had written in his Journal : " To
be the first man—not the Dictator—not the Sylla, but the Wash-
ington or the Aristides—the leader in talent and truth—is next
to the Divinity ! " The Greek adventure, fruitless as it proved,
placed Byron for the hour it lasted in that coveted position.
In that hour, he was brilliant, wise, and brave ; superbly generous
of gold ; genial, unselfish, compassionate. Every noble trait
in him was liberated, and showed itself as the real stuff of his
being. " His conduct seems to have come as a revelation to
his contemporaries ", says Mr. Richard Edgcumbe ; [1] but his
contemporaries, not wholly by their own fault, had all along
been blinded to the real Byron. It is easier for us to judge :
we see him whole, as it were. Brilliant always ; wise not often
hitherto in the practical affairs of life—though wise sometimes,
and eminently so in the acceptance of travellers' hardships,
as he had well shown in the earlier Greek adventure ; brave
unchangingly in all but social matters ; generous but prudent
(his avarice[2] was a mere passing whim), genial with companions
who pleased him, compassionate, he had always been. Un-
selfish ? Selfish only with women—and there were no women
at Missolonghi. With men, in later life at all events, he was
rarely anything but admirable. Everything that Byron showed
himself in Greece, he genuinely was at heart ; and there, despite
the mental and physical ravage of the days at Missolonghi, he
was for almost the first time in his maturer life doing something
that he really wanted to do. To win fame for deeds, not words,
had long been his wilful dream. " If I live ten years longer ",
he had written, " you will see that it is not over with me. I
don't mean in literature, for that is nothing, and—it may seem
odd enough to say so—I do not think it was my vocation ". If,

---

[1] *Byron, The Last Phase*, 1909.

[2] It must be recorded, in this connection, that in June 1823—after he
had engaged the *Hercules*, and knew that he should need all the money
he could come by—he refused a legacy of £2,000 left to him by Shelley.
This is attested by a letter to Leigh Hunt, dated June 28. " I state this
distinctly that—in case of anything happening to me—my heirs may be
instructed not to claim it " (Leigh Hunt, *Correspondence*, i. 203).

then, he dreamed for a moment of kingship—he would not have been Byron if he had not. To exchange a coronet for a crown, the laurels of a poet for those of a ruler ! On such an imagination such a dream must fasten ; yet on Byron's it fastened with no illusions. His ironic humour, often directed on kings, was directed no less on himself in such an office. The Dream and the Business : he was like us all, as he ever was—he saw the gulf between those two conceptions, yet dreamed on.

His spirit was superb. Not all the discouragements could damp him. Through the miserable February and March, he worked and played ; helped Parry, helped every one ; wrote countless letters, gay, brave, and wise ; even played his practical jokes on Parry and the immortal butt, Fletcher ; rode, fenced, practised with the beloved pistols, talked, read. But all the while he persisted in his suicidal abstinence—not now from fear of getting fat, but from fear of another seizure. He took meat in no form but that of weak broth, he refused to touch fish, one of the few things eatable in Missolonghi ; he lived on tea, toast, and vegetables ; and in that pestilential fever-hole, surrounded by every trouble that can attack the nerves and spirits, he dosed himself more drastically than ever with the violent medicines which had already worked havoc in his system.

Let us set forth, from Parry's quasi-diary, the tale of the last days in Greece.

February 19. Murder of the Swedish officer, Sass, by the Suliots.

February 20. Contract of the English mechanics who had come with Parry, broken, and the men sent to Zante.

February 21. Mutiny of the Suliots, and a "smart shock " of earthquake.

February 23. Mutiny of German officers ; trouble in the Ionian Islands about Stanhope's newspaper, and its circulation stopped at Zante.

Then about the middle of March came the plague-scare —luckily unfounded ; then urgent appeals from the Peloponnesus, and from Kolokotronis, to join the parties there ; while at Missolonghi suspicions of Mavrocordato arose among the Englishmen, who sought to colour Byron's mind with the same mistrust. At the end of the month he was informed of a plot to seize and confine his own person, and murder Mavrocordato. At the same time came the formal invitation from Odysseus to the Congress at Salona. He and Mavrocordato arranged to go ; but then arrived news of the appearance of the Turkish fleet before Missolonghi, and they resolved to remain. Next, applications were made to Byron for money to the amount of 50,000 dollars in one day. " The Greeks seemed to think he

28

was a mine from which they could extract gold at their pleasure ".

At length, on April 9 came the first good news he had had since his arrival. The Greek Loan had been floated. " I may almost say that this revived for a moment a spirit that was already faint and weary, and slumbering in the arms of death ". He rode out, and was caught in heavy rain. When he came back he complained of pain and fever, and Bruno proposed to bleed him. He refused to permit it, and Parry was of the same mind. " I was convinced that to bleed him would be to kill him ". Next day he rode again—the last ride of his life.

On the 11th he was very ill. " He talked a great deal . . . in rather a wandering manner ". Parry became alarmed for his safety, and earnestly begged him to go immediately to Zante for change of air and scene. He unwillingly consented, and vessels were prepared for his conveyance. But the 12th had to be spent in bed. On the 13th all was ready for departure ; but the pestilent sirocco wind began to blow ; torrents of rain fell, the region was flooded, and " Missolonghi became a complete prison. . . . It seemed as if the elements had combined with man to ensure Lord Byron's death ".

Hitherto he had got up during the day ; but after going to bed on April 14, he came out no more. He clung pathetically to Parry—but Parry (called artificer ; in reality man-of-all-work) was obliged to be much away from him. So early as this 14th of April, he was occasionally half-delirious. " I . . . deny ", writes Parry, " that the delirium arose from inflammation ; it was that alienation of the mind which is so frequently the consequence of excessive debility ". On the 15th he was alarmingly ill, but the doctors (Millingen had now been called in) declared that there was no danger. Parry was convinced that there *was*, and that Byron knew it. " He spoke of death with great composure, and, though he did not believe that his end was so very near, there was something about him so serious and so firm, so resigned and composed, so different from anything I had ever before seen in him, that my mind misgave me ". But Byron still had hopes of recovery, " and of retirement in England with my wife and Ada. [It] gives me an idea of happiness I have never experienced before ". Then, speaking of those immediately around him, he begged Parry to be with him as much as possible. " You may prevent me from being jaded to death ".

Outside, the dread sirocco was blowing, and rain was falling with tropical violence. Inside . . . but our hearts contract to a present impulse of sorrow and of anger as we seek to realise that interior. Let Parry's striking words depict it : " Lord Byron's apartment was such a picture of distress, and even anguish, during the last two or three days of his life, as I never before beheld, and wish never again to witness ". The incompetence of Bruno, the lack of self-control displayed both by him and Millingen—Bruno so much agitated that he became incapable of using whatever knowledge he might possess ; Millingen unable to restrain his tears, and therefore walking out of the room ; nobody invested with any authority, neither method, nor order, nor quiet ; no comforts, few necessaries ; and, above all, the ghastly confusion of tongues ! Bruno's English, in his agitation, unintelligible ; Fletcher's Italian equally bad ; Parry speaking nothing but English, Tita nothing but Italian, and the lower Greek servants incomprehensible to all. . . . The imagination turns in torment from the scene.

On the 16th he was almost constantly delirious. The doctors now began again the old quarrel about bleeding. Yesterday Byron had angrily refused ; to-day Millingen spoke out. Unless he would consent, neither of the doctors would answer for the consequences ; and not only life was in question. His life might persist, but his reason too was endangered. Millingen adds : " I had now touched the sensible chord, for, partly annoyed by our unceasing importunities, and partly convinced, casting at us both the fiercest glance of vexation, he threw out his arm, and said in the most angry tone : ' Come ; you are, I see, a d——d set of butchers. Take away as much blood as you will, but have done with it ".

On the 17th he was much worse, but notwithstanding was again bled twice, and both times fainted. Parry and Fletcher had the strongest doubts that the doctors understood the nature of the disease. Three days before, Fletcher had begged to be allowed to send to Zante for Dr. Thomas ; but Byron had refused, though he repeatedly said that he was sure the doctors did not know what was the matter with him.[1] On the 18th he at last consented to send for Dr. Thomas ; and on Fletcher's informing Messrs. Bruno and Millingen of this, " they said it was very right, as they now began to be afraid themselves ". Gamba saw Byron at noon on that day, when he actually did some business—translating a French letter into English without hesitation, and, though with more difficulty, making out some passages in Modern Greek. This was Easter Sunday. About four o'clock, there stood round his bed Tita,[2] Fletcher, and

---

[1] Fletcher's account of Byron's last moments is reprinted (from the *Westminster Review* for July 1824) in Medwin's Conversations, 1824. He brought his master's body to England ; visited Lady Byron, as we have seen, and was witness of her overwhelming emotion.

[2] After Byron's death, Tita was appointed to command a regiment of Albanians. In 1830–31 he travelled with Benjamin Disraeli in Greece, Turkey, and Egypt ; came to England in 1832, and became house-steward to Isaac Disraeli, remaining till his master's death in 1848. Benjamin

Millingen—all weeping. " Oh ! this is a fine scene ! " he exclaimed, in Italian. Directly afterwards he became delirious, crying, " as if he were mounting a breach in an assault . . . half in English, half in Italian : ' Forwards—forwards—follow my example—don't be afraid ! ' " When he came to himself Fletcher was with him. He began to talk of doing something for his servants ; but Fletcher cried, " For God's sake, my lord, never mind that now ; talk of something of more importance ". He answered : " It is now nearly over. I must tell you all without losing a moment ". Fletcher begged that he might be allowed to fetch pen and paper. " Oh, my God ! no ; you will lose too much time—mind you execute my orders ". He then continued, " Oh, my poor dear child—my poor Ada ! My God ! could I but have seen her. Give her my blessing—and my dear sister Augusta, and her children ; and you will go to Lady Byron, and say—Tell her everything ; you are friends with her."

Here his voice failed him, so that Fletcher could only catch a word at intervals ; but he continued muttering something very earnestly " for nearly twenty minutes, and would often raise his voice and say, ' Fletcher, if you do not execute every order which I have given you, I will torment you hereafter if possible ' ".[1] The valet could only distinguish a word here and there : " Augusta ", " Ada ", " Hobhouse ", " Kinnaird ". Byron then said, " Now I have told you all ".

" Here I told his lordship, in a state of the greatest perplexity, that I had not understood a word of what he said ; to which he replied, ' Oh, my God ! then all is lost, for it is now too late. Can it be possible you have not understood me ? ' ' No, my lord ', said I ; ' but I pray you try and inform me once more ' ". He then made several efforts to speak, but could only say two or three words at a time, such as " My wife—my child—my sister ! You must say all, you know my wishes "— The rest was unintelligible.

Two more doctors—one a German, to add to the confusion of tongues—had been called in ; yet when Parry returned, he found Byron in great pain, " gnashing his teeth, and saying *Ah, Christi* ! " The bandage round his head was causing this ;

Disraeli asked Hobhouse, then a member of the Government, for a messengership for Byron's old servant. Tita was by Hobhouse's influence appointed a messenger to the Board of Control. This Board was four years later abolished, and Tita, at Disraeli's request (the Conservatives were then in power), was made chief messenger at the India Office. He died in 1874, aged 76, and his widow received a pension from Lord Beaconsfield. Tita figures in *Contarini Fleming*.

[1] Galt says of this : " It cannot be questioned that the threat was the last feeble flash of his prankfulness " (p. 316).

Parry loosened it, and this simple device brought instant relief. After it was loosened, he shed tears. Parry, with a tenderness which even now dims our eyes, said : " My lord, I thank God. I hope you will be better now. Shed as many tears as you can ; you will then sleep and find ease ". He sighed faintly, took Parry's hand, " uttered a faint Good-night, and sank into a slumber ".

They thought he would awake no more ; but he did awake at half-past five on this Sunday afternoon. He tried to utter his wishes, but he was incapable ; there came only a few incoherent words. His eyes soon closed again ; he murmured, " I must sleep now ". Life did not leave him until six o'clock in the evening of April 19, 1824 (Easter Monday), when " he opened his eyes once, and then closed them "—for ever.[1]

So Byron died. In Parry's stern arraignment : " He was worried, and starved, to death ". " But though in my opinion ", Parry continues, " the primary cause of Lord Byron's death was the serious disappointment he suffered, I must not be understood to say that no art could have saved him. . . . He cannot now be recalled ; anger would only disturb his ashes ; but in proportion as we loved and valued him, must we be displeased at those whose conduct hastened his dissolution ".

The words were written in 1825 ; they echo in our hearts to-day. A thousand times we read the story of that room of anguish ; a thousand times utter the same outraged groan. But " he cannot now be recalled ". It happened thus, and we must bear it.

On the day of his death, Mavrocordato issued a proclamation to the Provisional Government of Greece, and decreed that seven-and-thirty funeral shots should be fired from the grand battery, " to-morrow morning, at daylight " ; that all the public offices, even the tribunals, should be closed for three days ; that shops should be shut, all Easter festivities suspended, and a general mourning observed for twenty-one days. Prayers and a funeral service were to be offered up in all churches. Similar honours were paid to his memory at many other places in Greece, notably at Salona, where the Congress he was to have attended had assembled. Stanhope, from Salona, wrote to John Bowring :

---

[1] " At the very moment he died there was," says Parry, " one of the most awful thunderstorms I ever witnessed ". The Greeks immediately cried (waiting for news as the whole town was) : " The great man is dead ! "

In 1910, Sir William Osler gave to Mr. Leonard Mackall of Savannah, Ga., U.S.A., his decided opinion that Byron's illness was meningitis, and that his life could not by any possible means have been saved. This information appeared for the first time in print in a letter from Mr. Mackall to the *Times Literary Supplement* of April 24, 1924.

" England has lost her brightest genius—Greece her noblest friend. . . . Had I the disposal of his ashes, I would place them in the Temple of Theseus, or in the Parthenon at Athens ". Byron himself, writing to Lord Blessington in April 1823, had said : " I should prefer a grey Greek stone over me to Westminster Abbey " ; but Parry had his last word on the subject. " If I die in Greece, and you survive me ", he had several times said, " do you see that my body be sent to England ". We have read long since how he wrote to Murray : *I would not even feed your worms.* Is this inconsistency ? No : but the very expression of him, all anger with and love for England as he was. Men feel two things at once, *are* two things at once, with every day that dawns—and Byron was (it cannot be too often repeated) the quintessence of humanity.

On April 22, deferred thus long by the continuous rain, a funeral ceremony took place at Missolonghi. His body had been embalmed. The coffin, says Gamba, " was a rude chest of wood ; a black mantle served for a pall, and over it we placed a helmet and a sword, and a crown of laurel. But no funeral pomp could have left the impression, nor spoken the feelings, of this simple ceremony. The wretchedness and desolation of the place itself ; the wild and half-civilised warriors around us ; their deep-felt, unaffected grief ; the fond recollections ; the disappointed hopes ; the anxieties and sad presentiments which might be read on every countenance ;—all contributed to form a scene more moving, more truly affecting, than perhaps was ever before witnessed round the grave of a great man.

" When the funeral service was over, we left the bier in the middle of the church, where it remained until the evening of the next day, and was guarded by a detachment of his own brigade. The church was crowded without cessation by those who came to honour and to regret the benefactor of Greece. In the evening of the 23rd the bier was privately carried back by his officers to his own house. The coffin was not closed till the 29th of the month. Immediately after his death, his countenance had an air of calmness, mingled with a severity that seemed gradually to soften ; for when I took a last look of him, the expression, at least to my eyes, was truly sublime ".

Parry, at last broken down after his manifold exertions, had been obliged to leave Missolonghi on April 21, and was now lying in hospital at Zante. Trelawny arrived four days after Byron's death from the Congress at Salona, which he had left on the 17th, carrying with him a letter from Stanhope to Byron : " Once more I implore you to quit Missolonghi, and not to sacrifice your health, and perhaps your life, in that bog ". . . . There, in that bog, Trelawny heard the tidings of April 19.

Fletcher at once led him up the stairs into a narrow room,
" with nothing in it but a coffin standing on trestles. No word
was spoken by either of us ; he withdrew the black pall and the
white shroud, and there lay the embalmed body of the Pilgrim
—more beautiful in death than in life. . . . Few marble busts
could have matched its stainless white, the harmony of its
proportions, and perfect finish. Yet he had been dissatisfied
with that body. . . . How often had I heard him curse it ! . . .
Where had he seen the face or form worthy to excite his envy ? "
But after the first look, sending Fletcher for a glass of water,
Trelawny fell from his estate as a gentleman. He turned back
the sheet, and uncovered Byron's feet. " I was answered—the
great mystery was solved. Both his feet were clubbed, and his
legs withered to the knee ".

It is not even true.[1]   Let us put this away, as one of the least
admirable things we know of any man—put it away as the poor
valet did, when returning, " without making any remark, he
drew the shroud carefully over the feet of his master's corpse ".[2]

---

[1] The quotation is from the *Recollections*, published in 1858. In the
Records of twenty years later (an enlarged form of the earlier work) the
description of the feet is different. " I uncovered the Pilgrim's feet, and
was answered—it was caused by the contraction of the back sinews . . .
that prevented his heels from resting on the ground. . . . Except this
defect, his feet were perfect ".

Mr. Richard Edgcumbe stated, in an article in *Temple Bar* of May 1890,
that the second account of Byron's form of lameness was supplied to
Trelawny by him (Mr. Edgcumbe). This information is given by Professor
Dowden in his Introduction to the edition of the *Recollections* published by
Henry Frowde in 1906. But see Trelawny's *Letters*, pp. 265-7.

[2] Trelawny wrote of Byron on April 28 to Stanhope :
" With all his faults, I loved him truly ; he is connected with every
event of the most interesting years of my wandering life. His everyday
companion, we lived in ships, boats, and in houses, together ; we had no
secrets, no reserve, and though we often differed in opinion, we never
quarrelled. If it gave me pain witnessing his frailties, he only wanted a
little excitement to awaken and put forth *virtues* that redeemed them all.
. . . This is no private grief ; the world has lost its greatest man, I my best
friend ".

The same day he wrote again to Stanhope :
" I think Byron's name was the great means of getting the loan. A
Mr. Marshall with £8,000 per annum was as far as Corfu, and turned back
on hearing of Byron's death ". And on April 29 : " The greatest man in
the world has resigned his mortality in favour of this sublime cause ; for
had he remained in Italy he had lived ! "

Four months later (when Trelawny was prisoner in a cave on Mount
Parnassus, and his friend Odysseus was persecuted by a Government
which they both thought to be inspired by Mavrocordato), the Cornishman
wrote thus to Mary Shelley, who had known and liked Mavrocordato at
Pisa : " [Byron] took part with, and became the paltry tool of, the weak,
imbecile, cowardly being calling himself Prince Mavrocordato. Five
months he [Byron] dozed away. By the gods ! the lies that are said in his

On April 24 Blaquiere arrived at Zante in the *Florida*, bringing the first instalment of the long-looked-for Greek Loan. Byron's body was embarked for Zante on May 2, under a mournful salute from the guns of Missolonghi. There it was finally decided to send it to England in the *Florida*, by which ship Stanhope (recalled to England by the military authorities) was sailing. The coffin was embarked at Zante on May 25 ; the *Florida* reached England on June 29. Stanhope at once addressed a letter to Byron's executors—Hobhouse and John Hanson. It contained the following passage :

" With respect to the funeral ceremony, I am of opinion that his Lordship's family should be immediately consulted, and that sanction should be obtained for the public burial of his body either in the great Abbey or Cathedral of London ".

I now turn to Hobhouse's statement, first printed in the *Edinburgh Review* for April 1871.

" On Thursday, July 1, I heard that the *Florida* had arrived in the Downs, and I went the same evening to Rochester. The next morning I went on board the vessel. There I found Colonel Leicester Stanhope, Dr. Bruno, and Fletcher, Byron's valet, with three others of his servants. Three dogs that had belonged to my friend were playing about the deck. I could hardly bring myself to look at them. We beat up the river to Gravesend. I cannot describe what I felt during the five or six hours of our passage. I was the last person who shook hands with Byron when he left England in 1816. I recollected his waving his cap to me as the packet bounded off on a curling wave from the

praise urge one to speak the truth. It is well for his name, and better for Greece, that he is dead. . . . I now feel my face burn with shame that so weak and ignoble a soul could so long have influenced me. It is a degrading reflection, and ever will be ". Trelawny was violently irritated at the moment, as he confesses later in the letter ; and, like all the Pisan circle, he was extreme in his expressions of anger. Byron had never joined the faction of Mavrocordato, or any other faction ; Trelawny had made the mistake of joining that of Odysseus. In the books published by him—the *Recollections*, which is the earlier, did not appear until thirty-four years after Byron's death (1858)—he wrote of the Pilgrim in the strain of his letters to Stanhope in April 1824.

Trelawny died in his 89th year at Sompting, on August 13, 1881. His body was cremated, and the ashes laid in a grave beside Shelley's at Rome. He is the old sailor in Millais' picture of The North-West Passage (Tate Gallery). " In the ashen colour of the face, the rough grey hair and beard, the hard, clear, aquiline profile, and the strong, masterful, searching grey eye, there was something both more distinguished and more formidable than is seen [in the likeness of the picture]—a likeness with which he himself was much dissatisfied " (" A Reminiscence of Trelawny ", *Pall Mall Gazette*, August 19, 1881).

Mary Shelley, in the Pisan days, had called him " a superb, half-Arab Englishman ".

pier-head at Dover, and here I was now coming back to England with his corpse.

. . . .

" On the following Monday I went to Doctors' Commons and proved Byron's will. Mr. Hanson did so likewise. Thence I went to . . London Docks Buoy, where the *Florida* was anchored. . . . After the removal of the corpse into the coffin, I accompanied the undertaker in the barge with the coffin. There were many boats round the ship at the time, and the shore was crowded with spectators. We passed quietly up the river, and landed at Palace Yard stairs. Thence the coffin and the small chest containing the heart were carried to the house in George Street,[1] and deposited in the room prepared for their reception. The room was decently hung with black, but there was no other decoration than an escutcheon of the Byron arms, roughly daubed on a deal board.

" On reaching my rooms at the Albany, I found a note from Mr. Murray, telling me that he had received a letter from Dr. Ireland, politely declining to allow the burial of Byron in Westminster Abbey ; but it was not until the next day that, to my great surprise, I learnt, on reading the doctor's note, that Mr. Murray had made the request to the Dean in my name. I thought that it had been settled that Mr. Gifford should sound the Dean of Westminster previously to any formal request being made. I wrote to Mr. Murray, asking him to inform the Dean that I had not made the request. Whether he did so, I never inquired ".[2] Later, Hobhouse learnt from Augusta that it was wished that the burial should be in the family vault at Hucknall Torkard.

The eagerness shown to get sight of anything connected with Byron was remarkable. General Lafayette sent a note requesting a sight of the dead poet for a young Frenchman who came over from Havre. The coffin had been closed, and the prayer had to be refused. Another young man " in very moving terms " made the same petition ; Hobhouse gave him a piece of the cotton in which the body had been wrapped. " He took it with much devotion, and placed it in his pocket-book ". Phillips the Academician, who had often painted Byron, applied for

---

[1] The house of Sir Edward Knatchbull-Hugessen, in Great George Street, Westminster.

[2] Jeaffreson well sums up this vexed question, saying that so long as the Deans of Westminster are required to decide on the award of the honour of burial in the Abbey, it will be unjust to accuse them of dull prejudice because their decisions are made with reference to matters which they are bound by their very office to think of paramount importance. " Byron's writings had not been uniformly favourable to religion and morality ". There was as much intolerance (he says) in the Byronic enthusiasts as in the Dean, by them accused of bigotry.

permission to take a likeness; but the features had been so disfigured by the means used to preserve the remains that Augusta, when she saw them (Hobhouse writes confusingly here), scarcely recognised them. Hobhouse says: " This was the fact : for I had summoned courage to look at my dead friend. So completely was he altered that the sight did not affect me so much as looking at his handwriting, or anything that I knew had belonged to him ".

The body lay in state during Friday and Saturday, July 9 and 10 ; on the following Monday the funeral procession took place. It left Westminster at 11 a.m. Passing up Highgate Hill, on the way to Nottingham, it passed a modest house in the windows of which stood Jane Williams and Mary Shelley. Outside the gate of Brocket Park came that unbelievable meeting with Caroline Lamb—the meeting which has made her story immortal. If Byron could have known of it, what a wonder it would have made for his imagination !

In the afternoon of July 16—a Friday—he was laid in the family vault in the village church of Hucknall Torkard.[1] On a white marble tablet in the chancel is this inscription :

IN THE VAULT BENEATH,
WHERE MANY OF HIS ANCESTORS AND HIS MOTHER ARE
BURIED,
LIE THE REMAINS OF
GEORGE GORDON NOEL BYRON,
LORD BYRON, OF ROCHDALE,
IN THE COUNTY OF LANCASTER,
THE AUTHOR OF " CHILDE HAROLD'S PILGRIMAGE."
HE WAS BORN IN LONDON ON THE
22ND OF JANUARY 1788.
HE DIED AT MISSOLONGI, IN WESTERN GREECE, ON THE
19TH OF APRIL 1824,
ENGAGED IN THE GLORIOUS ATTEMPT TO RESTORE THAT
COUNTRY TO HER ANCIENT FREEDOM AND RENOWN.

———

HIS SISTER, THE HONOURABLE
AUGUSTA MARIA [2] LEIGH,
PLACED THIS TABLET TO HIS MEMORY.

Thus, even in death half-betrayed by one who loved him and whom he loved, the author of *Don Juan* rests—beside the mother who tortured his childhood, and the daughter who never knew him. Lady Byron was asked if she had any wishes with regard

———

[1] Hobhouse said that the church was so crowded that it was difficult to follow the coffin up the aisle. It was still as full up to a late hour in the evening, so that the vault was not closed until next morning.

[2] So in Moore ; but the actual inscription has Mary, not Maria. The mis-spelling of Missolonghi is also in Moore.

to the funeral. Her answer was that "it might be left to Mr. Hobhouse". No message from her came to the grave at Hucknall Torkard—but what message could have come ?

*   *   *   *

Byron's tragedy resided in being so like, yet so much more than, the rest of us. It was almost impossible, we may say in defence of his world, for his world to understand him. Living in the blaze of his personality, they confused the aspects he presented to them ; they thought him more than themselves when he was not more, and less when he was. Idolised when he was merely finding himself, he was persecuted when he *had* found himself. He suffered apotheosis when, except for the accident of genius, he was like the rest ; he suffered outlawry when, except for the accident of publicity added to that of genius, he was like them still ; and when the outlawry had done its work, and he was *not* like them, but much more than they, and showed them to themselves in that great World-Poem,[1] his ironic *apologia pro vita sua*, which stands in our literature beside the works of Shakespere and of Milton . . . why then, more vehemently than man was ever told before, they told him that he was less. Glory and shame hung over him from the first, and descended upon him at the last. Only thirty-six ! " He could never have lived to be old ", they tell us—and that is true, but in a deeper sense than the surface one. To whatever age he had lived, he would not have been old. Weary and *ennuyé* as he thought himself, discouraged and worn as he was, Byron was the imperishable youth. Always something fresh sprang forth from him, always the spirit renewed its strength. When he died at Missolonghi, there began for him an immortality quite different from that which hitherto had seemed the obvious one. " I do not mean in literature, for that is nothing, and I do not think it was my vocation ". His vocation was greater than either of these, may we say ? It was to be the most splendid example we have of the struggling, winning and losing, enjoying and scorning, aspiring and falling, loving and hating, human spirit.

" *Es irrt der Mensch,*
  So lang er strebt ". . . .

---

[1] Dr. Brandès, the Danish critic, justly says that *Don Juan* is the only work of the nineteenth century which bears comparison with Goethe's *Faust*. Swinburne wrote of it : " Across the stanzas . . . we swim forward as over the ' broad backs of the sea ' ; they break and glitter, hiss and laugh, murmur and move like waves that sound or that subside. . . . There is about them a wide wholesome air, full of vivid light and constant wind, which is only felt at sea. Life undulates and death palpitates in the splendid verse. . . . This gift of life and variety is the supreme quality of Byron's chief poem ".

No other human being has incarnated that saying as Byron has.

The poet who was to be his only rival in wide popularity during life in the whole poetical history of England—Alfred Tennyson—was, at the time of Byron's death, a boy of fourteen. He heard the tidings from Missolonghi, and fled from his father's house to a favourite solitude. There, with head in hands and heart oppressed with sense of loss, he found himself over and over again repeating inwardly : " Byron is dead—Byron ". . . . What is it that makes in us, even now, as passionate and as present a sorrow, when we read of those last hours ? Other poets' deaths have been, in reality, sadder—Keats's death, Shelley's death. To them the world had given little, to him nearly all of what it has to give; yet neither wakes in us that quick emotion. Is it his fame, his beauty, his heroism, his youth ? None of these. It is his enthralling humanity. We are mourning for ourselves.

APPENDICES

APPENDIX I

MRS. BEECHER STOWE

IN 1856 Mrs. Harriet Beecher Stowe, still in the blaze of her fame as the author of *Uncle Tom's Cabin*, which had been published in 1850), visited England for the second time. She had already, during her first visit in 1853, made Lady Byron's acquaintance, and they had had some conversation and correspondence ; now in 1856 Lady Byron, who was ill and believed herself to be dying, requested Mrs. Stowe to give her a private interview on a subject of great importance. (She was then living on Ham Common, near Richmond.) A cheap edition of Byron's works was in view ; and Lady Byron, fearful of the wider circulation of his writings, doubted whether she " had not a responsibility to society for the truth ". It was on this point that she consulted Mrs. Stowe, for whom she had great affection and admiration. She wished to learn from an unprejudiced person what her duty appeared to be. Ought she to declare, at last, the truth ? (Augusta Leigh and Ada, Countess of Lovelace, were both at this time dead.) Lady Byron in this interview imparted to Mrs. Stowe the secret of Byron's relations with his half-sister. She gave Mrs. Stowe " a brief memorandum of the whole, with the dates affixed " ; and Mrs. Stowe, after two or three days' consideration, decided that " Lady Byron would be entirely justifiable in leaving the truth to be disclosed after her death, and recommended that all the facts necessary should be put in the hands of some person, to be so published ".

We have seen in Chapter XVI that in 1850 (six years previously) Lady Byron had done this, and had mentioned 1880 as the earliest possible date for " a discretionary disclosure ". She now acquiesced in Mrs. Stowe's opinion, but made no sort of mention of regarding Mrs. Stowe as the person empowered to make the disclosure. She did not die until 1860, and her will then contained the same provision as the document of 1850.

In 1869 there appeared in England the translation of the Countess Guiccioli's book about Byron, which was reviewed very favourably in *Blackwood's* for July 1869. The book contained nothing that the world did not already know ; but Mrs. Stowe cited it—and it alone —as her reason for the action which she now immediately took. She published in *Macmillan's* for September 1869, and simultaneously in

The Atlantic Monthly (an American magazine), an article entitled " The True Story of Lady Byron's Life ", in which she disclosed to the world what Lady Byron had told her in 1856.

The article brought down a storm of abuse upon Lady Byron's memory, notably in *Blackwood's*, to a less degree in the *Quarterly* ; and Mrs. Stowe then wrote her *History of the Byron Controversy*, published in 1870 by Sampson Low. In this book, which contained as an Appendix the original Macmillan article, the author gave as her reason for breaking silence in September 1869, the article in *Blackwood's* for July, reviewing the Guiccioli volumes. This article had not once been alluded to in Mrs. Stowe's first piece ; and the author of *A Vindication of Lady Byron* (Bentley, 1870) proves by the chronology of the two articles that Mrs. Stowe could have had no thought of *Blackwood's* when she wrote for *Macmillan's*. Yet she now declared that it was the *Blackwood's* " frantic slanders " (in the Guiccioli article) on Lady Byron, remaining unrefuted by Lady Byron's relatives, which had driven her—Mrs. Stowe—into print. She had not given those relations " one little day, not an hour ", in which to refute those slanders!

Writing thus a book to defend the publication of an article, Mrs. Stowe did Lady Byron's memory more injury than all the enemies had done it. Her story is related with such carelessness as amounts to disingenuousness ; she weaves together in one narrative (for her book) Lady Byron's own statement, and things before and since heard from others, or read, or conjectured—the result being a maze of contradictions, vague inferences, and false premisses. She may almost be said to have constructed a new story. To give one instance :— In the book Lady Byron is made to say that the incest was the cause of separation ; in the earlier article, she had not been made to say any such thing.

It may be observed that the author of *A Vindication of Lady Byron* takes the attitude with respect to the incest charge which most contemporary writers took : viz. that it was true, but that it was not the reason given to Dr. Lushington which caused him to declare that a reconciliation was impossible. That reason (it is clearly to be read between the lines) was, by the author of those papers and by many others, believed to be the offence apparently indicated in Campbell's unhappy article of 1830 in defence of Lady Byron. Apropos this point, there is in *Notes and Queries* for June 15 1867 (Third Series), an allusion to a suppressed poem by Byron, entitled *Don Leon*, which was bound up with an *Epistle from Lord Byron to Lady Byron*. (A copy now in the possession of Mr. T. J. Wise bears the date 1866 for *Don Leon*, and 1865 for the *Epistle*.) This was advertised in " several penny papers " (reputable newspapers at that time cost always more than a penny), and then suddenly withdrawn. " A friend " wrote to one S. Jackson (who asked in *N. & Q.* if the poem were authentic) that " it was owing to some interference of the Byron family that the poem had been burked ". . . . This is one of the *brochures* to which I refer in the opening paragraph of Chapter XVI. I do not for a moment believe it to be genuine ; but it has the interest

of showing the forms which rumour had taken.   It was in reviewing
Mrs. Beecher Stowe's article that the *Blackwood's* writer made the
infamous parallel between Lady Byron and " the lowest prostitute
that ever haunted the night-houses of the Haymarket ".   (See
Chapter XVI.)   This was in reference to the forbearance she had
shown to Mrs. Leigh.

Astarte has since borne out the story told by Mrs. Beecher Stowe,
but the two great errors committed by her remain.   She told her tale
without warrant, and she told it disingenuously.

Penny books, displaying a portrait on the cover of " Lord Byron's
half-sister, Augusta ", were hawked in the streets of London in 1869.
The portrait had already, on similar productions, done duty as Manon
Lescaut, Lola Montès, and Madeline Smith.

APPENDIX II

THE MEMOIRS

IN 1819–21 Byron wrote these Memoirs. They related particularly to his life in London after the publication of *Childe Harold* in 1812, and to his marriage and separation. He gave the first portion to Moore in October 1819 at La Mira, Venice, and continually added to the MS. during 1820-21. He authorised Moore to show the papers to " the Elect " ; and Moore did show them to many persons, both in Paris and at home. Byron wrote from Ravenna in December 1820 that if Moore could "make anything of them *now* in the way of *reversion* . . . I should be very glad ". They were absolutely Moore's property, by Byron's own desire. When Moore fell into pecuniary difficulties in 1821, an arrangement was made at Byron's suggestion whereby Murray bought from Moore these Memoirs for the sum of two thousand guineas, binding himself not to publish until after Byron's death. Moore, who had employed a person to copy them, gave Murray the copy as well as the original MS. when this agreement was made in November 1821. There was a stipulation that Moore should edit these papers, *and* supply an account of subsequent events in Byron's life as well ; so that the two thousand guineas paid by Murray was really, as Murray afterwards said, " a simple loan ". This agreement gave neither Byron nor Moore any powers of redemption.

Before long, Byron began to vacillate ; and when Lady Noel died in January 1822, and he had hopes of a reconciliation with his wife, he felt that he should like to be in a position to redeem the Memoirs from Murray. He had already, in January 1820, offered the perusal of the MS. to Lady Byron, and she had (in March) very decisively refused it. (See Chapter XVI.) The upshot of Byron's desire for a different position with regard to the MS. was that Murray consented to execute, and did execute on May 6, 1822, a deed giving Byron and Moore, or either of them, the power of redeeming the MS. *during Byron's life.*

In March 1824 Murray for the first time obtained possession of the original agreement of 1821 from Douglas Kinnaird. Kinnaird had thought the transaction an odd one, and had detained the paper until he should receive from Lord Byron positive orders as to whom he wished it to be delivered to. This ambiguous conduct had made Murray anxious to know where he stood ; and on obtaining the original agreement, he at once requested Moore either to exercise the power of redemption accorded by the second paper of 1822, or to cancel that paper. Moore declared that both he and Byron wished to redeem the MS., and that, by insuring his life, he intended to procure the sum necessary for doing so. He promised to come to town in a few days, and take all the necessary steps. He came to town, but he took none of the necessary steps ; he did not even call on Murray ; and before anything was done, there arrived on May 14, 1824, the news of Byron's death.

By that event, the MS. of the Memoirs became the absolute property of Murray ; for the deed of 1822 empowered Moore to redeem them *only during Byron's life.*

In the *Temple Bar* articles of 1869–70,[1] there is a long attack upon Mocre's conduct with reference to the news of Byron's death. No sooner had he heard than he hastened to Murray's (his own diary is the authority for his movements) and, failing to see the publisher, left a note urging him to " complete the arrangement agreed upon while I was last in town ". The *Temple Bar* writer continues : " Then he rushed up and down to Rogers, Kinnaird, Brougham, Hobhouse, Wilmot Horton, etc., striving to persuade them all that Murray ought to return the Memoirs to him ".

Meanwhile, Hobhouse was already in consultation with Sir Francis Burdett as to the best means of preventing the Memoirs from being published, for Hobhouse had from the first considered them foolish documents. On the same day that Hobhouse got the news from Missolonghi (May 14, 1824) Augusta Leigh also got it; and also on that day Captain George Byron (then seventh Lord) went down to Beckenham in Kent to inform Lady Byron.[2] Hobhouse, calling on Augusta that day, urged upon her the importance of this question of the Memoirs. On Saturday, May 15, he called again and told her that he had seen Moore, and that Moore had resolved to place the Memoirs at her disposal. Murray had already volunteered to do this. There was some uncertainty in everybody's mind as to the actual property in the Memoirs. Moore believed that he still retained some right in them ; he declared that he would deliver the MS. to Mrs. Leigh with his own hands ; " he would have the grace of this sacrifice himself ". But the Memoirs were now, in reality, Murray's absolute property.

It was proposed that Moore should meet Murray—Hobhouse and Wilmot Horton to be also present—at Augusta's house, and in her presence repay the two thousand guineas, receive the MS., and hand it over to her to be absolutely at her disposal. She, who had never read a word of the Memoirs, had by this time been convinced by Hobhouse that the right way to dispose of them was to burn them. He had been urgent on that from the first. All this was arranged between Friday and Saturday, May 14 and 15.

[1] Collected under the title *A Vindication of Lady Byron* (Bentley, 1870).
[2] Captain Byron told Hobhouse and Augusta that Lady Byron was in a distressing state. " She said she had no right to be considered, but she had her feelings, and would wish to see any accounts that had come of his last moments ". Hobhouse sent her his letters relating to the death by Captain Byron.

On Sunday, May 16, Moore and Kinnaird called on Hobhouse.
Moore announcing that he had obtained the two thousand guineas.
(He had got the sum from Messrs. Longmans.) On that day he for the
first time intimated to Hobhouse his dislike to burning the Memoirs ; he
said that he would not be present at the destruction. Next day there
came from him a letter, saying that his friends, who were Mr. Luttrell,
Samuel Rogers, and Lord Lansdowne, had suggested a modification.
The Memoirs were to be redeemed by him, and he was to peruse them
and make extracts for publication. Wilmot Horton later suggested
another compromise : they should be sealed and sent to the bank, so
that at some future time they might be discreetly edited.[1] Hobhouse
repudiated firmly both these plans, and Murray ultimately joined with
him in protesting that the MS. should at once be burned. *All* were still
under the impression that Moore still retained some property in them.

There was a heated discussion in Murray's room at Albemarle
Street, where all the parties, except Augusta, assembled on the Monday,
May 17. Colonel Doyle, representing Lady Byron, was also present.[2]
Every one but Moore acquiesced in the destruction of the MS. ; and
Wilmot Horton declared that they need not adjourn to Augusta's
house, for she had given him her authority to see it burned. Moore
protested against the burning, " as contrary to Lord Byron's wishes,
and unjust to himself ".

By this time the agreement of 1821 and the deed of 1822 had
been collated, and the MS. was at last perceived to be *Murray's
property alone.* Colonel Doyle and Mr. Horton then tore up the
MS. and Moore's copy of it, and put them both on the fire. Moore
then placed the two thousand guineas on the table. Murray refused
to take the money, saying that he had destroyed not Mr. Moore's
property but his own : " he would take no money for that ". Moore
insisted. Murray then consented to take the money ; but, retaining
Hobhouse after the others had left, urged upon him the propriety
of Lord Byron's family reimbursing Moore. Hobhouse, Horton,

---

[1] Lord Lovelace thought this the course that should have been taken.

[2] Though Colonel Doyle had been requested by Lady Byron to act for
her, if necessary, in the matter, his presence at this meeting was accidental ;
Wilmot Horton had called upon him and asked him to go. Moore had told
Colonel Doyle that he [Moore], in delivering the MS. to " Lord Byron's
family ", must be understood not to mean Lady Byron, or to include her.
At this meeting, the point in debate was what Mrs. Leigh might be disposed
to do with the MS. The question of its destruction had not been discussed
between, or even thought of by, Lady Byron and Colonel Doyle ; *their*
debate had been as to whether the MS. should be suppressed—or partially
published. " Lady Byron ", says Colonel Doyle in a letter to Wilmot
Horton of May 18, 1825, " certainly gave no consent to the destruction of
the manuscript, either directly or indirectly ". At this meeting, Colonel
Doyle, finding an entirely new point under discussion, " regarded himself "
(when the MS. *was* destroyed) " only as a witness, and not as a party to the
proceeding " (*Astarte*, App. A, pp. 327–8).
It will be noticed that in Hobhouse's narrative, from which my text
derives, Colonel Doyle is said to have been one of those who actually put
the MS. on the fire.

Luttrell, and Doyle all agreed with Murray. Augusta, who agreed
on the main point, was emphatic in declaring that Lady Byron could
not be asked to contribute : *" nothing was being done for her sake "*.
But Lady Byron had been already approached on the subject (by
whom we know not) ; and, on finding later that no member of the
Byron family except Augusta would pay, she " consented to a proposal
that she and Augusta should each provide one thousand guineas for
the purpose ".[1]

But this arrangement in the end fell through ; and it was not until
1828 that any kind of reimbursement to Moore was made.   In that
year Leigh Hunt's book came out, and John Murray became con-
vinced that a Life of Byron must be written.   He therefore arranged
with Moore to prepare the biography which was published in 1830.
For this commission Moore was paid £1600 ; but over and above that
sum, Murray discharged Moore's bond with his creditors (the Messrs.
Longman) for the two thousand guineas, together with the interest
thereon and other charges, amounting to £1020 more.   The total
sum paid by Murray was £4620.   Jeaffreson thinks that Murray should
be regarded as having discharged Moore's bond, with the interest
and costs, " with money placed in his hands for that purpose ".

Though the loss of any prose writings from Byron's hand must
be reckoned as acute, it is doubtful if in other respects the world has
lost much by losing the Memoirs.   That part of them which related
to the early London life was, in so far as it was fit for general circulation
at all, transferred by memory from Byron's MS. to Moore's Life—or
so at any rate Moore tells his readers.   He says that " on the mysterious
cause of the separation, [the MS.] afforded no light whatever ".   Byron
himself, while assuring Moore and Murray that his statement of this
case was written with the fullest intention to be faithful and true,
admitted that it was nevertheless *" not impartial "* ; and he added
passionately : " No, by the Lord !   I cannot pretend to be that while
I feel ".

As to the grossness, there are conflicting voices.   Murray attributed
to Gifford the opinion that " the Memoirs were of such a low, *Pot-
house* description " that a bookseller of repute could not possibly
publish them.   Lord Lovelace, in *Astarte*, declares that at most four
or five pages in the latter part were indelicate, and that they could
perfectly have been spared.   He cites as authorities for this opinion
Lord John Russell, Lady Holland, and other readers.   But again,
Lord Rancliffe, who had been among " the Elect ", told Hobhouse that
no one having read the MS., could have any excuse for wishing to
publish it, and that no decent person could have any wish but for its
destruction.   " The flames were the fit place for it ".

Was Augusta implicated ?   Lord John Russell said in 1869 that
she was not ; Lady Holland in 1843 (by no means so crucial a date)[2]
said she was.   Augusta never read, or heard read, a single word of

---

[1] Jeaffreson, p. 429.

[2] It was, however, to some extent crucial.   Medora Leigh—see
Appendix III.—was then in England, and there were rumours in the air
of blackmail by her servants.

the MS. ; and I can find no proof that she showed any eagerness to have it destroyed—indeed, only the urgency of Hobhouse induced her "very decidedly" to sanction the burning. Hobhouse's attitude was based on the fact that Byron had expressed to him in 1822 a desire that the Memoirs should not be published.

Lady Byron had been from the first (see Chapter XVI) strongly opposed to publication ; but she took no part whatever in the destruction, and did not approve when she heard of it (*Astarte*, pp. 122–3).

Moore, who has been universally blamed for the burning, very urgently protested against it. Jeaffreson declares that John Murray did so too ; but this does not appear either from Hobhouse's very detailed narrative in the *Recollections of a Long Life*, or from John Murray's letter of May 19, 1824, to Wilmot Horton, to be found in the Appendix to the English translation of Elze's *Life of Byron*.

It must be added that at the time, and ever afterwards, Moore assumed an attitude of magnanimity and sacrifice in the matter of allowing the Memoirs to be destroyed which was wholly unsanctioned by the facts. He had no property whatever in the MS. at the time of its destruction, and it was through his own deliberate dilatoriness that he had lost that property. In December of the same year (1824) he told Hobhouse, in writing, that he had "become a convert to [Hobhouse's] opinion about the propriety of the destruction, and of not making extracts for publication " (*Recollections of a Long Life*, vol. iii.).

APPENDIX III

MEDORA LEIGH

O N April 15, 1814, a daughter (the fourth) was born by Augusta Leigh, and was named Elizabeth Medora.

Ten days later Byron wrote to Lady Melbourne :—" Oh ! but it is 'worth while', I can't tell you why, and it is not an '*Ape*', and if it is, that must be my fault ". (The phrase : " It is not an Ape " is an evident allusion to the mediæval idea that the child of incest must be a kind of monster.) Byron goes on to say that he will positively reform, that " She and I will grow good. We are *now*, and shall be these three weeks or more ". (*Correspondence I.* 251.)

In the summer of 1843—nineteen years after Byron's death—there arrived in London from the South of France " a young lady with a pretty little daughter of nine or ten years old ".[1] She said that she was the fourth daughter of the Hon. Mrs. Leigh, and had come to England to urge a claim on Lady Byron, who had " long treated her with affection, but had suddenly withdrawn her favour ". This lady was Medora Leigh. During her stay in England she wrote out and placed in the hands of a friend an account of " *all* the circumstances of her life from her fifteenth year, painful and discreditable to herself as they were ". It was this narrative, and the friend's narrative of her proceedings in London, which the editor[2] of *Medora Leigh*, " after long doubt and hesitation ", decided to produce, and did produce through Messrs. Bentley in 1869, in the full tide of the Beecher Stowe revelations. The following notes are from Medora's autobiographical narrative.

When Medora was fifteen years old (1829) she was on a visit to her married sister, Georgiana, who was awaiting a confinement. The girl was much thrown into her brother-in-law's society—he was a distant cousin of the Byron family, a Mr. Henry Trevanion[3]—and he seduced her. She bore a child (1830) which died ; her sister knew the whole story, but her mother did not ; and she returned to her mother's house three months after the birth. She represents herself as having much disliked Henry Trevanion ; yet after her return home,

---

[1] *Medora Leigh : A History and an Autobiography.* Edited by Charles Mackay. Bentley, 1869.

[2] This was Charles Mackay, a well-known literary man of the period.

[3] In 1748 our Byron's grandfather, Admiral Byron, married his first cousin, Sophia Trevanion of Carhays in Cornwall.

he came " very often " to see her, and his visits were not discouraged.
Early in 1831 she found herself pregnant for the second time.   Tre-
vanion urged her to confide in her mother.   She did so ; and Augusta
" was at first very kind to me, though she afterwards became cruel ".
It was arranged between Mrs. Leigh and Georgiana Trevanion that
Medora should again go with the Trevanions into the country.   " This
was in March 1831 ".   The child seems to have been still-born.   In
June Colonel Leigh, Medora's supposed father,[1] heard the story.   It
had been kept from him by Medora's express desire ; she was his
favourite child, though " we were never, any of us, taught to love and
honour him."   He went to the house in the country.   (Medora said she
did not know in what part of the country this house was situated.)   He
carried away the girl, and placed her in what seems to have been a
private lunatic asylum.   At the end of a month she, by the connivance
of Trevanion and his wife (who had " promised me to procure a divorce,
so that then I could marry Henry if disposed to do so "), escaped from
the asylum and went with Trevanion to Normandy.

In 1833, after living with Trevanion for two years (under the.
assumed names of M. and Mme. Aubin), Medora wrote to Augusta,
begging to be enabled to go as a boarder to a convent in Lower Brittany.
Augusta, after long delay, engaged to allow her £60 a year, and she
entered the convent.   But after a month's residence (August 1833),
finding that for the third time she was about to become a mother,
she left, without her mother's knowledge, but with the consent of the
Abbess.   About April 1834, the daughter—Marie [2]—with whom she
appeared in London, was born ; *where* born she says not, but " Tre-
vanion was not under the same roof with me ".   Clearly, however,
they did rejoin one another; for she goes on : " We (Trevanion and
I) continued to live in an old château in a secret and unfrequented
spot, in great poverty, but as brother and sister ".   Thus, with one
absence of Trevanion's, passed five years of misery ; and in the spring
of 1838, " the hardships I had endured caused me to fall dangerously
ill ".   She then wrote to her mother, and to her mother's half-sister,
Lady Chichester,[3] imploring them to enable her to escape from Tre-
vanion's cruelty.   The means were given, and she went to a neigh-
bouring town.   For two years she received affectionate letters from
Augusta (1838 to 1840), who promised to allow her £120 a year ; but
this allowance did not, Medora says, continue.   Early in 1840 she found
herself in want, and was advised to sell her reversionary interest in a
Deed of Appointment which—probably about 1839, but the date is
nowhere afforded—Mrs. Leigh had given her.   This was a document
whereby £3000 was to be payable to Medora on the deaths of Mrs.
Leigh and Lady Byron.   She applied for advice about the sale to

---

[1] At this time she believed, though the Trevanions had told her the
contrary, that Colonel Leigh was her father.

[2] I do not think it is known what became of this daughter.

[3] It will be remembered that Augusta's mother was originally the wife
of the Marquis of Carmarthen, later fifth Duke of Leeds.   Lady Mary
Osborne, Augusta's half-sister by the mother's side, was married to the
Earl of Chichester.

Sir George Stephen, Lady Byron's solicitor. He must have told her that she could not sell until the Deed was in her possession. It was not, for Mrs. Leigh had kept it, to prevent the very thing which Medora now proposed to do.

Medora then, through Sir George Stephen, appealed to Lady Byron to use her influence with Mrs. Leigh to give up the Deed. (This was a period of estrangement between Lady Byron and Augusta.) Medora received "a most kind letter from Lady Byron, and money, with offers of protection for her and Marie". This was in August 1840. A meeting was arranged at Tours. Thence they went together to Paris, where the Countess of Lovelace and her husband were; and Ada received Medora "as a sister". "At Fontainebleau . . . Lady Byron informed me of the cause of the deep interest she felt and must ever feel for me. Her husband had been my father. . . . Her only wish, she said, was to provide for me according to Lord Byron's intentions respecting me, and according to my rank in life".

While Lady Byron with Medora Leigh was still in Paris, a Chancery suit was begun against Augusta to obtain possession of the Deed. In May 1842 this was concluded, and Medora obtained possession. By that time she was established in England with Lady Byron. No sooner had she obtained the Deed than she seems to have inaugurated a kind of blackmail upon Lady Byron. She complained that the Chancery suit had been concluded without consulting her, and that she had been sacrificed to her mother's interest. She determined to leave England, and asked for the means to do so. Lady Byron spoke of the necessity of her having a lady to live with her abroad; this she rejected: "I would not submit to any such restraint". In July 1842 she left, attended by a female servant, whose husband Lady Byron permitted to accompany them. They were to live at Hyères, and Lady Byron was to allow Medora £150 a year, and pay the wages of the female servant. To the two servants Medora told the secret of her birth. Lady Byron, who was evidently growing distrustful, arranged that the allowance should be paid to the maid, and that from the maid an account of the way the money was spent would be expected. The Deed was left in the care of Lord Lovelace; and in the care of Lady Byron's housekeeper was left a box of letters and papers belonging to Medora.

On their arrival at Hyères, already short of money (though Lady Byron had given them £40 for the journey), the maid's husband refused to leave, and prepared to profit by the secret that Medora had entrusted to him. Soon, too, Medora grew discontented with the amount of her allowance, and went to Paris to consult the famous advocate, M. Berryer, as to how she might obtain a more certain and suitable arrangement. This was in March 1843. Berryer did nothing. In May a Dr. King arrived, deputed by Lady Byron to offer Medora £300 a year on condition that she should resign "all control over myself and child" to Lady Byron. This Medora refused to do; and Dr. King said, "Sign, sign, you great fool!" She still refused, and Dr. King left Paris next morning.

A Captain de Bathe, R.N., whom Medora had known in the Mme.

Aubin days, now appeared : " he came to Paris, and called upon me ".
Apparently he found her in a state of destitution ; he interested him-
self in her case, and by his and Berryer's advice, and with means
supplied by de Bathe, Medora came to London, as we have seen, in the
summer of 1843.[1]

Medora's " claim " on Lady Byron was at this early stage confined
to one for some valuable family papers (see p. 455) which had been
stolen from Lady Byron's house by a valet—the servant who had
accompanied Medora to Hyères in 1842, and who was now in London,
blackmailing Lord and Lady Lovelace by threatening to reveal the
secret of Medora's birth.

Captain de Bathe introduced Medora to a firm of solicitors, one
of whom, Mr. S.——,[2] specially interested himself in the case. He
approached Dr. Lushington, who " received his statement as to
Medora's parentage as an understood fact ". Dr. Lushington wrote
to Lady Byron, and heard from her that " she would have no further
intercourse with Miss Leigh ; she was sorry for her, but could not
renew intercourse ".

Miss Leigh was in great need, and Captain de Bathe could not
support her any longer. Dr. Lushington, in an interview with Mr.
S——, advised him to apply to Sir George Stephen, saying : " There
may be others of the family to whom he has access—I cannot say
more ". Mr. S—— then had several interviews with Sir George
Stephen, who made three conditions to his helping Miss Leigh :

I. She must surrender the Deed of Appointment, " as a sacred
   provision to trustees—for her child ".[3]
II. She must send a written expression of her sincere contrition for
   her conduct to Lady Byron.
III. She must return to seclusion in France.

Miss Leigh consented to II. and III., but refused to surrender the
Deed. All negotiations proved fruitless ; and it was then that Medora
wrote, and placed in the hands of Mr. S——, her autobiographical
narrative.

Lady Byron's anger was caused by Medora's ingratitude and by
the way in which she had spread abroad the story of her birth. She
had told not only her servants, but M. Berryer, Mr. Bulwer of the
British Embassy in Paris, Captain de Bathe, and Mr. S——. Her
refusal to surrender the Deed was another reason for distrust ; more-
over, her blackmailing intentions were now evident. Already she
had sent and was sending letter upon letter to the Leeds family,
forcing her story upon them, and appealing for small sums of money.
She wrote also to her mother, who had refused to see her ; but the

---

[1] Captain de Bathe maintained her there for three months. He was
never reimbursed for his assistance to her, the Byron family regarding his
intervention as " wholly uninitiated by Lady Noel Byron and Lord
Lovelace ".

[2] Only initials given. This was the Mr. S—— who had met Byron in
Greece.

[3] Sir George Stephen had delivered it to Medora, from Lord Lovelace's
keeping, upon her arrival in London.

editor of *Medora Leigh* felt that this letter was " so haughty, unfilial; and cruel " that he could not admit it into his pages.

This was in August 1843. Captain de Bathe and Mr. S——now began to meditate extreme measures ; but while they were consulting on these, Medora Leigh disappeared, bearing with her little Marie and the Deed.

Nothing more was heard of her (she did not sell her reversionary interest) until in 1849 she died in France, having been married there some three or four years. She was supported during these years by a " maternal relative ". Lady Byron held no further direct communication with her ; but it is quite possible, and even (with what we know of Lady Byron) probable, that she was not unconcerned in the benevolence of the " maternal relative ".

This story was, like everything else, used in 1869–70 to defame Lady Byron, the *Quarterly Review* being particularly active.[1] In our own day, Byron's paternity of Medora Leigh is not questioned ; but there has arisen since 1909 a new theory as to her mother's identity. Mr. Richard Edgcumbe published in that year a book entitled *Byron : The Last Phase*, wherein, desiring to refute *Astarte*, he promulgated the following ideas.

1. Byron's boyish love for Mary Chaworth was the cause of his unhappiness with Lady Byron, and the reason for the cruel conduct which made her leave him.
2. In 1813–14 this passion had been renewed, and had resulted in the birth of the girl Medora.
3. Mrs. Leigh willingly inculpated herself in the manner shown in Chapter XVI of this book, and pretended that the girl Medora was her own child—to save the good name of Mary Chaworth.
4. Byron and Mrs. Leigh conspired together, for years after the separation, to persuade Lady Byron of the fact of their incestuous relations with one another—for the same purpose.

I reviewed Mr. Edgcumbe's book at the time of its publication, and said then what I still think—that only the strongest proofs could convince any reader of *Astarte* of so wild an assumption. Mr. Edgcumbe produced no proofs of any kind. He merely said that he " regretted being unable more precisely to indicate the source of the information embodied in the concluding portion of his work ", adding that " the reader might test the value of his statements by the light of citations which *seem* (!) amply to confirm them "—a feeble phrase if ever there was one ; and the more so because his citations are peculiarly ineffective. " At all events ", Mr. Edgcumbe continued, " I claim to have shown by analogy that Lord Lovelace's accusation against Mrs. Leigh is groundless "—a phrase still feebler than that already quoted. Mr. Edgcumbe sought to persuade his readers by the annotation of Byron's poems. So far as I was and am concerned,

---

[1] See *A Vindication of Lady Byron ;* article on Mrs. Stowe's book, pp. 206–336.

his failure is absolute. But the mere adoption of such a method, though it should be infinitely better carried out, is sufficient to annihilate such a case. Only documents—and irrefutable ones—will satisfy the student of these matters ; and those Lord Lovelace did produce. Here are some specimens of Mr. Edgcumbe's dealing with the *Astarte* documents.

"Augusta Leigh . . . assisted her brother to place the pack on a false scent". "Augusta avenged herself upon Lady Byron by heightening her jealousy ". Byron's letter of May 1819 was, according to Mr. Edgcumbe's theory, in reality written to Mary Chaworth, but sent through Augusta, and by Augusta sent to Lady Byron for the purpose of "heightening her jealousy ". "Augusta wished Lady Byron to believe that her brother was still making love to her ". "Mrs. Leigh seems to have enjoyed the wrigglings of her victim on the hook. . . . ". Yet this part of Mr. Edgcumbe's book is written in avowed championship of the woman—" the selfless martyr "—who could "enjoy " herself by means of such ugly malice !

To take another point. Compare the degrees of "social ruin " in the two cases. Mary Chaworth was a married woman already at odds with a flagrantly unfaithful husband ; and the morals of the age regarded adultery as the normal occupation of all men and most women. Augusta Leigh was Byron's half-sister ; and Lady Melbourne, who was very far from prudish, had told Byron in 1813 that incest was " a crime for which there was no salvation in this world, whatever there might be in the next ". Yet Augusta Leigh takes upon herself this crime, as well as that of adultery, to save the reputation of a woman who, if discovered, would have suffered merely the degree of ostracism which the world then assigned to adultery alone !

I cannot but think that Mr. Edgcumbe's theory is so manifestly feeble that unless he could produce documents (and these, in 1924, he has not yet produced) it would have been wiser to keep it to himself. Even if we could hold *Astarte* to be unproved, there would still remain the impossibility of believing *this* solution of the Byron Separation Mystery.

INDEX